The War on Drugs:
An International Encyclopedia

The War on Drugs:
An International Encyclopedia

Ron Chepesiuk

ABC-CLIO

Santa Barbara, California
Denver, Colorado
Oxford, England

For the Aranda Family of Bogotá, Colombia
For your support and love

Portions of this work are from *Hard Target: The United States War against International Drug Trafficking, 1982–1997.* © 1999 by Ron Chepesiuk. Used by permission of McFarland & Company, Inc., Publishers, Box 611, Jefferson, NC 38640 (www.mcfarlandpub.com).

Library of Congress Cataloging-in-Publication Data

Chepesiuk, Ronald.
  The war on drugs : an international encyclopedia / Ron Chepesiuk.
      p.   cm.
  Includes bibliographical references and index.
  ISBN 1-57607-037-9 (alk. paper)
      1. Narcotics, Control of—Encyclopedias. 2. Drug traffic—Encyclopedias. 3. Drug abuse—Prevention—Encyclopedias. I. Title.

  HV5804.C47 1999
  363.45'03—dc21   99-054389
03 02 01 00 99   10 9 8 7 6 5 4 3 2 1

ABC-CLIO, Inc.
130 Cremona Drive, P.O. Box 1911
Santa Barbara, California 93116–1911

This book is printed on acid-free paper ♾.

Manufactured in the United States of America

Foreword

Colombia has been at the very frontlines of the struggle described within the pages of this encyclopedia, facing down the drug cartels and their campaigns of bloody intimidation and terror, for which we have paid a high price, losing many of our finest citizens in the process. But with the end of the major drug cartels the business of narcotrafficking had become like a hydra, more fractured, more international, less public, and therefore more difficult to uproot.

Governments must focus significant attention on this problem and be determined to combat narcotics, which threatens the democratic institutions and the integrity of both consumer and producer nations. Increased efforts must be made, for example, to take away from the drug traffickers the money and properties obtained through the illegal trade, to fight money laundering of drug profits, and control the chemicals multinational companies knowingly send to Colombia that are vital to the cocaine and heroin production.

The narcotics trade, because of its huge profits and its destabilizing power, is one of the central factors generating violence in Colombia, Mexico, and the United States, and is a growing menace in other countries as traffickers seek new routes to spread their poison.

To defeat the drug trafficking menace demands a true alliance between countries both consuming and producing illegal drugs under the principle of joint responsibility, reciprocity, and fairness. We must move forward vigorously to meet the formidable challenge that the illegal drug trade poses. The future of countries in all parts of the world and the well-being of their citizens depends on it.

—Andres Pastrana Arango
President, Republic of Colombia

Contents

The War on Drugs: An International Encyclopedia

Preface

This encyclopedia is designed to provide easy access to the information it contains. There are 642 entries, covering the legal, political, social, economic, and environmental aspects of the international drug trade and the war on drugs. The encyclopedia begins with an introduction that puts the international drug trade and the War on Drugs in historical perspective and follows with a chronology of key historical events covered in the encyclopedia.

The entries are arranged alphabetically, and each attempts to cover the subject as clearly, succinctly, and informatively as possible. Entries cover a wide range of subject matter, including key historical events, major laws, significant terms, drugs trafficked, major organizations involved in drug trafficking and combating drug abuse, and important personalities involved in the drug trade or the drug issue. *See also* references provide access to entries of related interest, and each entry has references that lead the user to sources for further reading about the entry. Citations are provided for sources quoted within entries.

The list of ninety select websites will lead the user to the rich sources of information about the War on Drugs that can be found on the Internet. The book concludes with a comprehensive bibliography of sources used in compiling the encyclopedia.

Acknowledgments

Many relatives, friends, colleagues, experts, and sources for my writings on the international drug trade and the War on Drugs made this book possible, and I am deeply grateful. First, I would like to thank Mary Compton DeYoung for her skillful and professional editing and proofreading of this encyclopedia and helping me make the entries as accurate and clear as possible. I would like to thank my wife Magdalena for proofreading the manuscript, for sharing her insights on Colombian history and society, and above all, for her patience and understanding as I completed this big project.

Several relatives in Bogotá helped me bring this project to successful completion. They include Rosa Aranda Diaz for making available the use of her computer and for helping to set up a work area for me, and Jorge and Zahadya Cardona and their children Camilita and Danielito for the use of their Internet service and printer.

Professor and colleague Dr. Edward Lee of the Winthrop University faculty has always been supportive of my scholarly endeavors and I appreciate his support and long-time friendship. Several other colleagues at Winthrop helped to move this project along and furthered my knowledge of international drug trafficking and the War on Drugs. First, thank you to Gina Price White, my assistant at the Winthrop Archives, for her support over the years of my research interests. Archives Assistant Heather South helped proofread the manuscript and put it in order. Sara McIntyre, Ann Thomas, and David Weeks were patient and helpful with the numerous interlibrary loan requests I made. Lois Walker and Nancy White helped open up the riches of the Documents Department at the Winthrop University Library, and I appreciate their professional service.

Todd Hallman, my editor at ABC-CLIO, helped guide the project towards its completion. The staffs of the U.S. Drug Enforcement Administration Library in Arlington, Virginia; the York County Library in Rock Hill, South Carolina; the Library of Congress in Washington, D.C.; the Mecklenburg County Library in Charlotte, North Carolina; National Archives in Washington, D.C.; and the Central Colombo-American Library in Bogotá, Colombia, were extremely helpful in locating research materials.

Over the past ten years, several individuals have offered insights on the complex topic of international drug trafficking and the War on Drugs or helped to locate experts who could. They include, but are not limited to, Francisco Aranda, Gonzalo Aranda, Ramiro Aranda, Zahadya Aranda, Sonia Aranda, German Baquero, Luis Alberto Becerra, Tommy Burns, P. Sante Cervellin, Merrill Collette, Jan Crijiins, J. R. de Groot, Myriam Mejia de Godoy, Dario Diaz, Maria Jimena Duzan, Juan Ferro, Myles Frechette, Leonardo Gallego, Larry Gallina, Ely Rubio Gomez, Julio Orlando Gomez, Gustavo Gorriti, Jorge Graitman, Gary P. Keith, Terry Kneebone, Charles Intriago, Carlos Landeros, Rensselaer Lee, Victor T. Le Vine, Artur Madrigal, Maria Luisa Mejia, Oscar Arnulfo Mejia, Mike Marcial, Elsa Martinez,

Alfredo Molano, Clara Lopez Obregon, Andres Pastrana Arango, Charles Rangel, Alexandro Reyes, Fernando Brito Ruiz, Gustavo Ramirez Salgado, Obido Salinas, Ernesto Samper Pizano, Alexandro Saenz de Santamaria, Enrique Santos, Fernando Santos, Rafael Santos, Rosso Jose Serrano, Carlos Lemos Simmons, Jim Sutton, Juan Tokatlian, Alfonso Valdivieso Sarmiento, Giel Van Brussel, John Vance, Alfredo Vasquez, Bruce Wyrick, and Fernando Zarate.

Thank you all for your advice, information, guidance, consideration, and much more.

International Drug Trafficking and the War on Drugs: A Historical Overview

International drug trafficking is the world's second most profitable illicit business after arms trafficking, accounting for an estimated 8 percent of the world trade and taking in earnings estimated to be as high as $400 billion to $500 billion annually, according to the United Nations Drug Control Program. Heroin is believed to account for $200 billion of the total, cocaine for $100 billion, and the rest of the amount is divided among marijuana, hashish, and several psychotropic drugs. The United Nations says that at least 104 countries are involved in some way—through production, distribution, and laundering of illicit profits—in the criminal enterprise, and thousands of entrepreneurial criminals from all over the world are willing to risk death and/or jail to get a piece of the lucrative action.

The profits are so huge that drug traffickers find it difficult to hide, let alone to spend, them. The so-called dons, godfathers, drug lords, and kingpins who control the traffic regularly appear on *Forbes* magazine's annual list of the world's richest individuals (such as Pablo Escobar Gaviria, Carlos Lehder Rivas, and Jorge Ocho Vasquez), while the power and wealth of the trafficking networks they have created threaten the stability and social fabric of countries all over the world.

Each year, thousands of unfortunate people of all colors, ages, and classes die or have their lives wrecked or derailed because of international drug trafficking. According to the Office of National Drug Controlling, illegal drug use claims an estimated 40,000 lives in the United States annually, while in Europe between 500,000 and 1 million people are addicted to heroin. The problem, together with the criminality associated with the illegal trade in drugs, makes drug trafficking the Continent's number one problem. [1]

Much of the criminal attention is directed to the huge market in the United States, where experts say drug trafficking has become the country's largest source of illegally earned income. The illegal drug traffic has made drug abuse a problem of national concern, particularly since the early 1980s, when President Ronald Reagan declared the War on Drugs. After Reagan left the Oval Office in 1989, his two successors, George Bush and Bill Clinton, renewed the pledge to fight the War and spent more billions of dollars combating international drug trafficking.

Drug use itself, however, is not a modern phenomena. In fact, two major drugs of the international drug trade—opium and marijuana—have been in use for several thousand years. It is believed that opium was used as early as the fifth century B.C., while the ancient Chinese used marijuana as an anesthetic. The Indians of South America's Andes mountains began chewing the coca leaf as a way to stave off hunger and fatigue as early as 500 B.C., even though cocaine was not discovered until the nineteenth century.

The settlers who came to the New World brought drugs such as marijuana and opium with them, and by the late nineteenth century, it is not an overstatement to say that the United States had become one of the most drug-taking and drug-abusing nations in history. In fact, the use of opium, heroin, cocaine, and marijuana was widely prevalent in American society, and it was all legal. Chinese immigrants got the drug wagon rolling in the early nineteenth century when they brought opium with them to the United States. The Chinese had been smoking opium for at least a thousand years by the time the British opium trade with China began in the early nineteenth century.

Beginning about 1840, opium imports increased significantly, the result of the United States' opium trade with China, which—while dominated by the British—included participation by Americans. In the early 1800s the Chinese reacted by laying siege to the port city of Canton in China, and then confiscating and destroying the opium awaiting unloading from foreign ships. In retaliation, a British expedition attacked the Chinese, routing their weak and poorly organized troops and forcing them to pay $6 million for the opium they had seized and $2 million in compensation. By 1856, however, the balance of trade once again favored the Chinese and the Second Opium War began. This time, however, the French, Russian, and American forces joined the English and sacked Canton, forcing the Chinese Empire to pay $20,000 to offset the balance of trade. The British appointed a commission, which legalized and regulated the opium trade. [2]

In addition to its importation, the opium poppy was grown legally in many parts of the United States during the nineteenth century, especially in the southern states of Georgia, Florida, Louisiana, Virginia, Tennessee, and South Carolina. Doctors used opium regularly—without a second thought—as part of their regular practice to control and treat a variety of ailments and diseases, including fevers, dysentery, rheumatism, swellings, and broken limbs, and to ease the pain of the dying. [3]

About 1840, cannabis became popular in the treatment of ailments like insomnia, tetanus, migraine headaches, and venereal disease, and even as an antidote for strychnine poisoning. Some patients and doctors claimed cannabis was effective, although no scientific evidence yet exists to support those claims. In the 1870s cocaine, which is derived from the coca leaf grown in South America, began arriving in the United States and Europe, and within a decade, a number of famous personalities had hailed the "wonder drug." For example, Sigmund

Freud, the father of psychiatry, and his wife experimented with the drug, praising it as a cure for migraine headaches and alcohol addiction and claiming that the "user [has] absolutely no craving for further use of cocaine." [4] The American general and president Ulysses S. Grant used cocaine for energy to keep himself alive while he finished his memoirs, and U.S. President William McKinley, Pope Leo XIII, inventor Thomas Edison, and the king and queen of Norway enjoyed a popular drink called Vin Mariani, which consisted of wine mixed with cocaine. [5] Ordinary Americans used cocaine as well; in fact, many enjoyed a shot of whiskey laced with a pinch of cocaine. [6]

In 1898, Bayer Laboratories introduced heroin. thinking it would be a nonaddictive substitute for morphine, and doctors began to prescribe the drug to patients, using it as a cure for the worst coughs and chest pains. Made from opium, heroin was viewed as a powerful pain killer that did not have the addictive qualities of morphine, which had come into general use in the 1820s and was popular in medical treatment. The American Medical Association even endorsed the new drug as safe for respiratory ailments. [7]

In the late nineteenth century, however, the prevailing permissive attitude, easy access to narcotics, and the rising number of drug abuse cases became a cause of public concern. No one could be sure of the accuracy of the statistics, but surveys conducted by doctors and pharmacists during this period suggested that the number of drug addicts was in the range of 100,000 to 200,000. As H. Wayne Morgan explains, "The statistics can never be exact, but the divining [of the number of addicts] lent credence to the general fear that opium addiction and drug use was spreading and undermining American values." [8] When the physically and psychologically addictive qualities of the many thought-to-be-wonder drugs became apparent, politicians, religious leaders, pharmacists, doctors, and journalists spoke out for tighter controls on drug use.

The medical establishment warned that morphine, while itself not physically addictive, could become habit forming for people with "susceptible" minds. Freud began to have second doubts about the miracle nature of cocaine after one of his close friends died of an overdose, and in his lectures and scientific writings he began warning the public about the drug's addictive tendencies. By the early 1890s many doctors had abandoned heroin in the treatment of their patients, concerned that they were needing increasingly stronger doses of the drug.

The United States' move towards the regulation and, ultimately, the prohibition of drugs was largely guided by its foreign policy, especially its desire to open up the Chinese market, which Japan and the major European powers had cornered, as well as its acquisition of the Philippines in 1898 after winning a four-month war with Spain. The Spanish had allowed Chinese residents in the Philippines to purchase opium and taxed its sale, but drug addiction had spread to the native population, which began to use the drug for its constipative qualities and to stave off cholera. Under pressure from clergy and others in the growing and increasingly active U.S. antiopium movement, President William Taft formed the Philippines Commission to investigate the opium trade and report back to him. The Commission's conclusion that the opium trade was one of the most serious problems in the Orient led Congress to ban opium use in the Philippines in 1905. [9]

This was the beginning of an international antiopium crusade that lobbied successfully for a series of treaties restricting trade in the drug. In 1909 the United States and twelve other countries met in Shanghai, China, to examine the opium trade, and they agreed in principle that they should make a stronger effort to control opium and its derivatives, particularly morphine.[10] Meanwhile, in the United States the Progressive Era held sway. It was a time of reform and political change, and the growing fear of drug abuse created strong public support in the early twentieth century for passage of national legislation that would lead to the control of the domestic traffic in opium and cocaine.[11] In 1906 Congress passed the Pure Food and Drug Act, which made it illegal to sell food or medicine if the ingredients, including heroin and cocaine, were not stated on the label. Two years later, shipping cocaine and heroin from one state to another became illegal, although the sale of the drugs was still legal, as was the trafficking of drugs within states. In 1909 Congress passed another act that prohibited the importation and use of opium for other than medical purposes. Opium could still be imported for medical purposes, but only to twelve ports.[12] States with big urban populations like New York caught the Progressive

Era spirit and began to legislate and apply laws controlling the sale of drugs.[13]

After the Shanghai meeting of 1909, the United States continued to attend and support international antiopium conferences. In December 1911 a conference at The Hague in the Netherlands, held to sanction the resolutions adopted at Shanghai, led to the signing of the International Opium Convention of 23 January 1912. Signatories committed themselves to the enactment of laws that would suppress "the abuse of opium, morphine, cocaine, as well as drugs prepared or derived from these substances."[14]

The United States' strong support for international opium control, as well as the popular consensus against drug use and addiction, which had been building since the late nineteenth century, led to the passage in 1914 of the Harrison Narcotic Act, one of the most famous and important drug laws in U.S. history. Named after Representative Francis B. Harrison of New York state, who introduced the measure into Congress, the act was signed by Woodrow Wilson on 17 December 1914, and went into effect on 1 March 1915. It had the long-winded title of "an Act to provide for the registration of, with collectors of internal revenue, and to impose a special tax upon all persons who produce, import, manufacture, compound, deal in, disperse, sell, distribute, or give away opium or coca leaves, their salts, derivatives, or properties and for other purposes."

With the Harrison Act's passage, anyone selling, importing or dispensing drugs had to be registered with the U.S. government. Heroin and cocaine, moreover, could now only be obtained legally with a doctor's prescription. Marijuana was excluded from the law, and not until 1937 did lawmakers bring it under control. While intense lobbying by the U.S. drug industry stopped the total regulation of drugs, the Harrison Act became the cornerstone for U.S. domestic drug policy for the next sixty-five years.[15] More laws would follow in the belief that legislation at both the national and state levels could, if not eliminate, at least control the country's drug use. In the coming decades, however, drug abuse as a perceived social problem would not go away.

The crusade to regulate alcohol culminated in the passage of the Eighteenth Amendment to the U.S. Constitution in 1917 (ratified in 1919), and the total prohibition of the sale and manufacture of beverages exceeding 0.5% alcohol content went into effect in 1920. Little did the Amendment's proponents and supporters realize that their moralistic intentions would lead to the emergence of organized crime on a prodigious level and to the accumulation of huge illegal profits that would spur the growth of criminal activity.

It is true that organized crime did exist in the United States before Prohibition. Sicilian secret societies, which would spawn the Sicilian Mafia, were operating in most Italian American communities in the 1890s, while other ethnic gangs, including Jews, Japanese, Chinese, and Irish, were also involved in organized criminal activity. But as one scholar explained, "All of the living pre-prohibition mobsters, extortionists, racketeers, and criminals would have remained in the lower depths without the passage of the Eighteenth Amendment. Prohibition not only gave them opportunity, it gave them respectability and legitimacy. Prohibition not only provided a means of making vast sums of money, it created a need for organization, cooperation, and syndication." [16] And with their big bank accounts, the gangsters of the Prohibition era were able to corrupt public officials, such as police officers, attorneys, politicians, and prosecutors on a scale never seen before in American history.

Governments were no longer actively promoting drugs, but that didn't stop the emergence of new criminal syndicates in the major cities of Asia and the West to organize the underground traffic in illegal drugs. By 1924 many drug source countries were raising a demand that would become a constant refrain in the 1980s: the need for development assistance from the Western countries to help them control the production of drug. In 1923 Turkey, one of the major drug source countries, rejected a request by the United States to implement a crop substitution program, and within a decade that country had become one of the world's largest centers for heroin traffic. [17]

In the 1920s heroin trafficking, under the direction of Jewish gangs in New York City, became big business in the United States. Historians credit Jewish Prohibition-era gangster Arnold Rothstein with turning narcotics trafficking into a sophisticated operation. In describing Rothstein's role, one historian wrote:

He dispatched a number of employees with experience purchasing liquor in Europe to locate major sources of supply. They found that buying narcotics on the Continent was ridiculously easy. Legitimate pharmaceutical firms in France, Germany, and Holland were happy to see big orders of heroin, morphine and cocaine, no questions asked. Rothstein used his own people to arrange giant orders and overseas shipments to be sent back to the U.S. as innocuous sea freight. Once in the U.S., the drugs were distributed by Rothstein's people to the wide network of big-city Prohibition gangsters. [18]

The repeal of the Eighteenth Amendment in 1933 ended Prohibition, and many leading gangsters, such as Meyer Lansky, Frank Costello, Bugsy Siegel, and Lucky Luciano, who had been making huge profits in bootlegging, stayed in the liquor business legally, buying and establishing companies that sold wine, whiskey, and other spirits. Some of them, however, moved into narcotics trafficking and other lucrative kinds of criminal activity. By the mid-1930s, the Italian Cosa Nostra had joined Jewish organized crime groups in the international narcotics trade and was importing opium and heroin from Asia, France, and the Middle East.

During the 1920s and 1930s, the control of opiates and other narcotics at the international level became one of the most successful activities of the League of Nations. The League sponsored several opium treaties that were ratified by numerous countries, and its Permanent Central Control Opium Board supervised the legal international trade in opium and other drugs it considered dangerous, and applied effective sanctions against countries that exceeded estimates. [19]

With the outbreak of World War II, the problem of international drug trafficking was put on hold, as the United States and the Allies concentrated their energy and resources on defeating the Axis powers. Still, some important developments occurred with regard to international drug trafficking. In 1943, for example, the Allies announced that the system of opium smoking under government license would end with the return of the liberated territories to the countries that had colonial holdings. In June of the following year, the U.S. Senate and House passed a joint resolution sponsored by Walter Judd, a congressman from Minnesota and former missionary to China, authorizing the president to urge opium-producing countries to limit their production of opium strictly to meet the world's scientific and medical needs. [20]

With the defeat of the Axis powers in 1945, drug trafficking once again became the focus of international attention. The United Nations assumed the drug control functions of the defunct League of Nations and gave high priority to working for greater cooperation among the drug enforcement agencies around the world. The Federal Bureau of Narcotics (FBN), Uncle Sam's chief antidrug agency at the time, expanded its operation overseas into Europe and the Middle East. It looked as though the problem of international drug trafficking was well under control. To the casual observer, "the hope of finally stopping supplies and cutting production [sic] of new addicts seemed about to come true." [21] International drug trafficking, however, would continue to grow and expand as the result of two major developments in the late 1940s.

After World War II, La Cosa Nostra, under the leadership of godfather Charles "Charley Lucky" Luciano, took control of the U.S. heroin market. Luciano had been convicted of ninety-one counts of extortion and promoting prostitution in the 1930s and began serving a long prison sentence in New York state, but the U.S. government deported him to his native Italy in 1945, reportedly in payment for "services" he had performed for the United States during the war, the nature of which have never really been explained. Luciano quickly took advantage of his freedom, grabbing control of the local Mafia soon after arriving in Italy and developing a plan of action to ship heroin to the United States. During the war, drug traffickers had a difficult time importing heroin into the United States, and so, without access to the drug, many addicts had cured themselves. The FBN estimated that there were no more than 20,000 addicts in the entire country at the time, a figure that represented about a 0.13 percent addiction rate for the American population. [22]

Luciano's deportation to Italy changed that statistic dramatically. The federal authorities had underestimated the Mafia godfather, thinking that he was nothing more than a goon and a thug, but Luciano had much experience in the heroin trade, for in the 1930s he had led his fellow Italian mobsters into the illegal business as a way of controlling his prostitutes. After moving to Italy in the late 1940s and im-

posing his control over the Sicilian Mafia, Luciano began buying raw opium from the poppy fields in Turkey, Lebanon and other producing countries, setting up heroin-processing laboratories in Sicily, and developing a sophisticated drug-smuggling network that transported heroin to markets in the United States and Europe. By 1952 the FBN had revised its estimate of the number of addicts in the country, putting the figure at three times what it was before World War II.

The Italian government finally moved to stamp out heroin manufacturing in the early 1950s, when an investigation showed that heroin had been smuggled into the United States from Italy since 1948. That didn't deter the enterprising Italian mob, which devised a new system by which supplies of morphine base were refined to heroin in Marseilles, shipped to Montreal or Sicily, and then sent directly to the United States. This new arrangement became known as the French Connection, and it allowed the Italian Mafia to dominate the heroin trade from the 1950s to the early 1970s. At its peak, the French Connection supplied an estimated 95 percent of the heroin distributed to the United States.

The Chinese Revolution of 1948, which deposed Chiang Kai-Shek and brought the communists to power under Mao Tse-Tung, also gave international drug trafficking a boost. Chiang Kai-Shek's Fifth Kuomintang Army (KMI) fled China, going south across the border into Burma (present-day Myanmar). To get money for arms and materials, the KMI got involved in the local opium trade, helping to turn the Golden Triangle into one of the world's biggest producers of opium. As James Traub explained, "The KMI established a pattern: as the politics of Southeast Asia became more chaotic, more gangs sprang up to challenge governments, turning to opium for money and finally became very little different from bands of smugglers. The difference, in Southeast Asia, is that the drug trade is controlled by entire armies with thousands of troops and modern weapons." [23] There have been accusations that some of these armies also got a boost from the United States' Central Intelligence Agency (CIA), which, in the interest of fighting communism in the region, would ignore, or tacitly approve, the shady activities of these huge rogue armies. [24]

Opiates, more than any other narcotic substance, had dominated the attention of the U.S. antidrug movement in the first half of the twentieth century, but that focus changed in the 1960s, as heroin, marijuana, and cocaine became a part of the international trade in illegal drugs, and Americans from all walks of life began experimenting with a variety of drugs. Cheap and easy to find, marijuana was especially popular among white middle-class college students. Cocaine, which had declined in use after World War I, made a big comeback beginning in the late 1960s. The U.S. Customs Service impounded a mere three kilograms of cocaine in 1961, but that figure jumped to 29 kilograms in 1971. [25]

The drug known by its initials of LSD, a hallucinogenic and extremely powerful substance, became an integral part of the lifestyles of young people who joined the counterculture that emerged in the mid-1960s. Rejecting the values of mainstream America, members of the counterculture did such things as wear their hair long, eschew materialism, practice "free" love, live in communes, flock to rock concerts, embrace eastern mysticism, perform street theater, and, of course, take drugs. [26]

The huge demand for illegal drugs arising in the 1960s created the conditions that allowed international drug trafficking to expand and flourish. Until the 1960s, the cost of cocaine was so high that it was known as the "champagne of drugs," but, in the late 1960s drug traffickers responded to the strong demand for new drugs with which to experiment by persuading coca growers to plant more coca leaves. This, in turn, spawned the growth of the powerful Latin American drug-trafficking organizations that became known as cartels and produced increasing amounts of cocaine to meet demand. As the cocaine supply increased, the price decreased, making it possible for more people to buy cocaine. Thus, by the late 1960s cocaine had become the drug choice for many Americans and the United States had another kind of drug epidemic on its hands.

In 1961, the United Nations agreed to the Single Convention on Narcotic Drugs, which simplified and streamlined the international narcotics control machinery that had grown haphazardly since the first international treaty in 1912. [27] The Convention was hailed as a major international agreement, but in retrospect many of its articles proved to be impractical. For example, it declared that "the use of cannabis for other than medical or scientific purposes must be discontinued as soon as possible, but, in any case, within twenty-five years." This proclamation, of course, was made just a few years before marijuana use exploded on the world scene. The Convention also agreed to try and cut off heroin trafficking at the source, by paying off the growers not to plant poppy crops, but despite several subsequent initiatives during the past three decades, this strategy has proved to be a dismal failure. [28]

President John F. Kennedy, aware of growing national concern about drug abuse, convened the first White House Conference on Narcotics and Drug Abuse in 1962. This, in turn, led to the establishment of the President's Advisory Commission on Narcotics and Drug Abuse, the so-called Prettyman Commission, which recommended tougher measures against international drug trafficking. The Commission, for example, proposed that the U.S. government assign more federal agents to investigate the illicit importation and trafficking in narcotics, marijuana, and other dangerous drugs, and to control, by federal statute, all nonnarcotic drugs "capable of producing serious psychotropic effects when abused." The wide net of control was extended three years later with the passage of the Drug Abuse Control Amendments of 1965, which sought to control the diversion of depressant and stimulant drugs such as barbiturates and amphetamines from legal channels. To enforce the amendments, the federal government expanded the drug-fighting bureaucracy by creating the Bureau of Drug Abuse Control.

These federal initiatives did not relieve the public's worry about crime and drug abuse, and so, in 1966, President Lyndon B. Johnson established the President's Commission on Law Enforcement and Administration of Justice (the Katzenbach Commission) in order to undertake "a comprehensive study of the nation's crime problem and to provide recommendations to coordinate its eradication on all fronts." The Commission's recommendations sought to deal with both the supply and demand of drugs by increasing the enforcement staffs of the Federal Bureau of Narcotics (FBN) and the Bureau of Customs, while recommending that the National Institute of Mental Health develop and distribute educational materials about drugs. In response to the commission's recommendations, President Johnson restructured the federal government's drug law enforcement machinery. Among other changes, he abolished the FBN and shifted its responsibilities to the newly created Bureau of Narcotics and Dangerous Drugs. Johnson also gave the Department of Justice major responsibility for enforcing federal drug laws for the first time in its history.[29]

The U.S. government's efforts to structure and coordinate its forces in the emerging war on drugs culminated in the enactment, during Richard Nixon's presidency, of the Comprehensive Drug Abuse Prevention and Control Act of 1970, which was designed to put "diverse laws in one piece of legislation based upon new scientific information, the restructured federal law enforcement efforts under Reorganization Plan No I of 1968, and greater information concerning the scope of the problem."[30]

By the early 1970s marijuana had become the most popular illegal drug in America. Marijuana's ardent proponents considered the drug to be harmless and even beneficial, and, for an increasing number of Americans, "a stand of marijuana in the countryside, or in the window, was as comforting as homemade wine was to many older people."[31] Marijuana became so popular that public support for harsh sentences for marijuana users weakened. The federal government under Presidents Kennedy, Johnson, and Nixon reacted reflexively to the surge in marijuana use, increasing law enforcement efforts and passing tougher sentences. At the federal level, there were a mere 169 arrests relating to marijuana in 1960, but that figure climbed to 7,000 in 1965, and a year later, the figure had jumped to 50,000. Several states followed the federal government's lead and increased the sentences for first offense possession of marijuana from five to fifteen years at hard labor. In politically liberal Massachusetts, a person arrested in the company of someone possessing marijuana, or in a place where it was kept, could receive a five-year prison sentence.[32]

Despite the crackdown, widespread marijuana use had made drug trafficking a booming multibillion dollar business by the 1970s, and many criminal syndicates were eager to get a piece of the action. The Italian American Mafia had given other ethnic criminal organizations an opening when its leadership decided in the 1950s to prohibit its members from trafficking in the lucrative narcotics. The godfathers would later come to fear a new federal conspiracy law known as the RICO statute, which was passed in 1970. This statute allowed the federal government to prosecute the Mafia leadership for narcotics trafficking, even though they may not have handled drugs themselves.[33]

At the international level, Cuban criminals were the first to take advantage of the Italian American Mafia's decision. In Cuba during the corrupt regime of dictator Fulgencio Batista, the Italian American Mafia was given a free hand to run the casinos, brothels, loan-sharking operations, and other criminal activities, and to protect its thriving businesses, the Mafia put numerous government officials, policemen, businessmen, members of the military, and criminals on its payroll. The mob and many of their Cuban associates fled the island for the safety of the United States in 1959, when Fidel Castro overthrew Batista and established a communist dictatorship. During the early 1960s, the Cuban exiles conspired to overthrow the new Cuban dictator. The Italian American Mafia was involved in several plots to kill Castro, while many of its former Cuban associates joined the CIA's failed Bay of Pigs invasion of Cuba in 1961. In the wake of that disaster, Cuban criminals set up base in South Florida and organized La Compania, whose primary criminal activity was importing heroin and cocaine to the United States. Establishing its headquarters in Miami, with branch operations in California, Nevada, Arizona, and New Jersey, La Compania dominated the Latin American drug-trafficking trade during the 1960s and early 1970s.[34]

The ranks of the Cuban Mafia in the United States were bolstered by two more waves of Cuban immigration: the Camarioca boatlift, or "freedom flotilla," which brought 250,000 Cubans to the United States between 1965 and 1972, and the Mariel boatlift of 1980, in which U.S. officials estimated that about 2 percent of the immigrants were criminals, prostitutes, drug addicts, and vagrants. Although most Cubans who fled to the United States came in search of political freedom and the opportunity to build better lives, Cuban immigrant communities did become bases of operation for Cuban organized crime networks.[35]

The powerful Colombian cartels also got their start in the drug trade in the 1960s as the middlemen who bought raw coca from farmers in the Andean region of South America, turned the coca into cocaine, and then sold the finished product to the Cubans. The large number of Colombians who emigrated to the United States in the 1960s and settled in major cites like Miami, Chicago, New York, and Los Angeles gave the Colombian trafficking networks a solid, sympathetic, and helpful base for their operation. By 1965 the Colombians were supplying nearly all of the cocaine moving through Cuban trafficking networks. By the early 1970s, the Colombians had gained control over the cocaine producers in Peru and Bolivia and the refineries in Chile and were challenging the dominance of the Cubans in the U.S. drug trade. [36]

The Colombians bought cocaine paste from Bolivian and Peruvian suppliers and used chemicals manufactured and supplied by U.S. and European companies to refine the paste in clandestine laboratories hidden in remote areas of Colombia, before shipping the finished product to Florida and the U.S. market. The Colombians started small, paying individuals to carry cocaine on regular commercial flights in shoe heels or sewn into linings of coats or suitcases. By the 1970s they were revolutionizing the way drugs were smuggled into the United States from Latin America; in fact, so successful did the Colombians become in drug trafficking that, by the early 1980s, cocaine had supplanted coffee as Colombia's number one foreign exchange earner. [37]

Although marijuana was the most popular illegal drug of choice in the 1970s, and an increasing number of Americans had begun experimenting freely with cocaine, LSD, and other drugs known as psychedelic drugs, heroin use once again began to rise in the United States, spreading from the poor inner cities to the predominantly middle-class neighborhoods of suburbia and threatening to reach epidemic proportions. Between 1960 and 1970 the number of heroin users in the United States rose from 40,000 to 500,000. Among the users were many GIs who had become addicted to heroin while serving in Vietnam.[38] By 1971 an estimated 25,000 to 37,000 American soldiers in Vietnam were using heroin, and about 14 percent of them became addicted to the drug.[39]

High Vietnamese government officials, including Prime Minister Nguyen Kao Ky and his successor General Tran Thien Khiem, were reportedly involved in the heroin trade. "Periodic attempts by American agents to smash the elaborate smuggling network were thwarted by their superiors in the U.S. mission, since a crackdown would have exposed nearly every prominent member of the Saigon regime," wrote journalist Stanley Karnow. [40]

Critics of U.S. foreign policy charge that investigations have shown the U.S. government, through its Central Intelligence Agency (CIA), shares responsibility in the addiction to heroin of American soldiers in Vietnam. Not only was the CIA involved in covering up for their drug-trafficking allies in Southeast Asia, but the agency may have been actively engaged in the transportation and distribution of heroin. [41]

The heroin traffic in Southeast Asia centered in the Golden Triangle, an area of rugged terrain occupying parts of Laos, Thailand, and Myanmar, which today, says the federal Drug Enforcement Administration, supplies 70 percent of the world's heroin and opium. First the French, during their colonial rule of Southeast Asia, and then the CIA during the Vietnam War, supported the warlords in the area as allies and as a buffer against communist expansion in the region and turned a blind eye to their involvement in the cultivation and trafficking of the local opium crop.[42]

The 1964 coup that toppled South Vietnam leader Ngo Dinh Diem gave a big boost to the narcotics trade in the Golden Triangle, because corrupt South Vietnam government officials and generals were given a free hand to use Vietnamese and Laotian planes, which were paid for by the U.S. government, to ship heroin from the Triangle. Once the loads arrived in South Vietnam, the traffickers bribed corrupt customs officials not to inspect the bags and bundles carrying the heroin.[43] Later, after the U.S invasion of Cambodia in 1970, the heroin was carried from the Golden Triangle to Cambodia by mules and then flown or shipped to South Vietnam.[44]

Around 1968, Hong Kong chemists, under the protection of the CIA's local allies, including the commander-in-chief of the Royal Laotian Army, opened heroin laboratories in the Golden Triangle that produced large quantities of a new kind of 90 percent pure heroin called Number Four. This heroin was ideal for injecting and was superior in quality to the type of heroin being sold at the time in the United States, which was only 25 to 50 percent pure.

By the early 1970s, GIs were spending an estimated $88 million a year on heroin, and bringing their habit home with them when they finished their tours of duty. [45] A 1973 survey revealed that the U.S. heroin trade was worth $4 billion, making it the country's "single biggest consumer import." [46]

As late as 1971 the official U.S. response was to blame the communists for the drug trade in Southeast Asia, and during the past twenty-five years, the CIA has denied any involvement. Given the covert nature of the CIA, and the fact that there has been little government oversight of the agency, it has been difficult to prove the CIA connection to international drug trafficking. But as Alfred J. McCoy, author of the investigative study *The Politics of Heroin in Southeast Asia* explained:

Those who look for the CIA officers to actually dirty their hands with drugs during the line of duty are missing the point. In most covert actions, the CIA avoids direct involvement in combat or espionage and, instead, works through local clients whose success often determines the outcome of an ongoing operation. Thus the CIA's involvement in the drug trade revolves around the indirect complicity in the drug dealing of its assets, not in any direct complicity in the actual traffic.[47]

It would not be the last time that there would be accusations of "indirect complicity" on the part of the CIA in the international narcotics trade. Later, the agency would be accused of involvement in narcotics traffic in Afghanistan and Central America and of fueling the demand for crack in the United States, and critics such as Alfred J. McCoy and Gary Webb would continue to charge that the CIA, in the name of anticommunism, had become part of the problem, not the solution, in America's much vaunted War on Drugs.

The country's growing heroin epidemic did catch the attention of President Richard Nixon, who, on 17 June 1971 made a major television speech in which he said, "America has now the largest number of heroin addicts of any nation in the world. If we cannot destroy the drug menace in America, then it will surely destroy us."[48] Nixon's speech marked a major turning point for the U.S. government's attitude towards illegal drugs and international drug trafficking. As Catherine Lamour and Michael R. Lamberti explained, "Thereafter, the battle against narcotics was regarded by Washington as one of the most urgent items in the American political program, and concrete measures were put in hand so as to convince the country that the Republican administration was not simply making a promise."[49]

Initially, the Nixon administration did have some success, particularly against heroin. In 1971 the U.S. began pressuring Turkey, Mexico, and Southeast Asia's Golden Triangle to eradicate their opium crops. The famous French Connection, which was dominated by Sicilian and Corsican drug-trafficking organizations, supplied a huge percentage of the heroin entering the United States via a smuggling route stretching from Turkey to Marseilles and southern France. There, chemists working in hidden laboratories converted the raw opium to a type of heroin called "China White" before traffickers shipped the finished product to the United States. By 1973 the French government had shut down the laboratories in southern France, and Turkey, supported by $20 million in U.S. aid, had convinced its farmers to switch from poppies to alternative crops. The heroin sold in the U.S. dropped in purity to one-half of what it was, while the price of heroin in New York City, the drug's principal market, tripled, an indication that heroin was in short supply. In September 1973 Nixon told the American people: "We have turned the corner on drug addiction."[50]

Nixon's declaration proved to be premature, for the basic principle of supply and demand once again went to work. Trafficking syndicates in southeast Asia filled the gap left by the dismantling of the French Connection's laboratories, while opium production quickly shifted to new centers. As Alfred J. McCoy and Alan A. Block noted, "during the next ten years, drug trafficking syndicates simply shifted their resources—from Turkey to Southeast Asia to Mexico, and then to Southeast Asia (again)—remaining one step ahead of U.S. diplomats and drug agents."[51] Amsterdam replaced Marseilles as the center of the European heroin trade and new trafficking syndicates—the Triads, Colombians, and African Americans, among others—arose to fill the heroin distribution pipeline.

The heroin trade subsequently expanded in the United States to include not just New York City as the major distribution point, but also Miami, Chicago, and Los Angeles. Ironically, the French Connection may have revived during the late 1970s, when law enforcement officials noted that heroin-processing labs had reappeared in southern France, staffed by the same "employees" who worked in the original French Connection's labs a decade earlier.[52] Nixon's get-tough strategy had backfired. Demand increased and international drug trafficking continued to expand the supply network.

Presidents Gerald Ford and Jimmy Carter continued the nation's War on Drugs, but by 1980 Uncle Sam had little to show for its hard-line antidrug policy. During the Nixon administration, the budget for the U.S. antidrug program had increased significantly and drug enforcement infrastructure underwent a major reorganization to provide the leadership in the War on Drugs and to reduce interagency rivalries, but one of the federal agencies—the CIA—had allegedly helped fuel drug use in the United States by helping allies in Southeast Asia and possibly Afghanistan who were heavily involved in international drug trafficking. The federal government had tried eradication programs in Turkey and Mexico, but sources for heroin and marijuana had sprung up in other countries and drugs continued to flow freely into the United States.

During the 1970s, the U.S. government put antidrug policies in place in cocaine source countries, such as Peru and Colombia, and the transit countries of the Caribbean and Central America, but these efforts were small and ineffective. The United States concentrated most of its attention and resources on heroin during the decade. Meanwhile, by the early 1980s the ambitious criminal cartels based in the Colombian cities of Cali and Medellin were poised for their big entrance onto the international drug-trafficking scene in which they would make cocaine the drug of the 1980s. This abysmal record led the 1984 President's Commission on Crime to conclude that "the nation's drug problem at the end of the 1970s was as great, if not greater, than the problem in 1970."[53]

Despite the failures of the 1970s, the Reagan administration pushed ahead in the early 1980s with a hard-line military-oriented agenda for the War on Drugs. In launching his War on Drugs in 1982, Reagan reorganized the chain of command and sent an impressive array of military hardware, intelligence, and other resources to South Florida and the front lines in the drug battle. It was not a unilateral decision, for Congress strongly supported the Reagan administration's actions, and calls for a tougher stance in the War on Drugs came from a variety of legislative sources, including the powerful House Foreign Affairs Committee and the House Select Committee on Narcotics Control.

The Reagan administration concentrated on the interdiction of drugs in Latin America and shifted the focus of the War on Drugs from heroin to cocaine and marijuana, drugs that the administration believed Americans were using the most. But by the mid-1980s, the United States was having to deal with another dangerous drug. Crack, perhaps the most potent, addictive—and certainly the cheapest—form of cocaine, had begun appearing in the inner cities of Miami, Los Angeles, and New York City in the early 1980s, and its use was spreading across America. Crime rates soared to record levels in the inner cities, as gang warfare raged between drug dealers determined to protect their turf in the lucrative drug trade. This new development heightened the public's concern about the impact of illegal drugs and led President Reagan to react in a predictable fashion. He increased the funding for the drug war from $1.5 billion in 1981 to $2.75 billion in 1986, and pushed for the passage of the 1986 Antidrug Abuse Act, which not only authorized $1.7 billion in additional money to fight drug abuse, but also provided for prison sentences for drug dealers who either sold drugs near schools or recruited young people to peddle them.[54]

While the United States intensified its antidrug effort at home, the War on Drugs heated up overseas. During the 1970s, Colombian drug traffickers had operated throughout Colombia without much interference from the authorities, but by 1984 Colombia was under pressure from the United States to change its laissez-faire ways and begin to crack down on the traffickers. Reagan vowed that the United States would continue to interdict drugs trafficking, but at the same time, it would fight drugs on all fronts, "taking away drugs from the consumers through increased efforts to diminish the use and demand of drugs and by destroying crops abroad."[55]

Impressive raids followed. From July to November 1986 Bolivia, with the help of the U.S. military, launched a major assault against drug trafficking that became known as Operation Blast Furnace. Several cocaine-producing facilities were destroyed and the supply of cocaine was disrupted for several months. The amount of cocaine seized in raids rose, from just two tons of cocaine in 1981 to twenty-seven tons in 1986, and if statistics were the sole measure of success, it appeared that the forces for good were winning the drug war.

But once again, by 1988, Reagan's last year in office, the United States had little to show for its much-hyped War on Drugs. On the contrary, events and statistics showed that the war effort had been marked by inconsistent leadership, conflicting priorities, bureaucratic infighting, and inadequate resources.

Millions of Americans were still willing to risk jail and public disapprobation in their pursuit and use of illegal drugs. The United States still had an estimated 5.8 million regular users of cocaine, 20 million to 25 million marijuana smokers, and an estimated half a million heroin users, who were spending about $150 billion a year on illegal drugs.[56]

Government reports in 1987 by the General Accounting Office and the House Committee on Government Operations found the United States' drug policy to be "diffuse and overlapping."[57] Reagan's fiscal year 1988 budget request called for the elimination of nearly $1 billon from the budgeted drug war allocations, which meant that the United States' allies in the War on Drugs were not receiving adequate financial support from Uncle Sam.[58] "We're being left to fight the war alone," complained Francisco Bernal, head of Colombia's narcotics bureau in the office of the attorney general. "We're supplying the dead, the country is being destabilized, and what help are we getting?"[59]

By the late 1980s, a small but influential group of distinguished Americans began to criticize the objectives of the War on Drugs. The dissenters came from across the political spectrum and a variety of backgrounds and included economist Milton Friedman, writer and arch conservative William Buckley, Baltimore Mayor Kurt Schmoke, and the editors of the influential *Economist* magazine, among others.

These critics, however, did not sway the leaders of the War on Drugs, who continued to pursue a military solution and optimistically predicted that victory was just around the corner, if only American resolve remained firm and enough resources were applied to the drug problem. They pointed to the statistics that showed increased arrests, overflowing prisons, massive cocaine seizures, the killing or kidnapping of drug kingpins, and declining drug use, and insisted, in the words of drug czar William Bennett, that "the scourge is beginning to end."[60]

The United States did not win one lasting victory against international drug trafficking during the Reagan administration, but this did not deter the next U.S. president, George Bush, from publicly renewing the pledge to wage War on Drugs and continuing the same policy. Bush's pledge reflected the results of public opinion polls showing that the American public wanted their political leaders to get even tougher on illegal drugs and combat the increasing drug-related violence in many American cities. Congress responded to the public mood by adopting measures that further militarized the country's antidrug effort.

The U.S military was given a much broader role, despite continuing opposition from many military leaders, who felt the new policy would divert the armed forces from its primary role of defending U.S interests abroad against such forces as communism and terrorism. Congress approved and Bush appointed a "drug czar" as a kind of top-level commander in the War on Drugs who would have direct access to the president.

The first drug czar, William Bennett, a Democrat and former philosophy professor, revealed his antidrug plan in the summer of 1989. He called for an even tougher stance against the enemy: more federal agents, more prosecutors, more judges to hear more cases, and more federal prisons to hold more drug offenders. Instead of interdicting drugs at the border, Bennett proposed interdicting drugs in the countries where they were grown and on the streets of America where they were consumed. The Bennett plan called for $7 billion a year in funds, with which the czar projected that the U.S. could reduce drug use in the country by 10 percent over the next twenty-five months and by 50 percent in the coming decade.[61] How exactly that would happen was not spelled out.

In unveiling his National Drug Control Strategy in September 1989, Bush endorsed Bennett's plan of action and proposed that 70 percent of the $2.2 billion increase in additional money that was to be allocated to the drug issue over the next several years be spent on law enforcement. Bush also urged Congress to give more military and economic assistance to Andean countries to help stem the flow of cocaine to the United States. "In the past, programs have been hampered by the lack of importance given by this country to the drug issue as a foreign policy concern," Bush declared. "We must develop a broad, meaningful public diplomacy program in a manner that would increase the level of international influence for illicit drugs."[62]

The militarization of the War on Drugs, begun by

Reagan in 1982, reached a climax in the 1989 invasion of Panama and the capture of the country's dictator General Manuel Antonio Noriega, who had been indicted in a U.S. court for alleged involvement in international drug trafficking. The United States reportedly knew about the general's drug-smuggling activities, but had tolerated them because, as a paid employee of the CIA since the late 1960s, he had been a useful intelligence source. With a force of 24,000 troops, the United States launched Operation Just Cause—an invasion of Panama that led to the arrest of the former U.S. ally and his trial in the United States on drug trafficking charges.

One reason for the capture of Noriega was the United States' frustration over the refusal of many countries to extradite suspected drug traffickers to the United States. The United States insisted that extradition was an essential weapon in the War on Drugs, but Colombia, Mexico, Burma, and other source countries considered extradition to be a form of imperialism and an affront to their sovereignty. The legal strategy, moreover, was highly unpopular among the citizens of those countries.

In Colombia, the government of President Virgilio Barco Vargas was seriously considering unilaterally repudiating its 1979 extradition treaty with the United States, when Senator Luis Carlos Galan, presidential candidate for the 1990 Colombian elections and a strong opponent of drug trafficking, was killed at a Bogotá rally on 18 August 1989. Minutes after Galan's killing, Barco made a major television address in which he declared all-out war against the drug traffickers and said that he would begin extradition proceedings for Colombian drug traffickers wanted abroad. Six days later, Colombia changed its extradition policy, and the country's drug traffickers became nervous and angry about the possibility of being extradited to the United States.

The Medellin Cartel's members started calling themselves "the extraditables" and launched a vicious terrorist bombing campaign to force the Colombian government to change its policy. In the week following Barco's declaration, the Cartel exploded twenty small bombs in Bogotá, Colombia's capital, and it began targeting prominent Colombians—and their families—for assassination. By the end of October, there had been 200 bomb attacks that left ten people dead and 160 wounded or injured. [63]

On 6 September 1989 Eduardo Martinez Romero, suspected to be the Medellin Cartel's chief financial officer, was extradited to the United States under Colombia's new extradition policy. Two more members were to be extradited to the United States, but the courts freed them instead in September. Meanwhile, the terrorist attacks continued, culminating on 21 November 1989 with the bombing of a Bogotá-to-Medellin Avianca airlines jet that killed all 107 passengers and crew members aboard. [64] Under the relentless assault from the Medellin cartel, the Colombian government eventually wilted and changed its extradition policy.

By the beginning of the 1990s, the United States had escalated the War on Drugs to an unprecedented level. The country had begun to use its elite special forces, such as the Green Berets, in preemptive strikes against drug-trafficker enclaves in source countries like Peru and Colombia. The justification for such interventions rested on opinions issued by the U.S. Justice Department's Office of Legal Counsel that concluded that U.S military forces could go overseas and arrest drug dealers and other criminals, even without the consent of the host country. [65]

Congress—not just the president—wanted the military to play a more active role in the drug battles. The mood of the legislature was expressed by Representative Larry Hopkins (R-Ky), who told the Pentagon in early 1989, "We are serious about your active role in this war on drugs, even if it means we have to drag you screaming every step of the way." [66]

Bush's search for an effective strategy in the War on Drugs led to his administration's implementation of the so-called Andean Strategy. "The Andean strategy amounted to a broad, triadic program composed of military support, law enforcement advice, and economic assistance for the coca-growing and cocaine-producing countries of Bolivia, Colombia, and Peru," explained Raphael F. Pearl, drug policy analyst. "As first designed, the strategy represented the culmination of more than a decade of U.S. anti-coca efforts in the region. These various programs had been systematically impaired, however, by political instability—evident on occasion in each of the source countries by economic and social inequities, by a lack of will, by corruption, and also by dubious planning by policy makers in Washington, D.C." [67]

To get the support of the Andean countries for his antidrug program and to show that he was serious about his Andean initiative, Bush journeyed to Cartagena in February 1990 for a summit meeting with the leaders of Peru, Colombia, and Bolivia, a move that led to the formation of what has been called "the world's first antidrug cartel." [68] Participating nations at the summit vowed to attack international drug trafficking from every angle—economic, political, and military. Bush pledged to work hard to decrease the demand for drugs in the United States, while the Andean leaders said they would work equally hard to reduce drug-related corruption, strengthen the judiciary, and step up law enforcement efforts against the drug traffickers operating in their countries. The Andean nations urged Bush to create new trade opportunities that would provide more employment opportunities for workers displaced from the cocaine economy. This was sound advice, said many drug policy analysts, for without this kind of assistance, military interdiction would be counterproductive.

By the early 1990s, the Colombian cartels were no longer moving cocaine primarily through their home country to their U.S. and European markets. Instead, they were developing alternative routes through Brazil, Chile, Argentina, and Paraguay. By 1993 drug traffickers had expanded the Latin American distribution network to include Mexico and Central America. [69] In a short time, the amount of drugs the traffickers were able to move was as impressive ever. In one antidrug operation in 1994, for example, Nicaraguan authorities netted 606 pounds of cocaine in an initial raid and then uncovered another 386 pounds in a bakery on the outskirts of Managua, the country's capital. [70] One drug policy analyst described Nicaragua as a "black hole," because so many small planes carrying drugs landed there and the police couldn't trace them any farther. [71]

The lack of law enforcement resources and the poverty and high unemployment rates in those countries, no doubt, has helped create a ready labor market for the drug cartels, making it easy for them to ship drugs through the new distribution routes. In Nicaragua, where the unemployment rate was 54 percent, there were only about six full-time antidrug police in Managua (population 1.3 million) and no resources to patrol the country's Atlantic coast, which the Cali Cartel was using as a transportation point.

The new drug-smuggling distribution network also took advantage of people moving across the U.S.-Mexican border: illegal immigrants, some of whom were willing to make a little extra cash as drug couriers, and tourists, such as vacationing American citizens, who were tempted to smuggle larger shipments of drugs across the border in hidden compartments of their vehicles. With heroin, cocaine, and marijuana pouring into the United States from numerous directions and by every conceivable means of transportation, interdiction could not possibly make a significant dent in the traffic.

By the early 1990s, international drug trafficking had become a far different illicit enterprise than it had been in the early 1980s when President Reagan first declared War on Drugs. Traffickers had shown remarkable flexibility and imagination in responding to the challenge of the increasingly sophisticated interdiction methods of the world's biggest user of illegal drugs.

When U.S. law enforcement authorities had some success with the interdiction in South Florida, the traffickers changed their strategy, using trucks, private vehicles, and tractor trailers to smuggle the cocaine across the southwest border of the United States. The job of interdicting this movement of drugs involved guarding a 3,000-mile border that had thirty ports of entry through which daily passed 640,000 pedestrians and 240,000 cars, trucks and other vehicles. [72] By 1996 the U.S. government estimated that 70 percent of the cocaine smuggled into the United States came across the U.S.-Mexican border. [73] Meanwhile, traffickers were also using the longer, more expensive eastern shipping routes through the Caribbean on to the mid-Atlantic and the New England coast. [74] Given the billions of dollars at stake, the smugglers were more than willing to pay for the larger vessels and the sophisticated electronic equipment they needed.

By the time the 1992 presidential elections got rolling in the United States, the consensus of opinion among drug analysts was that the Bush administration's War on Drugs strategy, which focused primarily on supply and looked for a military solution, had not worked. The policy had also done little to alleviate drug-induced corruption, terrorism, and violence in the many countries that had been drawn into the War on Drugs.

During the 1992 presidential elections, Bill Clinton saw the opening provided by the disillusionment with the War on Drugs and pledged to change U.S.

policy, promising the American people that he would combine tough law enforcement while expanding antidrug treatment and prevention programs. Clinton also announced that he would shift the emphasis away from the interdiction of drugs towards a policy that would help countries fight drug trafficking both economically and militarily.

It was becoming obvious to America's allies, however, that war as usual was not working, and they started calling for a global effort to combat international drug trafficking, pointing out that the dynamics of the illegal trade cut across national boundaries and involved criminal organizations that were now operating like multinational corporations in the cutthroat world of international trade. In December 1996 members of the Organization of American States reached an agreement in Montevideo, Uruguay, that ratified a hemispheric antidrug plan. "This is a strategy that can lead to the reduction of drug consumption and supply through international multilateral strategies," said Diego Cardona, foreign affairs adviser to Colombian President Ernesto Samper.[75] The more than 100 countries around the world that were connected in some way to international drug trafficking would need to cooperate more and rethink strategy to combat the resources, money, and power of the international drug traffickers.

Yet, the United States has shown no indication that it will abandon its current policy initiatives. Uncle Sam continues to pressure producing countries to destroy drug crops at the source, wipe out drug laboratories wherever they exist, and help it intercept drugs before they enter the country. In light of the United States' current antidrug policy, foreign countries continue to view the superpower's antinarcotic policy as unfair, complaining that Uncle Sam has to make an effort to solve its own drug problems and stop blaming other countries that have far fewer resources. Meanwhile, the War on Drugs goes on without end.

End Notes

1. AFP. "Los Drugs Ganan Terreno en Europa." *El Tiempo* (Bogotá, Colombia), 9 October 1996; Alzate, Jorge Cardona. "Catarsis de una Epidemia." *El Espectador* (Bogota, Colombia), 20 October 1996; "Drugs $400 Billion; Second Only to Arms Trade." *Chicago Tribune*, 15 December 1994; Keating, Michael. "Breaking the Taboo on Drugs." *World Today* (July 1997): 178 (2pp.).

2. For background on the Opium Wars, *see* Stelle, Charles C. *America and the Chinese Opium Trade in the Nineteenth Century.* North Stratford, NH: Ayer, 1981; Lodwick, Kathleen L. *Crusades against Opium: Protestant Missionaries in China.* Lexington, KY: University Press of Kentucky, 1996; and Robson, Michael. *Opium: The Poisoned Poppy.* New York: Weatherhill, 1994.

3. Morgan, H. Wayne. *Drugs in America: A Social History, 1800–1980.* Syracuse, NY: Syracuse University Press, 1981, pp. 10–28.

4. Weir, William. *In the Shadow of the Dope Fiend.* New Haven, CT: Archon, 1995, p. 9.

5. Morgan, H. Wayne. *Drugs in America: A Social History, 1800–1980.* Syracuse, NY: Syracuse University Press, 1981, p. 16.

6. Stewart, Gail B. *Drug Trafficking.* San Diego, CA: Lucent, 1990, p. 11.

7. Morgan, H. Wayne. *Drugs in America: A Social History, 1800–1980.* Syracuse, NY: Syracuse University Press, 1981, p. 94.

8. *Ibid.*, p. 29.

9. *Ibid.*, p. 30.

10. President's Commission on Organized Crime. *America's Habit: Drug Trafficking and Organized Crime.* Washington DC: U.S. Government Printing Office, 1986, p. 195.

11. Morgan, H. Wayne. *Drugs in America: A Social History, 1800–1980.* Syracuse, NY: Syracuse University Press, 1981, p. 86.

12. President's Commission on Organized Crime. *America's Habit: Drug Trafficking and Organized Crime.* Washington, DC: U.S. Government Printing Office, 1986, p. 195.

13. Morgan, H. Wayne. *Drugs in America: A Social History, 1800–1980.* Syracuse, NY: Syracuse University Press, 1981, p. 30.

14. President's Commission on Organized Crime. *America's Habit: Drug Trafficking and Organized Crime.* Washington, DC: U.S. Government Printing Office, 1986, p. 195.

15. *Ibid.*, p. 196.

16. Kenney, Denis J., and James O. Finekenauer. *Organized Crime in America.* London: International Thompson, 1990, p. 144.

17. Traub, James. *The Billion Dollar Connection: The International Drug Trade.* New York: Julian Messner, 1983, p. 6.

18. Jonnes, Jill. "Founding Father: One Man Invented the Modern Narcotics Industry." *American Heritage* (February-March 1993): 48–49.

19. Walsh, Stephen. "Some Aspects of the International Drug Trade." In Dennis Rowe, ed. *International Drug Traffick-*

ing. Chicago: University of Illinois, International Criminal Justice, 1988, p. 102.

20. Moorhead, Alan Hovell. "International Narcotics Control, 1939–1946." *Foreign Policy Reports*, 1 July 1946, pp. 94–103.

21. Morgan. *Drugs in America*, p. 144.

22. Weir, William. *In the Shadow of the Dope Fiend*. New Haven, CT: Archon, 1995, p. 152.

23. Traub, James. *The Billion Dollar Connection: The International Drug Trade*. New York: Julian Messner, 1983, pp. 26–27.

24. McCoy, Alfred J. *The Politics of Heroin: CIA Complicity in the Global Trade*. Brooklyn, NY: Marlow, 1991.

25. Strong, Simon. *Whitewash: Pablo Escobar and the Cocaine Wars*. London: Macmillan, 1995, p. 37.

26. Chepesiuk, Ron. *Sixties Radicals, Then and Now: Candid Conversations with Those Who Shaped an Era*. Jefferson, NC: McFarland, 1995, p. 305.

27. President's Commission on Organized Crime. *America's Habit: Drug Trafficking and Organized Crime*. Washington, DC: U.S. Government Printing Office, 1986, p. 215.

28. Inglis, Brian. *The Forbidden Game: A Social History of Drugs*. New York: Scribner's, 1975, pp. 198–199.

29. President's Commission on Organized Crime. *America's Habit: Drug Trafficking and Organized Crime*. Washington, DC: U.S. Government Printing Office, 1986, p. 220.

30. *Ibid*. p. 229.

31. Morgan, H. Wayne. *Drugs in America: A Social History, 1800–1980*. Syracuse, NY: Syracuse University Press, 1981, p. 161.

32. Inglis, Brian. *The Forbidden Game: A Social History of Drugs*. New York: Scribner's, 1975, pp. 188–189.

33. Sterling, Claire. *Octopus: The Long Reach of the International Sicilian Mafia*. New York: W. W. Norton, 1990, p. 147.

34. Lyman, Michael D. *Gangland: Drug Trafficking by Organized Criminals*. Springfield, IL: Charles C. Thomas, 1989, p. 43; President's Commission on Organized Crime. *America's Habit: Drug Trafficking and Organized Crime*. Washington, DC: U.S. Government Printing Office, 1986, pp. 11–12.

35. Lyman, Michael D. *Gangland: Drug Trafficking by Organized Criminals*. Springfield, IL: Charles C. Thomas, 1989, p. 41; President's Commission on Organized Crime. *America's Habit: Drug Trafficking and Organized Crime*. Washington, DC: U.S. Government Printing Office, 1986, pp. 111–112.

36. President's Commission on Organized Crime. *America's Habit: Drug Trafficking and Organized Crime*. Washington, DC: U.S. Government Printing Office, 1986, pp. 77–78.

37. De Grazia, Jessica. *DEA: The War against Drugs*. London: BBC Books, 1991, p. 13.

38. Traub, James. *The Billion Dollar Connection: The International Drug Trade*. New York: Julian Messner, 1983, p. 27.

39. *Ibid*., p. 9.

40. Karnow, Stanley. *Vietnam: A History*. New York: Viking, 1983, p. 631.

41. For an in-depth study of this theme, see McCoy, Alfred W. *The Politics of Heroin: CIA Complicity in the Global Drug Trade*. Brooklyn, NY: Marlow, 1991, pp. 145–146.

42. Nash, Jay Robert. *World Encyclopedia of Organized Crime*. New York: Marlow, 1994, pp. 145–146.

43. Inglis, Brian. *The Forbidden Game: A Social History of Drugs*. New York: Scribner's, 1975, p. 196.

44. Weir, William. *In the Shadow of the Dope Fiend*. New Haven, CT: Archon, 1995, p. 64.

45. McCoy, Alfred W. "What War on Drugs? The CIA Connection." *Progressive* (July 1991): 24–26, at 26.

46. Weir, William. *In the Shadow of the Dope Fiend*. New Haven, CT: Archon, 1995, p. 116.

47. McCoy, Alfred J. "What War on Drugs? The CIA Connection." *Progressive* (July 1991): 24–26, at 26.

48. Lamour, Catherine, and Michael R. Lamberti. *The International Connection: Opium from Growers to Pushers*. New York: Pantheon, 1974, p. 60.

49. *Ibid*.

50. President's Commission on Organized Crime. *America's Habit: Drug Trafficking and Organized Crime*. Washington, DC: U.S. Government Printing Office, 1986, p. 237.

51. McCoy, Alfred J., and Allan A. Block. "U.S. Narcotics Policy: An Anatomy of Failure." In McCoy, Alfred W., and Allan A. Block, eds. *War on Drugs: Studies in the Failure of U.S. Narcotics Policy*. Boulder, CO: Westview, 1992, p. 14.

52. Traub, James. *The Billion Dollar Connection: The International Drug Trade*. New York: Julian Messner, 1983, p. 76.

53. President's Commission on Organized Crime. *America's Habit: Drug Trafficking and Organized Crime*. Washington, DC: U.S. Government Printing Office, 1986, p. 229.

54. "Drug War Begins." *C.Q. Researcher*, 19 March 1993, p. 257.

55. President's Commission on Organized Crime. *America's Habit: Drug Trafficking and Organized Crime*. Washington, DC: U.S. Government Printing Office, 1986, (Appendix), p. 9.

56. Bagley, Bruce. "The New Hundred Years War? U.S. National Security on the War on Drugs." *Journal of Interamerican Studies and World Affairs* (Spring 1988): 67.

57. *Ibid*., p. 168.

58. *Ibid*., p. 167.

59. *Ibid*., p. 173.

60. Inciardi, James A. "American Drug Policy and the Le-

galization Debate." In James Inciardi. *The Drug Legalization Debate.* Newbury Park, CA: Sage, 1991, p. 85.

61. Klare, Michael T. "Fighting Drugs with the Military." *Nation,* 1 January 1990, p. 8.

62. Nash, Jay Robert. *World Encyclopedia of Organized Crime.* New York: Marlow, 1994, p. 159.

63. *Ibid.*, p. 160.

64. Isenburg, David. "Military Options in the War on Drugs." In Bruce Bagley and Alan Block, eds., *War on Drugs: Studies in the Failure of U.S. Narcotics Policy.* Boulder, CO: Westview, 1992, p. 2.

65. *Ibid.*, p. 24.

66. Bagley, Bruce. "The New Hundred Years War? U.S. National Security and the War on Drugs." *Journal of Interamerican Studies and World Affairs* (Spring 1988): 171.

67. Baker, James. "Narcotics: Threat to Global Stability." *U.S. Department of State Dispatch,* 3 September 1990, p. 15.

68. *Ibid.*, p. 16.

69. Farah, Douglas. "Drug Traffickers Build Central American Route to U.S." *Washington Post,* 28 March 1993.

70. Dye, David R. "Nicaraguan Cocaine Bust Reveals New Cartel Route." *Christian Science Monitor,* 26 January 1994.

71. *Ibid.*

72. U.S. General Accounting Office. *Drug Control: Threats and Roles of Explosives and Narcotics Technology: Briefing Report to Congressional Requesters.* Washington, DC: U.S. Government Printing Office, 1986, p. 84.

73. *Ibid.*

74. President's Commission on Organized Crime. *America's Habit: Drug Trafficking and Organized Crime.* Washington, DC: U.S. Government Printing Office, 1986, p. 97.

75. "New Drug Strategy Needed." *Colombian Post,* 18–24 November 1996.

"We need to break the grower to user chains which stretch across five continents. To do so we must have a comprehensive program of international control."

—*Walter J. Stoessel, former U.S. secretary of state*

"It's like hitting mercury with a hammer."

—*U.S. State Department official*

"Stop the traffic on the ground and they take to the air. Control the air and they go by sea. It's a battle with no end."

—*Enrique Salgado Cordero, chief of the Mexican Police*

"The only law the narcoterrorists don't break is the law of supply and demand."

—*Virgilio Barco Vargas, former president of Colombia*

A

Abbell, Michael (c. 1939–)

A criminal defense lawyer indicted by the U.S. government along with two other lawyers for allegedly being members of a racketeering enterprise that centered on the Rodriguez-Orejuela branch of the Cali Cartel.

Abbell was the chief of the U.S. Justice Department's Office of International Affairs in the early 1980s. He left the Justice Department in 1984 with a waver of potential conflict of interest that allowed him to represent suspected drug traffickers Gilberto and Miguel Rodriguez Orejuela and Jose Santacruz Londono. The indictment charged that Abbell took false statements from cartel figures, accepted drug funds for attorney fees, and falsified documents.

Criminal defense attorney William C. Morgan was also named in the indictment, for, among other charges, revealing the identity of a government informant to a client. The informant was later murdered. Criminal defense lawyer Donald Ferguson, a former U.S. attorney in Miami in the 1990s, was also indicted, and he pled guilty to charges of conspiracy to obstruct justice and money laundering and agreed to cooperate with the government.

If convicted, Morgan and Abbell faced life sentences and the possibility of having their assets seized by the federal government as profits of the drug trade. Legal experts said the verdict also would have serious implications for the U.S. criminal defense bar. "Moran and Abbell are charged with being a part of a drug conspiracy in connection with their representation of clients," said Robert Fogelnest, a New York City-based lawyer and a past president of the National Association of Criminal Defense Lawyers. "The case may very well define the scope of what constitutes proper representation in drug cases." (Chepesiuk 1997)

In 1998 Moran and Abbell were found guilty, but Moran became a fugitive after he was last seen on July 17 in the Miami federal courthouse. Moran and Abbell's case was the highest profile example of a legal trend of the past decade: the U.S. government's decision to aggressively pursue lawyers whom they believe have crossed the line from simply representing their criminal clients to actually aiding and abetting them. The trend has disturbed many criminal defense lawyers, who question the government's move and tactics and charge that law enforcement is unfairly targeting and intimidating the criminal defense bar in an attempt to frighten lawyers away from representing drug suspects.

See also: Assets Forfeiture; Cali Cartel; Moran, William C.

References: Chepesiuk, Ron. 1997. "Guilty By Association." *Student Lawyer.* (December): 35+.

McGee, Jim. 1985. Ex Prosecutors Indicted in Cali Cartel Probe. *Washington Post,* 4 July.

Navarro, Mireya. 1998. Lawyers Weigh Effect of Conviction of Missing Colleague. *New York Times,* 9 August.

Abello Silva, Jose Raphael (c. 1954–)

Colombian drug trafficker who was arrested in Bogotá, Colombia, in October 1989 for a 1987 drug conspiracy indictment filed in federal court in the northern district of Oklahoma. Colombia extradited Abello Silva to the United States, where a federal district court in Tulsa, Oklahoma, tried and convicted him on two counts of conspiracy to bring drugs into the United States and sentenced him to 30 years in prison. Following his extradition to the United States, federal prosecutors described the drug trafficker as the number four man in the Medellin Cartel and said his trial was "one of the most significant narcotics prosecutions in the country." (Frieder 1990)

See also: Extradition
Reference: Frieder, Richard R. "The Abello Conspiracy." 1990. *ABA Journal*. December.

Acosta, Pablo (d. 1987)

American drug kingpin who was a criminal power along a 200-mile stretch of the United States—Mexican border, across from Big Bend County, Texas. Acosta became the mentor and business partner of Amado Carrillo Fuentes and established a working relationship with Colombian drug cartels. At his peak in the mid-1980s, Acosta controlled as much as 60 percent of the cocaine trafficked into the United States. Acosta cultivated a Robin Hood image by distributing money to the poor and contributing generously to civic projects, while using his wealth and power to corrupt local police and officials. His entrepreneurial skill and iron grip on his criminal organization began to slip when he himself became a cocaine addict. An international narcotics strike force that included FBI agents tracked Acosta down in 1987 and killed him.

See also: Carrillo Fuentes, Amado; Cocaine
Reference: Poppa, Terrance E. 1990. *Drug Lord: The Life and Death of a Mexican Kingpin*.

Air America

Charter airplane company that specialized in providing transport for U.S. government undercover operations, including those believed to be conducted by the CIA, during the Vietnam War, particularly in the 1960s. Many experts on international drug trafficking, in fact, contend that Air America transported opium and heroin for the agency during the Vietnam War. Sensitive to the drug trafficking charge, Air America claimed that it had installed a security program that was designed to prevent the smuggling of narcotics on their aircraft. Critics, however, remain doubtful. Air America is still in existence.

See also: Carter, James Earl; Heroin; Opium; United States Central Intelligence Agency
References: Freemantle, Brian. 1985. *The Fix*.
Lamour, Catherine, and Michael R. Lamberti. 1974. *International Connection*.

Alternative Development

According to the United Nations International Drug Control Program (UNDCP), alternative development can be defined as "a process to reduce, eliminate, or prevent the production of illicit crops through systematically designed rural development measures." (United Nations, 1997) Unlike crop eradication, which simply tries to wipe out illegally grown crops, alternative development attempts to ensure that local people who grow drug crops have other sources of income generation. Central to alternative development programs are crop substitution programs, which attempt to get farmers to stop growing illegal drug crops and grow legal ones, such as maize or potatoes. The UNDCP points out that "the reduction of rural poverty, particularly through sustainable natural resource management, is a typical claim by alternative development proponents." (United Nations, 1997)

See also: Associate High Valleys Project; Bush, George Herbert Walker; Crop Substitution; Eradication; Operation Blast Furnace; United Nations Food and Agriculture Organization
References: Clawson, Patrick, and Rennselaer, W. Lee. 1996. *The Andean Cocaine Industry*.
United Nations International Drug Control Program. 1997. *World Drug Report*.

American-Chinese Commercial Treaty of 1880

This measure and subsequent legislation attempted to put an end to opium smoking in the United States by prohibiting Chinese immigrants from importing opium into the country. The treaty was also an example of the United States' readiness to take action beyond its borders in order to eradicate opium smoking within the country. This treaty and subsequent legislation, however, "did not attain their objectives. American citizens continued to import opium that could be smoked, and they distributed it to Chinese people, who, in turn, sold it to both Chinese immigrants and American citizens, who had become addicted." (President's Commission on Organized Crime, 1986)

See also: Opium
Reference: President's Commission on Organized Crime. 1986. *America's Habit: Drug Trafficking and Organized Crime.*

American Civil Liberties Union (ACLU)

Founded in 1920, the American Civil Liberties Union (ACLU) champions the rights set forth in the Bill of Rights of the U.S. Constitution involving freedom of speech, due process of law, and fair trials. The ACLU's activities include litigation, advocacy, and public education. The organization maintains that the Fourth Amendment has become the principal casualty of the government's War on Drugs and has opposed such law and order tactics as asset forfeiture, wiretapping, drug testing, and the passing of laws that allow police to search automobiles stopped for minor traffic violations.

See also: Asset Forfeiture; Drug Testing
Reference: ACLU website at http://www.aclu.org.

American Council on Drug Education (U.S.)

Founded in 1977, the American Council on Drug Education (ACDE) is an independent nonprofit organization dedicated to the elimination of drug abuse through the shaping of societal and individual attitudes and the reinforcement of appropriate behaviors. Upon request, it will provide print and audiovisual materials on the abuse of marijuana, cocaine, and other drugs and respond to specific questions about drugs and drug prevention programming and intervention. The ACDE claims to reach more than 200 million people through the print, film, and broadcast media.

See also: Heroin
Reference: ACDE website at http://www.acde.org.

American Express Bank International

In 1993 a U.S. grand jury indicted two former employees of American Express Bank International for their alleged role in laundering some $30 million in drug profits. The 18-count federal indictment charged that Antonio Giraldi, a senior vice president in the Bank's Miami office, and Lourdes Reategui, a former official in the Bank's branch office in Beverly Hills, California, helped launder money from a northern Mexican drug cartel headed by Juan Garcia Abrego. The indictment accused the two of setting up international bank accounts for Ricardo Aguirre, a gas station owner from Matamoros, Mexico, who was named as a key money launderer for Abrego's drug organization. In August 1994 Giraldi was sentenced to 20 years in prison.

See also: Bush, George Herbert Walker; Cocaine; Garcia Abrego, Juan; Gulf Cartel; Money Laundering
References: "Banker Given Twenty Years in Drug Money Case." 1994. *Charlotte Observer*, 13 August.
Cole, Laurie P. 1993. "Bankers at American Express Affiliate Face Money-Laundering Investigation." *Wall Street Journal*, 8 November.

Amezcua Contreras, Jesus

Operating out of Guadalajara, Mexico, Jesus Amezcua Contreras, with the support of his brothers Adan and Luis, heads the drug trafficking organization that the Drug Enforcement Administration says is the world's largest supplier of ephedrine and producer of methamphetamine. In congressional testimony in March 1997 DEA administrator Thomas Constantine said, "With a growing methamphetamine abuse program in the United States, this organization's activities impact on a number of the major population centers in the U.S." (Senate Committee on Foreign Relations 1998)

The Amezcua Contreras organization uses contacts in Thailand and India to obtain large quantities of the chemical ephedrine, a necessary ingredient in methamphetamines, supplying it to methamphetamine laboratories in both Mexico and the United States.

In the fall of 1998 Jesus and Luis Amezcua Contreras were arrested by Mexican authorities in separate raids. Mariano Heran Salvetti, Mexico's top antidrug official, said, "This is the most important blow to the drug trade so far this year in Mexico." (Mexico Arrests Break Meth Cartel 1998, 20)

See also: Juarez Cartel; Methamphetamine; Precursor Chemicals
References: "Mexican Arrest Breaks Up Meth Cartel." 1998. *International Drug Report*. Fall.

U.S. Senate Committee on Foreign Relations. 1998. *International Organized Crime Syndicates and Their Impact on the United States: Hearings before the Subcommittee on Western Hemisphere, Peace Corps, Narcotics and Terrorism*, 26 February (statement of Thomas A. Constantine, U.S. Director, DEA.

Amphetamine

Amphetamine's therapeutic possibilities were first investigated in 1927, and the drug was synthesized in Germany in 1887. The first medical product containing amphetamine, the benzedrine inhaler, was marketed in 1936 to help asthmatics breathe and widen bronchial passages. Amphetamines first became available in tablet form in 1937, and were used extensively during World War II by Japan, the United States, Great Britain, and Germany to help troops and civilians in some countries fight fatigue and maintain alertness and energy levels. Medical use of amphetamines increased during the 1950s and 1960s, but the Controlled Substance Act of 1970 placed restrictions on the manufacture, distribution, and use of amphetamines.

The effect of the drug is similar to cocaine, meaning it can relieve fatigue, reduce the need for sleep, increase energy, and, in general, bring about physical and psychological exhilaration.

The Drug Identification Bible defines amphetamine as "a term given to a category of stimulant drugs having similar chemical formulas: amphetamine sulphate, amphetamine asparate, and dextroamphetamine sulphate, etc. These forms vary in their potency and manufacturing process." (Drug Identification Bible, p. 631)

See also: Ecstasy; Methamphetamine; Preludin; Ritalin; Synthetic Drugs; United Nations Convention on Psychotropic Substances; United States Comprehensive Crime Control Act of 1970; United States Drug Abuse Control Amendments of 1965; World War II; Yakuza
References: Marnell, Tim, ed. 1997. *Drug Identification Bible*. O'Brien, Robert, and Sidney Cohen. 1984. *The Encyclopedia of Drug Abuse*.

Analgesic

A drug used medically to relieve pain without causing a loss of consciousness. The most common controlled analgesic is codeine.

See also :Cocaine
Reference: O'Brien, Robert, and Sidney Cohen. 1984. *The Encyclopedia of Drug Abuse*.

Andean Strategy
See Bush, George Herbert Walker

Andean Trade Preference Act
See Bush, George Herbert Walker

Anderson, Robert A.

Anderson was a former U.S. Secretary of the Treasury, naval secretary, and deputy secretary of defense during the Dwight D. Eisenhower presidential administration (1952–1960). Upon retiring from government service, Anderson sat on the boards of directors of a number of major corporations and served as a consultant to the Reverend Sun Myung Moon's Unification Church. He also operated an illegal offshore bank in Antigua, known as the Commerce Exchange Bank and Trust, which not only lost $4.4 million of its investors' money, but laundered large amounts of cash for drug traffickers. In June 1987, Anderson was sentenced to one month in prison, five months of house arrest, and five months of probation for tax evasion and operating an illegal offshore bank.

See also: Offshore Financial Institutions
Reference: Ehrenfeld, Rachel. 1992. *Evil Money*.

Angel Dust
See PCP

Anslinger, Harry (1893–1975)

Commissioner of the United States Bureau of Narcotics from 1930 to 1962 and a major, but controversial, figure in the history of the United States' War on Drugs. Many admired Anslinger for his zealous attitude toward wiping out illegal drug trafficking. His critics deplored his harsh, unsympathetic attitude toward drug addicts.

Anslinger worked for the Ordinance Division of the U.S. War Department in 1917 and then joined the U.S. State Department in the Netherlands. After World War I he worked in the counselor service in Amsterdam, Venice, and the Bahamas, where he collaborated with local officials to combat the illegal alcohol trade with the United States during the 1920s. He then joined the Foreign Control Division of the Prohibition Unit before becoming commissioner of the United States Bureau of Narcotics in 1930.

President Kennedy presents retired Commissioner of Narcotics, H. J. Anslinger, an outstanding record citation at the White House, 27 September 1962. (Corbis-Bettmann/UPI)

During his tenure as commissioner, Anslinger was a hard-line advocate of harsh penalties for the sale and possession of all narcotic drugs and was instrumental in the passage of the Marijuana Tax Act of 1937. After the Act's passage, marijuana was virtually banned from medical practice, and its name was deleted from the Pharmacopeia of the United States. Presidents Herbert Hoover and Franklin D. Roosevelt named Anslinger a delegate to conferences on narcotic drugs that were held in several European cities during the 1930s.

During World War II, Anslinger tried to tie American drug use and abuse to Japanese aggression by claiming that much of the heroin coming into the United States could be traced to factories in Japan.

On 6 June 1946, Anslinger was appointed the U.S. representative to the United Nations Commission on Narcotic Drugs, which was organized to assume the work of the League of Nations Opium Advisory Commission. Anslinger continued to dominate the U.S. government's position toward illegal drugs until his retirement in 1962, and he remained a controversial figure throughout his tenure.

In assessing the legacy of Anslinger, historian H. Wayne Morgan wrote, "Supporters saw him as a stalwart opponent of the insidious drug traffic that threatened the nation's vitality. His belief in strong law enforcement won their approval, as did his opposition to what they saw as soft-minded theorists and humanitarians. Critics saw Anslinger as a persecutor of hapless addicts, foe of enlightened medical and psychological reforms and a builder of a tyrannical bureaucratic empire." (Morgan, 1981, 119)

See also: League Of Nations; Marijuana; Marijuana Tax Act of 1937; Prohibition; United States Bureau Of Narcotics
References: Courtwright, David T. 1982. *Dark Paradise*. Morgan, H. Wayne. 1981. *Drugs in America*.

Arce Gomez, Luis (c. 1929–)

A colonel in the Bolivian army who played an important role in the so-called 1980 Cocaine Coup that brought to power General Luis Garcia Meza with the backing of the country's leading and powerful coca growers and cocaine processors and smugglers. Arce Gomez also reportedly played a role in getting drug smugglers released from prison and enlisting them in a bodyguard unit for his cousin, drug kingpin Roberto Suarez Gomez, which was led by infamous Nazi Klaus Barbie. Arce Gomez was eventually arrested and convicted for his role in promoting Bolivia's drug trade and extradited to the United States, where he is expected to spend the rest of his life in prison.

See also: Extradition; Suarez Gomez, Roberto
References: Hargreaves, Claire. 1992. *Snowbirds*.
Weir, William. 1995. *In the Shadow of the Dope Fiend*.

Arellano Felix, Ramon (1964–)

Ramon and his brothers Benjamin, Francisco Javier, and Francisco Rafael head the Tijuana cartel, Mexico's most violent drug ring. Interestingly, the Arellano brothers are nephews of another noted drug trafficker, Miguel Felix Gallardo.

The cartel transports multiton loads of cocaine, marijuana, heroin, and methamphetamine into California from Tijuana, and the joint FBI-DEA task force in San Diego believes that gang members launder hundreds of thousands of dollars in drug profits annually from its U.S. operation, which has expanded in recent years into the Midwest and New York City.

In 1997 Ramon was charged with drug conspiracy in a sealed federal indictment. Meanwhile, the U.S. State Department posted a $2 million reward for Ramon's capture and conviction. This did not stop the Arellano Felix organization from posting a contract for the murder of a police officer—any police officer—in San Diego county, U.S.A., according to U.S. officials.

Ramon is also wanted in Mexico for alleged complicity in the May 1993 assassination of Cardinal Juan Jesus Posada Ocampo, and he is believed responsible for killing several top Mexican officials, including Ernesto Ibarra Santes, the head of Tijuana's federal judicial police. Ramon is also linked to the killing of 19 people near the U.S. border on 17 September 1998. Reports indicate that the victims were killed because Ramon Arellano Felix and other leaders of the Tijuana cartel were angry at a rival drug dealer who refused to pay them money owed in a marijuana deal.

See also: Cocaine; Felix Gallardo, Miguel Angel; Heroin; Logan Heights Calle 30; Marijuana; Methamphetamine; Posada Ocampo, Juan Jesus; Tijuana Cartel
References: Downie, Andrew. 1998. "Tijuana Massacre Traced To Drug Deal Gone Bad Between Rival Gangs." *Houston Chronicle*, 11 November.
Sniffen, Michael J. 1997. "U.S. To Post Reward for Drug Kingpin." *Seattle Times*, 24 September.
U.S. Senate Committee on Foreign Relations. 1998. *International Organized Crime Syndicates and Their Impact on the United States: Hearings before the Subcommittee on Western Hemisphere, Peace Corps, Narcotics and Terrorism*, 26 February (statement of Thomas A. Constantine, Director, DEA).

Arizabaleta-Arzayuz, Phanor (c. 1940–)

A top member of the Cali Cartel who has been accused of kidnaping, extortion, and processing and shipping tons of cocaine to the United States. He faces kidnapping charges in Colombia and is a fugitive from federal authorities in the eastern district of Louisiana, where he is wanted for a 1989 incident involving the seizure of 275 kilos of cocaine. He surrendered to Colombian authorities in Bogotá on 8 July 1995.

See also: Cali Cartel; Cocaine
Reference: "Six Top Colombian Traffickers Still at Large." 1995. Reuters. 10 June.

Arlacchi, Pino (1951–)

On 1 September 1997 Arlacchi was appointed Director General of the United Nations Office of Drug Abuse Control and Crime Prevention in Vienna. He had long been an advocate for the United Nations in the field of drug control.

Born in Gino Tauro, Reggio Calabria, Italy, on 21 February 1951 Arlacchi is a recognized expert on organized crime and has published several books and articles on the subject, including *Mafia Business: The Mafia Ethic and the Spirit of Capitalism*, 1987. Before officially joining the United Nations, Arlacchi worked in various capacities, as a university professor, a senior adviser to Italy's Ministry of the Interior, and a member of the Italian senate, among others. In 1989 he became president of the International Association for the Study of Organized Crime.

See also: United Nations International Drug Control Program

References: Arlacchi, Pino. 1987. *The Mafia Ethic and the Spirit of Capitalism.*
Wren, Christopher. 1998. "U.N. Aide Would Fight Drug with Better Life For Growers." *New York Times,* 7 June.

Assets Forfeiture

The U.S. government has determined that an effective way to fight drug trafficking is to seize the assets used by drug traffickers to facilitate the trade. In 1984 Congress inserted a section in the Comprehensive Crime Control Act that now allows for the civil forfeiture of a broad range of property, including residences, taverns, apartment and office buildings, undeveloped land, and improvements built on land. In 1985 the U.S. Department of Justice created the National Assets Seizure and Forfeiture Fund, which by 1990 had grown to $500 million. By that year, an additional $1.4 billion in real and personal property had been seized and was awaiting forfeiture. In the next five years, the Department almost doubled this intake.

Asset forfeiture, however, has raised questions about drug war tactics because it appears to be in conflict with the Fifth Amendment's protection against seizing property without due process of law. It has also been criticized as a graphic example of how federal and state government power could be widely abused. To cite one example: In 1993 Richard Lyle Austin was convicted of cocaine possession with intent to distribute and sentenced to seven years in prison by a South Dakota court. Although the offense in South Dakota could lead to a fine of $10,000 maximum, the court assessed Austin a fine 40 to 50 times larger. Moreover, the federal government confiscated Austin's mobile home and auto body shop, which was appraised at $400,000.

The federal government has confiscated property even in cases in which the owner was ignorant of the illegal use to which the property was put and even when no criminal charges were filed. The U.S. House Judiciary Committee has noted that in more than 80 percent of the civic asset forfeiture cases the property owner is not charged with a crime. Nevertheless, the government can keep the seized property. In December 1993 the U.S. Supreme Court gave a ruling that guaranteed owners the right to protest the prop-

erty seizure in court before it is confiscated. In an editorial, *The Christian Science Monitor* noted that the closeness of the 5–4 decision indicates "both the reluctance to weaken an anti-crime measure that has been at least somewhat successful, and the acknowledgment that seizure by law enforcement agencies of assets even suspected to be contraband may have been carried out in some instances with too little regard for basic civil liberties." ("Drugs and Civil Rights," 16 December 1993)

By the mid-1990s, many federal and local government agencies had done well with the cash obtained from forfeiture, using it for staff, equipment, and sometimes even for basic operating expenses. A 1992 U.S. General Accounting Office study revealed that one police department relied on forfeiture for 10 percent of its budget.

The U.S. Supreme Court has also ruled that the government's right to forfeiture extends to drug assets needed or used by a defendant to pay attorneys' fees. Thus, since the 1980s the government has used forfeiture laws to go after the lawyers of drug traffickers in an effort to destroy their criminal organizations.

In 1996 the U.S. Supreme Court ruled that the government may prosecute drug dealers and seize their property without violating the Fifth Amendment ban on double jeopardy. The decision was viewed as a victory for federal prosecutors in the War on Drugs.

Critics have charged that forfeiture may make it difficult for defendants in drug cases to pay fees to their attorneys, thus preventing them from receiving a fair trial. Many defendants in drug cases, moreover, have been able to negotiate lighter sentences by giving up hidden property or agreeing not to challenge forfeiture in court. Groups like the American Civil Liberties Union and the National Association of Criminal Defense lawyers have said that the practice favors the successful, powerful criminal over the lesser one and is injurious to the American legal system.

See also: Abbell, Michael; American Civil Liberties Union; Cocaine; Common Sense For Drug Policy; Moran, William C.; United States Crime Control Act of 1984; United States Crime Control Act of 1990; United States Marshal Service; Zero Policy Program
References: Chepesiuk, Ron. 1999. *Hard Target.*
"Drugs and Civil Rights," *Christian Science Monitor,* December 1993.

Colombian troops inspect the residence of Gonzalo Rodriguez Gacha, suspected leader of the Medellin Cartel, 20 August 1989. The ranch was seized after Colombian president Virgilio Barco passed tough new laws to combat drug trafficking. (David Robbins/Corbis)

Ivins, Molly. 1998. "War on Drugs Makes Some Cops Act Like Criminals." *Sacramento Bee*, 6 September.

McMurry, Kelly. 1996. "Supreme Court Upholds Civil Forfeiture in Drug Cases." *Trial*, 4 August.

Associate High Valleys Project

The Associate High Valleys (AHV) is an area adjacent to the Chapare Province, a major coca growing area of Bolivia. The AHV project is an attempt to stop the movement of migrant workers into the Chapare, where they become drug crop farmers, by instituting a series of development projects in the AHV to increase economic opportunities for the local population. The project has been modestly funded and has focused on making farm land available through irrigation and better soil management.

See also: Chapare Province (Peru)
Reference: Riley, Kevin. 1990. *Snow Job.*

B

Bandidos

Established in 1966, this motorcycle gang expanded in the 1970s to recruit members as far away as South Dakota and Washington State. Today, the gang has approximately 500 members and a network of 3,000 associates. United States law enforcement authorities report that the Bandidos are heavily involved in the manufacture, distribution, and sale of methamphetamine.

See also: Methamphetamine
Reference: Miller, Gary J. 1997. *Drugs and the Law*.

Bank of Commerce and Credit International (BCCI)

In 1988 the U.S. government charged several BCCI bankers plus dozens of other individuals with laundering $14 million for Colombia's Medellin Cartel. Two years later they were convicted. Launderers working for the drug traffickers put their cash profits into certificates of deposit in Bahamian, European, Panamanian, and Uruguayan branches of BCCI and then created loans using the certificates as collateral, a slick move that allowed the traffickers to withdraw their money through other branches. Loans were to be repaid with funds from certificates of deposit. BCCI, which closed on 5 July 1990, was called "the most pervasive money-laundering operation and financial supermarket ever created, a marathon swindle and steering service for [Colombian] drug traffickers to deposit hundreds of millions of contraband dollars outside the country." (Robinson, 1990, 76)

See also: Medellin Cartel; Money Laundering; Operation C-Note
References: Potts, Mark, et al. 1992. *Dirty Money: BCCI*. Robinson, Jeffrey. 1990. *The Laundrymen*.

Barbiturates

Known by several street names, including downers, good balls, and block busters, this drug acts on the central nervous system, creating a sedative (calming) or sleep inducing reaction. The first barbiturate was synthesized in 1864 and first manufactured and used in medicine in 1882. Barbiturates were being widely pushed in the United States by the 1930s, but in the next decade, when studies showed that these drugs were highly addictive and caused withdrawal symptoms, their use was stopped. States began passing laws against nonprescription barbiturates, but this move created a thriving black market in the drug.

By the 1950s barbiturates had become one of the most widely abused class of drugs in the United States, a situation that has continued into the 1990s. The U.S. government has estimated that today 20 percent of legally manufactured barbiturates are diverted to the illegal market. Most of the illegal supplies of barbiturates reach the U.S. black market via Colombia and Mexico through theft and smuggling. In the United States barbiturates are Schedule II drugs under the Comprehensive Crime Control Act of 1970. This includes drugs or substances that have a high potential for abuse, drugs or other substances that have a currently accepted use in the United

States or a currently accepted medical use with some restrictions, or drug in which its abuse may lead to severe psychological or physical dependence.

See also: Benzodiazepine; Hendrix, Jimi; Methaqualone; United Nations Convention Against the Traffic in Narcotic Substances and Psychotropic Substances of 1971; United States Comprehensive Crime Control Act of 1970; World War II

References: Abadinsky, Howard. 1990. *Organized Crime.* O'Brien, Robert, and Sidney Cohen. 1984. *Encyclopedia of Drug Abuse.*

Barco Vargas, Virgilio (1921–1997)

President of Colombia from 1986 to 1990. Barco Vargas earned degrees in civil engineering from the Massachusetts Institute of Technology and in the social sciences from Boston University and served in a variety of public service positions prior to his election as president, including mayor of Bogotá, a member of both houses of the national legislature, and ambassador to the United States and the United Kingdom. When elected president Barco Vargas had as his major priority eliminating the causes of the social unrest plaguing his country through economic and social reform, but his agenda was diverted by a United States-backed war against Colombia's powerful drug cartels that led to a terrorist campaign of bombings, kidnappings, and assassinations carried out by the country's powerful drug cartels.

In 1988 Barco Vargas intensified the war against drugs by declaring a state of siege, reimposing an extradition treaty with the United States, and ordering the pursuit and capture of several high-level traffickers. After leaving the presidency, Barco served as ambassador to the United Kingdom from 1990 to 1993. He suffered from Alzheimer's disease, which was diagnosed in 1990, and died of cancer in Bogotá in 1997.

See also: De Grieff, Monica; Extradition; Hoyos Jimenez, Carlos Mauro; Narcoterrorism; Palma, Manuel; Palma Molina, Manuel Julio; Roldan, Benardo

References: Chepesiuk, Ron. 1999. *Hard Target.* "Died—Virgilio Barco." 1997. *Time,* 2 June. Gugliotta, Guy, and Jeff Leen. 1990. *Kings of Cocaine.* Strong, Simon. 1995. *Whitewash.*

Barnes, Leroy "Nicky" (c. 1933–)

A colorful drug trafficker from Harlem who became a heroin kingpin in New York City in the mid-1960s. Barnes began his criminal career as a heroin pusher in Harlem for the Italian American Mafia before going on his own in 1964 with the Cosa Nostra's permission. In 1965 Barnes was given a 14-year prison sentence for extortion and sent to New York's Greenhaven Prison, where he formed a friendship with Mafia godfather Joseph "Crazy Joe" Gallo. Upon their release from prison, the two gangsters formed an alliance in which Barnes became the largest heroin dealer in Harlem, while cutting Gallo and his brothers in for a piece of the action.

Barnes set out to organize an African American Mafia on the Italian model by organizing other prominent black drug dealers into a seven-member council and dividing up the drug traffickers' territories around New York City. He established so-called heroin mills in which women, working naked to protect against theft, cut and bagged the heroin powder. The drug kingpin was ruthless with anybody who crossed him, but he became a legend for his wardrobe, chauffeur-driven Mercedes Benz limousines, and "pocket change" that often amounted to as much as $100,000.

Caught in a drug deal in 1978, Barnes was sent to prison and fined $125,000. In 1982 he became a federal informant and began working undercover and supplying the authorities with information that led to indictments against other top level drug dealers. Barnes had his sentence reduced to 35 years, but his former associates have allegedly put a $6 million bounty on his head. With time off for good behavior, Barnes was scheduled for release in October 1998.

See also: Heroin; Italian American Mafia
Reference: Kleinknecht, William. 1996. *New Ethnic Mobs.*

Barry, Marion (1936–)

Mayor of Washington, D.C., from 1979 to 1991, and from 1994 to 1998. In 1990 the FBI, acting on reports that Barry was using drugs, supplied the mayor's girlfriend with crack cocaine and then videotaped the mayor snorting the drug in a District of Columbia hotel room. Barry, who was in his third term as mayor, reportedly denied that he had ever taken drugs or had been involved in the international drug trade, but his arrest and the ensuing scandal seriously eroded his ability to fight the War on Drugs.

Popular and powerful, he was often called D.C.'s "mayor for life." However, that did not protect him from being convicted of drug charges and spending

Former Washington mayor Marion Barry celebrates after winning the Democratic primary, 13 September 1994. (Reuters/Corbis-Bettmann)

six months in jail. While in jail, Barry apparently could not keep out of trouble or the public eye. Prison officials investigated a report that a woman performed oral sex on him in the visiting facility at the federal prison in Petersburg, Virginia. An angry Barry denied the charge. When released from jail in 1991, the political pundits thought that Barry's political career was over, but he made a stunning comeback in a three-way democratic mayoral primary in September 1994 and then defeated the Republican candidate in the November 1994 election. In June 1998 Barry announced he would not run for a fifth term as Washington, D.C., mayor.

See also: Crack Cocaine

References: Dowd, Maureen. "Resurrection." 1994. *New York Times*, 11 September.

Morley, Jefferson. 1990. "Barry and His City: Crack in the Washington Culture." *The Nation*, 19 February.

Bartels, Jr., John R. (1934–)

On 4 October 1973 Bartels became the first head of the newly created United States Drug Enforcement Administration (DEA). He had served as acting administrator since the agency's formation in July 1973. Born in Brooklyn, New York, Bartels attended Phillips Exeter Academy in New Hampshire, earned a B.A. degree magna cum laude from Harvard (1956) and, after a year as a Fulbright Scholar at the University of Munich (1957), he entered Harvard Law School, where he graduated with a bachelor of law degree in 1960.

Prior to coming to the DEA, Bartels served as chief of the Justice Department's State Task Force Against Organized Crime in Newark, New Jersey, and as a U.S. assistant attorney. He also served as an official with the U.S. Office of Drug Abuse Law Enforcement before it merged to become part of the DEA.

Bartel's tenure as DEA administrator was plagued with controversy and scandal, and he resigned in

May 1975 under pressure, as a Senate investigating committee was about to open hearings into allegations of mismanagement, corruption, and a cover-up at the top levels of DEA's management.

See also: United States Drug Enforcement Administration
Reference: "Bartels Named to Head Drug Enforcement Administration." 1973. *International Narcotics Report.* July.

Basel Convention
Signed in December 1988 by the G-7 (Group of Seven Leading Industrialized Countries), plus Belgium, Sweden, the Netherlands, Switzerland, and Luxembourg, this declaration commits the central banks of the signatory countries to help identify customers and the source of their funds, to collaborate with criminal investigations as permitted by domestic legislation, and to report all transactions that involve suspicious funds. The declaration has been described as the first concerted action taken against money laundering in Europe.

See also: Money Laundering
Reference: Jamieson, Alison. 1994. *Terrorism and Drug Trafficking Europe in the 1990s.*

Basuco
A mixture of coca paste and tobacco that is smoked in Colombia, particularly in the big-city slums. Colombian drug rehabilitation officials have put the number of basuco smokers at between 300,000 and 3 million. The drug is extremely dangerous because it has also contained traces of ether, kerosene, sulfuric acid, leaded gasoline, and other chemicals, and has been known to cause brain damage.

Reference: Gugliotta, Guy, and Jeff Leen. 1990. *Kings of Cocaine.*

Beat Generation
See Beatniks

Beatniks
Refers to individuals who came of age in the 1950s and challenged the mainstream society and rejected its values. Beatniks were often writers or other artists and would-be artists. They experimented with their lives, often indulged in drugs, particularly marijuana and cocaine, and influenced by example the counterculture that followed in the 1960s.

Famous beatniks, or beats, as they are also known, included Allen Ginsberg, Neal Cassady, Lawrence Ferlinghetti, and William Burroughs.

See also: Burroughs, William S.; Counterculture; Ginsberg, Allen
References: Plummer, William. 1981. *The Holy Goof: A Biography of Neal Cassady.*
Tytell, John. 1976. *Naked Angels: The Lives and Literature of the Beat Generation.*

Belushi, John (1949–1982)
In 1971, a year after graduating from College of DuPage with an Associate of Arts Degree in General Studies, Belushi went to Chicago to perform for the famous Second City Improvisational Comedy Troupe, becoming at age 22 the youngest troupe performer ever. Belushi became the star of the troupe, working six days a week, but he also began experimenting with a variety of drugs, including marijuana, LSD, mushrooms, methamphetamines, and peyote.

From the Second City Improvisational Comedy Troupe, Belushi went on to fame as a performer in the popular television program "Saturday Night Live," and as an actor in several movies such as "National Lampoon's Animal House" (1978), "The Blues Brothers" (1980), and "Neighbors" (1981). Belushi never realized his enormous potential, for he died tragically of a drug overdose in 1982.

See also: Farley, Chris; LSD; Marijuana; Methamphetamines; Peyote; Psilocybin
References: Young, Charles M., "Son Of Samurai." *Rolling Stone*, 11 June 1992.
Bob Woodward. 1985. *Wired: The Short Life and Fast Times Of John Belushi.*

Bennett, William J. (1943–)
The first so-called drug czar, Bennett was the U.S. government's official leader in the country's War on Drugs, appointed by President George Bush to the post officially known as the Director of the Office of National Control Policy from 1989 until 1991. As an avowed conservative, Bennett assumed a high profile and took a tough stance against illicit drugs, strongly opposing the legalization of drugs and publicly advocating capital punishment for drug dealers. By the time he left office, Bennett claimed that he had made a positive impact on the drug war, noting that casual

drug use appeared to be declining. Critics of Bennett's tenure as drug czar, however, disputed his assessment and said there had been little change in the United States' War on the Drugs.

See also: Best Friends Program; Drug Czar; Friedman, Milton; Legalization; United States Office of National Drug Control Policy
References: Morgenthau, Tom, and Mark Miller. 1989. "The Drug Warrior." *Newsweek*, 10 April.
Sims, Jane. 1990. "William Bennett." *People Weekly*, 11 June.

Bensinger, Peter (1936–)

Administrator of the Drug Enforcement Administration from February 1976 to July 1981. Bensinger was educated at Phillips Exeter Academy and Yale University, where he received a B.A. degree in 1958. Bensinger worked for the Brunswick Corporation in Chicago before serving the state of Illinois in various administrative capacities, including director of the Department of Corrections (1970–1973); executive director of the Chicago Crime Commission (1973–1975); and chief of the Crime Victims Division (1975–1976).

During his tenure, Bensinger opposed the proposed absorption of the DEA by the FBI, spoke out for tougher penalties to control the proliferation of heroin and other hard drugs, targeted the Mexican drug trafficking connection and its involvement with heroin, worked hard to reduce interagency tensions that had marred the U.S. government's antidrug efforts, sought to end corruption within the DEA ranks, and, by confidential memo sent worldwide, ordered strict adherence to guidelines on the DEA's role abroad, which now prohibited its agents from engaging in direct political actions in any foreign country.

See also: Heroin; United States Drug Enforcement Administration
Reference: "Drug Busters' Aim: Hit The Big Boys." 1976. *National Observer*, 1 May.

Benzodiazepine

First developed as a sedative in the late 1950s, this drug replaced barbiturates, which were among the most widely prescription drugs in Western countries, but were associated with numerous overdoses. Benzodiazepine is highly effective in relieving anxiety and inducing sleep and much safer to use than barbiturates. However, it can also be addictive, and therefore, subject to abuse. Patients on methadone maintenance programs, especially in England, are reported to have supplemented their prescriptions with benzodiazepine, which they obtain illegally.

See also: Barbiturates; Methadone Maintenance Programs
Reference: Garretty, Deborah J., et al. 1997. "Benzodiazepine Misuse by Drug Addicts." *Annals of Criminal Biochemistry.*

Bernal Madrigal, Alejandro

Nicknamed "Juvenal," Bernal Madrigal is a Medellin-based drug trafficker allegedly responsible for coordinating large shipments of cocaine to the United States via Mexico and then moving the drug proceeds to Colombia via Mexico and Panama.

See also: Medellin Cartel
Reference: U.S. Senate Committee on Foreign Relations. 1998. *International Organized Crime Syndicates and Their Impact on the United States: Hearings before the Subcommittee on Western Hemisphere, Peace Corps, Narcotics and Terrorism*, 26 February (statement of Thomas A. Constantine, Director, DEA).

Best Friends Program (U.S.)

Elayne Bennett, wife of the former drug czar, William Bennett, started this program in 1987 as a school-based attempt to teach teenage girls the importance of avoiding drugs, as well as premarital sex. The program encouraged total abstinence, and stressed character building and the value of physical fitness and community service.

See also: Bennett, William J.
Reference: Toosi, Nahal. 1998. "Saying Yes and No." *Charlotte Observer*, 21 May.

Betancur Cuartas, Belisario (1923–)

Colombian president from 1982 to 1986. In 1986 Betancur Cuartas promulgated a series of decrees relating to narcotic drugs and, with the technical assistance provided by the United Nations, subsequently formed a national plan for Colombia to combat the illicit drug trade and the consumption of narcotic and psychotropic substances. Colombia also entered into an agreement under which the United Nations Fund for Drug Abuse Control, among other groups, provided for a plan to replace the coca-leaf crop in certain areas of the country with nonnar-cotic crops. Betancur Cuartas also conducted a crackdown on Colombia's drug traffickers after the assassination of Colombia's justice minister, Rodrigo Lara Bonilla in 1984, ordering the extradition to the United States of 20 suspected drug traffickers.

However, in April 1994, Gabriel Taboada, a former member of the Medellin cartel, testified before the U.S. Congress that Betancur Cuartas had received money from Colombian drug traffickers. The charges have never been substantiated.

See also: Extradition; Giraldo, Alberto; Gonzalez Parejo, Enrique; Lara Bonilla, Rodrigo; Ochoa Vasquez, Jorge Luis; Reagan, Ronald; Toboada, Gabriel; United Nations Fund For Drug Abuse Control
References: Cooper, Mary H. 1990. *The Business of Drugs*. Strong, Simon. 1995. *Whitewash*.

Bias, Len (1963–1986)

University of Maryland basketball star who died suddenly of cocaine intoxication in July 1986. Bias was in perfect health, but died the day after becoming the number two selection by the Boston Celtics in the pro National Basketball Association player draft. Bias's death shocked Americans and made them aware of the country's growing drug abuse problem.

See also: Cocaine
References: Leo, John. "How Cocaine Killed Len Bias." *Time*, 7 July 1986.
MacCallum, J. "College Star Len Bias Barely Misses Realizing His Two Biggest Goals." *Jet*, 17 July 1986.

Blackstone Rangers
See El Rukns

Blanco de Trujillo, Grisella

A major drug trafficker of the 1970s who collaborated with Colombian drug traffickers Pablo Escobar, Carlos Lehder, and the three Ochoa brothers (Jorge Luis, Fabio, and Juan David) and was considered more violent than any other drug trafficker of the era. Born in Cartagena, Colombia, the daughter of a prostitute, Blanco De Trujillo moved to Medellin as a teenager. There she worked as a pickpocket before entering the more lucrative criminal field of cocaine trafficking. She attracted the attention of Drug Enforcement Administration agents involved with Operation Banshee, the first major U.S. investigation of Colombian drug trafficking activities in the mid-1970s. The DEA discovered that Blanco de Trujillo was involved in the distribution of hundreds of kilograms of cocaine in New York City. She eluded capture, however, and was not heard from again for nine years, when she emerged as a leader of a violent Miami-based drug trafficking organization.

Blanco de Trujillo loved killing more than drug trafficking, and organized a group of assassins known as the Pistoleros, who earned their initiation into the group by killing somebody and cutting a body part off as proof of the act. Blanco De Trujillo reportedly used murder not only to get rid of rivals and wayward lovers, but also as a way of canceling debts. In 1977 she was linked to the notorious shootout that became known as the Dadeland Massacre. The increased drug trafficking competition in Miami led Blanco de Trujillo to move her drug business to California, but the DEA used a confidential informant to gather evidence and convict her of conspiring to import cocaine. In trials in Miami and New York City, she was given ten- and fifteen-year jail sentences respectively.

See also: Cocaine; Dadeland Massacre (Miami); Escobar Gaviria, Pablo; Lehder Rivas, Carlos; Ochoa Vasquez, Jr., Fabio; and Ochoa Vasquez, Jorge Luis
Reference: Traub, James. 1983. *The Billion Dollar Connection*.

Blancornelas, J. Jesus

Editor of *Zeta*, a Tijuana, Mexico, newspaper (circulation 100,000), Blancornelas published exposés about drug trafficking and corruption for eighteen years until his attempted murder in November 1997. Blancornelas focused his attention on powerful Tijuana-based Mexican drug trafficker Ramon Arellano Felix, and in November 1997 he published an exposé of David Barron, one of Arellano's lieutenants, in which he identified Barron as the mastermind behind the murder of two Mexican soldiers. A week later, ten gunmen pumped about 100 bullets into Blancornelas's car, killing the journalist's bodyguard, but Blancornelas incredibly survived. Barron, who was believed to have participated in the murder, was apparently killed by a stray bullet.

The brazen assassination attempt of Blancornelas shocked people on both sides of the United States-Mexican border. The Mexico City publication

Excelsior wrote that the assault clearly shows how "violent crime in this country is closely linked to organized crime. The police have evidence that showed clearly that this attack was ordered by the Arellano Felix family, chiefs of one of the most powerful drug cartels in the country." (Kowalski 1998, 12) Mexican prosecutors announced a $1 million reward for the capture of the Arellano Felix brothers. In April 1998 *World Press Review* honored Blancornelas as International Editor of the Year.

See also: Arellano Felix, Ramon; Media.
Reference: Kowalski, B. J. 1998. "Taking on the Drug Lords." *World Press Review*, 11 April.

Blandon Castillo, Jose

A former intelligence aide to General Manuel Noriega, Blandon Castillo provided evidence that helped U.S. federal prosecutors indict Noriega, the former dictator of Panama, for his involvement in the trafficking of drugs to the United States. Blandon Castillo also linked Cuba and its leader, Fidel Castro, to the drug trade, claiming that Castro acted as mediator between Noriega, the Medellin Cartel, and Colombia's M-19 guerrillas in an effort to keep drugs moving to the United States via Cuba. According to Blandon "His [Castro's] interests were political, they were economic, and there were interests linked to the war which was being waged with the U.S. Fidel Castro made Panama a window of opportunity for business in order to import Western technology and export some of his goods from Cuba." (Ehrenfeld, 1994, 43)

See also: Cuban Connection; Medellin Cartel; M-19; Noriega, Manuel Antonio
Reference: Ehrenfeld, Rachel. 1994. *Narcoterrorism*.

Bloods

A Los Angeles street gang that emerged from the bloody Watts riots of 1965 and today plays an important role in the domestic U.S. drug trade as traffickers in cocaine and crack cocaine. According to William Kleinknecht, "It is a misnomer to call them gangs. They are really federations made up of dozens of independent groups that each claim at most a few blocks of territory." (Kleinknecht, 1996, 225) Kleinknecht estimates that in the Los Angeles area alone there are eighty gangs of Bloods and 220 Crips gangs, with membership in the "tens of thousands." In the early 1980s the group began to spread across

the United States, recruiting members in Portland, Seattle, Denver, St. Louis, and at least forty other American cities, and setting up franchise operations for crack and cocaine trafficking. According to Mary H. Cooper, "The Bloods and Crips have ambiguous business relations, competing in certain areas of the trade while killing one another off in others." (Cooper, 1990, 41)

See also: Cocaine; Crack Cocaine
References: Cooper, Mary H. 1990. *The Business of Drugs*. Kleinknecht, William. 1996. *The New Ethnic Gangs*.

Body Packing

The method whereby mules, as people transporting illegal drugs are called, swallow small containers of drugs to smuggle them past customs officials. This is a method commonly employed by couriers working for Nigerian organized crime.

See also: Nigerian Organized Crime
Reference: Crook, Farrell. 1993. "Drug Smuggler Jailed 12 Months." *Toronto Star*, 24 June.

Bogotá Cartel (Colombia)

This group began its criminal enterprise as a smuggling operation for a wide variety of contraband, but then entered into drug trafficking after establishing contact with American criminal organizations in the 1980s. Although not receiving the same media attention that the Medellin and Cali Cartels have received, the Bogotá Cartel has established a powerful presence in Colombia, purchasing huge tracts of land and successfully buying protection from the country's establishment.

See also: Cali Cartel; Medellin Cartel; North Atlantic Coast Cartel
Reference: Miller, Gary J. 1997. *Drugs and the Law*.

Bonner, Robert C. (1942–)

Administrator of the United States Drug Enforcement Administration from August 1990 to December 1993. Born in Wichita, Kansas, Bonner graduated from the University of Maryland with a B.A. degree in 1963 and from Georgetown University Law School with a J.D. degree in 1966. Bonner served in the U.S. Naval Reserve from 1967 to 1977. Before becoming administrator of the DEA, he worked in the private practice of law with the firm of Kadison, Pfaelzer, Woodard, Quinn and Ross (1975–1984), as

U.S. attorney for the central district of California (1984–1989), and as U.S. district judge for the central district of California in Los Angeles.

Under Bonner's leadership, the DEA spearheaded several large investigations, putting drug traffickers from South America to Asia out of business and playing a key role in the arrest and prosecution of Panamanian dictator Manuel Noriega. It is believed that Bonner, a Republican and Bush appointee, would eventually have been forced to leave the DEA under Democratic President Bill Clinton, who entered office in 1993. Instead, Bonner resigned voluntarily.

See also: Bush, George Herbert Walker; Clinton, William Jefferson; United States Drug Enforcement Administration
Reference: Isikoff, Michael. 1995. "DEA Chief Has Harsh Words for Clinton's Anti-Drug Policy." *Washington Post* 6 June 6.

Boot Camps

Facilities in the United States that are used for the penal punishment of drug offenders and are ostensibly patterned after military basic training for new recruits. The first penal boot camp was opened in 1983. They have since become popular with both federal and state governments as a way to punish first-time nonviolent offenders, because they are cheaper than regular prisons and are believed to instill self-discipline in prisoners. Opponents of boot camps, however, point to studies that have shown that graduates of penal boot camps were as likely to be arrested again as other convicts. Despite the controversy, President Bill Clinton has remained an enthusiastic supporter of boot camps, making the concept an important feature of his 1994 crime bill.

See also: Clinton, William Jefferson
Reference: Weir, William. 1995. *In the Shadow of the Dope Fiend.*

Botero Zea, Fernando (c. 1957–   )

On 2 August 1995 Botero Zea resigned as Colombian defense minister amid charges that the Cali cartel had financed the electoral campaign of President Ernesto Samper Pizano. Botero Zea had served as manager of Samper Pizano's election campaign. Botero Zea denied that he had taken drug money but the week before his resignation Samper Pizano's campaign treasurer told Colombian government

prosecutors in secret testimony that both Botero Zea and Samper Pizano were directly involved. Botero Zea was given a three-year jail term and was released in February 1998. He also had to pay off a 2.231 million peso fine.

See also: Cali Cartel; Narcocassettes; Samper Pizano, Ernesto
Reference: Strong, Simon. 1995. *Whitewash: Pablo Escobar and the Cocaine Wars.*

Bourne, Peter (c. 1939–   )

Drug policy advisor to U.S. President Jimmy Carter (1976–1979). Bourne was forced to resign as director of the White House Office of Drug Abuse Policy in 1979 because of charges that he had used cocaine and had written an illegal prescription for one of his aides. As Carter's advisor, Bourne wrote that cocaine is "possibly the most benign of illicit drugs currently in widespread use" (Shannon 1989, 40) Bourne became a symbol for critics of Carter's antidrug policy, which they believed was soft.

See also: Carter, James Earl; Cocaine
References: Ehrenfeld, Rachel. 1994. *Narcoterrorism and the Cuban Circuit.*
Shannon, Elaine. 1989. *Desperadoes.*

Brent, Charles Henry (1863–1929)

Missionary and bishop who in the early twentieth century began a campaign against opium traffic and served on several important international commissions devoted to stamping out the international traffic in narcotics. Brent got interested in drugs and drug abuse in the Philippines, where he had been appointed the first Episcopal bishop in 1902.

For two years he was a member of the committee appointed by the Philippine government to investigate the local opium problem. Brent concluded that the system of regulation of opium by taxation employed in the Far East, especially by the British, was more concerned with making money than with reform, and he recommended that the Philippines would benefit from a general policy of prohibition. The U.S. Congress acted on the committee's report and in March 1905 passed a law declaring that the importation of opium into the Philippines other than for medical purposes would end as of March 1908, and that henceforth it would be illegal to sell nonmedical opiates to native Filipinos.

Brent also served as head of the American delegation to the 1909 International Opium Conference in Shanghai, becoming the Conference's president. He then served as chairman of the United States delegation to the International Opium Conference at the Hague in 1911, the following year, and became its president also. He was also a delegate to the second conference on the opium question, which was held in Geneva in 1924. The previous year, he had represented the United States at the meeting of the Advisory Board of the League of Nations on the matter of narcotic control. Brent declined three elections to bishoprics in the United States in order to continue his work in the Philippines, but he accepted the position of bishop of western New York in 1918. Bishop Brent served in that position until his death in 1929.

See also: League Of Nations; Opium; Prohibition; Spanish American War
References: Courtwright, David. 1982. *Dark Paradise*.
Morgan, H. Wayne. 1981. *Drugs In America: A Social History, 1800–1980*.

Brown, Claude (1937–)

An African American lawyer who wrote the book, *Manchild in a Promised Land* (1990), which eloquently describes the racism, segregation, and the breakdown of black culture in the rural southern United States during segregation. The book explains how this contributed to a loss of identity and self-destructiveness that led many young blacks in his community to experience heroin abuse.

Reference: Brown, Claude. 1990. *Manchild in the Promised Land*.

Brown, Lee (1938–)

Former director of the National Drug Control Strategy Policy, the so-called drug czar, for two-and-one-half years from 1993 to 1995. Brown had previously served as police chief of the city of Houston, Texas, from 1980 to 1990, and as New York City police commissioner from 1990 to 1993. During his term as drug czar, Brown focused his efforts on reducing the demand for illegal drugs and integrating antidrug programs into every federal department. Critics described him as a bureaucrat and charged that his appointment was a graphic example of President Bill Clinton's lack of commitment to the War on Drugs. After resigning as drug czar, Brown worked as a se-

nior fellow at the James A. Baker Institute for Public Policy and then became Houston's first African American mayor in 1997.

See also: Clinton, William Jefferson; Drug Czar; United States Office Of National Control Policy
References: "Drug Czar Lee Brown Resigns Post To Become Sociology Professor At Rice University In Houston." 1996. *Jet*, 8 January.
"Lee Brown Elected Houston's First Black Mayor." 1997. *Jet*, 22 December.
York, Byron. 1994. "Clinton's Phony Drug War." *American Spectator*. February.

Buckley, William F. (1925–)

Prominent conservative newspaper columnist, writer, publisher of the magazine *National Review*, and outspoken critic of the United States' War on Drugs. Like economist Milton Friedman, former U.S. Secretary of State George P. Schultz, and other prominent drug war critics, Buckley believes the current U.S. antidrug strategy is an invasion of privacy and threatens the constitutional rights of U.S. citizens. Buckley also believes that we should at least examine and consider the different approaches to the legalization of drugs.

See also: Friedman, Milton; Legalization; Schultz, George P.
References: Bertram, Eva, Kenneth Sharpe, and Peter Anders. 1996. *Drug War Politics: The Price of Denial*.

Buprenorphine

In early 1998 researchers were claiming that a drug called buprenorphine offered a breakthrough in the treatment of heroin addiction because it was an improvement on current methods using methadone. The researchers reported that buprenorphine gave only a mild "high" and was not addictive. The reports compared buprenorphine favorably to methadone, a drug that has been traditionally used as a substitute for heroin in the treatment of heroin addiction. Methadone is addictive and many addicts find the experience similar to heroin, making a cure difficult.

By January 1998 France had used buprenorphine for a year, and clinical trials, coordinated by the U.S. government and the drug's manufacturer, were being conducted at twelve hospitals around the United States. The trials were reported to be going well, but more research would have to be done. For one thing, researchers had not determined how long heroin addicts would have to take

Author William S. Burroughs sitting at his typewriter in Paris, 1962. (Corbis/Underwood & Underwood)

buprenorphine before they would be free of heroin addiction.

See also: Heroin and Methadone Treatment Programs
Reference: Cloud, John. 1997. "A Way Out for Junkies." *Time*, 10 October.

Burroughs, William S. (1914–1997)

The grandson of William Burroughs, the inventor of the adding machine, Burroughs became the noted experimental and unconventional author of such books as *Junkie* (1953), *Naked Lunch* (1959), and *The Soft Machine* (1961). Burroughs's first book, *Junkie: The Confessions of an Unredeemed Drug Addict* (1953), describes his life as a heroin and morphine addict, which began in 1944 and didn't end until 1957. During those years, he traveled widely and was an "example" of what a beat should be ("Cool, Man") for younger members of the Beat Generation, such as Jack Kerouac and Allen Ginsberg. His second and most celebrated novel, *Naked Lunch* (1959), survived a number of obscenity trials to become a widely read cult book for adherents to the 1960s countercultural lifestyle.

See also: Beatniks; Counterculture; Ginsberg, Allen; Heroin; Morphine

References: Miles, Barry. 1994. *William Burroughs: El Hombre Invisible: A Portrait*.
Tytell, John. 1976. *Naked Angels: The Lives and Literature Of The Beat Generation*.

Buscetta, Tommaso

Buscetta was a prominent member of Italian organized crime who testified in 1988 about the Mafia's involvement in the international heroin trade. Disillusioned by this drug connection, Buscetta quit the mob and fled to Brazil after the Mafia took revenge and killed ten of his relatives, including a son and two brothers. In July 1984 he was about to be imprisoned for drug trafficking offenses when he confessed to illegal drug dealings that implicated more than 350 mobsters in Italy and the United States.

In 1987 Buscetta became the Italian government's chief witness in a Palermo trial that focused on the war between the Sicilian crime families over control of the international heroin trade. Buscetta's testimony led to the conviction of twenty mafia bosses, including Michele Greco, for the 1982 killing of Carlo Alberto Dalla Chiesa, leader of Italy's crime task force, and the verdict of guilty for another one hundred defendants in absentia.

See also: Heroin; Italian Organized Crime
Reference: Sterling, Claire. 1990. *Octopus: The Long Reach of the International Sicilian Mafia*.

Bush, George Herbert Walker (1924–)

President of the United States from 1989 to 1993. Despite the sharp criticism of Ronald Reagan's antidrug policy, George Bush publicly renewed his predecessor's pledge to wage war on drugs and continued the same policy. Public opinion polls showed that the American public wanted their political leaders to get even tougher on illegal drugs and combat the increasing drug-related violence in many American cities. Congress, under George Bush's leadership, responded by adopting measures that further militarized the country's antidrug effort. The U.S. military was given a much broader role in the War on Drugs, despite continuing opposition from many military leaders, who felt the new policy would divert the armed forces from its primary role of defending U.S. interests abroad against such forces as Communism and terrorism.

Congress approved and Bush appointed a so-called drug czar as a kind of top level commander in the War on Drugs who would have direct access to the president. The first czar, William Bennett, a registered Democrat and former philosophy professor, revealed his antidrug plan in the summer of 1989. Bennett called for an even tougher stance against the enemy: more federal agents, more prosecutors, more judges to hear more cases, and more federal prisons to hold more drug offenders. Instead of interdicting drugs at the border, Bennett proposed intervening in the countries where narcotic crops were grown and on the streets of America where they were consumed. The Bennett plan called for $7 billion per year. The drug czar projected that with this funding the United States could reduce illegal drug use by 10 percent over the first twenty-five months and by 50 percent in the coming decade. How exactly that would happen was not spelled out.

In unveiling his National Drug Control Strategy in September 1989 Bush endorsed Bennett's plan of action and proposed that 70 percent of the $2.2 billion increase in additional money to be allocated to the War on Drugs over the next several years be spent on law enforcement. Bush also urged Congress to give more military and economic assistance to Andean countries to help stem the flow of cocaine to the United States. "In the past, programs have been hampered by the lack of importance given by this country to the drug issue as a foreign policy concern," Bush declared. "We must develop ... a broad, meaningful public diplomacy program in a manner that would increase the level of international influence for combating illicit drugs." (Klare 1990, 8)

The militarization of the War on Drugs, begun by Reagan in 1982, reached a climax in the 1989 invasion of Panama and the capture of that country's dictator, General Manuel Antonio Noriega, who had been indicted in a U.S. court for alleged involvement in international drug trafficking. With a force of 24,000 troops, the United States launched Operation Just Cause, an invasion of Panama that led to the arrest of the former U.S. ally and his trial in the United States on drug trafficking charges. United States officials defended this military incursion, arguing that kidnapping was a legitimate strategy that the U.S could use to improve its role in the War on Drugs.

"Some foreign governments have unfortunately failed to take steps to protect the United States from drug traffickers," said William P. Barr, a deputy attorney general in the U.S. Justice Department's Office of Legal Counsel. (Anderson 1991, 155–156) Critics of Operation Just Cause said the United States had actually kidnapped Noriega—a move that was in violation of international law. The United States shouldn't be breaking its own laws abroad, they admonished.

In late 1988 the Bush administration asked the military to "play a major role in helping to interdict drug traffic in the United States, to create an integrated intelligence and communications network, and to train foreign military personnel and both U.S. and foreign police forces." (Bagley 1988, 155–156) The United States had begun to use its elite special forces, including the Green Berets, in preemptive strikes against the drug-trafficker enclaves in source countries like Peru and Colombia. The justification for the operation was an opinion issued by the Justice Department's Office of Legal Counsel that concluded that U.S. military forces could go overseas and arrest drug dealers and other criminals, even without the consent of host country.

In September 1989 Secretary of Defense Dick Chaney issued a directive to all military commanders to develop policies and to play a major role against international drug trafficking. Under the new policy, the Department of Defense began to assume a new and bigger responsibility in the interdiction of illegal drugs at the United States' southern borders.

But Congress—not just the president—wanted the military to play a more active role in the drug battle. The mood of the legislature was expressed by Representative Larry Hopkins (R-Ky), who told the Pentagon in early 1989, "We are serious about your active role in this war on drugs, even if it means we have to drag you screaming every step of the way." (Isenberg 1990, 24)

Times had changed, though, and the military was no longer reluctant to assume more active participation in the United States' latest crusade. The Pentagon had changed its position, not just because of pressure from the president and Congress, but also for economic reasons. With the Soviet Union collapsing and becoming less of a threat to U.S. security, Secretary Chaney announced in November 1989 that the administration would be cutting the Department of Defense budget by $180 million over five years. The announcement sent shock waves through the military, which could not but conclude that the legislative trend was going to be continued reductions of military expenditures, manpower, and commitments worldwide. As David Isenberg explains, "Pentagon leadership began arguing that military manpower should not be reduced because Congress is mandating increased military involvement in drug interdiction efforts." (Isenberg 1990, 25)

Bush, like Reagan, called often for the need to reduce the demand for drugs at home, but, in reality, the United States' antidrug strategy during the 1980s and early 1990s focused heavily on reducing the supply of illegal drugs from abroad through border and off-shore interdiction efforts. By 1991 nearly 70 percent of the U.S. antidrug budget went towards reducing supply, particularly cocaine from South America.

Bush's search for a military solution to the War on Drugs was evident in 1989 when he unveiled the "Andean Strategy," a program in which the United States would provide some modest military assistance to the source countries of Peru, Colombia, and Bolivia, while encouraging them to involve their own militaries more in the War on Drugs. Annual U.S assistance to the Andean countries had been about $40 to $50 million, a minuscule amount compared to the billions generated by the region's drug trafficking industry, but, with the Andean Strategy in place, the United States' antidrug expenditures for South American source countries increased sevenfold from fiscal year 1989 to 1991.

To get the support of the Andean countries for his antidrug program and to show he was serious about his Andean initiative, Bush journeyed to Cartegena in February 1990 for a summit meeting with the leaders of Peru, Colombia, and Bolivia—a move that led to the formation of what has been called "the world's first antidrug cartel." Participating nations at the summit vowed to attack international drug trafficking from every angle; economic, political, and military. Bush pledged to work hard to decrease the demand for drugs in the United States, while the Andean leaders said they would work equally hard to reduce drug-related corruption, strengthen the judiciary, and step up law enforcement efforts against the drug traffickers operating in their countries. The Andean nations urged Bush to create new trade opportunities that would provide more employment

opportunities for workers displaced from the cocaine economy.

To meet his commitment at the Cartegena summit, Bush sent his Andean trade preference bill to Congress for ratification in July 1990. Signed into law on 4 December 1990, the Andean Trade Preference Act (ATPA) was designed to expand the economic alternatives for the source countries that had been fighting to eliminate the production, processing, and shipment of illegal drugs. Specifically, the Act gave the president the authority to grant duty-free entry to imports of eligible articles from countries designated as beneficiaries according to criteria set forth in the Act. This economic incentive program was to remain in effect for ten years.

By the time the 1992 U.S. presidential elections got rolling, the consensus among drug analysts was that the Bush administration's War on Drugs strategy, which focused primarily on supply and looked for a military solution, had not worked. "U.S. drug policy in much of the hemisphere was viewed not nearly as costly and ineffective, but as perversely counterproductive as well," explained Professor Bruce Bagley. (Bagley & Walker 1994, 69) Despite the assurances made by the U.S. government since 1982 that "the scourge was about to end," the supply of heroin, cocaine and other illegal drugs were still plentiful, while their cost had remained low. The Bush administration's antidrug strategy, moreover, may have actually led to more drug abuse and drug-related violence.

The policy had also done little to alleviate drug-induced corruption, terrorism, and violence in the many countries that had been sucked into the War on Drugs. "The Peruvian-American antidrug policy has failed," acknowledged Peruvian President Alberto Fujimori. "For ten years, there has been a considerable sum invested by the Peruvian government, and this has not led to a reduction in the supply of coca leaf offered for sale. Rather, in the ten years from 1980 to 1990, it grew tenfold." (Podesta & Farah 1993)

Senator Patrick Leahy (D-NH), the chairman of the powerful Senate Appropriations Subcommittee that oversees foreign operations, concurred with President Fujimori's assessment, and in an interview appeared to agree with the opinion of many drug-policy analysts who believed that the DEA should stop its support of raids on drug-trafficking operations in Peru. "We've spent over $1 billion down there so far and we've accomplished virtually nothing," Leahy explained. "We ought to realize it's not going to work." (Isikoff 1993)

See also: Alternative Development; Bennett, William J.; Cartegena Summit; Cocaine; Drug Czar; Heroin; National Narcotics Interdiction System; Noriega, Manuel Antonio; Reagan, Ronald; United States National Drug Control Strategy

References: Bagley, Bruce. 1989–1990. "Dateline Drug Wars Colombia: The Wrong Strategy." *Foreign Affairs* (Winter): 54.

———, and William O. Walker. 1994. "After San Antonio." In *Drug Trafficking in the Americas*.

Chepesiuk, Ron. 1999. *Hard Target*.

Isenberg, David. 1990. "Military Options in the War on Drugs." *USA Today*, 7 July.

Isikoff, Michael. 1993. "U.S. Considers Shift in Drug War." *Washington Post*, 16 September.

Klare, Michael T. 1990. "Fighting Drugs with the Military." *Nation*, 1 January.

Podesta, Don, and Douglas Farah. 1993. "Drug Policing in the Andes." *Washington Post*, 27 March.

C

Caicedo-Tascon, Giovanni

A major cocaine drug trafficker whose organization has ties to the Cali and North Valle Cartels and which is particularly active in the New York City area.

See also: Cali Cartel; Cocaine

Reference: U.S. Senate Committee on Foreign Relations. 1998. *International Organized Crime Syndicates and Their Impact on the United States: Hearings before the Subcommittee on Western Hemisphere, Peace Corps, Narcotics and Terrorism,* 26 February (statement of Thomas A. Constantine, Director, DEA.

Cali Cartel

A Colombian drug-trafficking organization that emerged as the world's leading purveyor of illicit drugs in the late 1980s, when the Medellin cartel engaged the Colombian government in a war of attrition. The Cali Cartel began supplying most of the cocaine consumed in the United States and Europe, a situation that eventually made Colombia the target of U.S. trade sanctions.

The Cartel took to establishing legitimate business ventures as a means of forging contacts with key people in business, politics, the law, and the press. It invested plenty of "narco-dollars" to establish an intelligence network that rivaled those of many South American governments and to keep them informed of the Colombian government's every move in the War on Drugs.

The low key, business-like style worked. Even the police began to speak of *Los Caballeros* (gentlemen) of Cali in contrast to *Los Hampones* (hoodlums) of Medellin. "The Cali Cartel will kill you if they have to, but they would rather use a lawyer," observed Robert Bryden, head of the Drug Enforcement Administration's New York City office. (Shannon 1991, 30) "They [the Cali Cartel] are much more astute than the leaders of the Medellin Cartel," explained Fernando Brito Ruiz, Director of DAS, Colombia's equivalent of the FBI. "They have economic power and they know how to use it." (Chepesiuk 1999, 16)

Los Hampones craved respectability; *Los Caballeros* enjoyed it. Many Colombians looked upon the godfathers from Cali as Horatio Alger–type success stories—who by brains, enterprise, and hard work had risen out of the slums of Cali and the backwater of the Cauca Valley. The chief executive officers of Cali Cartel, Inc., included Jose Santacruz Londono, a one-time hoodlum who had studied engineering and had transformed himself into the caballero Don Chepe, the billionnaire construction magnate; his close associate Gilberto Rodriguez Orejuela, who started out as a kidnapper, but ended up owning a vast network of business enterprises, which included La Rebaja, the biggest drug store chain in Colombia, as well as banks, car dealerships, apartment buildings, and Cali's talented America soccer team; Miguel Rodriguez Orejuela, Gilberto's handsome brother, who oversaw the business side of the criminal empire; Gilberto and Miguel's cousin Jamie, and his three brothers, prominent impresarios of concerts and sporting events, who travel frequently to New York City and have business offices in Los Angeles; and Helmer Pacho Herrera, believed to

Cocaine Colombian National police on a mission against drug traffickers. (Courtesy of the Colombian National Police)

be the son of Benjamin Herrera Zuleta, a legendary Afro-Colombian smuggler known as the Black Pope, who played a big role in the Cali Cartel's early development.

Unlike the Medellin Cartel, the Cali godfathers ran their criminal enterprise conservatively, much like other big corporate heads. It was a cerebral approach that depended more on planning, shrewd calculation, and the use of a boardroom, rather than dependence on the gun to do business.

If one played by the company rules and did not make mistakes, one could have a good life as a Cali corporate man or woman. It could be difficult, though, for those who screwed up or tried to sever ties. They weren't fired, they were discretely executed. As distasteful as violence was to the Cartel, it kept a gun in the desk drawer, just in case.

But while the organization was authoritarian——one that demands absolute discipline and loyalty—it still allowed for creativity. Under the chief executive officers and serving as the senior vice presidents of acquisitions, transportation, sales, finance, and enforcement were some of Colombia's best and brightest. They supervised and coordinated the logistics of importing, storing, and delivering the product and oversaw—through daily, and often, hourly phone calls—ambitious underlings in dozens of overseas branch offices, who moved the drugs to wholesalers.

Employees of Cali Cartel, Inc., whether executive officers or underlings, were expected to be conservative in their lifestyle: no flashy clothing or cars, no drinking or drug problems, and no loud parties and activities that could call attention to themselves.

Gilberto Rodriguez Orejuela, his brother Miguel, and friend Jose Santacruz Londono, who eventually became the three highest ranking members of the Cali Cartel, got their criminal start in the 1950s and 1960s as juvenile delinquents, kidnappers, petty criminals, enforcers, and couriers for drug traffickers. The ransom money they made from several kidnappings gave the young criminals the necessary capital to finance their entry in the early 1970s into what was becoming big-time cocaine smuggling.

In the mid 1970s, while the more powerful Medellin Cartel was establishing a strong base in Miami, the Cali Cartel moved into the New York City market. In 1975 Gilberto Rodriguez Orejuela sent Hernando Giraldo Soto, a close boyhood friend, to New York City to develop the Cali Cartel's Colombian contacts in the borough of Queens, and during the next three years, he refined and enlarged their cocaine distribution line to New York City. Meanwhile, in September 1975 the names of Gilberto and Miguel Rodriguez Orejuela had appeared as fifty-eighth and sixty-second respectively on a list of 113 top drug traffickers compiled by the intelligence section of Colombia's Customs Service. The Cali Cartel was on its way.

The Medellin Cartel developed a different, confrontational approach to drug trafficking than its Cali rival. The Medellin Cartel was not afraid of violent confrontation with anyone, including the Colombian government, and it would not hesitate to eliminate any threats to its interests. During the 1980s, the Medellin Cartel used bombings and terrorism and hired and trained hit men known as *sicarios* to kill thousands of people, including some of the most prominent figures in Colombian politics: Rodrigo Lara Bonilla, Colombian Justice Minister, in 1984; Jaime Gomez Ramirez, head of Colombia's National Police Anti-Narcotics Unit, in 1986; Guillermo Cano Isaza, the respected editor of *El Espectador* newspaper, in 1986; and Luis Carlos Galan, presidential candidate, in 1989—among others.

The Cali Cartel preferred the bribe to get business done, but no group gets to the top of the criminal underworld and becomes what has been described as the most powerful criminal organization in history on sophisticated style alone. The Cali Cartel showed that it could be as ruthless as any other mafia involved in international drug trafficking. "They are smart; the authorities never seem to find the bodies," one Bogotá-based journalist explained. "And they always seem to be floating in the river, of course, away from [the city of] Cali." (Chepesiuk 1999, 145)

Differences aside, the two Colombian cartels revolutionized cocaine trafficking, not just in the way the drug was transported to the United States, but also in how it was distributed there. The cartels established the drug trade on a business model with efficient, well-oiled smuggling, marketing, and money-laundering networks operating from coast to coast. By 1989 an estimated 300 Colombian trafficking groups and 20,000 Colombians were involved in the cocaine trade in the United States. At least 5,000 of the Colombians who worked for the cartels lived in the Miami area and another 6,000 in the Los Angeles area.

"The Colombians have the momentum by benefit of their early involvement in the cocaine trade," The President's Commission on Organized Crime concluded in 1986. "They have evolved from small, disassociated groups into compartmentalized organizations that are sophisticated and systematized in their approach to the trafficking of cocaine in the U.S." (President's Commission 1986, 78)

According to law enforcement reports, Colombian trafficking groups operate as self-centered cells of about five to fifty members with only a handful of the "managers" knowing all the cell's members. Top level managers both in Colombia and in the United States are recruited on the basis of blood and marriage, which helps to minimize the potential for theft or disobedience, because family members in Colombia are held accountable for drug deals gone bad. Middle managers are placed all over the United States and may include individuals who are not family members, but who may be friends of top-level *capos* (leaders or godfathers) or at least have roots in the same region the capos come from.

The third level consists of thousands of workers, both inside and outside the United States: accountants, couriers, chemists, lawyers, stash-house keepers, enforcers, bodyguards, launderers, pilots, and wholesale distributors. These individuals perform specialized tasks and may work for different groups at different times. While the cartels are predominantly Colombian in membership, they will go outside their group to hire specialists, such as pilots or lawyers, and will, when need be, cooperate with other criminal groups, including Mexicans, Italians, Jamaicans, and Nigerians.

Despite their brilliance in organizing the cocaine trade, the Medellin Cartel's emphasis on violence to fulfill its criminal objectives ultimately led to its decline and fall. From 1984 to 1993, the Medellin Cartel engaged the Colombian state in a war of attrition. The terror and death toll was largely of Pablo Escobar's making. "Every time there is a major assassination in Colombia, they [the Ochoas] send out word that they aren't behind it," revealed Maria Jimena Duzan, an investigative journalist and columnist with the Bogotá-based *El Espectador* newspaper. (Chepesiuk 1987)

The Medellin Cartel, however, paid for its violent ways. On 5 February 1987 an elite Colombian police unit captured Carlos Lehder twenty miles outside of Medellin, the heart of Colombia's cocaine industry and quickly extradited him to the United States, where he was convicted of drug trafficking and sentenced to a life sentence plus 135 years in prison. Jose Gonzalo Rodriquez Gacha, who matched Escobar in ruthlessness, was killed in a shootout with police in December 1989, while the three Ochoa brothers, seeing the writing on the wall, all turned themselves in and were sent to jail. Medellin's dominance of the cocaine trade ended when Colombian police killed Pablo Escobar in 1993. That left the Cali Cartel to rule supreme in the empire of cocaine.

During the late 1980s and early 1990s, while the Colombian government waged war with the Medellin Cartel, the Cali Cartel expanded its operation and extended its tentacles deeper into Colombia's tottering democracy in search of greater profits and more power. With the heat on in Colombia, Cali moved most of its cocaine-refining operations to Peru and Bolivia, and its transportation routes through Venezuela and Central America. The Cartel also began to muscle into the heroin trade, growing the opium itself in Colombia and then using its efficient cocaine distribution network to move the refined product.

The heroin the Cali Cartel peddled was both purer and cheaper than its chief competitor, the Southeast Asian variety. In 1994 a gram of Colombian heroin was selling for $80 to $150 per gram, compared to $300 to $400 for the type from Southeast Asia. One DEA report revealed that the Cali Cartel's share of the New York City heroin market had jumped from 22 to

60 percent during the early 1990s. "In the past five years, there has been a steady increase in the flow and purity of heroin in the U.S., suggesting that the taste for the drug is growing," a U.S. State Department report warned in 1994. (Farah 1994)

Although the Cali Cartel led the Colombian connection's move into big-time heroin trafficking, many other Colombian criminal organizations were involved as well, indicating that the nature of the drug trade was changing. By 1991 one cartel, led by the brothers Ivan and Julio Urdinola and based in the country's northern Cauca Valley, was making as much money in drug trafficking as the Cali Cartel. "By expanding from cocaine to heroin production, the (Urdinola) organization has the capacity to become the first true narcotics conglomerate, and it is already shipping mixed loads of the two drugs to the United States and Europe," the *Washington Post* reported. (Farah 1994)

Facing increasing competition and knowing that with the demise of the Medellin Cartel it would be the number one target of Colombian and U.S. officials, the Cali Cartel began to negotiate their exodus from international drug trafficking with the Colombian government. After a meeting with Pacho Herrera, Jose Olmedo Ocampo, and Juan Carlos Ramirez, three leaders of the Cali Cartel, Colombian Attorney General Gustavo de Grieff began pushing the Colombian government to accept an agreement with the Cartel that would have led to lenient terms of surrender for the drug traffickers. News of the meeting and what transpired caused a storm of controversy both inside and outside of Colombia. The United States charged that de Grieff's office had been infiltrated by the Cali Cartel and warned that any such agreement with the Cartel would seriously damage United States-Colombia relations.

Those relations deteriorated, largely because of accusations that Colombian President Ernesto Samper Pizano's 1994 presidential campaign had been infiltrated by the Cali Cartel. A stunned Colombia heard a cassette tape in which Cali Cartel leader Miguel Rodriguez Orjuela revealed that he had arranged to give millions to the Samper Pizano campaign. The "narcocassettes" were based on police wiretaps and intercepts and confirmed the Drug Enforcement Administration's long-time suspicions that Samper Pizano and key members of his Liberal Party were on the Cali payroll.

The Colombian Congress, which was dominated by the Liberal Party, eventually declared Samper Pizano innocent of any wrongdoing in the scandal, but several associates in his presidential campaign and in his administration went to jail. United States-Colombian relations reached rock bottom on 1 March 1996, the date the United States "decertified" Colombia as a helpful partner in the War on Drugs. The move placed Colombia with such pariahs as Iran, Syria, Nigeria, and Afghanistan.

Ironically, while these developments were unfolding, the Colombian government was having stunning success against the Cali Cartel. Between June and August 1995 Colombian police, with the help of the CIA and DEA, captured six of the top seven leaders of the Cali Cartel, including the brothers Rodriguez Orejuela and Jose Santacruz Londono. Authorities captured Gilberto Rodriguez Orejuela after searching a house in a middle-class neighborhood of Santa Monica and found him inside a secret vaulted closet with three pistols and between $100,000 and $200,000 in cash. One of the arresting officers told the press, "He was half asleep. He was very confused. He did not resist arrest." (Sheridan 1995)

U.S. officials predicted that Rodriguez's capture would be a "mortal blow" against the Cali Cartel. In October 1996 Gilberto Rodriguez Orejuela agreed to pay a fine of $105 million to the Colombian state and confessed to crimes involving narcotics trafficking and "illegal enrichment." He faced a maximum penalty of twenty-five years in jail. The arrest of other Cali Cartel leaders followed and in 1998 Helmer Pacho Herrera, who had turned himself in to the authorities in 1996, was murdered in a prison yard. Gilberto and Miguel Rodriguez Orejuela are currently in a Colombian jail, serving fifteen- and twenty-one-year terms respectively.

But will the stunning success against the Cali Cartel have any impact on Colombia's role as the linchpin in the Latin American drug trade? Drug war analysts believe that, just as it was business as usual after Escobar's death, there is no reason to expect that the situation will change because another powerful Colombian Cartel's tenure of leadership in the drug trade has ended. Indeed, destroying the Colombian connection might be even more difficult in the future, because instead of one monolithic cartel to deal with, law enforcement will have to confront and try to dismantle several "baby cartels," not just in Colombia, but in Mexico and other Latin American countries as well.

Rosso Jose Serrano, general director of Colombia's National Police, explained, "These smaller cartels won't have the corrupting capacity of the Cali cartel, nor will they easily have the organizational reach that made Cali such an international power." (Chepesiuk 1999, 151)

See also: Abbell, Michael; Arizabaleta Arzayz, Phanor; Cano Izaza, Guillermo; Cartelitos; Certification; Cocaine; Duzan Jimena, Maria; Escobar Gaviria, Pablo; Fonseca Carillo, Ernesto; Garcia, Edgar; Giraldo, Alberto; Grieff, Gustavo de; Guzman Lara, Joaquin; Henao Montoya, Jose Orlando; Heroin; Lara Bonilla, Rodrigo; Herrera Zuleta, Helmer "Pacho"; Rodrigo; Lehder Rivas, Carlos; Matta Ballesteros, Juan Ramon; Medellin Cartel; Carter, James Earl; Money Laundering; Moran, William C.; Narcocassettes; Narcoterrorism; Noriega, Manuel Antonio; Ochoa Vasquez, Jr., Fabio; Ochoa Vasquez, Jorge Luis; Ochoa Vasquez, Juan David; Operation Calico; Operation College Farm; Operation Dinero; Operation Green Ice II; Pastrana Arango, Andres; People Persecuted by Pablo Escobar (Pepes); Ramirez Gomez, Jaime; Rodriguez Orejuela, Gilberto; Rodriguez Orejuela, Miguel; Samper Pizano, Ernesto; Sanchez, Orlando; Santacruz Londono, Jose; Serrano Cadena, Rosso Jose; Toft, Joe; Urdinola, Ivan

References: Castillo, Fabio. 1988. *Los Jinetes de la Cocaina.* Chepesiuk, Ron. 1999. *Hard Target.*
———. 1987. "Kingpin's Trial: A Small Win in Losing War on Drugs." *Orlando Sentinel,* 4 October.
De Grazia, Jessica. 1991. *DEA: The War Against Drugs.*
Farah, Douglas. 1994. U.S.-Colombia Split over Cali Cartel. *Washington Post,* 8 March.
President's Commission on Organized Crime. 1986. *America's Habit: Drug Trafficking and Organized Crime.*
Shannon, Elaine. 1991. "New Kings of Cocaine." *Time,* 1 July.
Sheridan, Beth, et al. 1995. "Colombia Arrests Kingpin of Cali Cartel." *Miami Herald,* 10 June.
Strong, Simon. 1995. *Whitewash: Pablo Escobar and the Cocaine Wars.*

Califano, Joseph A. (1932–)

A former U.S. government official who has been a leader in the fight against drug abuse since the 1960s. As President Lyndon Johnson's White House liaison on domestic policy, Califano secured the first federal drug-rehabilitation funds. Today, as head of the National Center on Addiction and Substance Abuse, he is responsible for developing strategies that help keep young people from experimenting with illegal drugs. Califano has expressed strong opposition to the legalization of drugs, arguing that it would increase the number of addicts, worsen violent crime, and increase health-care costs.

See also: Johnson, Lyndon Baines; Legalization
Reference: Dreyfuss, Robert. 1997. "Hawks and Doves: Who's Who in the World of Drugs." *Rolling Stone,* 7 August.

Camarena Salazar, Enrique (1958–1985)

On 7 February 1985 U.S. Drug Enforcement Administration agent Enrique Camarena Salazar was kidnapped in broad daylight within a block of the American consulate in Guadalajara, Mexico. U.S. Ambassador John Gavin, concerned because another DEA agent had been kidnapped several months earlier, immediately demanded that Mexican authorities take strong and quick action to find Camarena. The Mexican authorities resisted and the U.S. government launched Operation Camarena along the Mexican border. Each car entering the U.S. was carefully searched for Camarena Salazar, a move that created bottlenecks on both sides of the United States-Mexican border.

The DEA suspected that Camarena Salazar's kidnapping had been orchestrated by powerful drug trafficker Rafael Caro Quintero. The Mexican authorities, under intense U.S. pressure, raided one of Caro Quintero's ranches and then issued an order for his arrest. The drug trafficker escaped to Costa Rico, however, and the mutilated body of Camarena Salazar was found in March 1985. Caro Quintero and Ernesto Fonseca Carillo, a drug trafficker and another suspect in Camarena Salazar's murder, were arrested in April 1985. A third suspect, Juan Jose Esparragoza Morena, was arrested in Mexico City in March 1986.

Camarena's colleagues at the DEA did not believe that Caro Quintero acted alone. They believed that prominent figures of Mexico's power elite were behind Camarena's murder. The U.S. government did all it could to bring the accomplices in Camarena's murder to trial in the United States, including what many Mexicans complained was the kidnapping of its citizens. Eight people were tried on charges that included murder, and seven of them were convicted. Raul Lopez Alvarez, the first to be convicted, was a member of the Guadalajara homicide squad and became the first person ever convicted in the United States under a 1984 racketeering law that added new penalties for violence in connection with criminal acts. Jurors saw a tape of Lopez telling authorities about the torture of Camarena on orders from Mexican drug lord Rafael Caro Quintero.

Camarena's murder highlighted a contentious issue between the United States and Mexico. The U.S government has long argued that its drug agents need to carry weapons to protect themselves against violent drug traffickers while on missions on Mexican soil. Mexico has repeatedly rejected the request, seeing armed DEA agents operating in Mexico as a threat to their country's sovereignty.

In August 1998 U.S. Senator Mike Dewine (R-Ohio) and Representative Bill McCollum (R-FL) introduced a bill that would have included an offer of helicopters for Mexico to fight the War on Drugs if the country allowed U.S. drug agents to carry weapons there. A top Mexican official responded, "The government of Mexico has repeatedly and emphatically indicated that it will not grant such permission." (Mexico Rejects New Plans to Arm U.S Drug Agents. 1998)

See also: Caro Quintero, Rafael; Operation Colombus
References: "Justice for Camarena." 1998. *Time*, 3 October.
McPhee, John. 1996. "Death of an Agent." *New Yorker*, 29 January.
"Mexico Rejects New Plans to Arm U.S. Drug Agents." 1998. *Miami Herald*, 27 August.
Shannon, Elaine. 1989. *Desperadoes*.

Campaign against Marijuana Planting (CAMP)

The Campaign against Marijuana Planting (CAMP) is an antidrug operation that was set up in 1983 by the state of California and involves many federal, state, and local law enforcement officials. As a result of CAMP, law enforcement has arrested many marijuana growers and destroyed hundreds of thousands of marijuana plants, but critics charged that the program was too costly and ineffective in deterring marijuana cultivation. According to a report of the National Drug Enforcement Policy Board, "CAMP has displaced some of the problems to Oregon. The remaining commercial growers tend to view CAMP as a cost of doing business and take a variety of measures to minimize associated costs. Production has increased and product availability appears to have remained unchanged." (National Drug Enforcement Policy Board 1996, 118)

References: Cooper, Mary H. 1990. *The Business of Drugs*.
National Drug Enforcement Policy Board. 1996. *The Cannabis Problem—Historical Overview: An Analysis Of The Domestic Cannabis Problem and the Federal Response*. August.

CAMP
See Campaign against Marijuana Planting

Cannabis Buyer's Club

Founded in 1991, this club was started by Dennis Peron in San Francisco to provide AIDS and cancer patients with marijuana. Peron had led a successful citywide initiative that allowed marijuana to be sold for medical purposes. All the club's 12,000 members needed to buy marijuana was a doctor's note. The club also offered drug counseling.

Selling marijuana is a federal offence, but San Francisco officials did nothing to stop the club's operations. On 4 August 1996 however, agents from the California Bureau of Narcotics raided the club and confiscated 150 pounds of marijuana and $60,000 in cash. No one was arrested but state officials obtained a restraining order to keep the club closed. The authorities also moved to close other marijuana buyers' clubs in California.

See also: Marijuana; Medical Marijuana
Reference: Rist, Curtis. 1996. "Weed the People." *People Weekly*, 21 October.

Cano Izaza, Guillermo (1925–1986)

Editor-in-chief of *El Espectador*, Colombia's second largest newspaper, who wrote frequently about drugs in his editorial page column "Libreta de Apuntes" (Notebook), calling for tougher laws against the country's drug traffickers. He was disturbed that several prominent Colombians opposed extradition of criminals to the United States and wanted to legalize drugs as a way to avoid drug-related violence. On 17 December 1986 Cano was killed by an assassin traveling on a motorcycle in busy downtown Bogotá traffic. In early 1988, the Colombian authorities announced that they had solved Cano's murder, revealing that it was a contract killing carried out by a Medellin Cartel assassination squad known as Los Priscos.

See also: Cali Cartel; Extradition; Legalization; Medellin Cartel; Media; Rodriguez Gacha, Jose Gonzalo

Guillermo Cano, assassinated editor of the Colombian newspaper El Espectador (Courtesy of Ron Chepesiuk)

References:
Gugliotta, Guy, and Jeff Leen. 1990. *Kings of Cocaine.*
Strong, Simon. 1995. *Whitewash: Pablo Escobar and the Co-caine Wars.*

Cardona, Libia

The so-called Cocaine Queen who was involved with the cocaine trafficking business in the mid-1960s. Cardona met with Luis Gaviria, a convicted robber, and the two became lovers, as well as partners in setting up a cocaine distribution network that consisted mainly of relatives. By the late 1960s, the network employed 150 people in Latin America and the United States and was earning an estimated $60 million annually in income. The organization, however, began to unravel when two of its drug couriers were arrested in Houston in 1977. Gaviria was murdered, but Cardona continued in the cocaine business. In 1980 Cardona was arrested in Miami and released on $1 million bail. She escaped to the Bahamas and later returned to Bogotá.

See also: Cocaine
Reference: Traub, James. 1983. *The Billion Dollar Connection: The International Drug Trade.*

Caribbean Financial Action Task Force (CFATF)

This regional organization comprises twenty-four nations and is supported financially by five other nations, including the United States. The CFATF is an example of the regional antimoney-laundering organizations that are springing up around the world to deal aggressively with the technologically sophisticated ways with which criminals are stealing, moving, and hiding money.

See also: Money Laundering
Reference: "International Crime Control Strategy Report." 1998. *Transnational Crime* (Fall): 86.

Caro Quintero, Rafael (1952–)

A former head of the Guadalajara drug cartel, which in the mid-1980s controlled most of the powerful drug empire in Mexico that centered on smuggling tons of cocaine and marijuana into the United States. Enrique Camarena Salazar was murdered on 7 February 1985 outside Guadalajara, and the drug trafficker was arrested in connection with the murder. In December 1989, he was found guilty of killing Camarena.

See also: Camarena Salazar, Enrique; Cocaine; Marijuana
Reference: Shannon, Elaine. 1989. *Desperadoes.*

Carrillo Fuentes, Amado
(c. 1953–1997)

Leading Mexican drug trafficker who, at the time of his mysterious death in July 1997, was the country's most powerful drug trafficker. Nicknamed the Lord of the Skies for his use of Boeing 727s and other large planes to transport tons of cocaine from Colombia to Mexico, Carrillo Fuentes headed the Juarez Cartel, which was associated with Colombia's Cali Cartel, and he had numerous regional bases in northern Mexico that served as storage locations for drugs later smuggled across the U.S. border.

Like his Colombian associates, Carrillo Fuentes used sophisticated technology and state-of-the-art communication devices to conduct his illegal trade in cocaine, heroin, methamphetamine, and marijuana. A fugitive from U.S. justice for nine years before his death, the Lord of the Skies had been the subject of more than twenty-five separate U.S. and Mexican investigations and had been indicted twice in Miami (1988 and 1996) and in Dallas, Texas, (1993) on charges that included conspiracy to distribute cocaine, heroin, and marijuana. The drug trafficker had numerous ties to Mexican law enforcement and the political establishment. As a sign of his power, Carrillo Fuentes is believed to have had Jesus Gutierrez Rebello, who held the position that is Mexico's counterpart to the U.S. drug czar, on his payroll until Gutierrez's arrest in 1997.

The scope of Carrillo Fuentes's organization was staggering. Reportedly, it spent from $20 to $30 million on each drug smuggling operation and generated weekly profits in the tens of millions of dollars. In early 1998 the Drug Enforcement Administration reported that Carrillo Fuentes's organization was beginning to make inroads into the U.S. distribution of cocaine on the East Coast, principally in New York City, the traditional U.S. base of the Cali Cartel's smuggling operation. At the time of his death the Lord of the Skies was attempting to consolidate control over drug trafficking operations along the border of northern Mexico.

Under intense pressure from Mexican and U.S. law enforcement authorities, Carrillo Fuentes made efforts to disguise his appearance through cosmetic surgery and to relocate some of his operations and resources to Chile. He died in Mexico City on 4 July 1997 while undergoing plastic surgery. Spanish language reports suggested that the drug kingpin was either murdered or victimized by gross medical negligence. His postoperative recovery was apparently proceeding normally when he was supposedly injected with Dormicum, which is described as a "postoperatory medicine." This evidently caused contraction of the blood vessels and a fatal heart attack. After Carillo Fuentes's death, a violent struggle broke out in Juarez, Mexico, for control of the drug kingpin's empire.

See also: Cali Cartel; Certification; Cocaine; Garcia Abrego, Juan; Gutierrez Rebello, Jesus; Heroin; Juarez Cartel; Marijuana; Methamphetamine; Pallomari, Guillermo Aleandro "Reagan"
Reference: U.S. Senate Committee on Foreign Relations. 1998. *International Organized Crime Syndicates and Their Impact on the United States: Hearings before the Subcommittee on Western Hemisphere, Peace Corps, Narcotics and Terrorism,* 26 February (statement of Thomas A. Constantine, Director, DEA.

Carillo Fuentes, Vincente

Brother of the late, powerful drug trafficker Amado Carillo Fuentes, Vincente was indicted in federal court for the western district of Texas and had a drug-trafficking warrant issued for his arrest in 1993. Mexican authorities captured Vincente in October 1998.

See also: Carillo Fuentes, Amado
Reference: Constantine, Thomas A. 1998. *International Organized Crime Syndicates and Their Impact on The United States.*

Carrera Fuentes, Adrian

Head of Mexico's Federal Judicial Police, an antidrug police agency from 1992 to 1993, who admitted taking a bribe of $1 million from drug trafficker Amado Carrillo Fuentes (no relation) to look the other way. He was sentenced to six years in prison on 31 August 1998 for money laundering. Carrera Fuentes said he used the money to establish more than a dozen floor-tile stores, but he denied having turned over some of the money to former Deputy Attorney General Mario Ruiz Massieu.

See also: Massieu, Mario Ruiz; Carrillo Fuentes, Amado
Reference: "Ex Mexican Police Chief Sentenced." 1998. Associated Press, 1 September.

Cartegena Summit

On 15 February 1990, U.S. President George Bush journeyed to Cartagena, Colombia, to meet with leaders of Peru, Bolivia, and Colombia and work out an aggressive strategy to combat international drug trafficking. The summit countries agreed to attack drug trafficking from every angle in a concerted effort to put the Latin American drug traffickers out of business. President Bush also expressed his determination and commitment to reduce the demand for drugs.

In an address before the National Governor's Association on 26 February 1990 U.S. Secretary of State James Baker said, "By going to Cartegena, the President demonstrated our country's absolute determination to fight the drug war for however long it takes. We have assured our partners that we will not fail to support them in the drug fight." (Baker 1990, 15) To show its support for the agreement reached at Cartegena, the Bush administration increased the international component of its drug budget sevenfold from fiscal year 1987 to 1991.

See also: Bush, George Herbert Walker
References: Bagley, Bruce, and William O. Walker. 1994. *Drug Trafficking in the Americas.*
Baker, James. 1990. *Narcotics: Threat to Global Security.* U.S. Department of State Dispatch, 3 September.

Cartel

In the business sphere, the term refers to a combination of independent commercial enterprises designed to limit competition. In the War on Drugs, the term is used to describe large drug-trafficking organizations, such as the Medellin Cartel or Tijuana Cartel. The cartels are actually a loose association of drug traffickers who usually conduct their illicit business independently but will work together when it is mutually beneficial. According to Jeff Leen and Guy Gugliotta, the term cartel was first used in 1983 in an Operation Fountain report analyzing cocaine seizures.

See also: Bogotá Cartel; Cali Cartel; Caro Quintero, Rafael; Cartelito; Galeano Murcia, Cristobal; Gulf Cartel, Juarez Cartel; Lara Nauza, Jaime Orlando; Medellin Cartel; North Atlantic Coast Cartel; Orlandez Gamboa, Jaime; Quintero-Payan, Emilio, and Quintero-Payan, Juan Jose; Sonora Cartel; Tijuana Cartel
Reference: Gugliotta, Guy, and Jeff Leen. 1990. *Kings of Cocaine.*

Cartelito

From a Spanish diminutive form of the English word *cartel*, meaning "little cartel," the term *cartelito* is used by law enforcement authorities and the press to describe the type of drug-trafficking organization that began to spring up after the stunning success the law enforcement authorities had against the Cali Cartel in the mid-1990s. At that time the organization's top leadership was either surrendering or being captured and put in prison. The authorities began to notice a trend. The drug-trafficking industry was downsizing.

In the future, instead of confronting huge drug-trafficking organizations, or cartels, the authorities believe they will have to deal with many smaller cartelitos or "baby cartels", not just in Colombia, but also Mexico and other Latin America countries. Many authorities predict that this will make the job of combating drug trafficking more difficult in the future. Instead of large, cumbersome, easy-to-identify organizations, many will be small, mobile, and more elusive.

See also: Cartel; Cali Cartel
Reference: Chepesiuk, Ron. 1999. *Hard Target.*

Carter, James Earl (Jimmy) (1924–)

United States president from 1977 to 1981. Early in the Carter administration the federal government's antidrug policy changed. At the March 1977 House of Representatives hearings on decriminalization, the chief of the Department of Justice testified that the federal government could no longer effectively prosecute marijuana and admitted, "nor do we, in any conceivable way, in the Federal Government, have the resources to do so." (De Grazia 1991, 12). The Carter administration also softened the government's position on cocaine. Dr. Peter Bourne, the President's Director of the Office of Drug Policy Abuse, described cocaine as "probably the most benign of illicit drugs currently in widespread use. At least as strong a case could be made for legalizing it as for legalizing marijuana. Short acting—not physically addicting, and acutely able—cocaine has found increasing favor at all socioeconomic levels." (De Grazia, 12)

During the Carter administration, cocaine, like

heroin and marijuana before it, was beginning to hit the American mainstream in a big way. Many musicians, intellectuals, artists, politicians, and even government bureaucrats saw nothing wrong with snorting the drug. In 1978 the White House was embarrassed by a story in the *Washington Post* alleging that the president's drug policy adviser, Peter Bourne, himself used cocaine at a party. The good doctor resigned, but before leaving his post he had set the tone for the Carter administration's drug policy. "Deciding that imprisonment was worse than narcotics use and that international intervention would not slow the drug flow, the Carter White House adopted a more cautious policy." (McCoy & Block 1992) Alfred McCoy and Alan Block explained, "With the exception of comparatively modest suppression operations against opium in Mexico, Carter deemphasized the CIA and restrained its covert operations during his first three years in office." (McCoy & Block 1992, 9)

By December 1979, however, the Carter administration was worrying about the Soviet invasion of Afghanistan, and it began shipping arms to the Mujahideen guerrillas. Not all Carter officials agreed with the administration's Afghanistan policy. Dr. David Musto and Joyce Lowinson, members of the White House Strategy Counsel on Drug Abuse, wrote an editorial opinion article for the *New York Times*, expressing their concern about the growing of opium poppies in Pakistan and Afghanistan by rebel tribesmen. "Are we erring in befriending these tribes as we did in Laos where Air America (chartered by the Central Intelligence Agency) helped transport crude opium from certain tribal areas?" (Musto & Lowinson 1979, 26) Alfred McCoy believed the answer was "yes." He believed that evidence showed that Afghan heroin had begun flooding the U.S. market in 1979, substantially increasing the number of hard-core addicts, as well as overdose deaths. "Although the drug epidemic of the 1980s had complex causes, the growth in the global heroin supply could be traced in large part to two key aspects of U.S. policy: the failure of the DEA interdiction efforts and the CIA's covert operations. . . . [J]ust as the CIA support of nationalist Chinese troops in Shan States had increased Burma's opium crop in the 1950s, so the agency's aid to the Mujahideen guerrillas in the 1980s expanded opium production in Afghanistan and linked Pakistan's nearby heroin laboratories to the world market. After a decade as the sites of major CIA covert operations, Burma and Afghanistan ranked respectively as the world's largest and second largest suppliers for illicit heroin in 1989." (McCoy 1991, 22)

By 1980 and the end of the Carter administration, many were questioning whether the United States' antidrug policy had produced any tangible results. During the Nixon administration, the budget for the United States' antidrug program had increased significantly and drug enforcement infrastructure underwent a major reorganization to provide the leadership in the War on Drugs and to reduce interagency rivalries, but critics charged that one of the federal agencies, the CIA, had helped fuel drug use in the United States by helping allies in Southeast Asia and possibly Afghanistan who were heavily involved in international drug trafficking.

The federal government had tried eradication programs in Turkey and Mexico, but sources for heroin and marijuana had sprung up in other countries and drugs continued to flow freely into United States. During the 1970s the U.S. government put antidrug policies in place in cocaine source countries, such as Peru and Colombia, and the transit countries of the Caribbean and Central America, but they were small and ineffective, since the United States concentrated most of its attention and resources on heroin during the decade. Meanwhile, the ambitious criminal cartels based in the Colombian cities of Cali and Medellin were poised for their big entrance on the international drug trafficking scene when they would make cocaine the drug of the 1980s. This record led the President's 1984 Commission on Crime to conclude that "the nation's drug problem at the end of the 1980s was as great, if not greater, than the problem in 1970." (President's Commission on Organized Crime 1984, 229)

See also: Air America; Bourne, Peter; Cali Cartel; Cocaine; Decriminalization; Eradication; Heroin; Marijuana; McCoy, Alfred W.; Medellin Cartel; Musto, David; Narcoguerrillas; Opium; United States Central Intelligence Agency; United States President's Commission on Organized Crime

References: De Grazia, Jessica. 1991. *DEA: The War Against Drugs.*
McCoy, Alfred W. 1991. The CIA Connection. *The Progressive* (July).
McCoy, Alfred W., and Alan A. Block. 1992. "U.S. Narcotics Policy: An Anatomy of Failure" in *War on Drugs: Studies in the Failure of U.S. Anti Narcotic Policy.*

Morgan, H. Wayne. 1981. *Drugs in America: A Social History, 1800–1980.*

President's Commission on Organized Crime. 1986. *America's Habit: Drug Trafficking and Organized Crime.*

Casas de Cambio

These currency exchange houses operate on both sides of the United States-Mexico border and are used by drug traffickers to launder money. The major legitimate function of the houses is to change U.S. dollars into pesos or vice versa for tourists, businessmen, and workers, but they perform numerous other services as well, such as selling money orders and cashier checks and wiring transfers of funds, all of which are used by drug traffickers. The houses have proven to be rich ground for money-laundering activity because they are virtually unregulated.

See also: Money Laundering; Operation Green Ice II
Reference: Shannon, Elaine. 1996. "Narco-Gnomes of Mexico: Where Drug Money Goes To Hide." *Washington Post*, 17 March.

Castano, Fidel and Carlos

Colombian ranchers and large land owners who Colombian authorities suspect of being the heads of a paramilitary group calling itself the Self-Defence of Uruba and Cordoba (ACCU). In the 1990s the Castanos became heavily involved in the country's civil war and, under the guise of fighting the local guerrillas, they drove thousands of peasants off their land and then redistributed the land to themselves and other wealthy landowners. The Castanos are believed to be involved in the Colombian drug trade in collaboration with traffickers from Medellin and other centers in Colombia.

See also: Henoa Montoya, Jose Orlando; Human Rights; M-19; Revolutionary Armed Forces of Colombia (FARC)
References: Brooke, James. 1991. "Gaviria's Gamble." *New York Times,* Oct. 13.
Diebel, Linda. 1998. "Cocaine Trade Goes Low Key." *Toronto Star*, 6 June.

Castro, Jorge

A high-ranking member of the Mexican Arellano Felix drug-trafficking organization and one of the highest level narcotics traffickers ever arrested in the United States. In July 1998 a federal grand jury in Los Angeles indicted Castro in a conspiracy to smuggle narcotics from Mexico to the United States.

After a year-long wiretap investigation of Castro and his associates, nearly four tons of cocaine and more than $15 million in narcotics proceeds were seized.

See also: Cocaine; Felix Arellano, Ramon
Reference: "U.S. Crime Notebook: California." 1998. *Global Crime Update*, 27 July, 8.

CENTAC
See Central Tactical Units

Center For Substance Abuse Research (U.S.) (CESAR)

Located at the University of Maryland at College Park, the Center for Substance Abuse Research (CESAR) is dedicated to addressing the problems that substance abuse causes individuals and society and seeks to fulfill its mission by conducting research, training students in substance abuse research methods and policy analysis, and providing technical assistance to agencies and organizations working in substance abuse fields.

Reference: Center's web site at http://www.cesar.umd.edu/main.docs/mission.htm

Central Intelligence Agency
See United States Central Intelligence Agency

Central Tactical Units (CENTAC)

The Drug Enforcement Administration instituted the Central Tactical Units (CENTAC) program in 1974 to concentrate law enforcement resources on conspiracy investigations of high-level drug-trafficking targets. By the mid-1980s CENTAC was staffed by personnel not only from the DEA but also the Internal Revenue Service, the Customs Department, and state and local agencies, which were charged with pursuing criminal conspiracy cases under the Continuing Criminal Enterprise and RICO statutes. The U.S. General Accounting Office (GAO) released ambivalent reports about the effectiveness of the CENTAC program. A 1990 report criticized CENTAC for not achieving "the overall objective... complete immobilization of the targeted trafficking organizations." (President's Commission on Organized Crime 1986, 244–245). But another GAO report issued three years later concluded that the CENTAC program should be expanded.

See also: RICO; United States General Accounting Office
References: Mills, James. 1986. *The Underground Empire: Where Crime and Justice Embrace.*
President's Commission on Organized Crime. 1986. *America's Habit: Drug Trafficking and Organized Crime.*

Certification (U.S.)

Each year since 1986 the president of the United States gives to the U.S. Congress an annual assessment of thirty-two major drug-producing countries. This "certification" process is required by law under the Foreign Assistance Act of 1961 § 490, as amended, which mandates the president to prepare a list and assessment of the major illicit drug-producing and transit countries.

Under the law, the president must take sufficient steps to ensure that each of the thirty-two countries have complied "fully" with the United States on drug-trafficking matters and have implemented adequate measures to meet the goals and objectives of the 1988 United Nations Convention Against Illicit Traffic in Narcotic Drugs and Psychotropic substances.

If the listed countries are found not to have complied fully on drug-trafficking matters, the president may withhold foreign assistance from them. According to the U.S. State Department's Bureau of International Narcotics and Law Enforcement, "The purpose of the law is not to punish any particular country, rather it is to hold every country to a minimum standard of cooperation." (Clawson & Lee 1996) The U.S. State Department acknowledges that many countries resent the certification process, but adds that "they know that the President of the United States based the determination on sound, objective evidence, and he must defend his decisions before the U.S. Congress." (Clawson & Lee 1996)

Nevertheless, certification has become one of the most controversial aspects of U.S. drug control strategy. Many countries, which are on the list or are allies of the United States, as well as the critics of U.S. drug policy, have questioned whether certification is doing more harm than good in the War on Drugs. Many consider the process to be hypocritical and arrogant. They charge that the process is an excuse for the United States to blame foreign countries for its inability to curb demand for drugs at home. They have further argued that, despite the United States' claims to objectivity in applying certification, politics often dominates the process.

In recent years the comparative certification status of Mexico and Colombia has been used to make their point. In 1997, for example, Mexico was certified and Colombia was not. The United States had sought to punish Colombia since 1994, the year that Colombian President Ernesto Samper Pizano was accused of accepting money from the Cali Cartel for his presidential campaign. Ironically, in an effort to stave off certification, Samper had moved to crack down on the Cali Cartel and had put most of its top leadership in jail. To many observers, Colombia appeared to be doing enough to be certified as a helpful drug war ally. In terms of drug-related corruption, they saw no difference between the situations in Mexico and Colombia.

In defending its decision, the Clinton administration presented to Congress statistics on drug busts and arrests made by the Mexican government and evidence that it had passed new drug laws, which it said showed that the United States' major ally in the War on Drugs was cooperating "fully." Clinton administration officials, however, warned that decertification of Mexico would impact negatively on United States-Mexico relations and undermine mutual cooperation on a host of important issues, including immigration and the viability of the North American Free Trade Agreement (NAFTA). But to many other countries, the U.S. government had ignored the strong evidence that the Mexican government at all levels was rife with drug-related corruption and had become a major transit point for heroin, cocaine, and methamphetamine. Meanwhile, just before President Clinton announced that Mexico would be certified and Colombia would not, General Jesus Gutierrez Rebello, Mexico's drug czar, was arrested on drug-trafficking and corruption charges and for cooperating with Amado Carrillo Fuentes, who, at the time, was Mexico's top drug trafficker.

The certification of Mexico led to fierce debate in Congress. The House voted to overturn the certification of Mexico and impose sanctions if the country's drug-fighting performance didn't improve in ninety days. The Senate reached a compromise with the Clinton administration in which it issued a resolution censuring Mexico's efforts as "inadequate" and requiring President Clinton to report back later in the year to see if it had improved.

In the end, the Clinton administration's certification decision stood. Mexico was home free and

Colombia was on a decertified list with such pariahs as Iran, Syria, and Afghanistan.

See also: Cali Cartel; Carillon Fuentes, Amado; Clinton, William Jefferson; Pastrano Arango, Andres; Rebello Gutierrez, Jesus; Samper Pizano, Ernesto; United Nations Convention against Illicit Traffic in Narcotic Drugs and Psychotropic Substances of 1988.

References: Bertram, Eva, and Kenneth Sharpe. 1997. "The Drug War's Phony Fix: Why Certification Doesn't Work." *The Nation*, 28 April.

Clawson, Patrick, and Rensselaer W. Lee. 1996. *The Andean Cocaine Industry.*

Cooper, Mary H. 1990. *The Business of Drugs.* Drugs, Latin America and The United States. 1998. *The Economist*, 7 February.

U.S. Department of State Website, http://www.state.gov/.

Chamber Brothers

One of the violent new African American drug gangs that appeared in the 1980s. Based in Detroit, Michigan, the gang at its height controlled about 200 crack houses, supplied crack to about 50 more, and pulled in about $1 million a week. Authorities busted and successfully prosecuted the gang in 1988.

Reference: Kleinknecht, William. 1996. *The New Ethnic Mobs: The Changing Face of Organized Crime in America.*

Chapare Province (Bolivia)

The principle coca growing area in Bolivia, where an estimated 70 percent of the crop is grown in the region's semitropical lowlands. Authorities believe that almost the entire population may be involved in coca production because the local leaf is unsuitable for chewing. Drug traffickers either move into the area and process the coca leaf into cocaine themselves or sell the crop to the Colombian traffickers who refine it into the finished cocaine product and move it through Argentina and Brazil to the United States and European markets. By 1990 the United Nations Drug Abuse Control Program had begun introducing programs for alternative and economic development programs in the Chapare.

See also: Alternative Development; Associated High Valley Project; Cocaine; United Nations International Drug Control Program

Reference: Jamieson, Alison. 1994. *Terrorism and Drug Trafficking in Europe in the 1990s.*

Chemical Bank of the United States (New York City)

In February 1977 Chemical Bank became the first U.S. financial institution to be indicted under the Bank Secrecy Act of 1970. At the time of the indictment, Chemical Bank was the sixth largest commercial bank in the United States with 244 branches in the New York City area. Three of the bank's officers were indicted for laundering money for several narcotics dealers, including Frank Lucas, an Italian American Mafia associate, by exchanging smaller denomination bills for larger ones.

The indictment charged Chemical Bank with failing to report $8.5 million on more than 500 cash transactions. In exchange for the court's dismissal of felony charges, the Bank pled guilty to more than 200 misdemeanors and was fined $200,000 plus court costs. Two of the bank's officers pled guilty to failing to report the cash payments they received in payment for laundering the narcotics dealers' money.

See also: Italian America Mafia; Money Laundering; United States Bank Secrecy Act

Reference: President's Commission on Organized Crime. 1984. *The Cash Connection: Organized Crime, Financial Institutions and Money Laundering.*

Chemical Precursor Agreement

Signed in May 1997, this agreement between the United States and the European Union provides for "advance notification of chemical shipments between parties so that the impacting country can verify the legitimacy of the proposed end use and end user." (International Crime Control Strategy 1998, 51) The agreement also provides for information exchange on suspected shipments of precursor chemicals to third countries and forbids the shipment of some chemicals if it has not been authorized by the importing country.

See also: Precursor Chemicals

Reference: International Crime Control Strategy. 1998. *Transnational Crime* (Fall).

China White

The nickname for heroin 4, a type of powerful heroin that American addicts usually like to use by injecting it into the veins. China White is refined into a solid cake substance. As with powdered heroin, the flakes can be granulated and then mixed with water and injected, as well as snorted, smoked, or taken orally.

See also: Heroin; Nixon, Richard Milhous; Vietnam War
Reference: Marnell, Tim, ed. 1997. *Drug Identification Bible.*

CIA
See United States Central Intelligence Agency.

Chloral Hydrate
Known popularly as a "knockout" drug, this sedative was invented in 1869 and remained in widespread medical use until it was found to be addictive.

Reference: Rose, Jonathan. 1985. "The Sorry History of Drug Abuse in the U.S." *Scholastic Update,* 10 May.

Clinton, William Jefferson (Bill) (1946–)
United States president from 1993 to 2001. During the 1992 presidential election, Bill Clinton sensed that the American public was disillusioned with the War on Drugs and pledged to change U.S. policy, promising the American people that he would combine tough law enforcement with more antidrug treatment and prevention programs. Clinton also announced that he would shift the emphasis away from the interdiction of drugs towards a policy that would help countries fight drug trafficking both economically and militarily.

In February 1993, the month after Clinton's inauguration as president, Lee Brown, the former police chief of New York City who was Clinton's choice for the new drug czar, said at his confirmation hearings that, if Congress approved his nomination, he would develop a "comprehensive and balanced" antidrug strategy, although he did not provide substantive details. In February 1993 Clinton also announced his plan to cut the support staff in the drug czar's office from 146 to twenty-five, a number fewer than half the size of the White House's communications staff.

Supporters of the move took this as a sign that the Clinton administration was serious about placing the emphasis of the drug policy on reducing demand. Critics, on the other hand, said that Clinton's announcement reflected the typical lack of commitment that has been exhibited by the president all throughout the drug war. The following month,

March 1993, the group called the U.S. Policy on International Counter Narcotics in the Western Hemisphere presented a strategy for combating cocaine production and trafficking that, among other things, called for a "gradual" shift in focus away from the transit countries of Mexico, the Caribbean, and Central America and to the cocaine source countries of Peru, Colombia, and Bolivia.

At her confirmation hearings in May 1993, attorney general nominee Janet Reno said that the U.S. antidrug policy should focus on prevention and treatment and not on combating drug trafficking abroad. In October 1993 the U.S. Defense Department announced that the military would cut spending on drug interdiction, which accounted for 71 percent of the $1.17 billion drug budget, by eleven percentage points, while increasing the amount spent on training and equipment for source countries to 16 percent, an increase of five percentage points. The following month, the executive branch announced that, within 120 days, it would develop a separate strategy to combat the heroin trade, because heroin use was reportedly increasing.

The Clinton administration finally released its "new" drug control strategy on 8 February 1994 at a briefing for foreign ambassadors in Washington, D.C. The following day, Robert S. Gelbard, assistant secretary for international narcotics matters, said that the strategy "recognizes that America's first line of defense against drugs is to reduce the drug abuse here at home. We are the world's largest illegal drug market—nothing at all to be proud of—but definitely we should shoulder our share of the responsibility for combating the drug scourge." (Wren 1994, 89)

Gelbard went on to list the key elements of the Clinton administration's drug control strategy: "We will help to build democratic institutions—the courts, law enforcement, community and political organizations—institutions strong enough to resist the reach of the drug trade. We will help drug-producing countries create economic alternatives to narcotics and advance applications for sustainable development. We will fight the multinational cartel...with a multinational effort." (Wren 1994, 89)

As the Clinton administration made public the objectives of its antidrug policy, critics began questioning Clinton's commitment to the War on Drugs and his seriousness about changing U.S. drug policy. In a candid interview with the *New York Times,* outgoing DEA head Robert C. Bonner said that he had reservations about whether Clinton really wanted to "develop... a drug strategy" and whether he "has the will to move Congress and the American people." (Teaster 1993) Some observers looked at the Clinton administration's fiscal year 1994 budget, which it had submitted to Congress in March 1993, and noticed only a slight shift of priorities towards demand reduction programs. Both Democratic and Republican legislators, as well as independent experts, criticized the Clinton administration for not giving any indication on how specifically the budget would be reapportioned.

The disenchantment grew during the year after Clinton's inauguration, and by early 1994 the Republican-controlled Congress was ready to abolish the office of the drug czar. "If at the end of this trial year (1994), we have not seen a... substantial improvement, we will vote to eliminate the office," warned Representative Jan Keyll. "Nobody is happy with the administration's lack of support." (York 1994) Meanwhile, Congress rejected Clinton's proposal to cut the drug czar's office staff and budget and actually doubled the office's allocation from $5.8 million to $11.1 million, while increasing its office staff to forty from the twenty-five proposed by Clinton.

Statistics showed that funding for drug interdiction did decline during Clinton's first term of office—from about $1 billion to $569 million—resulting in fewer ships, flight hours, and ground-based radar stations devoted to drug interdiction. Cocaine seizures in the transit zone dropped from 70,336 kilograms in 1992 to 37,181 in 1995. The proposed increased funding for source countries never did materialize.

Studies showed that heroin use was on the rise again in the early 1990s, and in November 1993 the Clinton administration announced that within 120 days it would have a plan in place to combat the growing heroin trade. However, as of June 1995—nineteen months later—the administration still had not developed a heroin control strategy. "Delays involving the strategy were due in large part to the difficulties in balancing U.S. objectives in Burma—the primary source of heroin," noted one government report. (U.S. General Accounting Office 1986, 2) As has happened often in the War on Drugs, the administration subordinated its antidrug strategy to other foreign policy objectives.

While heroin was making a strong comeback among American upper classes, a government study called the National Household Survey on Drug Use, released by the U.S. Department of Health and Human Services in August 1996, reported that between 1992 and 1995 teenage use of marijuana, cocaine, and LSD rose an average of 105 percent. The report became political fodder for both the Republicans and Democrats during the 1995 election. The Republicans accused the Clinton administration of creating a "lost generation" of American youth by cutting the drug budget and failing to exercise strong leadership on the issue. The Democrats countered that the apparent surge in teenage drug use had begun well before Clinton came into office, and they tried to link the rise to the Republican leadership on the War on Drugs under Ronald Reagan and George Bush, who, they charged, had made things worse by cutting the antidrug budget.

Robert Dole, the Republican candidate for president in 1996, unveiled his antidrug message, "Just Don't Do It," an obvious copy of Nancy Reagan's famous slogan of the 1980s, "Just Say No," and kept telling the American public how tough he would be on the War on Drugs. Not to be outflanked, Clinton promised that by 30 September 1996 he would give $75 million worth of helicopters, planes, arms, and other military equipment to the governments of Colombia, Peru, Bolivia, Venezuela, and the Caribbean region, a strong indication that it was going to be the drug war as usual if Clinton were re-elected. Dole called drug abuse "the most important news story of out time," but voters remained unimpressed. (Bayona Vargas 1996) According to opinion polls, drugs ranked fifth among the issues that most concerned the voters.

In the climate of heated rhetoric over the poll results regarding teenage drug use, both presidential candidates weren't listening to the experts who said that the reasons for teenage drug use were complex and advised the candidates not to make the drug issue so politically partisan. "Kids are not getting the strong messages they got in the 1980s," explained Diane Barry, communications director for Join Together, a Boston-based national resource center for communities fighting substance abuse. "When you look at those messages, it's no wonder that these kids are willing to start with marijuana. There's got to be leadership for the entire industry and there's got to be leadership for parents." (Toner 1996).

Many drug policy analysts believed there had to be leadership in the White House and Congress as well. Dr. Rensselaer Lee called the Dole-Clinton debate on national drug policy "artificial" and said that "[n]o good ideas have come out of this campaign, either from [the Clinton] administration or Dole." (Cavalier Castro 1996)

Clinton defeated Dole easily and as he began his second term of office, it became obvious that there would be no new direction in the War on Drugs. The United States would continue to seek a military solution to the drug problem in a stubborn effort to stop the supply, while paying lip service to decreasing the demand for drugs. As a result, international drug trafficking would expand to more and more countries and the drug abuse, violence, and corruption, fueled by the enormous profits generated by the trade, would continue.

Some sources in the media began speaking out for new, more creative approaches to the drug problem. In a November 1996 editorial, the conservative *National Review* concluded that the War on Drugs was lost and called for the legalization of drugs. Another editorial in the *San Francisco Chronicle* declared, "We are not saying that all drugs be summarily legalized, but every option—including decriminalization—should be considered in dealing with this complex problem that combines crime, public health, and social disintegration." (Clinton Pushing Anti-Drug Plan 1996)

It was also becoming obvious to America's allies that war as usual was not working, and they started calling for a global effort to combat international drug trafficking, pointing out that the dynamics of the illegal trade cut across national boundaries and involved criminal organizations that were now operating like multinational corporations in the cutthroat world of international trade. In December 1996 members of the Organization of American States reached an agreement in Montevideo, Uruguay, which ratified a hemispheric antidrug plan. "This is a strategy that can lead to the reduction of drug consumption and supply through international multilateral strategies," said Diego Cardona, foreign affairs adviser to President Ernesto Samper Pizano. (New Drug Strategy Needed 1996)

See also: Bonner, Raymond C.; Brown, Lee; Certification; Cocaine; Cuevas Ramirez, Nelson; Decriminalization; Drug Czar; Heroin; Just Say No; Legalization, LSD; Marijuana; Mathews, Frank; National Household Survey on Drug Abuse; Organization of American States; United States Office of National Drug Control Policy

References: Bayona Vargas, Mauricio. 1996. "Bayona: Clinton Reparte Los Dolores." *El Espectador*, 25 September.
Cavalier Castro, Andre. 1996. "Droga: Debate Artificiel In E.U." *El Tiempo*, 14 September.
"Clinton Pushing Anti-Drug Plan." 1992. *Miami Herald*, 2 December, International Satellite Edition.
"New Drug Strategy Needed." 1996. *Colombia Post*, 18–24 November.
Teaster, Joseph A. 1993. "Exiting Drug War Chief Warns of Cartels." *New York Times*, 31 October 1993.
Toner, Robin. 1996. "Parties Seek to Cast Blame for Rise in Teenage Drug Use." *New York Times*, 22 August.
United States General Accounting Office. 1996. *Drug Control: U.S. Interdiction Efforts In Caribbean Decline.*
Wren, Christopher. 1994. *New International Drug Strategy Needed To Combat Drugs.* United States Department of State Dispatch, 21 February.
York, Byron. 1994. "Clinton's Phony War." *American Spectator* (February).

Coca-Cola

The original formula for the popular soft drink we know today was developed in 1887 by John Styth Pemberton, a patent medicine manufacturer. Pemberton had noted the success of Vin Mariani, a drink that mixed wine and coca, and developed a product that he registered as "French Wine Coca—Ideal Nerve and Tonic Stimulant." Its ingredients included coca, a plant that grows exclusively in the Andean mountains of South America, primarily in the countries of Peru, Bolivia, and Colombia. The plant itself can be used to produce a high or stimulation, but once harvested the leaves are dried and put through a chemical process to extract the cocaine.

Asa Griggs, an American manufacturer and philanthropist, bought the formula from Pemberton and, after improving its quality, he devoted himself full-time to its production and sale. But from 1909 to 1919, Griggs's company was the defendant in a federal court case under the Pure Food and Drug Act, regarding the contents of the beverage. The case was settled after the Coca-Cola Company assured the U.S. government that the formula had been changed to exclude coca.

See also: Cocaine; United States Pure Food and Drug Act; Vin Mariani

Reference: Pendergrast, Mark. 1999. *For God, Country and Coca-Cola.*

A Bolivian campesino chews coca leaves as he and about 50 other people begin a hunger strike to protest the signing of an anti-drug agreement between Bolivia and the United States, 1987) (Corbis/Reuters)

Cocaine

A powerful drug is contained in the leaves of the coca shrub, a plant grown primarily in the South American countries of Peru, Bolivia, and Colombia. Archeologists have found coca leaves in Peruvian grave sites dating from approximately a.d. 500, along with other items that the culture considered essential for the afterlife. The Indians who live in mountains of the Andean region have chewed the coca leaves for thousands of years as a way to diminish hunger, lessen fatigue, and help them gain endurance to work at high altitudes. When the Spanish arrived in South America in the sixteenth century, they disapproved of coca use, but they were the first to introduce the plant to Europe.

Cocaine was first extracted from coca leaves in Germany in 1855 by a chemist named Friedriche Gaedecke, who named the ingredient erythroxyline. Four years later, Albert Niemann isolated the compound and renamed it cocaine. Soon after, cocaine quickly became a "wonder drug." Sigmund Freud, for example, published a paper titled "On Coca" in which he praised cocaine. The drug was believed to help reduce a number of ailments, including asthma, digestive disorders, and morphine addiction, and it was often used as an anesthetic in minor surgery. Cocaine was also used in a new, popular drink called Vin Mariani, which was drunk by kings, queens, and a number of other famous people, and as an active ingredient in a new drink called Coca-Cola.

By the late 1800s, however, the unrestrained enthusiasm for the "wonder drug" began to be tempered by a realization that it also had addictive qualities. Even Sigmund Freud now warned of the drug's dangers. Meanwhile, its easy availability was leading to widespread abuse. Growing concerns about cocaine's dangers led to restrictions on its use when the U.S. Congress passed and President Woodrow Wilson signed the Harrison Act of 1914. From 1914 until the early 1970s, cocaine use went underground, and was largely confined to movie stars, jazz musicians, and thrill seekers. As an illegal drug, cocaine was expensive, and amphetamine was a cheaper, legal substitute.

The so-called psychedelic revolution of the 1960s revived interest in cocaine, and once again, the drug

Seized materials after the Colombian National Police make a drug bust (Courtesy of the Colombian National Police)

became viewed as a safe high. In the 1960s cocaine was viewed as "the champagne of drugs," meaning that it was the drug of choice for the rich and famous. Statistics show that by the late 1970s and the 1980s, cocaine use had skyrocketed. By the mid-1980s cocaine was not only the drug of the affluent. In 1972 one in eleven eighteen– to twenty-five-year-old Americans had used cocaine. Ten years later that figure was up to one in four. In 1982 the National Institute on Drug Abuse reported that approximately 22 million Americans had used cocaine at least once, a figure that was up from 5 million in 1974. In 1984 one study found that 69 percent of the individuals arrested for drug-related offenses in East Harlem had traces of cocaine in their urine, while only half of the urine samples obtained were positive for other narcotic drugs such as heroin or methadone. By the mid-1980s a cheaper form of cocaine called crack was being used in the United States.

The increased demand for cocaine led to the rise of powerful cocaine-trafficking organizations such as Colombia's Medellin and Cali Cartels. Criminals were attracted by the enormous profits that could be made at each level of the cocaine-trafficking business. Critics of U.S. drug policy say that, in concentrating interdiction efforts in the 1990s on stopping the importation of marijuana from Mexico and heroin from the Far East, the U.S. government may have inadvertently helped to make cocaine use popular.

By the 1990s Colombian cartels, and to an increasingly larger extent, Mexican organizations, were handling most of the cocaine that was being distributed in the United States, while the Colombians were working closely with the Italian Mafia and Russian organized crime to traffic the drug in Europe. The collapse of the Soviet Union opened up many new markets for cocaine in Eastern Europe and routes to hide and smuggle the cocaine shipments. However, by 1997 the number of cocaine users in the United States had declined from an estimated 6 million a decade previously to about 2.1 million.

Today, cocaine is a Schedule II drug under the U.S. Controlled Substances Act, meaning that it has legitimate uses, but also a high potential for abuse. Cocaine is still used medically as a local anesthetic for ear, nose, and throat surgery.

See also: Acosta, Pablo; American Council on Drug Education; Amphetamines; Arce Gomez, Luis; Arizabaleta-Arzayuz, Phano; Arellano Felix, Ramon; Assets Forfeiture; Blanco De Trujillo, Griselda; Bush, George Herbert Walker; Caicedo-Tascon, Giovanni; Cali Cartel; Cardona, Libia; Carillo Fuentes, Amado; Caro Quintero, Rafael; Carter, James Earl; Castro, Jorge; Chapare Province (Bolivia); Coca-Cola; Constantine, Thomas A.; Controlled Substance; Crack Cocaine; Cuban Connection; David Nasser, Julio; Drug Testing; Escobar Gaviria, Pablo; Free Trade; Freud, Sigmund; Galeano Murcia, Cristobal; Harrison Act; Herrera Zuleta, Helmer "Pacho"; Italian Organized Crime; Jamaican Posses; Junior Black Mafia; Legalization; Lehder Rivas, Carlos; Luciano, Charles; Medellin Cartel; Methadone Treatment Programs; Miami River Cops Scandal; Montoya Sanchez, Diego; Morphine; Nigerian Organized Crime; Norman's Cay; Ochoa Vasquez, Jr., Fabio; Ochoa Vasquez, Jorge Luis; Ochoa Vasquez, Juan David; Operation Blast Furnace; Operation Blue Lightning; Operation Calico; Operation Chemcon; Operation Colombus; Operation Blue Thunder; Operation Cornerstone; Operation Desert Stop; Operation Fountainhead; Operation Frontier Lace; Operation Greenback II; Operation Hat Trick I; Operation Limelight; Operation Mars; Operation Padrino; Operation Polar Cap; Operation Primavera; Operation Reciprocity; Operation Steeple; Operation Swordfish; Operation Thunderbolt; Operation Zorro; Outlaws; Perez, Augusto; Phelps, Johnny; Pinochet Ugarte, Augusto; Precursor Chemicals; Pryor, Richard; Ramos, Jose Manuel; Reagan, Ronald; Romero Gomez, Alphonso; Russian Organized Crime; Sanchez, Orlando; Santacruz London, Jose; Rodriguez Orejuela, Gilberto; Rodriguez Orejuela, Miguel; UCLA Drug Abuse Treatment Center; United States Act of 8 March 1946; United States Comprehensive Crime Control Act Of 1970; United States Drug Abuse Control Amendments of 1965; United States Institute on Drug Abuse; United States Pure Food and Drug Act; Vaughn, Federico; Vin Mariani

References: Abadinsky, Howard. 1990. *Organized Crime.*

Chepesiuk, Ron. 1999. *Hard Target.*

Marnell, Tim, ed. 1997. *Drug Identification Bible.*

Miller, Gary J. 1997. *Drugs and the Law—Detention, Recognition and Investigation.*

Cocaine Anonymous (CA)

Founded in Los Angeles in 1982, Cocaine Anonymous is a fellowship of, by, and for cocaine addicts seeking recovery. Today, the organization has chapters in the United States and Europe. As of 1996 it had an estimated 30,000 members in over 2,000 groups. The group's program of recovery was adopted from the program developed by Alcoholics Anonymous (AA) in 1935, and like AA, CA uses a twelve-step recovery method. There are no dues or fees for membership, and the organization is totally self-sufficient, supporting itself through members' volunteer contributions.

See also: Cocaine; Crack Cocaine

Reference: Cocaine Anonymous's Website at http://www.ca.org.

Codeine

A narcotic analgesic used to relieve mild to moderate pain. The most common side effects are nausea, confusion, drowsiness, and vomiting. Physical dependence is common. Codeine also goes by the street names of "pops" and "school boys." In the 1960s the U.S. government put tighter control over the drug when it was discovered that many addicts of harder drugs began to use codeine syrup to get high. Under the U.S. Controlled Substances Act, codeine is a Schedule II drug. This includes drugs or substances that have a high potential for abuse, drugs or other substances that have a currently accepted use in the United States or a currently accepted medical use with some restrictions, or drug in which its abuse may lead to severe psychological or physical dependence. According to O'Brien and Cohen, death from codeine is very rare and the lethal dose has not been determined.

See also: Analgesic; United States Comprehensive Crime Control Act of 1970; Vietnamese Gangs.

References: Cooper, Mary H. 1990. *The Business of Drugs.*

O'Brien, Robert, and Sidney Cohen. 1984. *The Encyclopedia of Drug Abuse.*

College on Problems of Drug Dependence (CPDD)

The College on Problems of Drug Dependence (CPDD) is a professional organization of scientists who conduct research in order to understand drug abuse and addiction better. As a group of scientists, the CPDD believes it is in a position to provide information from the best available scientific data on which sound drug policy can be based.

Reference: College on Problems of Drug Dependence website at http://views.vcu.edu/epdd

Colombo Plan

Based in Sri Lanka, and comprising twenty Asia-Pacific jurisdictions, this regional organization has a

Colombia Plan Drug Advisory Program that attempts to balance the demand and supply sides of the international drug problem by developing drug prevention programs that complement bilateral U.S. assistance to the region. The United States is an active participant in the program.

Reference: "International Crime Control Strategy." 1998. *Transnational Crime* (Fall): 49.

Colosio Murrieta, Luis Donaldo (1948–1994)

A Mexican politician and government official who was a member of the Institutional Revolutionary Party (PRI) and served in the Mexican government as a legislative representative, senator, party head, and social development secretary under President Carlos Salinas de Gortari. He resigned to run for president in 1994 as Salinas's chosen successor, but was assassinated in Tijuana. The reason for Colosio's death still remains a mystery, but many observers suspect drug traffickers, who have a strong presence in Tijuana.

Evidence from video photos at Colosio's rally in Tijuana led to the arrest of five men and the search for two others, but no one has ever been convicted for his murder, and it looks as if it will never be solved. Comparisons have been made to John F. Kennedy's assassination because twelve officials who investigated that case have themselves been inexplicably murdered.

See also: Salinas de Gortari, Carlos; Tijuana Cartel
References: "Mexican Acquittal." 1996. *MacLean's*, 19 August. "On Colosio, Back to Square One." 1996. *World Press Review* (November).

Common Sense for Drug Policy

Founded in 1995 and based in Falls Church, Virginia, this organization seeks to reform national drug policies, particularly in the areas of asset forfeiture, marijuana policy, mandatory sentencing for drug-related offenses and needle exchange programs. To realize its objectives, the CSDP provides local drug reform organizations with speakers and technical assistance.

See also: Asset Forfeiture; Marijuana; Needle Exchange Programs
Reference: Common Sense for Drug Policy website at http://www.csdp.org

Community Action Coalition of America (CACA)

Funded mostly by private sources, the Community Action Coalition of America (CACA) is the nerve center for a network of 4,300 community groups in all fifty states, which are attempting to fight the War on Drugs at the local level. The group also serves as a clearinghouse for community groups and represents their interests in working with the director of the Office of National Drug Control Policy and key members of Congress.

See also: United States Office of National Drug Control Policy
Reference: Dreyfuss, Robert. "Hawks and Doves." 1997. *Rolling Stone*, 7 August.

Community Action Coalition of America (U.S.)

Established in 1976, the Community Action Coalition of America consists of twenty-one epidemiologists from major metropolitan areas, and its purpose is to provide "on-going community-level surveillance of drug use through the collection and analysis of epidemiological and ethnographic (culture-related) data. Changes in drug use patterns are often captured by the organization through its use of law-enforcement data, street surveillance, and other local public health drug detention sources." (U.S. General Accounting Office 1998, 6)

See also: United States National Institute on Drug Abuse
Reference: U.S. General Accounting Office. 1998. *Emerging Drug Problems.*

Constantine, Thomas A. (1938–   )

Administrator of the Drug Enforcement Administration from 1994 to the present. Born in Buffalo, New York, Constantine obtained a B.A. degree from the State University College at Buffalo and a master's degree from the State University of New York at Albany. From 1960 to 1962, Constantine worked for the Erie County (New York) Sheriff's Department before joining the New York State Police as a uniformed officer. He held several administrative posts with the state police before being appointed superintendent of the New York State Police by Governor Mario Cuomo.

After Constantine's appointment to the position of DEA Administrator, the press reported that "well-

Five Contras decipher codes for their radio communication during a patrol in Southern Zelaya Province, Nicaragua, 1988. These soldiers were suspected of trafficking drugs for arms. (Corbis/Reuters)

informed sources" said he planned a basic shift in strategy, moving away from an almost exclusive concentration on battling major cocaine drug-trafficking organizations in favor of focusing on street-level trafficking, drug-related violence, and violent drug gangs. Constantine's appointment put to rest speculation that the DEA would be eliminated and its duties merged with the FBI. During his tenure with the DEA, the agency added 1,200 new agents, increasing the agency to a complement of 4,550. He is also credited with revamping and computerizing the DEA's intelligence operations and revising the drug agency's standards for hiring, training, and internal integrity.

See also: Cocaine; United States Drug Enforcement Administration; United States Federal Bureau of Investigation
References: Savage David G. 1994. "New York Police Chief To Head DEA." *Los Angeles Times*, 14 January.
Skornek, Carolyn. 1994. "New York State Police Chief Picked To Head DEA." Associated Press, 13 January.

Contras

While calling for resolve in the War on Drugs during the early 1980s U.S. President Ronald Reagan was still much concerned about the Cold War and the threat of communist expansion. By 1986 his administration was heavily involved in covert operations to topple the Marxist Sandinista regime in Nicaragua, which had taken power in 1979, through training and financing the Nicaraguan rebels known as the Contra forces. To justify his Central American policy, the president tried to link the two wars. "The link between the governments of such Soviet allies as Cuba and Nicaragua and international narcotics trafficking and terrorism is becoming increasingly clear," Reagan told the American people. "These twin ends—narcotics trafficking and terrorism—represent the most insidious and dangerous threats to the hemisphere today." (Weir 1995, 83)

By the mid-1980s there appeared to be no quick end to the fighting in Nicaragua and increasing U.S. involvement had raised fears about a Vietnam-style war. Certain that Congress would cut military aid to the Contras, the Reagan administration began developing covert sources of money and arms to the Contras. Oliver North, a staff member of the National Security Council, created an operation called The Enterprise, which used various U.S. And Latin American connections to funnel arms and equipment to the Contras.

Rumors circulated about weapons shipments being flown to the Contras and how, on return flights from Nicaragua, drugs were being sent to the United States, no questions asked. Southern Air Transport, a Miami-based cargo airline that had ties to the CIA, was suspected of involvement in the Contra arms-for-drugs network. In press interviews, drug smugglers claimed they had worked with the Contras. Smuggler Jorge Morales, who had been indicted in March 1989, said that the CIA had approached him with a deal in which they would take care of his legal problems and allow him to fly drugs into the United States, if he would fly arms to the Contras.

Public pressure for an investigation of the allegations mounted, and the Subcommittee on Terrorism, Narcotics and International Operations of the Senates's Foreign Relations Committee initiated hearings under the leadership of Senator John F. Kerry (D-Mass). In the so-called Kerry Commission hearings, evidence once again came to light that the U.S. government had turned a blind eye to the involvement of their anticommunist allies in the drug trade and that CIA-sponsored covert operations were "entangled" with criminal activities such as drug smuggling. The subcommittee found "substantial evidence of drug smuggling through the war zones on the part of individual countries, Latin suppliers, Contra pilots and mercenaries who worked with the Contras and Contra supporters throughout the region" and concluded that "U.S. officials involved in Latin America failed to address the drug issue for fear of jeopardizing the war efforts against Nicaragua." (U.S. Senate Subcommittee 1994, 41) Once again, critics charged, the objectives of the War on Drugs had been subordinated to other foreign policy interests.

See also: Kerry, John F.; Narcoterrorism; Noriega, Manuel Antonio; Reagan, Ronald; Vietnam War; Webb, Gary
References: Scott, Peter Dale, and Jonathan Marshall. 1995. *Cocaine Politics: Drugs, Armies and the CIA in Central America.*
U.S. Senate Subcommittee on Terrorism, Narcotics and International Operations. 1994. *Report: Drugs, Law Enforcement and Foreign Policy.*
Weir, William. 1995. *In the Shadow of the Dope Fiend.*

Controlled Substance

The term used to identify a drug substance, the use, sale, and distribution of which has been regulated by the federal government or a state entity. The U.S. Comprehensive Crime Control Act of 1970 lists specific controlled substances, such as cocaine, heroin, LSD, and PCP, which have been classified by the federal government.

See also: Cocaine; Heroin; LSD; Marijuana; PCP; United States Controlled Substances Analogue Enforcement Act of 1986; United States Comprehensive Crime Control Act of 1970
Reference: Karch, Steven B., ed. 1998. *Drug Abuse Handbook.*

Convention for the Suppression of the Illicit Traffic in Illegal Drugs

As its last action before World War II, the Opium Advisory Board of the League of Nations adopted this convention in 1936, setting stiff penalties for international drug trafficking through the establishment of extradition procedures to bring traffickers to justice. Each of the signatory countries was required to establish a central office to supervise and coordinate the Convention's enforcement. Forty-two governments sent representatives to the Convention, but only twenty-six signed the accord. As it had done at earlier conventions, the U.S. government refused to sign the convention on the grounds that it did not go far enough and contained too many loopholes.

See also: Extradition; League of Nations
References: Stares, Paula B. 1996. *Global Habit: The Drug Problem in a Barbarous World.*
Taylor, Arnold H. 1969. *American Diplomacy and Narcotics Trafficking, 1900–1939.*

Corruption

"Corruption caused by drug trafficking is certainly the most widespread form of corruption found in the world today," asserted Victor T. LeVine, professor of political science at Washington University, St. Louis Missouri, and author of *Political Corruption: The Ghana Case.* (Chepesiuk 1999, 232)

Corruption in which drug-trafficking criminals give money to politicians in return for favors has involved the highest levels of government, including heads of state, military leaders, judges, police chiefs, and other officials in every country touched by the drug trade. This has been particularly true of nations like Bolivia, Mexico, Burma, Pakistan, and Colombia, which all have thriving narcotics industries.

In the early 1980s, the Bolivian military under General Luis Garcia Meza joined with the country's drug traffickers to organize what has been described as the country's first official "narcocracy." Journalist Simon Strong described what subsequently happened: "Colonel Luis Arce Gomez, the head of military intelligence and relative of Roberto Suarez, then Bolivia's biggest coca-paste trafficker and supplier of Pablo Escobar, was appointed minister of the interior. Not only did he and General Garcia Meza organize the army's systematic extortion of protection money from major drug traffickers—recalcitrants were murdered—but they also used paramilitary squads to stamp out the smallest dealers in Santa Cruz, the commercial heart of the cocaine trade. The squads were set up with the assistance of Nazi Klaus Barbie." (Strong 1995, 162)

Colombia has been called a "narco democracy" after strong evidence suggested that the Cali Cartel financed Ernesto Samper Pizano's successful 1994 political campaign with millions of dollars. Relations between Mexico and the United States were seriously strained after the United States learned about the widespread corruption that has riddled Mexico's top drug-fighting unit. In the 1990s, many top Italian officials, including Guilio Andreotti, seven times a prime minister, went on trial on charges of conspiring with the Mafia. Meanwhile, fifty municipal councils in four regions of Sicily have had to be dissolved on the grounds that they were infiltrated by the Mafia. Corruption is widespread among law enforcement officials in Burma, the world's largest producer of the opium crop, and international narcotics agents have warned that Pakistan could become another Colombia because the meager resources of the Pakistani state are no match for the power and wealth of the country's drug traffickers.

Drug-related corruption is growing in Mexico, a development that is seriously threatening U.S.-Mexico relations. Corruption Mexican style has been called "a rattlesnake pit that could destabilize Mexico politically, undermine NAFTA, and poison U.S.-Mexican relations." (Sweeney 1997)

A study by the National Autonomous University of Mexico estimates that Mexican drug cartels spend $500 million a year in bribes, an amount that goes a long way—considering that a military commander in the Mexican army makes only $900 a month and a regular policemen, $300. A customs official on the U.S.-Mexican border can now command as much as $1 million for simply looking the other way when drug traffickers try to sneak a truckload of drugs across the border to the United States. In testifying before the U.S. Senate in 1997, DEA Director Thomas Constantine revealed that a Mexican general had offered a Tijuana judicial official $1.5 million if he would scale down his efforts against drug trafficking.

In addition to the corruption in countries involved with growing and processing narcotics, many other countries are caught in the net of international drug trafficking as money-laundering centers and transit points in smuggling routes leading to the United States and Europe. For example, there have been several cases involving drug shipments to Russia and Eastern Europe from Peru, Venezuela, and other Latin American countries by traffickers trying to take advantage of the lax customs regulations and weak law enforcement in the region.

Attempts to stamp out the drug traffic often exacerbate the problem and make hard-fought gains in the War on Drugs short-lived. This is because cocaine, heroin, and marijuana are easy to produce, refine, transport, and sell, and the profits are enormous, which means there will always be an ambitious criminal or criminal organization willing to try to get the illegal product to the market.

The cultivation of opium is no longer confined to Mexico, the Golden Triangle, and the Golden Crescent, but is now also grown in Latin American countries like Colombia and Guatemala, Eastern Europe (Poland and Ukraine), and the central highland republics of the former Soviet Union (Kazakhstan, Turkmenistan, and Tajikstan). Today, coca is cultivated in Brazil, Ecuador, and Venezuela, as well as Peru, Bolivia, and Colombia. Law enforcement authorities now bust cocaine-processing laboratories in Italy, Spain, and Portugal as well as Latin America. New areas of marijuana cultivation include Brazil, Siberia in the former Soviet Union, and Togo, Rwanda, and Nigeria in Africa. To meet the surging demand for synthetic drugs, secret laboratories have sprung up to manufacture amphetamine (Poland), "ice" (nickname for a smokable, highly pure form of amphetamine) (Taiwan and South Korea), and methaqualone or mandrax (India and South Africa).

Since 1982 and the beginning of the modern crusade against international drug trafficking, every country in the Caribbean region and Latin America has become involved in some way in the drug trade. In the early 1990s, when authorities began to put pressure on transportation routes through Mexico and Central America, the drug traffickers shifted their routes to go through the Barbados, Antigua, Monserrat, and the other small countries of the Eastern Caribbean. By 1996 the United Nations Drug Control Program's Caribbean regional office estimated that the Barbados accounted for 180 tons or 10 to 20 percent of Europe's supply of cocaine.

A 1996 report by eight European experts called drug trafficking "the single biggest threat to the economic and social development of the countries of the region" and concluded: "With their weak economies, high unemployment, meager resources and inadequate law enforcement, the islands of the eastern Caribbean provide easy targets for the international drug traffickers." (Lee 1989, 25) It may be too late, however, to stop the assault. Various U.S. officials have said that corruption induced by drug trafficking is widespread throughout the Caribbean, where poorly paid public servants find it difficult to resist payoffs and those that do make it difficult for honest officials to ferret out corruption.

The Caribbean assessment reflects a worldwide pattern. The people who allow traffickers to conduct business without obstacles or fear of arrest are everywhere in the drug distribution chain. They could be top government officials like the prime minister of the Barbados, or the presidents of Panama and Colombia, or customs officers on the border between the United States and Mexico or Burma and Thailand, or police officers in Palermo, Sicily, or Managua, Nicaragua. Invariably, the drug traffickers find a way to get their help through bribes or intimidation. Manuel Noriega reportedly made millions of dollars for helping drug traffickers launder their money. In Bolivia, drug traffickers reportedly paid police officers between $20,000 and $25,000 for a "seventy-two-hour window of opportunity" for moving major drug shipments by air, land, and sea.

Meanwhile, an increasing number of American officials and law enforcement officers on the front lines of the war are being arrested and incarcerated for drug trafficking. Police officers have been caught selling information about drug investigations or offering protection to the criminals. They have reportedly cheated drug dealers and have even become major drug dealers themselves.

Kenneth Kennedy, assistant special agent in charge of the Drug Enforcement Administration's Miami Office, said that "the massive profits generated by narcotics trafficking have had a tremendous corrupting influence, permeating all environs of the criminal justice system." (Kennedy 1998, 26) In early 1997 three Miami police officers and two U.S. customs agents were arrested for drug dealing and other charges that included the theft of narcotics and extortion of drug dealers. According to prosecutors, one of the officers, a twenty-five–year veteran of the customs office, used his authority to direct cocaine shipments through the inspection process. All five defendants pleaded guilty and faced prison terms that could reach thirty-five years.

In their book *The Cocaine Wars*, Paul Eddy and his coauthors estimated that one out of ten Miami police officers were "on the take."

In cities such as Miami, Chicago, Atlanta, New York, Philadelphia, and New Orleans many drug cases have been overturned or thrown out of court because testifying officers have been convicted of corruption charges. As a result of one corruption investigation in Philadelphia, the police commissioner transferred some 200 officers to new positions in the 6,000-member department and reassigned seven top internal affairs commanders.

Corruption has been especially serious along the U.S.-Mexican border, where in the mid-1990s at least thirty-nine U.S. local, state, and federal officials were convicted in federal court on drug corruption charges, according to the U.S. Justice Department. Speaking before the U.S. Senate in May 1997, Thomas Constantine, the head of the U.S. Drug Enforcement Administration (DEA) revealed that drug traffickers had offered one U.S. official working along the Mexican border an $18 million bribe.

The U.S. government and a number of states have moved to address the problem. In 1997 two congressional panels conducted hearings on drug-related corruption of U.S. border officials, while the FBI asked Congress for sixty-seven more officials so it could conduct more border corruption investigations. In 1996 California formed an anticorruption task force, and several other states are considering similar moves. In February 1997 Arizona announced the creation of a task force of three federal agencies in the state to combat drug corruption.

Lawyers and judges are being corrupted as well. Several lawyers were arrested in 1995 on a drug-smuggling conspiracy charge involving the Cali Cartel, which included allegations of obstruction of justice, money laundering, and conspiracy to import cocaine. "Lawyers have a license to practice law, but they don't have a license to be above the law," James Milford, special agent in charge of the DEA's Miami field office, told the press.

Given the power of drug trafficking organizations and the money at their disposal, law enforcement officials do not expect any abatement in the spread of corruption.

See also: Abbell, Michael; Acosta, Pablo; American Express Bank International; Anderson, Robert A.; Arce Gomez, Luis C.; Asset Forfeiture; Bank Credit and Commercial International; Barry, Marion; Bartels, John R.; Bensinger, Peter; Botero Zeta, Fernando; Cali Cartel; Carillo Fuentes, Amado; Cartel; Casa De Cambio; Certification; Currency Transaction Reports; Escobar Gaviria, Pablo; Extradition; Financial Action Task Force; Fonseca-Carillo, Ernesto; Franklin Quintero, Colonel Waldemar; Garcia Meza, Luis; Garfield Bank; Giraldo, Alberto; Great America Bank; Grieff, Gustavo De; Guillot-Lara, Jaime; Gutierrez Rebollo, Jesus; Italian Organized Crime; Lisboa Medgar, Juan Carlos; Mara Mosquera, Eduardo; Medellin Cartel; Miami River Cops; Michelsen Lopez, Alfonso; Money Laundering; Moran, William C.; Narcocassettes; Narcodemocracy; Navarro Lara, General Alfredo; Nigerian Organized Crime; Noriega, Manuel Antonio; Norman's Cay; Ochoa Sanchez, Orlando; Offshore Financial Centers; Operation Bahamas, Turks and Caicos; Operation Casablanca; Operation C-Chase; Operation C-Note; Operation College Farm; Operation Cornerstone; Operation Fountainhead; Operation Greenback; Operation Polar Cap; Operation Raccoon; Operation Swordfish; Orazco-Prado, Eduardo; Orlandez Gamboa, Alberto; Palaez, Luis Fernando; Pallomari, Guillermo Alejandro "Reagan"; Pastrana Arango, Andres; People's Liberty Bank; Pindling, Lyndon; Pizza Connection; Reagan, Ronald; Rico; Romero de Vasco, Flavio; Romero Gomez Alfonso; Ruiz Massieu, Mario; Russian Organized Crime; Salinas De Gortari, Carlos; Salinas De Gortari, Raul; Samper Pizano, Ernesto; Summit Of The Americas; Summit Of The Americas Ministerial Conference on Money Laundering; Taboada, Gabriel; Tijuana Cartel; Toft, Joe; United States Central Intelligence Agency; Valdivieso Sarmiento, Alphonso; Vesco, Robert; Weinig, Harvey

References: Center for Strategic and International Studies. 1993. *The Transnational Drug Challenge.*

Craig, Richard B. 1989. "Are Drug Kingdoms South America's New Wave?" *World and I* (November).

Kennedy, Kenneth. 1998. "Drug Corruption in South Florida." *The Narcofficer* (January-February).

Lee, Rensselaer W. 1989. "South American Cocaine: Why the U.S. Can't Stop It." *Current History* (June).

"The Sicilian Mafia: A State within a State." 1993. *The Economist*, 24 April 24.

Sweeney, John. 1997. "A Culture of Corruption." *The World and I.* (August): 34–39.

U.S. General Accounting Office. 1996. *Drug Control: U.S. Heroin Program Encounters Many Obstacles in Southeast Asia.*

Corsicans

Natives of the island of Corsica, which is a department of France located in the Mediterranean Sea southeast of France. Corsicans played an important role in the development of the French Connection drug smuggling organization in the 1960s and early 1970s. They smuggled base heroin from Turkey to France and then exported heroin to the United States. In their 1971 special report, American Congressmen Morgan M. Murphy and Robert H. Steele say that "Over the past ten years, every narcotic case in Marseilles (France) has involved one or more of four Corsican families: the Venturi brothers (Jean and Dominic), Marcel Francisci, Antoine Guerini and Joseph Orsini." (Lamour & Lamberti 1974, 29)

See also: French Connection; Heroin; Nixon, Richard Milhous

Reference: Lamour, Catherine, and Michael R. Lamberti. 1974. *The International Connection: Opium from Growers to Pushers.*

Counterdrug Technology Assessment Center (U.S.)

Established in 1991 under the Office of National Drug Control Policy, the Center serves as the central drug enforcement research and development organization of the federal government. The Counterdrug Technology Assessment Center's responsibilities include overseeing and coordinating counterdrug technology initiatives with the related activities of other federal departments and agencies, preventing unnecessary duplication of research and development

Two curious teens inspect a graffiti-covered wall at an open-air drug market in New Jersey where police had arrested 28 crack dealers, thanks partially to the graffiti, 1986. (UPI/Corbis-Bettmann)

efforts, and funding counterdrug research projects to help federal agencies develop technology.

See also: United States Office of National Drug Control Policy

Reference: U.S. General Accounting Office. 1998. *Planned Activities Should Clarify Counterdrug Technology Assessment Center's Impact.*

Counterculture

The distinct subculture that emerged in the mid-1960s from the involvement of youth in politics. Rejecting the values of mainstream America, counterculture members did such things as wear their hair long, eschew materialism, practice free love, live in communes, flock to rock festivals, practice Eastern mysticism, perform street theater, and take drugs.

See also: Beatniks; Burroughs, William S.; Grateful Dead; *High Times;* Kesey, Ken; Leary, Timothy; LSD

References: Chepesiuk, Ron. 1999. *Hard Target.*
———. 1995. *Sixties Radicals: Then and Now.*

Crack Cocaine

A refined form of cocaine that is produced when cocaine is dissolved in water, mixed with baking soda, and then heated until the water evaporates. Crack can be smoked in a glass pipe, an empty aluminum can, or any means by which heat can be directly applied to vaporize the drug. A building in which crack cocaine is manufactured is called a crack factory. The drug is often distributed, sold, and used in fortified structures known as crack houses.

Crack cocaine is produced in the form of off-white solid chunks called rocks. According to the *Drug Identification Bible,* the term *crack* refers to "either the crackling sound that is heard when it is smoked, or the process of cracking larger sections of the drug into smaller units of sale (rocks)." (Marnell 1997, 644)

Crack is easy to make, cheap, and every bit as addictive as heroin, which helps explain its popularity in both the United States and Europe and its evolution into the most sought-after illegal drug on the street, with the widespread involvement of organized crime. Unlike cocaine, crack will not dissolve in water, which means that crack cannot be snorted into the nostrils in order to be ingested. Crack is much more addictive than cocaine and of much higher quality than powdered cocaine, between 70–90 percent pure. Crack is cheaper than cocaine, too. A "rock," or piece of cocaine, can cost between $5 to $10. Traditionally, a gram of cocaine in powder form has cost about $100 per gram. The inexpensive price tag of crack has made it a popular drug among drug traffickers to market, since whole new retail markets for dealers have opened up, including children and adolescents.

Introduced in the early 1980s, authorities report that crack is available today in every large American city and its use is spreading. Among the serious health-related problems are so-called crack babies born to crack-addicted women. One of the most dangerous trends of the 1990s is the use of crack, cocaine, and methamphetamine by pregnant women. Research done by Brown University estimates that up to $34 million annually will be spent on special addiction programs for children born after being exposed to crack. Although there are many variables to consider in evaluating the health of infants born to women who use drugs like crack cocaine, many scholars believe that the drugs target the same areas in the fetus as they do in adults. These areas include the central nervous system, and extended drug use may result in neurological, cognitive, and behavioral problems. It has made women liable for abusing a fetus by taking drugs in South Carolina, for example, and the state supreme court has ruled that the fetuses are subject to protection under the child abuse statutes if the mother takes drugs while pregnant.

See also: Barry, Marion; Cocaine; Freebase Smoking; Jamaican Posses; Methamphetamine; Webb, Gary

References: Marnell, Tim, ed. 1997. *Drug Identification Bible.*

Scherer, Jane. 1988. *Crack: The Rock of Death.*

Crips
See Bloods

Crop Substitution
Introduced in the 1970s, crop substitution is a supply reduction strategy that aims to replace illicit crops like coca and opium poppies with legal crops such as maize or a variety of other vegetables. According to the United Nations Drug Control Program, "the rationale for crop substitution is that eliminating the economic imperative to grow an illicit crop would, within a reasonable period of time, lead to the elimination of the illicit crop within the targeted area. The activity would then spread to adjoining growing areas and eventually cover the entire zone of illicit cultivation."

The areas for which this hypothesis was felt to be appropriate were primarily traditional growing areas where subsistence economies prevailed. (United Nations Drug Control Program 1997, 222) The problem with the premise for crop substitution is that, if the policy works in one area, drug traffickers can always introduce the drug crops in nontraditional areas to meet the growing demand. In many instances, the farmers who grow the illegal crops have not been able to make nearly as much money from legal, substituted crops. Government officials, moreover, often do not build the infrastructure needed to make a crop substitution program work. Crop substitution has been tried in Burma, Colombia, Peru, and Bolivia, among other countries.

See also: Alternative Development; Eradication

Reference: United Nations Drug Control Program. 1997. *World Drug Report.*

Cuban Connection
During the corrupt regime of Cuban dictator Fulgencia Batista, who was in power from 1933 to 1959, the Italian American Mafia was given a free hand to run the casinos, brothels, and loan-sharking operations, and to establish other criminal activities on the island. To protect its thriving businesses, the Mafia put numerous Cuban government officials, policemen, businessmen, members of the military, and local criminals on their payroll. The Mafia and many of their Cuban associates fled the island for the safety of the United States in 1959, when Fidel Castro overthrew Batista and established a communist dictatorship. During the 1960s, these same individuals conspired to overthrow the new Cuban dictator. The Italian American Mafia was involved in several plots to kill Castro, while many of their former Cuban associates joined the CIA's failed Bay of Pigs invasion of Cuba in 1961.

In the wake of that disaster, Cuban criminals set up base in South Florida and organized La Compania, an organization the primary criminal activity of which was importing heroin and cocaine to the United States. Establishing its headquarters in Miami with branch operations in California, Nevada, Texas, Arizona, and New Jersey, La Compania dominated the drug-trafficking trade in heroin, cocaine, and marijuana from South America during the 1960s and 1970s.

The ranks of Cuban organized crime in the United States were bolstered by two more waves of Cuban immigration: the Camarioca boatlift, or "freedom flotillas", which brought 250,000 Cubans to the United States between 1965 and 1972, and the so-called Mariel boatlift of 1980, in which U.S. officials estimated that 2 percent of the immigrants were criminals, prostitutes, drug addicts, and vagrants. While most Cubans fled to the United States in search of political freedom and the opportunity to build better lives, Cuban immigrant communities did become bases of operation for Cuban organized crime networks.

Some of the Mariel immigrants formed criminal groups, including large drug-trafficking organizations, or began working for larger, more established Cuban criminal groups, such as La Compania, as collectors of drug money and enforcers in drug operations. According to the 1984 President's Commission on Organized Crime, "Marielito groups . . . are most often involved in cocaine trafficking, along with murders and assaults, which are part of its illicit narcotics trade (President's Commission on Organized Crime 1984, 113–114)

During the 1960s, the Colombian cartels also got their start in the drug trade as the middlemen who bought raw coca from farmers in the Andean region of South America, turned the coca into cocaine, and then sold the finished product to the Cubans. By 1965 the Colombians were supplying nearly all the cocaine moving through Cuban trafficking networks. By the early 1970s, the Colombians had gained control over the cocaine producers in Peru and Bolivia and refineries in China and were challenging the dominance of the Cubans in the U.S. trade.

The alleged role of Fidel Castro and his communist regime in the drug trade has been the most controversial aspect of the Cuban connection. U.S. officials have accused the Cuban government of abetting the drug trade as a matter of policy. Drug smuggling operations have received the support and protection of high-ranking officials in the Castro regime, as shown by the Arnaldo Ochoa Sanchez case, in which Ochoa and thirteen Cuban senior military and Interior Ministry officials were convicted of embezzlement and helping Colombia's Medellin Cartel smuggle six tons of cocaine into the United States. Researchers warn that the Colombian cartels have worked out deals with highly placed Cuban officials in which the latter have agreed to facilitate the movement of drug shipments in exchange for bribes.

In February 1988, for example, a seventeen-member drug ring with ties to the Medellin Cartel was charged with smuggling cocaine into the United States by way of Cuba. In early 1993 federal prosecutors in Miami considered indicting the entire Cuban government, including the military, as a criminal enterprise. Ultimately they did not do so, apparently because the evidence to be presented in court, which relied primarily on the testimony of convicted drug dealers, including Carlos Lehder Rivas, was shaky.

The controversy over the alleged Cuban drug connection has led to political problems between Cuba and the United States. For example, the United States has refused to cooperate with Cuba on drug issues, a policy that many experts believe has been damaging to relations between the two countries.

See also: Cocaine; Heroin; Italian American Mafia; Lehder Rivas, Carlos; Medellin Cartel; Ochoa Sanchez, Arnaldo; United States President's Commission on Organized Crime

References: Ehrenfeld, Rachel. 1994. *Narcoterrorism.*
Lee, Rensselaer W. 1996. "Drugs: The Cuban Connection." *Current History* (February).
President's Commission on Organized Crime. 1986. *America's Habit: Drug Trafficking and Organized Crime.*

Cuevas Ramirez, Nelson (1934–)

Drug trafficker extradited to the United States from Colombia in December 1989, pursuant to an indictment the previous October on a conspiracy charge to import and distribute approximately 330 pounds of cocaine. Cuevas was the first person extradited after a bomb killed dozens of people in front of the Colombian national police headquarters as part of a violent campaign of intimidation against extradition by Colombian drug traffickers.

See also: Cocaine; Extradition; Narcoterrorism
References: "Cocaine Extradition." 1989. Associated Press,
    16 December.
"U.S. Brings Colombian to New York on Drug Charges." 1989.
    United Press International, 15 December.

Currency Transaction Reports (CTRs)

A U.S. government financial procedure instituted as a result of the U.S. Bank Secrecy Act of 1970 that initially attempted to make banks, savings and loans, and other financial institutions report on transactions over $1,000 to the Internal Revenue Service. The introduction of CTRs was a government effort to deter money laundering. The ceiling for cash transactions has since been raised to $10,000, and over the years, the law has been broadened to include nonbank types of institutions, such as car dealers, travel agencies, check-cashing businesses, and money wire services.

See also: Cocaine; Money Laundering; People's Liberty
    Bank (U.S.); United States Bank Secrecy Act of 1970
References: Powis, Robert E. 1992. *The Money Launderers*.
Robinson, Jeffrey. 1990. *The Laundrymen*.

Customs Cooperation Council
See World Customs Organization.

D

Dadeland "Massacre" (Miami, Florida)

Bloody and shocking killings of two drug dealers carried out by Colombian hit men with machine guns on 11 July 1979 at the Dadeland Mall in Dade County, Florida. The shootouts made national headlines and introduced the term "cocaine cowboys" into the English language. According to journalists Guy Gugliotta and Jeff Leen, the Dadeland Massacre was part of a trend that showed how "the Colombians would transform Miami into the cocaine Casablanca of the 1980s. Metropolitan Dade County would become for a time the murder capital of the nation, and South Florida would see an unprecedented federal police effort against drug smuggling...." (Gugliotta & Leen 1990, 19)

See also: Blanco De Trujillo, Grisella
Reference: Gugliotta, Guy, and Jeff Leen. 1990. *Kings of Cocaine.*

Dangerous Drug Act

Enacted by the British government in 1868, this statute provided the legislative framework for the criminalization of drugs in the United Kingdom.

Reference: De Grazia, Jessica. 1991. *DEA: The War against Drugs.*

DARE

See Drug Abuse Resistance Education

DAS

See Department of Administrative Security (Colombia)

Dass, Baba Ram (1941–)

Born Richard Alpert, Dass became a prominent and controversial figure in the turbulent 1960s. After Harvard fired him in 1963 for experimenting too liberally with LSD, Dass (Baba is Hindi for "respected father") changed his name and went to India to study under a religious guru. When he returned, he became a spiritual leader to the Hippie movement.

"Once I started to learn the eastern methods of arriving at the same place, the drugs became uninteresting," Dass told *People Weekly* magazine in 1987. "If you're in Detroit, you don't need to take a bus to get to Detroit." (Sugden 1987)

But Dass did admit to taking LSD occasionally because "I am part of an old explorer's club, and I think it shows me things I have forgotten." (Sugden 1987) In the late 1990s Dass retained his interest in and commitment to eastern religions.

See also: Hippies; Kesey, Ken; Leary, Timothy; LSD
References: Dass, Baba Ram. 1974. *Be Here Now, Remember.*
Dass, Baba Ram, and Stephen Levine. 1977. *Grist For The Mill.*
Sugden, James. 1987. "Ram Dass, Veteran Guru and Former LSD Prophet, Leads a New Kind of Vision Quest." *People Weekly*, 28 September.

Davidow, Jeffrey (1944–)

A career U.S. diplomat with much experience in Latin America who supports Clinton's antidrug policy, Davidow was appointed U.S. ambassador to Mexico in June 1998. At the time of his appointment he was serving as U.S. assistant secretary of state for inter-American affairs. The post in Mexico had been vacant for a year after William Weld withdrew his name for consideration in the face of strong opposition from Senator Jesse Helms (R-NC), the chairman of the Senate Foreign Relations Committee. Unlike Weld, Davidow had no trouble winning Senate confirmation.

See also: Weld, William
References: Deveney, Paul S. 1998. "U.S. Fills Posting In Mexico." *The Wall Street Journal*, 29 June.
Phelp, Shanon. 1998. "Clinton Picks a Career Diplomat for Disputed Mexican Vacancy." *The New York Times*, 29 April.

DAWN

See Drug Abuse Warning Network

De Dios Uanue, Manuel

In March 1992 De Dios, the publisher of *El Diario-La Prensa*, New York City's largest Spanish-language newspaper, was gunned down. It is believed the attack was in retaliation for a series of investigative articles he published about the impact of the Cali Cartel on his community in Queens. Alexandro Wilson Mejia Velez was found guilty of De Dios's murder in early 1994 and was sentenced to prison without parole. U.S. authorities, however, believed Jose Santacruz Londono, a Cali Cartel kingpin, was the real mastermind behind the murder. He was angry that De Dios had published stories exposing the Cali Cartel's connection to the drug trade in New York City. Santacruz Londono could not be extradited to the United States from Colombia, however, because, at the time, the Colombian constitution forbid extradition. Colombian police later killed the drug trafficker after he had escaped from prison.

See also: Cali Cartel; Media; Santacruz Londono, Jose
References: Berkeley, Bill. 1993. "Dead Right." *Colombian Journalism Review* (March-April): 36.
"Solving a Journalist's Murder." 1993. *Editor and Publisher*, 5 May.

De Grieff, Gustavo

Colombian attorney general during the presidential administration of Cesar Gaviria Trujillo (1990–1994) who angered the United States by his public support of legalizing drugs and for his relations with the leaders of the Cali Cartel. The U.S. Drug Enforcement Administration suspected that De Grieff had made a deal with the cartel so he could use its intelligence to help hunt down drug trafficker Pablo Escobar Gaviria.

Although De Grieff claimed that he never met Cali Cartel leaders Gilberto and Miguel Rodriguez Orejuela, the attorney general's signature appeared in a document relating to an airline that he and the two drug traffickers apparently coowned in 1987. In February 1994 the U.S. Justice Department stopped sharing intelligence with De Grieff's office after learning that someone in his office had threatened some of the witnesses against the leaders of the Cali Cartel. During the presidential administration of Ernesto Samper Pizano (1994–1998), De Grieff served as ambassador to Mexico.

See also: Cali Cartel; Escobar Gaviria, Pablo; Gaviria Trujillo, Cesar; Legalization; Rodriguez Orejuela, Gilberto; Rodriguez Orejuela, Miguel
Reference: Strong, Simon. 1995. *Whitewash: Pablo Escobar and the Cocaine Wars.*

De Grieff, Monica

Colombian minister of justice during the administration of President Virgilio Barco Vargas (1986–1990) who fled the country with her family to the United States as a result of a terror campaign waged by Pablo Escobar against the state, during which De Grieff was warned: Leave the country or die. She returned to Colombia after Escobar's death in 1993. During the 1994 presidential campaign, she served as Ernesto Samper Pizano's campaign treasurer, and then later, during his scandal-ridden administration, as an advisor on international affairs.

See also: Barco Vargas, Virgilio; Escobar Gaviria, Pablo
References: Bugliosi, Vincent. 1991. *Drugs In America*.
Strong, Simon. 1995. *Whitewash: Pablo Escobar and the Cocaine Wars.*

De La Cuesta Marquez, Jorge

Personal pilot of Pablo Escobar Gaviria who was arrested by Colombian police in October 1989 and then extradited to the United States to stand trial on drug charges. According to the indictment filed in Jacksonville, Florida, De La Cuesta piloted or was aboard aircraft that smuggled more than 9,500 pounds of cocaine from Colombia to the Bahamas. After Virgilio Barco Vargas, Colombia's president, began an offensive against the country's cartels after the assassination of Luis Carlos Galan, leading presidential candidate for the 1990 elections, De La Cuesta Marquez became the ninth person extradited from Colombia.

See also: Barco, Virgilio Vargas; Medellin Cartel; Escobar Gaviria, Pablo; Galan, Luis Carlos
Reference: Wells, Tom. 1989. "Pilot Of Pablo Escobar Captured." Associated Press, Oct. 19.

De Lorean, John Z. (1925–   )

An American entrepreneur whom the FBI arrested in October 1992 on a drug-smuggling charge. De Lorean was the general manager of the General Motors Corporation when he left the company in 1973 to make stainless steel gull-winged automobiles bearing his name at a factory in Belfast, Northern Ireland. By 1982, however, De Lorean's company was in serious financial difficulty. The FBI charged that De Lorean needed to raise $100,000 in three days in order to buy cocaine so he could sell it and save his sports car empire.

At De Lorean's trial in 1984, the FBI produced a video recording that was made at the Sheraton Plaza Hotel in Los Angeles. De Lorean could clearly be heard telling FBI undercover agents that cocaine was "as good as gold." (Freemantle 1985, 140). By that time De Lorean's company had gone bankrupt. The jury in De Lorean's trial concluded that the FBI had entrapped the entrepreneur and he was cleared.

References: Freemantle, Brian. 1985. The Fix.
Martin, Justin. 1995. "John De Lorean: In the Rough in Bedminister." Fortune, 25 December.

De Quincey, Thomas (1785–1859)

The English writer of essays, criticisms, and the famous Confessions of an Opium Eater. De Quincey began using opium in 1804 to relieve acute neuralgic pains, and by 1813 had become a regular user of the drug, although—according to his biographers—he was able to limit and control its use until about 1817. London Magazine published "The Confessions of an English Opium Eater" in 1820, and the following year it appeared in book form. The largely autobiographical work gives an account of the writer's literary life and describes the growth and effects of his opium habit. The book became a best-seller.

See also: Opium
References: DeLuca, V. H. 1980. Thomas De Quincey: The Prose Of Vision.
Snyder, Robert L. 1986. Thomas De Quincey: Bicentenary Studies.

Death to the Kidnappers
See Ochoa, Marta Nieve

Declaration on Enhanced Regional Cooperation for Drug Abuse Control for Asia; The Pacific

This declaration resulted from a meeting about drug abuse issues of senior officials from the Asian and Pacific regions, hosted by the Economic and Social Commission for Asia and the Pacific (ESCAP) and held in Taipei in February 1991. The declaration called for the development of regional and subregional antidrug programs and encouraged a proposal that would organize a coordinating antidrug center with the help of the United Nations Drug Control Program.

Reference: United Nations Drug Control Program. 1997. World Drug Report.

DEA
See United States Drug Enforcement Administration.

Decriminalization

An approach to dealing with the drug problem that calls for reduced criminal sanctions against drug use, while maintaining sanctions against drug trafficking. Drug use would be tolerated under decriminalization, but law enforcement would still attempt to put pressure on drug traffickers, their organizations, and other suppliers.

As decriminalization advocate and mayor of Baltimore Kurt Schmoke explained, "Decriminalization is not legalization of all drugs. Drugs will not simply be made available to anyone who wants them, as is the case with the drug nicotine. Decriminalization is in effect 'medicalization,' a broad public health strategy led by the surgeon general, not the attorney general...designed to relieve the harm caused by drugs by pulling addicts into the public health system." (Schmoke 1990, 28)

The strongest push for decriminalization in the United States came during the 1970s when legislators in 11 states decriminalized marijuana. Critics said that decriminalization contributed to the high rise in adolescent drug use throughout the 1970s. Parents' groups led by the National Federation of Parents for Drug-Free Youth, an umbrella group formed to support their interests in Washington and Capitol Hill, moved to defeat a pending federal decriminalization bill that would have removed criminal penalties for the possession of one ounce of marijuana. Congress voted down the bill and rejected decriminalization for good.

See also: Carter, James Earl; Clinton, William Jefferson; Drug Policy Foundation; Harm Reduction; Legalization; Lindesmith Institute; Nadelmann, Ethan; National Commission On Marijuana; Prohibition; Schmoke, Kurt; Shultz, George P.
References: Riley, Kevin Jack. 1996. *Snow Job? The War Against International Drug Trafficking.*
Schmoke, Kurt. 1990. "Back to the Future." *The Humanist* (September-October).

Del Cid, Luis (1943–   )

A lieutenant colonel in the Panamanian Defense Forces, which was headed by Manuel Antonio Noriega. Del Cid was accused of smuggling cocaine for the Medellin Cartel and was jailed in Florida in December 1989, after surrendering in Panama. Del Cid was one of fifteen Noriega associates named in a 5 February 1988 indictment filed in Miami. According to the indictment, Del Cid acted as a liaison and money carrier between the Medellin Cartel and Noriega.

See also: Medellin Cartel; Noriega, Manuel Antonio
Reference: Warren, Michael. 1989. "Panama-Del Cid." Associated Press, 12 December.

Demerol S
See Meperidine

Department of Administrative Security, Bogotá, Colombia (DAS)

More commonly known by the acronym DAS, this Colombian government agency operates as a detective force and is roughly equivalent to the FBI in the United States. DAS has played a major role in Colombia's antidrug campaign.

References: De Grazia, Jessica. 1991. *DEA: The War against Drugs.*
Gugliotta, Guy, and Jeff Leen. 1990. *Kings of Cocaine.*

Depressants

Drugs, such as barbiturates and tranquillizers, that slow down or reduce the activity of the central nervous system and lead to a decline in bodily activity, especially that of the brain. Taken as prescribed by a physician, depressants can be beneficial for the relief of anxiety, irritability, and tension, and for the treatment of insomnia, but they also cause a high state of intoxication that is very similar in effect to that of alcohol. Like alcohol, the effects vary not only from person to person but also from time to time in the same individual.

Low doses can produce mild sedation, but higher doses can produce a temporary sense of well-being or perhaps apathy and mild depression. Abusers are unaware of the dangers of increasing dependence and will often increase the dose up to ten to twenty times the recommended therapeutic level. The supply's source may be no further than the family medicine cabinet, but supplies can also be obtained by theft, illegal prescription, or purchases on the black market.

See also: Barbiturates; Inhalants; Opium; Tranquillizers
Reference: Cooper, Mary H. 1990. *The Business of Drugs.*

Designer Drugs

A synthetic drug so-named because it is produced by making a small change in the chemical structure of the parent drug. The designer drug can be several times more potent than the drug it was patterned after. According to the Drug Identification Bible, "Hundreds of designer drugs have been produced, but only a few have the unique combination of physical and psychoactive effects that have made them popular with the drug culture." (Marnell 1997, 557)

These drugs became popular in the 1980s as an alternative to banned drugs such as heroin and cocaine because they can easily replicate their effects; however, designer drugs are extremely potent and dangerous and their abuse can cause death. The U.S. Anti-Drug Abuse Act of 1986 banned designer drugs, but according to Mary H. Cooper, "They continue to be a major component of the traffic in dangerous drugs. Their distribution is far less widespread than that of cocaine and heroin, but in some areas they are among the most dangerous on the illicit market." (Cooper 1990, 93)

See also: United States Controlled Substance Analogue Enforcement Act of 1986

References: Abadinsky, Howard. 1990. *Organized Crime*. Cooper, Mary H. 1990. *The Business of Drugs*. Karch, Stephen, ed. 1998. *Drug Abuse Handbook*. Marnell, Tim. 1997. *Drug Identification Bible*.

Diablos

An American outlaw motorcycle gang founded in 1964 that, among other criminal activities, is involved in drug trafficking. In 1997 the press reported that the gang was headed by national president John Baltas and had chapters in Springfield, Massachusetts; Connecticut; Terre Haute, Indiana; and San Bernardino, San Diego, and the San Fernando Valley in California, among other cities. Ten gang members, including Baltas, were arrested in October 1996 following an FBI sting operation. They were indicted on charges of racketeering, drug trafficking, murder for hire, firearms offenses, and the interstate transportation of stolen vehicles.

Reference: "Murder Charges Added to Racketeering Indictment." 1997. *Business Wire*, October.

Diacetylmorphine
See Heroin

Diaz Vega, Baltazar (c. 1951–)

At the time of his arrest in 1991, Diaz Vega was suspected of being the mentor and principal financier of drug kingpin Miguel Angel Felix Gallardo during his years in prison from 1989 to 1991. According to U.S. authorities, Diaz Vega accumulated as much as $300 million per shipment in drug deals operated by Felix Gallardo from his Mexico City prison cell. Diaz Vega is believed to have helped finance Felix Gallardo's early entry into cocaine trafficking and he himself reportedly accumulated a fortune of $500

million from his key role in the Colombian-Mexican cocaine trade. To avoid capture, Diez Vega underwent plastic surgery, but he was arrested at his home in Culiacan, a city in northwestern Mexico that serves as Felix Gallardo's home base.

See also: Felix Gallardo, Miguel Angel
Reference: Darling, Juan. 1991. "Accused Mentor of Imprisoned Drug Kingpin Arrested." *Los Angeles Times*, 28 March.

Diazepam
See Valium

Dihydromorphinone
See Dilaudid

Dilaudid

Also known as hydromorphone and dihydromorphinone, Dilaudid is made from morphine and can be as potent as heroin. Legal as an analgesic, Dilaudid can be used by heroin addicts to substitute for, or as a supplement to, heroin. Dilaudid's potency is almost eight times that of morphine, and chronic use will produce tolerance and dependence. Its side effects include constipation and difficulty in breathing. It is one of the most widely used and effective drugs for moderate to severe pain. Mary H. Cooper, in *The Business of Drugs,* states that "although hydromorphone use has declined since the mid-1980s, nationally, Washington D.C. remains an active market for the drug." (Cooper 1990, 91)

References: Cooper, Mary H. 1990. *The Business of Drugs*. O'Brien, Robert, and Sidney Cohen. 1984. *The Encyclopedia of Drug Abuse*.

Dominican Gangs

The tough New York City neighborhood of Washington Heights is reported to be the center of the Dominican dominance over cocaine trafficking in dozens of cities in the northeastern United States. Dominicans act as middlemen who receive cocaine from Colombian cartels and then sell it to other drug gangs. Washington Heights includes dozens of money-wiring houses known as envios de valores, which are used by the Dominican drug traffickers to ship the drug money to the Dominican Republic.

According to William Kleinknecht, "The gravitation of the Dominicans to the drug trade was inevitable. Dominicans are natural entrepreneurs, opening small businesses and restaurants, no matter where they settle. Turning those skills towards cocaine has been hard to resist for a certain percentage of the Dominican population. After all, the neighborhood they have chosen as the promised land has always been a major source of drugs." (Kleinknecht 1998, 258)

Several Dominican gangs have risen to prominence in Washington Heights. Gang leader Santiago Luis Palanco-Rodriguez, for example, who is known in the local street parlance as Yayo, began in the cocaine trade in 1982, and by 1985 his gang had become among the first to market crack in any significant quantity. Two years later, Yayo's gang was selling about 10,000 vials of crack a day on the street corners throughout Washington Heights and the South Bronx. In July 1987 authorities arrested nearly all the members of Yayo's organization, but the leader himself has never been caught.

The Jheri-Curls gang was prominent in drug trafficking between 1989 and 1991, but it became a target of a federal-state task force that imprisoned twenty-three members by October 1993. Another Dominican gang, known as the Wild Boys, spawned a crack enterprise that grossed $20 million annually.

Now major players in the international drug trade, the Dominican gangs have branched out from Washington Heights and set up drug distribution networks in several northeastern cities, including Allentown and Reading in Pennsylvania; Lewiston, Maine; and Hartford and New Haven in Connecticut.

Reference: Kleinknecht, William. 1996. *The New Ethnic Mobs: The Changing Face of Organized Crime in America.*

Dover's Powder

A form of medical opium developed by Thomas Dover, an assistant to Thomas Sydenham, the noted seventeenth-century teacher who originated the formula for laudanum, another early and popular opium-based medicine. Dover's Powder contained a mixture that included one ounce of opium, ipecac (the dried roots of a tropical creeping plant), and licorice, combined with wine, tartar, and saltpeter. Introduced in England in 1709, Dover's Powder made its way to the United States, where for nearly two centuries it was one of the most popular opium

preparations. Opium-based medicines like Dover's Powder were used for many illnesses and disorders, including bronchitis, tuberculosis, pain, syphilis, malaria, and chronic headache.

The introduction of Dover's Powder in the United States started a trend and by the latter half of the eighteenth century, patent medicines containing opium were readily available throughout urban and rural America. They were sold in groceries, pharmacies, general stores, and at traveling medicine shows and through the mail.

See also: Opium; Syndenham, Thomas
Reference: Inciardi, James. 1984. *The War On Drugs: Heroin, Cocaine, and Marijuana in Public Policy.*

Doyle, Sir Arthur Conan (1859–1930)

British writer and the creator of the fictional detective Sherlock Holmes, possibly the best-known character in English literature. In 1891 Doyle quit his medical practice to devote himself full-time to writing, publishing more than sixty stories about the Holmes character. In some of the stories, Holmes would smoke opium as he contemplated the details of a case, and historians say that this is a graphic example of the relaxed attitude in the nineteenth century toward the use of drugs that are illegal today.

See also: Opium
Reference: Higham, Charles. 1996. *The Adventures of Conan Doyle: The Life of the Creator of Sherlock Holmes.*

Dr. Snow

The nickname for Larry Lavin, who headed a major cocaine distribution network based in Philadelphia. Lavin had begun dealing drugs in college, and before graduating from dental school he was netting about $60,000 a month in cocaine profits. By the time he was indicted on drug-trafficking charges in 1985, the twenty-six-year-old dentist had made an estimated $6 million from his illegal activities. After his indictment, Dr. Snow fled to Virginia where he adopted a new identity but was captured eighteen months later. Lavin pleaded guilty to five counts of drug conspiracy and received twenty-two years in prison, along with another twenty years for tax evasion.

Reference: Bowden, Mark. 1987. *Doctor Dealer.*

Lothar, The Phantom, Flash Gordon, and Chief Daryl Gates of the L.A. police department all make appearances at an anti-drug rally in Westwood, California sponsored by the DARE organization, 1986. (Corbis/Bettmann-UPI)

Drug Abuse Resistance Education (DARE)

Introduced in Los Angeles in 1983, DARE is an educational program that seeks to assist young people to avoid drugs by helping them overcome personal problems, such as low self-esteem, which makes them more vulnerable to the lure of drugs. DARE's main program uses uniformed police officers to teach seventeen hour-long weekly lessons to fifth and sixth graders about how to resist drugs. DARE has received millions of dollars in federal, state, and local funds and, as the United States' most widely used drug prevention program, it is offered in three-fourths of U.S. schools.

By 1994, however, several studies had questioned DARE's effectiveness. For example, a team of researchers at the Durham, North Carolina, Research Triangle Institute concluded that DARE had limited influence on adolescent drug use, even given the program's popularity and prevalence, and was taking the place of other, more beneficial drug-abuse curricula that adolescents could be receiving.

References: Mason, Julie. 1998. "Study Questions DARE Program." *Houston Chronicle,* 27 August.

Chip Rowe. 1998. "Just Say No." *Playboy* (October): 44.

Drug Abuse Treatment Outcome Study (DATOS)

The National Institute on Drug Abuse initiated DATOS in 1990 as an effort to study drug abuse treatment outcomes and emerging treatment issues in the United States. Its overall goal is to advance scientific knowledge about the effectiveness of drug abuse treatment as it is typically delivered in the United States. The research plan for DATOS is based on studies and findings about drug abuse treatment outcomes over the past thirty years.

In 1995 four collaborating research centers were funded to pursue independent, but coordinated, programs of research based on DATOS. They include the National Development and Research Institutes in North Carolina, Texas Christian University in Fort Worth, the University of California at Los Angeles, and the National Institute on Drug Abuse Services Research Branch in Washington, D.C.

See also: United States National Institute On Drug Abuse
Reference: Drug Abuse Treatment Outcome Study website
   at http://www.datos.org

Drug Abuse Warning Network (DAWN)

A government-supported network that identifies and evaluates the scope and magnitude of drug abuse in the United States. DAWN identifies drugs currently being abused, monitors drug abuse trends, detects new abuse conditions, and provides data for the assessment of health hazards and the data needed for the rational control and scheduling of drugs of abuse. More than 900 hospital emergency rooms and medical examination facilities nationwide supply data to the program.

See also: United States National Institute On Drug Abuse
Reference: Cooper, Mary H. 1990. *The Business of Drugs.*

Drug Courts (U.S.)

Special judicial proceedings that are generally used for nonviolent drug offenders and provide periodic drug testing and supervised treatment. Some states and local jurisdictions set these courts up in the late 1980s to handle the proliferation of drug cases on the judicial dockets, the result of the increasingly tougher statutes against drug trafficking and drug use. Title V of the Violent Crime Act (Violent Crime Control and Law Enforcement Act of 1994) authorized the awarding of federal grants for drug court programs that include supervised drug treatment. Between 1989 and 1992 forty-two drug court programs were started; by April 1997 that figure had jumped to 161. In a 1997 report the U.S. General Accounting Office concluded that for several reasons, "it could not draw any firm conclusions on the overall impact of drug court programs or on certain specific issues raised by Congress about the programs or their participants." (U.S. General Accounting Office 1997, 6) While there have been no rigorous studies of the drug court system, preliminary results published in 1993 indicate drug court participants have less frequent rearrests, lower incarceration rates, and longer times between rearrests.

References: Bertram, Eva, Kenneth Sharpe, and Peter
   Anders. 1996. *Drug War Politics: The Price of Denial.*
United States General Accounting Office. 1997. *Drug Courts:
   Overview of Growth, Characteristics, and Results.*

Drug Czar

The popular name for the leader of the United States War on Drugs. Although not occupying a cabinet-level position, the drug czar sits with the president's cabinet. The first drug czar was William Bennett, who assumed the position in 1989. As of December 1998 the drug czar was Barry McCaffrey. In 1998 Colombia's incoming president, Andres Pastrana Arango, also created a new antidrug office that was headed by Augusto Perez. That country's press referred to Perez as the drug czar.

See also: Bennett, William; Brown, Lee; Clinton, William
   Jefferson; Martinez, Bob; McCaffery, Barry; Pastrana
   Arango, Andres; Perez, Augusto; United States Anti-Drug
   Abuse Act of 1988; United States Office of National Drug
   Abuse Control Policy
Reference: United States Office of National Control Policy
   Website at http://www.whitehousedrugpolicy.gov.

Drug Enforcement Agency
See United States Drug Enforcement Administration

Drug Free Zones

A well-defined area within the vicinity of a U.S. school in which a drug dealer who is caught selling drugs receives severe penalties under the law. For example, those found dealing drugs within 1,000 feet of school property usually receive a prison term without parole. Many urban cities have set up the zones to protect children and young people against the lure of the drug trade.

Reference: Cooper, Mary H. 1990. *The Business of Drugs.*

Drug Policy Foundation (U.S.)

Created in 1987 and based in Washington. D.C., the Foundation promotes alternatives to current U.S. drug policy through debates and seminars on drug policy issues. Topics such as legalization, decriminalization, and medicalization of currently illegal substances, including marijuana and heroin, and ways to curb further drug abuse while protecting the rights of the individual have been considered in these forums. Other activities of the foundation include assisting in litigation that involves federal drug possession laws and maintaining the Medical-Legal Advisory Project to provide legal aid in cases involving law and medicine. The Foundation

While in Miami to participate in a drug raid, Federal drug czar William Bennett stops at a local middle school to speak with the students, 18 May 1989. (Corbis/Bettmann-UPI)

strongly opposes urine tests for employees and believes that the legalization of drugs (making drugs available to adults in a regulated market, similar to U.S. alcohol laws) and effective drug treatment would greatly improve the health of addicts, decrease crime, and slow the spread of AIDS.

The Foundation is a central clearinghouse for drug policy information, and it has a grant program available to support drug reform-minded organizations, such as research centers, needle exchange programs, harm reduction groups, and legal action organizations. George Soros gave $6 million to the foundation in 1993, and he remains the organization's biggest financial backer. The Foundation has an international membership of 20,000.

See also: Decriminalization; Drug Tests; Legalization; Needle Exchange Programs; Soros, George
Reference: Drug Policy Foundation Website at http://www.drugpolicy.org.

Drug Strategies Institute (U.S.)

This Washington, D.C.based nonprofit research institute promotes the search for more effective approaches to the nation's drug problems and supports public and private initiatives that reduce demand for drugs through prevention, treatment, and law enforcement. Among other activities, Drug Strategies conducts an annual review of federal drug control spending; identifies promising prevention, education, and treatment programs; produces in-depth studies of alcohol, tobacco, and other types of drug abuse in seven states; and prepares a comprehensive assessment of the forty-seven most widely used drug education programs in the United States.

See also: Soros, George
Reference: Drug Strategies Institute website at http://www.drugabuseprevention.com/ds/.

Drug Testing

As a form of drug prevention, drug testing is now used in several countries, in many different occupations, and even in secondary schools and colleges in such countries as Great Britain and Malaysia. Drug testing has also been controversial. Critics oppose drug testing on various grounds, including that it is unconstitutional, costly, and ineffective. They also claim that drug testing is an invasion of personal privacy. Proponents, however, argue that drug testing promotes drug deterrence and the enforcement of the laws.

See also: American Civil Liberties Union; Cocaine; Drug Policy Foundation (U.S.); Lindesmith Institute
References: Cooper, Mary H. 1990. *The Business of Drugs.* United Nations International Drug Control Program. 1997. *World Drug Report.*

Drug Use Forecasting (U.S.) (DUF)

Known as DUF, this survey was launched in 1987 under the auspices of the U.S. National Institute of Justice and conducts urine tests and follow-up interviews with those arrested for serious crimes, first in a dozen cities and then in twenty-four. The program attempts to measure drug use among that part of the U.S. population likely to be missed in surveys of school and household populations. According to the *Encyclopedia of Drugs and Alcohol,* "The DUF findings have been used by local jurisdictions to promote the funding of drug intervention programs and to focus policymakers on the drug problems among convicted criminals. The DUF findings have helped to define the estimates of cocaine consumption in the United States. . . ." (*Encyclopedia of Drugs and Alcohol* 1995, 434)

Reference: Jonnes, Jill. 1996. *Hep-Cats, Narcs and Pipe Dreams.*

Drug Watch International

Founded in the 1970s, this Omaha, Nebraska–based volunteer, nonprofit information network and advocacy organization promotes the creation of "healthy drug-free cultures in the world" and opposes the legalization of drugs. Its purpose is to provide the public, policy makers, and the media with current drug information, factual research, expert resources, and countermeasures aimed at drug legalization. Its mission, as stated on its website, is to help assure a healthier and safer world through drug prevention by providing accurate information on both illicit and harmful psychoactive substances, promoting sound drug policies based on scientific research.

See also: Legalization
Reference: Drug Watch International website at http://www.drugwatch.org.

Dubose, Hampton C.

An American missionary in China who was instrumental in initiating the antiopium campaign in the Philippines and then in China in the early twentieth century. DuBose was one of the most important Christian missionaries in the Far East, and he helped shape public opinion against the use of opium in China. As historian Arnold H. Taylor writes, "Believing that the United States had a higher responsibility in the matter [of opium], he set forth the principal which was to become the basic tenet of American foreign policy throughout the international antiopium movement, that there can be no judicious use of opium save administered by a physician." (Taylor 1969, 32)

See also: Opium
Reference: Taylor, Arnold H. 1969. *American Diplomacy and Narcotics Trafficking, 1900–1939.*

Dublin Group

This organization includes Austria, Australia, Belgium, Canada, Denmark, France, Finland, Germany, Greece, Iceland, Italy, Japan, Luxembourg, the Netherlands, Norway, Portugal, Spain, Sweden, the United Kingdom, and the United States and meets annually in small regional groupings sponsored by individual host countries. The Group provides a forum for host countries to examine their antidrug programs and to identify areas for improvement. The United States uses the Group to disseminate information about its antidrug program and to solicit support for them.

Reference: International Crime Control Strategy. 1998. *Trends In Organized Crime* (Fall).

DUF

See Drug Use Forecasting

Duzan, Maria Jimena

A reporter for *El Expectador,* Colombia's oldest and one of its most respected newspapers, who spent the period from the early 1980s to the mid-1990s covering the war on drugs in her country. As a result of her investigative work, Duzan was under a constant threat of death. In 1985 her house was bombed after she spent several days interviewing M-19 guerrillas, who for decades have been involved in a guerrilla war with the Colombian government. In 1990 her sister and colleague, Sylvia Duzan, was shot to death while on assignment in the Magdalena River valley region, the power center of the country's paramilitary groups. In 1994 Maria Jimena Duzan published an autobiography entitled *Death Beat: A Colombian Journalist's Life inside the Cocaine Wars*, in which she chronicles and meditates on the havoc caused by the drug trade in her country. One reviewer noted that Jimena Duzan "regards the drug traffickers, not the armed forces or their Colombian accomplices, as the principal threat to society... [and] as outsiders who have corrupted her homeland with their money." (Jimenez 1994, 246)

See also: Cali Cartel; Media

References: Duzan, Maria Jimena. 1994. *Death Beat: A Colombian Journalist's Life inside the Cocaine Wars*.
Jimenez, Michael J. 1994. "Review of *Death Beat: A Colombian Journalist's Life inside the Cocaine Wars*, by Maria Jimena Duzan." *The Nation*, 5 September.

E

Easy Rider

A low-budget film released in 1969 and starring Peter Fonda and Dennis Hopper. Its plot follows two pot-smoking motorcyclists who travel around the country and find a meaningless death. As writer Jill Jonnes explained, "*Easy Rider* reflected a growing experience with altered states of consciousness while further popularizing that interest." (Jonnes 1996, 257)

Reference: Jonnes, Jill. 1996. *Hep-Cats, Narcs and Pipe Dreams.*

Ecstasy

This drug was created in the early 1980s by underground drug designers who wanted to increase the potency of amphetamine while changing its chemical composition to make it legal. Ecstasy itself, however, was made illegal in 1985. A 1993 study by the

Dennis Hopper (L) and Peter Fonda (R) in a scene from the cult movie "Easy Rider" filmed in 1969. (UPI/Corbis-Bettmann)

University of Michigan found that the drug's use was most prevalent among people in their twenties, but as it is easy to obtain, Ecstasy also has become the drug of choice for teenagers who attend dance parties known as "raves," or "rave parties." These large gatherings of young people are held in a large structure like a warehouse, where music and psychedelic lighting provide the setting for all-night dancing. Users of Ecstasy claim that the drug heightens their sex drive while giving them a sense of tranquillity, but a 1995 Johns Hopkins study, published in the November 1995 issue of the *Journal of Neuroscience,* revealed that the drug causes permanent damage to the parts of the brain that produce the chemical serotonin, which controls mood, appetite, and sexual functions.

See also: Amphetamine; Perez, Augusto; Synthetic Drugs
References: Cooper, Mary H. 1990. *The Business of Drugs.* "Ecstasy May Cause Irreversible Brain Damage." 1995. *International Drug Report* (November–December).

Edwards, Delroy

Edwards was the head of the largest and most efficient Jamaican drug distribution ring ever to operate in the United States and is believed to be the first major trafficker of crack cocaine. Edwards began selling crack and marijuana in 1985 from his home base in the Bedford Stuyvesant area of Brooklyn, New York, but soon branched out to Washington, D.C., Baltimore, and Philadelphia as well. He peaked as a drug trafficker in 1988, the year when he reportedly earned nearly $100,000 weekly. On 1 December 1989 Edwards was sentenced to seven consecutive life terms plus fifteen years in prison and was fined $1 million for six murders, seventeen assaults, one kidnapping, and an assault and a shooting that resulted in the paralysis of an innocent victim.

Reference: Kleinknecht, William. 1996. *The New Ethnic Mobs: The Changing Face of Organized Crime in America.*

El Paso Intelligence Center (EPIC)

Established in 1974 as an intelligence unit on the U.S.-Mexican border, EPIC soon grew into a round-the-clock intelligence center, with worldwide ability to collect, process, and disseminate information about illicit drug trafficking, as well as the smuggling of aliens and weapons. The Center provides a valuable resource for law enforcement at the federal, state, and local levels. The Center is staffed by personnel from the FBI, IRS, DEA, the Coast Guard, the Immigration and Naturalization Service, the Bureau of Alcohol, Tobacco and Firearms, the Federal Aviation Administration, and the U.S. Marshals Service.

Reference: President's Commission on Organized Crime. 1986. *America's Habit: Drug Trafficking and Organized Crime.*

El Rukns

Organized in the 1960s as the Blackstone Rangers, this Chicago street gang has been described as perhaps the best-known black organized crime group in America. When Jeff Fort, the gang's founder, was released from prison in 1970 after serving two years of a five-year sentence, he resumed control of the gang and renamed it the El Rukns. They subsequently took over drug trafficking in much of Chicago's South Side and earned a reputation for viciousness.

In 1987 Fort was again sent to prison, this time for eighty years, for his role in a plot to unleash terrorist activities in the United States on behalf of Libyan President Moammar Gadhafi. He was later convicted of the 1981 murder of a rival who refused to share his profits from a drug deal. Fort is currently in jail, but, according to law enforcement officials, he is believed to still head the El Rukns gang, which retains a powerful presence in Chicago drug-trafficking activities.

References: Abadinsky, Howard. 1990. *Organized Crime.* Kleinknecht, William. 1996. *The New Ethnic Mobs: The Changing Face of Organized Crime in America.*

Elders, Joycelyn (1933–   )

Controversial U.S. surgeon general during the first term of President Bill Clinton. Elders was confirmed to the post of surgeon general in 1993 but was fired the following year for suggesting that schools should consider teaching masturbation. The surgeon general also ignited a firestorm of controversy when she suggested publicly that legalization of drugs should be studied as a policy issue. After her resignation, Elders spoke out for the expansion of clean needle programs for drug users.

See also: Clinton, Bill; Legalization; Needle Exchange Programs

The War on Drugs often has a terrible impact on the environment as can be seen from this picture taken in Colombia. (Courtesy of the Colombian National Police)

References: Colford, Stephen W. 1993. "New Surgeon General Backs Condom Ads: Elders Wants TV Networks To Abandon Prohibition." 1993. *Advertising Age*, 11 January.
Heald, Bonnie. 1997. "Former Surgeon General Speaks Out At Local Conference." Knight Ridder Tribune News Service, 13 February.

Environment

In addition to the human costs of drug trafficking, the illicit trafficking in drugs has played a deleterious role on our natural environment in a number of ways. Illicit cultivation and processing of coca and poppy crops causes deforestation, the extent of which depends upon how and where drug producers grow crops, how they process them and how they dispose of the waste products. As *The World Drug Report* explained, "[T]he most widely used method, commonly referred to as 'slash and burn' agriculture, involves the felling and burning of trees. This deforestation practice leaves no remaining vegetative matter to replenish the soils, thus rendering them sterile." (United Nations International Drug Control Program 1997, 147)

The greatest environmental harm from illegal drug production, however, may not come from deforestation but from the powerful chemicals used to refine drugs. In cocaine manufacturing, cultivation also involves the use of powerful herbicides, pesticides, and fungicides to release the cocaine alkaloids and then to purify the drug in order to ensure higher value. No one is sure about the amount of chemical by-products released into the environment, but the effects are clear. It is estimated that 20 million liters of chemicals are dumped each year in the Colombian jungle, while in Bolivia some 38,000 tons of toxic waste relating to drug trafficking are dumped annually in the Chepare and Yungus regions.

Synthetic drugs like methamphetamine have created an environmental problem as well. Methamphetamine laboratories, in fact, have become known in U.S. law enforcement as "the hazardous waste sites of the drug trade." In California, where methamphetamine manufacturing is largely centered, hospital admissions due to "meth" use rose 360 percent between 1986 and 1996. These patients included victims of fires, chemical spills, explosions, and the inhalation of toxic fumes.

Hydriodic acid and red phosphorus, the most dangerous chemicals used in methamphetamine production, can produce toxic phosphine gas and hydriodic acid vapors, while inhalation of ether can cause respiratory damage, chemical burns, and even death. Red phosphorus, a by-product of the manufacturing process, poses additional problems because it is unstable and flammable and can cause explosions if exposed to a flame or spark. The post-manufacturing phase poses the additional problem of what to do with the hazardous waste generated in methamphetamine production. Cleaning up such hazardous waste sites is expensive, too, varying in cost from case to case and site to site. Responsibility for cleanup costs is one of the biggest issues regarding methamphetamine.

See also: Alternative Development; Cocaine; Crop Substitution; Eradication; Ford, Gerald R.; Methamphetamine; Revolutionary Armed Forces of Colombia; Operation Condor/Trigo

References: Chepesiuk, Ron. 1998. The Threat of Meth. *Environmental Health Perspectives Journal* (April).
Gatjanis, Greg. 1995. Cocaine's Latest Victim: "The Water Runs Red." *U.N. Chronicle* (June).
United Nations International Drug Control Program. 1997. *World Drug Report.*
U.S. Congress. Senate. Committee on Governmental Affairs. *Cocaine Production, Eradication; Environment: Policy Impact, Options.* Report prepared for the Permanent Subcommittee on Investigations.

Eradication

An antidrug control strategy that has as its objective the disruption of the supply chain bringing the plant-based drug from the field to the consumer by decreasing the supply of illegally cultivated crops. Eradication can either be done by burning, by mechanical means that involve slashing or burning the crops, or by applying chemicals, such as herbicides. The process can either be accomplished through force, which is often the case in areas in which there has been no tradition of growing illicit drug crops, or through measures that provide compensation to the growers. In some countries, most notably Peru and Bolivia, eradication efforts have been met with strong and sometimes violent resistance.

Governments of drug-producing countries have disapproved of the use of herbicides as well. In October 1998 Colombia's new president, Andres Pastrana Arango, told the press that the U.S.-backed aerial eradication program in Colombia has not worked, and that the policy is simply pushing peasants deeper into the jungle. Pastrana added that he would like to see the U.S government spend more on development to lure coca-growing farmers out of the drug trade and less on forcible eradication.

Eradication is difficult to carry out because the drug crops are often grown in inaccessible areas. In some of the locations heavily armed guerrilla groups guard the illicit crops. Despite the media attention that eradication has received in the 1990s, this strategy has been implemented in a relatively small percentage of the illicitly cultivated areas.

See also: Alternative Development; Carter, Jimmy; Crop Substitution; Environment; Operation Condor/Trigo; Operation Vanguard; Operation Wipeout; Pastrana Arango, Andres; United Nations Conference On Drug Control

References: Clawson, Patrick, and Rensselaer W. Lee. 1996. *The Andean Cocaine Economy.*
Johnson, Tim. 1998. "Pastrana Cool To Coca Policy." *Miami Herald*, 16 October.
United Nations International Drug Control Program. 1997. *World Drug Report.*

Escalante, Ramon

A Wisconsin produce dealer who became prominent in drug trafficking in the 1920s, smuggling drugs from Mexico to the United States. He attached packets of marijuana to burros and then taught them to cross the Rio Grande River at night in search of feed. U.S. customs agents uncovered the ploy and arrested smugglers working for Escalante. They helped the authorities to nab their leader.

Reference: Roark, Garland. 1964. *The Coin of Contraband: The True Story of United States Customs Investigator Al Scharff.*

Escobar Gaviria, Pablo (1949–1993)

One of history's most powerful drug traffickers, who helped found the Medellin Cartel. At the height of his power in the late 1980s Escobar Gaviria was one of the world's richest individuals. Born the son of a night watchman and a school teacher on 1 December 1949 in Rionegro, Colombia, a town twenty-five miles from Medellin, Escobar grew up in the tough blue-collar suburb of Envigado, a place that would later become his refuge when the Colombian authorities were in hot pursuit of him. In a shrewd effort to create a positive public image, Escobar often portrayed himself as coming from a poor, deprived background; in reality, his life was middle class (by Colombian standards), and he was a high

Pablo Escobar Gaviria, founder and leader of the Medellin Cartel (Courtesy of the Colombian National Police)

school graduate—no small feat for someone from Envigado.

Escobar's first known criminal activity is believed to have been the stealing of gravestones. He would then sell them to the recently bereaved relatives of the deceased. In the early 1970s he worked as a thief and bodyguard, who made a quick $100,000 on the side by kidnapping and ransoming a Medellin business executive. In 1976 police arrested Escobar for possessing thirty pounds of cocaine, but he never went to trial. Later, the drug trafficker had gunmen murder the two arresting officers in what was the beginning of a vicious pattern that he would follow throughout his criminal career: kill anyone who crossed him, stood in his way, or posed a threat.

By the late 1970s as the cocaine trade began to boom in response to American demand, Escobar was moving about thirty-five tons of cocaine annually out of Colombia. He was making so much money, in fact, that he even invested in U.S. real estate, including an $8 million apartment complex in Florida. In Colombia, Escobar financed race cars and

sponsored a team in the local competitions. Over the gate of his well-protected 7,000-acre estate in Puerto Triunfo, called Hacienda Napoles, Escobar arrogantly displayed an aircraft that was reported to be the vehicle that had carried his first load of cocaine. The estate also had a zoo, twenty-four lakes, and a country house that could accommodate 100 guests.

Escobar cultivated an image as a generous benefactor by developing such projects as "Medellin without Slums." During this period, he played a leading role in organizing the Medellin Cartel. In deference to his position in the organization, other Cartel members began referring to him as *El Padrino* ("the godfather")—a sign of respect that made him the boss of bosses within the cartel.

In 1982 Escobar was elected to Congress as an alternate representative, but he was forced out of office in 1984 when his criminal dealings were revealed by Justice Minister Rodrigo Lara Bonilla. Escobar got his revenge by killing Lara Bonilla, a move that incurred the wrath of the Colombian government and instigated a violent seven-year internal struggle in Colombia.

Escobar said he would dismantle his empire in exchange for amnesty for himself and his associates and even offered to help pay off Colombia's $13 billion foreign debt. The Colombian government, however, rejected his offer and Escobar went into hiding. El Padrino continued to conduct his violent campaign against law enforcement officials and politicians who supported the extradition to the United States of Colombian drug kingpins. In addition to the assassination of Lara Bonilla, Escobar was also linked to the murders of Jaime Gomez Ramirez, head of the Antinarcotic Unit Colombia's National Police, and Guillermo Cano Isaza, the respected editor of *El Espectador*, Colombia's second largest newspaper.

As the Medellin Cartel's power increased, the United States learned more about the powerful drug lord. On 18 November 1986 Escobar and nine other men were indicted in Miami on charges that included racketeering and smuggling of at least sixty tons of cocaine into the United States. By the early 1990s Escobar was feeling the intense heat of the campaign against him, and he surrendered to authorities in June 1991 after Colombian President Cesar Gaviria Trujillo authorized legal changes that would bar extradition to the United States of drug traffickers who surrendered and confessed their crimes. Escobar was incarcerated in a luxury prison that he was permitted to build for himself.

Escobar continued to conduct his drug business from jail, but learning that the Colombian authorities were moving to curtail his freedom, Escobar and several of his associates walked out of the "prison" in July 1992. A massive manhunt for Escobar ensued, and he was eventually tracked to Medellin, where on 2 October 1993 he was killed in a roof-top shoot-out with authorities. By then the Cali Cartel had become the dominant power in the Colombian drug trade, and Escobar's death had little impact.

See also: Blanco De Trujillo, Griselda; Cali Cartel; Cano Isaza, Guillermo; Cocaine; De Grieff, Gustavo; De Grieff, Monica; De La Cuesta Marquez, Jorge; Escobar Gaviria, Roberto; Escobar, Severo; Extradition; Gaviria Trujillo, Cesar; Gomez Ramirez, Jaime; Herrera, Father Rafael; Lara Bonilla, Rodrigo; Lopez Michelsen, Alfonso; Low Murtra, Enrique; Medellin Cartel; Medellin Without Slums; Mermelstein, Max; Narcoterrorism; Ochoa Vasquez, Jr., Fabio; Ochoa Vasquez, Jorge Luis; Ochoa Vasquez, Juan David; People Persecuted By Pablo Escobar (Pepes); Ramirez Gomez, Jaime; Seale, Barry; Turbay Ayala, Diana; Vaughn, Federico
References: Castillo, Fabio. 1988. *Los Jinetes De La Cocaina*. Chepesiuk, Ron. 1999. *Hard Target*.
———. 1989. "Colombian Drug Lord Trying to Turn Wealth into Respect." *Orlando Sentinel*, 10 March.
Gugliotta, Guy, and Jeff Leen. 1990. *Kings of Cocaine*.
Strong, Simon. 1995. *Whitewash: Pablo Escobar and the Cocaine Wars*.

Escobar Gaviria, Roberto

The older brother of Medellin Cartel drug kingpin Pablo Escobar Gaviria. As a young man, Roberto became a sports cyclist and studied electronics before setting up a bicycle shop in the city of Manizales, which is about six hours by car from the city of Medellin. When Roberto became involved much later in brother Pablo's lucrative and growing drug-trafficking enterprise, he was described as his brother's "right-hand man and his administrative brains." (Strong 1995, 23) Roberto reportedly organized his brother's communications network, which allowed him to keep his criminal enterprise going while he battled the state. In April 1992 Pablo told brother Roberto and some of his other fellow fugitives to turn themselves in to Colombian authorities. A year later, Roberto, on orders from Pablo, was about to turn over documents to the U.S. authorities

that implicated the brothers Gilberto and Miguel Rodriguez Orejuela in the drug trade, but prison officials raided his cell and took the documents away.

See also: Escobar Gaviria, Pablo; Medellin Cartel
Reference: Strong, Simon. 1995. *Whitewash: Pablo Escobar and the Cocaine Wars*.

Escobar, Severo (1959–   )

Nicknamed "Junior", Severo is a nephew of deceased drug kingpin Pablo Escobar Gaviria and was a leading drug trafficker in Europe during the late 1980s. Severo was arrested in a police raid on a Swiss luxury hotel in December 1989 in which seven pounds of pure cocaine were seized prior to the planned delivery by the drug trafficker and his associates of 440 pounds to the Swiss and Italian markets. Escobar was said to operate a smuggling network that transported huge loads of cocaine to supply the Swiss, German, and Dutch markets. His father, Severo, Sr., was convicted of drug charges in 1984 and sentenced to thirty years in prison.

See also: Escobar Gaviria, Pablo; Medellin Cartel
Reference: "Nephew of Pablo Escobar Gaviria Arrested." 1989. Associated Press, 6 December.

European Cities on Drug Policy (ECDP)

Organized in 1991, this organization's work is based on the concept of harm reduction in the field of drug control, and it seeks to use the power of government and community leadership in a constructive attempt to reduce the harm caused by the inevitable presence of drugs in a society. The ECDP's basic political documents are the Frankfurt Resolution (1990) and the Declaration of the ECDP, which was passed in May 1998 at the organization's seventh general assembly. To become a member, a city has to have a local council decision in support of the Frankfurt Resolution and the Declaration of the ECDP.

See also: Frankfurt Resolution; Harm Reduction
Reference: European Cities on Drug Policy website at http://www.ecdp.net/.

European Committee to Combat Drugs

The heads of state of the twelve nations of the European Community (EC) set up this committee in December 1989 as a body that would be responsible for coordinating the fight against drug trafficking in the EC.

See also: European Cities on Drug Policy; Frankfurt Resolution
Reference: Jamieson, Alison. 1994. *Terrorism: Drug Trafficking in Europe in the 1990s.*

European Community Directive on the Prevention of Money Laundering

A measure passed by the European Union in 1991 that put into place legislative procedures designed to attack the financial basis of drug-trafficking syndicates. Procedures included taking steps to confiscate the proceeds from drug trafficking and implementing reporting requirements on financial institutions to help detect and investigate transactions suspected of involving illegal drugs.

See also: Money Laundering
Reference: Anderson, Malcolm, and Monica De Boer. 1995. *Policing the European Union.*

European Monitoring Centre for Drugs and Drug Addiction

Established by the European Commission in 1993, the Centre was organized with the hope of providing a vital resource in gathering and analyzing of information about drug-related activity. The Centre undertakes such activities as supporting research into the causes of drug-related diseases, disseminating health education information, and providing financial assistance to producer countries to help them make crop substitutions.

See also: Crop Substitution
Reference: Anderson, Malcolm, and Monica De Boer. 1995. *Policing the European Union.*

Europol

Formerly known as the European Drugs Intelligence Center, Europol is the principal coordinating body for exchanging criminal intelligence concerning illicit drug trafficking and money laundering. In 1994 the European Commission adopted a European Plan of Action to Combat Drugs, which was to be in effect for the period from 1995 to 1999. In providing for a new framework for drug control strategy, the Plan contained three key elements: action at the international level, the reduction of drug trafficking, and the prevention of drug dependency. Europol was officially opened on 1 October 1998.

Reference: United Nations International Drug Control Program. 1997. *World Drug Report.*

Extraditables

This was the name that Colombian drug traffickers from the Medellin Cartel gave themselves in the 1980s as they fought back against a North American-inspired crackdown against them that included pressure on the Colombian government to extradite drug traffickers to the United States for trial. The motto of the Extraditables was "Better in a grave than a jail in the United States," and they waged a terrorist campaign against the Colombian state that included murder and car bombings. Among their targets were Carlos Mauro Hoyos Jiminez, Colombia's attorney general, and Andres Pastrana Arango, the mayor of Bogotá, who became Colombia's president in 1998.

Pastrana was kidnapped on 18 January 1988, but was freed by police after a manhunt to find the killers of Hoyos, who had been abducted in the Medellin airport. An anonymous caller, who said he represented the Extraditables, told police they could find Hoyos in a field. The location was a few miles from where Pastrana was being held. Hoyos had been shot eleven times in the face. But the most shocking act of terrorism attributed to the Extraditables occurred on 27 November 1989, when an Avianca jet was bombed out of the sky, killing the crew members and all 107 passengers on board.

The Extraditables eventually did get what they wanted when the Colombian legislature banned the extradition of its citizens in 1991. In 1997, however, the Colombian Congress passed a new law that allowed for the extradition of its citizens. A group calling itself the Extraditables then claimed responsibility for the murder of President Ernesto Samper's chief press spokesman, although a guerrilla group also claimed credit. Colombia braced itself for another terrorist campaign by the Extraditables.

See also: Extradition; Hoyos Jiminez, Carlos Mauro; Medellin Cartel; Pastrana Arango, Andres
References: Gugliotta, Guy, and Jeff Leen. 1990. *Kings of Cocaine.*
Strong, Simon. 1995. *Whitewash: Pablo Escobar and the Cocaine Wars.*

Extradition

The act of surrendering or turning over an alleged criminal, usually under the provisions of a treaty or statute, by one state or jurisdiction to another, to try the charge. Forty-three members of the United Nations signed an international convention against drug trafficking and drug abuse, which contains a provision guaranteeing that all signatories will extradite suspected drug dealers and confiscate their assets.

The United States has tried to have important drug dealers extradited for trial in the United States, where it believes there will be a greater likelihood of conviction, as well as tougher sentencing. While the United States considers extradition to be an essential weapon in the War on Drugs, Colombia, Mexico, Myanmar, and other countries that produce the illicit drugs consider extradition to be a form of imperialism and an affront to their sovereignty. Moreover, drug crops provide an important source of income for many poor farmers, and they regard the illegal drug trade as vital to their survival.

Moves to extradite traffickers has sparked strong protest and even violence in many countries. For example, people staged anti- American protests on the streets of Tegucigalpa when drug trafficker Juan Ramon Matta Ballesteros was extradited to the United States in 1988. Drug traffickers, moreover, have taken the initiative and have tried to intimidate governments and influence popular opinion. In November 1985, for example, the Medellin Cartel reportedly paid guerrillas in M-19 (the April 19 Movement, a Colombian guerrilla group that has been fighting the Colombian government for more than three decades) between $1 and $5 million to take over the Palace of Justice in Bogotá, destroy records that could be used in extradition proceedings, and hold the Colombian Supreme Court justices hostage.

When Senator Luis Carlos Gala, the leading candidate in the 1990 Colombian presidential election and a strong opponent of drug trafficking, was killed at a Bogotá rally in August 1989, Colombian President Virgil Banco Argas made a major television speech in which he said he would begin extradition proceedings of Colombian traffickers wanted abroad. Six days later, when Colombia changed its extradition policy, members of the Medellin Cartel started calling themselves the Extraditables and launched a vicious terrorist bombing campaign to force the Colombian government to change its policy.

Under the intense pressure the Colombian government wilted and changed its position in the mid-1990s. In 1997 the Colombian government restored extradition, but prevented it from being applied retroactively. The move has prevented the extradition to the United States of Calli Cartel godfathers, the brothers Gilberto and Miguel Rodriguez Orejuela. U.S. Attorney General Janet Reno had made a formal request to the Colombian government for the godfathers' extradition.

See also: Abello Silva, Jose Rafael; Arce Gomez, Luis; Bentacur Cuertas, Belasario; Cano Izaza, Guillermo; Convention on the Protection of Financial Interests in the Community; Convention on the Suppression of the Illicit Traffic in Illegal Drugs; Customs Information Systems Convention; Escobar Gaviria, Pablo; Extraditables; Galan, Luis Carlos; Hoyos Jiminez, Carlos Mauro; Khun Sa; Lara Nauza, Jaime Orlando; Lehder Rivas, Carlos; Low Murtra, Enrique; Martinez, Ramero Eduardo; Matta Ballesteros, Juan Ramon; Mera Mosquera, Eduardo; M-19; Narcoterrorism; National Latin Movement; Ochoa Vasquez, Jorge Luis; Palace of Justice (Bogotá, Colombia); Palma, Manuel; Palma Molina, Manuel Julio; Perafan, Justo Pastor; Parejo Gonzalez, Enrique; Revolutionary Armed Forces of Colombia; Rodriguez Orejuela, Gilberto; Rodriguez Orejuela, Miguel; Roldan, Bernardo; Romero Gomez, Alfonso; Ruiz Massieu, Mario; Turbay Ayala, Diana; United Nations Conference on Drug Control; Vivas, Raul Silvo

References: Chepesiuk, Ron. 1999. *Hard Target*.
Cooper, Mary H. 1990. *The Business of Drugs*.
"Extraditables." 1997. *The Economist*, 20 September, 36–37.

F

Families against Mandatory Minimums

Sparked by Julia Stewart, a former employee of the Libertarian Cato Institute in Washington, D.C., this group consists of a nationwide network of prisoners in jail because of drug charges and their families. Its focus is to challenge the mandatory sentence laws. The group has about 33,000 members, including 10,000 inmates in federal and state prisons.

Reference: Moore, John W. 1995. "A Lobbyist Who Packs Real Passion." *National Journal*, 25 February.

Farley, Chris (1964–1997)

A popular comedian who starred in the television show "Saturday Night Live" and such movies as "Tommy Boy," "Beverly Hills Ninja," "Coneheads," and "Wayne's World," and then died from a drug overdose. A woman with him at the time of his death pleaded guilty to involuntary manslaughter and drug charges for giving him "speedball" injections of heroin and cocaine. The press noted that the 6-foot 1-inch, 296-pound comedian followed the life pattern and fate of his idol, comedian John Belushi, who lived a life of excess and died from a drug overdose in 1982.

See Also Belushi, John; Speed Balling
References: Medegaard, Erik. "Chris Farley, 1964-1997," *Rolling Stone*, 5 February 1998.
Tresniowski, Alex. "Requiem For A Heavyweight," *People Weekly*, 12 January 1998.

"Fat Albert"

The nickname for a balloon-shaped NORAD radar installation that was set up 10,000 feet above Key West, Florida, in 1983 as part of President Ronald Reagan's decision to allow civil authorities to use military resources, particularly technology and equipment, in the War on Drugs. The radar installation is designed to help monitor aircraft flying to the United States and the Caribbean and South America.

Reference: Chepesiuk, Ron. 1999. *Hard Target*.

Felix Gallardo, Miguel Angel (c. 1946–   )

At the time of his capture in Guadalajara by the Mexican government in April 1989, Felix Gallardo was described as Mexico's leading cocaine trafficker. The U.S. Drug Enforcement Administration had identified him as the head of an international drug-trafficking ring responsible for shipping two tons of cocaine into the United States each month. American officials believed that Felix Gallardo was involved in the killing of American drug agent Enrique Camarena Salazar in Guadalajara in 1985, although the Mexican government doubted their suspicions. Felix Gallardo's capture was hailed as a major political accomplishment for President Carlos Salinas, who had taken office four months earlier. Interestingly, Felix Gallardo is the uncle of the powerful drug-trafficking Arellano Felix brothers.

See also: Arellano Felix, Ramon; Camarena Salazar, Enrique; Diaz Vega, Baltazar; Garcia Abrego, Juan; Guzman, Joaquin; Matta Ballesteros, Juan Ramon; Operation Padrino; Salinas De Gortari, Carlos
References: "Mexico Arrested Alleged Godfather of Drug Traffic." 1989. *Los Angeles Times*, 10 April.
Rohter, Larry. 1989. "Mexicans Arrest Top Drug Figure and 80 Police." *New York Times*, 11 April.

Fighting Back Program (U.S.)

Sponsored by the Robert Wood Johnson Foundation, this antidrug program operates in at least fourteen American cities, including Richmond, Virginia; Santa Barbara, California; Kansas City, Missouri; and Worcester, Massachusetts. It encourages community prevention and treatment efforts by building local citizen networks that embody public health rather than punitive features.

See also : Robert Wood Johnson Foundation
References: Bertram, Eva, Kenneth Sharpe, and Peter Anders. 1996. *Drug War Politics: The Price of Denial.*
Fighting Back Program website at http://www.pbs.org/wnet/closetohome/policy/html/fighting.html

Financial Action Task Force (FATF)

Set up in Paris in July 1989, the FATF is composed of G-7 countries (group of seven leading industrialized countries), as well as Austria, Belgium, Sweden, the Netherlands, Spain, Australia, Switzerland, and Luxembourg. Its objectives are to analyze the money-laundering business, assess the utility of national and international programs that are being used to combat the phenomenon, and recommend appropriate actions. Drug traffickers are the biggest users of money-laundering techniques to hide their profits.

See also: Money Laundering
Reference: Financial Action Task Force website at http:// www.oecd.fr/fatf

Financial Crimes Enforcement Network (FINCEN)

Formally established on 25 April 1990 FINCEN is a U.S. Department of Treasury organization that primarily serves and assists other law enforcement agencies to identify, investigate, and prosecute money-laundering activity. To do this FINCEN has a staff of about 200 employees who analyze and disseminate a variety of data, mostly financial in nature, which has been collected and processed by federal, state, and local authorities, as well as foreign official sources. FINCEN also provides strategic intelligence analyses in the form of reports that identify and track trends and issues related to money laundering and are used by law enforcement and regulatory agencies for many purposes.

See also: Money Laundering
Reference: U.S. General Accounting Office. 1993. *Money Laundering: Progress Report on Treasury's Financial Crimes Enforcement Network.*

Flores, Fernando Jose (c. 1961–   )

Nicknamed "Fatso," Flores, a Venezuelan and longtime associate of Cali Cartel godfathers Miguel and Gilberto Rodriguez Orejuela, was arrested in Bogotá in August 1998. During the three months prior to his capture, Flores had visited the Rodriguez Orejuela brothers several times in Bogotá's La Picota prison, where they had been held since their capture in 1995. Flores was expected to be extradited or expelled to the United States, where he is wanted on drug-trafficking charges. There is also speculation that Flores can provide testimony that could result in the extradition of the Rodriguez Orejuela brothers to the United States for trial, where they are wanted on a number of drug trafficking charges.

See also: Cali Cartel; Rodriguez Orejuela, Gilberto; Rodriguez Orejuela, Miguel
Reference: Kotler, Jared. 1998. "Fatso May Be Big Break against Cali Cartel Bosses." *Seattle Times*, 28 May.

Fonseca Carrillo, Ernesto (1931–   )

Nicknamed "Don Neto" or "Sir Good Price," Fonseca Carrillo had become one of the biggest cocaine traffickers in Mexico by the late 1970s. In December 1982 Fonseca Carrillo was indicted for his part in an alleged money-laundering scheme that involved smuggling large amounts of cash between Rancho Sante Fe, California, and his base of operation in Mexico.

Fonseca Carrillo fled his base and remained a fugitive until 7 April 1985, when Mexican police caught him by chance at the vacation resort of Puerto Vallarta. Don Neto was later implicated in the murder of DEA agent Enrique Camarena Salazar earlier in the year. A federal jury in Los Angeles indicted him for Camarena's murder, and discussions were held about extraditing the drug dealer to the United States for trial. However, he remained in a Mexican jail on drug-trafficking and related charges. In 1989 he was convicted by a Mexican court of killing Camarena.

See also: Camarena Salazar, Enrique
References: "Mexican Probe Reportedly Links Military, Drugs." 1997. Reuters. 28 July.
Oppenheimer, Andres. 1997. "Are More Generals in Mexico Focus of Drug Probe?" *Seattle Times*, 28 July.

Ford, Gerald R. (1913–   )

President of the United States from 1974 until 1977 (the first vice president to succeed to the office because of the resignation of a president). The Ford administration continued the interdiction strategy begun by Richard Nixon. From the 1930s to 1975, Mexico supplied nearly all the marijuana used in the United States, but in a joint effort, U.S. and Mexican authorities began using the potent herbicide paraquat to fumigate and eradicate the Mexican crop. The program created an uproar in the United States because paraquat poisoned—but did not destroy—the marijuana crop and many Americans who used Mexican marijuana got sick. The program did prove successful, though, in that many American marijuana users became reluctant to smoke Mexican marijuana, and its overall use declined. By 1979 Mexico supplied about 11 percent of the marijuana for the U.S. market, a figure that declined to just 4 percent by 1981.

Ford differed from his predecessor, Richard Nixon, in opposing the creation of an executive-level office pertaining to drug abuse prevention. But, as the President's Commission on Organized Crime later pointed out, "Ford did not veto the 1976 amendment creating ODAP (Office of Drug Abuse Policy). However, President Ford did not staff ODAP, even though a specific line-item authorization had been made for it." (President's Commission on Organized Crime 1986, 251). The ODAP came into being in 1977 under Ford's successor, President Jimmy Carter.

See also: Environment; Marijuana
References: Chepesiuk, Ron. 1999. *Hard Target*.
President's Commission on Organized Crime. 1986. *America's Habit: Drug Trafficking and Organized Crime*.

Frankfurt Resolution

A resolution signed by the city councilors of nine European cities in 1990, which has as its objective the reduction of the harm caused by drug use and abuse, as well as the perceived harm caused by the illegal status of drugs. The resolution proposed that neither the possession nor the consumption of drugs for purely personal use be promoted, that cannabis should be treated differently than other drugs under the law, that the use, purchase, and possession of cannabis should be decriminalized, and that the prescription of drugs to addicts under medical supervision should be considered. During the 1990s several cities in Eastern and Western Europe have implemented these proposals. The Frankfurt Resolution has also led to the formation of an alternative association known as the European Cities on Drug Policy, which opposes any relaxation of existing laws.

See also: European Cities on Drug Policy; Harm Reduction; Marijuana; Medical Marijuana
Reference: United Nations International Drug Control Program. 1997. *World Drug Report*.

Franklin Quintero, Colonel Waldeman

The head of the police force in Antioquia, Colombia, who was murdered in August 1989 within two days of the killing of Luis Carlos Galan, the leading candidate in Colombia's 1990 presidential campaign. Authorities believed that Pablo Escobar had ordered the hit, but he denied it. Four months earlier, however, Franklin Quintero had raided one of Escobar's biggest cocaine-processing laboratories and seized four tons of cocaine. Carlos Arturo Casadiego, the deputy commander of the national police, replaced Franklin Quintero, but about a year later, he was forced to resign after he was arrested for passing information to Escobar.

See also: Galan, Luis Carlos
Reference: Strong, Simon. 1995. *Whitewash: Pablo Escobar and the Cocaine Wars*.

Frechette, Myles (1936–   )

U.S. ambassador to Colombia from 1994 to 1997, a posting considered to be the most difficult U.S. foreign service assignment in Latin America. As ambassador, Frechette's atypical, blunt diplomatic style

Myles Frechette, former United States ambassador to Colombia (Courtesy Ron Chepesiuk)

Free Base Smoking

A dangerous kind of cocaine abuse in which a chemically treated form of cocaine is smoked to produce an intense high. Free basing involves removing hydrochloride salt from street cocaine. The "freed" cocaine is then mixed with a solvent, such as ether, and heated, resulting in purified crystals, which are crushed and smoked. The introduction of crack cocaine in the 1980s in U.S. society led to a significant rise in free base smoking.

See also: Crack Cocaine
Reference: Du Lac, J. Freedom. 1995. "Free Fall." *Sacramento Bee*, 19 February.

Free Trade

This economic term means trade or commerce conducted without such restrictions as trade quotas, import licenses, import duties, and domestic production subsidies. After World War II strong attitudes developed throughout the world against protection and high tariffs and in favor of free trade. As a result, several new trade organizations developed worldwide, including the North American Free Trade Association (NAFTA) in 1992 and the European Community (EC) in 1993.

Some critics of free trade have argued that with few or almost no border regulations, free trade has become highly beneficial to organized crime, particularly drug traffickers, who can smuggle their illicit goods more easily. According to one report, U.S. law enforcement officials working along the Rio Grande river, which divides Mexico and the United States, refer to NAFTA as the "North American Free Drug Trafficking Agreement." (Payne 1997, 59)

See also: Money Laundering
References: Estrada, Richard. 1998. Drug War Alliance with Mexico Has Its Limits. *Dallas Morning News*, 25 September.
Hall, Kevin J. 1998. Truckers: Business As Usual. *Journal of Commerce*, 22 October.
Payne, Douglas W. Why Drug Traffickers Love Free Trade. 1997. *Dissent* (Summer).

made him a controversial figure in Colombia. "Colombians aren't used to foreigners talking about them publicly, especially someone like me, who is not afraid to tell them what they don't want to hear," Frechette explained in an interview. (Chepesiuk 1997, 34)

Frechette grew up in Chile and learned to speak French, Spanish, and Portuguese fluently. He graduated in 1958 from the University of British Columbia in Vancouver, Canada, with a degree in English and French, and earned an M.A. degree in Latin American Studies from UCLA in 1972. He worked at the international level in the private sector with Hanover Trust Company (1987–1988), served as U.S. ambassador to Cameroon (1983–1987), and as assistant U.S. trade representative for Latin America, the Caribbean, and Africa (1990–1993). Frechette's candor and role as U.S. point man on the War on Drugs made him the object of several death threats.

See also: Human Rights; Ochoa Vasquez, Jorge Luis; Toft, Joe
Reference: Chepesiuk, Ron. 1997. "Myles Frechette—in the Eye of the Storm." *UBC Alumni Chronicle* (Summer).

French Connection

One of the largest and most important heroin-trafficking rings ever established. Founded by French criminal Jean Jehan, this French-Italian drug syndicate operated from the 1930s to the 1970s and was responsible for supplying an estimated 95 percent of the heroin to U.S. streets. According to the arrangement, the Italian criminals guaranteed the American market to the French, promising to stay out of drug trafficking if the French criminals restricted their heroin sales to their Italian American counterparts in the United States. Marseilles, France, was the base of operation for the French Connection's heroin laboratories, which converted the raw opium base imported from Turkey into heroin before it was smuggled into the United States by French Corsican gangsters, members of the Sicilian Mafia, and Italian American Mafia counterparts.

A concerted international law enforcement effort smashed the French Connection in 1973, but many believed it continued to operate. As evidence, authorities pointed to the number of clandestine heroin laboratories in France and Italy that they uncovered until 1980. In that year, French police arrested the eighty-two-year-old Jehan in Marseilles, but released him in December 1980 for health reasons.

See also: Corsican Connection; Italian Organized Crime; Luciano, Charles

References: Chepesiuk, Ron. 1999. *Hard Target*. Moore, Robin. 1972. *The French Connection*.

Freud, Sigmund (1856–1939)

A pioneer in the science of psychiatry and a leading advocate of cocaine use in the late 1800s, Freud initially hailed cocaine as a "magic drug," believing it would cure alcoholism and opium addiction. Freud himself took cocaine and gave it to his wife and coworkers. In one of his first scientific papers, entitled "Coca and Its Salts," he claimed that "Cocaine is a stimulant that is particularly adapted to develop the working ability of the body, without any dangerous results." (Freud 1974, 79) But he also detailed the dangerous effects of cocaine, describing how users hallucinated and suffered wild mood changes that went from happiness and confidence to insecurity and melancholia. Freud hoped to use cocaine as a cure for the morphine addiction of his colleague Ernst Von Fleischl-Marxow, but instead Freud watched him deteriorate to a state of "cocainist" delirium before dying in 1891. According to drug expert David Musto, Freud withdrew his support for cocaine's use as a treatment for morphine addic-

Austrian neurologist and founder of psychoanalysis, Sigmund Freud, 1922. Early in his career, Freud advocated the use of cocaine in the treatment of patients, but later changed his mind when he saw the harmful effects of the drug. (Corbis/Bettmann)

tion, but he never publicly renounced other uses of the drug.

See also: Cocaine

References: Freud, Sigmund. 1974. *The Cocaine Papers*. Musto, David F. 1989. "America's First Cocaine Epidemic." *Washington Quarterly*. Storr, Anthony. 1989. *Freud*.

Friedman, Milton (1912–)

A prominent American conservative economist and professor emeritus of the University of Chicago who has been an outspoken critic of the U.S. government's War on Drugs. Friedman argues that the War on Drugs threatens constitutional rights and is an invasion of privacy. In an open letter in 1989 to U.S drug czar William Bennett, he chastised Bennett for "failing to recognize that the very measures you favor are a major source of the evils you deplore" and that "drugs are a tragedy for addicts, but criminalizing their use converts that tragedy into a disaster for society, for users and nonusers alike." (Friedman,

1989) Friedman is joined in his criticism of U.S. drug policy by other conservatives, including George P. Shultz, former secretary of state in the Reagan administration, and William F. Buckley, a columnist and writer.

See also: Bennett, William J.; Buckley, William F.; Decriminalization; Schultz, George P.

References: Bertram, Eva, Kenneth Sharpe, and Peter Anders. 1996. *Drug War Politics: The Price of Denial.* Friedman, Milton. 1989. "An Open Letter to Bill Bennett." *Wall Street Journal,* 7 September.

G

Galan, Luis Carlos (1943–1989)

Galan's political star rose like a meteor after he founded the New Liberal Party in Colombia in 1979. An idealist, he had written an editorial in the publication *New Frontier,* denouncing the drug mafia in his country and the infiltration of drug money into Colombian society. In the 1980s many Colombians looked to Galan as the politician who would morally rejuvenate the country, but critics such as Rachel Ehrenfeld contended that "in contrast to the American media portrait of him, the Liberal Party leader was not an ardent enemy of the cartels." (Ehrenfeld 1994, 89) Ehrenfeld also noted that Galan opposed extradition of drug traffickers to the United States on nationalistic grounds.

Galan was the leading presidential candidate for Colombia's 1990 elections when he was assassinated on 17 August 1989. The reason is not officially known, but many Colombians believe the country's drug traffickers were behind Galan's assassination.

See also: Extradition; Narcoterrorism; Lopez Michelsen, Alphonso

Reference: Ehrenfeld, Rachel. 1994. *Narcoterrorism.*

Luis Carlos Galen, assassinated Colombian presidential candidate (Courtesy of the Colombian National Police)

Galeano Murcia, Cristobal

The suspected head of the Llano Cartel, whose existence the Colombian police discovered in December 1995. According to the Colombian authorities, the cartelito consisted of about twenty individuals and operated in the Colombian areas of Vichada, Vaupes, Guaviare, and Meta. Galeano Murcia was suspected of being the owner of seven tons of cocaine confiscated by Colombian police in 1998. He was captured in Bogotá in December 1998.

See also: Cartelitos; Cocaine

Reference: "Cayo El Duano De Los Siete Toneladas De Coca." 1998. *El Tiempo,* 15 December.

Gambino Family

One of the five Italian American families based in New York City that has been linked to international drug trafficking. In 1985, as a result of a five-year investigation, Gambino family godfather Paul Castellano was one of several Mafia leaders to be indicted on charges of running a criminal enterprise. The year before, Castellano was arrested and charged, along with twenty-five other Mafia figures, with murder, extortion, and drug trafficking. In his investigation of international drug trafficking, journalist Brian Freemantle reported that the Gambino family was involved in the smuggling of heroin to Sicily via Turkey. In 1998 as a result of Operation Caesar, Gambino family members were among sixty-five members of three leading mob families (the other two being the Spatola and Inzerrillo families) who were given jail sentences totaling 400 years as a result of their participation in drug trafficking.

See also: Italian American Mafia; Italian Organized Crime
References: Freemantle, Brian. 1985. *The Fix*.
Sterling, Claire. 1990. *Octopus: The Long Reach of the International Sicilian Mafia*.

Gamma-vinyl-gaba (GVG)

After twelve years of research, a group of scientists published findings in the scientific journal *Synapse* on 5 August 1998 revealing that gamma-vinyl-gaba (GVG), a drug being used in Europe and Canada to combat leprosy, might also be used to curb the craving for cocaine. Scientists at the Brookhaven National Laboratory hoped to begin human testing in the fall of 1998 after testing the drug on monkeys. If approved by the U.S. Food and Drug Administration, GVG will be marketed in the United States under the brand name Sabril.

See also: Cocaine
Reference: "Drug Found to Cut Craving for Cocaine." 1998. *Charlotte Observer*, 6 August.
Sheriman, Dick. 1998. "Prof, Crew May Have Key to Unlock Drug Addiction." *New York Daily News*, 21 August.

Ganga

See Jamaican Posses; Marijuana

Garcia, Edgar

The so-called accountant of Cali Cartel leader Jose Santacruz Londono, who was responsible for managing and laundering profits of the godfather's drug-trafficking empire. The U.S. Drug Enforcement Administration uncovered Garcia's role through an investigation of the Interamerican Bank of Panama, which the Cali Cartel owned. Authorities arrested Garcia in Luxembourg in June 1990 and charged him with money laundering and conspiring to distribute cocaine.

See also: Santacruz Londono, Jose
Reference: De Grazia, Jessica. 1991. *DEA: The War against Drugs*.

Garcia Abrego, Juan (1945–)

Garcia's arrest in January 1996 was seen as the most important drug arrest in Mexico since the capture of drug kingpin Miguel Angel Gallardo in 1989. In fact, Garcia was the first international drug trafficker to make the FBI's Ten Most Wanted List. Garcia Abrego was the head of the Juarez Cartel, which he had made into one of Mexico's most powerful drug-trafficking organizations. His organization moved drugs through the Texas border region, principally in the Matamoros-Brownsville area and along the Gulf coast.

The personal fortune of Garcia Abrego, nicknamed "the doll" because of his youthful appearance, was placed at $2 billion, and he was said have owned eighty-six homes. U.S. authorities claimed that the Gulf Cartel had been responsible for transporting an estimated 100 tons of cocaine across the U.S.-Mexican border since the late 1980s.

At the time it occurred, U.S. officials said privately that Garcia Abrego's arrest could produce embarrassing revelations about Mexican government corruption. Later, when Garcia Abrego was brought to trial, the evidence against him revealed that he had received ample support from Mexico's government to run its operations. The evidence also revealed that the drug lord had much control with the former President Carlos Salina's government and corrupt immigration officials. According to press reports, Garcia Abrego had close ties to top Mexican politicians, including Raul Salinas de Gortari, the brother of former Mexican president Carlos Salinas de Gortari. Salinas was said to have been seen at a lavish party given by Garcia Abrego in 1992 at his ranch near Monterrey.

Because he was an American citizen, Garcia Abrego was deported to the United States to stand trial. At the time authorities said that the Mexican drug trafficker Amado Carillo Fuentes ("Lord of the Skies") had the most to gain from Garcia Abrego's conviction. In October 1996 Garcia Abrego was convicted on federal drug-trafficking charges in Houston, Texas, and given a life sentence.

See also: Gallardo, Miguel Angel; Salinas De Gortari, Carlos; Salinas De Gortari, Raul; Gulf Cartel
References: Oppenheimer, Andres. 1996. "Mexican Drug Lord Deported To U.S." Knight-Ridder/Tribune News Wire Service, 15 January.
"Convicted, Juan Garcia Abrego." 1996. *Time*, 28 October.

Garcia Herreros, Father Rafael

The Colombian priest who brokered Pablo Escobar's 1991 surrender to Colombian authorities. Escobar was then incarcerated in a prison he built especially for himself.

See also: Escobar Gaviria, Pablo
Reference: Dermota, Ken. "Where You Can Order Steak— And a Stallion." 1995. *Business Week*, 27 March.

Garcia Meza, Luis

A Bolivian general who started a coup in 1980 as the country was about to hold a democratic election. The 189th coup in Bolivia's 154–year history was called the Cocaine Coup because it was widely reported in the American press that Garcia had been backed by the Santa Cruz mafia. In the words of journalist Elaine Shannon, "Garcia Meza and his generals made Bolivia the world's pariah." (Shannon 1989, 358)

The general's move to employ Nazis, including the infamous former Gestapo commander Klaus Barbie, to run right-wing death squads prompted U.S. President Jimmy Carter to cut off all economic aid to Bolivia, and, under intense international pressure, Garcia Meza made a feeble effort to crack down on the country's drug traffickers. There was a report, however, that the general was paid $50 million to end the operation. Several officials of the Garcia Meza regime were indicted in the United States on charges of cocaine trafficking, but none of them was ever brought to trial. Garcia Meza was deposed in September 1981.

See also: Carter, James Earl; Santa Cruz Mafia
Reference: Shannon, Elaine. 1989. *Desperadoes*.
Strong, Simon. 1995. *Whitewash: Pablo Escobar and the Cocaine Wars*.

Garfield Bank

This Los Angeles bank was involved in a money-laundering scheme that led to a federal grand jury indictment of several individuals, including its chairman and two former vice presidents. Over a two-year period, authorities were able to track twenty-nine illegal transactions, ranging in size from $36,020 to $491,790 and totaling more than $3.3 million. Undercover IRS agents infiltrated the conspiracy in 1980 and were able to implicate bank officials, who were found guilty on all counts on 15 December 1981.

See also: Money Laundering
Reference: President's Commission on Organized Crime. 1984. *The Cash Connection: Organized Crime, Financial Institutions and Money Laundering*.

Gaviria Trujillo, Cesar (1947–)

President of Colombia from 1990 to 1994. Born in the Andean town of Pereira, Gaviria Trujillo graduated at the top of his class from the University of Los Andes, where he studied economics. His political ascent began in 1973 when he was appointed the mayor of Pereira. By the late 1980s he had become minister of government, a post that allowed him to serve as acting president when President Virgilio Barco Vargas traveled abroad. In winning the May 1990 presidential election, Gaviria became the youngest president in the country's history.

In an attempt to make inroads in reducing the power of Colombia's drug traffickers, Gaviria Trujillo pursued a policy reflecting his belief that accommodation would resolve the drug problem more smoothly than confrontation and repression. He implemented a surprising series of moves to meet his objective, but, in the process, he gave up significant concessions to the drug cartels. For example, he convinced powerful drug traffickers, the Ochoa brothers (Jorge, Fabio, and Juan David), to give themselves up. In return, he promised them lighter sentences and a promise not to extradite them to the United States. The moves proved popular with the Colombian people, though, who were tired of years of drug-related terrorism, and the Colombian authorities did seize huge amounts of cocaine. But at the end of Gaviria Trujillo's term, the drug cartels remained a strong presence in Colombia. After leaving office, Gaviria Trujillo headed the Organization of American States.

See also: Barco Vargas, Virgilio; Narcoterrorism; Organization of American States; Turbay Ayala, Diane
References: Brooke, James. 1990. "Strong Drug Foe Wins in Colombia by Wide Margin." *New York Times*, 28 May.
———. 1991. "Gaviria's Gamble." *New York Times*, 13 October.

Geneva International Opium Convention of 1925

Thirty-six countries attended this landmark antidrug convention, the first one to be concluded under the auspices of the League of Nations. The provisions of the Hague Convention of 1912 were strengthened by putting the supervision of the narcotics trade in the hands of a Permanent Control Board, which "was given extensive powers of inquiring into an unsatisfactory situation in any country, of bringing such a situation to the attention of the contracting parties, and of the Council and the League, and of recommending that no further export of narcotic substances be made to the country concerned until the Board of Regents reports that it is satisfied as to the situation of that country."

The United States and China withdrew from the Convention because they believed no real effort was being made toward seriously limiting the manufacture of illegal drugs. The United States was acting on the joint resolution adopted by the U.S. Congress on 15 May 1924, which stipulated that "the representatives of the United States should sign no agreement which does not fulfill the conditions necessary for the suppression of the narcotic drug trade as stipulated in the preamble of the convention." The Convention's preamble actually stated the aim of devising ways internationally of "bringing about a more effective limitation of the production or manufacture" of narcotic substances, but the goal was not achieved. The Convention came into force in 1930, and by 1952, sixty-two countries had ratified it.

Reference: Courtwright, David T. 1982. *Dark Paradise*.

GHB (Gamma Hydroxy Butyrate)

A white powdery drug that creates a sedating effect, gamma hydroxy butyrate (GHB) was developed as an anesthetic in the 1980s. Initially, GHB was used as an alternative anesthetic for surgery and other medical procedures, but the medical community stopped using the drug because of its unpredictable nature and side-effects, which can lead to overdoses. It was then promoted for muscle growth and weight loss, and caught on in a big way with the body-building community. Before long every health food store in the United States was carrying a good supply of the drug.

Because of the dangers to consumers, in 1990 the U.S. Food and Drug Administration (FDA) banned the drug's sale, and the following year restricted its use to licensed researchers. It also became a misdemeanor to possess it. According to the *Drug Identification Bible*, GHB is "easily synthesized using two readily available chemicals: butyrolactone and sodium hydroxide." (Marnell 1997, 184–185)

Reference: Marnell, Tim, ed. 1997. *Drug Identification Bible*.

Ginsberg, Allen (1926–1997)

Noted American poet who became the first "beat" poet to gain popular attention when he delivered a performance of his epic poem *Howl* at a poetry reading in 1955. As a beatnik, Ginsberg became obsessed with drugs. In the 1960s, as a member of the hippie scene, he worked with Timothy Leary to publicize the psychedelic drug LSD and participated in Ken Kesey's Acid Test Festivals in San Francisco.

See also: Beatniks; Burroughs, William S.; Hippies; Kesey, Ken; Leary, Timothy; LSD
Reference: Rosenberg, Anton. 1998. "A Hipster Ideal Dies at 71." *New York Times*, 22 February.

Giordano, Henry L. (1914–   )

The director of the U.S. Bureau of Drug Abuse Control from 1966 to 1969. Born in San Francisco, California, Giordano graduated from the University of California in 1934, but first practiced as a registered pharmacist in San Francisco before entering government service as an agent at the Federal Bureau of Narcotics at Seattle, Washington. Giordano entered military service in 1943 with the United States Coast Guard and, upon discharge in 1946, returned to the Board of Narcotics. Giordano held various appointments at the Bureau before his selection as director on 7 April 1968. Giordano's bureau was merged with the Bureau of Drug Abuse Control and the Department of Health, Education, and Welfare and put under the administration of the Department of Justice.

See also: United States Bureau of Drug Abuse Control
Reference: "Associate Director H. L. Giordano Retires as Head of U.S. Narcotics Bureau." 1969. *New York Times*, 1 March.

Allen Ginsberg leads a group of demonstrators outside the women's House of Detention in New York City's Greenwich Village, 11 February 1965. (Corbis/Bettmann-UPI)

Giraldo, Alberto

On 22 December 1998, after a year and two months of freedom after a drug-trafficking conviction, Giraldo was sent back to prison, convicted of a charge of illicit enrichment from drug trafficking. Giraldo's punishment was eight years in jail and a fine of 1.438 million pesos. Giraldo was tried in front of one of Colombia's so-called faceless judges, whose identity was hidden from the public during the trial for the judge's protection.

Colombian authorities considered Giraldo to be a key link to the Rodriguez Orejuela brothers, Gilberto and Miguel (leaders of the Cali Cartel), and to have crucial knowledge regarding the 1994 Colombian presidential campaign in which the future Colombian president Ernesto Samper Pizano was accused of accepting money from the Cali Cartel. Colombian authorities said checks in Giraldo's name connected businesses owned by the Cali Cartel to Samper's campaign. A former press secretary to Belasario Betancur Cuartas during his presidential campaign in 1982, Giraldo was considered to be an outstanding journalist with an expert grasp of international affairs before his legal problems began.

See also: Cali Cartel; Rodriguez Orejuela, Gilberto; Rodriguez Orejuela, Miguel; Samper Pizano, Ernesto
Reference: "Ocho Anos de Prision para Alberto Giraldo." 1998. *El Tiempo*, 23 December.

Golden Crescent

Located in Iran, Afghanistan, and Pakistan, the Golden Crescent has been one of the world's most active opium-growing and producing areas since the late 1970s. Several reasons account for the area's importance to the international drug trade. The Golden Crescent produces a type of heroin that is high in purity and low in price, and the large addict population in the region, which has been put at half a million souls, guarantees a large market. The Golden Crescent is also largely controlled by antigovernment tribesmen scattered throughout the region, who are known as exceptional warriors. The opium

Poppy growers making incisions on poppy heads to extract opium from their crop in a tribal area near the Buner district of Pakistan's northwestern Frontier province. The tribal areas of northern Pakistan and Afghanistan produce the second largest heroin crop in the world. (Corbis/Reuters)

has served as a cash crop that has allowed them to buy guns and ammunition. The opium is moved out of the Golden Crescent to Europe and the United States through India and Turkey, via commercial aircraft and cargo ships.

Reference: Jamieson, Alison. 1994. *Terrorism and Drug Trafficking in Europe in the 1990s.*

Golden Triangle

A thriving area of opium cultivation in Southeast Asia that is a major source of the world's opium and heroin supply. The amount of opium cultivated in the Golden Triangle has been put at 70 percent of the world's supply, but no one knows for sure the exact amount. The Golden Triangle covers an area of about 150,000 square miles (about the size of Greece), extending from Myanmar's Chin Hills in the west, north into China's Yunan province, east into Laos and Thailand's northwestern province, and south into Myanmar's Kayah state. The Golden Triangle offers ideal conditions for opium cultivation, including excellent climate, fertile soil, cheap labor, and a ready market for a crop that is easy to sell. In addition, opium use is an integral part of the local culture and serves both medicinal and recreational purposes. The Triangle is heavily infiltrated by as many as 40,000 armed insurgents who are involved in the opium drug trade, a development that makes antidrug efforts by the authorities difficult.

Historically, France's intelligence service and the CIA in the United States are believed to have helped foster the growth of the Golden Triangle economy by encouraging and supporting the area's independent warlords as a buffer against the extension of communism in the region. Over the years the Burmese government has tried to eliminate the opium crop through a campaign known as Operation Hellflower, which has employed thousands of soldiers, police, and civilian personnel to manually destroy the opium, but it has had limited effectiveness. The opium is marketed to the world via the powerful Chinese criminal connection known as the Triads.

See also: Heroin; Khun Sa; Kuomintang; Opium; Triads; United States Central Intelligence Agency; Vietnam War
References: Jamieson, Alison. 1994. *Terrorism and Drug Trafficking in Europe in the 1990s.*
Wiant, Jon. 1985. "Narcotics in the Golden Triangle." *Washington Quarterly* (Fall): 125–140.

Gomeros

The Spanish name for gum makers, which is what the Mexican poppy growers have often been called.

Reference: Shannon, Elaine. 1989. *Desperadoes.*

Gomez-Bustamante, Luis Hernando

A major Colombian drug trafficker from the Norte Valle who is allied with the Henao-Montoya brothers. Gomez-Bustamante owns farms in the Valle del Cauca region, which Colombian officials believe are used to hide his cocaine-processing laboratories. Gomez-Bustamante is also wanted on drug-trafficking charges in the United States.

See also: Henao-Montoya, Jose Orlando
Reference: U.S. Senate Committee on Foreign Relations. 1998. *International Organized Crime Syndicates and Their Impact on the United States: Hearings before the Subcommittee on Western Hemisphere, Peace Corps, Narcotics and Terrorism,* 26 February (statement of Thomas A. Constantine, Director, CIA).

Gomez-Patino, Denis

A long-time Colombian drug trafficker who Colombian officials say smuggles cocaine base from Bolivia and Peru to Colombia. He was allied with brothers Gilberto and Miguel Rodriguez Orejuela, leaders of the Cali Cartel, but since their capture he has established ties with the Henao-Montoya brothers.

See also: Henao-Montoya, Jose Orlando; Rodriguez Orejuela, Gilberto; Rodriguez Orejuela, Miguel
Reference: U.S. Senate Committee on Foreign Relations. 1998. *International Organized Crime Syndicates and Their Impact on the United States: Hearings before the Subcommittee on Western Hemisphere, Peace Corps, Narcotics and Terrorism.* 26 February (statement of Thomas A. Constantine, Director, CIA).

Gonzales Calderoni, Guillermo (1948–)

Known as "the Commandante," Gonzales Calderoni was head of the Mexican Federal Judicial Police (MFJP), Mexico's equivalent of the FBI, until he fled to the United States in February 1993. He is credited with hunting down members of an alliance of Mexican drug-trafficking organizations known as the Mexican Federation, but he was also known to have contacts in the higher echelons of the Mexican drug trade.

Born in Reynosa, Mexico, the Commandante had grown up with Jose Garcia Abrego, the younger brother of Juan Garcia Abrego, head of the Gulf Cartel. U.S. officials charged that while pursuing some Mexican drug traffickers, Gonzales Calderoni was protecting others. Federal prosecutors in San Diego claimed that the Commandante had received about $1 million from Joaquin Guzman (El Rapido), the head of Sonora Cartel, for helping his brother, Arturo, get released from a Mexican prison.

Gonzales Calderoni was never charged in either case, and he was even appointed head of the MFJP's San Antonio office in 1991. In the fall of that year he began to talk with federal prosecutors in Dallas about Mexican drug matters, but the Mexican government ordered him back to Mexico. The Commandante was kicked out of the MFJP on charges of torturing prisoners, and he fled to Texas in January 1993, where he obtained a resident alien card with the help of high-ranking DEA and FBI officials.

See also: Garcia Abrego, Juan; Fuentes Carillo, Amado; Mexican Federation; Sonora Cartel

Reference: Bierderman, Christine. 1997. "The Commandante." *Texas Monthly* (July): 18.

Grateful Dead

Major rock-and-roll music group that got its start in the early 1960s as the Warlocks and then went on to phenomenal success during a thirty-year career in which they recorded 25 albums. Between 1992 and 1995, the year that bandleader Jerry Garcia died at age 53, the group earned about $162 million. Garcia experienced years of drug abuse and was often in poor health. The group's fans were called Deadheads, and they were known to smoke marijuana, use other drugs, and follow the group across the country from concert to concert.

See also: Kesey, Ken

References: Dougherty, Steve. "What A Long Strange Trip," *People Weekly*, 21 August 1995.

West, Woody. "A Farewell To The Dead," *Insight On The News*, 1 September 1995.

Great American Bank (Florida)

As a result of Operation Greenback, a federal grand jury indicted the Great American Bank of Dade County, Florida, and three of its employees for processing $94 million from January 1980 through February 1981 without filing the Currency Transaction Reports (CTRs) to the Department of the Treasury as required by U.S. law for deposits over $10,000. The depositors of the money were also indicted. The indictments were handed down between December 1982 and April 1984. All of the defendants who had not become fugitives also pleaded guilty to various charges. This case is another example of the growing power of drug money.

See also: Operation Greenback

Reference: President's Commission on Organized Crime. 1984. *The Cash Connection: Organized Crime, Financial Institutions and Money Laundering*.

Guillen Davila, General Ramon

See Romero Gomez, Alfonso.

Guillot-Lara, Jaime

On 15 November 1986 a U.S. federal grand jury indicted this drug trafficker along with four Cuban officials, all members of that country's ruling Communist Party. According to the indictment, Guillot-Lara was part of a drugs-for-arms operation with Colombian drug-trafficking organizations, which were smuggling arms and money to the Colombian M-19 guerrillas, who are battling the government. Guillot-Lara was arrested in Mexico, but released, after which he fled to Spain and eventually, Cuba. The publicity surrounding Guillot-Lara's arrest led to charges that Cuba was heavily involved in drug trafficking, but Fidel Castro, the country's leader, denied the charge.

See also: Cuban Connection; Herran, Mariano Salvatti; Narcoguerrillas

Reference: Ehrenfeld, Rachel. 1994. *Narcoterrorism*.

Gulf Cartel

This organization was the undisputed leader of Mexican drug-trafficking organizations until about 1994 when its head, Juan Garcia Abrego, was forced to go into hiding. The cartel moved drugs primarily through the Texas border region around the Matamoros-Brownsville area, and along the coastal shores of the Gulf of Mexico. Abrego was arrested in Mexico in January 1996 and deported to the United States for trial on drug-trafficking charges.

See also: American Express Bank International; Garcia Abrego, Juan; Mexican Federation

Gutierrez Rebello, Jesus

In February 1997, just two months after being appointed head of the National Institute to Combat Drugs, Mexico's top drug-fighting agency, General Rebello was fired from his job, dismissed from the army, and was imprisoned on drug corruption charges. He was accused of smuggling cocaine and accepting large bribes from leading drug trafficker Amado Carillo Fuentes in exchange for protection. A well-respected military commander of the Guadalajara district, Gutierrez Rebello had been in the military for forty-two years when he was appointed Mexico's drug czar.

Gutierrez Rebello claimed he was a political prisoner who was jailed because he was about to crack down on drug lords who enjoyed the protection of his superiors. However, when police searched Gutierrez Rebello's plush apartment after arresting him, they found not only cellular phones with scramblers and $10,000 in U.S. currency, but also a photo of drug kingpin Amado Carillo Fuentes. In the fall of 1997 forty military officers were arrested as part of the Gutierrez Rebello investigation, but, as of December 1998 none of them have been brought to trial. On 3 March 1998 Gutierrez Rebello was convicted of abuse of authority and weapons charges and sent to jail for thirteen years.

See also: Carillo Fuentes, Amado; Certification
Reference: Padgett, Tim. 1997. "Getting Off Drugs." *Time*, 10 March.

Guzman-Lara, Joaquin

Guzman-Lara played an important role in the Miguel Felix-Gallardo organization, but he eventually went out on his own to become a powerful drug-trafficking godfather. In its heyday, the Guzman-Lara organization transported cocaine from Colombia through Mexico to the United States for the Medellin and Cali Cartels and has also been implicated in the storage and distribution of marijuana in the United States. Guzman-Lara has been indicted several times on drug-trafficking charges, and on 9 June 1993 Mexican authorities arrested him in Talisman, Mexico, on murder and drug-trafficking charges. He is currently imprisoned in Almoya de Juarez Security Prison in Toluca, Mexico.

In congressional testimony in March 1997 DEA Administrator Thomas A. Constantine stated that "Guzman-Lara's organization has not been dismantled or seriously affected by Guzman-Lara's imprisonment because his brother Arturo Guzman-Lara has assumed the leadership." (U.S. Senate Committee on Foreign Relations 1998)

See also: Cali Cartel; Felix Gallardo, Miguel; Medellin Cartel
Reference: U.S. Senate Committee on Foreign Relations. 1998. *International Organized Crime Syndicates and Their Impact on the United States: Hearings before the Subcommittee on Western Hemisphere, Peace Corps, Narcotics and Terrorism.* 26 February (statement of Thomas A. Constantine, Director, DEA).

H

Hague Convention of 1912

This convention, the first international venture in the field of drug control, was organized under the direction of the United States as a follow up to the Shanghai Conference of 1909. The Hague Convention incorporated a number of the general principles adopted at the Shanghai Conference, although it provided no administrative mechanism to implement those principles. It also bound the contracting parties to adopt provisions for the control and regulation of raw opium, prepared opium, and the manufacture of cocaine and diacetylmorphine (heroin). On 11 February 1915 the Convention went into force for China, the Netherlands, and the United States, the first three countries to agree to apply the provisions, although it did not come into general application until after the end of World War I. By 1952 seventy countries had become parties to the Convention.

Reference: Renborg, Bertie A. 1947. *International Drug Control: A Study of International Administration by and through the League of Nations.*

Haight-Ashbury

See Hippies

Hallucinogens

Also known as a psychedelic drug, a hallucinogen can be either a natural drug, such as peyote or psilocybin mushrooms, or a synthetic drug, such as LSD or PCP, that, when ingested, causes hallucinations or a sensory experience seeming to happen outside the mind. The user can experience flashbacks, if a hallucinogen is used recurrently. According to the *Drug Identification Bible*, "Although other drugs, such as marijuana and alcohol may produce hallucinations if a very high dose is used, they are not classified as hallucinogens because this is not the usual effect expected or experienced." (Marnell 1997, 654)

See also: Huxley, Aldous; Kesey, Ken; Leary, Timothy; LSD; Marijuana; PCP; Peyote; Psilocybin
Reference: Marnell, Tim, ed. 1997. *Drug Identification Bible.*

Harm Reduction

One approach to dealing with the twin problems of drug abuse and international drug trafficking is harm reduction, an alternative that lies behind the current prohibitionist policy in place in most countries and the alternative policy that favors the legalization of drugs. Its advocates maintain that harm reduction should be the overriding focus of all drug laws and drug-control policy, but it remains one of the most controversial topics in the field of substance abuse prevention and treatment.

Harm reduction emphasizes treatment and rehabilitation, rather than criminalization and punishment, and focuses on specific strategies that reduce both personal and social harm done by illegal drugs. The approach has been in operation in Australia; Liverpool, England; and Amsterdam, Holland, and has been endorsed by drug experts in other European countries. Since the 1980s harm reduction proponents in the United States have offered it as an alternative to the punitive policy that has been in place since Ronald Reagan launched the War on Drugs in 1982.

In 1994 more than 100 physicians, including fifteen members of the California Academy of Family Physicians board of directors, signed a resolution by the National Coalition of Drug Policy calling for the establishment of a federal commission to rewrite drug laws to "recognize drug use and abuse as the medical and social problems they are." (Cotton 1994)

Writing in JAMA, the *Journal of the American Medical Association*, Dr. Paul Cotton said, "Dealing with drug addiction was once primarily the purview of physicians. But since the initiation of prohibition in the early part of this century, and especially since the 'war on drugs' was declared in the 1970s, drug use, abuse, and addiction have been treated primarily as crimes and only secondarily as a public health problem. Critics say this makes public health problems worse." (Cotton 1994)

Advocates of harm reduction believe that society should accept the fact that a drug-free society is unrealistic and that trying to make it so is counterproductive. Further, they accept what they say is reality—that millions of people will continue to use and abuse drugs, no matter how severe the punitive sanctions society attempts to impose. So, as a part of an enlightened antidrug policy, addicts should have access to drugs under a doctor's supervision, and they should be provided with clean needles to prevent the spread of AIDS. Every effort should be made to change the addict's behavior, but such efforts should be done with compassion and virtually on demand.

Advocates of harm reduction see many benefits of the policy for society and for the drug abuser: for example, a decrease in substance abuse related to illness, diseases, and death; a decline in the need for massive, large scale law enforcement and prison facility infrastructure that currently support antidrug policy; safer streets and neighborhoods, the result of a decrease in violent crime to sustain drug usage; and less government interference with individual choices.

Initiatives that harm reduction advocates have suggested include reversing drug-funding policy priorities to emphasize treatment and not punishment, expanding the available treatment centers, stopping the practice of imprisoning pregnant drug users, making medical marijuana available to seriously ill patients, and appointing a national commission similar to the 1972 National Commission on Marijuana and Drug Abuse to examine seriously alternatives to the current prohibitionist policy.

Critics of harm reduction, legalization or any alternative that liberalizes current policy warn that if drug laws are relaxed or repealed, there may be a possible rise in drug use and abuse and that changing the policy may create public health problems and concerns that will far outweigh those created by the current prohibitionist policy. As Arnold S. Trebach and James A. Inciardi have written, "Although drug prohibition policies have been problematic, it would appear that they have managed to keep drugs away from most people...the numbers at risk are dramatically fewer than is the case with legal drugs. Or stated differently, there is a rather large population who might be at risk if illicit drugs were suddenly available." (Trebach & Inciardi 1993, 203)

See also: Decriminalization; European Cities on Drug Policy; Frankfurt Resolution; Legalization; Lindesmith Institute; Medical Marijuana; Nadelmann, Ethan; National Commission on Marijuana And Drug Abuse; Needle Exchange Programs; Prohibition

References: Concar, David, and Laura Spinney. 1994. "The Highs and Lows of Prohibition." *New Scientist* 1 October.
Cotton, Paul. 1994. "Harm Reduction Approach May Be Middle Ground." *Journal of the American Medical Association* (June).
Lindesmith Institute website at http://www.lindesmith.org.
Trebach, Arnold S., and James A. Inciardi. 1993. *Legalize It? Debating American Drug Policy*.

Harrison Narcotic Act (U.S.)

One of the most important drug laws in U.S. history, the Harrison Act was named after Representative Francis B. Harrison of New York, who introduced the measure in the U.S. Congress. Woodrow Wilson signed the Act into law on 17 December 1914, and it went into effect on 1 March 1915. With the act's passage, anyone selling, importing, or dispensing drugs had to register with the government, and heroin and cocaine could now be obtained legally only with a doctor's prescription. Marijuana was excluded from the law and did not come under government regulation until 1937. The U.S. government adopted the Harrison Act as part of its support for international opium control, and it represented a popular consen-

Undated image of a man dying and stripping hemp in the Philippines (Grant Smith/Corbis)

sus against drug use and addiction that had been building since the 1870s. Although intense lobbying from the drug industry stopped the total regulation of drugs, the Harrison Act, nevertheless, became the cornerstone of U.S. domestic narcotics policy for the next sixty-five years.

See also: Cocaine; Marijuana; Opium; Rothstein, Arnold; *United States v. Behrman*; *United States v. Jim Fuey Moy*; Wright, Dr. Hamilton
References: Courtwright, David T. 1982. *Dark Paradise*.
Morgan, H. Wayne. 1981. *Drugs In America: A Social History, 1800–1980*.

Hashish

From an Arabic word meaning "dry grass," hashish is the resinous extract of the female marijuana plant and is the most potent form of cannabis. The drug is reportedly eight times stronger than marijuana. It can be eaten or ingested, and its effects, like marijuana, depend upon the usage and dosage. The possible effects are accelerated heart rate, elevated blood pressure, and reddening of the eyes. The major supplying countries are Morocco, Nepal, Lebanon, Pakistan, and Afghanistan. Because of its potency and reputation as an aphrodisiac, hashish attracted the attention of hippies in the 1960s, although it did not gain the popularity of marijuana as it was much more difficult to obtain.

See also: Hippies; Ludlow, Fitzhugh; Marijuana; Operation Thunderbolt
Reference: O'Brien, Robert, and Sidney Cohen. 1984. *The Encyclopedia of Drug Abuse*.

Hemp

According to the *Drug Identification Bible*, the term *hemp* is used to "describe cannabis plants or products of those plants that have a low THC content and are cultivated for the fiber from the stalks or the oil contained in the seeds." (Marnell 1997, 605) Hemp is coveted in the skin-care industry for its fatty acids, and in all has about 28,000 uses—from producing "veggie burgers" and BMW brake pads to fabrics, paper, fuel, pain-relievers, and plastic substitutes. Controversy has raged over how closely related hemp is to marijuana, and it is illegal to grow hemp in the United States. Thus, all of the hemp products sold there are made from imported hemp, which increases the store prices substantially. Twenty-five countries, including Canada, England, France, Germany, and China, currently produce industrial hemp.

See also: Marijuana; United States Single Convention on
Narcotic Drugs of 1961
References: Marnell, Tim, ed. 1997. *Drug Identification
Bible.*
Price, Mark. 1998. "Redemption of Hemp: Weed To Wear-
ables." *Charlotte Observer*, 11 October.

Henao Montoya, Jose Orlando (c. 1953–)

A major Colombian drug trafficker who, with his
brother Arcangel de Jesus, ran the most powerful organization operating out of the country's Northern
Valle del Cauca region. In September 1997 Henao
Montoya surrendered to authorities in Bogotá. Three
days prior to this Bogotá's *El Tiempo* newspaper ran
a photograph of Henao Montoya at a church baptism
in which he was identified as "the new king of drug
trafficking in Colombia" and "the capo of capos."
(Reputed Drug Lord Turns Himself in to Colombian
Police. 1997). Authorities held the drug kingpin
without bail.

Henao Montoya had declared war on Cali Cartel
leaders Gilberto and Miguel Rodriguez Orejuela
after their arrest in 1995, and he was believed to have
carried out the 1996 attempted assassination in a
Cali restaurant of Miguel Rodriguez Orejuela's son
Miguel, who was seriously wounded. Six of the son's
bodyguards and lunch companions were shot dead.
According to the U.S. DEA, Henao Montoya also has
close ties with the paramilitary group run by Carlos
Castano, who himself was suspected of being a
major drug trafficker.

See also: Cali Cartel; Castano, Carlos; Castano, Fidel;
Rodriguez Orejuela, Gilberto; Rodriguez Orejuela,
Miguel; Urinola Grajales, Ivan
References: "Reputed Drug Lord Turns Himself into
Colombian Police." 1997. *Orange County Register*, 30
September.
U.S. Senate Committee on Foreign Relations. 1998.
*International Organized Crime Syndicates and Their
Impact on the United States: Hearings before the
Subcommittee on Western Hemisphere, Peace Corps, Nar-
cotics and Terrorism*, 26 February (statement of Thomas
A. Constantine, Director, DEA).

Hendrix, Jimi (1942–1970)

Electrifying guitar player from the United States and
a major 1960s rock star whose musical style combined blues and psychedelic music. In 1966, Hendrix
found success in England with his band The Jimi

*Efrain Hernandez, dead Colombian drug trafficker (Cour-
tesy of the Colombian National Police)*

Hendrix Experience. Returning to the United States,
Hendrix made his American debut on 18 June 1967
at the Monterrey Pop Festival in a virtuoso performance that saw him set his guitar afire at the end of
the show. In 1968, Hendrix's album "Are You Experienced?" climbed the record charts, and *Rolling Stone*
magazine named him Performer of the Year. On 18
September 1970, in London, Jimi Hendrix became
another major star of the 1960s rock music scene to
die from drug abuse: "an inhalation of vomit due to
barbiturate intoxication," according to the coroner's
report. (Shapiro 1995, 147)

See also: Barbiturates
References: Shapiro, Harry, and Caesar Glebbek. 1995. *Jimi
Hendrix: Electric Gypsy.*
John Burks. "An Appreciation." *Rolling Stone*, 15 October
1970, p. 8.

Hernandez Ramirez, Efrain Antonio

A leading Colombian drug trafficker referred to as
"Don Efra" whom assassins murdered in Bogotá in
November 1996. In the weeks following Hernandez's
death, the Colombian newspapers contained several

12-year-old Phor Sae-Yang inhales the smoke of the "white powder" with a pipe as his brother, Koo Sae-Wang, prepares the cup for his turn, 9 May 1991. Heroin use is spreading at an alarming rate among the hill tribes of northern Thailand. (Reuters/Corbis-Bettmann)

reports about Hernandez's fortune that Colombian authorities said was larger than that of the brothers Gilberto and Miguel Rodriguez Orejuela, godfathers of the Cali Cartel. The Colombian police had heard little of Hernandez; yet, with the money from his drug-trafficking empire, Don Efra was able to buy more than thirty businesses in Colombia.

See also: Rodriguez Orejuela, Gilberto; Rodriguez Orejuela, Miguel

References: Chepesiuk, Ron. 1999. *Hard Target.* "La Fortuna de 'Don Efra.'" 1996. *El Espectador,* 8 November.

Heroin

A semisynthetic narcotic drug that is produced by treating morphine with a highly reactive substance called acetic anhydride. The addictive form of the drug is not the heroin base but the heroin salt that is produced after the heroin is further treated. It takes about ten kilograms of morphine to make one kilogram of heroin. Morphine is ten times stronger than opium and heroin is 25 times more powerful than morphine. In 1874 an English chemist named Alder

Wright synthesized diacetylmorphine (heroin), and in 1898 Bayer Chemical Company introduced diacetylmorphine as a medicine and renamed it "heroin."

Upon its introduction, heroin was first hailed as a wonder drug more potent than morphine. It was used as medicine to relieve such ailments as pain, diarrhea, and coughing spasms, and as a cure for morphine addiction. The American Medical Association even endorsed heroin as safe for the treatment of respiratory ailments. However, by 1910 doctors were realizing that heroin was at least as addictive as morphine. Four years later, the Harrison Act taxed the manufacture, importation, and distribution of heroin, and from then on it could only be obtained legally with a doctor's prescription. In 1922 medical doctors were no longer permitted the common practice of providing heroin to addicts. Two years later, heroin production in the United States was outlawed.

In the 1940s and 1950s the world began to recognize the dangers of heroin, and by 1963 it was being used medically in only five countries and manufactured in only three. By then, though, heroin had largely replaced opium and morphine as the illegal drug of choice on the street. An international black market with underground laboratories and a well-organized trafficking network was flourishing. Being more potent than opium and morphine and smaller in bulk, heroin became attractive to pushers and dealers and helps explain its continued easy availability to users. Most illegal heroin, though, is only about 5 percent pure because by the time it reaches the streets, the drug has been cut from twenty to one hundred times with quinine, milk, sugar, baking powder, or some other kind of dilutant. This make heroin more dangerous because the user does not know what substance has been mixed with the heroin or the purity of the remaining heroin.

In 1970 the U.S. Comprehensive Crime Control Act established heroin as a Schedule I drug. Schedule I drugs are those with a high potential for abuse, or have no currently accepted medical use in treatment in the United States, or where there is a lack of accepted safety for use of the drug or other substance under medical supervision. The U.S. Office of National Drug Control Policy estimated that in 1997 about 600,000 Americans used heroin as their drug of choice. As evidence of how popular the drug had become in the 1990s, the number of emergency room admissions relating to heroin use doubled between 1990 and 1995. According to U.S. government reports, in 1996 the worldwide seizures of morphine base and heroin amounted to about twenty-three metric tons, with 1.5 metric tons of that amount seized in the United States. Today, heroin is legally manufactured in England, with small amounts produced in France and Belgium.

Heroin is typically injected intravenously, but it can also be sniffed like cocaine and even smoked like marijuana. The ability to use heroin without injecting it and the corresponding fear of HIV infection from dirty needles have been the major reasons that heroin is more popular than ever today. In 1996 the newspaper *USA Today* reported that cocaine had been the drug of choice on Wall Street in the 1980s, but that in the 1990s heroin was much more affordable and offered a high that allowed users to function, at least initially, at work. Two years later, the American media was reporting that heroin was becoming a problem with young people living in suburbia.

Mexico, Colombia, the Middle East, and Southeast Asia are the principal areas where heroin is produced today. Southeast Asia (principally Myanmar) and the Middle East (Afghanistan, Lebanon, Pakistan, and Turkistan) have traditionally supplied most of the heroin used in the United States. By the 1990s Colombian and Mexican drug-trafficking organizations had largely taken over the heroin distribution in the United States from Asian traffickers, whose share of the market had plummeted from 90 percent to 28 percent. Mexico had become the largest heroin source for the U.S. market, and the purity of Mexican heroin had increased sixfold between 1996 and 1998. Meanwhile, heroin production had become a growth industry in Colombia. During the 1990s Colombian traffickers had contacted Italian and Asian crime syndicates to acquire the seeds and to learn the know how to cultivate poppies in the Andes region and to process it.

See also: Air America; Arellano Felix, Ramon; Barnes, Leroy "Nicky"; Bensinger, Peter; Buprenorphine; Burroughs, William S.; Buscetta, Tommaso; Cali Cartel; Carillo Fuentes, Amado; Carter, James Earl; Clinton, William Jefferson; Corsican Connection; Golden Crescent; Golden Triangle; Harrison Act; Italian American Mafia; Italian Organized Crime; Khun Sa; Lara Nausa, Jaime Orlando; Legalization; Maspeth Federal Savings And Loan Association (New York City); McCoy, Alfred J.; Medellin Cartel; Meperidine; Methadone Treatment Programs; Methamphetamine; Morphine; Nasser David, Julio Cesar; National Alliance For Methadone Advocates; Nigerian Organized Crime; Nixon, Richard Milhous; Operation Blue Thunder; Operation Chemcon; Operation Condor/Trigo; Operation Cooperation; Operation Desert Stop; Operation Global Sea; Operation Green Ice II; Operation Thunderbolt; Opium; Pizza Connection; Oxycodone; Perez, Augusto; Ricorde, Auguste; Rothstein, Arnold; Tijuana Cartel; United States Comprehensive Crime Control Act of 1970; United States Narcotic Control Act of 1956; United States Narcotic Drug Import and Export Act; United States Pure Food and Drug Act; Triads; Vietnam War; World War II; Yakuza

References: Abadinsky, Howard. 1990. *Organized Crime.*

Lowry, Tom. "Chasing the Dragon." 1996. *USA Today*, 9 August, pp. A1 and A2.

Marnell, Tim, ed. 1997. *Drug Identification Bible.*

O'Brien, Robert, and Sidney Cohen. 1984. *The Encyclopedia of Drug Abuse.*

Miller, Gary J. 1997. *Drugs and the Law—Detention, Recognition and Investigation.*

Schemo, Diana Jean. 1997. "Heroin Is Proving a Growth Industry for Colombia." *Colombian Post*, 21–27 April.

Herrera Family

A cartel consisting of six interrelated families that dominated the drug trade in Mexico from shortly before World War II into the 1980s. Headquartered in Durango, Mexico, and operating in the United States out of Chicago, the organization had an estimated 5,000 members, with at least 2,000 of them related by blood and marriage. By the 1980s, the Herrera organization had struck alliances with several other traffickers who had married into the clan. Federal authorities, however, began to move in on the Herrera's U.S. operation, and by 1987 215 members of at least eight separate Herrera-related distribution rings had been arrested, while many more had become fugitives.

References: Lupsha, Peter A., and Kip Schlegel. 1980. *The Political Economy: Drug Trafficking: The Herrera Organization (Mexico and the United States).* Shannon, Elaine. 1989. *Desperadoes.*

Herrera Vasquez, Hugo

The reputed head of a Cali-based drug-trafficking organization that smuggles large shipments of cocaine to the United States via Central America and Mexico. According to the DEA, Herrera Vasquez's organization uses cash, wire transfers, and other means to launder their drug proceeds from the United States southwest border area first to Colombia and then through Mexico to Panama.

References: U.S. Senate Committee on Foreign Relations. 1998. *International Organized Crime Syndicates and Their Impact on the United States: Hearings before the Subcommittee on Western Hemisphere, Peace Corps, Narcotics and Terrorism,* 26 February (statement of Thomas A. Constantine, Director, DEA).

Herrera Zuleta, Benjamin

Pioneering Colombian drug trafficker and father of the Cali Cartel's godfather Helmer Pacho Herrera, who has the nickname of "the Black Pope." In the early 1970s Herrera used a base in Georgia to begin distributing cocaine in the United States. He was arrested in 1973 at the Miami International Airport for the possession of one kilogram of cocaine and sent to prison. After his parole, Herrera Zuleta returned to Georgia, where he was arrested a second time in Atlanta, but he skipped bail and returned to Cali, Colombia, where he set up a cocaine-processing and distribution center to ship cocaine to the United

States. Caught a third time, he served a short prison sentence, but in about 1989 he was arrested again in Fort Lauderdale, Florida, on a Las Vegas drug-trafficking warrant. His son Helmer "Pacho" took over his father's drug-trafficking organization, eventually making it an integral part of the powerful Cali Cartel.

See also: Cali Cartel; Herrera, Helmer Pacho
References: Castillo, Fabio. 1998. *Los Jinetes de la Cocaina.* Gugliotta, Guy, and Jeff Leen. 1990. *Kings of Cocaine.*

Herrera Zuleta, Helmer "Pacho" (c. 1951–1998)

One of the highest ranking members of the Cali Cartel who surrendered to the Colombian National Police on 1 September 1996. Helmer began his criminal career in the early 1970s, selling small amounts of cocaine in New York City. He was arrested twice in 1975 and 1979, but by the 1980s he had become a major supplier of cocaine for both New York and southern Florida. Herrera used clandestine airports in Colombia to ship cocaine from the country's northern ports through the Caribbean to various U.S. ports of entry.

According to the U.S. Drug Enforcement Administration, he also had a close working relationship with various Colombian guerrilla groups, including the M-19 and FARC groups, which protected his cocaine laboratory sites in remote parts of Colombia. To facilitate the return of cocaine drug profits to Colombia, Herrera operated one of the Cali Cartel's most sophisticated money-laundering operations in New York City. In the mid-1980s, he played a key role in the Cali Cartel's secret alliance with the Colombian government to wipe out the more violent Medellin Cartel.

In September 1996 Herrera surrendered to Colombian authorities, telling reporters that he was tired of running and thought he would be safer behind bars. At the time of his surrender, Herrera was the subject of two indictments: one in New York and the other in Florida. He was convicted of drug trafficking in March 1997 and sentenced to six years and eight months in prison, after incriminating at least twenty former associates. Herrera continued to seek sentence reductions by providing evidence against his half brother, but in September 1997, his sentence was increased to fourteen years, following an appeal from prosecutors.

In November 1998 Herrera was slain while watching a soccer game in a prison yard. He was shot at least five times in the face by a man who gained entry to the prison by claiming he was a lawyer for another inmate. The killer turned out to be a member of Herrera's own organization. The assassin told police that Herrera had threatened to kill members of his family if he didn't agree to kill some people whom the godfather wanted dead.

See also: Cali Cartel; M-19; Medellin Cartel; Revolutionary Armed Forces Of Colombia (FARC)
Reference: Bajak, Frank. 1998. "Colombian Drug Lord Is Slain." *Charlotte Observer*, 6 November.

High Intensity Drug Trafficking Areas (HIDTAs)

This program operates under the direction of the Office of National Drug Control Policy (ONDCP), and is authorized under the Anti-Drug Abuse Act of 1988. Its purpose is to designate places in the United States as high intensity drug trafficking areas, or "HIDTAs," for the purpose of providing increased federal assistance to alleviate drug-related problems. Current HIDTAs are New York City, Newark, Miami, Houston, Los Angeles, and the southwest border region with Mexico. Two new HIDTA initiatives have been approved for Puerto Rico and the Washington/Baltimore area as well.

In fiscal year 1996, HIDTAs partners (DEA law enforcement agencies) were empowered to coordinate their efforts by creating joint systems to work together and share resources. Typically, an HIDTA's administrative personnel consists of an executive committee of sixteen members, about equally divided among local, state, and federal officials, and a major task force consisting of 100 to 300 law enforcement employees. The various HIDTAs usually establish regional joint centers and information-sharing networks, which can sustain their law enforcement efforts. The 1996 budget for the HIDTA program was $102.9 million.

See also: United States Drug Enforcement Administration; United States Federal Bureau of Investigation; United States Office of National Control Policy
Reference: HIDTA Website http://www.usdoj.gov/deas/pubs/briefing/3_11.htm.

Susan Manca has her face painted by her friend William Fuller at a casting call in Greenwich Village in hopes of being selected as an extra for the movie "For Love of Ivy" starring Sidney Poitier. Over 300 authentic hippies responded to this call. (UPI/Corbis-Bettmann)

High Times

Founded in 1974, *High Times* is a monthly magazine that covers marijuana use and the counterculture. Its circulation in 1998 was about 250,000.

See also: Counterculture; Marijuana
Reference: Jonnes, Jill. 1996. *Hep-Cats, Narcs and Pipe Dreams.*

Hippies

Members of the youth movement of the 1960s and early 1970s that started in the United States and spread to Canada, Great Britain, and many other countries. The hippies rejected the customs and style of mainstream middle-class society and tried to develop one of their own. The hippy movement was born sometime in the fall of 1966 in the Haight Ashbury District of San Francisco, California, and by the following year, the Haight neighborhood and its residents were internationally known. The Haight's hippy community consisted largely of adolescents from the suburbs who were rebelling against their conservative backgrounds.

According to scholars who have studied the hippie movement, its members were alienated and distrustful of social and political institutions and had strong beliefs about the appropriateness of aggressive personal behavior. The hippies adapted their own look: often unkempt long hair, bowler hats, colorfully designed clothing, and Victorian shawls, among other costumes. They wore flowers in their hair, painted their bodies like Easter eggs and took drugs, especially LSD, calling themselves acid heads. Many sold marijuana joints and acid tabs (LSD).

The Haight Ashbury hippie scene deteriorated soon after it had reached international fame. To a certain extent the hippy message and lifestyle has become institutionalized and is now part of the system its proponents rebelled against. For example, the hipster image of rebellion has been used in advertising to entice consumers. Still there has been an effort to keep the hippy ideal alive. Each year since 1971 an informal network of hippies and anarchists have used computers and word of mouth to organize the Rainbow Gathering, a modern-day counterculture gathering.

See also: Dass, Baba Ram; Ginsberg, Allen; Hashish; Leary, Timothy; LSD
References: Chepesiuk, Ron. 1995. *Sixties Radicals, Then and Now: Candid Conversations with Those Who Shaped an Era.*
Sterne, Jane, and Michael Sterne. 1990. *Sixties People.*

Hirsch, Robert
See Weinig, Harvey.

Hobson, Richard P. (d. 1937)
American hero of the Spanish-American War and a temperance lecturer and organizer who in the early 1920s became a crusader against narcotic drug use, particularly heroin. Although Hobson often made outrageous claims about the extent of the drug problem and the number of addicts, he became a powerful force in the era's antidrug movement by using radio and the lecture circuit to get his message to the American public. Among other activities, he helped organize the International Narcotics Defense Association in 1923 and the World Narcotic Defense Association in 1927. David Courtwright writes that "Hobson continued agitating until his death in 1937, and his mix of questionable statistics and pseudoscience was instrumental in persuading Americans that addiction was both pervasive and malignant." (Courtwright 1982, 33)

See also: International Narcotic Defense Association; World Narcotics Conference; World Narcotics Defense Association
References: Courtwright, David T. *Dark Paradise.*
Morgan, H. Wayne. 1981. *Drugs In America: A Social History, 1800–1980.*

Hodoyan Palacios, Alfredo
A top operative of the Mexican Felix-Arellano drug-trafficking organization, who was wanted in connection with the assassination of leading Mexican drug prosecutor Ernesto Ibarra Santes. Mexico secured Hodoyan's extradition from the United States, and he pled guilty to weapons charges in Mexican court.

See also: Felix-Arellano, Ramon
Reference: U.S. Senate Committee on Foreign Relations. 1998. *International Organized Crime Syndicates and Their Impact on the United States: Hearings before the Subcommittee on Western Hemisphere, Peace Corps, Narcotics and Terrorism,* 26 February (statement of Thomas A. Constantine, Director, DEA).

Hoyos Jiminez, Carlos Mauro
Colombian attorney general who was ambushed by drug traffickers in January 1988 near the Medellin airport in Rionegro, Colombia. Hoyos's bodyguard and chauffeur were killed immediately and Hoyos was dragged bleeding from the limousine, put in a car and driven away. Colombian President Virgilio Barco Vargas ordered a manhunt, and in combing the area, security forces found and freed another kidnapping victim, Andres Pastrana Arango, a Conservative Party candidate for mayor of Bogotá. Police found Hoyos's body a few miles from where Pastrana had been kept captive. Pastrana revealed that his captors said they had planned to kidnap Hoyos and others to dramatize their opposition to Colombia's extradition treaty.

See also: Barco Vargas, Virgilio; Extradition; Pastrana Arango, Andres
Reference: Gugliotta, Guy, and Jeff Leen. 1990. *Kings of Cocaine.*

Human Rights
In their pursuit of enormous profits and formidable power, drug traffickers often violate human rights. In fact, they have shown that they will kill anyone

who gets in their way, whether they be law enforcement officials, members of the judiciary, the press, a good citizen, or even a clergyman. In 1974, for example, an Italian priest in Naples was murdered in his church as he was preparing for mass by drug traffickers angry that he was telling his parishioners to shun their criminal organization.

The drug-related abuse of human rights has taken many forms: murder, beatings, kidnappings, and intimidation. In Colombia alone, by April 1997, sixty-seven journalists had been murdered.

In some countries, most notably Colombia, there has been concern about a possible alliance between drug traffickers, the military, and landowners, who all share a rabid anticommunism and a hatred of leftists and are willing to work together to establish a reactionary social order. In 1989 the Washington Office on Latin America charged that a "marriage of convenience" had formed between the three groups in which "all are bent on eliminating subversive elements" and that "this alliance manifests itself in death squads that have the power of mini-armies, and is the driving force behind Colombia's escalating political violence." (Washington Office on Latin America 1989)

In 1996 Amnesty International, a human rights group, charged that Colombian armed forces and units linked to the military have been responsible for the deaths of 20,000 suspected leftists since 1986. The group produced three documents it said supported its claim that U.S. military equipment had been used not to combat drug trafficking, but rather to combat insurgency, a development that has led to human rights abuses. The leaked documents, said William P. Schultz, Amnesty International's director, offered proof that U.S. tax dollars have been used to supply the Colombian armed forces with military equipment that "equip thugs in uniform who murder other people who were simply inconvenient to the Colombian military." (Gedda 1996)

The U.S. ambassador to Colombia at the time, Myles Frechette, said that the United States has an "in-use monitoring program to keep a check on the military equipment given to the Colombian military," but he conceded that the program is not completely secure. "That would be unrealistic, although we remain satisfied that the aid we give is being used for anti-narcotics efforts," the ambassador added. (Chepesiuk 1999, 253)

Human rights groups have also been critical of governments around the world, several of which, they contend, have violated human rights in the pursuit of antidrug policy objectives. In 1998 Human Rights Watch charged that "efforts to curtail the sale and consumption of illegal drugs continued to rely on excessive punishment, exacerbated prison overcrowding, distorted criminal justice systems, and weakened protection of civil liberties. In countries with vastly different political, social, and economic systems and traditions, anti-narcotic strategies included tactics inconsistent with human rights." (Human Rights Watch 1998) Among the countries of which Human Rights Watch has been critical are Vietnam, the People's Republic of China, Singapore, Thailand, Colombia, Brazil, Bolivia, and the United States.

See also: Frechette, Myles; Media
References: Chepesiuk, Ron. 1999. *Hard Target.*
Gedda, George. 1996. "Amnesty: U.S. Military Aid to Colombia Used for Repression." *Miami Herald*, 30 October, International Satellite Edition.
Human Rights Watch website at http://www.hrw.org.
Washington Office on Latin America. 1989. *Colombia Besieged: Political Violence and State Responsibility.*

Hurtado, Rendon

One of drug kingpin Jose Gonzalo Rodriguez Gacha's bodyguards, who was believed to be the number eight figure in the Medellin Cartel. In December 1989, Hurtado was killed along with Rodriguez Gacha in a gun battle with police in Colombia.

See also: Medellin Cartel; Rodriguez Gacha, Jose Gonzalo
Reference: Coleman, Joseph. 1989. "Police: Slain Bodyguard Was Drug Cartel Leader." Associated Press, 19 December.

Huxley, Aldous (1894–1963)

Noted British essayist, novelist, and author of forty-seven books, Huxley's best-known works include the futuristic *Brave New World* and *Brave New World Revisited.* In the 1950s Huxley became famous for his interest in and experimentation with psychedelic or mind-exploratory drugs, such as mescaline and LSD, which, according to his biographers, he took at least a dozen times over the course of ten years. Huxley wrote two nonfiction books based on his experiences using mescaline under supervision: *The Doors of Perception* (1954) and *Heaven and Hell* (1956). Another Huxley book concerning drugs was *Islands*

(1962) in which he described a drug—half tranquilizer and half intoxicant—that produces an artificial happiness that helps people cope with their lack of freedom.

A number of readers took these books as Huxley's approval of the liberal experimentation with drugs, but Huxley warned about the dangers of such experiments. He died on the same day U.S. President John F. Kennedy was assassinated.

See also: LSD; Mescaline; Psychedelic Drugs
References: Bedford, Sybille. 1974. *Aldous Huxley: A Biography*.
Watts, Harold W. 1969. *Aldous Huxley*.

Hydromorphone
See Dilaudid

I

ICE
See Methamphetamine

Inciardi, James
Director of the Center for Drug and Alcohol Studies
and professor of sociology at the University of
Delaware, and an adjunct professor of epidemiology
and public health at the University of Miami School
of Medicine. Dr. Inciardi received his Ph.D. in sociology from New York University and has extensive research, training, and law enforcement experience in
substance abuse, criminology, and criminal justice.
He has also published numerous books and articles
in the areas of substance abuse, criminology, and
criminal justice, several of which have been critical
of efforts to legalize drugs.

See also: Legalization

References: Sondheimer, Adrian. 1998. "Cocaine-Exposed
  Infants: Social, Legal and Public Health Issues (Book Re-
  view)." *Journal of the American Academy of Child and
  Adolescent Psychiatry* (April): 453.
Trebach, Arnold S., and James A. Inciardi. 1993. *Legalize It?
  Debating American Drug Policy.*

Inhalants
Inhalants are substances giving off fumes and vapors that are inhaled for their intoxicating or other
sensory and mood-altering effects. They are found
in everyday household products, including propane,
paint thinner, fabric protector, and the scented pro-
pellants from air freshener. Inhalants are cheap,
legal, and easy to get—especially for teenagers—

*Two Filipino children sit along Manila's main avenue as
they sniff fumes of glue solvent in plastic bags. The use of
inhalants has become a dangerous form of drug abuse
worldwide. (Corbis/Reuters)*

and their use is difficult to detect because, unlike cocaine and marijuana, there is no physical evidence of
their use in the bloodstream. Inhalants, however, are
dangerous and can kill by cutting off the oxygen
supply or creating an irregular heart beat, as well as

101

causing damage to many organs, including the brain, liver, and kidneys. Hundreds of inhalant-related deaths are documented annually in the United States. According to the National Institute on Drug Abuse, the use of inhalants rose significantly between 1975 and the mid-1990s. In 1993 sixty youths in the United States died from sniffing inhalants. Among children age 14 to 17, inhalants are the most abused drug after alcohol, tobacco, and marijuana.

References: Deangelis, Mary Elizabeth. 1995. "Teen Dies after Inhaling Chemical." *Charlotte Observer*, 21 June. Marnell, Tim, ed. 1997. *Drug Identification Bible.*

Interamerican Drug Abuse Commission

See Organization of American States.

Interdiction

A drug prevention strategy that has dominated U.S. antidrug policy and tries to stop drugs from reaching the streets by preventing their distribution to local dealers. As part of the interdiction strategy, a law enforcement effort is made to disrupt the drug-producing activities in other countries. The rationale behind interdiction is to make the price of drugs go up by limiting their supply.

See also: Bush, George Herbert Walker; Carter, James Earl; Ford Gerald R.; Clinton, William Jefferson; Nixon, Richard Milhous; Reagan, Ronald

References: Clawson, Patrick, and Rensselaer W. Lee. 1996. *The Andean Cocaine Industry.* Mica, John. 1996. "Did the Clinton Administration Drop the Ball on Drug Interdiction Policy?" *Insight on the News*, 4 November.

International Education Association

Organized in 1923 and based in the United States, this crusading antidrug organization was one of several similar organizations that sprang up during the 1920s. It was premised on the belief that the key to fighting illegal drugs was through education and tough law enforcement. To achieve its objectives, the Association lobbied the U.S. government for federal funds to support its antidrug efforts and provided speakers and printed antidrug literature for distribution to schools, churches, and other organizations throughout the United States. But as historian H.

Wayne Morgan explained, "These groups cared little for sophisticated theories about the treatment of addicts. . . . [C]ritics attacked their statements about the effects of opiates and cocaine, and their estimates of the number of users." (Morgan 1981, 122–123)

See also: World Narcotics Conference; World Narcotics Defense Association

Reference: Morgan, H. Wayne. 1981. *Drugs in America: A Social History, 1800–1980.*

International Law Enforcement Academy (ILEA)

Established in April 1995 in Budapest, Hungary, ILEA organizes U.S. training and technical assistance to countries to help their efforts to combat narcotics trafficking and other criminal activities, including nuclear smuggling and financial crime. More than 12,000 law enforcement officers and prosecutors attended ILEA in just one two-year period.

Reference: The United States International Crime Control Strategy. 1998. *Trends in Organized Crime* (Fall): 1–87.

International Narcotic Research Conference (INRC)

Founded in 1968, the INRC is an annual meeting designed to bring together drug abuse researchers from around the world to present their latest results on the basic mechanisms of narcotic drug effects and important advances in the molecular, cellular, and behavioral aspects of narcotic actions. Attendance is open.

Reference: International Narcotic Research Conference website at http://osu.okstate.edu/irnrc/index/htm/.

International Narcotics Board of the United States

Established in 1968, the board is composed of thirteen members responsible for the continuous evaluation of drug control treaties and their implementation by governments. The organization also assesses annual estimates of lawful drug requests submitted by governments and monitors the lawful movement of psychotropic drugs, and when treaties are breached, requires governments to adopt remedial measures.

See also: Entries under United Nations
References: Osmanczyk, Edmund Jan. 1985. *Encyclopedia of the United Nations and International Agreements.*
United Nations Department of Public Information. 1986. *Everyman's United Nations.*

Interpol (International Criminal Police Organization)

Founded in 1923, Interpol helps law enforcement agencies conduct investigations that transcend international borders. Interpol's general secretariat, which acts as the agency's coordinator and point of contact, has its headquarters in Lyon, France. Currently, there are 176 member countries. The agency has a division dedicated to coordinating and dispensing information on drug-trafficking activities, and its Financial and Economic Crime Unit investigates and monitors money-laundering schemes, which often involve drug trafficking. About 20 percent of the budget is dedicated to fighting drug trafficking.

References: Abadinsky, Howard. 1990. *Organized Crime.*
INTERPOL website at http://193.123.144.14/interpol-pr.
Jamieson, Alison. 1994. *Terrorism and Drug Trafficking in Europe in the 1990s.*

Italian American Mafia

Founded in the 1930s by Italian immigrant families, *La Cosa Nostra* ("Our Thing") dominated organized crime for nearly sixty years, functioning independently of the Sicilian Mafia, although the two crime syndicates have interacted and cooperated on a number of criminal enterprises of mutual interest, including drug trafficking. That a powerful Italian American Mafia existed did not become public knowledge until a U.S. Senate committee headed by Senator Estes Kefauver (D-TN) began investigating it in 1951. J. Edgar Hoover, the long-time head of the Federal Bureau of Investigation (FBI), remained skeptical that such an organization existed until 1957, when on November 14 of that year law enforcement authorities stumbled upon a meeting of sixty or so Italian American mobsters in the Appalachian Mountains of New York state. Congressional testimony by Joe Valachi, a former soldier in the mob, in 1963 shed further light on what was until then the mysterious workings of the world's most powerful criminal organization.

By the early 1980s, when the U.S. government under President Ronald Reagan decided to target the La Cosa Nostra, much was known about the Mafia, thanks to law enforcement investigations and congressional hearings. In 1986, the President's Commission on Organized Crime revealed that there were twenty-four mob families nationwide, containing about 1,700 members.

La Cosa Nostra is under the control of a so-called National Commission, which "Godfather" Lucky Luciano established in 1931. The exception is the oldest and most well-established family in New Orleans, which works independently of the National Commission in most matters. The Commission includes the bosses of the five New York mob families, as well as the heads of La Cosa Nostra branches in several major cities, including Detroit, Philadelphia, Chicago, and Buffalo. The National Commission represents joint ventures between families, intervenes in family disputes, governs the initiation of new members, and controls relations between the U.S. and Sicilian branches of the La Cosa Nostra.

Each mob family has a typical organizational structure that includes the boss, or head of the family; under bosses, who serve as the bosses' right hand men; *consiglieri* or "counselors"; *capos* or "captains," who advise the bosses and supervise the family's day-to-day criminal operations; soldiers, who comprise the basic ranks of the family; and associates, such as politicians, police, lawyers, and accountants.

Unlike many of today's other organized crime groups, which tend to focus on drug trafficking, the Italian American Mafia is engaged in a wide range of criminal activities, which, in addition to drug trafficking, include prostitution, extortion, loan sharking, money laundering, illegal gambling, auto theft, embezzling, and labor racketeering, among others.

Historically, the Italian American Mafia has never adapted well to the emergence of the international drug trade. In 1993 Salvatore ("Sammy the Bull") Gravano testified before a federal district court in New York City that, during the 1970s and 1980s the Gambino crime family of New York City, for whom he had worked as an underboss, had strict rules against drug trafficking and anybody in the crime family who got involved with the trade risked death. "Our policy was against drugs," Gravano told the court in testifying against John and Joseph Gambino, who were accused of running a major heroin distribution operation. (Lubasch 1993, 2B)

With such an attitude, it is easy to understand

Charles "Lucky" Luciano and his nine alleged lieutenants are marched into court under heavy guard and handcuffs, 21 May 1936. Luciano later played a major role in organizing the French Connection, the world's first major heroin trafficking network. (Corbis/Bettmann-UPI)

why the five crime families of New York City never got control of the lucrative local heroin market and why they were never big players in the emergence and growth of the cocaine trade. Scholar Peter Reuter explained the mob's missed opportunity in the heroin trade, "Mexican-source heroin became available when the heroin market first expanded in the early 1970s, and the Mafia was never able to prevent its distribution in New York City, the home of perhaps one-third of the nation's heroin addicts. It's early control of the market apparently rested on its domination of the New York docks, through the longshoremen's union, as well as its connections with southern European processors. By the late 1980s, the traditional circuitous route for Southeast heroin through Sicily, Southern Italy, and France, had primarily been replaced by direct importation, via the West Coast, by Chinese and Vietnamese entrepreneurs. The Mafia proved helpless to deal with any of these incursions on its traditional territories." (Reuter 1995, 91)

La Cosa Nostra reportedly has made money indirectly off the international drug trade. The Sicilian

Mafia has paid their American cousins "monetary tribute" in return for the approval of certain Italian American families prior to initiating a major heroin-smuggling operation. As the 1986 Commission on Organized Crime explained, "Sicilian organizations supply LCN (Italian American Mafia) affiliates with heroin; LCN networks either distribute the drug themselves or sell it in large quantities to major distributors." (President's Commission on Organized Crime 1986, 126)

Two years later, another commission on organized crime revealed that reports had linked the Russian mafia to the Genovese La Cosa Nostra family in drug deals and insurance frauds. According to experts on La Cosa Nostra, the high legal risks involved with heroin and cocaine trafficking has encouraged the Italian American Mafia to shy away from drug-related criminal activities. Furthermore, they have not been willing to engage in the kind of violence that is necessary to maintain hegemony in the world of cocaine and heroin trafficking.

The Italian American Mafia may have little direct involvement in the international drug trade, but that did not stop the U.S. government from targeting the mob in the early 1980s. The political momentum to do something about the mob had been building since 1970, when the U.S. Congress expanded federal powers against the underworld by passing the Organized Crime Control Act of 1970, which among other measures, set up federal government task forces against organized crime, expanded a federal witness protection program set up in the late 1960s, gave prosecutors more latitude with witnesses, and most importantly, initiated the RICO statute (Racketeer Influenced and Corrupt Organizations Act), which allowed prosecutors to go after entire criminal organizations, not just individuals, who may have been associated with it.

By the early 1980s, federal prosecutors had become highly sophisticated in their use of RICO and it became a major weapon against organized crime. The 1986 President's Commission on Organized Crime reported that there were 600 approved RICO prosecutions from 1970 through 1985, but that two-thirds of them occurred after 1981. During the 1980s, the leaders of some twenty-five major Mafia families were indicted on criminal charges, including such well-known New York godfathers as Carmine Persico of the Colombo family, Fat Tony

Salerno of the Genoveses, and Tony Ducks Corallo of the Luccheses. Between 1981 and 1987 there were more than a thousand convictions of Italian American organized crime mobsters, not just in New York but also in Boston, Chicago, Philadelphia, New Orleans, Kansas City, and Los Angeles.

The relentless pursuit of La Cosa Nostra continued into the 1990s and culminated in the biggest catch in the modern era of the mob: John Gotti, reportedly the most powerful mafia leader in New York City and the most famous godfather since Al Capone. By 1996, the heads of the Italian American Mafia families in Chicago, Detroit, Boston, Newark, Cleveland, and Philadelphia had all been indicted and convicted of racketeering under the RICO statute.

By the mid-1990s, the Mafia in some cities, most notably Philadelphia, had become its own worst enemy. A mob war that broke out in the City of Brotherly Love in the 1990s left several Mafia members dead, some turning informant, and many arrested and put in jail—developments that seriously weakened the local La Cosa Nostra. Evidence of how the mob had changed was the fact that Sicilian-born mobster John Stanfa, the Philadelphia godfather, was unable to control the young members of his gang from going on a killing rampage and triggering a senseless gang war.

La Cosa Nostra has been seriously weakened, but U.S. law enforcement is not ready to write its epitaph just yet, given the organization's experience and tradition. The mob is still considered a force in at least a dozen American cities, and even though hundreds of mafiosi have been put behind bars, the FBI reports that the number represents only 10 percent of La Cosa Nostra's total membership. It's doubtful, though, that the Italian American Mafia will ever again regain its preeminence in the world of organized crime, especially since it has left much of the trafficking in illegal drugs to the Chinese, Colombians, Russians, and other increasingly powerful ethnic groups. While many of these gangs now use modern business techniques to conduct their illegal activities, the Italian American Mafia "languishes in suspicion of such sophistication, with nary a computer in sight." (Reuter 1995, 97)

See also: Barnes, Leroy "Nicky"; Chemical Bank of the United States (New York City); Cuban Connection; Gambino Family; Heroin; Italian Organized Crime; Junior Black Mafia; Luciano, Charles; Mathews, Frank; Mexican Mafia; President's Commission on Organized Crime; Racketeer Influenced and Corrupt Organizations Act (RICO); Russian Organized Crime; Trafficante, Jr., Santo; Triads

References: Anastasia, George. 1994. "The Last Civil War." *Playboy* (September): 66–68.

Fox, Stephen. 1989. *Blood and Power: Organized Crime in Twentieth-Century America*.

Kelly, Robert J., ed. 1986. *Organized Crime: A Global Perspective*.

Lubasch, Arnold H. 1993. "Drug Dealing Was Banned by Mob, U.S. Witness Says." *New York Times*, 15 April.

President's Commission on Organized Crime. 1986. *The Impact of Organized Crime Today*.

Reuter, Peter. 1995. "The Decline of the American Mafia." *Public Interest* (Summer): 89–99.

Italian Organized Crime

Organized crime, Italian style, has come primarily in two varieties: the Sicilian Mafia, the so-called Octopus, which is an alliance of semiautonomous crime organizations based in the Italian state of Sicily, and the Italian American Mafia, which is also an alliance of semiautonomous crime groups, but is not a branch of the Sicilian Mafia. U.S. law enforcement authorities knew little about the existence of the Sicilian Mafia's drug-trafficking activity in the United States until the Justice Department launched one of its most important crime investigations in the 1980s. The Pizza Connection investigation, which the DEA and FBI conducted jointly, ran for almost three years and targeted the Joseph Bonanno mob family in New York City and its laundering of millions of dollars in revenue from heroin sales through pizza parlors owned by the family and other Sicilian Mafia members. In the United States the investigation led to thirty-four indictments against the Sicilian Mafia members and the first important appearance of its members in U.S. court. U.S. authorities scored another first, gathering the first hard evidence that the Sicilian Mafia had a large and powerful presence in the U.S drug-trafficking scene.

The pizza parlor network was a part of a criminal empire that was mind-boggling in scope, one that spanned the globe to include not just the United States but other countries as well, such as Brazil, Canada, Spain, Switzerland, and several in Southern Asia, the major source of the poppy plant used in heroin production. Claire Sterling, an investigative

This 1928 photo shows a selection of alleged members of some of the most dreaded Italian secret societies or "Mafia" handcuffed and securely behind bars in Palermo, Italy. (Corbis/Bettmann-UPI)

journalist who studied the Sicilian Mafia extensively, has put the annual income of the Sicilian Mafia in the early 1990s at $30 billion, a figure three times the total budget of the Sicilian regional government and one that would make the Mafia the twentieth richest "nation" on earth. In 1989 the Rome-based Census Research Institute put the annual income of the Sicilian Mafia at $95 billion or 12 percent of Italy's gross national product, and called the Octopus the most important private industry in Italy, even bigger than Fiat or Olivetti companies.

The huge U.S. market nourished La Cosa Nostra's criminal empire. By the time the Pizza Connection trial opened in 1985, the FBI had established that, from 1982 to 1985, the New York branch of the Sicilian Mafia transferred $40 million in cash from New York to Sicily via Switzerland. Three years later, the agency estimated that Octopus had transferred $20 billion in drug profits from the U.S in the previous fifteen years.

As a result of the Pizza Connection trial, the Sicil-ian Mafia became the target of U.S. law enforce-ment's attention, and the FBI began using infor-mants, surveillance, electronic "overhears," and in-formation from Italian law enforcement agencies to investigate. The FBI estimated that there were at least twenty-five Sicilian Mafia members operating in the United States, although several more Sicilian Mafia members were suspected of being in the country. That figure seemed to reveal more about the FBI's knowledge of the Sicilian Mafia than it did about the size of the Mafia. Claire Sterling has put the number of Sicilian Mafia members operating in the United States at about 1,700. According to the FBI, the Sicilian Mafia obtained the approval of cer-tain Italian American Mafia families prior to initiat-ing a major heroin-smuggling operation in the United States and is rumored to pay monetary trib-ute for their sanction, which could be up to $5,000 for each smuggled kilogram of heroin.

The Sicilian Mafia may have been news to U.S law enforcement authorities, but the crime syndicate had played a seminal role in organized crime in the United States since the early twentieth century and had dominated the international heroin trade since the 1950s. Mafia gangs were operating in Sicily early in the nineteenth century, and, by the turn of the twentieth century, they had become the de facto rulers of Sicily, infiltrating all branches of government and eliminating anybody who got in their way. Sicilian Mafia members began emigrating to the United States in the early 1890s, settling in greatest numbers in New Orleans, where they dominated and terrorized the city's Italian American population and corrupted the local government. Within a few years, the growing crime syndicate had established bases in such cities as Chicago, Detroit, Newark, New York, Kansas City, and St. Louis.

In the 1920s almost 500 members fled to the United States as the result of a purge by Italian dictator Benito Mussolini. Among the new arrivals were such future godfathers as Carlos Gambino, Joseph Profaci, and Joseph Bonanno, who would comprise the leadership of organized crime in the United States during the next forty years. When Charles "Lucky" Luciano took over in 1931, "Sicily acquired its exclusive heroin concession, and the drugging of America began." (Sterling 1990, 53)

Luciano launched the modern era of the Sicilian Mafia, helping to establish the so-called French Connection, which by the 1970s was responsible for 80 percent of the heroin smuggled into the United States. Working together, American, Italian, and French law enforcement agencies managed to break the French Connection in the early 1970s, a development that led to the shift of heroin laboratories from southern France to Sicily and northern Italy, and the purchase of morphine base from suppliers in Jordan, Syria, Lebanon, and other Eastern Mediterranean countries. By 1987 the Sicilian Mafia controlled the trafficking of processed heroin from both Southeast and Southwest Asia to the United States. Couriers wore body bags (bags on their bodies that could hide drugs) of two- to three-kilogram quantities of heroin or stored the drug in a wide variety of items, including mail, furniture, film canisters, shoes, clothing, provolone cheese, and even cases of baby powder.

To disguise the billions of dollars in profits earned through its worldwide drug-trafficking operation, the Sicilian Mafia has made huge investments in legitimate businesses, buying cafes, bakeries, restaurants, auto dealerships and, of course, pizza parlors in both the United States and Italy. In response to the increased pressure of Italian law enforcement, the Sicilian Mafia went on a murder spree in the early 1980s, but the Italian authorities began to have some success against the difficult target. In 1984, 460 members and associates of the Sicilian Mafia were arrested. They were put on trial in Palermo in 1986. The so-called Maxi-Trial has been described as a "collage" of all the mafia investigations from 1970 to 1984. Totaling forty volumes and 8,632 pages, the indictment described murders, numerous kidnappings, and the use of torture chambers by the Sicilian Mafia. It called the crime syndicate "a very dangerous criminal association, [that through] violence and intimidation has sown terror and death." (McWeeney 1997, 9) Informants such as Tommaso Buscetta and Salvatore Contorno gave invaluable insights into the workings and activities of the Italian La Cosa Nostra.

Italian investigators succeeded in convicting 338 of the defendants, including Michele Greco, who was suspected of being the godfather of the Sicilian Mafia, sentencing them to a total of 2,700 years in prison. Many of its leaders were in jail, but the powerful La Cosa Nostra went to work. Most of those convicted eventually had their sentences reduced or overturned, and by 1992, only fifty were still in jail.

The brave and tenacious chief prosecutor in the trial, Giovanni Falcone, resigned his judicial post at Palermo, complaining of political interference. A national hero because of his work in the Maxi-Trial, Falcone became the object of professional jealousy and a character assassination campaign, and he was passed over for the post of Palmero's chief prosecutor. Falcone narrowly escaped an assassination attempt in 1989, and when many associates intimated that he had fabricated the incident, Falcone quit his Palermo post and moved to Rome, going to work for the Justice Department. He was planning another judicial attack on the Mafia when he was murdered on 7 April 1992.

Claudio Martelli, the Italian Minister of Justice, said Falcone's murder would prove to be "the Mafia's worst mistake," and the government's quick and tough response seemed to back up his word. (Stille 1993, 66) The Italian parliament enacted a package of anti-Mafia measures, which set up an American-style witness-protection program, gave the police special powers to investigate Mafia suspects, and established new rules for taking evidence at Mafia trials. The government sent several thousand police officers to Sicily, where they set up roadblocks and searched for Mafia suspects. By November 1992 Italian law enforcement had arrested 241 suspected Mafia members and seized Mafia assets said to be worth $1.4 billion. Meanwhile, more than 250 gang members had become informants and were revealing some of the mob's biggest secrets.

In 1992 the Italian government launched Operation Clean Hand, one of the biggest criminal investigations in the country's history. Scores of politicians, including thirty-four members of parliament and three cabinet ministers, were arrested on corruption charges.

Italy had won some big battles against the Sicilian Mafia, but the war was far from over. The Octopus was wounded, but it was still capable of spreading terror and mayhem. In July 1993 a bomb killed six people in Florence, wrecking the Uffizi Gallery, one of the world's great art museums, and Italy began to fear that it was about to relive the urban terror that had paralyzed the nation in the 1970s. Some viewed the attack as an effort by the Sicilian Mafia to punish Pope John Paul II for his condemnation of the Mafia during a recent visit to Sicily, while many analysts predicted it was going to be a part of a Mafia terrorist campaign that would retaliate for the arrest of Salvatore (Toto) Riina, the suspected godfather of the Sicilian Mafia. The Mafia, however, didn't follow up in any substantial way until two years later when it went on another killing rampage, murdering several people who were related to Mafia turncoats.

Meanwhile, the Sicilian Mafia has formed strategic alliances with other major drug-trafficking groups, particularly the Colombians and the Russians, and has remained a powerful force in international drug trafficking. "The Sicilian Mafia, pronounced dead by certain American enthusiasts, was rated officially with its American offspring as the country's 'most serious crime problem,'" wrote Claire Sterling. "According to the FBI, it's bringing in thousands of fresh troops to rejuvenate, if not replace, American Mafia's geriatric leadership." (Sterling 1994, 43)

See also: Buscetta, Tommaso; French Connection; Heroin; Italian Mafia; Luciano, Charles; Pizza Connection; Russian Organized Crime

References: Arlacchi, Pino. 1993. *Men of Dishonor: Inside The Sicilian Mafia: An Account of Antonio Calferone.*
"The Mafia Again." 1995. *The Economist*, 11 March.
McWeeney, Sean M. 1987. "The Sicilian Mafia and Its Impact on the United States." *FBI Law Enforcement Bulletin* (February): 1–10.
President's Commission on Organized Crime. 1986. *The Impact of Organized Crime Today.*
Sterling, Claire. 1990. *Octopus: The Long Reach of the International Sicilian Mafia.*
———. 1994. *Thieves' World: The Threat of the New Global Network of Organized Crime.*
Stille, Alexander. 1993. "The Mafia's Biggest Mistake." *New Yorker* 1 March.

J

Jamaican Posses

Jamaican criminal gangs, which are known as "Posses," are among the most powerful drug-trafficking organizations in the United States, dominating the crack cocaine trade in cities all over the American landscape. Initially based in Jamaican-immigrant communities on the East Coast, in Miami, New York City, and Washington, D.C., the Posses have since spread to other large cities, including Dallas, Chicago, Cleveland, Denver, Rochester, Boston, Buffalo, and Long Island, as well as many smaller locations in the Midwest and elsewhere in the country. Suspected Posse members have been spotted as far away as Anchorage, Alaska.

All Jamaican Posses are believed to be the offshoots of two original gangs named Shower and Spangler. Other Posses' names include Tel-Aviv, Super Banton, and Waterhouse Riverton City, the last two of which are named after Jamaican neighborhoods. The Shower is said to have gotten its name from its "showering" of its enemies with gunfire, while the Waterhouse Posse's grizzly habit of setting its victims on fire earned it the alternate name of Firehouse.

Posse members are natives of Kingston, West Kingston, and other tough Jamaican urban shanty towns, and their migration to the United States and powerful role in the country's drug trade can largely be attributed to Jamaican politics. In the 1970s the island's politicians recruited young thugs from the shanty towns to coerce and intimidate voters, as local politics became increasingly divided along two party lines: the People's National Party under Michael Manley and the Jamaican Labor Party under Edward Seaga. The violence in Jamaican politics reached its zenith in the 1980 elections in which 700 people were killed. Seaga's Jamaican Labor Party (JLP) won the election, but the bitter contest destroyed the Jamaican economy. Seaga was left with the potentially explosive situation of having well-armed enforcers mulling around with no jobs and nothing to do. The JLP had no money to keep them on the payroll, so the party began sending their hired help to the United States. As the Jamaican economy continued to decline in the early 1980s, more and more of the young thugs from both political parties made their way to the United States and began organizing themselves into Posses.

The Posses began their U.S. crime careers by smuggling marijuana. In 1984 the U.S. government persuaded Colombia to implement a marijuana eradication program, which led to marijuana supplies drying up. The enterprising Posses stepped in with potent sensimilla, a type of marijuana that could be purchased in Jamaica for $20 a pound and sold in the United States for $1,200 a pound. The ambitious criminal entrepreneurs discovered that more money could be made from selling crack cocaine, a new and lucrative source of illegal drug revenue, and they quickly gained a large share of the crack cocaine market, establishing themselves as major drug traffickers. Federal authorities have estimated that the Posses now control 40 percent of the country's cocaine distribution, principally crack.

The number of Jamaican Posses has been put at thirty to forty and its membership at about 10,000, although the Jamaican government has questioned these figures, saying that some Posse members may actually be other West Indians mistakenly thought to be Jamaicans. Federal authorities, however, have stood by their statistics.

Law enforcement officials describe the Posses as a cunning, vicious, and sophisticated criminal organization, presently operating in international drug trafficking, and say that between the mid-1980s and 1990, they may have been responsible for more than 1,400 murders nationwide. A 1990 Pennsylvania Crime Commission report explained that the Posses have "a well-deserved reputation for violence, even by the standards of an unusually violent business. This brutality stems in part from their belief that violence is an occupational necessity. Their choice of name 'posse' testifies to their fascination with the Hollywood image of the outlaw gunslingers of the 'Wild West.'"

Disciplined as well as violent, the Posses are a tight-knit group and, like the Italian Mafia, are shrouded in secrecy and bound by old-country ties. Because members of a particular gang come from the same neighborhood and are often related by blood and marriage, they can easily be kept in line by threats to loved ones back home. The gangs hire local helpers to open a crack house in a new city, but the core group is always from Jamaica and no outsiders are allowed to penetrate its higher echelons. Masters of forged documentation, the Posses give new members entering the United States authentic-looking false passports, social security numbers, and driver's licenses.

The police have difficulty tracking the Posses because they are highly mobile and move their members every few months. When detained, Posse members will use a code from the spoken language of Rastafarian to confuse the police. The word "Babylon," for example, is used to refer to the "outside world," while "baldness" means "an undesirable outsider" and "beast," a police officer.

During the past decade, U.S. law enforcement has tried to crack down on the Posses, arresting and imprisoning several gang members, but the organized crime syndicate has continued to grow. Scotland Yard has reported increased Posse activity in England, where they are known by the name of "Yardies."

See also: Crack Cocaine; Marijuana; Operation Caribbean Cruise; Operation Rum Punch
References: Chepesiuk, Ron. 1999. *Hard Target.*
Harrison, Faye V. 1990. "Jamaica and the International Drug Economy." *Transafrican Forum* (Fall): 49–57.
Kleinknecht, William. 1996. *The New Ethnic Mobs: The Changing Face of Organized Crime in America.*
"True Confessions: A Gang Member's Story." 1988. *U.S News and World Report*, 18 January.
Weir, William. 1995. *In the Shadow of the Dope Fiend.*

Japanese Organized Crime
See Yakuza

Johnson, Lyndon Baines (1908–1973)
U.S. president from 1964 to 1969. Public concern about drugs had been dormant during the 1950s and early 1960s, but during President Johnson's administration, it flared up and again pressure increased for federal initiatives to do something about the issue. Acting upon the Prettyman Commission's final report, which had been submitted to President Kennedy in November 1963, the U.S. Congress enacted the Drug Abuse Control Amendments of 1965 to deal with the perceived serious problems associated with the diversion of depressant and stimulant drugs from legal channels. Among other measures, the act mandated record keeping and inspections for depressant and stimulant drugs, especially for barbiturates and amphetamines. To enforce the provisions of the amendments, a new agency, the Bureau of Drug Abuse Control (BDAC) was created within the Food and Drug Administration (FDA). In 1966 Congress passed another significant piece of legislation: the Narcotics Addict Rehabilitation Act, which emphasized medical and rehabilitative measures over a punitive solution to illegal drugs and led to an increased focus on research and experimentation with treatment for drug abusers.

In response to the growing public concern over crime in general, and drug abuse in particular, Johnson also established the President's Commission on Law Enforcement and Administration of Justice (the Katzenbach Commission) in 1966 to "undertake a comprehensive study of the nation's crime problem to provid(e) recommendations to coordinate its eradication on all fronts." (President's Commission on Organized Crime 1986, 220) By February 1968

Janis Joplin performing at the Festival for Peace held in Shea Stadium in New York, 6 August 1970. (Corbis-Bettmann)

President Johnson sent a reorganization plan to Congress that restructured the federal drug enforcement effort. Among other significant provisions of the plan was the abolition of the Bureau of Drug Abuse Control and the Federal Bureau of Narcotics (FBN) and the creation within the U.S. Justice Department of the Bureau of Narcotics and Dangerous Drugs, which gave the Justice Department major responsibility for the enforcement of federal drug laws for the first time in its history. Despite the flurry of congressional activity, drug use and abuse in the United States did not abate, and illegal drugs became one of the major issues of the 1968 presidential campaign.

See also: Califano, Joseph A.; Drug Abuse Control Amendments; Katzenbach Commission; National Addict Rehabilitation Act of 1966; Prettyman Commission; United States Bureau of Drug Abuse Control; United States Bureau of Narcotics and Dangerous Drugs

References: Chepesiuk, Ron. 1999. *Hard Target.*

Morgan, H. Wayne. 1981. *Drugs In America: A Social History, 1800–1980.*

President's Commission on Organized Crime. 1986. *America's Habit: Drug Trafficking and Organized Crime.*

Join Together

Based at the Boston University School of Public Health and funded by the Robert Wood Johnson Foundation, this organization was founded in 1991 to serve as a national resource center for communities working together to reduce substance abuse. The group believes that the communities need to employ comprehensive strategies that respond to the problems created by substance abuse, including crime, unemployment, domestic violence, gun violence, and the loss of workplace productivity.

References: Bertram, Eva, Kenneth Sharpe, and Peter Anders. 1996. *Drug War Politics: The Price of Denial.*

Join Together's website at http://www.jointogether.org.

Joplin, Janis (1943–1970)

A blues and rock singer who was enormously popular in the late 1960s, but who was emotionally unstable and abused drugs. Joplin burst on the scene in 1967 at the Monterrey Pop Festival as a member of the band Big Brother and the Holding Company. She and Big Brother earned a gold record in 1968 with their album "Cheap Thrills," but later that year, she quit Big Brother. The next year, Joplin joined the group Kosmic Blues Band and earned another gold album, "Got Dem Ol' Kosmic Blues Again Mama." Joplin died of a heroin overdose in 1970.

References: Amburn, Ellis. 1992. Pearl: *The Obsessions and Passions Of Janis Joplin: A Biography.*
Dalton, David. 1985. *Piece of My Heart: The Life, Times, and Legend of Janis Joplin.*

Juarez Cartel

This cartel was headed by Amado Carillo Fuentes, who took over its leadership in 1993. The cartel operates primarily in the Juarez-El Paso areas, extending along the west Texas and New Mexico borders and into Arizona from Hermosillo, Mexico. The cartel reportedly maintains a close relationship with the Amezcua Contrera organization and is believed be responsible for shipping the more than 650 pounds of methamphetamine seized in Las Cruces, New Mexico, in February 1995. After Carillo Fuentes's bizarre death in 1997, the territory of the Juarez Cartel became the scene of a vicious struggle for power, a battle that is still being played out.

See also: Amezcua Contreras, Jesus; Carillo Fuentes, Amado; Methamphetamine; Mexican Federation; Munoz Talavera, Rafael
Reference: "The Southwest Border Initiative 12 March 1997" (Remarks of Thomas A. Constantine, Director, DEA).

Junior Black Mafia

An African American criminal organization located in Philadelphia, Pennsylvania, which specializes in cocaine and heroin trafficking. The group models itself after the Italian American Mafia, and its leaders are said to be obsessed with the movie *The Godfather,* memorizing its lines and following the lifestyle exhibited by the movie's gangster characters. Gang members drive customized Volvos, are known to wear signature rings (gold, engraved with the initials 'JBM'), and are required to pay the group's $1,000 initiation fee.

In the 1980s the Junior Black Mafia developed a reputation for ruthlessness and violence that involved many vicious drive-by shootings. In 1989 one gang member shot to death a sixteen-year-old youth who had thrown a snow ball at his car, and, in an-

other, the Junior Black Mafia killed a drug dealer who refused to pay a "street tax" by shooting him thirteen times, including, according to a police report, ten times in the head at close range and after he was already on the ground. Gang members have also fired at rival groups in front of Philadelphia City Hall. The Junior Black Mafia was hurt, but not destroyed, by a 1991 drug bust in which twenty-six of its members were sent to jail for distributing more than 2,000 pounds of cocaine in Philadelphia.

See also: Cocaine; Italian American Mafia
Reference: Kleinknecht, William. 1996. *The New Ethnic Mobs: The Changing Face of Organized Crime in America.*

Just Say No Campaign

Nancy Reagan, the wife of U.S. President Ronald Reagan, started this campaign in 1985 as a way of educating young Americans about the dangers of drugs and drug abuse. Mrs. Reagan's idea was to show the nation's youth that even though drug traffickers were powerful, young people were powerful, too, and could simply tell those who urged them to take drugs: "no." By doing so, the logic went, the demand for drugs would decrease and so would the supply. "Frankly, it is easier for the United States to focus on coca fields grown by 300,000 campesinos in Peru than to shut down the dealer who can be found on the street corners of our cities," Nancy Reagan said. (Lewis 1988)

In 1988 Mrs. Reagan told a committee of the United Nations General Assembly, "We need a generation to just say 'no' to drugs." (Lewis 1988) Inspired by Nancy Reagan's message, thousands of "Just Say No" clubs were established across America to help young people resist the temptation of drugs. The verdict on the clubs is mixed. Its supporters say that the clubs got the message out: Drugs are bad for you. The program's critics say the clubs had little impact on the War on Drugs.

See also: Reagan, Ronald
References: Cooper, Mary H. 1990. *The Business of Drugs.*
Lewis, Paul. 1988. "Nancy Reagan at the U.N. Says U.S. Must Do More to Combat Drugs." *New York Times,* 26 October, p. A1.

K

Katzenbach Commission

Officially titled the President's Commission on Law Enforcement and Administration of Justice, this Commission was established by President Lyndon Johnson in 1966 in response to the public's growing concern about crime in general and drug abuse in particular. Its charge was to undertake a comprehensive study of the nation's crime problem and to provide recommendations to coordinate crime's eradication on all fronts. The Commission issued a report, which has a chapter on drug abuse. Among its recommendations: significantly increase the enforcement staffs of the Federal Bureau of Narcotics and the Bureau of Customs, allow courts and correctional officials to deal flexibly with violations of drug laws, and provide more educational and informational material relating to drugs and drug abuse.

See also: Johnson, Lyndon Baines; United States Federal Bureau of Narcotics and Dangerous Drugs
References: President's Commission on Organized Crime. 1986. *America's Habit: Drug Trafficking and Organized Crime.*
Scott, Peter Dale, and Jonathan Marshall. 1999. *Cocaine Politics, Drugs, Armies and the CIA in Central America.*

Kerry, John F. (1943–)

Democratic senator from Massachusetts (1984 to the present), who served as chairman and ranking Democrat on the U.S. Senate Subcommittee on Terrorism, Narcotics, and International Operations from 1987 to January 1997. Kerry graduated from Yale University in 1966 with a bachelor's degree and then served in the U.S. Navy, where he became an officer on a gunboat in the Mekong Delta in Vietnam. He also graduated from Yale Law School in 1976 and is a former lieutenant governor of Massachusetts (1982–1984).

As a senator, Kerry investigated White House efforts to aid the Contras and the private network that sent funds to the rebels. The Contras are Nicaraguan guerrilla fighters, funded by the Reagan administration, who tried to oust the democratically elected government of the country run by the Marxist Sandinistas. To supporters of Reagan's policy, the Contras were "freedom-fighters"; to opponents they were terrorists. Kerry issued a report in 1986 that documented illegal administration involvement in Nicaragua and human rights violations by the U.S.-backed Contras. This led to a full-scale investigation of the so-called Iran-Contra affair. The Iran-Contra affair resulted from the secret U.S. government agreement to provide funds to the Nicaraguan Contra rebels from profits gained by the selling of arms to Iran. Aid to the Contras had been prohibited by the U.S. Congress, and discovery of this arrangement in 1986 shook the administration of Ronald Reagan. A number of convictions later resulted, including those of Marine Lt. Col. Oliver North and Adm. John Poindexter, but both convictions were overturned on appeal on technical grounds. As chairman of the Senate Foreign Relations Subcommittee on Terrorism, Narcotics and International Operations, Kerry also probed allegations that profits from Colombian drug cartels were being funneled to the Contras.

FBI agents finally arrested author Ken Kesey in San Francisco for felony possession of marijuana after returning from Mexico, 10 October 1966. The 31-year-old author had fled the country after facing a similar charge in January of the same year. (UPI/Corbis-Bettmann)

at the hospital where the drug experiments took place became the inspiration for *One Flew over the Cuckoo's Nest.*

In 1964 Kesey joined a group of free spirits who called themselves the Merry Pranksters and left Honda, California, for New York City on an LSD-sodden trip aboard a psychedelically painted school bus driven by noted beatnik Neal Cassady and bearing a destination sign reading "Furthur." The trip became legendary in the 1960s counterculture. In 1990, to mark the twenty-fifth anniversary of the occasion, Kesey published a book titled *Further Inquiry.* According to *Publisher's Weekly,* the book had the cooperation of several major figures from the 1960s counterculture, including Allen Ginsberg, Timothy Leary, Baba Ram Dass, Jerry Garcia, and Hunter Thompson. "The cooperation was extraordinary, practically everybody said, 'God, this a great idea, all the participants are dying off,'" Kesey told the publication. (McQuade 1990)

See also: Counterculture; Dass, Baba Ram; Ginsberg, Allen; Leary, Timothy; LSD; Psychedelic Drugs
References: Kesey, Ken. 1990. *Further Inquiry.*
Leeds, Barry. 1981. *Ken Kesey.*
McQuade, Molly. 1990. "On the Bus with Kesey, Viking and Thunder's Mouth." *Publisher's Weekly,* 15 June.

As relations between the United States and the Soviet Union thawed under Soviet President Mikhail Gorbachev, Kerry proposed that military bases slated for closing be used as detention centers for first-time drug offenders. Kerry also headed the Senate's investigation into the drug-corrupted Bank of Commerce and Credit International (BCCI).

See also: Bank of Commerce and Credit International; Contras; Reagan, Ronald; United States Central Intelligence Agency; Vaughn, Federico
References: Kerry, John F. 1997. *National Security and the Globalization of Crime.*

Kesey, Ken (1935–)

A prominent American literary figure who wrote the celebrated novels, *One Flew over the Cuckoo's Nest* (1962) and *Sometimes a Great Notion* (1964). In 1961 Kesey volunteered for a series of U.S. government-sponsored experiments with what were called psycho-mimetic drugs. Those experiences and his work as a security night attendant on the psychiatric ward

Ketamine

An anesthetic for human and veterinarian use that is often known on the streets as "K" or "Special K." Because ketamine's synthesis is complicated, its only known source in illegitimate trade is from the diversion of the drug from legal channels. A chemical relative of PCP, ketamine is used as a preoperative general anesthetic. Drug users say ketamine produces a better "high" than PCP or LSD because the effects of PCP and LSD last an hour or less, but ketamine can affect the senses, judgment, and coordination for eighteen to twenty-four hours. With repeated daily exposure, users can develop tolerance and psychological dependence.

Veterinarian clinics have been burglarized for ketamine, and in 1997 the U.S. Drug Enforcement Administration reported that its abuse and trafficking was increasing. Ketamine use has been reported at so-called Rave parties, while law enforcement agencies are encountering the problem when stopping drivers for what appears to be driving while intoxicated. These have been among the factors that prompted the DEA to reevaluate the drug's control status and priority in 1997.

References: Cloud, John. 1997. "Is Your Kid on K?" *Time*, 20 October.

Farley, Dixie. 1996. "Illegal Use of Vet Drug Results in Fine, Probations." *FDA Consumer* (April): 28.

Khun Sa (1934–   )

A powerful opium drug trafficker and self-styled Shan freedom-fighter in Myanmar (Burma). Khun Sa is nicknamed "Money Tree" by his supporters and "Prince of Death" by his detractors. Born in eastern Myanmar to a Chinese father and Burmese mother, Khun Sa, whose Chinese name is Chang Fi-fu, was a Shan guerrilla fighter before entering the narcotics trade in the 1960s. He reportedly began smuggling while he was an officer in the Myanmar army in 1963, but he left the military to form his own private army and become a warlord.

In 1967 Khun Sa came into conflict with drug-trafficking Chinese Kuomintang forces in the area, which led to the so-called Opium Wars. The struggle destroyed Khun Sa's army. The Myanmar authorities arrested Khun Sa in 1969 and detained him until 1974. When Lo Hsing-Han, the dominant drug lord in the area, was arrested, Khun Sa filled the vacuum and became so powerful in the Golden Triangle that he was able to build up a private army that at one time was reported to be 20,000 strong. Khun Sa was powerful enough to form a de facto autonomous state. At the height of his power, he is believed to have controlled half of the approximately 600 tons of opium produced annually in the Golden Triangle.

In January 1996, Khun Sa surrendered to Myanmar troops, but the country has refused the United States' repeated requests to extradite him to the United States on drug-trafficking charges. The Myanmar government has announced that Khun Sa is under close government supervision and that it will deal with the drug kingpin under its own antidrug laws. Meanwhile, the United States has offered a $2 million reward for his capture. Press reports indicate that, although Khun Sa suffers from diabetes, his vast legal commercial empire is thriving.

See also: Extradition; Golden Triangle; Heroin; Kuomintang; Opium

References: Lintner, Bertil. 1994. "Khun Sa: Asian Drug King on the Run." *Far Eastern Economic Review*, 20 January.

———. 1995. "The Noose Tightens: Khun Sa Faces a Day of Reckoning." *Far Eastern Economic Review*, 19 October.

Kintex

In the mid-1980s, an import-export firm known as Kintex was identified by Western officials as being involved with drugs and terrorism. Its trade ostensibly dealt with sports and hunting equipment, as well as explosives for mining and construction work, but the company was believed to be an arm of Dajanavna Sigurnost, the Bulgarian secret intelligence unit, which was believed to be a major facilitator of drug transport through Belgium. The U.S. Drug Enforcement Administration estimated at the time that 75 percent of all illicit drugs entering Europe did so through Kintex and Bulgaria.

One Bulgarian law enforcement official told writer Brian Freemantle that, "We do not consider that the Americans or any other drug enforcement authority have satisfactorily made out any case to prove our involvement in either drugs or gun running. Kintex is a respectable government agency, not a criminal organization." (Freemantle 1985, 186)

Reference: Freemantle, Brian. 1985. *The Fix*.

Klein, Yair (c. 1946–   )

Israeli mercenary and retired Israeli lieutenant colonel who allegedly provided training and mercenary services to the Medellin Cartel in Colombia in the late 1980s. Klein acknowledged to the press that he led a team of "instructors" in Puerto Boyaca, Colombia, in early 1988, but claimed that he was there to help local ranchers defend themselves against government attacks and had no involvement with drug traffickers. In August 1989, however, the Israeli and Colombian governments began investigating Klein because of reports that Colombians he had trained assassinated Luis Carlos Galan, the leading presidential candidate in the 1990 elections.

See also: Galan, Luis Carlos; Medellin Cartel

Reference: Robinson, Eugene. 1989. "Israeli Mercenary Allegedly Provided Training and Services to the Medellin Cartel." *Washington Post* Foreign Service, 29 August.

Kuomintang (KMT)

After the communists defeated General Chiang Kai-Shek's Chinese nationalist forces in 1949, the gen-

eral's Third and Fifth armies took flight for the remote southern Chinese province of Yunan and escaped over the mountains to the safety of the Shan
states of Myanmar. Numbering about 12,000 men,
the KMT had become a power in the southern part
of the Shan states by 1952, and after attempts to retake China failed, they settled down in Myanmar and
became active in the local opium trade.

The Myanmar military was unsuccessful in
pushing the KMT out of the country, but in 1965
they finally forced them into the Thai portion of the
Golden Triangle. In the 1960s the United States air-
lifted KMT troops to Taiwan and the remaining
troops became known as the Chinese Irregular
Forces (CIF). Experts say that while the KMT always
dabbled in opium, the drug has now become the sole
support of the CIF.

See also: Golden Triangle; Khun Sa; Triads

References: Abadinsky, Howard. 1990. *Organized Crime.*
Lamour, Catherine, and Michael R. Lamberti. 1974. *The
    International Connection: Opium from Growers to
    Pushers.*

L

La Mina
See Operation C-Note

Land Carrier Initiative Program
See United States Customs, Department of

Lara Bonilla, Rodrigo (c. 1946–1984)

In early 1983 Colombian President Belasario Betancur appointed the thirty-eight-year-old Rodrigo Lara Bonilla to the post of justice minister. In terms of responsibility this was a position equivalent to the U.S. attorney general. The diligent Lara Bonilla began to investigate the influence of the Medellin Cartel in the Colombian political system, despite death threats from the Cartel and its offer of bribe money. His investigation led to the discovery that thirty politicians had taken drug money in municipal elections. He also conducted a series of raids that led to the seizure of several airplanes and much equipment owned by the Medellin Cartel, which disrupted its smuggling operations. Meanwhile, Lara Bonilla publicly denounced Pablo Escobar Gaviria as a drug trafficker, humiliating the drug kingpin and driving him from his office in the Colombian Congress.

An angry Escobar, in turn, bitterly denounced Lara Bonilla as a stooge of U.S. imperialism and ordered his assassination. U.S. officials in Colombia warned Lara Bonilla about the danger, but he downplayed the threat. When Lara Bonilla found out that the Medellin Cartel was bugging his phones, however, he began to take the threats more seriously. For his safety, the Colombian government made the decision in April 1984 to send Lara Bonilla to Czechoslovakia as Colombian ambassador, but the transfer would take place in thirty days. On 30 April 1984, Lara Bonilla was assassinated in heavy traffic as he headed in his Mercedes Benz limousine to a fashionable neighborhood in north Bogotá.

See also: Betancur Cuertas, Belisario; Escobar Gaviria, Pablo; Medellin Cartel; Ochoa Vasquez, Jorge Luis
References: Eddy, Paul, Hugh Sabogal, and Sarah Walden. 1988. *The Cocaine Wars.*
Gugliotta, Guy, and Jeff Leen. 1990. *Kings of Cocaine.*

Lara Nausa, Jaime Orlando

The U.S. Drug Enforcement Administration and FBI accused Lara Nausa of being one of the principal godfathers of a drug-trafficking ring that shipped heroin from Colombia to the New York City area. In December 1998 Colombian authorities captured Lara Nausa and quickly extradited him to the United States, making Lara Nausa the first Colombian extradited in eight years. His extradition was made possible because he was accused of having trafficked in drugs after 17 December 1997. Under the current Colombian law, extradition does not extend to crimes committed before that date.

See also: Extradition; Heroin
Reference: *:*"Se Reanuda la Extradition." 1998. *El Tiempo,* 15 December.

Laudanum

Refers to opium preparations that were used extensively in the late nineteenth and early twentieth centuries as a tonic and cure-all and sold in shops, by mail order, and at traveling medicine shows—until society found out laudanum was addictive. Paracelsus first compounded laudanum in the sixteenth century.

Reference: O'Brien, Robert, and Sidney Cohen. 1984. *Encyclopedia of Drug Abuse.*

Lavin, Larry
See Dr. Snow

Lawn, John C.

Administrator for the Drug Enforcement Administration from 1985 to 1990. Born and raised in New York City, Lawn received a bachelor's degree from St. Francis College in Brooklyn in 1957 and a master's degree from St. John's University in 1964, before beginning a fifteen-year career with the FBI in 1967 as an agent based in the Savannah, Georgia, office. In 1982 Lawn became the deputy administrator of the DEA after serving as acting administrator for the agency.

In early 1990 Lawn announced his intention to resign as administrator of the DEA. He gave an interview to *Narcotics Control Digest* in which he reflected on the War on Drugs. He said, "Despite success in nearly all aspects of narcotics control, a victory in the War on Drugs is out of sight and the country has a long way to go before the problem is under control Drug abuse in the world will never be eliminated, but it can be reduced to a manageable irritant." (An Interview with John C. Lawn 1990)

See also: United States Drug Enforcement Administration
References: "An Insider's Look at Drug Enforcement." 1985. *Scholastic Update,* 19 May.
"An Interview with John C. Lawn." 1990. *Narcotics Control Digest,* 28 March.

League of Nations

An international organization formed after World War I as a way to promote international cooperation and to achieve world peace and security. Based in Geneva, Switzerland, the League functioned from 1920 until it dissolved in 1946. Eventually, sixty-three governments joined the League, although total membership at any one time never exceeded more than fifty-eight, a figure reached in 1934.

The League established the Advisory Committee on Traffic of Opium and Dangerous Drugs to elicit and disseminate information; a Permanent Control Opium Board in 1925 to supervise a system of international licensing of the import, export, and transport of opium and its derivatives; and a clearinghouse to gather statistics on drug movements. Although most historians consider the League a failure, they have also given it credit for success in the area of drug control, particularly that of opium.

See also: Anslinger, Harry A.; Convention for the Suppression of the Illicit Traffic in Illegal Drugs; Opium
Reference: Gilbert, Murray. 1948. *From the League of Nations to the U.N.*

Leary, Timothy (1920–1996)

Major figure of the 1960s counterculture who advocated the use of drugs, particularly LSD. Rebellious from an early age, Leary was expelled from high school, the U.S. military academy at West Point, and the University of Alabama before earning a Ph.D. degree in psychology from the University of California at Berkeley. Leary began a promising academic career that led to his appointment to the Harvard University faculty in 1960, but he discovered psychedelic drugs while on a trip to Cuernavaca, Mexico, and his life changed forever.

Leary consumed psilocybin, or magic mushrooms, and he experienced what he described as an enlightening, mystical revelation. He also began experimenting with LSD at Harvard before being fired in 1963. But the emerging counterculture provided Leary with a big audience for his message, and he put together a traveling light-and-sound show and toured the country expounding on the virtues of psychedelic drugs.

Leary became the so-called high priest of LSD and urged people to "tune in, turn on, and drop out." He also founded the League of Spiritual Discovery, which he dedicated to altering consciousness and exploring mysticism through psychedelic drugs, particularly LSD. But in 1970 he was jailed for possession of a small amount of marijuana, and President Richard Nixon called Leary "the most dangerous man alive."

Leary escaped from jail and fled the country, first for Algeria, where Black Panther Eldridge Cleaver,

Timothy Leary stands under the Village Theatre marquee where he's giving a talk in which he explains his League of Spiritual Discovery, which he called an orthodox psychedelic religion that hopes to be allowed to use LSD and marijuana as sacraments. (Corbis/Bettmann-UPI)

himself on the run, also thought him a dangerous man and put him under house arrest. Leary ended up in Kabul, Afghanistan, where he was arrested and deported to the United States. In all, the drug guru spent forty-two months in jail.

In the 1980s Leary became a leader of the futurist movement, which looked at trends in the future as they related to technology, and president of Futique, a company that designs highly interactive software programs for personal computers. Meanwhile, he remained an advocate of drug experimentation.

Leary died of prostate cancer on 31 May 1996. He was cremated and his ashes, along with twenty-three other individuals, were put aboard a rocket that was launched in the Canary Islands.

See also: Burroughs, William S.; Counterculture; Dass, Baba Ram; Ginsberg, Allen; Halucinogen; Hippies; Kesey, Ken; LSD; Nixon, Richard Milhous; Psilocybin

References: Chepesiuk, Ron. 1995. *Sixties Radicals, Then and Now: Candid Conversations with Those Who Shaped an Era.*
Leary, Timothy, and William S. Burroughs. 1997. *Flashbacks.*
Lee, Martin, and Bruce Schlain. 1985. *Acid Dreams, the CIA, LSD, and the Sixties Rebellion.*

Legalization

The War on Drugs has no more controversial issue than legalization. Proponents of drug legalization, which now include a diverse group of scientists, social workers, economists, and other leaders in society, see the underground economy arising from illicit drug use as the main source of drug-related crime and contend that legalizing drugs like heroin and cocaine will make it easier for drug abusers to receive the treatment they need for addiction. Opponents, on the other had, contend that drug legalization would promote a lifestyle and culture that would be disastrous for society.

Proponents argue that legalization would make the problems associated with illegal drugs more manageable and easier to control and urge that society should debate the issue of legalization. Opponents counter that legalization would open up a Pandora's box of headaches for society that would exacerbate the drug problem and not alleviate it. Although proponents argue that the use of drugs is a civil liberties issue and that it involves the right of adults to decide whether they want to use drugs, critics of drug legalization counter that if drugs were legalized, it would be the children who choose and society would find it impossible to keep drugs away from them.

Both sides have plentiful statistics to bolster their positions. The controversial Netherlands drug policy is a case in point. The coffeehouses of Amsterdam are nationally controlled drug distribution centers, which, in effect, makes for a legalized drug program. To the Dutch and their supporters, criticism of that policy is unjustifiable because the policy's success is demonstrated and supported by its results. For example, they say that the number of addicts in the Netherlands is low when compared to other countries. According to their statistics, about 1.6 percent of the people in the Netherlands are addicted to hard drugs, mostly heroin. These figures compare with 2.5 percent of the population in France, 1.5 percent in Germany, and 3 percent in Italy. "About fifty people a year die of drug-related causes in the Netherlands: the lowest rate in the Western World," said Bob Keijzer, a senior drug policy advisor in the Netherlands Ministry of Health. (Gross 1997)

But statistics from Joseph Califano, director of the Center on Alcohol and Drug Abuse at Columbia University, present a different picture. "Anyone over the age of 17 can drop into a marijuana 'coffee shop,' and pick types of marijuana like one might chose flavors of ice cream," he wrote in *USA Today Magazine*. "Adolescent pot use jumped nearly 200 percent while it was dropping by 66 percent in the U.S." According to Califano, "Dutch persistence in selling pot has angered European neighbors because its wide-open attitude toward marijuana is believed to be spreading pot and other drugs beyond the Netherlands' borders." (Califano 1997)

The critics and supporters of Dutch policy disagree sharply over the reason why the number of coffee shops where marijuana is sold legally has been cut back. To Califano, the cutback was in response to complaints from Dutch citizens about "the decline in their quality of life." Supporters, on the other hand, say it's because the economic and monetary unification of Europe has forced the Netherlands to conform to the laws and mores of its neighbors.

The differences over legalization have also affected the medical marijuana issue. Opponents charge that medical marijuana is a "insidious' way to legalize drugs. "Knowing that most Americans won't countenance outright legalization, many promoters

Thousands of people gathered at the University of Wisconsin Madison campus for a march to the State Capital calling for the legalization of marijuana, 30 September 1990. (Corbis/Bettmann-UPI)

deceitfully profess their goal is to help the seriously ill," charged Steve Forbes. (Forbes 1997)

Despite the rhetoric on both sides, no one knows for sure what the health costs or social and economic implications would be if drugs were legalized. Many questions are unanswered. For example, which drugs should be legalized? All? Some? How would legalization be implemented? Who would be responsible for overseeing legalization? Where would the drugs be sold? Would legalization, if accompanied by adequate regulations, lead to a safer product? What potency levels should be permitted? What age limits?

Despite the controversy and uncertainties surrounding the legalization issue, one country has boldly tackled the issue dead on. In November 1998 Switzerland took one of its most ambitious proposals to a referendum: the legalization of the use and sale of such drugs as marijuana, cocaine, and heroin.

Critics said that, if the referendum passed, it would go the way of the country's previous radical experimentation with drug legalization in 1995. That's when police allowed drugs to be sold in open-air drug markets in Zurich and Bern, and the laissez-faire policy led to problems, as the markets attracted drug users and dealers from across Europe. Supporters hoped that legalization would put an end to the black market for drugs by putting the state in control of the supply of both hard and soft drugs. The state would issue a type of smart card, they said, that would prevent drug binging, as well as keep foreigners and children from taking part. The Swiss overwhelmingly rejected the proposed constitutional amendment to legalize drugs by a margin of 74 to 26 percent.

See also: Bennett, William J; Buckley, William F.; Califano, Joseph; Cano Izaza, Guillermo; Clinton, William Jefferson; Cocaine; Decriminalization; Drug Watch international; Harm Reduction; Heroin; Inciardi, James A.; Lindesmith Institute; Marijuana; National Association for the Reform of Marijuana Laws; National Families in Action; Shultz, George P.; Sweet, Rober

References: Califano, Joseph. 1997. "Legalization of Narcotics: Myths and Realities." *USA Today Magazine* (March): 46.

Concar, David, and Laura Spinney. 1994. "The Highs and Lows of Prohibition." *New Scientist*, 1 October.

"Drugs in Switzerland." 1998. *The Economist*, 28 November.

"Equity and Addiction." 1995. *Nature*, 30 March.

Forbes, Steve. 1997. "Deadly Deceit." *Forbes*, 8 September.

Gross, Richard C. 1997. "Dutch Claim Drug Policy Works, But Agree to Stricter Enforcement." *Insight on the News*, 17 March.

Trebach Arnold S., and James A. Inciardi. 1993. *Legalize It? Debating American Drug Policy*.

Lehder Rivas, Carlos Enrique (1947–)

Founding member of the drug-trafficking organization known as the Medellin Cartel, which at its height of power was responsible for supplying as much as 80 percent of the cocaine entering into the United States, according to the U.S. Drug Enforcement Administration.

Lehder Rivas was born in the Colombian coffee-growing region of Armenia, but his parents brought him to the United States at an early age. By age fifteen he was dealing in cocaine. Three years later he was arrested and convicted of importing 200 pounds of marijuana into the United States. Lehder served a two-year prison term and was deported to Colombia in 1976, where he returned to the drug-trafficking business, learned to fly, and organized a distribution ring that specialized in aerial drug drops and eventually evolved into the Medellin Cartel.

In a 1983 interview with the Colombian magazine *La Semana*, Lehder described the Medellin Cartel's early beginnings. He had a predilection for flying, Lehder recalled, and with the money he managed to bring with him after being kicked out of the United States he went to the Bahamas and bought his first airplane. By buying, repairing, and selling old planes, Lehder boasted of making his first million dollars by age twenty-three. For $4.5 million he bought Norman's Cay, a small island in the Bahamas, where he built a radar-equipped airstrip that he used to smuggle drugs into the United States via the short final hop to the Florida coast.

Lehder's operational base became his home town of Armenia, where he founded a political movement, the National Latin Movement; built a five-star hotel with a landmark statue of slain Beatle John Lennon and a condominium complex with a total area of 80,000 square meters; and established a newspaper, *Quindio Libre*, which published techniques on how to increase marijuana production.

The arrest of Colombian drug trafficker Carlos Lehder Rivas (Courtesy of the Colombian National Police)

The U.S. government filed an indictment against Lehder Rivas in Tampa, Florida, but when the Bahamian government police raided Norman's Cay, he was gone. However, he was captured and extradited to the United States in February 1987, after an elite twenty-man Colombian police unit received a phone tip and surrounded one of his mansions located about twenty miles from Medellin.

After a seven-and-a-half-month trial, a jury found Lehder Rivas guilty on eleven counts, ranging from cocaine possession to running a continual criminal enterprise. In July 1988 he was sentenced to life imprisonment without parole, plus 135 years, and fined $350,000.

See also: Blanco De Trujillo, Griselda; Cali Cartel; Cocaine; Cuban Connection; Extradition; Marijuana; Medellin Cartel; National Latin Movement; Norman's Cay; Noriega, Manuel Antonio; Ochoa Vasquez, Jr., Fabio; Ochoa Vasquez, Jorge Luis; Ochoa Vasquez, Juan David; Operation Caribe

References: Gugliotta, Guy, and Jeff Leen. 1990. *Kings of Cocaine*.

Strong, Simon. 1995. *Whitewash: Pablo Escobar and the Cocaine Wars*.

Limitation Convention of 1931

Signed at Geneva on 31 July 1931, this convention limited the manufacture, regulation, and distribution of narcotic drugs. In effect, world manufacture of drugs was now restricted to medical and scientific needs and limits were placed on the quantity of drugs available for use in each country or territory. The limitation was enforced through a supervising board, an international body of experts set up by the Convention that mandated governments to provide the administrating body with estimates on annual drug requirements. The 1931 Convention came into full application on 1 January 1934. By August 1952 sixty-three countries had signed it. It is no longer in effect.

Reference: Renborg, Bertie A. 1947. *International Drug Control: A Study of International Administration By and Through the League of Nations.*

Linder v. United States

Linder was a prominent physician who gave one tablet of morphine and three tablets of cocaine to an addict and was charged with breaking the law. This 1925 U.S. Supreme Court decision (No. 83, U.S. Supreme Court 268; U.S. submitted 9 March 1925, decided 11 April 1925) reversed an earlier decision in *United States v. Behrman* of the same year. The Behrman decision declared that a narcotic prescription for a drug addict was unlawful, even if the drugs were prescribed as part of a cure program. Linder v. United States held that addicts were entitled to medical care, just like other patients, but as was noted, "[t]he ruling had almost no effect. By that time, physicians were unwilling to treat addicts under any circumstances and well-developed illegal drug markets were catering to the ranks of the addict population." (Trebach & Inciardi 1993, 183)

See also: Cocaine; Morphine; *United States v. Behrman*
Reference: Trebach, Arnold, and James A. Inciardi. 1993. *Legalize It? Debating American Drug Policy.*

Lindesmith, Alfred

A sociologist and a member of the Indiana University faculty who was an early critic of the emerging drug control policy formulated by the U.S. government. As a graduate student at the University of Chicago in the 1930s, Lindesmith wrote a doctoral dissertation that was the first systematic study of drug addiction in the field of sociology. He did research at the United States Public Health Service Hospital in Lexington, Kentucky, which led him to the conclusion that the use of criminal sanctions was inappropriate for drug-abusing patients. As a doctor who favored medical treatment for drug addiction, Lindesmith was ahead of his time.

Through his writing and publishing, Lindesmith attacked the federal drug policy. As was noted, "[a]lthough a direct call for the legalization of drugs was not apparent in Lindesmith's early work, it was clearly implied. Moreover, it would appear that he was the first member of the academic community to venture into the political arena of drug-policy debate, and the criticisms of his work were fierce." (Trebach & Inciardi 1993, 146) The Federal Bureau of Narcotics (FBN) attempted to intimidate Lindesmith, stifle his research, and interfere with his writings, which criticized U.S. government antidrug policy. The efforts at intimidation and harassment continued over three decades. Today, the Lindesmith Institute bears Alfred Lindesmith's name.

See also: Harm Reduction; Legalization; Lindesmith Institute; United States Federal Bureau of Narcotics
References: Galliher, John F., David P. Keys, and Michael Elsner. 1998. "Lindesmith Versus Anslinger: An Early Government Victory in the Failed War on Drugs." *Journal of Criminal Law and Criminology.* (Winter): 661–683.
Trebach, Arnold S., and James A. Inciardi. 1993. *Legalize It? Debating American Drug Policy.*

Lindesmith Institute

This New York City-based research policy center was founded in 1994 and is named for Alfred R. Lindesmith, a prominent early critic of the U.S. government's antidrug policy. The Institute's purpose is to broaden the debate on drug policy and related issues. Its guiding principal is harm reduction, an initiative that offers an alternative to current drug policy by focusing on minimizing the adverse effects of drug abuse. The Institute also makes an effort to study the drug policies of other countries.

To fulfill its mission the Institute maintains a library and information center. It organizes conferences and seminars that bring the media, government, and scholars together, and supports special projects on timely topics, such as methadone policy reform and alternatives to drug testing in the workplace.

See also: Drug Testing; Harm Reduction; Lindesmith, Alfred; Nadelmann, Ethan; Needle Exchange Program
Reference: Lindesmith Institute website at http://www.lindesmith.org.

Lisboa Medgar, Juan Carlos (1954–)

In the late 1980s Lisboa Medgar was considered one of Bolivia's top drug traffickers and the owner of the biggest cocaine-processing laboratories ever uncovered in the country. In November 1989 Lisboa Medgar was arrested during a raid on a home in Santa Cruz, a drug-trafficking center 335 miles southeast of La Paz. But in early December the Bolivian Supreme Court freed him. In response Bolivian Prime Minister Gonzalo Torrico charged that some of the country's judges and prosecutors were showing "too much weakness in confronting crime" and suggested reforms for the judicial system.

See also: Cocaine
Reference: "Bolivian 'Fat Fish' Cocaine Trafficker Freed." 1989. United Press International. 9 December.

Liu Chong Hing Bank (Hong Kong and San Francisco)

This bank was implicated in a U.S. government undercover investigation in which two IRS agents pursued four employees of the Bank who were involved in the laundering of $1.5 million in illegal drug-trafficking profits. In September 1983 the four individuals were indicted on conspiracy and false statement charges, as well as currency transaction violations relating to the money that had been laundered. Aaron Lee, the owner of Canada Asia Financial Group, LTD of Vancouver, British Colombia, who coordinated the operation, was given a six-month sentence.

See also: Currency Transaction Reports (CTRs); Money Laundering
Reference: President's Commission on Organized Crime. 1984. *The Cash Connection: Organized Crime, Financial Institutions and Money Laundering.*

Loaiza-Ceballos, Henry

Initially, Loaiza-Ceballos was a hit man and bodyguard for the Cali Cartel, but he worked his way up the organization's hierarchy to assume a top leadership position as the Cartel's military leader. He is accused of involvement in one of Colombia's worst massacres: the chainsaw murders of 107 persons who refused to cooperate with the Cali Cartel. He is also believed to be involved in a June 1995 bombing in Medellin that killed twenty-two people. Loaiza-

Ceballos surrendered to Colombian authorities in June 1995.

See also: Cali Cartel
References: Fedarko, Kevin. 1995. "Outwitting Cali's Professor Moriarty." *Time*, 17 June.
"Six Top Colombian Traffickers Still at Large." 1995. Reuters, 10 June.
U.S. Drug Enforcement Administration website at http://www.usdoj.gov/DEA/pubs/briefing.

Logan Heights Calle 30

An assassination gang that has carried out killings and provided security for the Mexican drug-trafficking organization known as the Tijuana Cartel, which is headed by the Arellano Felix brothers. In one incident allegedly perpetrated by the group on 11 December 1996, Fernando Jesus Gutierrez was shot five times in the face in rush-hour traffic in the upscale Silver Strand neighborhood in Coronado, California, as the result of a dispute over drugs. In March 1997, DEA Director Thomas Constantine told the U.S. Congress that the Narcotics Task Force in San Diego had arrested forty-nine members of the Logan Heights Calle 30 on a variety of charges involving drug trafficking.

See also: Arellano Felix, Ramon; Constantine, Thomas A.; Tijuana Cartel
Reference: U.S. Senate Committee on Foreign Relations. 1998. *International Organized Crime Syndicates and Their Impact on the United States: Hearings before the Subcommittee on Western Hemisphere, Peace Corps, Narcotics and Terrorism*, 26 February (statement of Thomas A. Constantine, Director, DEA).

Lopez Michelsen, Alfonso (1913–)

Colombian president from 1982 to 1986, who was also suspected of receiving a $400,000 contribution for his presidential campaign from drug kingpin Pablo Escobar Gaviria in 1981. Carlos Lehder Rivas reportedly wrote a letter to Lopez Michelsen in which he referred to the presidential candidate as the Medellin Cartel's "protector." In 1984 Lopez Michelsen met with Escobar and Jorge Luis Ochoa in a Panama City hotel. The drug traffickers asked the former Colombian president to relay their offer to the Colombian government. In return for amnesty, Escobar and the Ochoa brothers said the Medellin Cartel would abandon its involvement in the drug trade. The Colombian government rejected the offer.

In December 1998 Gloria Pachon de Galan, the widow of Luis Carlos Galan, who was assassinated in 1989, sent Lopez Michelsen a letter in which she accused the former Colombian president of accepting support from Pablo Escobar Gaviria during his campaign for the presidency in 1982. Lopez Michelsen told the newspaper *El Tiempo* that he would study the letter before responding publicly to it.

See also: Escobar Gaviria, Pablo; Galan, Luis Carlos; Lehder Rivas, Carlos; Ochoa, Jorge Luis
References: "Lopez Acepto Los Aportes De Escobar." 1998. *El Tiempo,* 26 December.
Strong, Simon. 1995. *Whitewash: Pablo Escobar and the Cocaine Wars.*

Low Murtra, Enrique (d. 1991)

Colombian justice minister who in January 1991 incurred the wrath of the Medellin Cartel drug lords Pablo Escobar, Jose Rodriguez Gacha, and the Ochoa brothers (Jorge, Fabio, and Juan David) by issuing arrest warrants for them with the intention of having them extradited to the United States. On 30 April 1991 assassins believed to be working for Escobar murdered Low Murtra. The killing was seen as an attempt by Escobar to influence the Colombian Constituent Assembly's vote on extradition. On 19 June 1990, less than two months after Low Murtra's murder, the Assembly outlawed extradition by a vote of 50 to 13.

See also: Escobar Gaviria, Pablo; Extradition; Ochoa Vasquez, Jr., Fabio; Ochoa Vasquez, Jorge Luis; Ochoa Vasquez, Juan David; Rodriguez Gacha, Jose Gonzalo
References: Gugliotta, Guy, and Jeff Leen. 1990. *Kings of Cocaine.*
Strong, Simon. 1995. *Whitewash: Pablo Escobar and the Cocaine Wars.*

LSD

The abbreviation for lysergic acid diethymalide, LSD is produced from lysergic acid, a substance derived from the ergot fungus found in morning glory seeds. Two Swiss scientists first synthesized the drug in 1938, and five years later, Dr. Albert Hoffman, one of its codiscoverers accidently ingested some of the drug and began experiencing what later became known as "a trip"—that is, a feeling of vertigo, restlessness, and dizziness. When Hoffman closed his eyes, he had fantastic visions of extraordinary vividness accompanied by a kaleidoscopic play of colors,

A scientist at Les Laurentides Mental Hospital in Quebec injects LSD into a spider to study the effects of harmful drugs on its web making abilities. (UPI/Corbis-Bettmann)

a condition that lasted for about two hours. LSD was introduced to the United States in 1949 by the Boston Psychopathic Hospital. The U.S. Army began testing the drug for use as a possible brainwashing agent and as a way of making prisoners talk more readily. It was also stockpiled for possible use against enemies of the United States.

Psychologists began using LSD on themselves and on staff members of mental hospitals in an effort to better understand mental illness. The CIA also became interested in LSD for a short while as a possible truth serum. By 1962 the drug was available on the black market, and concerned authorities began calling for its regulation.

In 1963 Timothy Leary left Harvard University under a cloud of scandal resulting from his use of and research on LSD, and he became the most prominent proponent of the drug in the emerging counterculture of the 1960s, urging people to "tune in, turn on, and drop out." LSD became widely used during the decade. Although its popularity declined after the sixties decade, there are indications that its illicit use is once again on the rise. But while LSD use and experimentation in the 1960s was largely confined to college students and members of the counterculture, studies have shown that its use and abuse have come to include people in a variety of occupations, such as mechanics, plumbers, and longshoremen.

LSD is usually sold in the form of tablets, thin squares of gelatin or impregnated paper (blotted paper). The average effective oral dose is thirty to fifty milligrams, although the amount per dosage amount varies greatly. Tolerance, however, develops rapidly, and the effect of high doses can persist from as long as ten to twelve hours. Street names for LSD include acid, blotter, blue heaven, big D, dose, and microdot, among others.

See also: Clinton, William Jefferson; Controlled Substance; Counterculture; Dass, Baba Ram; Hallucinogens; Huxley, Aldous; Kesey, Ken; Leary, Timothy; United Nations Convention on Psychotropic Substances; United States Comprehensive Crime Control Act of 1970; United Nations Convention Against Illicit Traffic in Narcotic Drugs and Psychotropic Substances
References: Abadinsky, Howard. 1990. *Organized Crime*. Marnell, Tim, ed. 1997. *The Drug Identification Bible*. Schlain, Bruce. 1985. *Acid Dreams*.

Luciano, Charles "Lucky" (1897–1962)

A godfather of the Italian Mafia and one of history's most powerful criminals. Luciano was the founder and the "Boss of Bosses" of a national organized crime syndicate in the 1930s that later became famous as the Italian American Mafia. After World War II, La Cosa Nostra, under the leadership of Luciano, took control of the U.S. heroin market.

In 1935 Luciano was convicted of ninety-one counts of extortion and prostitution and began serving a long prison sentence in New York state. According to some historians, the U.S. government deported him to his native Italy in 1945, reportedly for "services" he had performed for the United States during World War II from his cell. The nature of those services has never been explained, but it is believed that in return for being deported, Luciano agreed to recruit his Mafia friends and colleagues in Sicily and get their help for the allied invasion of Italy.

U.S. authorities had underestimated the Mafia godfather, thinking that he was nothing more than a hood and a thug. Luciano actually had much experience in the heroin trade. In the 1930s he had led his fellow Italian mobsters into the illegal business as a way of controlling his prostitutes. After moving to Italy in the late 1940s and imposing his control over the Sicilian Mafia, Luciano began buying raw opium

from the poppy fields in Turkey, Lebanon and other producing countries, setting up heroin-processing labs in Sicily, and developing a sophisticated drug-smuggling network that transported heroin to markets in the United States and Europe. By 1952 the Federal Bureau of Narcotics (FBN) had revised its estimate of the number of addicts in the country, putting the figure at three times what it was before World War II.

The Italian government finally banned the manufacture of heroin in the early 1950s, when an investigation showed that heroin had been smuggled into the United States from Italy since 1948. That didn't deter the enterprising Italian mob, which devised a new system in which supplies of morphine base were refined to heroin in Marseilles, shipped to Montreal or Sicily, and then sent directly to the United States. This new arrangement became known as the French Connection, and it allowed the Italian Mafia to dominate the heroin trade from the 1950s to the early 1970s. At its peak, the French Connection supplied an estimated ninety-five percent of the heroin distributed to the United States. Luciano died of a heart attack in 1962 in Italy.

See also: French Connection; Heroin; Italian Organized Crime; Morphine; World War II
References: Chepesiuk, Ron. 1999. *Hard Target*. Federa, Sid. 1986. *The Luciano Story*. Weir, William. 1995. *In the Shadow of the Dope Fiend*.

Ludlow, Fitzhugh (1836–1870)

Known as the "hashish eater," Ludlow revealed his experiences with hashish in a book of that title that he published in 1857. Ludlow became famous in the literary world and the drug underworld of the time with his graphic descriptions of his hallucinatory experiences with hashish. According to historian H. Wayne Morgan, despite "the public fascination with his confessional writing friends and critics remembered him as an example of the creative mind that drug use defeated, a warning against experimenting with drugs of enchantment." (Morgan, p. 15)

See also: Hashish
Reference: Morgan, H. Wayne. 1981. *Drugs in America: A Social History, 1800–1980*.

Lupsha, Peter

Lupsha is a professor of political science at the University of New Mexico, where he has taught since

1972. He received his Ph.D. from Stanford University and is an expert in international drug trafficking, as well as political corruption, organized crime, and political violence and terrorism. Lupsha has conducted research and published widely in the field of international drug trafficking. His books include *War on Drugs: Studies in the Failure of U.S. Narcotics Policy* (1981), and (with Kip Shlegel) *The Political Economy of Drug Trafficking: The Herrera Organization (Mexico and the United States)* (1980).

References: Lupsha, Peter. 1981. "Drug Trafficking: Mexico and Colombia in Comparative Perspective." *Journal of International Affairs* (Spring/Summer): 95–115.
———. 1992. *War On Drugs: Studies in The Failure of U.S. Narcotics Policy.*

M

Magic Mushrooms
See Psilocybin

Man with the Golden Arm
This 1955 film is considered Otto Preminger's best directorial effort and Frank Sinatra's best role. It deals with a drug addict who is cured of his addiction and then becomes a jazz drummer, but under life's pressures, he is driven back to his drug habit. With the help of a loyal girl friend, played by actress Kim Novak, Sinatra experiences a difficult rehabilitation and at the film's end begins a new life.

Reference: Sadoul, George. 1972. *Dictionary of Film.*

Mandrax
See Methaqualone

Marijuana
A mixture of leaves, stems, and flowering tips of the hemp plant (*Cannabis sativa*), which contains the psychoactive substance tetrahydrocannabis. Today, the hemp plant grows wild throughout most of the world and can be cultivated in any area having a hot season. Marijuana is considered the world's oldest cultivated nonfood plant and has been used by man for recreational, medical, and religious purposes for thousands of years. Archeologists have found references to marijuana in a Chinese pharmacology treatise dated about 2737 B.C. The hemp plant was introduced to the New World in Chile in 1545 and by 1611 it was being cultivated in Virginia.

In 1850 the U.S. Pharmacopeia listed marijuana as a recognized medicine. By about 1875 "hasheesh houses" modeled after opium dens began to appear. Marijuana was not included in the regulations established by the 1914 Harrison Narcotic Act, and in the 1920s the traffic in marijuana for recreational use began to increase.

The attitude toward marijuana in the U.S. began to change in the 1930s when efforts were made to link the drug to crime. The press published sensational stories about the alleged harmful effects of marijuana. In 1937 the U.S. Congress passed the Marijuana Tax Act, which outlawed the untaxed possession or sale of the drug. Two years later, all legal medical marijuana products were removed from the market. Ironically, the same year, a commission report in New York cleared the drug of the charge of being "criminogenic" and attested to its relative harmlessness.

In 1941 marijuana was dropped from the U.S. Pharmacopeia and the U.S. National Formulary, the two official compendiums of drugs in the United States. During World War II marijuana was cultivated as part of U.S. government policy because Japan had cut off the U.S. supply of hemp fiber from the Philippines in 1942. By 1943, 350,000 acres of marijuana were under cultivation.

Marijuana use continued on a limited scale until the 1960s, when a sharp rise in its use occurred, and there was widespread acceptance of marijuana as harmless when compared to other drugs.

In 1970 federal legislation in the United States re-

A man smoking marijuana, 1984. The U.N. has estimated that there may be as many as 200 million marijuana smokers worldwide. (UPI/Corbis-Bettmann)

duced the penalty for first-time possession of the drug from a felony to a misdemeanor, punishable by less than a year in jail. That same year, the Controlled Substances Act of 1970 made marijuana a Schedule I drug and, even though the sale of it is still a felony, possession of it became a misdemeanor. A Schedule I drug is one that has a high potential for abuse and has no currently accepted medical use in the United States, or where there is a lack of accepted safety for use by someone not under medical supervision. By the 1980s marijuana use had spread to Americans in all states and age groups. Today it is the fourth most abused drug in the world after caffeine, nicotine, and alcohol, and, despite its illegal status, the number of regular users in the United States has been put at about 17 million. By conservative estimates, one-third of the American population over the age of eleven has smoked marijuana at least once.

In the United States much of the attention toward illegal drugs has focused on cocaine and heroin trafficking from abroad. Meanwhile, the domestic pro-

duction of marijuana has quietly flourished. Indeed, marijuana's easy availability has increased substantially in the 1990s, according to the Drug Enforcement Administration. In 1995, the federal agency reported that domestic production of marijuana totaled about 528 tons, up from 129 tons the year before. The value of the United States marijuana crop is staggering, with estimates between $4 billion and $24 billion.

See also: American Council on Drug Education; Arellano Felix, Ramon; Camarena Salazar, Enrique; Camp; Caro Quintero, Rafael; Carter, James Earl; Clinton, William Jefferson; Common Sense for Drug Policy; Controlled Substance; Cuban Connection; Ford, Gerald R.; Frankfurt Resolution; Hallucinogens; Harrison Narcotic Act; Hemp; Legalization; Lehder Rivas, Carlos; Marijuana Tax Act; National Association for Reform of Marijuana Laws (NORML); National Commission on Marijuana and Drug Abuse; Operation Blue Lightning; Operation Cooperation; Operation Hat Trick I; Operation Limelight; Operation Mars; Operation Red River; Operation Reciprocity; Operation Swordfish; Operation Thai-in; Operation Thunderbolt; Operation Vanguard; Opium; Reagan, Ronald; *Reefer Madness*; Steinberg, Donald; Tijuana Cartel; United States Act of 8 March 1946; United States Boggs Act; United States Comprehensive Crime Control Act of 1970

References: Auld, John. 1981. *Marijuana Use and Social Control.*
Gold, M. S. 1989. *Marijuana.*
Schlosser, Eric. 1994. Reefer Madness. *Atlantic Monthly,* August.

Martinez, Bob (1934–   )

Director of the Office of National Drug Control Policy (the drug czar) during the Bush administration from 1991 to 1993. Earlier, Martinez served as mayor of the city of Tampa, Florida, and as Florida's first Hispanic governor from 1987 to 1991. He is now a business development consultant and head of Pro Tech Martinez Company, a Palm Beach-based company that sells satellite systems used to monitor inmates under house arrest.

See also: Drug Czar; United States Office of National Drug Control Policy
References: Dumas, Kitty. 1991. "A Quiet Changing of the Guard." *Congressional Quarterly Weekly Report,* 6 April.
"The Last Czar." 1993. *New Republic,* 1 March.

Martinez Romero, Eduardo (1955–)

At the time of his capture by Colombian authorities in August 1989, Martinez was believed to be a key figure in Medellin Cartel money-laundering operations. The previous March he had been indicted as part of Operation Polar Cap. The seventy-five-page indictment charged that Martinez had acted as a broker in negotiating with money-laundering groups about the cost of laundering the Medellin Cartel's drug proceeds. On 7 September 1989 Colombia extradited him to the United States.

See also: Medellin Cartel; Money Laundering; Operation Polar Cap

Reference: Strobel, Warren. 1989. "U.S. Moves to Extradite Drug Trafficker." *Washington Times*, 23 August.

MAS (Muerte a Secuestradores)

See Ochoa, Marta Nieves

Maspeth Federal Savings and Loan Association (New York City)

This drug money laundering investigation occurred in the early 1980s and involved the smuggling of heroin from Palermo, Sicily, into the United States. Maspeth Savings and Loan was cleared of any criminal wrongdoing, but four employees were convicted in the case. The investigation showed that the Savings and Loan was ignorant of U.S. government regulations regarding individual bank deposits in excess of $10,000. The institution had kept a hand-written record of all transactions over $10,000 since 1957, and this helped authorities to reconstruct evidence that led to the successful prosecution of the defendants. Later, the IRS concluded that Maspeth Federal records were complete and equivalent to government regulatory requirements.

See also: Heroin; Money Laundering

Reference: President's Commission on Organized Crime. 1984. *The Cash Connection: Organized Crime, Financial Institutions and Money Laundering.*

Mathews, Frank

At the height of his power in 1972, when he was just twenty-eight years old, Mathews operated several illegal drug factories in Harlem and Brooklyn and employed at least fifty people. Mathews's base was the "Ponderosa," an apartment building at 925 Prospect Place in Brooklyn that became the nerve center for an extensive drug-trafficking network covering most of the East Coast.

Although Frank Mathews never became a household name like Al Capone or John Gotti, his high-profile lifestyle made him one of the drug world's most interesting characters. Mathews was not afraid to step on the toes of the powerful Italian Mafia, which dominates the crime scene in New York City. He once told members of the powerful Gambino mob family, "Touch one of my people and I'll load my men into cars and drive down Mulberry Street and shoot every wop [Italian] I see." (Kleinknecht 1996) This brashness earned Mathews a place in criminal history as the first African American drug dealer to circumvent the Italian mob's drug distribution network and import his own heroin.

Mathews's brilliant criminal career didn't last long, though. In 1973 he was arrested on drug conspiracy charges after authorities busted some of his associates who were carrying twenty-five pounds of cocaine bound for his operation. The law, however, made the mistake of letting Mathews out on $325,000 bail, and he disappeared with a reported $20 million. The drug trafficker has not been seen since.

See also: Cocaine; Italian American Mafia

Reference: Kleinknecht, William. 1996. *The New Ethnic Mobs: The Changing Face of Organized Crime in America.*

Matta Ballesteros, Juan Ramon (c. 1944–)

A Honduran national who at the time of his arrest in 1988 was wanted by U.S. law enforcement as a leading international drug trafficker who had close ties to the Cali and Medellin Cartels. He and another drug trafficker named Miguel Angel Gallardo are believed responsible for introducing Colombian cocaine refiners to Mexican smugglers and helping to shift the cocaine-smuggling routes in the early 1980s from Florida to California.

Matta Ballesteros grew up in Tegucigalpa, Honduras, and at age sixteen made his way to the United States, where as an illegal immigrant he worked as a farm laborer in Texas and as a supermarket clerk in New York City. He was reportedly deported five times from the United States on charges ranging from pickpocketing to passport fraud to drug trafficking.

U.S. authorities are unsure when Matta Ballesteros started his involvement in drug trafficking, but the first known drug charge against him was filed as early as 1974 in San Diego. He was accused of operating a cocaine laboratory in Honduras and then exporting the semirefined paste to California and Florida.

In Honduras, Matta Ballesteros cultivated the image of a successful businessman who invested large amounts of money in legitimate enterprises, including hotels, factories, and cattle ranches. He operated a tobacco plantation and processing plant that employed several hundred people. In several interviews, Matta Ballesteros denied being a drug trafficker.

Efforts to capture Matta Ballesteros intensified after he was indicted for the murder of Enrique Camarena Salazar, a DEA agent in Mexico, who was abducted off the streets of Guadalajara in 1985. He was one of the four top suspects in the case. U.S. federal authorities thought they had nabbed Matta Ballesteros in May 1985 when he was arrested and jailed in Colombia, but he escaped after paying a bribe estimated to be between $1 million and $2.5 million. He returned to Tegucigulpa, where he bought a house and moved openly in public.

Honduras has no extradition treaty with the United States, but in April 1988, Matta Ballesteros was seized by Honduran military officials and put on a plane bound for the Dominican Republic. The authorities there then put him in the custody of U.S. marshals, who put him on a commercial flight for New York. Later it was revealed that the associate director of the U.S. Marshals Service had traveled secretly to Tegucigulpa to negotiate the plan with senior Honduran military officials that led to the deportation of Matta Ballesteros to the United States.

Matta Ballesteros's arrest and deportation sparked three days of rioting in Honduras. Five people died and the U.S. embassy in the city was burned. In 1990 Matta Ballesteros became the first person convicted for Camarena's murder when he was found guilty of conspiracy to kidnap, torture, and murder the DEA agent. The following year, a federal court sentenced the drug kingpin to three life sentences in prison.

See also: Cali Cartel; Camarena Salazar, Enrique; Extradition; Felix Gallardo, Miguel Angel; Medellin Cartel
References: Collier, Robert. 1985. "Matta, The Honduran Hero." *St. Petersburg (Florida) Times*, 10 April.
"Honduran Trafficker First U.S. Conviction for DEA in Camarena Case." 1990. Associated Press, 27 July.
Rohter, Larry. 1988. "Seized Honduran: Drug Baron or Robin Hood?" *New York Times*, 16 August.
Shannon, Elaine. 1989. *Desperadoes*.

McCaffrey, Barry (1942–)

On 29 February 1996 the U.S. Senate unanimously confirmed McCaffrey as Director of the White House Office of National Drug Control Policy (ONDCP), a position more commonly known as the Drug Czar. Prior to his confirmation, McCaffrey was commander-in-chief of the U.S. Armed Forces Southern Command, which coordinates the United States' national security operations in Latin America. After beginning his military career as a seventeen-year-old cadet at West Point, McCaffrey served the military in various capacities, including as a participant in four combat operations to Vietnam (twice), Iraq, and the Dominican Republic, and as a Joint Chiefs of Staff assistant to General Colin Powell.

As Drug Czar, McCaffrey is a member of the President's Cabinet and is the principal administrative spokesman on matters relating to illicit drug use. His primary duty is to heighten national awareness about the dangers of illicit drugs and to encourage public support for resisting drugs at all levels of society.

See also: Drug Czar; United States Office of National Drug Control Policy; United States Southern Command
References: Barry R. McCaffrey. 1997. *Current Biography* (July): 31.
Office of National Drug Control Policy webpage at http://www.whitehouse.drug.policy.gov/.
Witkin, Gordon. 1997. "The Troubled Reign of the Nation's Drug Czar: The Elusive Quest for Real Power and Respect." *U.S. News and World Report*, 8 September.

McNamara, Joseph

A former police chief of San Jose, California, who has been an outspoken critic of U.S. drug policy, declaring it to be ineffective. McNamara believes prohibitive measures, such as incarceration, and efforts to create drug-free workplaces have created problems for society and led to corruption, tremendous costs, and the erosion of civil liberties. McNamara has recommended that "we should declare the war over," suggesting that "we need to step back," and appoint a national commission to "see how Americans can be more law abiding." (McNamara 1997)

Reference: McNamara, Joseph. 1997. "The Drug War; Violent, Corrupt, and Unsuccessful." *Vital Speeches*, 15 June.

Medellin Cartel

Named after the Colombian city of Medellin (population 1.5 million), the capital of Antioquia province, the Medellin Cartel was the country's most powerful drug-trafficking organization from the mid 1970s to the late 1980s, when it was crippled by the massive manhunt for its godfather, Pablo Escobar Gaviria. The Cartel kept a high profile in its approach to drug trafficking and, in addition to Escobar, it included a number of godfathers or capos who became world famous in the 1980s: Jose Rodriguez Gacha, Carlos Lehder, and the Ochoa brothers (Fabio, Jorge Luis, and Juan David), among the most prominent.

Historically, Medellin had a reputation as a smuggling center for liquor and cigarettes from the United States and stereos, radios, and television sets from the many ports of the Panama Canal Zone. Medellin began to play an important role in the international drug trade in 1973 when Chilean General Augusto Pinochet overthrew Marxist President Salvador Allende and either jailed or deported from Chile numerous drug traffickers who had made Chile the center of the emerging U.S. cocaine trade, although at the time the market for cocaine was small. The trade then moved to Colombia, where criminals like Pablo Escobar and Fabio Ochoa, Sr. (the father of the Ochoa brothers) were eager to expand the cocaine distribution network.

Fabio Ochoa, Sr., who got his start in crime by smuggling whiskey and home electronic appliances, is credited with founding the Medellin cartel around 1978, when Pablo Escobar convinced Fabio to use his well-established and connected smuggling routes for the more profitable drug business. The date of 18 April 1981 may be considered the key date for the Medellin Cartel's establishment. Several drug traffickers, including Jorge Luis Ochoa, Fabio Ochoa, Jr., Pablo Escobar, and Carlos Lehder met at the estate owned by the Ochoa clan to discuss ways to transport cocaine to the United States. By year's end,

the Medellin cartel had supervised at least thirty-eight shipments to the United States, containing about nineteen tons of cocaine. As business picked up other family members and relatives joined the Cartel. The three Ochoa brothers, for example, took over from their father when he decided to retire.

What the Medellin Cartel needed, though, to expand their operation and stay ahead of the competition was a fast, cheap transportation system. That was provided by Carlos Lehder, a flamboyant, unpredictable criminal of Colombian-German background who got his start in crime in the United States. Lehder revolutionized the way drugs were smuggled into the United States and established a monopoly for the Medellin Cartel by retaining a fleet of small cargo planes and high-speed boats that eliminated the middleman or "mule" who had traditionally smuggled cocaine into the United States. The Cartel established routine air corridors in South and Central America and fuel stops in the islands of the Caribbean and Mexico. Transit sites included the Bahamas, Turks, Caico Islands, Jamaica, Mexico, and Nicaragua, which were protected by Cartel employees or independent organizations, including those headed by local government officials.

The planes blended in with the traffic over the Florida Keys, and upon reaching their destination, they either dropped their drug cargos to waiting boats or landed at clandestine air strips in Florida, Georgia, or Alabama. Lehder directed the transportation network from his command post at Norman's Cay in the Bahamas. Once safely in the United States, cocaine shipments were taken to warehouses or stash houses and then distributed and sold to the Cartel's clients.

For a big "service" fee based on weight of the shipment, independent dealers not affiliated with the Medellin Cartel could use the transportation system to get their drugs to the United States. Gilberto Rodriguez Orejuela, a founding member of the Cali Cartel, used his boyhood friendship with Jorge Luis Ochoa to ship an undetermined amount of cocaine through the system to Florida, where he would hire trucks to ship the cocaine to the Cali Cartel's prime market, New York City.

The Medellin Cartel was not afraid of violent confrontation with anyone, including the Colombian government, and it would not hesitate to eliminate any threats to its interests. During the 1980s, the

Pablo Escobar Gaviria, head of the Medellin Cartel and Colombia's most notorious drug dealer, and three of his lieu-tenants are driven in a convoy of jeeps to the Enviagada prison after they surrendered to authorities. (Corbis/Reuters)

Medellin Cartel used bombings and terrorism and hired and trained hit men known as *sicarios* to kill thousands of people, including some of the most prominent figures in Colombian politics: Rodrigo Lara Bonilla, Colombian justice minister, in 1984; Jaime Gomez Ramirez, head of Colombia's National Police Anti-Narcotics Unit, in 1986; Guillermo Cano Isaza, the respected editor of *El Espectador* newspaper, in 1986; and Luis Carlos Galan, presidential candidate, in 1989; among others. The Cali Cartel, on the other hand, diligently cultivated an image as a kinder, gentler mafia that preferred to use the bribe rather than the bullet in doing business. As James Sutton, a Mexico City-based security consultant, explained, "The saying goes that the Medellin Cartel confronts; Cali corrupts." (Chepesiuk 1999, 144)

Differences aside, the Medellin and Cali cartels helped to revolutionize cocaine trafficking, not just in the way the drug was transported to the United States, but also in how it was distributed within the United States. Both cartels established the drug trade on a business model with efficient, well-oiled smuggling, marketing, and money-laundering networks operating from coast to coast in the United States. By 1989 an estimated 300 Colombian trafficking groups and 20,000 Colombians were involved in the cocaine trade in the United States. At least 5,000 of the Colombians who worked for the cartels lived in the Miami area and another 6,000 in the Los Angeles area.

"The Colombians have the momentum by benefit of their early involvement in the cocaine trade," the President's Commission on Organized Crime concluded in 1986. "They have evolved from small, disassociated groups into compartmentalized organizations that are sophisticated and systematized in their approach to the trafficking of cocaine in the U.S." (President's Commission on Organized Crime 1986, 78) According to law enforcement reports, the Medellin Cartel and other Colombian trafficking groups operate as self-centered cells of about five to fifty members with only a handful of the "managers" knowing all the cell's members. Top level managers, both in Colombia and in the United States, are recruited on the basis of blood and marriage, which helps to minimize the potential for theft or disobedience because family member in Colombia are held accountable for drug deals gone bad. Middle managers are placed all over the United States and may include individuals who are not family members, but who are the friends of top-level capos or at least have roots in the same region the capos come from. The third level consists of thousands of workers, both inside and outside the United States—accountants, couriers, chemists, lawyers, stash house keepers, enforcers, body-guards, launderers, pilots, and wholesale distributors—who perform specialized tasks and may work for different groups at different times. Although the cartels are predominantly Colombian in member-

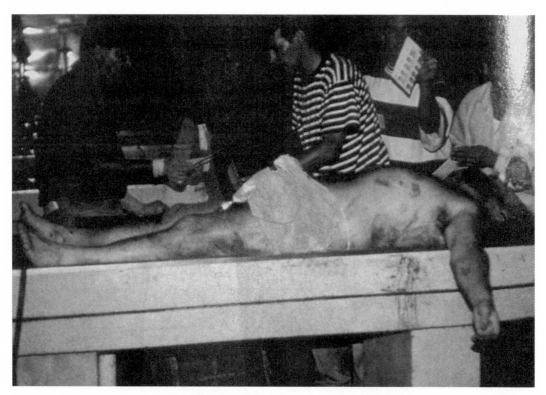

Famous Colombian drug kingpin Pablo Escobar lies dead in the morgue. (Courtesy of the Colombian National Police)

ship, they sometimes go outside their group to hire specialists, such pilots or lawyers, and when need be, do cooperate with other criminal groups, including Mexican, Italian, Jamaican, and Nigerian criminal organizations.

Despite its brilliance in organizing the cocaine trade, the Medellin Cartel's emphasis on violence and narcoterrorism to fulfill its criminal objectives ultimately led to its decline and fall. From 1984 to 1993 the Cartel engaged the Colombian state in a war of attrition. The terror and death toll was largely of Pablo Escobar's making. "Every time there is a major assassination in Colombia, they (the Ochoas) send out word that they aren't behind it," revealed Maria Jimena Duzan, an investigative journalist and columnist with the Bogotá based *El Espectador* newspaper. (Chepesiuk 1987)

The Medellin Cartel, however, paid for its violent ways. On 5 February 1987 an elite Colombian police unit captured Carlos Lehder twenty miles outside of Medellin, the heart of Colombia's cocaine industry and quickly extradited him to the United States, where he was convicted of drug trafficking and given a life sentence plus 135 years in prison. Jose Gonzalo Rodriquez Gacha, who matched Escobar in ruthlessness, was killed in a shootout with police in December 1989, while all three Ochoa brothers, seeing the writing on the wall, turned themselves in and were sent to jail. Medellin's dominance of the cocaine trade ended when Colombian police killed Pablo Escobar in 1993. That left the Cali Cartel to rule supreme over the Empire of Cocaine, until its organization too began to fall apart in the mid-1990s.

In early 1998 the press began reporting about a revival of organized drug activity in the Medellin region by a number of loosely knit, small drug-trafficking groups that—unlike the original Medellin Cartel—shun a high-profile presence, are computer literate, and establish legitimate businesses to front for their illegal operations. Authorities, however, are not calling these organizations cartels. "They go around in taxis, meet in normal places," said Colombian National police chief Rosso Jose Serrano. "You don't see armed people, or those dressed the way they used to, with rings and big chains. They are very subtle." ("Medellin Revives the Drug Trade")

See also: Bank of Commerce and Credit International;
   Blanco De Trujillo, Griselda; Blandon Castillo, Jose; Cali
   Cartel; Cano Izaza, Guillermo; Carter, James Earl;
   Cartelitos; Duzan, Maria Jimena; Escobar Gaviria, Pablo;
   Extraditables; Extradition; Galan, Luis Carlos; Guzman
   Lara, Joaquin; Jamaican Posses; Klein, Yair; Lara Bonilla,
   Rodrigo; Los Quesitos; Mera Mosquera, Eduardo; Mer-
   melstein, Max; Money Laundering; M-19; Mule; Nar-
   coterrorism; Noriega, Manuel Antonio; Norman's Cay;
   Ochoa Vasquez, Jr., Fabio; Ochoa Vasquez, Jorge Luis;
   Ochoa Vasquez, Juan David; Ochoa Vasquez, Marta
   Nieves; Operation Chemcon; Operation College Farm;
   Operation Fountainhead; Operation Polar Cap; Pallo-
   mari, Guillermo Alejandro "Reagan"; Parejo Gonzalez,
   Enrique; Pinochet, Augusto Ugarte; Ramos, Jose Luis;
   Rodriguez Gacha, Jose Gonzalo; Rodriguez Orejuela,
   Gilberto; Roldan, Benardo; Sicarios; Tranquilandia;
   Turbay Ayala, Diana
References: Abadinsky, Howard. 1990. *Organized Crime*.
Castillo, Fabio. 1988. *Los Jinetes De La Cocaina*.
Chepesiuk, Ron. 1999. *Hard Target*.
———. 1987. "Kingpin's Trial Small Win in Losing War on
   Drugs." *Orlando Sentinel*, 4 October.
Eddy, Paul, Hugh Sabogal, and Sarah Walden. 1988. *The
   Cocaine Wars*.
Gugliotta, Guy, and Jeff Leen. 1990. *Kings of Cocaine*.
Strong, Simon. 1995. *Whitewash: Pablo Escobar and the
   Cocaine Wars*.

Medellin without Slums

The name of a social action program started by drug
trafficker Pablo Escobar Gaviria in 1982 to gain him
respectability. The program, Escobar announced,
would lead to the building of a 1,000-unit low-in-
come housing project in a north Medellin landfill to
be known as Barrio Pablo Escobar. It was a shrewd
public relations gimmick that endeared Escobar to
many poor people in Medellin and gave Don Pablo
the status of a folk hero. The outpouring of grief was
so great at Escobar's funeral in December 1993 that it
had to be canceled when an emotional crowd of 5,000
pushed so hard to get into the mortuary to see the late
drug kingpin's body that they shattered the windows.

See also: Escobar Gaviria, Pablo
References: Chepesiuk, Ron. 1999. *Hard Target*.
Gugliotta, Guy, and Jeff Leen. 1990. *Kings of Cocaine*.

Media

Since the early 1980s, deadlines for journalists in
several countries, especially those in Latin America,
have often been literal. According to the Miami-
based Interamerican Press Association, which monitors the media throughout the Western Hemisphere,
drug traffickers and their paramilitary forces are effectively suppressing press freedom in ten countries:
Bolivia, Chile, Colombia, El Salvador, Guatemala,
Guyana, Haiti, Mexico, Paraguay, and Peru. In
Colombia alone, at least sixty-seven journalists were
murdered since the early 1980s. Some of the more
prominent journalists killed by drug traffickers include Diana Turbay, Jesus Blancornelas, Guillermo
Isaza Cano, Manuel De Dios Uanue, and Manuel
Buendia.

Drug-related terrorism of the media has taken
many forms: journalists have been threatened,
beaten, kidnaped. and murdered. Advertisers have
been intimidated, and physical plants and administration centers bombed. Those who have been intimidated include columnists, reporters, publishers,
radio commentators, and television anchormen and
women. Many articles relating to drug trafficking,
especially controversial ones, have appeared without
author attribution. Colombian reporters have re-
sorted to a roundabout technique when they want to
inform the public about drug-related corruption
without incurring the drug lords' wrath. They pass
the information to U.S. colleagues in the hope that it
will be published in newspapers or aired on television there. Once that happens, the Colombian press
picks up the story.

In Colombia journalists have charged that the
Colombian government has violated their press freedom. In the fall of 1996, for example, television news
editors complained that the government ban on television coverage of coca farmers smacked of revenge
for news reports of the drug corruption scandal
plaguing President Ernesto Samper Pizano, who had
been accused of financing his 1994 presidential
campaign with a $6 million "contribution" from the
Cali Cartel.

See also: Blancornelas, Jesus; Buendia, Manuel; Cano Isaza,
   Guillermo; De Dios Unanue, Manuel; Human Rights;
   Turbay, Diana; Webb, Gary
References: Chepesiuk, Ron. 1997. "Colombian Press Under
   Siege." *Editor and Publisher*, 11 May.
———. 1990. "Undermining Democracy: Drug Lords versus
   the Press in Latin America." *New Leader*, 30 April.

Medical Marijuana

Although most people believe that marijuana is a
dangerous drug that should be severely suppressed,

Andrea Nagy, owner of the Ventura County Cannabis Center, tends plants in her indoor nursery where marijuana is grown for medical purposes. Medical marijuana has become a controversial issue in the United States in the 1990s. (Agence France Presse/Corbis-Bettmann)

a growing number of people say physicians should be able to recommend the use of marijuana to patients with life-threatening and debilitating diseases, such as cancer and AIDS. In fact, many doctors are now on record as saying that marijuana has legitimate medical uses. For example, it appears to relieve symptoms of multiple sclerosis, and it helps to reduce nausea and vomiting in cancer patients undergoing chemotherapy. It also stimulates the appetites of those who have lost their desire to eat, such as people suffering the last stages of AIDS, and it may also help those suffering from the eye disease glaucoma, which can cause blindness.

The controversy over medical marijuana use has led to a fierce debate in the United States. Opponents of marijuana as medicine argue that the scientific proof of marijuana's safety and its effectiveness is lacking. Proponents point out that marijuana has been used as medicine over the last millennium.

Opponents counter that the arguments for using marijuana as medicine are seductive and a ploy to lead society through a back door to the legalization of marijuana for recreational use. Proponents answer that it is a cruel and compassionless society that won't allow marijuana to be available to very sick people and to those near death, whose pain and discomfort conventional medicines have failed to relieve. Opponents dismiss that argument, countering that marijuana, unlike other drugs proposed to be used as medicine, has not been put through rigorous scientific trials monitored by the Food and Drug Administration. Proponents say this is nonsense. There is plenty of evidence from doctors and patients who confirm from their own experience that marijuana can help relieve certain forms of suffering when others have failed and the law should not stand in the way.

In the United States the marijuana as medicine issue reached a head in the 1996 elections with the passage of Ballot Proposition 215 in California and Proposition 200 in Arizona. Other states and areas of the country were expected to follow the Arizona and California examples and offer their own initiatives. Washington, D.C., for example, had an initiative on the ballot for the November 1998 election that faced stiff opposition. Washington D.C. Police Chief

Charles H. Ramsey told the press, "Legalizing marijuana under the guise of medicine is a sure-fire prescription for more marijuana on the streets of D.C., more trafficking and abuse, and more drug-related violence in our neighborhoods." (Morgenthau 1997)

After the California and Arizona initiatives passed, General Barry McCaffrey, the U.S. drug czar, publicly warned doctors not to break federal laws by prescribing marijuana. This prompted a group of California physicians to file a lawsuit, claiming that their rights to advise their patients were being infringed upon.

During the 1990s so-called marijuana buyers clubs sprung up to distribute marijuana to members who claimed to be sick. Critics charged that the marijuana clubs were just another scheme to provide a safe place off the street for people to buy marijuana. The U.S. Justice Department brought legal action against six of the clubs for violating the federal law against the distribution of marijuana.

A public health emergency was declared in Oakland, California, after a federal court closed the city's only medical marijuana club, the Oakland Cannabis Buyer's Cooperative, leaving 2,200 patients with no legal source for the drug they claimed quells the pain of AIDS and cancer. In a five-to-four vote, the Oakland City Council allowed officials to develop other means of selling marijuana to people who could no longer get the drug at the club. By October 1998 the Justice Department had closed all but two of California's buyers clubs.

See also: Cannabis Buyer's Club; Frankfurt Resolution; Harm Reduction; Medical Marijuana; National Organization for the Reform of Marijuana Laws (NORML); Soros, George

References: Annas, George J. 1997. "Reefer Madness: The Federal Response to California Medical Marijuana." *New England Journal of Medicine*, 7 August.

Morgenthau, Tom. 1997. "The War Over Weed." *Newsweek*, 3 February.

Rist, Curtis. 1996. "Weed the People." *People's Weekly*, 21 October.

World, Frank S. 1998. "Oakland Marijuana Club Closed By Feds." Associated Press, 15 October.

Meese, Edwin (1931–)

As a counselor to the president (1981–1985) and as the seventy-fifth attorney general of the United States (1985–1988), Meese was one of President Ronald Reagan's staunchest supporters and closet advisors. Meese played an important role in the early history of the War on Drugs as chairman of the Domestic Policy Council and the National Drug Policy Board. Currently, he holds the Ronald Reagan Chair of Public Policy at the Heritage Foundation, a public policy research and education institution and is a distinguished fellow at the Hoover institution.

See also: Ronald Reagan

References: "The Days Dwindle Down for Edwin Meese." 1988. *U.S. News and World Report*, 11 April.
"The Meese Record." 1988. *National Review*, 5 August.

Mejia-Munera, Miguel and Victor

These identical twins, nicknamed "The Twins" or "Los Mellizos," are major Colombian drug traffickers with ties to the Cali and North Valle drug organizations. According to the Drug Enforcement Administration's Thomas A. Constantine, the "DEA believes that the Mejia brothers are 'up and coming' traffickers who will attempt to fill the void created by the arrest of the Rodriguez-Orejuela brothers." ("Organized Crime Syndicates and Their Impact on the United States")

See also: Cali Cartel; Rodriguez Orejuela, Gilberto; Rodriguez Orejuela, Miguel

Reference: U.S. Senate Committee on Foreign Relations. 1998. *International Organized Crime Syndicates and Their Impact on the United States: Hearings before the Subcommittee on Western Hemisphere, Peace Corps, Narcotics and Terrorism*, 26 February (statement of Thomas A. Constantine, Director, DEA).

Mejia Pelaez, Luis Fernando

A Colombian who is believed to have headed a drug-trafficking network that laundered as much as $50 million for the Medellin Cartel through the use of two peso-exchange houses, three auto dealerships, and banks in Tampa, Miami, New York City, and the country of Panama. U.S. Customs agents arrested Mejia Palaez on 12 November 1989, after acting on a 207–count indictment that charged him with laundering $36 million in drug money. Another thirteen people were also arrested on money-laundering charges as the result of the investigation.

See also: Medellin Cartel; Money Laundering

Reference: Anderson, Helmer. 1989. "Alleged Colombian Launderer Captured." United Press International, 1 November.

Meperedine

Better known by the brand name Demerol, meperedine is the first synthetic narcotic ever made. Legally, it is used to control pain, but illegally it has often been used by heroin addicts when the street supply of heroin is low. Chronic users can develop tolerance and dependence for the drug. Classic symptoms include sweating, muscle tremors, vomiting, nausea, and abdominal cramping.

See also: Heroin

References: Marnell, Tim, ed. 1997. *Drug Identification Bible.*

President's Commission on Organized Crime. 1986. *America's Habit: Drug Trafficking and Organized Crime.*

Mera Mosquera, Eduardo (c. 1953–)

A Colombian who was suspected of being an accountant for drug kingpin Jose Gonzalo Rodriguez Gacha. According to Colombian press reports, Mera Mosquera had been convicted in February 1984 of taking part in a drug-trafficking ring operating in the United States, but that he had been released from jail by a bureaucratic error. Two years later Mera Mosquera was arrested in Bogotá but released again when a judge ruled that the authorities had not finished the paper work for his extradition to the United States in the time allotted by law. Colombian police captured Mera Mosquera again in October 1989 at his apartment in Cali.

See also: Extradition; Medellin Cartel; Rodriguez Gacha, Jose Gonzalo

Reference: Yarbro, Stan. 1989. "Authorities Capture Drug Trafficker." Associated Press, 15 October.

Mermelstein, Max

From 1978 to 1985 Mermelstein played a key role in Colombian cocaine trafficking, helping to move a reported fifty-six tons of the drug and $300 million in cash back to Medellin in Colombia. He was the only non-Latino to work as a key advisor to the top kingpins of the Medellin Cartel: Pablo Escobar and the Ochoa brothers.

Mermelstein grew up in a working-class Jewish family in Brooklyn, and was an engineer who earned a good living before getting involved with drug trafficking, trapped by the allure of the money to be made. Mermelstein decided to turn against the Medellin Cartel after he had failed to follow through on an order from his bosses to murder drug informant Barry Seale in 1986. Mermelstein feared for his and his family's lives and entered the Federal Witness Protection Program, becoming a chief government witness against the Cartel.

See also: Escobar Gaviria, Pablo; Medellin Cartel, Ochoa Vasquez, Jr., Fabio; Ochoa Vasquez, Jorge Luis; Ochoa Vasquez, Juan Luis; Seale, Barry Alderman

Reference: Mermelstein, Max. 1990. *The Man Who Made It Snow.*

Mescaline

This drug is found in the peyote cactus, which grows in Mexico and the southwestern United States, and it can also be synthesized in the laboratory. Mescaline is usually taken orally, but it can also be inhaled or ingested. It continues to be used in rituals by the Native American Church. Members of the church can also harvest peyote after first properly documenting their intent with the Texas Department of Public Safety. Street names include buttons, cactus, mescal, mescalito, and dry whiskey. Physical effects include increased heart rate, salivation, respiration, and perspiration, as well as nausea, vomiting, headache, dilated pupils, and lack of coordination, among others. The main dangers associated with the drug are largely psychological in nature and include mood changes and anxiety or panic attacks.

See also: Huxley, Aldous; Peyote

Reference: O'Brien, Robert and Sidney Cohen. 1984. *The Encyclopedia of Drug Abuse.*

Methadone Treatment Programs

Dr. Vincent P. Dole and Marie Nyswander together developed methadone maintenance treatment at Rockefeller University in the 1960s. These programs involve the substitution of the drug methadone, a synthetic narcotic, for heroin in the hope that the drug's user will eventually become free of heroin's dependency.

This approach in drug treatment has been highly controversial from its start because a patient can develop psychological and physical dependency on methadone. Critics say that the treatment merely replaces one addiction with another. Supporters, on the other hand, say the drug helps to stabilize the addict's condition, allowing him or her to relieve the

A nurse at the Interim Clinic in Harlem watches a heroin addict take methadone, 1988. The experimental clinic had such promising results that the federal government gave it permission to operate on a permanent basis. (Corbis/Reuters)

craving in a safe, legal environment where he or she can have access to rehabilitative services and even overcome the addiction.

See also: Benzodiazepine; Buprenorphine, Cocaine; Heroin; Lindesmith Institute; Synthetic Drugs; UCLA Drug Abuse Research Center; United States Comprehensive Crime Control Act of 1970; United States Narcotic Addict Treatment Act of 1971

References: Cooper, Mary H. 1990. *The Business of Drugs.* O'Brien, Robert, and Sidney Cohen. 1984. *The Encyclopedia of Drug Abuse.*

Methamphetamine

Also known as methedrine, methamphetamine is a drug that has stimulant effects on the central nervous system similar to amphetamine, but which are much more pronounced. According to O'Brien and Cohen, methamphetamine "can cause increased activity, increased talkativeness, more energy, less fatigue, decreased food intake, and a general sense of well-being. Injecting the drug intravenously results in the production of a 'rush,' described by some as the best part of the drug effect." (O'Brien & Cohen 1984, 678)

Methamphetamine may also be smoked, snorted, or swallowed. It is legally manufactured as the prescription drug Desoxyn, which is used to treat obesity and attention deficit disorder. Common street names for methamphetamine include meth, crank, speed, crystal meth, and crystal tea.

During World War II Japan made large quantities of methamphetamine available to its troops to keep them alert, but the drug was also released for sale to the Japanese public, and this led to an epidemic of drug abuse that may have involved more than a million users. The first U.S. methamphetamine epidemic occurred in the 1960s in the San Francisco Bay area when a number of physicians prescribed the drug to treat heroin addiction by substituting it for heroin. The availability of illegal synthesized methamphtamine began to become a public health problem in the 1960s when the drug became subject to regulatory controls and the availability to retail pharmacies was curtailed.

The availability of illegal methamphetamine was reduced significantly in the 1970s, but that trend changed in the 1980s as pockets of meth abuse began forming across the United States. In 1988 and 1989 so-called ice began appearing on the illicit drug market. Ice is a potent, smokable form of methamphetamine that gets its name because it resembles rock candy or chips of ice. Ice is smoked in a similar fashion to crack cocaine, and like crack, it provides the user with an immediate, intense high and increased alertness. Ice, however, has resulted in serious adverse effects, addiction, and even death. Researchers say much still needs to be learned about the drug.

Throughout most of its history, methamphetamine has remained a "blue-collar" drug enjoyed by lower classes of blue-collar type workers, and with limited appeal among active drug users. Its manufacture and distribution was largely confined to outlaw motorcycle gangs, but during the 1990s, Mexican cartels began to dominate the illicit trade. United States law enforcement authorities estimate that as of 1998 about 80 percent of the methamphetamine now sold in the United States is either manufactured by Mexican cartels in the United States or made in secret laboratories in Mexico and transported across the border by them. The Juarez Cartel and the Amezcua-Contreras organization have been prominent Mexican groups involved in methamphetamine trafficking. The U.S. labs are primarily located in remote areas of southern or northern California.

Methamphetamine is cheap and easy to make and its manufacture is only limited by the ingenuity of the chemists or "cooks" who make it. Mexican methamphetamine manufacturing labs are reportedly making thirty to sixty pounds of the drug at a time, while the output of the outlaw motorcycle gangs is limited to about ten pounds at a time, which helps to explain the dominance of the Mexican cartels.

Historically, ice distribution and abuse in the United States has been largely confined to Hawaii. The Japanese Yakuza were responsible for servicing the illicit ice market in Hawaii and also for introducing the drug to Japan. United States law enforcement investigations in the late 1990s, however, uncovered a sophisticated group of Philippine nationals who were manufacturing and distributing ice along the East Coast. Although several conspirators have been arrested, the pipeline has remained open. Mexican cartels are also entering the ice-making business. In fact, they were the masterminds of the biggest ice-manufacturing operation ever uncovered on the U.S. mainland.

According to Jeffrey M. Ferguson of the Orange County (California) District Attorney's Office, "The illicit manufacture, distribution and level of abuse of methamphetamine now rivals that of cocaine in our communities on the West Coast (of the U.S.). Meth's spread throughout the U.S., possibly overtaking cocaine, may not be far behind." (Ferguson 1998, 17)

Meanwhile, methamphetamine manufacturing is a highly dangerous activity because the chemicals used in the process are toxic, highly reactive, and often explosive. The waste, moreover, can pose a problem. This has sparked concern about methamphetamine's impact on the environment.

See also: Amezcua Contreras, Jesus; Amphetamine; Bandidos; Arellano Felix, Ramon; Carillo Fuentes, Amado; Crack Cocaine; Environment; Heroin; Juarez Cartel; Operation Desert Stop; Pagans; Synthetic Drugs; Tijuana Cartel; United States Bureau of Narcotics and Dangerous Drugs; United States Domestic Diversion Control Act of 1993; Yakuza

References: Ferguson, Jeffrey M. 1998. "Investigation and Prosecution of Methamphetamine Manufacture." *NarcOfficer* (January–February): 17–22.

Marnell, Tim, ed. 1997. *Drug Identification Bible.*

O'Brien, Robert, and Sidney Cohen. 1984. *The Encyclopedia of Drug Abuse.*

U.S. Drug Enforcement Administration website at http://www.usdoj.gov.DEA/.

Methaqualone

A synthetic depressant first synthesized in 1951 in India as an antimalarial drug and introduced to the American medical market in the mid-1960s for treating insomnia and anxiety. Users initially thought that the drug offered a safe high, but subsequent scientific studies have shown that it has the potential for abuse. The effects can be the same as for alcohol or barbiturates and can lead to death by overdose. A large illegal market for the drug has resulted because doctors have taken note of its potential for abuse and have stopped prescribing it. Large amounts of illegal methaqualone have arrived in the United States from Colombia.

See also: Barbiturates; Quaaludes; Synthetic Drugs; United States Domestic Diversion Control Act of 1993

References: Cooper, Mary H. 1990. *The Business of Drugs.*

O'Brien, Robert, and Sidney Cohen. 1984. *The Encyclopedia of Drug Abuse.*

Methcathinone

A methamphetamine analog (a drug similar to another drug but different in chemical makeup) that goes by "cat," "goob," and a variety of other street names. The drug stimulates the central nervous system, has various negative health effects, and can cause anxiety, paranoia, sleeplessness, convulsions, and visual and audio hallucinations. Methcathinone can either be snorted or taken intravenously.

In early 1991 the Michigan state police made the first seizures of the drug when they busted five illegal laboratories. The following year another six labs were seized. By June 1994 Michigan authorities reported that fifty-two people had been arrested, forty-four had pled guilty, and thirty-two had been sentenced for manufacturing and distributing the drug.

One Drug Enforcement Administration special agent described methcathinone as a "made in Michigan product; it was developed and pushed in Michigan, and spread from there." The DEA moved quickly to address the new drug threat, temporarily putting the drug into Schedule I of the U.S. Controlled Substances Act in 1992 on an emergency basis. Schedule I includes drugs such as LSD, marijuana, and heroin, which the U.S. government considers to have a high potential for abuse and no recognizable medical use. The following year methcathinone was permanently scheduled.

See also: United States Comprehensive Crime Control Act
References: Marnell, Tim, ed. 1997. *Drug Identification Bible.*
U.S. Drug Enforcement Administration website at http://www.usdoj.gov.DEA.

Methedrine
See Methamphetamine

Mexican Federation (La Federation)

A term used by the U.S. Drug Enforcement Administration to refer collectively to the four main drug-trafficking organizations in Mexico (the Juarez Cartel, the Sonora Cartel, the Tijuana Cartel, and the Gulf Cartel) and about a dozen small drug-trafficking groups. Together they gross an estimated $10 to $30 billion annually in drug sales in the United States.

The Federation operates much like a board of directors and somewhat like the "Commission" does for the Italian American Mafia. With the death of Amado Carillo Fuentes in 1997, the Arellano Felix organization (Tijuana Cartel) became the most powerful member of the Federation. According to one source, the Mexican cartels "depend upon *sindicatos familias*, who operate informal, fluid service organizations that join their staffs and resources as they see fit. It is very difficult to track these family cadres, since they shift alliances frequently, and develop a rigid command structure, and operate in a very entrepreneurial fashion." (Ferguson 1998, 18)

See also: Gonzales Calderon, Guillermo; Gulf Cartel; Italian American Mafia; Juarez Cartel; Sonora Cartel; Tijuana Cartel
References: Ferguson, Jeffrey M. 1998. "Investigation and Prosecution of Methamphetamine Manufacture." *NarcOfficer* (January–February): 17–22.
U.S. Drug Enforcement Administration website at http://www.usdoj.gov/DEA/pubs/briefing.

Mexican Mafia

Reported to be the most powerful prison gang in the United States, the Mexican Mafia is primarily composed of convicts and ex-convicts from the barrios of Latino East Los Angeles. Ostensibly, the group took its name out of respect for the Italian American Mafia. Experts say the group's origins can be traced to 1957, when twenty young Mexican Americans from the Maravilla area of East Los Angeles formed a self-protection organization. However, they soon became involved in criminal activities, including narcotics trafficking. The authorities have tried to break the power of the Mexican Mafia by transferring gang members to different prisons, but that has only increased the gang's growth. Authorities estimate that the Mexican Mafia has about 650 members today.

See also: Italian American Mafia
Reference: President's Commission on Organized Crime. 1986. *The Impact of Organized Crime Today.*

Miami River Cops Scandal

In 1985 officers from the Miami Dade Police Department were involved in a scheme to steal cocaine from drug dealers who were off-loading drugs from boats they had anchored on the Miami River. The police would then split up the cocaine among themselves and sell it for a profit, which—during the course of their thievery—amounted to hundreds of thousands of dollars.

In one incident on 28 July 1985, the police surprised six drug dealers off-loading hundreds of kilos of cocaine. The dealers jumped from the boat and three of them drowned. The discovery of the bodies led to an investigation by the Miami Police Homicide Division and the subsequent federal trial of eight Miami police officers, who became known as "the Miami River Cops."

See also: Cocaine
Reference: Eddy, Paul, Hugh Sabogal, and Sarah Walden. 1988. *The Cocaine Wars.*

Michelsen Uribe, Jaime (d. 1998)

A prominent banker and cousin of former Colombian president Alfonso Lopez Michelsen who laundered drug money for the Medellin Cartel. Colombian authorities uncovered a letter in which drug trafficker Carlos Lehder Rivas acknowledged using Michelsen's bank branches to transfer $20 million annually out of Colombia for the Cartel. Michelsen Uribe's banking empire eventually collapsed and the Colombian government took over the administration of the organization's flagship bank, the Bank of Colombia. The banker fled the country for Panama, but he was eventually arrested and sentenced to jail in connection with unlawful activities relating to his bankrupt banking empire. Michelsen Uribe died of cancer in 1998.

See also: Lopez Michelsen, Alfonso; Medellin Cartel; Lehder Rivas, Carlos; Money Laundering
Reference: Strong, Simon. 1995. *Whitewash: Pablo Escobar and the Cocaine Wars.*

M-19 (Movimiento de 19 Abril) (Colombia)

This group, which takes its name from the disputed Colombian election of 1970, was founded in 1974 by Carlos Toledo Plata and Jaime Bateman Cayon as an organization that would promote revolution in Colombia. M-19's goal has been to destabilize the Colombian state through robberies, assassinations, and kidnappings for ransom. However, by the mid-1980s, M-19 had formed a close relationship with Colombian drug-trafficking organizations, and the authorities in the United States and Colombia believed that M-19 was trying to raise funds for its cause through drug smuggling. Its most high profile attack on the Colombian state was the assault on the Palace of Justice in Bogotá in November 1985. It is widely believed that the Medellin Cartel paid M-19 rebels to attack the Palace and burn the extradition case files in the court archives. M-19 remains an active guerrilla group in Colombia battling its government.

See also: Blandon Castillo, Jose; Guillot Lara, Jaime; Herrera Zuleta, Helmer "Pacho"; Medellin Cartel; Narcoguerrillas; Ochoa Vasquez, Marta Nieves; Palace of Justice; Revolutionary Armed Forces of Colombia (FARC)
References: Chepesiuk, Ron. 1997. "Guerrillas in the Midst." *National Review,* 1 September.
Ehrenfeld, Rachel. 1994. *Narcoterrorism.*

Mobile Defense Units (U.S.)

These units are tactical quick-response teams from the U.S. Drug Enforcement Administration, which at the request of a sheriff, police chief, or district attorney are deployed to work in concert with local authorities to dislodge violent drug offenders from the community. In coordination with state and local agencies, the units conduct surveillance, collect intelligence, pursue investigations, and work to obtain arrests. They provide not only agents to support local drug investigations, but also financial assistance and technical support for investigations. The DEA began assigning these units to its divisions across the country in early 1975. In fiscal year 1995 the DEA allocated $3 million to train, equip, and support nineteen teams. About 200 DEA special agents are assigned to the program.

See also: United States Drug Enforcement Administration
References: U.S. Drug Enforcement Administration website at http://www.usdoj/gov/DEA/programs/.

Money Laundering

Money laundering has been defined as "the process through which the existence, illegal source, and unlawful application of illegal gains is concealed or disguised to make the gains appear legitimate, thereby helping to evade detection, prosecution, seizure and taxation." (U.S. General Accounting Office 1991) Drug trafficking has been a big reason why money laundering has become a highly lucrative and extensive global enterprise. No one knows for sure how much dirty drug money is laundered through the world's banking system, but the FBI has put the annual figure at $300 billion worldwide, one-third of which is collected in the United States. Virtually all payments made for drugs are in cash and must be laundered or cleaned so that drug traffickers can create the illusion that the money comes from legitimate sources.

Money laundering can best be described as the nervous system of the international drug trade. "Not all money laundering involves cash from drug sales," explained Robert E. Powis, the author of *The Money Launderers* (1992), "[h]owever, almost all drug sales require some form of money laundering." (Powis 1992, 239)

This is not an easy task, considering the huge amounts of cash involved. In fact, moving the money can be a lot harder than moving the drugs, given the heavy weight and shear bulk of the cash bills. About 450 paper bills weigh one pound, and the money made from a cocaine deal can weigh as much as fifteen to thirty times the weight of its equivalent value in the drug.

In the 1960s and 1970s, when the profits were not as huge as they became later, drug traffickers used couriers known as "smurfs," a nickname based on popular cartoon characters that reflected the couriers' relative unimportance in the Colombian cocaine trade. The smurfs simply deposited the money, most of which came from street-level deals, in a nearby bank. In 1970 the federal government made its first effort to detect large cash deposits by passing the

Families of employees from the Bank of Credit and Commerce International in London protest outside Britain's High Court, 30 July 1991. The BCCI became involved in one of history's biggest money laundering scandals. (Corbis/Reuters)

Bank Secrecy Act of 1970, which requires banks and other financial institutions to report large domestic transactions of more than $10,000 to the U.S. Treasury Department. Failure to do so by a financial institution can lead to prosecution and confiscation of the money. Since 1970 enforcement of the Act in the United States has been progressively tightened. In 1980, for example, the Treasury rules were changed, requiring all banks to file Currency Transaction Reports (CTRs) with the U.S. government.

Not until the mid-1980s, however, did the financial institutions begin to take the legal change seriously. That happened after several highly publicized cases, most involving drug money, that gave prominent banks widespread and unfavorable notoriety.

Remarkably, money laundering was not a crime until 1986, a watershed year in money laundering history, when, as part of the Anti-Drug Act, the U.S. Congress passed the Money Laundering Control Act of 1986 as an effort to close the loophole that allowed financial institutions to avoid the reporting requirements. Also in 1986 President Reagan stepped up his offensive against drug trafficking by signing Na-

tional Security Decision Directive Number 221, which made drug enforcement a national security issue and put drug trafficking on the international agenda. Banks, corporations, and individuals who operated in money-laundering haven countries like Panama, Aruba, Hong Kong, and the Turks and Caicos Islands learned that their assets could be subject to freezing and forfeiture. Two years later the so-called Kerry Amendment to the Anti-Drug Abuse Act of 1988 brought all financial institutions, wherever located, under the umbrella of the U.S. currency transactions reporting system set up under the 1970 Bank Security Act.

Between 1986 and 1992 a total of 290 accountants, 151 certified public accountants, and 225 attorneys were charged with laundering drug money. Most were convicted and the U.S. banking community realized that under the new money-laundering legislation banking officials were courting trouble if they failed to recognize or allowed transactions that might involve money laundering activity. Consequently, banks became more vigilant, training employees to spot suspicious transactions and developing deterrence measures like "Know Your Customer" programs that provide for identification of individuals who make use of the bank's services. By 1992 it was costing U.S. banks as much as $136 million annually to complete currency transaction reports for the government. The tougher legislation was costing drug traffickers, too. Experts estimated that by the mid-1980s, the cost of full-service money laundering of drug money had risen from 6 percent to a maximum of 26 percent.

The crackdown forced the drug traffickers to change their money-laundering practices and become more sophisticated. No longer did the traffickers employ the bold practice of hauling sacks of money into banks. Being the innovative entrepreneurs they are, the drug lords simply changed their modus operandi of doing business. The major drug-trafficking organizations began to turn to money-laundering specialists, money brokers, or independent contractors, who knew the methods and techniques needed to move large sources of cash, but who were not necessarily involved in drug trafficking. Many of these specialists are white-collar professionals—bankers, lawyers, and accountants—who often don't have criminal records and don't consider themselves part of a criminal drug-trafficking syndicate.

The Cali Cartel reportedly uses ambitious money brokers in Colombia who bid competitively for the right to move large amounts of cash from cocaine sales to Colombia. The brokers have to show that they are bonded; that is, that they have enough financial resources to reimburse the drug traffickers if their cash load is stolen by competitors or seized by the police.

David Andelman describes how a typical contract might work: "Each time a million dollars has to be moved from a particular city in the United States, bids are taken. For a lot of $1 million, the money launderers guarantee the cartel's accountant $900,000, or whatever bid is fixed. The launderer delivers the $900,000 to Bogotá, generally in Colombian pesos or perhaps in merchandise that is quickly sold for pesos, and later takes possession of the dollars in New York or Los Angeles or Miami. It is then up to the launderer to get the full million dollars out of the U.S. His profit is $100,000 minus expenses." (Andelman 1994, 94)

By the late 1980s the drug traffickers were using a variety of different money-laundering schemes, many of which were able to avoid banks. They included dummy corporations at home and abroad, postal money orders, international transfer of funds, letters of credit for off-shore banks, dollar-exchange houses, and a shadow banking system of cash-laundering outlets. Drug traffickers, moreover, now electronically launder much of their money, making use of the Internet.

Keeping track of this movement of money is complicated, given the size and scope of the transactions. In 1990 the Clearing House Interbank Payment System, the primary wholesale international electronic funds transfer system, processed about 37 million money transfers valued at $222 trillion between the United States and international banks.

Mexico, more than any country, has been a major conduit for the money-laundering activities of Latin American drug-trafficking syndicates. It's a natural relationship, given the country's proximity to the U.S. border, its high level of corruption, and the fact that money laundering is not a crime there. Traffickers have used aging airplanes to fly money out of the United States to Mexico, slipped money through tunnels under the border, employed trucks and cars that bring drugs into the United States and then are used to transport laundered cash from stash houses to Mexico, and exploited the numerous, mostly unregulated Mexican dollar-exchange houses, the *casas de cambio*, which are located along the border. According to the U.S. Treasury Department's Financial Crime Enforcement Network (FINCEN), as much as $10 billion, 75 to 90 percent of the Latin American drug traffickers' annual revenue, passes through Mexico annually.

Nearby Caribbean countries—Aruba, the Bahamas, and the Cayman Islands, for example—have long been the target of U.S. scrutiny and investigation. Several islands in other parts of the world, including the Channel Islands and the Isle of Man off the coast of England, also operate as money-laundering havens for drug traffickers. At least fifty countries have tight secrecy on their financial transactions, a feature that makes them prime havens for money laundering. As big economic and political changes swept the globe in the 1990s, many other countries, especially those in eastern Europe, have become easy money-laundering targets for drug traffickers.

Although tight bank secrecy has been a problem in combating money laundering, at least one major banking country has changed its policy. In 1994 Switzerland's legislature passed a law that would allow the country's banks to report suspected illegal transactions without fear of breaking bank secrecy laws.

To combat drug trafficking, the United States has established bilateral treaties and arrangements with several countries since the 1980s, which has led to the exchange of valuable information on money-laundering investigations. In October 1996 Mexico and Texas signed a unique agreement in which they pledged to combat money laundering together. Among other measures, the agreement designated Mexican representatives in Texas to serve as official liaisons with Texas authorities. The agreement reflected the growing concern of Mexico and the United States about the challenges they were going to face in the years ahead, as the remaining trade barriers between the two countries are phased out under the North American Free Trade Agreement (NAFTA).

In October 1995 the United States announced that it would freeze the assets of individuals and companies in the United States that it identified as being associated with the Cali Cartel. Among those identified were four principal figures in the Cali Cartel, three businesses, and forty-three other individuals. By April 1997 the number had reached 416 businesses and individuals that the U.S. government said were connected to the Cartel.

For years the United States had suspected the Colombian cartels operating in New York City of sending millions of dollars a year back to Colombia through the store-front shops known as *casas de cambio*. The U.S. government looked upon the federal requirement that transactions of more than $10,000 be reported as a hindrance to its efforts to combat money laundering. So in May 1997 the government announced that the 25,000 casas de cambio in the United States would have to inform the federal government of any transaction over $750. The United States has also joined with other countries to seize assets and shut down operations of banks suspected to be involved with money laundering.

The United States' lead and its influence have certainly pushed the international community to move forcefully against drug money laundering and

has led to more effective cooperation today among law enforcement agencies internationally than a decade ago. The cost of doing business for the drug cartels, moreover, has gone up substantially. Still, the criminal entrepreneurs have managed to adapt to tougher times, using the new technology and cyberspace to track their drug profits and launder it more efficiently.

See also: Anderson, Robert A.; Bank of Commerce and Credit International; Bank Secrecy Act of 1970 (U.S.); Basel Convention; Cali Cartel; Carrera Fuentes, Adrian; Casas De Cambio; Chemical Bank of the United States (New York City); Cocaine; Currency Transaction Reports; Financial Crime Enforcement Network; Free Trade; Garfield Bank; Liu Chong Hong Kong Bank (Hong Kong and New York); Maspeth Federal Savings and Loan Association (New York City and Hong Kong); Medellin Cartel; Mejia Pelaez, Luis Fernando; Michelsen Uribe, Jaime; Money Laundering Control Act of 1986; Moran, William C.; Nasser David, Julio; Nigerian Organized Crime; Offshore Centers; Operation Casablanca; Operation C-Chase; Operation College Farm; Operation Dinero; Operation Greenback; Operation Polar Cap; Operation Royal Flush; Operation Tradewind; Operation Wipeout; Organization of American States; Outlaws; Palma, Manuel; People's Liberty Bank (U.S.); Pizza Connection; United Nations Convention against the Illicit Traffic in Narcotic Drugs and Psychotropic Substances of 1988; United Nations Prevention and Criminal Justice Division; United Nations Vienna Convention; United States International Narcotics Control Act of 1992; Weinig, Harvey; Yakuza

References:

Andelman, David A. 1994. "The Drug Money Maze." *Foreign Affairs* (July): 94–108.

Ehrenfeld, Rachel. 1992. *Evil Money.*

Florez, Carl P., and Bernadette Boyce. 1990. "Laundering Dirty Money." *FBI Law Enforcement Bulletin* (April): 22–25.

Powis, Robert E. 1992. *The Money Launderers.*

President's Commission on Organized Crime. 1984. *The Cash Connection: Organized Crime, Financial Institutions and Money Laundering.*

Robinson, Jeffrey. 1990. *The Laundrymen.*

U.S. General Accounting Office. 1991. *Money Laundering: The U.S. Government Is Responding to the Problem.*

Monitoring the Future Study (U.S.)

Established in 1978, the Monitoring the Future (MTF) study is a drug use research mechanism used by the National Institute of Health to determine and analyze drug use and abuse trends in the United States. The study involves a national representative survey that is administered annually to twelfth-grade students. The MTF survey inquires about the students' drug use, attitudes toward drugs, and perceptions about drug availability and harm. The survey covers past month, past year, and lifetime use of more than ten drugs.

References: U.S. General Accounting Office. 1998. *Emerging Drug Problems.*

Montoya Sanchez, Diego

The reputed head of the North Valle drug-trafficking organization in Colombia, who the U.S. Drug Enforcement Administration says transports cocaine base from Peru to Colombia and produces large quantities of cocaine for export to the United States and Europe. As of 1998 the DEA considered Montoya Sanchez one of Colombia's most important drug traffickers.

See also: Cocaine
Reference: U.S. Senate Committee on Foreign Relations. 1998. *International Organized Crime Syndicates and Their Impact on the United States: Hearings before the Subcommittee on Western Hemisphere, Peace Corps, Narcotics and Terrorism,* 26 February (statement of Thomas A. Constantine, Director, DEA).

Moran, William C. (1939–   )

A criminal defense lawyer who was named in a U.S. government indictment (along with two other criminal defense lawyers, including a former high-level U.S. Justice Department official and fifty others) and charged with being a member of a racketeering enterprise that centered on the Rodriguez Orejuela branch of the Cali Cartel. Moran was named in the indictment for, among other charges, revealing the identity of a government witness to his client. The informant was later murdered. After his conviction in August 1998 Moran became a fugitive, but was apprehended in Mexico and is awaiting trial.

See also: Abbell, Michael; Assets Forfeiture; Cali Cartel; Money Laundering; Rodriguez Orejuela, Gilberto; Rodriguez Orejuela, Miguel
References: Chepesiuk, Ron. 1997. "Guilty By Association?" *Student Lawyer.*
McGee, Jim. 1995. "Ex-Prosecutors Indicted in the Cali Cartel Probe." *Washington Post,* 4 July.

Morphine

A narcotic analgesic and the principal alkaloid of opium, morphine was first isolated in 1803 by a German pharmacist named Serturner, who named the drug after morpheus, the Greek god of sleep and dreams. Morphine is many times more powerful than opium; in fact, it takes ten parts of opium to produce one part of morphine. Still, morphine was once thought to be a cure for opium addiction that didn't produce negative side effects.

In 1853 the hypodermic needle was introduced and used to inject morphine. The American Civil War popularized morphine when doctors used the drug intravenously and indiscriminately to treat battlefield casualties, creating an estimated 400,000 addicts. In the 1870s the Franco-Prussian War in Europe created more addicts. By that time, morphine was being carried in pharmacies and general stores in the United States, and it became widely popular for the treatment of ailments ranging from toothaches to consumption.

In 1889 Henrich Dresser isolated heroin from morphine. Heroin was initially thought to be less addictive than morphine, but by the late 1920s addicts were favoring its use over opium because of its high potency and easier illegal availability. In 1970 prescriptions containing morphine were classified as Schedule II and III under the Controlled Substances Act of 1970. Schedule II drugs are those having a high potential for abuse, a currently accepted use in treatment in the United States, or currently accepted medical use with severe restrictions, or where the abuse of the drug will lead to psychological and physical dependence. Schedule III drugs have less potential for abuse than drugs on Schedules I and II, the drug has currently accepted medical use in treatment in the United States, and abuse of the drug will lead to low physical dependence or high psychological dependence. By the 1980s morphine rarely appeared on the illegal market, and people addicted to the drug were usually members of the medical and hospital establishments.

See also: Burroughs, William S.; Heroin; Cocaine; *Linder v. United States*; Opium; Oxycodone; Rothstein, Arnold; Spanish American War; United States Comprehensive Crime Control Act of 1970; Weinig, Henry
References: Cooper, Mary H. 1990. *The Business of Drugs.*
Musto, David. 1991. "Opium, Cocaine and Marijuana in U.S. History." *Scientific American* (July): 40.

Morrison, Jim (1943–1971)

Leader and creative force behind the influential 1960s rock band The Doors. Morrison became known for his outrageous behavior at concerts and for his reckless lifestyle that was marked by drug and alcohol abuse. On 3 July 1971, Morrison died of heart failure in the bathtub of his home in Paris, France. Morrison's death was one of the high-profile examples of the consequences of the drug excesses of the 1960s.

Reference: Hopkins, Jerry, and Danny Sugerman. 1980. *No One Gets out of Here Alive.*

Movimiento 19 Abril (Colombia)

See M-19

Mule

A person who carries drugs illegally and on his person from one country to another. This method of drug trafficking has become less important with the increased sophistication in the way traffickers can transport drugs via sea and air.

See also: Medellin Cartel; Nigerian Organized Crime; Santacruz Londono, Jose
Reference: Chepesiuk, Ron. 1999. *Hard Target.*

Mullen, Frances (1943–   )

Director of the U.S. Drug Enforcement Administration from July 1981, when he was named acting administrator by Attorney General William French Smith, until March 1985. He was then nominated for that position by President Ronald Reagan and confirmed by the U.S. Senate on 7 October 1983. Mullen served in the U.S Air Force from 1953 to 1957 before returning to school and earning a bachelor of science degree in history and education from Central Connecticut State College. Mullen joined the FBI as a special agent in 1962, and by 1980 he had risen to executive assistant director of investigations, one of the FBI's top three management positions. His responsibilities involved supervision over all of the FBI's intelligence and criminal investigative operations.

FBI Director William Webster convinced Mullen to leave that position to head the DEA and coordinate the government's new plan to share responsibility between the two agencies in the drug enforcement area.

Mullen had a difficult time in the confirmation process because of his handling of the Abscam investigation and the FBI background check of Raymond J. Donovan, who became U.S. Secretary of Labor. Mullen, however, is credited with getting closer cooperation with the FBI on such matters as wiretaps and criminal investigations.

See also: Reagan, Ronald; United States Drug Enforcement Administration; United States Federal Bureau of Investigation
Reference: Lardner, George. 1982. "FBI Withholds Files It Had on Donovan." *Washington Post,* 6 June.

Munoz Talavara, Rafael

Described by the U.S. Drug Enforcement Administration as an emerging drug kingpin, Munoz Talavara was believed to be a top associate of the Arellano Felix gang, although he repeatedly denied he was a drug trafficker. Munoz Talavera was vying to replace Amado Carillo Fuentes as head of the Juarez Cartel when he was found slumped in the back seat of a Jeep Cherokee in a Ciudad Juarez suburb on 10 September 1998. He had been shot four times in the head and heart.

In 1996 Mexican authorities angered the DEA when they released Munoz Talavera from jail after he had only served three-and-a-half years of a fifteen-year sentence. Munoz Talavera's murder prompted fears of a possible blood bath between rival Mexican drug gangs.

See also: Arellano Felix, Ramon; Carillo Fuentes, Amado; Juarez Cartel
Reference: "Slaying Ignites Fear of Mexican Drug War." 1998. *Miami Herald,* 12 September.

Musto, David F. (1936–   )

Professor of psychiatry at the Child Study Center, professor of history of medicine at Yale University, and a leading authority on the history of drugs, which he began studying in the 1960s while working at the National Institute of Mental Health. He has served as a consultant for several national organizations, including the President's Commission on the HIV Epidemic. Musto is author of *The American Disease: Origins of Narcotic Control.*

See also: Carter, James Earl
References: Musto, David F. 1987. *The American Disease: The Origin of Narcotic Control*
———. 1991. "Opium, Cocaine and Marijuana in American History." *Scientific American* (July): 40.

Mutual Legal Assistance Treaty

This treaty between the U.S. and Mexico enables each country to obtain information from the other in a form that allows it to be admissible in their respective court systems. According to Harold Wankel, chief of operations at the U.S. Drug Enforcement Administration, "This streamlined process permits swifter exchange of evidence than is possible through other mechanisms of international evidence sharing." (Wenkel 1996)

Reference: Wankel, Harold D. 1996. "Drug Control along the U.S. Border." Testimony before U.S. House Judiciary Committee, U.S. Drug Enforcement Administration website, http://www.usdoj/dea/pubs/cngrtest.

N

Nadelmann, Ethan (c. 1953–)

A former professor of politics and public policy at Princeton University, Nadelmann is today a prominent and crusading advocate for harm reduction, the alternative approach to the War on Drugs that seeks to decrease the harm caused by drug abuse and drug trafficking. From 1984 to 1985, Nadelmann served as a narcotics policy consultant to the U.S. State Department, but in June 1987 he shocked a drug policy conference at Bolling Air Force base, near Washington, D.C., by comparing current U.S. drug policy to the prohibitionist policy toward alcohol in the 1920s. In 1996 he became an important consultant to the successful Arizona and California medical marijuana election initiatives.

In 1997 Nadelmann told *Rolling Stone* magazine, "We [opponents of U.S. drug policy] are like the gay-rights movement was in the early to mid-1990s, where the Civil Rights movement was in the 1960s. Nevertheless, there is a rising sense of frustration." (Dreyfuss 1997, 50)

See also: Harm Reduction; Lindesmith Institute; Medical Marijuana; Prohibition
Reference: Dreyfuss, Robert. 1997. "Hawks and Doves: Who's Who in the War on Drugs." *Rolling Stone*, 7 August.

NAFTA
See Free Trade

Narcocassettes

Cassette recordings consisting of Colombian police intercepts and wiretaps on which Miguel Rodriguez Orejuela, a leader in the Cali Cartel tells an associate that he has arranged to give millions of dollars to Ernesto Samper Pizano's presidential campaign. In effect, one of the two leading candidates in Colombia's 1994 presidential elections was apparently being financed by drug-trafficking money. After Samper squeaked to victory in the closest presidential vote in Colombia's history, the tapes were leaked to a Colombian television station and played on the air on 20 June 1994. The tapes became infamous across Colombia as the "narcocassettes."

See also: Botero Zea, Fernando; Cali Cartel; Pastrana Arango, Andres; Toft, Joe
References: Chepesiuk, Ron. 1997. "Narco-Paralysis in Colombia: A War on Attrition." *New Leader*, 13 January.
———. 1996. "Colombia, Still There." *The Economist*, 1 June.

Narcodemocracy

A term used to describe democratic countries, most notably Colombia and Mexico, whose economic, political, and social institutions have been penetrated, corrupted, and damaged by the influence, money, and power of drug-trafficking organizations. In 1994, for example, a senior U.S. official told *Time* magazine that the United States was deeply worried about a narcodemocracy developing in Colombia. The official was responding to reports that the Cali

The scene after a truck loaded with explosives blew up in front of a police station in Fontibon, west of Bogotá in Colombia, leaving 8 people dead and 10 wounded, 16 June 1997. (Agence France Presse/Corbis-Bettmann)

Cartel was trying to channel money into the Colombian presidential campaigns of candidates Ernesto Samper Pizano and Andres Pastrana Arango. Over the years, Mexico and Bolivia have also been described as narcodemocracies.

See also: Cali Cartel; Pastrana Arango, Andres; Samper Pizano, Ernesto; Toft, Joe
Reference: "Birth of a Narcodemocracy?" 1994. *Time*, 11 April.

Narcoguerrillas

A term used to refer to guerrilla groups actively engaged in the international drug trade. Examples of narcoguerrilla groups include the Kurdish Worker's Party, M-19, Revolutionary Armed Forces of Colombia, and the Shining Path Guerrilla Movement.

See also: Carter, James Earl; Kurdish Worker's Party; M-19; Revolutionary Armed Forces of Colombia (FARC); Shining Path Guerrilla Movement; Vietnam War
Reference: Chepesiuk, Ron. 1997. "Guerrillas in the Midst." *National Review*, 1 September.

Narcoterrorism

The term used to describe the violent action of drug-trafficking cartels against governments that seek to disrupt their criminal activities. The most graphic example of narcoterrorism occurred in Colombia in the 1980s when the Medellin Cartel, principally under the direction of Pablo Escobar Gaviria and Jose Gonzalo Rodriguez Gacha, launched a terrorist campaign against the Colombian government that involved the assassination of police, judges, and journalists, and the bombing of government buildings. The drug traffickers hoped to prevent its members from being tried and prosecuted in the Colombian court system and from being extradited to the United States for trial.

See also: Barco Vargas, Virgilio; Contras; Cuevas Ramirez, Nelson; Escobar Gaviria, Pablo; Extradition; Medellin Cartel; Rodriguez Gacha, Jose Gonzalo; Sicarios
Reference: Ehrenfeld, Rachel. 1994. *Narcoterrorism and the Cuban Circuit.*

Narcotics Anonymous

Founded in 1953 in New York City, this self-help organization helps individuals to recover from drug addiction by encouraging its members to follow a 12–step rehabilitation similar to the one used by Alcoholics Anonymous (AA). But although its origins and strategies reflect those employed by AA, it has developed its own path to dealing with drug addiction. As the group spread from New York City to other cities, it developed a strategy that encouraged cooperation but not affiliation with AA.

Reference: Cooper, Mary H. 1990. *The Business of Drugs.* Narcotics Anonymous website at http://www.wsoinc.com/.

Nasser David, Julio Cesar

The head of a major drug-trafficking and money-laundering organization, which was based on Colombia's north coast. Nasser David's organization was known for using containerized cargo ships to smuggle huge amounts of cocaine and marijuana. Colombian National Police arrested Nasser David in April 1997.

See also: Cocaine; Heroin; Money Laundering
Reference: U.S. Senate Committee on Foreign Relations. 1998. *International Organized Crime Syndicates and Their Impact on the United States: Hearings before the Subcommittee on Western Hemisphere, Peace Corps, Narcotics and Terrorism,* 26 February (statement of Thomas A. Constantine, Director, DEA, before the Foreign Relations Committee on Western Hemisphere, Peace Corps, Narcotics and Terrorism (DEA website: http:/www.usdoj.gn/dea/pubs/cngrtest).

National Alliance for Methadone Advocates (U.S.)

Based in New York City, this organization's objective is to promote methadone maintenance treatment as the most effective procedure for treating heroin addiction and to destigmatize methadone maintenance as a way of combating heroin addiction.

See also: Heroin; Methadone Treatment Programs
Reference: National Alliance for Methadone Advocates website at http://www.methadone.org/.

National Association of Alcohol and Drug Abuse Counselors (NAADAC)

Founded in 1972, the NAADAC is the largest national organization for alcoholism and drug abuse professionals in the United States. The organization's objectives are to increase general awareness about alcoholism and drug abuse and to improve the care of people through treatment, education, and prevention programs. Its basic philosophy is that drug dependency must be treated primarily as a public health problem. The NAADAC has played an important role in U.S. public health policy and its leaders have been consulted for their opinions on legislation and public policy issues of importance to the drug treatment field.

Reference: National Association of Alcohol and Drug Abuse Counselors website at http://www.naadac.org/.

National Clearinghouse for Alcohol and Drug Abuse Information (U.S.)

This is the information service of the Center for Substance Abuse Prevention, which is located in the Substance Abuse and Mental Health Services Administration of the U.S. Department of Health and Human Services. As the world's largest resource of current information and materials concerning substance abuse, this federal agency is the focal point for information on drugs and other substance abuse and provides information through publications and a computerized information service that is tailored for use by parents, teachers, youth, communities, and prevention/treatment professionals.

Reference: National Clearinghouse for Alcohol and Drug Abuse Information website at http://www.health.org.

National Commission on Marijuana and Drug Abuse (U.S.)

Sponsored by Representative Ed Koch (D-NY) as a provision of the Comprehensive Control Act of 1970, this commission consisted of thirteen members, nine of whom were appointed by Richard Nixon, and was organized as a response to reports in the media and in congressional hearings that marijuana was not addictive and that the penalties for its use were too harsh. In its March 1973 report, the Commission challenged the government's current marijuana policy, arguing that "there is no evidence that experimental or intermittent use of marijuana causes physical or psychological harm. The risk lies instead in the heavy, long-term use of the drug, particularly the most potent preparations. Marijuana does not lead to physical dependency. No brain damage has been documented leading to marijuana use, in contrast to the well-established damage of chronic alcoholism."

The Commission recommended that possession of marijuana be decriminalized, while growing and selling marijuana for profit should remain a criminal offense. Several prominent organizations endorsed the Commission's proposals, including the Consumers Union, the American Academy of Pediatrics, the American Medical Association, the National Education Association, the American Bar Association, and the American Public Health Association.

See also: Decriminalization; Harm Reduction; Legalization; Marijuana; United States Comprehensive Crime Control Act of 1970

References: Anderson, Patrick. 1981. *High in America: The True Story Behind NORML and the Politics of Marijuana.* Himmelstein, Jerome L. 1983. *The Strange Career of Marijuana: Politics and Ideology of Drug Control in America.*

National Council on Alcoholism and Drug Dependence, Inc. (NCADD)

Founded in 1944, the NCADD is a volunteer health organization with a national network of affiliates that provides education, information, and assistance in the battle against alcoholism and other drug addictions. As the United States' major public health advocate for the prevention and treatment of alcohol and other drug problems, it works through hundreds of local affiliate councils and state councils. NCADD has established a reputation as an important force in the nation's development of service systems and health policy related to drug problems.

Reference: National Council on Alcoholism and Drug Dependence website at http://www.ncadd.org.

National Drug Control Strategy (U.S.)

Developed and published by the Office of National Drug Control Policy (ONDCP), this report outlines a ten-year conceptual framework to reduce illegal drug use and availability in the United States. The goal is a fifty percent reduction by the year 2007.

See also: United States Office of National Drug Control Policy

Reference: Office of National Drug Control Policy website at http://www.whitehouse.drug.policy.gov/.

National Drug Enforcement Officers Association (NDEAO)

The U.S. Bureau of Narcotics and Dangerous Drugs (BNDD) graduated its first national academy class

for state and local officers in 1970. The same year, graduates of the first National Drug Academy class founded the Law Enforcement Officers Alumni Association (LEOAA) to develop a network for sharing intelligence information, to maintain friendships that evolved during training, and to foster interagency development at all levels of government. While the BNDD evolved into the Drug Enforcement Administration and the LEOAA into the NDEAO, the organization's original objectives have remained the same.

See also: United States Bureau of Narcotics and Dangerous Drugs; United States Drug Enforcement Agency

References: National Drug Enforcement Officers Association website at http://www.ndeoa.org/.

National Drug Trade Conference

An ad hoc United States-based lobbying group active in the early twentieth century that kept close watch on U.S. government regulation of the narcotics market and worked to eliminate the provisions of the bill leading to the enactment of the 1914 Harrison Narcotic Act, which they considered too stringent.

See also: Harrison Narcotic Act

Reference: Courtnay, David. 1982. *Dark Paradise.*

National Families in Action

Founded in 1977, this group consists of parents and other adults who are concerned about drug use and want to prevent drug abuse. The group has the following objectives: to educate parents, children, and others in the community about drug use; to seek ways to stop drug use; and to look for ways to counteract the social pressures contributing to drug use. To promote its objectives, the organization maintains a collection of 500,000 documents, films, and videos relating to drug abuse.

In 1995 this group collaborated with Atlanta mayor Bill Campbell to produce the Atlanta Resolution, a nonbinding agreement signed by 300 U.S. mayors in which they declared their opposition to all forms of drug legalization. National Families in Action also led a boycott of Calvin Klein products, maintaining that the designer glamorizes drugs through the promotion of his products. The group is credited with playing a pivotal role in helping drug use diminish in the 1970s. Citizens from other countries wanting to develop prevention groups increasingly call upon this group for help.

See also: Legalization
Reference: Dreyfuss, Robert. 1997. "Hawks and Doves: Who's Who in the World of Drugs." *Rolling Stone*, 7 August.

National Household Survey on Drug Abuse (NHSDA)

First conducted in 1971, the NHSDA is a national probability sample of household members twelve years and older in which respondents are interviewed about their current and past use of a wide sample of legal and illegal drugs, including alcohol. The Substance Abuse and Mental Health Services Administration supports the survey. Statistics from the survey are used by the federal government to plan future policy and establish funding priorities related to substance abuse. The survey's primary purpose is to estimate the prevalence of illegal drug use (the number of people using illegal drugs) in the United States.

See also: Clinton, William Jefferson
Reference: Travis, Jeremy. 1998. "National Institute of Justice: Research in Brief." *NarcOfficer* (March/April).

National Inhalant Prevention Coalition (NIPC)

The NIPC was founded in 1992 by Synergies, a nonprofit organization based in Austin, Texas, and is funded in part by the Robert Wood Johnson Foundation. This organization grew out of a statewide prevention project in Texas called the Texas Prevention Partnership, which began in 1990. The NIPC's purpose today is to promote public awareness of what it considers to be the underpublicized problem of inhalant abuse. To achieve its objective, the coalition serves as a clearinghouse and referral center and provides training and technical assistance.

See also: Inhalants; Robert Wood Johnson Foundation
Reference: National Inhalant Prevention Coalition website at http://www.inhalants.org.

National Institute on Drug Abuse (U.S.)

Established in 1974, the National Institute on Drug Abuse (NIDA) aims to lead in bringing the power of science to bear on addiction and drug abuse by supporting and undertaking research across a broad spectrum of disciplines. Among its accomplishments, NIDA has demonstrated that successful drug abuse treatment reduces criminality, as well as relapses to addiction, and has shown the value of treating drug abusers' depression and other disorders to improve the results of addiction therapy. In 1981 NIDA's mission changed when Congress initiated the block grant program to give states more control over prevention services and drug abuse treatment. In 1992 NIDA became part of the National Institute of Health, the world's leading biomedical and behavioral research organization.

Reference: National Institute on Drug Abuse website at http://www.nida.nih.gov/.

National Inter-Agency Civil-Military Institute (U.S.)

Headquartered at Camp San Luis Obispo, California, the NICI specializes in teaching military and civilian agencies how to work together more effectively. As a part of its mission, the NICI directly supports the United States' National Drug Control Strategy and the Federal Response Plan by fostering partnerships that address critical domestic issues.

Reference: National Inter-Agency Civil-Military Institute website at http://www.nici.org/.

National Latin Movement (Colombia)

Colombian drug trafficker Carlos Lehder Rivas founded this movement in March 1983 as an instrument to get rid of the U.S.-Colombian extradition treaty. At that time, Lehder was second on a list of 100 suspected Colombian drug traffickers that the United States wanted extradited, but U.S. authorities indicated that he was the country's number one target. The movement was based in Armenia, the capital of Colombia's Quindio Department, where the party newspaper *Quindio Libre* operated with a press run of 60,000. As evidence of the movement's neo-Nazi orientation, Lehder claimed that an "incorrect" image had been spread about Germany and that international Zionism was behind "terror and terrorism" committed in Latin America. This was an example of the growing power of drug traffickers in

Colombia, who were able to use money and influence generated from the drug trade to finance their political objectives. The movement died with Lehder's capture and extradition to the United States in February 1987.

See also: Extradition; Lehder Rivas, Carlos
Reference: Gugliotta, Guy, and Jeff Leen. 1990. *Kings of Cocaine.*

National Narcotics Border Interdiction System (NNBIS)

Established in 1983, the National Narcotics Border Interdiction System's purpose was to "monitor suspected smuggling activity originating outside the national borders and coordinate agency seizures of contraband and arrests of person involved in illegal drug importation." (Shannon 1989, 98) It eventually consisted of thirteen different task forces that used personnel from various federal and state agencies around the country to coordinate their activities in combating drug trafficking.

See also: Bush, George Herbert Walker; Operation Blue Lightning
References: Cooper, Mary H. 1990. *The Business of Drugs.* Shannon, Elaine. 1989. *Desperadoes.*

National Narcotics Intelligence Consumers Committee (U.S.)

NNICC is a federal agency that was formed in 1978 to coordinate information on illegal drugs gathered by all the federal agencies in drug enforcement activities.

Reference: Cooper, Mary H. 1990. *The Business of Drugs.*

National Organization for the Reform of Marijuana Laws (NORML)

Founded in 1970, this group has an estimated 250,000 members and seeks to change U.S. laws regarding marijuana by lobbying for legislative reform, providing speakers, and distributing educational material. In the 1970s, NORML played a role in promoting the decriminalization and legalization of marijuana. Eleven states had decriminalized possession of small amounts of marijuana by 1979. In the 1990s, NORML made a big effort to make marijuana legal for medical purposes, even bringing

legal action against the U.S. Drug Enforcement Administration.

See also: Decriminalization; Legalization; Marijuana; Medical Marijuana; United States Drug Enforcement Administration
Reference: Bertram, Eva, Kenneth Sharpe, and Peter Anders. 1996. *Drug War Politics: The Price of Denial.* National Organization for the Reform of Marijuana Laws website at http://www.norml.org/.

National Youth Anti-Drug Media Campaign (U.S.)

A five-year antidrug media campaign launched in 1998 by the federal government, the National Youth Anti-Drug Media Campaign is the largest media campaign ever undertaken by the U.S. government. Phase I of the campaign began in January 1998 when the Office of National Drug Control Policy and the Partnership for a Drug Free America initiated a $195 million bipartisan media effort in twelve pilot cities.

The campaign focuses on youngsters, particularly middle school students and the adults who influence them, including parents, teachers, coaches, and mentors, and through advertising and other forms of communication, attempts to educate and help young people reject drugs. On 9 July 1998 the campaign went national, and the third and final phase, which was launched in October 1998, involved implementing a fully integrated strategy that included advertising; media outreach; corporate sponsorship; internet and interactive media; partnerships with community, civic, and professional groups; and entertainment and special industry initiatives.

See also: Partnership for a Drug Free America; United States Office of National Drug Control Policy
Reference: "National Youth Anti-Drug Media Campaign Launched." 1998. *International Drug Report* (July/August/September).

Navarro Lara, General Alfredo

Mexican authorities indicted this brigadier general in March 1997 on charges that he had tried to bribe a top Baja law enforcement official with a promise of monthly payments of $1 million in exchange for the official's cooperation in allowing illegal drugs to pass across the border into the United States. Navarro Lara reportedly threatened the official, warning him that the Tijuana Cartel would kill him

George Clark of Prevention Point, the United States' largest needle exchange program, hands over fresh hypodermic needles to an intravenous drug user in San Francisco's Mission District, 2 May 1991. Clark and his group hand out over 3,000 needles a week to addicts in an effort to curb the spread of AIDS. (Corbis/Reuters)

if he didn't accept the bribe. The general received a fifteen-year jail sentence.

See also: Tijuana Cartel
Reference: De Palma, Anthony. 1998. "Mexico: General Tied to Drugs Gets Fifteen Years." *New York Times*, 26 October, p. A8.

Needle Exchange Programs

These programs allow drug users to trade the dirty needles they use to inject drugs for clean ones. The purpose is to stop the spread of AIDS and other blood-borne diseases among intravenous drug users, and through them, to their sexual partners.

Needle exchange programs are the most prominent example of the harm reduction approach to drug control. Opponents of needle exchange programs contend that they do not discourage drug use and may actually encourage it.

Australia, Holland, and Great Britain have taken the lead in adopting needle and syringe exchange programs, while the United States has lagged behind. In 1994, for example, Australia, a country with one-fourteenth the population of the United States has sixty times as many syringe outlets as the United States. In 1998 New York became the first U.S. city to use public money to fund a needle exchange program, but the

following year the federal government imposed a ban on its funding of needle exchange programs.

In June 1997 more than forty major health advocacy and minority groups, including the National Urban League and the American Public Health Association wrote a letter to President Clinton, urging him to lift the ban. The letter came at a time when the respected medical journal *Lancet* reported that as many as 10,000 Americans could have avoided HIV infection between 1987 and 1995 if needle exchange programs had been in place, and that caring for the sick people cost the nation $500 million.

On 1 July 1998 delegates at the World AIDS Conference in Geneva, Switzerland, urged that the number of needle exchange programs worldwide be increased to halt the rising spread of the AIDS virus through intravenous injections. In 1997 the World Health Organization reported that 116 countries reported cases of intravenous drug use and 96 of those reported HIV cases connected to drug injection.

See also: Common Sense for Drug Policy; Harm Reduction; North American Syringe Network; Schmoke, Kurt; World Health Organization.
References: Sternberg, Steve. 1997. "Funding Urged for Needle Exchanges." 1997. *USA Today*, 13 July.
United Nations Drug Control Program. 1997. *World Drug Report*.

Newman, Robert G. (c. 1938–)

President of the Beth Israel Medical Center in New York City and the leading proponent in the United States of the use of methadone for the treatment of heroin addiction. Newman began setting up a network of methadone clinics in New York City in 1970, which today are run by the city's Department of Health and provide places for 35,000 heroin addicts. The methadone clinic at Beth Israel Medical Center, the world's largest, treats about 8,000 patients annually.

See also: Methadone Treatment Programs; North American Syringe Network
Reference: Dreyfuss, Robert. 1997. "Hawks and Doves: Who's Who in the World of Drugs." *Rolling Stone*, 7 August.

Nigerian Organized Crime

Nigerian nationals have been identified as the architects of a complex network of couriers that smuggle heroin into the United States and Europe from

Southeast and Southwest Asia. Testifying before U.S. Congress in 1992, Melvyn Levitsky, the assistant secretary for the Board of International Narcotics, Department of State, noted that "We are beginning to see an increase in Nigerian smuggling of cocaine from South America to markets in the U.S. and Europe. As far as we can tell, the Nigerian trafficking organizations are more loosely organized than their American counterparts, and therefore more difficult to penetrate. There are no clear hierarchies and no unambiguous chain of command. Nevertheless, they are sophisticated organizations capable of quickly adapting to changes in U.S. law enforcement activities." (U.S. Senate Committee on Foreign Relations 1992, 7)

Nigerian traffickers are, by most estimates, responsible for smuggling as much as 40 to 50 percent of the heroin entering the United States and are firmly entrenched in such American cities as Atlanta, Chicago, Baltimore, and Washington, D.C. From 1979 to September 1991 more than 15,000 Nigerians worldwide were arrested for drug trafficking. Nigerian traffickers and their associates accounted for most of the heroin seized at U.S. airports. In one year alone, fiscal 1991, 31 percent of the 756 heroin seizures at U.S. airports by the U.S. Customs Service involved Nigerian nationals and 11 percent other Africans, most likely couriers working for Nigerian drug trafficking.

The Nigerians buy their heroin in the Golden Crescent of India, Pakistan, and Afghanistan and the Golden Triangle of Laos, Myanmar, and Thailand, where there is a large Nigerian and West African population. The Nigerians control all facets of the trade—the purchase, transportation, and distribution—from their suppliers in Asia to the dealers on the streets of U.S. and European cities. Often, the drugs are shipped in containers hidden in freighters to Lagos, Nigeria's capital, where they are stored and later transported to their destination. The Nigerians have begun using other African countries as transit points as well, including Ghana, Benin, Senegal, and South Africa.

The couriers working for the Nigerian drug traffickers have been known to use everything imaginable, including their own bodies, to smuggle the drugs into the United States: shampoo, deodorant, children's toys, cans of food, even coat hangers (broken and then relaquered). Most are "swallowers" who carry the drugs in their digestive systems or "stuffers," who hide the drugs in their body cavities. Swallowers put the drugs in condoms, which are often wrapped in carbon paper or black electrical tape, making it difficult to spot the drugs in an x-ray machine because the carbon looks like any other body part. Given the poverty and unemployment in Africa, the Nigerian traffickers have no trouble recruiting couriers, who are willing to risk death.

The growing influence of the Nigerian connection in international drug trafficking has created serious drug problems for many African countries. Not only has drug trafficking taken root in Africa, but drug dependence, as well as drug-related crime, such as prostitution, robbery, and even gang warfare, has become widespread in such African countries as Liberia, Benin, Senegal, and South Africa, transit countries for drugs destined for the United States and Europe. South African police estimate that as many as 120 gangs in South Africa may be involved in drug trafficking.

Corruption has been a big factor in Nigeria's rise as a major conduit for drug trafficking. The Federal Military Government of Nigeria has taken a strong public stance against narcotics trafficking, but U.S. officials acknowledge that its effort leaves a lot to be desired. In 1994, Bill Olsen, former deputy assistant secretary of state for Narcotics, told Congress, "Nigerian public institutions are thoroughly penetrated by criminal groups who operate into and through Nigeria and through West Africa with virtually no effort by government to control them." (U.S. Senate Committee on Foreign Relations 1994, 124)

The corruption in Nigeria has taken many forms. Couriers, for example, have been able to obtain A-2 visas, which make them diplomatically "untouchable" as they move through customs in their destination countries. Many government officials are suspected of taking a percentage of the value of the drugs making their way through the country, while several drug-trafficking suspects have escaped from jail before they went to trial, thanks to the bribes given to officials. Compounding the problem are lax banking regulations and a cash-transaction based economy, a practice that encourages money laundering.

In 1989 the Nigerian government created the National Drug Law Enforcement Agency, which is modeled after the U.S. Drug Enforcement Administration. In 1992 about 350 of its employees were fired because of corruption, and the head of the agency was replaced on suspicion of having accepted bribes to stop pursuing drug traffickers.

The U.S. government has moved to assist Nigeria to clean up its act and make a dent in the narcotics trade by helping to improve the legal and investigative capabilities of Nigerian law enforcement and providing the country with law enforcement equipment and training. In 1991 and 1992, for example, the United States provided $100,000 in communication assistance and an additional $20,700 in DEA- and U.S. Customs-assisted law enforcement training. In 1989 Nigeria sent a ten-member interagency delegation to the United States to meet with DEA, Customs, and State Department officials about drug-related issues. Nigeria has also cooperated with the United States in the extradition of suspected drug traffickers from Nigeria to the United States to face drug-related charges, but U.S. officials admit that the Nigerian government has moved much more slowly than they would like.

U.S. officials have concluded that the Nigerian connection will continue to play a significant role in international drug trafficking in the years ahead. Nigerian organized crime is expanding to the South American countries of Colombia, Brazil, Peru, and Bolivia, becoming an important link in the cocaine and heroin pipeline to the United States and Europe.

See also: Body Packing; Extradition; Golden Crescent; Golden Triangle; Heroin; Money Laundering; Mule

References: Bake, Allen. 1995. "Drugged to the Eyeballs." *New African* (June): 16–18.
Chepesiuk, Ron. 1999. *Hard Target.*
Farah, Douglas. 1996. "Nigerian Cartels Widening Drug Operations." *Charlotte Observer*, 23 June.
"The Nigerian Connection." 1991. *Newsweek*, 19 October (Asian Edition) p. 19.
U.S. Department of State. "Treaty between the U.S. and the Federal Republic of Nigeria on Mutual Assistance in Criminal Matters." 20 May 1992. TREATY DOC. 10226.
U.S. Senate Committee on Foreign Relations. Subcommittee on Terrorism. *Narcotics and international Operations, Recent Developments In Transnational Crime Affecting Law Enforcement And Foreign Policy.*

Nixon, Richard Milhous (1913–1994)

President of the United States from 1969 until 1974, when he resigned because of the Watergate scandal.

Watergate involved a break-in of the Democratic party headquarters in July 1972 by agents of Nixon's presidential reelection committee. The agents were arrested, but there was a subsequent coverup, and this led to the downfall of Richard Nixon and his resignation as president on 9 August 1974. During the Nixon administration, the federal budget for the U.S. antidrug program increased significantly and the drug enforcement infrastructure underwent a major reorganization in an effort to provide leadership in the War on Drugs and to reduce interagency rivalries.

The country's growing heroin epidemic grabbed the attention of President Nixon, and on 17 June 1971 he made a major television speech in which he said, "America has now the largest number of heroin addicts of any nation in the world. If we cannot destroy the drug menace in America, then it will surely destroy us." (McCoy 1991, 26) Nixon's speech marked a major turning point in the U.S. government's attitude toward illegal drugs and international drug trafficking. As Catherine Lamour and Michael R. Lamberti explain, "Thereafter, the battle against narcotics was regarded by Washington as one of the most urgent items in the American political program, and concrete measures were put in hand so as to convince the country that the Republican administration was not simply making a promise." (Lamour & Lamberti 1974, 60)

Among the several measures implemented, Nixon established a Cabinet Committee on International Narcotics Control (CCINC) and a narcotics policy program within the Internal Revenue Service (IRS). Chaired by the secretary of state, the CCINC had responsibility for "developing a strategy to check the illegal flow of narcotics into the U.S. and coordinating the efforts undertaken abroad by involving federal departments and agencies to implement that strategy." (Lamour & Lamberti 1994, 60)

The following year Nixon established an Office for Drug Abuse Law Enforcement (ODALE) within the Justice Department under a director who was to advise the president on how to improve the effectiveness of federal antidrug enforcement and help state and local government improve their counterdrug efforts. Several months later, the president established the Office of National Narcotics Intelligence (ONNI) within the Justice Department to collect and disseminate narcotics intelligence to federal, state, and local officials who had a "legitimate official use" for it. (President's Commission on Organized Crime 1986, 234) In 1969 Nixon created the Bureau of Narcotics and Dangerous Drugs with only 60 agents and a budget of $14 million. By the end of 1972 the number of agents had tripled and the budget had increased fourfold. The following year Nixon reorganized the federal law enforcement machinery and established the Drug Enforcement Administration (DEA), which was to become the point agency in America's War on Drugs.

At the international level, Nixon summoned his ambassadors from France, Turkey, and Mexico and told them to help their foreign counterparts move more aggressively against international drug trafficking. He also signed the 1971 Convention on Psychotropic Substances, which extended control measures over hallucinogens, amphetamines, barbiturates, and tranquillizers not previously covered by international treaties.

Congress reacted to Nixon's call for a war on drugs by supporting passage of the Drug Abuse and Treatment Act of 1972, which its supporters touted as an important milestone in the history of drug abuse legislation because it "called for a balanced response to the problem of drug abuse by adding a vigorous prevention and treatment program to the existing law enforcement effort." But as the 1984 Federal Commission on Organized Crime later pointed out, "although commitments to the 'balanced' response were enshrined in the 1972 Drug Abuse Office Act they have not generally been translated into action, as measured by budget authorizations and expenditures." (Lamour & Lamberti 1994, 104)

Initially, the Nixon administration did have some success, particularly against heroin. In 1971 the United States began pressuring Turkey, Mexico, and Southeast Asia's Golden Triangle to eradicate their opium crops. The famous French Connection, which was dominated by Sicilian and Corsican drug-trafficking organizations, supplied about 80 percent of the heroin entering the United States via a smuggling route stretching from Turkey to Marseilles in southern France, where chemists, working in hidden laboratories, converted the raw opium to a type of heroin called "China white" before traffickers shipped the finished product to the United States.

By 1973 the French government had shut down the laboratories in southern France, and Turkey—

supported by $20 million in U.S. aid—had convinced its farmers to switch from poppies to alternative crops. The heroin sold in the United States dropped in purity to one-half of what it was, while the price of heroin in New York City, the drug's principal market, tripled, an indication that heroin was in short supply. In September 1973 Nixon told the American people: "We have turned the corner on drug addiction." (President's Commission on Organized Crime 1986, 234)

Nixon's declaration proved to be premature, for the basic principle of supply and demand once again went to work. Trafficking syndicates in southeast Asia filled the gap left by the dismantling of the French Connection's laboratories, while opium production quickly shifted to new centers. As Alfred J. McCoy and Alan A. Block noted, "During the next ten years, drug-trafficking syndicates simply shifted their resources—from Turkey to Southeast Asia to Mexico, and then to Southeast Asia again—remaining one step ahead of U.S. diplomats and drug agents." (McCoy & Block 1992, 14)

Amsterdam replaced Marseilles as the center of the European heroin trade and new trafficking syndicates—the Triads and Colombians, among other criminal groups—arose to plug the heroin distribution pipeline. The heroin trade subsequently expanded in the United States to include not just New York City as the major distribution point, but also Miami, Chicago, and Los Angeles. Critics said Nixon's get-tough strategy had backfired. Demand increased and international drug trafficking continue to expand its supply network.

See also: China White, Corsicans; French Connection; Heroin; Leary, Timothy; McCoy, Alfred J.; National Commission on Marijuana and Drug Abuse; Shultz, George P.; United States Bureau of Narcotics and Dangerous Drugs; United States Convention on Psychotropic Substances of 1971; United States Drug Enforcement Administration; United States National Narcotic Information Board; United States Office of Drug Abuse Law Enforcement

References: Lamour, Catherine, and Michael R. Lamberti. 1974. *The International Connection: Opium from Growers to Pushers*.

McCoy, Alfred J. 1991. "What War on Drugs? The CIA Connection." *The Progressive* (July): 20–26.

McCoy, Alfred J., and Alan A. Block, eds. 1992. *War on Drugs: Studies in the Failure of U.S. Narcotics Policy*.

President's Commission on Organized Crime. 1986. *America's Habit: Drug Trafficking and Organized Crime*.

Noriega, Manuel Antonio (1938–)

Panamanian general and commander of the Panamanian Defense Force (PDF) from 1983 to 1989. Noriega was also an operative for the Central Intelligence Agency. He was indicted in U.S. federal court for alleged involvement in the international drug trade. According to testimony before the U.S. Congress, the United States knew about Noriega's drug-smuggling activities for nearly two decades, but tolerated them because he was a paid employee of the U.S. government (from at least 1967) and a valuable intelligence source. Norman Bailey, a former National Security Council official, testified before Congress in 1989 that "clear and incontrovertible evidence was at least ignored, at worst hidden and denied by many different agencies and departments of the [U.S.] government in such a way as to provide cover and protection for Noriega's activities. (Strong 1995, 52)

While maintaining these ties to the CIA, Noriega also had a long and friendly relationship with the Medellin Cartel. At his trial in 1988, drug kingpin Carlos Lehder Rivas testified that the Cartel paid Noriega $1,000 per kilogram of cocaine to allow the drug to be shipped through Panama and on to Costa Rica and Florida, or to Mexico and then to Los Angeles. In January 1988 the U.S. government urged Noriega to step down from power, but he refused. Following the murder of a U.S. marine on the streets of Panama City, President Bush launched Operation Just Cause and sent a force of 24,000 soldiers to Panama. Noriega was hunted down, arrested, and whisked back to the United States for trial.

The United States defended the invasion, contending that it was a way to strengthen the fight against international drug trafficking. Critics, however, charged that the United States had actually kidnaped the general in violation of international law. In April 1992 Noriega was convicted of drug trafficking, money laundering, and racketeering and was sentenced to forty years in jail.

After the trial, the tactics that the U.S. government had used to get Noriega's conviction were questioned. Federal prosecutors admitted that they had negotiated with a lawyer from the Cali Cartel to win the testimony of a key witness in the case. They also acknowledged that the Cartel may have paid the witness, Ricardo Blotnick, $1.25 million to testify. The U.S. government admitted the incident was em-

Panamanian military leader Manuel Noriega waving to supporters from behind a barred window, following his successful crushing of an attempted coup. (Corbis/Reuters)

barrassing, but insisted that it was not sufficient reason for a new trial for Noriega. In 1997 Noriega wrote and published his memoirs in which he said he had been demonized by the United States because its leader, George Bush, wanted to invade Panama.

See also: Bonner, Robert C.; Bush, George Herbert Walker; Cali Cartel; Contras; Lehder Rivas, Carlos; Medellin Cartel; Ochoa Vasquez, Jorge Luis; Ochoa Vasquez, Marta Nieves; United States Central intelligence Agency

References: Eisner, Peter. 1997. *America's Prisoner: The Memoirs of Manuel Antonio Noriega.*

U.S. Senate Committee on Foreign Relations. Subcommittee on Terrorism, Narcotics and International Operations. *Report: Drugs, Law Enforcement and Foreign Policy.* Hearings before the Subcommittee on Terrorism, Narcotics and International Operations of the 1989 Committee on Foreign Relations, U.S. Senate, first session, 29–31 August and 1 September.

Norman, Mabel (1892–1930)

Major movie actress of the silent screen era who starred in such films as "Over the Garden Wall" and "Tillie's Punctured Romance." Norman's career was ruined by drug abuse, and she is a graphic example of the widespread use and abuse of drugs in the film community of the time.

Reference: Jonnes, Jill. 1996. *Hep-Cats, Narcs and Pipe Dreams.*

Norman's Cay

An island in the Bahamas that is approximately four and one-half miles long and located forty miles southeast of the capital city of Nassau and 200 miles from Miami, Florida. Norman's Cay became a major transhipment point for cocaine from Colombia to the United States in the late 1970s. Beginning in 1978 drug trafficker Carlos Lehder Rivas bought property on the island and upon arriving, forced many people, including several who had been on the island for years, to move out. When visitors arrived to fish or yacht in the area, they were intimidated into leaving. There were numerous complaints to the police, but nothing happened. Meanwhile, in a little more than six months after arriving on the island, Lehder's smuggling operation had grown to such an extent that he had five to seven pilots and more than a dozen planes to smuggle cocaine to the United States.

In September 1979 the Bahamian authorities raided Norman's Cay as part of Operation Raccoon. Launched in 1979, Operation Raccoon involved more than thirty members of the Royal Bahamian Defense and Police Forces in a raid of Norman's Cay, the island that served as a drug-trafficking base for Carlos Lehder Rivas and the Medellin Cartel. Prior to the raid Lehder had been under police surveillance for a long time, and authorities were concerned that the drug traffickers had taken over the island. Lehder was arrested after he fled Norman's Cay by powerboat.

In all, the Bahamian officials arrested thirty people, but Lehder was allowed to go free. Later, however, all of Lehder's arrested associates were released on $2,000 bail. Only one person was convicted as a result of the operation a Bahamian, for carrying an unregistered gun. It is believed that Lehder had bribed the Bahamian authorities.

Soon it was business as usual on Norman's Cay. Bahamian authorities conducted more raids on the island in 1980 and 1981, but Lehder was always tipped off and escaped capture, although several of his associates were arrested. Lehder left the island in September 1981, but in the early 1980s he continued to use it as part of his smuggling operation, despite the fact that Bahamian authorities put a permanent police station on Norman's Cay.

See also: Cocaine; Lehder Rivas, Carlos; Medellin Cartel; Operation Caribe; Operation Raccoon; Pindling, Lyndon
References: Gugliotta, Guy, and Jeff Leen. 1990. *Kings of Cocaine.*
Strong, Simon. 1995. *Whitewash: Pablo Escobar and the Cocaine Wars.*

North American Free Trade Agreement
See Free Trade.

North American Syringe Network

A U.S.-based organization that is dedicated to the creation, expansion, and continued existence of syringe exchange programs as a proven method of stopping the transmission of blood-borne pathogens, especially the HIV virus, in the intravenous drug-using community.

See also: Needle Exchange Programs; Newman, Robert G.
Reference: North American Syringe Network website at http://www.nasen.org.

North Atlantic Coast Cartel (Colombia)

Based in Colombia's coastal cities of Cartagena, Barranquilla, Santa Marta, and Rio Hacha, this is the smallest of the country's major drug cartels. In the United States it has operations in Atlanta, Boston, New York, Miami, Jacksonville, Gainsville, Los Angeles, and San Diego, among other cities. The Cartel began with marijuana smuggling but then moved into cocaine trafficking when it began to help the Medellin and Bogotá Cartels distribute the drug.

See also: Bogotá Cartel; Cali Cartel; Cocaine; Marijuana; Medellin Cartel
Reference: Miller, Gary J. 1997. *Drugs and the Law: Detection, Recognition and Investigation.*

North, Oliver
See Contras.

O

Observatoire Geopolitique des Drogues

Based in Paris, France, the Observatoire is one of the world's most important monitoring organizations for international drug trafficking, and its reports are used extensively by drug analysts and scholars. The organization publishes *Geopolitical Drug Dispatch,* a monthly update from which its annual report is synthesized.

Reference: Observatoire Geopolitique des Drogues website at www.ogd.org/.

Ochoa Sanchez, Arnaldo

A popular and much decorated Cuban war hero who fought alongside Fidel Castro in the revolution that toppled dictator Fulgencio Batista in 1959. Before becoming chief of the Cuban military mission in Angola, Ochoa Sanchez commanded the victorious Cuban forces in Ethiopia in its war with Somalia that began in 1978.

Ochoa Sanchez was among fourteen Cuban senior military and Interior Ministry officials who were convicted in Cuba of embezzlement and helping Colombia's Medellin Cartel smuggle six tons of cocaine into the United States, causing embarrassment to Cuba when word leaked out. Some say Castro viewed Ochoa Sanchez as a potential rival and wanted to get rid of him. The Cubans allegedly allowed the Cartel to use Cuba as a transhipment point for drugs in return for a reported $3.5 million in bribes. The Cuban officials were also convicted of black marketeering and smuggling diamonds, sugar, fine woods, manufactured goods, and U.S. dollars. Ochoa Sanchez confessed to his crimes and said at the four-day trial, which was shown nightly on Cuban national television, that "one pays for treason with one's life." (Cuban War Hero, 23 Others Executed by Firing Squad 1989) Ochoa and three other senior military officers were executed by firing squad on 13 July 1989.

See also: Cocaine; Cuban Connection; Medellin Cartel
References: "Cuban War Hero, 3 Others Executed by Firing Squad." 1989. *Los Angeles Times,* 14 July.
Oppenheimer, Andres. 1993. *Castro's Final Hour: The Secret Story Behind the Coming Fall of Communist Cuba.*
Uhlig, Mark A. 1989. "Cuba Replaces Top Security Officer." *New York Times,* 30 June.

Ochoa Vasquez, Fabio, Sr.

Father of one-time leading Colombian drug traffickers, Jorge Luis, Fabio Jr., and Juan David Ochoa Vasquez. Fabio Sr. was a founder of the Medellin Cartel and one of Colombia's great horse breeders. He retired from the drug trade in the early 1980s, and in 1991 he reportedly convinced his three sons to turn themselves in to Colombian authorities.

See also: Lehder Rivas, Carlos; Medellin Cartel; Ochoa Vasquez, Fabio, Jr.; Ochoa Vasquez, Jorge Luis; Ochoa Vasquez, Juan David; Ochoa Vasquez, Marta Nieves
Reference: Dermota, Ken. 1995. "When You Order a Steak—and a Stallion." *Business Week,* 27 March.

Fabio Ochoa Restrepo, father of three drug lords (Fabio, Jorge Luis and Juan David), autographs his book on horses, which he plans to send to the Pope, 2 September 1989. (Corbis-Reuters)

Ochoa Vasquez, Jr., Fabio (c. 1958–)

Youngest brother of Jorge Luis Ochoa Vasquez and Juan David Ochoa Vasquez and a prominent member of the Medellin Cartel. During the late 1970s Fabio lived for a time in Miami, where he headed the Ochoa family's drug distribution network. In the early 1980s he was implicated in the murder of drug informant Barry Seale. He surrendered to Colombian authorities in December 1991. In September 1996 he was the last Ochoa brother to be released from Colombian jail after serving sixty-nine months of an eight-and-a-half-year sentence for drug trafficking.

See also: Blanco De Trujillo, Griselda; Cali Cartel; Lehder Rivas, Carlos; Low Murtra, Enrique; Medellin Cartel; Ochoa Vasquez, Sr., Fabio; Ochoa Vasquez, Jorge Luis; Ochoa Vasquez, Juan David; Seale, Barry Alderman

References: "Colombia." 1996. *Miami Herald*, 17 September, p. 4.

Gugliotta, Guy, and Jeff Leen. 1990. *Kings of Cocaine.*

Ochoa Vasquez, Jorge Luis (1950–)

A founding member of the Medellin Cartel who was mainly responsible for transforming his family's business into a modern drug-trafficking organization. Born in Cali, Colombia, and raised in Envigado, Jorge Luis was the second of three sons of Fabio Ochoa Resrepo and Margot Vasquez. The U.S. Drug Enforcement Administration first discovered Ochoa's role in drug trafficking in 1977 when they confiscated sixty pounds of cocaine in Miami. Ochoa had ostensibly gone to Miami as a manager of an import-export firm, but, in reality, he was a cocaine distributor for his uncle Fabio. Although indicted, Ochoa escaped to Medellin, Colombia, where together with his father, Fabio, and brothers Fabio, Jr., and Juan David, he continued to operate the family's cocaine-smuggling business. In the early 1980s the DEA office in Bogotá reported that Ochoa "had become one of the most powerful traffickers in Medellin and the northern coast of Colombia, and is continuing to introduce one hundred to two hundred kilos of cocaine into the U.S. by several unknown methods."(Gugliotta & Leen 1997, 7)

Following the kidnapping of his sister, Marta Nieves Ochoa Vasquez, on 12 November 1981 and her subsequent release, Ochoa established a close working relationship with fellow drug traffickers Pablo Escobar Gaviria and Carlos Enrique Lehder Rivas in an organization that became known as the Medellin Cartel. As part of the arrangement, Ochoa provided assassins and helped pay off judges, police, and politicians. After the murder of Rodrigo Lara Bonilla, Colombia's justice minister in 1984, Colombian President Belisario Betancur Cuartas put pressure on the country's drug kingpins and drove them out of Colombia. The Ochoa brothers and other key leaders of the Medellin Cartel fled to Panama, where they were protected by Panamanian President Manuel Antonio Noriega for a fee reported to be between $4 and $7 million.

Ochoa moved to Madrid, Spain, but was arrested by Spanish police on 15 November 1984 and extradited to Colombia. On 13 May 1986, however, just a few weeks after his extradition, a judge in Cartagena released Ochoa. He was arrested again on 30 December 1987, but another judge from Bogotá, Andres Montanez, authorized his release, and he walked out of prison.

Ochoa turned himself in to Colombian authorities in January 1991. In explaining his decision, the drug lord told a Colombian television station, "I turned myself in because I believe in justice and the government in Colombia." (Colombian Drug Baron Surrenders under Offer of Lenient Treatment 1991)

In July 1996 Jorge Luis became the first of the Ochoa brothers to be released from jail. U.S. Ambassador Myles Frechette and other U.S. officials expressed anger at the Colombian government's decision to grant the Ochoa brothers early release from prison.

See also: Betancur Cuertas, Belisario; Blanco De Trujillo, Griselda; Cali Cartel; Cocaine; Extradition; Escobar Gaviria, Pablo; Frechette, Myles; Lara Bonilla, Rodrigo; Lehder Rivas, Carlos; Low Murtra, Enrique; Medellin Cartel; Noriega, Manuel Antonio; Ochoa Vasquez, Sr., Fabio; Ochoa Vasquez, Jr., Fabio; Ochoa Vasquez, Marta Nieves; Operation Fountainhead; Restrepo Ochoa, Fabio

References: "Colombian Baron Surrenders Under Offer of Lenient Treatment." 1991. *New York Times*, 16 January.

Eddy, Paul, Hugh Sabogal, and Sarah Walden. 1988. *The Cocaine Wars*.

Gugliotta, Guy, and Jeff Leen. 1990. *Kings of Cocaine*.

Ochoa Vasquez, Juan David (c. 1949–)

The older brother of former drug traffickers Fabio and Jorge Luis Ochoa Vasquez and one of the founders of the Medellin Cartel. Juan David and his brothers were introduced to the cocaine trade by their uncle Fabio Restrepo Ochoa, one of Colombia's pioneer smugglers. In 1986 Juan David and his two brothers were charged with several crimes, including conspiracy to smuggle sixty tons of cocaine into the United States. In 1987 the U.S. government seized $20 million of property owned by Juan David, Pablo Escobar, and other Medellin Cartel drug traffickers, which included Juan David's horse ranch in central Florida and thirty-nine of his prize caballos de paso walking horses. In February 1991 after feeling the heat of the war between Pablo Escobar and the Colombian government, Juan David became the last of the Ochoa brothers to surrender to authorities. The Ochoas were incarcerated in a jail near Medellin city. In January 1996, as the result of a sentence plea bargain with the Colombian state, Juan David was released from jail after serving five-and-half-years in prison.

See also: Blanco De Trujillo, Griselda; Cali Cartel; Escobar Gaviria, Pablo; Low Murtra, Enrique; Medellin Cartel; Ochoa Vasquez, Sr., Fabio; Ochoa Vasquez, Jr., Fabio; Ochoa Vasquez, Jorge Luis; Ochoa Vasquez, Marta Nieves; Restrepo Ochoa, Fabio

References: Gugliotta, Guy, and Jeff Leen. 1990. *Kings of Cocaine*.

Strong, Simon. 1995. *Whitewash: Pablo Escobar and the Cocaine Wars*.

Ochoa Vasquez, Marta Nieves (1954–)

The youngest sister of the Ochoa Vasquez brothers (Fabio, Jr., Jorge Luis, and Juan David), who are major figures in Colombia's Medellin Cartel. On 12 November 1981, M-19 guerrillas kidnapped Marta Nieves from the campus of the University of Antioquia and demanded $12 to $15 million in ransom from the Ochoa family. The family, however, had no intention of paying the ransom, and called a meeting of more than 220 top drug traffickers in Colombia. The drug traffickers agreed to organize a group known as Death to the Kidnappers (Muerte a Secuestradores (MAS)) and issued a communiqué on 13 December 1981 that was distributed in Cali, Colombia's third-largest city. The communiqué stated that MAS was offering a $330,000 reward leading to the capture of the kidnappers and guaranteed that those involved "will be hung from the trees in a public park or shot and marked with the sign of our group—MAS." (Gugliotta & Leen 1990, 91)

MAS also kidnapped relatives of the M-19 guerrilla group and reportedly killed or turned in to authorities more than 100 guerrillas or their sympathizers within six weeks of the group's formation, while holding some others hostages. On 6 February 1982 MAS issued another warning, "Our patience is wearing thin." (Gugliotta & Leen 1990, 94) The guerrillas finally released Marta Nieves unharmed on 17 February 1982 and the next day MAS freed five of the M-19 hostages. Although not confirmed, it is believed that the Ochoa family paid a ransom of $535,000 or more after talks between the guerrillas and drug traffickers were held in Panama with the approval of the country's dictator, Colonel Manuel Noriega.

See also: Medellin Cartel; M-19; Noriega, Manuel Antonio; Ochoa Vasquez, Sr., Fabio; Ochoa Vasquez, Jr., Fabio; Ochoa Vasquez, Jorge Luis; Ochoa Vasquez, Juan David

Reference: Gugliotta, Guy, and Jeff Leen. 1990 *Kings of Cocaine*.

Offshore Financial Centers

These centers have been defined as "financial systems whose banks have external costs and liabilities that are out of proportion to the current account transactions of their domestic economies and where the ratio of bank external assets to exports of goods and services is more than three times the world average." (United Nations 1997, 140)

Offshore financial centers can play a legitimate role in the international economic system, but they can also be used by money launderers as a point for the transfer of money, as a secret institution for financial transactions, and as a tax haven. In 1993 banks worldwide had $1.5 trillion of private money (20 percent of the total money in private hands) invested in these centers. How much of that amount is derived from drug trafficking is uncertain, but as the United Nations International Drug Control Program's *World Drug Report* states, "The amount may be marginal in comparative terms, but is probably large in absolute terms." (United Nations 1997, 141). The International Monetary Fund has identified the following countries as being major offshore centers: Antilles, the Bahamas, Bahrain, the Cayman Islands, Hong Kong, the Netherlands, Panama, and Singapore.

See also: Anderson, Robert A.; Money Laundering
Reference: United Nations International Drug Control Program. 1997. *World Drug Report.*

Operation Alliance

Launched in early 1986, this operation targeted the southwest border of the United States and was modeled on Operation Blue Fire, which began early in 1986. Operation Alliance involved every law enforcement agency in the southwest United States. According to Elaine Shannon, "Even before the federal government launched the operation, it was a standing joke among DEA and Customs Service personnel, who recognized a public relations gimmick when they saw one and called it 'Operation Dalliance.' They believed that the [Reagan] administration's move in pushing the plan was mainly defensive—to prevent congressional Democrats from taking full credit for defending the southwest border from drug traffickers, gun runners, and terrorists." (Shannon 1989, 432)

See also: Operation Blue Fire
Reference: Shannon, Elaine. 1989. *Desperadoes.*

Operation Autumn Harvest

A joint interdiction program of the U.S. Customs Service and the National Guard that was launched in September 1987 along the Arizona-Mexican border. According to reports, the program was a dismal failure that resulted in no arrests. A U.S. General Accounting Office report criticized the operation as being "not adequately coordinated and that [sic] Customs was not sufficiently involved in the planning." (U.S. General Accounting Office 1989)

See also: United States Customs, Department of; United States General Accounting Office; United States National Guard
Reference: U.S. General Accounting Office. 1989. *Drug Interdiction: Operation Autumn Harvest: A National Guard-Customs Anti-Smuggling Effort.*

Operation Bahamas, Turks, and Caicos (Opbat)

A joint United States-Bahamas drug interdiction project that operated in the late 1980s as part of the United States' stepped-up campaign to combat drug trafficking in the Caribbean. Bahamian Prime Minister Lyndon Pindling had committed police to the operation in an effort to counter corruption charges against himself and his aids and to diffuse pressure on Congress to decertify the Bahamas as a helpful ally in the United States' War on Drugs. Pindling also allowed U.S. Customs Department planes access to Bahamian airspace and Customs radar balloons to be deployed on Grand Bahama Island.

See also: Pindling, Lyndon; United States Customs, Department of
Reference: Shannon, Elaine. 1989. *Desperadoes.*

Operation Banshee

See Blanco De Trujillo, Griselda

Operation Blast Furnace

Launched in July 1988, Blast Furnace was the first U.S. antidrug operation to be directed on foreign soil. Its objective was to target cocaine laboratories in Bolivia and to reduce the supply of drugs by disrupting the drug-refining process in that country. The U.S. State Department began considering such an operation in 1985 after it determined that roughly 80,000 acres of coca was under cultivation.

The operation began when several giant U.S. Air Force transport planes landed in central Bolivia and unloaded six Army Black Hawk helicopters and 160 pilots, communications experts, and ground support crew. The Americans planned to raid thirty-five cocaine refining laboratories, landing strips, and warehouses, but because of advanced publicity, the drug traffickers were long gone when they arrived. Few traffickers or cocaine laboratories were found.

American and Bolivian authorities claimed the operation a success, but critics questioned the accuracy of that assessment. The U.S. government hoped to use the operation to drive up the price of coca leaves and force the coca farmers to find a more profitable, legal crop to grow. However, the only thing the operation did was to disrupt the Bolivian economy. On 30 July 1986 the Bolivian government asked the United States for a $100 million loan to make up for the revenue lost because of Operation Blast Furnace.

See also: Alternative Development; Cocaine; United States Department of State
References: De Grazia, Jessica. 1991. *DEA: The War against Drugs*
Gugliotta, Guy, and Jeff Leen. 1990. *Kings of Cocaine.*

Operation Blue Fire
The U.S. government began this operation in 1986 to strengthen drug interdiction efforts along the United States-Mexican border by coordinating the antidrug activities of all U.S. law enforcement agencies. For example, a radio network was to link all Customs units, sheriffs' offices, and police departments along the entire border. The operation turned out to be a failed effort that did little to slow the movement of drugs across the Mexican border into the United States.

See also: Operation Alliance; United States Customs, Department of
Reference: Shannon, Elaine. 1989. *Desperadoes.*

Operation Blue Lightning
Coordinated from the Office of the National Narcotic Border Interdiction System (NNBIS) regional center in Miami, Florida, this operation, which was launched in the early 1980s, attacked drug smuggling in two geographical areas: the Bahamas archipelago and the area west of the Bahamian archipel-

ago. Participants in Blue Lightning included sixteen state, county, and city law enforcement agencies; the U.S. Drug Enforcement Administration; the U.S. Customs Service; the Coast Guard; the Department of Defense, and the National Park Service, in addition to the government of the Bahamas. According to the U.S. government, more than 33,000 pounds of marijuana, 6,000 pounds of cocaine, and $1.5 million worth of cash, boats, aircraft, and trailers were seized in the operation.

The President's Commission on Organized Crime assessed that "the raids by the Bahamian authorities forced smugglers to move their drugs into the U.S. immediately, where law enforcement units were positioned to intercept them. Additionally, interdiction techniques were tested and refined, heightening the ability of authorities to conduct coordinated international and interagency operations. (President's Commission on Organized Crime 1986, 312)

See also: Cocaine; Marijuana
Reference: President's Commission on Organized Crime. 1986. *America's Habit: Drug Trafficking and Organized Crime.*

Operation Blue Thunder
A major national drug operation coordinated in the mid eastern United States in September 1994 that resulted in the arrest of twelve suspected drug dealers and the confiscation of several hundred plastic bags, capsules, and vials of heroin and crack cocaine having a street value of at least $25,000.

Reference: Irvin, Richard. 1994. "12 Busted in E. Baltimore Raids." *Baltimore Sun*, 8 September.

Operation C Chase
C Chase stood for "currency chase" and was an operation that the U.S. Customs Service launched in 1986 to uncover drug-money activities in the United States. An elaborate sting was put in place in which business offices were set up in several cities, undercover customs agents were given false papers so that they could act as money launderers for drug dealers, and arrangements were made with banks to allow the customs agents to make large currency deposits. The operation was based in Tampa, Florida, but several successful undercover money-laundering operations were set up in Chicago, New York, Detroit, Philadelphia, Houston, and Los Angeles.

According to money-laundering expert Robert E. Powis, "All of the goals of Operation C Chase were met and there was an additional bonus: a corrupt banking organization and a number of its officers were convicted of money laundering activities. That bank was the Bank of Commerce and Credit International, S.A. (BCCI)." (Powis 1992, 193) But Powis added, "The Customs operation had gone about as far as it could with BCCI." (Powis 1992, 235) Several media reports, however, were critical of Operation C Chase, charging that the U.S. government stopped the operation before it could embarrass the U.S. government.

See also: Bank of Commerce and Credit International (BCCI); Money Laundering; United States Customs, Department of
Reference: Powis, Robert E. 1992 *The Money Launderers.*

Operation C-Note

In 1988 the U.S. Customs Department launched this large money-laundering sting operation (the letter "C" standing for currency) in several American cities, including Detroit and New York City. In the sting that evolved, money launderers gave drug money to Customs agents, who placed it in U.S. banks. The money was then transferred to Panama and several off-shore locations, where Colombian drug traffickers could get access to it.

When the U.S. government decided to shut down the operation in October 1988, agents seized financial ledgers in the New York City area that indicated the receipt and distribution of over $35 million between April and October 1988 in La Mina, another important drug-laundering operation. Operation C-Note also launched a five-year investigation of the Bank of Credit and Commerce International (BCCI), which was conducted under the auspices of the Organized Crime Drug Enforcement Taskforce, a joint IRA, DEA, FBI operation, and led to the conviction in 1990 of several BCCI bankers and dozens of individuals on drug-trafficking and the money-laundering charges.

See also: Bank of Credit and Commerce International (BCCI); Operation Polar Cap
References: Powis, Robert E. 1992. *The Money Launderers.* Robinson, Jeffrey. 1990. *The Laundrymen.*

Operation Calico

In 1987 the U.S. Drug Enforcement Administration created a Special Enforcement Operation to go after Colombia's powerful Cali Cartel. The Operation included a special budget for DEA agents to travel across the United States and in foreign countries, more analysts at DEA headquarters to track Cali Cartel activities, and a directive to DEA regional offices that gave greater priority to cases involving the Cali Cartel. In the months following its creation, Operation Calico had a series of successes against the Cartel. In March 1988, for example, $7.8 million was seized, while a few months later, 5,000 pounds of cocaine were seized in Jackson Heights, Queens. According to Jessica De Grazia, "These successes [proved] to distant but still skeptical supervisors both the magnitude of the [Cali] Cartel and that Operation Calico was necessary. But they also underscored law enforcement's weakness." (De Grazia 1991, 130)

See also: Cali Cartel; Cocaine
Reference: De Grazia, Jessica. 1991. *DEA: The War against Drugs.*

Operation Camarena

See Camarena Salazar, Enrique.

Operation Caribbean Cruise

See Jamaican Posses.

Operation Caribe

An antidrug operation that Drug Enforcement Administration agents in Florida mounted in the late 1970s to investigate drug trafficking in the Bahamian archipelago, which the agency believed to be a major transshipment point for drugs, and to identify the Medellin Cartel as a major transporter of drugs from Norman's Cay. By 1981 DEA agents had gathered enough evidence against Carlos Lehder, one of the Medellin Cartel leaders, to file an indictment in federal court in Jacksonville, Florida. Operation Caribe caused a scandal in the Bahamas, and local police raided Norman's Cay twice. Lehder had fled, however, warned, DEA agents believe, by corrupt Bahamian authorities on the drug lord's payroll.

See also: Lehder Rivas, Carlos; Medellin Cartel; Norman's Cay
Reference: Shannon, Elaine. 1989. *Desperadoes.*

Operation Casablanca

In May 1998 the U.S. government announced that it had completed a three-year undercover investigation by arresting seven leading Mexican bankers and seizing about $50 million in laundered drug money. The elaborate sting, however, had been done without the knowledge of the Americans' counterpart in Mexico. U.S. authorities tricked the Mexican bankers into laundering money through their banks and then convinced nearly two dozen of them to come to the United States for what the bankers thought would be a weekend of festivity. Instead, they were arrested.

In all, 100 people, including about thirty Mexican and Venezuelan bankers, as well as three large Mexican banks, were charged with laundering more than $100 million in narcotics proceeds. Mexico was angered that the operation took place on their soil without their knowledge, but American officials said they did not notify the Mexican authorities in order to protect the undercover agents and secret informants involved in the operation. Mexico said it would demand the extradition of American officials who held meetings in Mexico as part of the operation and would put them on trial.

American officials described Operation Casablanca as the most successful operation of its kind ever undertaken by U.S. law enforcement.

See also: Money Laundering
References: "Mexico Wants To Charge U.S. Agents in Probe." 1998. *Charlotte Observer*, 4 January.
"Yankee Drug Busters Head South." 1998. *The Economist*, 23 May.

Operation Chemcon

An innovative program begun in 1984 by the Drug Enforcement Administration to track large orders of chemicals used in cocaine and heroin refining. A variety of methods were used, including interviewing informants, documenting, and, in certain cases, tagging barrels with beepers that sent signals to authorities. This operation was largely responsible for one of the biggest drug busts ever at Tranquilandia, a cocaine-processing complex in remote Colombia that was run by the Medellin Cartel.

See also: Cocaine;Heroin; Medellin Cartel; Precursor Chemicals; Tranquilandia
Reference: Shannon, Elaine. 1989. *Desperadoes*.

Operation Clean Hand
See Italian Organized Crime

Operation Clean Sweep

An aggressive strategy adopted in 1986 by the U.S. government to disrupt the supply of illegal drugs in Washington, D.C. By March 1989 the operation had netted 46,000 arrests, but at a cost of $6 million in overtime pay to participating police officers.

Reference: Gugliotta, Guy, and Jeff Leen. 1990. *Kings of Cocaine.*

Operation College Farm

Initiated in April 1990, this money-laundering investigation culminated on 25 September 1992 as part of a joint multioffice investigative effort involving the FBI, the IRS, and the Drug Enforcement Administration. The two other investigations were Operation Pacific Estates and Operation Green Harvest in Los Angeles and New York City respectively.

The three investigations monitored the movement and laundering of $36 million in drug-related proceeds given to drug trafficker Antonio Nunez and his organization by the Cali and Medellin drug cartels. On 28 September 1992 FBI Director William Sessions revealed that the three investigations had resulted in the arrest of twelve individuals and the seizure of $4.4 million and ninety bank accounts in the United States. The investigations were originally scheduled to conclude in August 1992, but they were held in abeyance to allow the DEA to complete the Operation Green Ice investigation.

See also: Cali Cartel; Medellin Cartel; Money Laundering; Operation Green Ice; United States Drug Enforcement Administration (DEA); United State Federal Bureau of Investigation (FBI)
Reference: United States Drug Enforcement Administration. Public Affairs Office. 1992. News Release. 12 December.

Operation Columbus

The Drug Enforcement Administration launched this operation in the mid-1980s after the murder of DEA agent Enrique Camarena Salazar in order to gather information about the case, as well as drug trafficking in Mexico. It was considered a long-term project involving the dispatch of informants from U.S. border offices into Mexico. The operation did lead to a number of cocaine seizures but, according to journalist Elaine Shannon, "it did not bring the DEA any closer to finding out what happened to Camarena. The central suspects in the murder of Camarena remained out of reach." (Shannon 1989, 396)

See also: Cocaine; Camarena Salazar, Enrique
Reference: Shannon, Elaine. 1989. *Desperadoes.*

Operation Condor/Trigo

Under U.S. pressure, the Mexican government initiated this opium crop eradication program in November 1975, using aerial spraying instead of manual uprooting of the poppy plants. The Mexican government named the program Operation Condor, while the U.S. Drug Enforcement Administration called its side of the program Operation Trigo (short for tri-zone).

The results were impressive. Mexico's share of the U.S. heroin market subsequently dropped from 75 percent in 1976 to 24 percent in 1980. Mexican officials described the Operation as a "model program" and expressed the hope that other countries would adopt similar programs. Critics, however, pointed out that the program had only short-term success. As journalist Elaine Shannon, explained, "The fittest of the traffickers not only survived but prospered. Operation Condor did them a great service by weaning out the competition." (Shannon 1989, 412)

See also: Environment; Eradication; Heroin
Reference: Shannon, Elaine. 1989. *Desperadoes.*

Operation Cooperation

In 1969 Operation Intercept had caused much controversy and outrage in Mexico, because the Mexican government objected to the border searches. The U.S. government launched Operation Intercept along the U.S.-Mexican border in September 1969 to halt the flow of marijuana, heroin, and other dangerous drugs into the United States, but critics charged that the operation was an effort by the Nixon administration to force Mexican compliance with U.S. antidrug policy. In a diplomatic move, Mexican President Gustavo Diaz Ordaz sent his Deputy General Franco David Rodriguez to Washington to negotiate an end to the border searches. The result was Operation Cooperation, a U.S.-Mexico cooperative effort that would allow American agents to be stationed in Mexico so they could monitor the country's poppy and marijuana fields. The operation, however, did

little to slow down the drug trade. As Drug Enforcement Administration agent Jaime Kuykendall later explained, "The traffickers got the message for a little while that we were serious and they slowed down. But it didn't last. We quit showing we were serious, so they figured everything was hunky-dory. They saw right through us, and they went around behind us." (Shannon 1989, 57)

See also: Heroin; Marijuana
Reference: Shannon, Elaine. 1989. Desperadoes.

Operation Cornerstone

This initiative began in 1991 when U.S. law enforcement authorities seized 12,000 kilograms of cocaine that was being smuggled into the United States inside concrete fence posts. The authorities learned that Cali Cartel kingpin Gilberto Rodriguez Orejuela was moving the cocaine through his South Florida distributor, Harold Ackerman. As a result of Operation Cornerstone, the Drug Enforcement Administration's Miami Division seized more than 29,000 kilograms of cocaine from the Orejuela organization and uncovered evidence that led to the indictment of several prominent U.S. attorneys for the Rodriguez Orejuela family, including Michael Abbell and William Moran, as well a former chief of the Office of International Affairs at the U.S. Justice Department, two former assistant U.S. attorney generals, and fifty-six other individuals. Ackerman was sentenced to a life term in April 1992 for smuggling twenty-two tons of cocaine.

See also: Abbell, Michael; Cali Cartel; Cocaine; Moran, William C.; Rodriguez Orejuela, Gilberto; Rodriguez Orejuela, Miguel
Reference: Duffy, Brian. 1995. "The Old Man and the Seizures: A Key Informant and Good Police Work Produce the Biggest Case Against the Cali Cartel." *U.S. News and World Report*, 19 June.

Operation Desert Stop

A multistate drug bust involving the Drug Enforcement Administration and the FBI that targeted Mexican-based suppliers of heroin, cocaine, and methamphetamine in Louisville, Kentucky; Atlanta, Georgia; and Los Angeles, California. The operation culminated in November 1997, with charges being filed against eighty-two defendants and the seizure of $500,000 in cash and $750,000 worth of illegal

Hundreds of cars and pedestrians wait in line on the Mexican side of the border as Operation Intercept, designed to throttle the flow of dangerous drugs into the United States, was put into effect, 21 September 1969. (Corbis/Bettmann-UPI)

drugs and drug-making chemicals. Most of the arrests were made in Los Angeles.

See also: Cocaine; Heroin; Methamphetamine
Reference: "Probe Targets Network." 1997. *CNN Interactive,* 18 November.

Operation Dignity

This 1996 operation was a reaction on the part of Mexico to economic chaos created by the U.S. drug interdiction exercise known as Operation Intercept, which had tried to stop drug trafficking at the Mexican-American border. More than 4.5 million individuals and their belongings were ultimately inspected by U.S. officials at the border. Traffic backed up for miles and the daily routine of life in Mexican border cities was radically altered. Launched by the Mexican Confederation of National Chambers of Commerce, the campaign urged Mexicans not to cross the border into the United States. Many Mexican citizens heeded the call and refused to cross the border. This led to economic repercussions on the American side when U.S. businesses were hurt by the boycott. What amounted to a boycott was called off with the end of Operation Intercept.

Reference: Shannon, Elaine. 1989. *Desperadoes.*

Operation Dinero

A 1994 criminal investigation that the U.S. Internal Revenue Service and Drug Enforcement Administration conducted jointly with authorities in Spain, Cuba, and Italy. The target was an international money-laundering operation connected to the Cali Cartel. The operation resulted in the arrest of 116 suspects and the seizure of $54 million in cash and assets. Thomas A. Constantine, the head of the U.S. DEA, told the press that Project Dinero clearly showed that Colombia's Cali Cartel had forged alliances with the Russian and Italian Mafias, as well as Spanish and Croatian criminal organizations.

See also: Cali Cartel; Constantine, Thomas A.; Money Laundering
Reference: U.S. House of Representatives Judiciary Committee. *Hearings before the Subcommittee on Crime.* 24 July 1997 (statement of Raymond V. Kelly).

Operation Fountainhead

Launched in 1982, this DEA program used computers to attempt to break the codes that drug traffickers put on kilogram-sized packages transported by Latin American drug traffickers. Dozens of cocaine shipments were traced to Colombia and Jorge Ochoa Vasquez, a leader in the Medellin Cartel. The Operation revealed the sophisticated connections existing between cocaine-smuggling organizations, and as a result, the word "cartel" was introduced in 1983 to describe this connection.

See also: Cocaine; Medellin Cartel; Ochoa Vasquez, Jorge Luis
Reference: Gugliotta, Guy, and Jeff Leen. 1990. *Kings of Cocaine.*

Operation Frontier Lace

As a result of Operation Frontier Shield's success in drug interdiction in the waters around Puerto Rico, drug traffickers shifted their routes in the Caribbean from Puerto Rico to Haiti, prompting the government to redirect its resources to the waters surrounding Haiti and the Dominican Republic for ninety days. In the three-month period from March to June 1997, the U.S. Coast Guard, in conjunction with Haitian and Dominican officials, seized more than 2,500 pounds of cocaine. Operation Frontier Lace was terminated on 1 June 1997.

According to a letter sent to President Clinton by

a group of U.S. Congressmen addressing the subject of drug interdiction in the Caribbean, the termination of Operations Frontier Shield and Frontier Lace couldn't have come at a worse time. According to acting U.S. Customs Commissioner Samuel Banks, "Drug trafficking patterns have unmistakably shifted from the southwest border region back to the Caribbean. This shift will be further exploited unless we work to restore Coast Guard presence in the area. It is imperative to provide additional funding to restore the successful USCG [U.S. Coast Guard] Caribbean drug interdiction initiatives." (Drug Interdiction in the Caribbean and Other Areas 1998, 40)

See also: Cocaine; Operation Frontier Shield; United States Coast Guard
Reference: "Drug Interdiction in the Caribbean and Other Areas." 1998. *International Drug Report* (April/May/June).

Operation Frontier Shield

Initiated in the fall of 1997 under the direction of the U.S. Coast Guard, this operation focused on drug interdiction in the waters around Puerto Rico and was a response to the large amount of drugs flowing into the United States. The campaign lasted ninety days, and according to the U.S. government, led to a 60 percent reduction in the amount of cocaine passing through the area.

See also: Cocaine; Operation Frontier Lace; United States Coast Guard
Reference: "Drug Interdiction in the Caribbean and Other Areas." 1998. *International Drug Report* (April/May/June).

Operation Gateway Sea

See United States Coast Guard.

Operation Global Sea

Begun in 1995, this eighteen-month operation was a cooperative effort of the U.S. Drug Enforcement Administration, the FBI, and the Customs Service and led to the dismantling of a major Nigerian-run drug-trafficking network that had smuggled at least $26 million worth of high-grade Southeast Asian heroin from Bangkok to Chicago. The Global Sea Operation marked the first time that U.S. federal authorities were able to immobilize a major Nigerian drug-trafficking organization operating from its major source

in Bangkok to its primary U.S. distribution center. By spring 1997 the operation had resulted in the arrest of forty-four defendants. DEA Administrator Thomas A. Constantine said, "This investigation demonstrates that Nigerian criminal organizations are no longer involved in heroin trafficking only as a couriers, but have developed into major heroin traffickers in their own right." (Operation Global Sea Nets Big Fish in Heroin Traffic 1997, 7)

See also: Constantine, Thomas A.; Heroin; Nigerian Organized Crime; United States Customs, Department of; United States Drug Enforcement Administration (DEA); United States Federal Bureau of investigation (FBI)
Reference: "Operation Global Sea Nets Big Fish in Heroin Traffic." 1997. *DEA World* (May): 7.

Operation Godfather

See Operation Padrino.

Operation Green Clover

One of two successful U.S. Department of Defense operations (the other being Operation Laser Strike) that were coordinated in the mid-1990s and played an integral part in training and providing intelligence information to Colombian and Peruvian law enforcement authorities fighting drug trafficking. According to Defense Department testimony before the U.S. Congress, during these two operations the United States for the first time worked side by side with countries throughout the Andean region to assist them in developing and implementing operational plans against drug traffickers.

Reference: Hearing before the Subcommittee on National Security, International Affairs, and Criminal Justice committee, Serial No. 105-7L, 105th Congress, second session (testimony of Robert Newberry, U.S. Defense Department Director of Drug Enforcement Policy and Support, before U.S. Congress on 9 July 1997).

Operation Green Harvest

See Operation College Farm.

Operation Green Ice II

A spinoff from the first Green Ice investigation, which ended in 1992. Green Ice II led to the arrest of 109 individuals and the seizure of 13,882 pounds of cocaine, 126 pounds of heroin, and $11.6 million in cash. This second phase of the operation focused on the Cali Cartel's money brokers and cocaine distribution networks from Mexico to the United States and led to the arrest of high-ranking Cali Cartel dealers and money brokers in the United States.

As part of the operation, the Drug Enforcement Administration set up several *casas de cambio* (money exchange houses) along the southwest border of the United States to launder the drug money. More than eighty individuals were indicted.

In the wake of the operation, the DEA said that Green Ice II allowed it to "gain a wealth of knowledge on wire transfers, bank accounts and money courier/brokers." (Green Ice II: Money Launderers Caught 1995, 215)

See also: Cali Cartel; Casas De Cambio; Cocaine; Heroin
Reference: "Green Ice II: Money Launderers Caught." 1995. *DEA World* (Spring/Summer): 214–215.

Operation Green Sweep

A raid on marijuana fields conducted in the King Range National Conservation Area in California in August 1990. This marked the first time the government used active-duty soldiers to mount operations against marijuana growing in the United States. Fifty-eight soldiers equipped with M-16 rifles, led by officials of the Interior Department's Board of Land Management, destroyed marijuana crops and made arrests.

The operation resulted in protests and a lawsuit by local residents and civil libertarians. Some demonstrators described the raids as U.S. military terrorism. (Isikoff 1990) U.S. government officials said similar raids would be launched in Oregon, Hawaii, Kentucky, and possibly other marijuana-producing states.

See also: Marijuana.
Reference: Isikoff, Michael. 1990. "War On Drugs Mobilizes National Guard: Raiders Attack Domestic Marijuana Boom in Remote Patches." *Washington Post*, 14 August.

Operation Greenback

Organized in Miami, Florida, in 1980, this operation was a response to the tremendous increase in money-laundering activity in the late 1970s. This was the result of an explosion in drug use in south Florida that made the region a key center of money-laundering activity. In 1979, for example, the Federal Reserve Bank conducted a study showing a $5.5 billion cash surplus of currency in Florida, while the rest of the country was showing currency deficits. Believing that a large part of the surplus came from drug money, the U.S. Treasury Department reviewed Currency Transaction Reports (CTRs) from Miami banks and discovered that about $350 million in currency transactions had been reported by thirty business and individual accounts.

The U.S. Treasury Department convinced the U.S. Justice Department to participate in the multiagency taskforce that became known as Operation Greenback. Staffed primarily by Justice Department prosecutors and IRS agents, the Operation's purpose was to investigate any unusual currency transactions in south Florida in order to see if any Bank Secrecy Act violations had occurred and to determine if the money was connected to drug-trafficking syndicates. A number of major money launderers were subsequently prosecuted, including Alberto Barrera, Hernan Botero Moreno, and Isaac Katten, and the Operation was deemed a success.

See also: Money Laundering; Operation College Farm; United States Bank Secrecy Act of 1970
References: Freemantle, Brian. 1985. *The Fix.*
Gugliotta, Guy, and Jeff Leen. 1990. *Kings of Cocaine.*

Operation Grouper

A drug investigation sponsored by the Drug Enforcement Administration in the early 1980s in which federal agents posed as off-loaders working on the Texas coast. The agents would complete an unloading job for drug traffickers and then wait to arrest them later in order to protect the operation. In twenty-two months, the operation arrested 155 suspected drug traffickers and seized $1 billion worth of drugs, $1 million in cash, two airplanes, and thirty ships.

References: Executive Intelligence Review. 1992. *Dope, Inc.*
Traub, James. 1983. *The Billion Dollar Connection: The International Drug Trade.*

Operation Hard Line

See United States Customs, Department of

Operation Hat Trick I

A sixty-day operation that began in 1984 under the direction of the National Narcotic Border Interdiction System (NNBIS) that was designed to achieve two objectives: stopping the transport of the fall harvest of marijuana from Colombia, while at the same time interrupting the flow of any cocaine shipped during the Operation. Involved in the Operation were the U.S. Department of Defense, the U.S. Customs Service, and the U.S. intelligence community. The NNBIS reported that over 600,000 pounds of marijuana and 6,000 pounds of cocaine were seized by the participating U.S. agencies during the Operation. According to the President's Commission on Organized Crime, "Operation Hat Trick has come to be viewed as a prototype effort in that it initiated improvements in planning, communications security, in-country efforts, air operations, intelligence, and resource support." (President's Commission on Organized Crime 1986, 309)

See also: Cocaine; Marijuana; Operation Hat Trick II; National Narcotic Border Interdiction Service (NNBIS)
References: Cooper, Mary H. 1990. *The Business of Drugs.* President's Commission On Organized Crime. 1986. *America's Habit: Drug Trafficking and Organized Crime.*

Operation Hat Trick II

Drawing on the experience of Operation Hat Trick I, the National Narcotics Border Interdiction System (NNBIS) launched Hat Trick II in November 1985. It was an ambitious effort to disrupt drug traffic in the United States by tightening surveillance along the U.S. border with Mexico and surveillance of known air and ocean supply routes from South America and other Caribbean countries. This operation involved the participation of all civilian drug enforcement agencies and all branches of the military.

See also: Operation Hat Trick I; National Narcotics Border Interdiction System
Reference: President's Commission On Organized Crime. 1986. *America's Habit: Drug Trafficking and Organized Crime.*

Operation Hell Flower
See Golden Triangle

Operation Intercept
See Operation Dignity.

Operation Jalisco

Launched in 1986, this operation was the brainchild of William Von Raab, U.S. Customs commissioner, who wanted the United States to pursue a get-tough response to the torture and murder of Drug Enforce-

ment Administration agent Victor Cortez by Mexican police in Guadalajara, Mexico. Immediately after Cortez's murder, Von Raab tried to convince the Reagan administration to allow him to take an aggressive stand against drug-trafficking along the Mexican border. According to Von Raab's plan, until Cortez's torturers were in jail, U.S. Customs agents would selectively inspect all cars and trucks with Jalisco plates that appeared at U.S.-Mexican border crossings, while the Federal Air Administration would cancel the landing rights of all airplanes flying out of Guadalajara International Airport. The plan was presented to a crisis subcommittee within the Reagan administration, but it was rejected because of fears that the operation could provoke retaliation against DEA agents in Guadalajara.

See also: Reagan, Ronald; United States Drug Enforcement Administration (DEA)
Reference: Shannon, Elaine. 1989. *Desperadoes.*

Operation Just Cause
See Noriega, Manuel Antonio.

Operation Laser Strike
See Operation Green Clover.

Operation Limelight

One of the major drug busts (the other being Operation Reciprocity) against the drug-trafficking organization of Amado Carillo Fuentes. Conducted by federal, state, and local antidrug teams in August 1977, the Operation resulted in the seizure of 4,012 kilograms of cocaine, 10,846 pounds of marijuana, $7.3 million in currency, and the arrest of fifty-eight people.

Limelight focused on the Alberto Beltran transportation and distribution cell, which was an important part of the Carillo Fuentes organization. Authorities believed that the Beltran cell, located in Mexico, was responsible for the monthly shipment of at least 1.5 tons of cocaine, which was transported across the U.S. border by Mexican nationals, usually in crates of fruits and vegetables.

See also: Carillo Fuentes, Amado; Cocaine; Marijuana; Operation Reciprocity.
Reference: Green, Eric. 1997. "Constantine Warns of New Drug Menace in the United States." U.S.I.A. Press Release, 2 September.

Operation Mars

The Mexican Army launched this operation in 1987 against the strongholds of the country's drug traffickers in the wake of the death of U.S. Drug Enforcement Administration agent Enrique Camarena Salazar. The operation was an effort by the Mexican government to get tough on drug trafficking, but this operation, like the reform measures of the Mexican government to clean up drug corruption, was largely cosmetic, and Mexico retained its position as the number-one source of marijuana and the major conduit for marijuana and cocaine entering the United States.

See also: Camarena Salazar, Enrique; Cocaine; Marijuana
Reference: Shannon, Elaine. 1989. *Desperadoes*.

Operation Offsides

Convinced that the Cali Cartel was expanding its European network, the U.S. Drug Enforcement Administration launched this initiative in 1990 in collaboration with the law enforcement and intelligence services of Italy, Colombia, and Argentina. The operation targeted for capture some twenty suspected fugitive drug traffickers who had fled Colombia after being charged or convicted in the United States. The authorities hoped to snare many of the Cali Cartel's top leaders during the soccer World Cup competition in Italy in the summer of 1990, but they failed in their objective.

See also: Cali Cartel
Reference: De Grazia, Jessica. 1991. *DEA: The War against Drugs*.

Operation Pacific Estates

See Operation College Farm

Operation Padrino

A U.S. Drug Enforcement Administration operation in Mexico that began in 1982 and targeted the Miguel Angel Felix Gallardo cocaine drug-trafficking organization. The operation, however, had little success, and it appears that by 1984 Felix Gallardo knew about the investigation. The DEA was able to tie up only $13 million of the drug trafficker's money, a figure that one DEA agent called "pocket change."

See also: Cocaine; Felix Gallardo, Miguel Angel

Reference: Shannon, Elaine. 1989. *Desperadoes*.

Operation Polar Cap

A thirteen-month federal operation that led to the arrest of the leaders of a billion dollar money-laundering scheme that involved the movement of cocaine profits through jewelry stores to California banks and then to drug dealers in Colombia. The laundering activity was so efficient and lucrative that the Colombian drug traffickers who kept it going from 1986 to 1989 called it La Mina, the "gold mine."

According to federal officials, La Mina laundered more than $1.2 billion in cocaine profits from the leading members of the Medellin Cartel. The cocaine from Colombia was sold on the streets of New York City and the proceeds packed into boxes labeled as jewelry, which were then delivered by armored car to New York's La Guardia airport and shipped to Los Angeles. Another armored car in Los Angeles took the boxes from the airport to a store in the city's jewelry district, where high-speed cash-counting machines counted and repacked the currency. The money was then delivered to city banks and deposited as if it were the proceeds from jewelry sales. To further muddy the trail, the money was then wire-transferred to unsuspecting banks in New York City, which were then directed to wire the drug money to other New York banks, before it was finally wired to Colombia.

See also: Cocaine; Martinez Romero, Eduardo; Medellin Cartel; Money Laundering; Operation C-Note
Reference: Woolner, Ann. 1994. *Washed in Gold: The Story Behind The Biggest Money-Laundering Investigation in U.S. History*.

Operation Primavera

A ten-day campaign conducted by the Colombian government in February 1989 designed to destroy the huge cocaine-processing industry that thrived in Colombia's jungles. Police confiscated about 1.3 tons of base and processed cocaine and seized unprecedented quantities of the precursor chemicals used in cocaine manufacturing, including nearly 418 gallons of ethyl ketone and 95 tons of potassium permanganate. It was enough chemicals to make about 104 tons of cocaine, or one-third of the estimated annual output of Colombia, Bolivia, and Peru combined. At the time, Colombian officials boasted that the operation was the most successful bust of cocaine laboratories in the country's history.

See also: Cocaine; Precursor Chemicals
Reference: Doerner, William R. 1989. "The Chemical Connection." *Time*, 20 February.

Operation Raccoon

Launched in 1979, this operation involved more than thirty members of the Royal Bahamian Defense and Police Forces in a raid of Norman's Cay, the island that served as a drug-trafficking base for Carlos Lehder Rivas and the Medellin Cartel. Prior to the raid, Lehder had been under police surveillance for a long time and authorities were concerned that the drug traffickers had taken over the island. Lehder was arrested after he fled Norman's Cay by powerboat.

In all, the Bahamian officials arrested thirty people, but Lehder was allowed to go free. Later however, all of Lehder's arrested associates were released on $2,000 bail. Only one person was convicted as a result of the operation—a Bahamian for carrying an unregistered gun. It is believed that Lehder had bribed the Bahamian authorities.

See also: Lehder Rivas, Carlos; Medellin Cartel; Norman's Cay
Reference: Gugliotta, Guy, and Jeff Leen. 1990. *Kings of Cocaine.*

Operation Reciprocity

One of two major drug sweeps (the other being Operation Limelight) against the Amado Carillo Fuentes drug-trafficking organization that was conducted in August 1997 by federal, state, and local antidrug teams. The operation resulted in fifty-six indictments for violation of federal antidrug laws in El Paso, Texas; Grand Rapids, Michigan; and Tucson, Arizona. It revealed that traffickers were transporting cocaine in the New York City area in false compartments in the roofs of tractor trailers, and in hollowed-out stacks of plywood.

The operation resulted in the seizure of seven tons of cocaine, 2,800 pounds of marijuana, and more than $11 million in U.S. currency. Authorities said that the two busts showed that Mexican drug-trafficking cartels were expanding across the United States. At the time of his death in July 1997, Carillo Fuentes was considered the most powerful drug trafficker in Mexico.

See also: Carillo Fuentes, Amado; Cocaine; Marijuana; Operation Limelight
Reference: Green, Eric. 1997. "Constantine Warns of New Drug Menace in the United States." U.S.I.A. Press Release, 12 August.

Operation Red River

Launched in 1992 and involving the U.S. Drug Enforcement Administration and several state law enforcement agencies, this operation began in northwest Texas and southeast Oklahoma and followed the Red River Along the Texas, Oklahoma, and Arkansas state lines. The operation required nearly two years of planning and intelligence efforts by federal and state agencies and targeted more than 714 suspected plots of cultivated marijuana. The operation's objective was to destroy the cultivation of domestic marijuana on public and private lands along the Red River. Described as "the largest multiagency operation ever spearheaded by the DEA in the U.S." (Operation Red River Completed First Phase 1992, 7), Operation Red River led to the seizure of nearly 40,000 marijuana plants during the first twenty days of operation.

See also: Marijuana; United States Drug Enforcement Administration
Reference: "Operation Red River Completed First Phase." 1992. *DEA World* (October): 7–8.

Operation Royal Flush

The U.S. government launched this operation in 1992 as a way of identifying and neutralizing the approximately 150 money launderers who at the time were providing the money for the Colombian cartels to operate.

See also: Money Laundering
Reference: Andelman, David A. 1994. "The Drug Money Maze." *Foreign Affairs* (July–August): 94–108.

Operation Screamer

A big antidrug sting operation of the early 1980s that had as its goal the infiltration of a network of mercenary pilots who were flying shipments of drugs into the United States. One of them was Barry Seale, whom a federal grand jury indicted in March 1983 in Fort Lauderdale, Florida, for smuggling 200,000 quaaludes into the United States. Facing a possible sentence of sixty-one years, Seale agreed to work as an informant for the government and go undercover. Operation Screamer led to the arrest of seventy-five suspects.

See also: Quaaludes; Seale, Barry Alderman
Reference: Gugliotta, Guy, and Jeff Leen. 1990. *Kings of Cocaine.*

Operation Screaming Eagle

First tried in 1986, this program was a joint effort by the U.S. Drug Enforcement Administration and Bolivian authorities that took advantage of the Bolivian legal code, which allowed authorities to seize and keep evidence for twenty-one days without having to prove that a crime had been committed. A team of DEA experts went to Bolivia and vacuum-cleaned and searched planes that had been confiscated for what authorities believed was use in drug trafficking. In the initial operation, twelve aircraft were vacuum-cleaned, and the authorities found evidence of cocaine in six of them. The Bolivian authorities initiated the program and a Bolivian team of chemists trained by the DEA to examine planes became known as the "Screaming Eagles."

See also: Cocaine; United States Drug Enforcement Administration (DEA)
Reference: De Grazia, Jessica. 1991. *DEA: The War against Drugs.*

Operation Snowcap

Begun in 1987, this operation was the biggest antidrug operation ever launched in Latin America. It involved nine countries, including the United States, and cost the U.S. Drug Enforcement Administration $8 million annually. Initially, about 140 agents were assigned to the operation, but the U.S. government expected that figure to rise to 180. The DEA agents received twelve weeks of jungle training, five weeks of tactical training, and Spanish-language training before being assigned to three-to-four-month rotations accompanying police forces in the Latin American countries involved in the project.

In Bolivia, where many of Snowcap's activities took place, the press reported that the DEA agents had "crossed the line" from being simply advisors to running the entire operation of the Bolivian antinarcotic militia. The press also reported that the escalation of Snowcap activities in Peru was causing concern among senior U.S. officials who worried that

U.S. drug agents would become combatants in a civil war between Shining Path guerrillas and the Peruvian government.

In June 1990, the DEA announced plans to scale back Operation Snowcap and begin a "phased withdrawal" of its agents assigned to accompany Peruvian and Bolivian police on antidrug raids of laboratories, airstrips and drug trafficker strongholds.

See also: Shining Path Guerrilla Movement; United States Drug Enforcement Administration
References: U.S. House Committee on Foreign Affairs. *Operation Snowcap: Its Present and Future Flow of Cocaine With Operation Snowcap. Is It Working?* 1990. 101st Congress, 2nd Session, 23 May.
U.S. House Committee on Government Operations. *Stopping The Flow of Cocaine With Operation Snowcap. Is It Working?* 1990. House Report, 101st Congress, 2nd Session, 101-673.

Operation Steeple

A study conducted by the U.S. Drug Enforcement Administration in which agents examined the Colombian imports of ether and acetone to determine the size of the Colombian cocaine industry. The study took place from January 1978 to July 1981, and was completed on 14 December 1981. The report of the study concluded that while acetone had a fairly wide industrial application in Colombia, ether did not, and perhaps as much 98 percent of the imported ether was destined for illicit uses. The DEA report concluded that the authorities could "effect major change of the Colombian cocaine processing industry through the denial of selected precursors, namely acetone and ether." (Gugliotta & Leen 1990, 123) The report also showed the DEA that the Colombian cocaine trade was much larger than they had previously believed.

See also: Cocaine; Precursor Chemicals; United States Drug Enforcement Administration
Reference: Gugliotta, Guy, and Jeff Leen. 1990. *Kings of Cocaine.*

Operation Swordfish

On 15 October 1982 the U.S. government culminated an eighteen-month investigation and crackdown on a major drug-smuggling and money-laundering operation by indicting four bankers, three attorneys and doctors, and several residents of Miami and Colombia. In all, Operation Swordfish gathered enough evidence for a federal grand jury to indict sixty-seven people on drug-related charges. In addition, more than $1 million in cash, bank accounts, vehicles, and real estate were seized, along with 500,000 quaalude pills, seventy-six kilograms of cocaine, and a sizable amount of marijuana.

The first major money-laundering investigation launched by the U.S. Drug Enforcement Administration, Operation Swordfish set up a bogus investment counseling firm called Dean International Investment, Inc., to launder drug traffickers' money. Although no banks were charged with illegal activity in the indictments, DEA agents funneled $19 million through the "firm" and on to forty-two U.S. and five foreign bank accounts. Investigative journalist David McClintick wrote a book entitled *Swordfish,* in which he alleged that drug agents used unethical tactics in the operation.

See also: Cocaine; Marijuana; Money Laundering; United States Drug Enforcement Administration (DEA)
References: Cody, Edward. 1982. "Sunfish Avoids A Net Set By Boss." *Washington Post,* 16 October.
McClintick, David. 1993. *Swordfish.*

Operation Tandem

Launched in 1989 as a joint U.S. and Bolivian anti-narcotics police initiative, this program targeted Yayo Rodriguez, a major drug trafficker. A surprise raid on the city of San Ramon in Bolivia led to the capture of much of Rodriguez's communication system and the disruption of the Colombian side of his organization, which needed Bolivian coca for their cocaine laboratories. The operation, however, proved to be largely symbolic and did little to diminish San Ramon's role as a major center of drug-trafficking activity.

See also: United States Drug Enforcement Administration (DEA)
Reference: De Grazia, Jessica. 1991. *DEA: The War against Drugs.*

Operation Thai-In

This operation targeted the marijuana-smuggling operation of Bangkok-based Brian Daniels, who had lived in the city since the early 1970s. Daniels brokered marijuana to U.S. groups, an illicit business that reportedly cleared him $2 million per ton. In 1989 alone, Daniels reportedly cleared $35 million, in October 1990, Daniels pled guilty to the charges of smuggling more than 190 tons of marijuana into the

United States, and was sentenced to 25 years in prison and a fine of $6.25 million. Another 250 individuals were also arrested and assets worth $96 million seized. The U.S. Drug Enforcement Administration has described Operation Thai-In as the biggest marijuana operation it ever undertook.

See also: Marijuana; United States Drug Enforcement Administration (DEA)
Reference: "$96 Million in Assets Seized." 1991. *DEA World* (May-June) 1991, p. 16.

Operation Thunderbolt

Conducted in the latter part of 1981, this antidrug operation lasted ninety days and resulted in the capture of forty-five aircraft, along with the seizure of a sizable amount of pills, cocaine, marijuana, and hashish. The operation is considered historic because the military was used for the first time in the War on Drugs. The use of personnel from the U.S. Customs Service and the U.S. Navy was made possible by an amendment to the U.S. Defense Appropriations Act, which was signed by President Ronald Reagan in December 1981 and allowed the U.S. government to break a 103–year prohibition against using the military as posse comitatus.

See also: Cocaine; Hashish; Heroin; Marijuana; United States Posse Comitatus Act
Reference: Hellman, Peter. 1982. "Reagan Gets Tough on Drugs." *Rolling Stone,* 15 April.

Operation Tiger Trip

A two-year investigation conducted by a joint task force of Thai police, military, and antidrug agents in collaboration with the U.S. State Department, Drug Enforcement Administration, and the Immigration and Naturalization Service. The task force methodically tracked down the drug-trafficking network of the powerful Myanmar drug lord Khun Sa, and in November 1994, ten of the organization's leading lieutenants were arrested. After the investigation, U.S. and Thai officials continued to work together toward the goal of dismantling Khun Sa's entire operation. Khun Sa is himself in custody of the Myanmar government.

See also: Khun Sa
Reference: Tutsathit, Tapin, and Yinder Lertcharoechok. 1994. "Khun Sa Network Dismantled." *Sunday Nation,* 18 December.

Operation Trigo
See Operation Condor

Operation Trinity
A U.S. Drug Enforcement Administration operation of the early 1980s that was based in New York City and targeted the city's violent street distribution gangs for arrest and incarceration. The operation spent two years investigating a street gang headed by Walter Tyrone Smith, a vicious and violent gangster who operated in Harlem. Operation Trinity was able to attribute twelve murders to Smith, and he was sentenced to two life terms in prison.

Reference: De Grazia, Jessica. 1991. *DEA: The War Against Drugs.*

Operation Vanguard
Launched in 1984, this operation involved the U.S. government asking the Mexican government to allow Drug Enforcement Administration observers to fly over Mexican poppy and marijuana fields in order to verify the Mexican government's claims that it was eradicating these drug crops by spraying them with herbicide. The U.S. had difficulty getting Mexico to approve the plan but finally in October 1984 the Mexican attorney general agreed to the U.S. terms. "The airplanes were produced around November 1," writes Elaine Shannon in Desperadoes. "The DEA agents who were taken aloft confirmed the worst suspicions of agents in Guadalajara. There was more marijuana and opium growing out there than anyone imagined." (Shannon 1989, 215)

See also: Eradication; Marijuana; United States Drug Enforcement Administration
Reference: Shannon, Elaine. 1989. *Desperadoes.*

Operation Wipeout
The U.S. Drug Enforcement Administration has described this operation, which began in 1990 and focused on Hawaii, as one of the most successful eradication programs ever undertaken by the agency. Phase One of the Operation destroyed 85 to 90 percent of the summer marijuana crop, eradicated more than 750,000 plants and led to the arrest of more than 600 individuals. The spraying technique employed in the eradication campaign used an herbicide identical to a household weed killer known as Round-Up. According to the DEA, the success of Operation Wipeout's spot spraying campaign encouraged other states in the United States to consider using the technique.

See also: Environment; Eradication; Marijuana; United States Drug Enforcement Administration
Reference: Operation Wipeout. 1991. *DEA World* (July–August).

Operation Zorro
An eight-month multiagency investigation of the 1990s, the result of the Southwest Border initiative, a joint DEA-FBI program in which their special agents work together to disrupt Mexican drug-trafficking organizations and jail their leaders. For the first time, law enforcement authorities succeeded in dismantling not only the U.S. infrastructure of a Colombian cocaine-producing organization, but also that of the organization responsible for transporting the drug. The operation led to the arrest of 136 people and the seizure of over $17 million in cash and 5,600 pounds of cocaine. During the course of the investigation, law enforcement officers shared information they planned to use for ninety court-ordered wiretaps.

According to congressional testimony by Harold Wankel, chief of operations of the DEA, "On a larger scale, the DEA, FBI, and U.S. Customs Service, working through our representatives at the Embassy in Mexico City, share drug and drug-related law enforcement information with our counterparts in Mexico on a regular basis utilizing CENDRO, the Mexican Center for handling drug intelligence." (Wankel 1996)

See also: Cocaine; Southwest Border initiative
Reference: Wankel, Harold D. 1996. "Drug Control along the Southwest Border." Testimony before U.S. House Judiciary Committee, U.S. Drug Enforcement Administration, website http://www.usdoj/dea/pubs/congrtest.

Opium
This drug comes from the juice of the poppy plant *Papaver somniferum* and is obtained by cutting the seed of the poppy plant and then scraping the residue from the incised plant. Both heroin and morphine are made from opium. Evidence seems to indicate that opium has been used since prehistoric times, but in the modern age opium became the world's most popular drug largely as a result of national policy. By the early 1800s Great Britain had

Typical scene of an opium den in Chinatown, New York, 12 April 1926. (UPI/Corbis-Bettmann)

become the largest drug trafficker in history by targeting the large Chinese market. Opium importation into China from India increased tenfold between 1840 and 1880, from 200 to 2,000 tons.

The use of opium to treat ailments such as pain or dysentery became popular in the nineteenth century, and many famous people, including Samuel Taylor Coleridge, William Wordsworth, Sir Arthur Conan Doyle, and Thomas De Quincey, became devotees of the drug. But by the end of the nineteenth century, addiction had become a problem. In the United States alone, an estimated 200,000 Americans had become addicted to opiates derived from opium. Laws were passed in the United States making opium and its derivatives (heroin, for example) available only though prescription, but by the 1920s, opium dens were operating in most U.S. cities. In 1942, the Opium Poppy Control Act prohibited cultivation of the plant in the United States except under license. In 1970 the Controlled Substances Act classified medicines containing opium as Schedule II, III, and V drugs, available only through prescription.

Today, the opium poppy is grown all over the world in countries such as China, Mexico, Turkey, Lebanon, Colombia, and several places in Southeast Asia, but it does not pose the drug-trafficking threat that its derivative, heroin, does. Opium eating and opium smoking are the most common ways of using the drug. As it has been for hundreds of years, opium is also used as a remedy for pain and other medical problems.

The United States and its allies in the War on Drugs are involved in a number of worldwide poppy eradication programs with several countries in the hope that the supply of heroin, morphine, and other narcotics derived from opium will be reduced.

See also: Air America; Anslinger, Harry A.; Carter, James Earl; De Quincey, Thomas; Doyle, Sir Arthur Conan; Heroin; Kuomintang; League of Nations; Marijuana; Morphine; Opium Wars; Golden Triangle; Golden Crescent; Spanish American War; United States Comprehensive Crime Control Act of 1970; United States Opium Extension Act; Vietnam War; World War II; Wright, Dr. Hamilton; Yakuza
Reference: Courtwright, David T. 1982. *Dark Paradise.*

Opium Wars

Two conflicts between Great Britain and China that lasted from 1839 to 1842 and then again in 1856. Great Britain was looking for a way to end the restrictions China had put on foreign trade when China took action to enforce its prohibition against opium importing, destroying a British ship laden with opium at the harbor of Canton. Concerned about its opium trade, Britain retaliated, destroying several coastal cities and easily defeating China. Through the treaty of Nanking, Great Britain won trade concessions from China, and, within a few years, other foreign powers gained the same, in effect making China a colony of foreign powers.

In 1856 a second opium war broke out following the Chinese seizure of another British ship. British and French troops took Canton and Tientsin and forced the Chinese to accept the treaty of Tientsin, to which Russia and the United States were also parties. As a result of the treaty, China agreed to legalize the importation of opium. Groups of Protestant missionaries and non-Chinese physicians in China initiated the movement to suppress the opium trade in China. International conferences and conventions in 1909, 1918, and 1930 ultimately led to the restriction and prohibition of traffic in opium and opium derivatives, including heroin, morphine, and codeine.

See also: Opium
References: Fay, P. W. 1975. *The Opium War, 1840–1842.*
Greenburg, Michael. 1951. *British Trade and the Opening of China, 1800–1842.*

Organization of American States (OAS)

In 1988 the Organization of American States established the 34–member Inter-American Drug Abuse Commission (CICAD) with the purpose of promoting multinational cooperation within the organization against the illegal international drug trade. The CICAD meets twice yearly and is attended by the most senior drug control authorities of the member states. The OAS's mandate in the drug control area includes the adoption of measures that will lead to the development of preventive education programs in the workplace and for school children, the adoption of legislation on money laundering, and the establishment of a drug surveillance monitoring system that collects and analyzes data from selected emergency rooms and detention centers in Central America.

See also: Clinton, William Jefferson; Money Laundering; Summit of the Americas

Reference: United Nations International Drug Control Program. 1997. *World Drug Report.*

Organized Crime Task Force (U.S.)

Implemented by U.S. Assistant Attorney General Rudolph Giuliani after President Ronald Reagan took office in 1980, the task force targeted the leadership of major Italian Mafia syndicates. The program pooled the resources of the FBI, Drug Enforcement Administration, Justice Department, International Revenue Service, Customs Department, and metropolitan and state police departments. The Task Force's work led to the uncovering of the Pizza Connection, an Italian Mafia heroin-trafficking and money-laundering operation, and by 1987 valuable data on at least a thousand Mafia members.

See also: Pizza Connection; Reagan, Ronald; United States Customs, Department of; United States Drug Enforcement Administration (DEA); United States Federal Bureau of Investigation (FBI)
Reference: Sterling, Claire. 1990. *Octopus: The Long Reach of the International Sicilian Mafia.*

Orlandez Gamboa, Alberto

Nicknamed "Caracol," Orlandez Gamboa is believed to head the most powerful drug-trafficking organization on the north coast of Colombia, known as the Coast Cartel, and is said to be responsible for smuggling multiton shipments of cocaine to the United States via air and sea routes by way of Haiti, the Dominican Republic, Puerto Rico, and other Caribbean islands. He works closely with drug-trafficking organizations in Mexico and Central America and is reported to have several front companies to launder millions of dollars in drug proceeds. Orlandez Gamboa was captured in June 1998, but he had also been indicted in south Florida on drug-related charges. While Colombia considers whether to extradite him to the United States for trial, he is in jail in Colombia. Colombian authorities consider the dismemberment of the Coast Cartel one of its major successes in 1998.

References: "Alleged Drug Boss Captured in Colombia." 1998. *Charlotte Observer,* 8 June.
"A Prision La Nueva Generacion De La Mafia." 1998. *El Tiempo,* 31 December.

Orozco-Prada, Eduardo

In 1983 Orozco-Prada became involved in one of the first big money-laundering cases in U.S. history. Orozco-Prada was the owner of Cirex International, a Colombian coffee-importing company based in New York City, and he worked with partners in Boston, Seattle, and Washington, D.C., to launder $150 million in drug money over a four-year period. The laundered money was delivered in $20 bills to Orozco-Prada's office in New York City, where it was counted and deposited in a New York City Citibank branch. Then, with the help of the branch's manager, Fred Gamble, the money was subsequently transferred to eighteen different bank accounts in Colombia, Panama, and Switzerland.

See also: Money Laundering
Reference: Ehrenfeld, Rachel. 1992. *Evil Money*.

Outlaws

Founded in 1959, the Outlaws merged with the Canadian motorcycle gang Satan's Choice in 1977 to become the largest motorcycle gang in the United States and Canada. Today, the Outlaws have thirty-nine chapters (six in Canada) and an estimated 1,200 to 1,500 members. Law enforcement reports that the gang is involved in cocaine-trafficking largely through their Florida chapters, many of which have established ties with Cuban and Colombian drug traffickers.

See also: Cocaine; Cuban Connection
Reference: Miller, Gary J. 1997. *Drugs and The Law—Detention, Recognition and Investigation*.

Oxycodone

A semisynthetic opioid analgesic that is used to relieve moderate or moderately severe pain, oxycodone is similar in effect to codeine, but it is more potent with a higher dependence potential. Legally, oxycodone is used as a pain reliever that can be either taken orally or in combination with other drugs. Physical dependence can occur, but is not as common as with some of the other semisynthetic opioids, such as heroin or morphine.

See also: Codeine; Heroin; Morphine; Synthetic Drugs
Reference: Marnell, Tim, ed. 1997. *Drug Identification Bible*.

P

Pagans

This motorcycle gang was founded in 1959 in Prince George County, Maryland. Its largest chapter is based in Philadelphia and it operates mainly in the northeastern United States, where it dominates the PCP and methamphetamine drug trade. In July 1998, two men who were members of the Amish, a strict anabaptist religious sect that shuns most worldly ways and affects plain garb, were charged, along with eight members of a Pagan motorcycle gang, with selling cocaine. In June 1999 seven of the arrested were sentenced in Philadelphia to terms ranging from home confinement to prison.

See also: Methamphetamine; PCP
Reference: Miller Gary J. 1997. *Drugs and the Law—Detention, Recognition and Investigation.*

Palace of Justice (Bogotá, Colombia)

At 11:40 a.m. on 6 November 1985, approximately thirty-five heavily armed M-19 guerrillas stormed into the Colombian Palace of Justice, located on Bogotá's central Plaza de Bolivar. Within minutes the guerrillas had 250 hostages, including Alfonso Reyes Echandia, chief justice of Colombia's Supreme Court, and many of the court's twenty-five Supreme Court justices. For the next twenty-six hours, hundreds of Colombian soldiers and police tried to retake the building, but the guerrillas were heavily armed and well entrenched, and they fought off their attackers. When the government launched a final assault, twenty-five hostages in the Palace died, including Chief Justice Reyes, eleven of the twenty-four justices, and apparently all of the guerrillas.

It is widely believed that drug traffickers paid the M-19 guerrillas to attack the Palace of Justice and burn the extradition case files in the court archives. The twenty-four justices, many of whom were believed to be in favor of upholding the extradition treaty with the United States, were scheduled to vote in the near future on the issue. When the Colombian Supreme Court finally voted on the extradition treaty's ratification, the Colombian law implementing the treaty was found to be unconstitutional by one vote.

See also: Extradition; M-19
References: Carrigan, Ana. 1993. *The Palace of Justice: A Colombian Tragedy.*
Gugliotta, Guy and Jeff Leen. 1990. *Kings of Cocaine.*

Palaez Roldan, Benardo (c. 1954–)

A key figure in the Medellin Cartel, who was extradited to the United States in October 1989 with two other accused drug traffickers (Ana Elena Rodriguez Tamayo and Robert Peter Carlini). At the time of Palaez Roldan's extradition, Stephen Markman, U.S. attorney general for the western district of Michigan, said, "This is a major victory in bringing a leading participant in the Colombian cartels to justice." (Colombian Drug Lord Extradited to the U.S. 1989)

Palaez Roldan's capture was the result of a war against drug trafficking launched by Colombian President Virgilio Barco Vargas three months earlier.

Palaez Roldan had been one of twenty-eight people indicted in November 1983 on charges that, between 1975 and 1983, he belonged to a drug-trafficking organization, sold more than 600 pounds of cocaine, and received $6 million in drug proceeds. During the first week of his trial, however, he disappeared while free on $200,000 bond. But the trial continued, and he was convicted in absentia the following year. In November 1989 Palaez Roldan was sentenced to fifteen years in prison.

See also: Barco Vargas, Virgilio; Extradition; Medellin Cartel
Reference: "Colombian Drug Lord Extradited to Detroit."
    1989. United Press International, 15 October.
"Extradited Colombian Gets Fifteen Years in 1989 Conviction." 1989. United Press International, 7 November.

Pallomari, Guillermo Alejandro "Reagan"

Chilean-born accountant, bookkeeper, and security expert for the Cali Cartel who was at the nerve center of the drug-trafficking organization during the height of its power in the early 1990s and oversaw the organization's most important area: payoffs. In 1994 the Colombian police raided Pallomari's office, located in the city of Cali, and found evidence of Cartel payoffs to Colombian politicians, military officers, and other leading Colombians. Pallomari fled to the United States in August 1995, in fear for his life after learning that somebody had ordered his assassination. In the safe custody of U.S. law enforcement officials, he volunteered to talk about the Cali Cartel's operation.

U.S. officials described Pallomari as "the best witness they ever had" (Fed's Big Catch: Man at the Center of Cali Cartel 1995), and he began testifying in drug cases in U.S. courts. The Colombian magazine *Semana* reported that Pallomari told U.S. officials the Cali Cartel had contributed at least $6 million to Ernesto Samper Pizano's 1994 presidential campaign. Samper denied the charge, and the U.S. government declined to comment.

Pallomari was also one of three individuals who, in 1996 and 1997, presented evidence in the investigation of Raul Salinas de Gortari, brother of former Mexican President Carlos Salinas de Gortari. The questioning was done by a Swiss government attorney and Mexico's antinarcotics chief in U.S. jails in the presence of three U.S. officials. Pallomari and the two other witnesses told Swiss prosecutors that the

cartels they worked for (the Cali and Medellin Cartels) paid off members of the Salinas family, including the former president, for protecting their drug-trafficking activities in Mexico.

Pallomari claimed that the Cali Cartel paid up to $5 million a month to Carlos and Raul Salinas and other top Mexican officials. The accountant said that the money was paid to drug trafficker Amado Carillo Fuentes, who then gave the money to Raul Salinas so it could be passed on to his brother. In a hand-written letter to the *Miami Herald*, Raul Salinas said emphatically, "I have never had any relations with drug trafficking," and according to the *Herald*, "reinterated his previous assertions that his Swiss deposits came from legitimate business deals." (Oppenheimer 1998) In December 1998 Pallomari was sentenced to seven years in a U.S. prison.

See also: Cali Cartel; Carillo Fuentes, Amado; Medellin Cartel; Ramos, Jose Manuel; Salinas De Gortari, Carlos; Salinas De Gortari, Raul
References: "Fed's Big Catch: Man at the Center of Cali Cartel." 1995. *Miami Herald*, 6 October.
Oppenheimer, Andres. 1998. "Swiss Pursue Links to Drug Money." *Miami Herald*, 14 July.

Palma, Manuel (1950–)

A Colombian drug trafficker who was captured in the coastal city of Barranquilla on 11 October 1989 and who, with another drug trafficker named Robert James Sokolowski Salah, was extradited to the United States in November 1989 as part of a crackdown waged by President Virgilio Barco Vargas against the country's drug cartels. On 17 April 1989 Palma had been named in an indictment, which charged him with drug trafficking and money laundering.

See also: Barco Vargas, Virgilio; Extradition; Money Laundering; Sokolowksi Salah, Robert James
Reference: Coleman, Joseph. 1989. "Colombia Extradites Two More," United Press International, 18 November.

Parejo Gonzalez, Enrique

Parejo Gonzalez succeeded the assassinated Rodrigo Lara Bonilla as Colombia's justice minister in 1984, and he proved to be just as tough on drug trafficking as his predecessor. Parejo Gonzalez believed that extradition was the best way to combat the Colombian drug trade, and so in November 1984, he submitted to Colombian President Belisario Betancur Cuartas the paperwork for the extradition of five key drug traffickers. The president approved the extraditions, and by September 1985 six Colombians had been extradited to the United States, nine more were in custody, and 105 U.S. "Requests for Provisional Arrests" were active in Colombia. By the end of 1986 Colombia had extradited thirteen people to the United States, all but one for alleged drug-related crimes.

Parejo Gonzalez, however, had angered the Medellin cartel leaders, and he received word that they were planning to kill him. To protect Parejo Gonzales, the Colombian government sent him to Hungary, where it was thought that he would be safe behind the Iron Curtain. The former Colombian justice minister, however, began to receive a number of death threats, warning him that wherever he hid, his enemies would get him. In January 1987 assassins working for the Medellin Cartel caught up with Parejo in a blizzard on a Budapest street and shot him five times. Parejo survived, thanks to the surgical skills of Hungarian doctors who performed two operations to remove the bullets. Parejo Gonzalez eventually returned to Colombia, where he ran unsuccessfully for president in 1994.

See also: Belisario Betancur Cuartas; Extradition;   Medellin Cartel
References: Gugliotta, Guy, and Jeff Leen. 1990. *Kings of Cocaine.*
Strong, Simon. 1995. *Whitewash: Pablo Escobar and the Cocaine Wars.*

Parker, Charles (1920–1955)

Prominent American jazz musician who was a legendary saxophonist and composer of the bebop style of jazz. Parker's brilliant improvisational style of performing earned him the admiration and accolades of his fellow musicians and aficionados, but he had a serious heroin problem, which led to his early death.

See also: Heroin
Reference: Jonnes, Jill. 1996. *Hep-Cats, Narcs and Pipe Dreams.*

Partnership for a Drug Free America

Founded in 1986, the Partnership is a nonprofit coalition of professionals in the communications industry whose mission is to reduce the demand for illegal drugs by using the media to change public attitudes about drug use and experimentation. Through its State/City Alliance Program, the Partnership has striven to help states and cities across the United States replicate its national advertising organization on the state and local levels.

See also: National Youth Anti-Drug Media Campaign
Reference: Partnership for a Drug Free America website at http://www.drugfreeamerica.org/.

Pastrana Arango, Andres (c. 1955–)

Former mayor of Bogotá, Colombia, who was elected president of the country in 1998. In January 1988 Pastrana was campaigning as the Social Conservative Party candidate for the mayor of Bogotá when ten armed men, believed to be working for the Medellin Cartel, walked into his campaign headquarters in Bogotá and kidnapped him. Pastrana was put aboard a helicopter and whisked away to the Medellin province.

Gunmen then kidnapped Carlos Mauro Hoyos Jiminez, Colombia's attorney general, but they botched their mission and killed him. In the massive manhunt that ensued for Hoyo's killers, authorities stumbled upon Pastrana and freed him. Pastrana announced he was still a candidate for mayor. He had been losing the campaign, but he won the March 1988 election in a close vote.

In 1994 Pastrana ran for the presidency of Colombia, but lost the election in the closest vote in Colombian history. Pastrana's campaign charged that Cali Cartel drug money had helped finance the campaign of his opponent, Ernesto Samper Pizano. Pastrana gave cassette tapes to the U.S. embassy in Bogotá, which seemed to implicate the Samper campaign. On the tape, Cali Cartel godfather Miguel Rodriguez Orejuela could be heard saying that he had given more than $3.5 million to Ernesto Samper's campaign. Given to Pastrana by an anonymous source from the city of Cali, the tapes became known as the "narcocassettes."

Public knowledge of the cassettes did not change the election result, but they did chill relations between Colombia and the United States and led to the decertification of Colombia and U.S. pressure on Samper to resign from office (the United States decided in its annual review in March 1998 that Colombia was not a helpful ally in the War on

Drugs). In June 1998 Pastrana was elected Colombian President, and the United States took that to be a positive development for its War on Drugs and its relationship with Colombia.

See also: Cali Cartel; Drug Czar; Certification; Eradication; Hoyos Jiminez, Carlos Mauro; Narcocassettes; Narcodemocracy; Perez, Alberto; Samper Pizano, Ernesto
References: "Change in Colombia." 1998. *MacLean's*, 6 July. "Colombia Looks for a Change." 1998. *The Economist*, 27 June.
Farah, Douglas. 1996. "The Crack Up." *Washington Post Magazine*, 21 July.
Kendall, Sarita. 1994. "Colombia Poll Victor Denies Drug Cartel Link." *Financial Times (London)*, 23 June.
Strong, Simon. 1995. *Whitewash: Pablo Escobar and the Cocaine Wars.*

Patino-Fomeque, Victor (c. 1958–   )

A former Colombian police officer who became a top member of the Cali Cartel. Patino-Fomeque was accused of processing and shipping tons of cocaine to the United States. He surrendered in Bogotá to Colombian authorities in June 1995, and in February 1996 he was sentenced to eighteen years in prison.

See also: Cali Cartel
References: "Six Top Colombian Drug Traffickers Still At Large." 1995. Reuters, 10 June.
U.S. Drug Enforcement Administration website at http://www.usdoj.gov/dea/pubs/briefing.

PCP

Technically, this drug is known as phencyclidine. PCP is the most common street name for the drug, but it is also known as "tic," "shermans," "angel dust," "crystal super weed," "animal tranquillizer," "rocket fuel," "peace pill," and "dead on arrival." Synthesized as early as 1926, the drug was introduced by the Parke-Davis Company in 1957 for use as a general anesthetic. PCP became popular in 1967, the year it was first used at a festival in the San Francisco Bay area, but it was taken off the market when its hallucinogenic properties were identified. Users typically report mood elevation, heightened or altered perception, and a dreamy, carefree state, but higher doses can induce catatonia, delirium, and hallucinations. The drug is dangerous, and using large amounts of it can cause convulsions, coma, and even death. PCP can be taken orally, by snorting it, or by taking it in eye drops. It is manufactured only in illegal laboratories within the United States, principally in the Los Angeles area. Efforts to control PCP have been difficult, because the huge profits that can be made from the sale of the drug as it moves along the distribution chain, from the laboratory to consumer, has made it attractive to criminals.

See also: Hallucinogens; Pagans
References: Cooper, Mary H. 1990. *The Business of Drugs.* Marnell, Tim, ed. 1997. *The Drug Identification Bible.*

People Persecuted by Pablo Escobar (PEPES)

When drug traffickers Gerardo Moncada and Fernando Galeano visited Pablo Escobar at Cathedral, the prison at which he was being held, in July 1992 Escobar's bodyguards ostensibly murdered the two and, in Moncada's case, tortured him for ostensibly withholding money from the drug lord. During the next two weeks, sicarios (assassins) employed by Escobar hunted down and killed about two dozen members of the Galeano-Moncada crime organization. The victims' families had to pay Escobar money to have their bodies returned.

In retaliation, the Moncada and Galeano families helped organize the paramilitary group People Persecuted by Pablo Escobar (PEPES) to hunt down Escobar after he escaped from prison. The group carried out bombing attacks on Escobar's family and property with the financial strategic support of Escobar's bitter rivals in the drug trade, the Cali Cartel. The PEPES played an important role in the destruction of Escobar's drug-trafficking empire, killing most of his key people by September 1993 and providing tips to the authorities that led to the arrest of several more. When authorities finally cornered and killed Escobar on 2 December 1993, he had a lone bodyguard with him.

See also: Cali Cartel; Escobar Gaviria, Pablo
Reference: Strong, Simon. 1995. *Whitewash: Pablo Escobar and the Cocaine Wars.*

People's Liberty Bank (U.S.)

In 1983 this bank located in Covington, Kentucky, became part of an international scheme to launder money for Colombian drug trafficker Luis Pinto. Operating the illegal scheme from Colombia, Pinto deposited large amounts of money, as much as

$300,000 at a time, in his personal and business accounts at the central branch of People's Liberty Bank. To circumvent filing CTRs (Cash Transaction Reports) under the Bank Secrecy Act of 1970, Pinto often made withdrawals of $1,000 from several different branch locations on a single day and had the money transferred to Colombia, where it appeared as legal profits in shell companies that the drug trafficker owned and operated in the Covington, Kentucky, area. People's Liberty Bank officials never notified local or federal authorities about Pinto's suspicious bank activities, as required by law, even though they often found counterfeit bills among the deposited money, a good sign to the authorities that the bank transactions included drug-related money.

See also: Currency Transaction Reports (CTRs); Money Laundering; United States Bank Secrecy Act of 1970
Reference: President's Commission on Organized Crime. 1984. *The Cash Connection: Organized Crime, Financial Institutions and Money Laundering.*

PEPES
See People Persecuted by Pablo Escobar.

Perafan, Justo Pastor
A leading Colombian drug lord who was known as "the Boss," "the Pilot," and "the Shepherd of Cocaine" because of his success as a drug trafficker and was considered the godfather of the Bogotá Cartel. Perafan was suspected of smuggling thirty tons of cocaine into the United States over a six-year period and hiding his profits in a vast empire of businesses ranging from coffee exports to hotels to metallurgic companies. The Colombian government offered a reward of $500,000 for information leading to his arrest.

Perafan was captured in Venezuela in 1996 and extradited to the United States for trial, which took place in Uniondale, New York, from March to May 1998. Perafan was found guilty on all eight counts of the indictment, which had charged him with engaging in a continuous criminal enterprise and conspiracy to import and distribute illegal narcotics. The court was expected to hand down Perafan's sentence in the fall of 1998. Although the charges carried a penalty of death or life in prison, Perafan will not have to serve more than thirty years because the extradition agreement between the United States and Venezuela prohibits the death penalty for individuals extradited to the United States.

See also: Bogotá Cartel; Extradition
Reference: Justor Pastor Perafan. "Guilty!" 1998. *Global Crime Update*, 27 July.

Percodan
See Oxycodone.

Perez, Augusto
The Colombian drug czar, a new position created in 1998 by incoming president Andres Pastrana Arango to confront the country's growing drug problem. Perez took charge of a new government office titled Confrontation Against the Consumption of Drugs (PPACD). Perez began his work against drug addiction as an aide to Pastrana when he was mayor of Bogotá from the 1980s to the early 1990s. When Perez went to work as Drug Czar, the Colombian press reported that the country had 200,000 drug addicts and that 500,000 Colombians between the ages of 12 and 45 had used marijuana, heroin, cocaine, and synthetic drugs like ecstasy.

See also: Cocaine; Drug Czar; Ecstasy; Heroin; Marijuana; Pastrana Arango, Andres; Synthetic Drugs
Reference: Gutierrez, Edwin. 1998. "Colombia: 500,000 Consumadores de Drogas." *El Tiempo*, 21 December.

Peyote
A spineless cactus found in northern Mexico and the southern part of Texas. The top of the cactus, which is called a button, contains a hallucinogenic substance, and three or four of such buttons can produce hallucinogenic effects in users that are similar to those experienced with LSD. During the 1950s and 1960s, peyote's easy availability led to abuse, especially among college students. Today, adherents of the Native American Church can use peyote regularly and legally as a sacrament or as part of the dance ritual, which is a component of their religious ritual to help the sick, for birthdays, and as part of marriage ceremonies, making it the only drug legally sanctioned by the U.S. government. Efforts have been made, however, to have the drug outlawed.

An important U.S. Supreme Court ruling impacted significantly on the issue of whether peyote could be used in a limited way as an institutional right to freedom of religion. In 1990 a U.S. Supreme Court case, the *U.S. Department of Human Resources vs. Smith* ruled that an individual was not beyond the law simply because peyote was used for religious purposes. Believing that this ruling endangered the free practice of religion for all Americans, Congress signed the Native Free Exercise of Religion Act of 1994, which gave full protection to Native American Church members to use peyote in religious ceremonies.

Peyote has a bitter taste, and the areas in which it can be grown are limited, which help explain why it has never been as popular in the drug subculture as other hallucinogens. Peyote is not known to be addictive, but its use can bring a change to visual perception, leading to significant mood changes.

See also: Hallucinogens; LSD; Mescaline
References: Marnell, Tim, ed. 1997. *The Drug Identification Bible*.
O'Brien, Robert, and Sidney Cohen. 1984. *The Encyclopedia of Drug Abuse*.

Phelps, Johnny (c. 1944–   )

A U.S. Drug Enforcement Administration agent who was sent to Colombia in 1981 and did important work for the federal agency until his departure from that country in 1984. Phelps was able to identify many of Colombia's most important drug traffickers, determine the nature and size of the Colombian cocaine trade, and alert his superiors in Washington, D.C., to the growing threat of Colombia's drug cartels. By the mid-1980s, Phelps was at the DEA headquarters in Washington, D.C., heading the desk that monitored cocaine trafficking.

See also: Cocaine
References: Gugliotta, Guy, and Jeff Leen. 1990. *Kings of Cocaine*.
Shannon, Elaine. 1989. *Desperadoes*.

Phencyclidine
See PCP

Phoenix House

A pioneer organization in the development of modern drug treatment, treating nearly 70,000 people in the United States since its beginning in 1967. Today, as one of the country's largest private, nonprofit providers of substance abuse treatment and education, Phoenix House provides residential and outpatient treatment for nearly 3,000 adults and adolescents in New York, Texas, California, and New Jersey. All of Phoenix House's programs rely on self-help

methods in a group setting and view drug abuse as a disorder affecting the whole person. Phoenix House aims to integrate their clients into society as drug-free, productive, and socially mobile citizens.

Reference: Phoenix House website at http://www. phoenixhouse.org/.

Pindling, Lyndon Oscar (1930–   )

The first black prime minister of the Bahamas, who served in the position from 1967 to 1992. Pindling's political party, the Progressive Liberal Party, lost the national election in 1992, and he became leader of the opposition in Parliament, remaining the Bahama's longest-serving elected government member.

From 1983 to 1994, however, Pindling was investigated for links to the international drug trade, and he was accused by the U.S. government of accepting bribes from drug traffickers. Specifically, in August 1994 it was discovered that the prime minister had spent eight times his official salary during the previous seven years. This led to suspicion that Pindling had good reason to ignore air flights out of Norman's Cay, a Bahamian island less that 100 miles from the United States that was owned by Colombian drug trafficker Carlos Lehder. At Lehder's trial in Jacksonville, Florida, in 1988, the evidence presented revealed that Pindling had received hundreds of thousands of dollars from Lehder and the Medellin Cartel.

See also: Medellin Cartel; Norman's Cay; Operation Tradewind; Lehder Rivas, Carlos
Reference: "A Kingpin Falls." 1988. *U.S. News and World Report*, 30 May.
"Pot Shots over a Drug Inquiry." 1984. *Time*, 13 February.

Pinochet Ugarte, Augusto (1915–   )

The Chilean general who launched a campaign in 1973 that overthrew the legally elected Marxist government of Salvador Allende. Up until the Pinochet-led coup, Chile had dominated the South American traffic of illegal drugs, but within three months of taking over the country, Pinochet, in an effort to improve relations with the U.S. government, deported twenty traffickers to the United States and arrested and imprisoned several more. Many of the remaining chemists involved with the manufacture of cocaine moved to Colombia, and Chile began to lose its important position in the drug trade.

By the middle of 1974, Colombians were beginning to cultivate and process the coca leaves themselves instead of merely distributing the finished product. That year, when U.S. Customs seizures of cocaine reached just 320 kilograms, a survey by the U.S. National Institute on Drug Abuse showed that five million North Americans had used cocaine at least once. By 1982 that figure had jumped to 22 million. This was seen as a graphic example of how the Colombian cartels had expanded and refined the cocaine pipeline to the United States since the days when Chile dominated the South American traffic of illegal drugs.

See also: Cocaine; Medellin Cartel
Reference: Strong, Simon. 1995. *Whitewash: Pablo Escobar and the Cocaine Wars.*

Pistoleros

Spanish term used in Mexico for the hired gunmen who often work for drug-trafficking organizations.

Reference: Shannon, Elaine. 1989. *Desperadoes.*

Pizza Connection

Name given by U.S. federal investigators to the heroin-trafficking and money-laundering operations of the Italian Mafia, including the suspected criminal activities of the America-based Bonanno crime family. In the Pizza Connection, the Italian Mafia used pizza parlors in the United States to import heroin from Southeast Asia's Golden Triangle and then transfer the drug profits through New York City to Switzerland and finally to Italy, where it was used to buy more heroin. U.S. authorities estimated that at least $25 million was laundered in this manner between October 1980 and September 1982.

According to the President's Commission on Organized Crime, the Pizza Connection case "provided new evidence of the extent to which elements of the La Cosa Nostra and the Italian mafia had jointly participated in narcotics trafficking and the laundering of narcotics proceeds through financial institutions in the United States." (President's Commission on Organized Crime 1984, 32) However, the money launderers in the Pizza Connection case were not the sophisticated handlers of drug money that the Colombian drug cartels were later to become. As Robert Powis noted, "The Pizza Connection launderers were frequently bumbling and lacking in knowl-

edge about how to move large quantities of cash inconspicuously." (Powis 1992, 29)

See also: Heroin; Italian Organized Crime; Money Laundering; Triads
References: Powis, Robert. 1992. *The Money Launderers.*
President's Commission On Organized Crime. 1984. *The Cash Connection: Organized Crime, Financial Institutions and Money Laundering.*

Pompidou Group

Consisting of about twenty European counties, this organization is the main policy forum in Europe with respect to all aspects of drug trafficking abuse involving law enforcement and demand reduction policy.

Reference: Jamieson, Alison. 1994. *Terrorism and Drug Trafficking in Europe in the 1990s.*

Posada Ocampo, Juan Jesus

Cardinal Posada of Mexico was fatally shot forty-five times at close range at the Guadalajara airport on 24 May 1993. The cardinal's chauffeur and five other people were also killed. Mexico's attorney general attributed Posada's murder to a gangland vendetta perpetrated by the Tijuana Cartel. The intended target appeared to be Joaquin "El Chapo" Guzman Loera, the leader of the rival Sinaloa-based syndicate.

The Mexican government reported that gunmen allegedly hired by the Arellano-Felix brothers, the heads of the powerful Tijuana Cartel, confused the cardinal with El Chapo. Many people, however, found that scenario hard to believe, given that Cardinal Posada was dressed in full religious regalia and wore a crucifix when he was shot in the thorax from five feet away.

In February 1998 members of a San Diego street gang were indicted on charges that the Tijuana Cartel hired them as hitmen to kill El Chapo. According to the indictment, in the ensuing gunfight, the cardinal, who was sitting in the car that was parked in front of Guzman's armored car, was shot to death. Still, no one knows whether the cardinal was also targeted because of his public stance against the drug cartels in Mexico or if he was killed by accident.

See also: Arellano-Felix, Ramon, And The Tijuana Cartel
References: Miller, Marjorie, and Juanita Darling. 1993. "Thousands Honor Slain Cardinal." *Los Angeles Times*, 26 May.
"San Diego Street Gang Members Indicted In Connection With Cardinal's Murder." 1998. *CNN Interactive,* 1 February.

Posse Comitatus Act

See United States Posse Comitatus Act.

Precursor Chemicals

Cocaine manufacturing requires a number of so-called precursor chemicals, such as methyl ethyl acetone and potassium permanganate. Without these key ingredients cocaine could not be made and trafficking in the drug could not flourish. Roughly half the precursor chemicals shipped to Andean drug-source countries came from the United States during the period from 1982 to 1988. In 1988 the U.S. Drug Enforcement Administration estimated that as much as 10,000 tons of precursor chemicals had been shipped to Peru, Bolivia, Ecuador, and Colombia the previous year.

The absence of universal, uniform regulations and the lack of adequate chemical control laws within many countries have been two of the big reasons precursor chemicals have been getting through to drug-source countries. In 1988, however, the United States, Europe, and the United Nations moved to address the problem. The United States, for example, passed the Chemical Diversion and Trafficking Act of 1988 to monitor and halt the flow of legitimate chemicals into illegal uses by requiring chemical manufacturers, importers, and exporters to maintain records on all transactions involving chemicals considered necessary for cocaine manufacture. Also in 1988, the United Nations adopted the U.N. Convention Against Illicit Traffic in Narcotic Drugs and Psychotropic Substances, which established procedures for controlling twelve of the most important chemicals in the manufacture of illegal drugs. Meanwhile, the European Community adopted communitywide chemical control regulations based on the U.N. Convention.

Despite these positive moves, reports continued to persist that chemicals manufactured by U.S. chemical companies were getting through to drug-source countries. In February 1990, about two weeks before the Cartagena Summit, representatives of the U.S. chemical industry went before the U.S. Congress to defend industry's efforts to stop the diversion of chemicals. In their testimony, spokesmen for the Chemical Manufacturing Association and the Synthetic Manufacturers Association admitted that some U.S.-manufactured chemicals were getting into the hands of drug traffickers, but they disagreed about the amount of such chemicals for which the U.S. chemical industry was responsible. "The U.S. chemical industry does not do business with criminals," Don Coticchia, a spokesman for the Chemical Manufacturers Association, told the U.S. Senate. (CMA Defends Industry on Drug Charges 1990, 3) The DEA agreed with Coticchia-—up to a point. "Although it is impossible to determine the exact percentage of U.S. chemicals used in the manufacture of cocaine, trade records and intelligence reports indicate that the U.S. is by far the largest exporter of chemicals to Latin America," David L. Westrate, a DEA operations assistant administrator told *Chemical and Engineering News* (Hanson 1990, 18)

Nearly a decade later, nothing has changed. Drug traffickers continue to have no problem getting the precursor chemicals they need to make cocaine.

See also: Amezcua Contreras, Jesus; Cocaine; Operation Chemcon; United Nations Convention against Illegal Traffic in Narcotic Drugs and Psychotropic Substances; United States Chemical Diversion and Trafficking Act of 1992; United States Chemical Diversion Control Act of 1993; United States International Narcotics Control Act of 1992

References: "CMA Defends Industry on Drug Charges." 1990. *Chemical Marketing Reporter*, 12 February.
Cooper, Mary H. 1990. *The Business of Drugs*.
Hanson, David J. 1990. "Chemical Industry, Drug Agency Sort Out Chemical Diversion Issues." *Chemical Engineering News*, 29 January.

Preludin

A prescriptive diet pill that is similar in effect to amphetamines. Preludin is highly addictive, and its abuse can cause serious psychological and physiological problems, which can lead to hallucinations and social dysfunction.

See also: Amphetamine
Reference: O'Brien, Robert, and Sidney Cohen. 1984. *The Encyclopedia of Drug Abuse*.

Prettyman Commission (U.S)

This commission, which was officially known as the President's Advisory Commission on Narcotics and Drug Abuse, was the result of the 1962 White House Conference on Narcotics and Drug Abuse. The Prettyman Commission's final report, which was sent to President Kennedy in November 1963, had twenty-

United States federal agents pour choice wines into the gutter in front of the Federal Building in Los Angeles, 26 October 1920. Over 900 gallons of alcohol were destroyed on this day as "mourners" looked on. During the period of alcohol prohibition, the modern era of drug running began with Arnold Rothstein. (UPI/Corbis-Bettmann)

five recommendations, including two advising that the enforcement and investigative function of the Federal Bureau of Narcotics relating to illicit transactions in narcotic drugs and marijuana be transferred from the Department of the Treasury to the Department of Justice and that the number of federal agents assigned to the investigation of illicit importation and trafficking in narcotics and dangerous drugs be increased. The Prettyman Commission's recommendations were not implemented until later in Johnson's first full term of office because of President Kennedy's assassination and because the incoming Lyndon B. Johnson presidential administration had other priorities.

See also: United States Federal Bureau of Narcotics; United States Narcotic Addict Rehabilitation Act; White House Conference on Narcotics and Drug Abuse

Reference: President's Commission on Organized Crime. 1986. *America's Habit: Drug Trafficking and Organized Crime.*

Prohibition

Traditionally, this term has been used to mean the forbidding by law of the manufacture, transportation, and sale of some or all types of alcoholic beverages. In the United States, the term has been used historically to describe the period between January 1920 and December 1933, during which the Eighteenth Amendment to the U.S. Constitution prohibited the sale and manufacture of alcoholic beverages. Critics of current government drug policies, especially those in the United States, have often labeled government efforts to wage war on drugs by outlawing their manufacture, distribution, and sale as "drug prohibition," and they compare the impact of these policies to what they say were the negative consequences of alcohol prohibition between the period from 1920 to 1933.

The critics contend that pursuing a policy of "drug prohibition" will not lead to a drug-free society but, rather, to one that is plagued by corruption, a high crime rate, the growth of organized crime, a clogged criminal justice system, the waste of billions of dollars, the erosion of minority rights, and the invasion of personal privacy. Some of the critics argue that drugs should be legalized; others that they be decriminalized. All the critics, however, believe that the United States and its allies in the War on Drugs should debate the merits of what they believe should be a more enlightened antidrug policy.

See also: Anslinger, Harry; Brent, Charles Henry; Decriminalization; Harm Reduction, Legalization; Rothstein, Arnold

References: Behr, Elwood. 1997. *Prohibition.*
Etheridge, Eric. 1994. "The Drug War Fails Again." *Rolling Stone,* 11 August.
Nadelmann, Eathan A. 1989. "Drug Prohibition in the United States: Costs, Consequences and Alternatives." *Science,* 1 September.
Trebach, Arnold S., and James A. Inciardi. 1993. *Legalize It?: Debating American Drug Policy.*

Project Craft (U.S.)

Sponsored by the University of New Mexico's Center on Alcoholism, Substance Abuse, and Addictions (UNM-CASAA), Project CRAFT (Community Reinforcement and Family Training) involves several treatment outcome studies that teach skills to help loved ones of resistant substance abusers to convince the abusers to accept treatment for drug and alcohol problems. CASAA's treatment division annually provides substance abuse services to more than 2,000 New Mexicans.

Reference: Project Craft website at http://www.unm.edu/~craft.

Pryor, Richard (1940-)

Pryor began his career as a nightclub comedian, but he became noted as the first black movie comic to achieve great fame, starring in such films as "Silver Streak" (1976), "Which Way Is Up" (1977), and "Stir Crazy" (1980). Pryor also had a well-publicized problem with cocaine substance abuse that derailed his professional career and nearly killed him.

See also: Cocaine; Free Basing
References: "Richard Pryor's Accident Spotlights Dangerous Drug Craze: Free Basing," *People Weekly,* 30 June 1980.
Williams, Dennis A. "When Cocaine Can Kill," *Newsweek,* 23 June 1980.

Psilocybin

A chemical compound derived from the mushroom *psilocybemexicana,* sometimes called the "magic" mushroom, this drug is one of the most rapidly acting hallucinogens and has been used ritually among Indians in Mexico and Central America from at least 1100 B.C. In 1958 the compound was first isolated and replicated in the laboratory. Psilocybin played a prominent role in the drug culture of the 1960s. For example, Timothy Leary, while on the faculty of Harvard University, administered the drug to Harvard theology students and to prison inmates at the Massachusetts Correctional Institute.

Today, authorities say it is difficult to tell how much illicit psilocybin is available to users. There are a reported one hundred species of mushrooms that contain hallucinogenic properties, qualifying them as "magic." Although in the United States psilocybin mushrooms are a Schedule I drug (listed in the U.S. Comprehensive Crime Control Act of 1970 as drugs that have a high potential for abuse, have no currently accepted medical use for treatment in the United States, or accepted safety for use of the drug), the spores of the mushroom are not. According to the *Drug Identification Bible,* magic mushrooms that are cultivated indoors can bring a price of $60 to $200 an ounce on the illicit drug market.

See also: Hallucinogens; Leary, Timothy
Reference: Lee, Martin, and Bruce Schlain. 1985. *Acid Dreams: LSD and the Sixties Rebellion.*
Marnell, Timothy, ed. 1997. *The Drug Identification Bible.*

Psychedelic Drugs
See Hallucinogens; Psychotropic

Psychotropic

Mind-affecting or altering in nature. Other popular names for psychotropic drugs are psychedelic and hallucinogenic drugs. Examples of this type of drug include LSD, PCP, and mescaline. Many psychotropic drugs are naturally occurring and have a long history of use for medical, religious, and social purposes.

See also: Hallucinogens; LSD; PCP; United Nations Convention Against Traffic in Narcotic Drugs
Reference: Marnell, Timothy, ed. 1997. *The Drug Identification Bible.*

Pulse Check

Conducted quarterly since 1992 and semiannually since the beginning of 1996 by the Office of National Drug Control Policy (ONDCP), this drug-use and drug-trend survey gathers information from telephone interviews with fifteen to twenty ethnographic sources, ten to fifteen police agencies, and fifty to sixty drug treatment providers from across the country. *NarcOfficer* magazine says that "while not a probability sample, it is nevertheless a timely report from persons working on the front lines of law enforcement and drug abuse research and treatment." (Travis 1998, 36)

Reference: Travis, Jeremy. 1998. "National Institute of Justice: Research in Brief." *NarcOfficer* (March–April).

Q

Quaaludes

A brand name under which the synthetic depressant methaqualone has been sold. Once thought to be nonaddictive, quaaludes were originally prescribed for daytime sedation and to help people sleep. In the early 1980s, quaaludes were removed from the market because of their widespread abuse. Subsequently, they became harder to obtain in the United States because of controls that included a 1984 law making their possession illegal except for research purposes. Quaaludes are still being used legally in many countries as a hypnotic and sedative agent.

See also: Methaqualone; Operation Screamer; Seale, Barry Alderman

References: Cooper, Mary H. 1990. *The Business of Drugs.*
O'Brien, Robert, and Sidney Cohen. 1984. *The Encyclopedia of Drug Abuse.*

Quintero-Cruz, Luis Carlos

The accused killer of DEA informant Barry Seale, who was gunned down in New Orleans, Louisiana, on 19 February 1986. Witnesses say they saw Quintero-Cruz shoot Seale with a silenced MAC-10 gun. Quintero-Cruz was arrested and brought to trial on 6 April 1987, along with three other members of an alleged conspiracy to kill Seale.

The trial began in Baton Rouge, but an impartial jury could not be selected, and it was moved to Lake Charles, 170 miles away. The star witness against Quintero-Cruz and the other defendants was Max Mermelstein, the former accountant of the Medellin Cartel, who had turned informant. It took the jury thirty minutes to convict Quintero-Cruz of Seale's murder.

See also: Mermelstein, Max; Seale, Barry Alderman
References: Gugliotta, Guy, and Jeff Leen. 1990. *Kings of Cocaine.*
Mermelstein, Max. 1990. *The Man Who Made It Snow.*

Quintero-Payan, Emilio, and Quintero-Payan, Juan Jose

Uncles of prominent Mexican drug trafficker Rafael Caro Quintero and active members of the Guadalajara Cartel. Emilio and Jose were big-time drug traffickers from the 1960s to the 1980s who were implicated in the abduction and murder of U.S. Drug Enforcement Administration special agent Enrique Camarena Salazar. While investigating Camarena's murder, Mexican federal agents stormed Emilio Quintero-Payan's ranch outside Guadalajara, but found only his servants.

After a 1985 DEA investigation that resulted in the seizure of $33 million of the assets of the Quintero brothers, the two were indicted by a Houston grand jury. They became fugitives, but still remained active in the production and distribution of heroin and marijuana.

See also: Camarena Salazar, Enrique; Caro Quintero, Rafael
Reference: Shannon, Elaine. 1989. *Desperadoes.*

Quito Declaration against Traffic in Narcotic Drugs

An agreement signed in 1984 by Ecuador, Bolivia, Panama, Nicaragua, Colombia, and Venezuela, which recommended that the traffic in narcotic drugs be viewed as "a crime against humanity." The agreement encouraged the United Nations in the same year to adopt a Declaration on the Control of Drug Trafficking and Abuse, which declared that drug trafficking was an illegal criminal activity, "demanding the most urgent attention and maximum priority" and urged member states to intensify their antidrug efforts and to coordinate their strategies with other member states.

Reference: United Nations Department of Public Relations. 1986. *Everyman's United Nations.*

R

Racketeer Influenced and Corrupt Organizations Act
See RICO

Ramirez Gomez, Colonel Jaime

Appointed head of the Colombian government's new Anti-Narcotics Unit in December 1982, Ramirez Gomez was a member of the National Police who is credited with launching the country's first real initiative against its powerful drug traffickers. Although highly respected by the U.S. Drug Enforcement Administration and the U.S. Embassy in Bogotá, he received little support from the Colombian government. As journalist Simon Strong writes, "His fellow New Liberals, never mind the government itself, cowered away from the heat." (Strong 1995, 93)

The Medellin Cartel tried to bribe him, and, when that tactic failed, it threatened to kill him. He began receiving approximately ten death threats a week. Ramirez was officially relieved of his post as head of the Anti-Narcotics Unit on 31 December 1985, and after forty days of leave, he returned to active duty with the National Police. In the three years he had served as head of the Anti-Narcotics Unit, he was credited with seizing twenty-seven tons of cocaine; arresting 7,941 men and 1,405 women; and confiscating 2,783 trucks, 1,060 cars, eighty-three boats, and 116 planes.

Colonel Ramirez became the star member of Colombian law enforcement. As Guy Gugliotta and Jeff Leen write, "At the beginning of 1986, he was undeniably the most famous narc in the world—a legend in his own country, revered by the DEA, sought for his counsel by the police from Lima to Washington." (Gugliotta & Leen 1990, 282)

But Ramirez had also angered the Medellin Cartel, and the group's godfather, Pablo Escobar Gaviria, put a contract out on his life. On 17 November 1986 assassins machine-gunned the Colonel to death in front of his wife. A move to posthumously honor Colonel Ramirez for his antinarcotics work was denied by the Colombian Defense Ministry.

See also: Escobar Gaviria, Pablo; Medellin Cartel; Tranquilandia
References: Gugliotta, Guy, and Jeff Leen. 1990. *Kings of Cocaine.*
Strong, Simon. 1995. *Whitewash: Pablo Escobar and the Cocaine Wars.*

Ramos, Jose Manuel

Known as *El Jefe* (the Boss), Ramos was convicted by a Houston, Texas, court in 1991 of cocaine smuggling and is currently serving a life sentence. Questioned in 1996 and 1997 by Swiss prosecutors investigating Raul Salinas de Gortari, the brother of former Mexican president Carlos Salinas de Gortari, Ramos told them that in the late 1980s he paid huge amounts of money on behalf of the Medellin Cartel to Raul Salinas in return for permission to land cocaine-laden planes in the northern state of Tamaulipar.

El Jefe claimed that he received more than $80 million as his part of the deal in which the Medellin Cartel paid $300,000 per landing. Ramos acknowledged, however, that he had no direct dealing with Carlos Salinas de Gortari. In July 1998 Raul Salinas's lawyer described Ramos's accusation as an "aberration." (Swiss Pursue Links to Drug Money 1998)

See also: Cali Cartel; Medellin Cartel; Pallomari, Guillermo Alejandro "Reagan"; Salinas de Gortari, Carlos; Salinas de Gortari, Raul

Reference: "Swiss Pursue Links to Drug Money." 1998. *Miami Herald*, 14 July.

Rand's Drug Policy Research Center (U.S.)

Established in 1989, the Drug Policy Research Center conducts empirical research, policy analysis studies, and public outreach to help community leaders and officials develop effective strategies for dealing with the drug problem. To attain its objectives, the Center conducts conferences and issues publications, briefings, and videotapes. It is supported by a grant from the Ford Foundation and receives additional support from individuals, corporations, foundations, and government agencies.

Reference: Drug Policy Research Center website at http://www.rand.org/centers/dprc.

Reagan, Ronald Wilson (1911–)

The modern era of the U.S. war against international drug trafficking began early in the first term of President Ronald Reagan when he told the American public that drug abuse was "one of the gravest problems facing us as a nation" and vowed to establish a foreign policy that "vigorously seeks to interdict and eradicate illegal drugs, wherever cultivated, processed, and transported." ("The Campaign Against Drugs," p. 30) Nineteen days before the 1982 congressional elections, with Republicans in need of votes, Reagan made a radio address in which he announced that he had "a bold confident plan to stop international drug trafficking." (Mills 1986, p. 1,120) Reagan said he intended to hire 900 new agents, 200 federal prosecutors, establish special task forces in twelve major cities, and build new prisons at a cost of $150 million.

Reagan responded to the reports of growing crisis in Florida and the visit of a Miami delegation of leading citizens by creating the South Florida Task Force to coordinate efforts against drug trafficking in southern Florida. He named Vice President George Bush to head the Task Force and made it operational on 15 March 1982. In explaining the rationale for the initiative, Reagan told the press, "The nearly two million people in South Florida are unfairly burdened financially in addition to being denied their constitutional right to live in peace without fear and intimidation." (Gugliotta & Leen 1990, 89)

True to his preelection words, Reagan sent a veritable flood of federal law enforcement officials to southern Florida to bolster the front lines of defense in the War on Drugs. The Drug Enforcement Administration sent seventy-three agents and support staff to its Miami office; the FBI, forty-three new agents; and the Customs Service, which was given the added responsibility of investigating drug-related crimes, 145 more agents. The Bureau of Alcohol, Tobacco and Firearms added forty-five more agents and declared it would concentrate on stopping the proliferation of automatic weapons, while the IRS pledged to crack down on money laundering. In addition, the Coast Guard, the U.S. Marshals, and the U.S. Border Patrol were all recruited to fight civilian crime in southern Florida. To handle the anticipated increase in federal prosecutions of drug-related cases, Bush said that the federal government would provide as many federal prosecutors as were needed.

In a major policy shift, the Reagan administration reorganized the chain of command in the War on Drugs, putting the FBI, for the first time in its history, in charge of drug enforcement and investigation. The DEA had to report to the director of the FBI, who now had the added responsibility of supervising drug law enforcement officials and policies.

To further coordinate federal drug enforcement efforts, Reagan also issued two executive orders. One on 24 June 1982 strengthened the Office of Policy Development to help the president perform his duties under the Drug Abuse, Prevention, and Treatment and Rehabilitation Act, and the second, which was issued on 9 December 1981, authorized agencies of the U.S intelligence community to "participate in law enforcement activities to investigate or prevent international narcotics activities and to render assistance and cooperation to law enforcement authorities not otherwise precluded by law." (*The Cash Connection*, p. 260)

Nancy Reagan greets local members of the "Just Say No" club at the White House 22 May 1986. In the mid-1980s, Nancy Reagan's "Just Say No" campaign put her at the forefront of the Reagan administration's campaign against drug abuse. (UPI/Corbis-Bettmann)

Meanwhile, the U.S. Congress lent its support to the War on Drugs, amending a law known as the Posse Comitatus, which had been on the books since the American Civil War and prohibited military involvement in civilian affairs. Congress, in its zeal to pursue the War on Drugs, authorized the U.S. Department of Defense to provide military training, intelligence, and equipment to civil law enforcement agencies and allowed members of the army, navy, air force, and marines to operate military equipment for civilian agencies responsible for enforcing the nation's laws.

For the first time in American history, U.S. naval vessels began directly to interdict drug-smuggling ships in international waters. The move sparked a fierce debate in Congress, as some congressmen and women questioned the wisdom of using the military as posse comitatus. Nevertheless, Reagan signed the new law in December 1981, allowing civilian authorities to use in the War on Drugs an impressive array of military technology, intelligence resources, and a sophisticated network of Navy E-2C, so-called mini AWACKs, radar planes, which operated out of Jacksonville, Florida.

Within weeks of its formation, the South Florida Task Force began to score some stunning successes. Even before the first year had ended, it appeared that the ever resourceful drug traffickers were shifting the battlefield in the War on Drugs, bringing to other parts of the country the violence, the drug addiction, the corruption, and the dirty money that had plagued South Florida. In response to the shifting crime scene, the federal government set up task forces modeled on the South Florida Task Force wherever a new drug-smuggling route seemed to be developing. The so-called El Dorado units soon began operations in Chicago, Houston, Philadelphia, New York, and Los Angeles.

After its initial response and outlay of resources, the Reagan administration pushed further antidrug measures through Congress. The 1982 Department of Defense Authorization Act contained a provision titled "Military Cooperation With Civilian Law Enforcement Officials," which was designed to codify the cooperative practices that had developed between the military and civil law enforcement authorities. Specifically, the provision clarified precisely the kind of assistance the military could give to civilian drug enforcement agencies and the type of military equipment those agencies could use.

Ostensibly, the rational for the provision, which substantially increased the potential interdiction capability of federal drug law enforcement agencies, was to "maximize" the degree of cooperation between the military and civilian law enforcement because "only through the additional work of all federal, state, and local law enforcement agencies can we begin to stem this tide." (Drug War Begins 1993, 251)

Although the legislation's sponsors cautioned that "we must recognize the need to maintain the traditional balance of authority between civilian and the military," the focus of the U.S antidrug policy had changed significantly. (President's Commission on Organized Crime 1986, 196) As Professor Bruce Bagley explained, "The criteria for this policy shift were no longer based purely on health concerns but on criminal factors where significant profits were being 'earned' by criminal organizations." (Bagley 1988, 164)

In 1984 Congress passed the Comprehensive Crime Control Act, an important piece of legislation containing several provisions designed to strengthen the interdiction efforts of U.S. law enforcement authorities. The Aviation Drug Trafficking Control Act, for example, amended the Federal Aviation Act of 1958 and allowed the Federal Aviation Administration (FAA) to revoke the pilot's license of anyone caught violating federal and state law relating to controlled substances, except for offenses involving possession of drugs. The Controlled Substances Registration Protection Act of 1984 made it illegal, among other measures, to steal controlled substances from pharmacists. "The effective regulation of the commerce in controlled substances has resulted in very high prices for drugs on the black market," the President's Commission on Organized Crime wrote, in explaining the act's rationale. (President's Commission on Organized Crime 1986, 269)

Other provisions of the comprehensive crime legislation package included the Bail Reform Act of 1984, which made it more difficult for accused drug offenders to stay out on bail; the Comprehensive Forfeiture Act of 1984, designed to "eliminate limitations and ambiguities . . . [that] have significantly impaired the full realization of forfeiture's potential as a powerful law enforcement tool"; the Controlled

Substances Amendment Act; the Dangerous Drug Division Control Act; and the Currency and Foreign Transactions Reporting Act Amendments. (President's Commission on Organized Crime 1986, 272–273 and 276–280)

The Reagan administration put forth a policy that emphasized the interdiction of drugs in Latin America, and the focus of the War on Drugs shifted from heroin to cocaine and marijuana, drugs the administration believed Americans were using the most. But by the mid-1980s, the United States was having to deal with another dangerous drug. Crack, perhaps the most potent and addictive—and certainly the cheapest—form of cocaine, had began appearing in the inner cities of Miami, Los Angeles, and New York and was spreading across America to other cities. Crime rates were beginning to soar to record levels in the inner city, as gang warfare raged between drug dealers determined to protect their turf in the lucrative drug trade.

This new development heightened the public's concern about the impact of illegal drugs and led President Reagan to increase the funding for the drug war from $1.5 billion in 1981 to $2.75 billion in 1986, and to push for the passage of the 1986 Anti-Drug Abuse Act, which not only authorized $1.7 billion in additional money to fight drug abuse, but also provided for prison sentences for drug dealers who either sold drugs near schools or recruited young people to peddle them.

While the United States intensified its antidrug effort at home, the War on Drugs heated up overseas. During the 1970s, Colombian drug traffickers had operated throughout Colombia without much interference from the authorities, but by 1984 Colombia was under pressure from the United States to change its laissez-faire ways and begin to get tough on the traffickers. A war of attrition erupted between the Colombian state and the country's powerful drug cartels. In a show of solidarity, Reagan and Colombian President Belisario Betancur Cuartas met in April 1985 and agreed to "fight against drug trafficking at all levels." (President's Commission on Organized Crime 1986, 9) Reagan said that the United States would continue to interdict drug trafficking, but at the same time, it would fight drugs on all fronts.

More impressive raids on drug-trafficking enclaves followed. From July to November 1986 Bolivia, with the help of the U.S. military, launched a major assault against drug trafficking that became known as Operation Blast Furnace. Several cocaine-producing facilities were destroyed and the supply of cocaine was disrupted for several months. The amount of cocaine seized in raids rose, from just two tons of cocaine in 1981 to twenty-seven tons in 1986, and if statistics were the sole measure of success, it appeared that the forces for good were winning the drug war.

The death of college basketball star Len Bias in 1986 from a cocaine overdose shocked the United States, riveted public attention on drug abuse, and sent Congress in the months leading up to the 1986 elections into a get-tough posture on drugs. The increased attention on drug abuse also spurred the Reagan administration to step up its antidrug offensive. In a major television address on 14 September 1986 the president called for "zero tolerance" towards everyone involved with drugs, including casual users of any illegal drug. Casual users shared responsibility for the violence and crime resulting from the international drug trade, Reagan told the American public. In October 1986 Congress passed—and Reagan signed—the 1986 Anti-Drug Abuse Act, which authorized $1.7 billion in additional money to fight drug abuse and international drug trafficking and increased once again the prison sentences for dealers by providing for mandatory sentences for drug dealing.

While calling for resolve on the War on Drugs, Reagan was still much concerned about the Cold War and communist expansion. By 1986 his administration was heavily involved in covert operations to topple the Marxist Sandinista regime in Nicaragua, which had taken power in 1979, through the training and financing of the Nicaraguan rebels known as Contra forces.

Rumors circulated about weapons shipments being flown to the Contras and how, on return flights from Nicaragua, drugs were being sent to the United States, no questions asked. Public pressure for an investigation of the allegations mounted, and the Senate Subcommittee on Terrorism, Narcotics, and International Operations of the Foreign Relations Committee initiated hearings under the leadership of Senator John F. Kerry (D-Mass).

In the so-called Kerry Commission hearings, evidence came to light that the U.S. government had turned a blind eye to the involvement of their anti-communist allies in the drug trade and that CIA-sponsored covert operations were "entangled" with criminal activities such as drug smuggling. The subcommittee found "substantial evidence of drug smuggling through the war zones on the part of individual countries, Latin suppliers, Contra pilots, and mercenaries who worked with the Contras and Contra supporters throughout the region." (Senate Committee on Foreign Relations 1989, 41)

By 1988, Reagan's last year in office, critics charged that the United States had little to show for its much hyped War on Drugs. On the contrary, they said, events and statistics revealed that the war effort had been marked by inconsistent leadership, conflicting priorities, bureaucratic infighting, and inadequate resources. Despite the tough penalties, many Americans were willing to risk jail and public disapprobation in the pursuit of illegal drugs. The United States still had an estimated 5.8 million regular users of cocaine and 20 to 25 million marijuana smokers, and another half a million heroin users, who were spending about $150 billion a year on illegal drugs. The U.S prison population rose from 329,821 in 1980 to 627,402 in 1988, making the country the world's leader in terms of the proportion of its population kept behind bars.

The authorities were confiscating more cocaine than ever, but between 1981 and 1988 the price of a kilogram of pure cocaine had actually fallen, a development that showed supply was still strong. Government reports in 1987 by the General Accounting Office and the House Committee on Government Operations found the U.S. drug policy to be "diffuse and overlapping." (Bagley 1988, 168) Reagan's fiscal year 1988 budget request called for the elimination of nearly $1 billion from the budgeted drug war allocations, which, to the United States' allies in the War on Drugs, meant that they would not be receiving adequate financial support from Uncle Sam.

Critics of the War on Drugs noted the huge gap between action and result and concluded that the effort had failed badly to attain its objectives. "No president has spent more against drugs than President Reagan," wrote Bruce Bagley. "No president has signed more antidrug treaties or spent more money to stem the flow of drugs into this country. But as the Reagan years drew to a close, American law enforcement officials acknowledge that they are losing ground in the fight against a new generation of drug smugglers who have the business skill—and capital—to threaten not only the streets of America but even the stability of countries long friendly to the United States." (Bagley 1988, 167)

By 1988 a small but influential group of distinguished Americans began to criticize the objectives of the War on Drugs. The dissenters came from across the political spectrum and a variety of backgrounds and included economist Milton Friedman, writer and archconservative William Buckley, Baltimore mayor Kurt Schmoke, and the editors of the influential *Economist* magazine, among others, who advocated legalization, decriminalization, or a combination of both.

The critics, however, did not sway the leaders of the War on Drugs, who continued to pursue a military solution and optimistically predicted that victory was just around the corner, if only American resolve remained firm and enough resources were applied to the problem. They pointed to the statistics that showed increasing arrests, overflowing prisons, massive cocaine seizures, the killing or kidnapping of drug kingpins, declining drug use, and insisted, in the words of drug czar William Bennett, that "the scourge is beginning to end." (Blair 1990, 7)

See also: Betancur Cuartas, Belisario; Buckley, William F.; Bush, George Herbert Walker; Contras; Crack; Fat Albert; Friedman, Milton; Just Say No Campaign; Mullen, Frances; Operation Jalisco; Organized Crime Task Force (U.S.); Posse Comitatus; Schmoke, Kurt; Shultz, George P.; South Florida Task Force; United States Central Intelligence Agency

References: Bagley, Bruce. 1988. "The New Hundred Years War?: U.S. National Security and the War on Drugs." *Journal of Interamerican Studies and World Affairs* (Spring): 164+.

Blair, Doniphan. 1990. Drug War Delusions: Unrealistic, Infeasible and Logistical Nightmare. *Humanist* (September-October): 7+.

Drug War Begins. 1993. *CQ Researcher*, 19 March.

Gugliotta, Guy and Jeff Leen. 1990. *Kings of Cocaine*.

Hellman, Peter. 1982. Reagan Gets Tough on Drugs. *Rolling Stone*, 15 April.

Mills, James. 1986. *The Underground Empire: Where Crime and Justice Embrace.*

President's Commission on Organized Crime. 1984. *The Cash Connection: Organized Crime, Financial Institutes, and Money Laundering.*

President's Commission on Organized Crime. 1986. *America's Habit: Drug Trafficking and Organized Crime.*

Starr, Mark. 1982. Reagan's War on Drugs. *Newsweek*, 9 August.

U.S. Senate Committee on Foreign Relations. Subcommittee on Terrorism, Narcotics, and International Operations. 1989. *Report: Drugs, Law Enforcement and Foreign Policy.*

Reed, Jack Carlton (1930–   )

A member of Carlos Lehder Rivas's drug-trafficking organization who in the early 1980s was found guilty by a U.S. federal grand jury in Jacksonville of conspiracy to distribute cocaine and with helping to operate a criminal enterprise. Reed was already serving a fifteen-year sentence after being convicted with Lehder on cocaine distribution charges the previous year. Prosecutors argued that the conspiracy dated back to 1974, when Lehder first proposed establishing a cocaine-trafficking enterprise while serving time in a U.S. prison. Also found guilty with Reed of helping to operate a continuing criminal enterprise were codefendants Barry Kane, a Hyannis Port, Massachusetts, attorney, and Donald Kenneth Lady, a Pomona, California, contractor.

See also: Lehder Rivas, Carlos
Reference: Gugliotta, Guy, and Jeff Leen. 1990. *Kings of Cocaine.*

Reed, William (1891–1923)

Hollywood actor, writer, and director, who starred in numerous films including "The Birth of a Nation" and "Too Many Millions." Reed developed a cocaine dependence after suffering an injury in a train wreck. After his death, his wife, actress Dorothy Davenport, made a film about a drug trafficker in remembrance of her husband's battle against drug addiction.

Reference: Jonnes, Jill. 1996. *Hep-Cats, Narcs and Pipe Dreams.*

Reefer Madness

A movie made by the U.S. Federal Bureau of Narcotics in the 1930s in which a middle-class man turns violent and abusive after a puff of marijuana and ruins his life. *Reefer Madness* reflected the prevailing attitude toward marijuana in the 1930s. In the 1960s, however, *Reefer Madness* became a cult movie among young drug users and abusers when they saw that the movie's content was so completely at odds with the effect that they said marijuana actually had on them.

The Colombian military battle for the hearts and minds of the citizens in its war against the country's guerillas. (Courtesy of the Colombian National Police)

See also: Marijuana; United States Federal Bureau of Narcotics
Reference: Goode, Erich, ed. 1969. *Marijuana.*

Restrepo, Ochoa Fabio

Leading Colombian drug trafficker of the early 1970s and a member of the Ochoa family, who was deposed from his prominent position in 1976 by his nephew Jorge Luis Ochoa Vasquez.

See also: Ochoa Vasquez, Jorge Luis
Reference: Gugliotta, Guy, and Jeff Leen. 1990. *Kings of Cocaine.*

Revolutionary Armed Forces of Colombia (FARC)

More commonly known by its Spanish acronym, FARC, this Marxist guerrilla group is Colombia's largest active guerrilla organization. Founded in 1966, FARC maintained close ties with the Soviet Union, which financed their Colombian comrades, but that support disappeared with the end of the Cold War in the 1990s.

FARC has since turned to various criminal activ-ities to finance its revolutionary activities, including kidnapping, extortion, and drug trafficking. FARC has worked with the country's drug traffickers, guarding their coca fields, laboratories, and clandes-tine airstrips, and even imposing a 10 percent tax on drug shipments moving through their territory. They also have supervised coca cultivation and have run their own cocaine-processing and distribution operations in remote parts of the country. In recent years, FARC is believed to be playing a major role in poppy cultivation, Colombia's newest growth indus-try, a development that has made the country one of the world's top three heroin-processing centers and raised concerns in the United States about a possible heroin epidemic.

When the Colombian government launched an aerial spraying and fumigation campaign in 1996, the guerrillas fought back, attacking workers in-volved with the project and orchestrating riots throughout the country in an attempt to influence public opinion against fumigation. The money that the Colombian guerrillas have made from the drug trade has increased their power considerably, and, today, they have control of large parts of the country.

"In certain areas, they are the law and authority," said Juan G. Tokatlian, a sociology professor at the National University of Bogotá and an expert in Colombian politics. (Chepesiuk 1997, 234)

See also: Environment; Herrera, Helmer "Pacho"; M-19; Narcoguerrillas

References: Chepesiuk, Ron. 1997. "Guerrillas in the Midst." *National Review*, 1 September.

Ehrenfeld, Rachel. 1994. *Narcoterrorism and the Cuban Circuit*.

Villamarin, Polido, and Luis Alberto. 1996. *El Cartel de las FARC*.

Ricorde, Auguste

Prominent French drug trafficker from the Marseille underworld, who was active in the trade in the 1960s and early 1970s. Ricorde fled France for Argentina after World War II because he faced a death sentence for collaborating with the Nazis. He went back to his old criminal activities, working in narcotics and prostitution.

In 1968, after some problems with Argentine authorities, he left for Paraguay, where he opened a motel and restaurant. U.S. authorities discovered, however, that Ricorde was operating a heroin drug ring in which it was estimated that he had been responsible for smuggling 5.5 tons of heroin into the United States between 1967 and 1972. In 1972 the United States demanded Ricorde's extradition, but Paraguay decided that he should serve his prison sentence in their country instead. The United States, however, threatened to decrease its foreign aid to Paraguay if Ricorde was not extradited, and the country relented. In 1972 Ricorde was extradited to the United States, where he was sentenced to prison.

See also: Extradition; Heroin

Reference: Lamour, Catherine, and Michael Lamberti. 1974. *The International Connection: Opium from Growers to Pushers*.

RICO (Racketeer Influenced and Corrupt Organizations Act)

Part of the Racketeer Control Act of 1970, RICO is considered today to be the most important piece of legislation ever enacted in the United States against organized crime. RICO has made it a crime to belong to an enterprise engaged in racketeering activities. Under the law, it is not necessary that a defendant actually commit a crime, only that he or she belong

to an enterprise that does. RICO, moreover, defines racketeering in a very broad manner and encompasses offenses that ordinarily do not violate any federal statutes. This includes gambling and dealing in narcotics or other dangerous drugs offenses that are chargeable under state law and punishable by imprisonment for more than one year. The criminal and civil sanctions under RICO are severe: imprisonment of up to twenty years to life, fines ranging from $25,000 to $500,000, as well as forfeitures, injunctions, and damage relief. RICO has generally been credited with being an effective law enforcement tool. For example, it has played a major role in weakening the power of Italian organized crime.

See also: Central Tactical Units (Centac); Italian American Mafia; Moran, William C.

References: Abadinsky, Howard. 1990. *Organized Crime*.

Fox, Stephen R. 1989. *Blood and Power: Organized Crime in Twentieth-Century America*.

President's Commission on Organized Crime. 1986. *The Impact of Organized Crime Today*.

Ritalin

A type of amphetamine, Ritalin is the brand name for methylphenidate, a drug made by Ciba Geneva Corporation that has been used for about forty years to calm restlessness, reduce impulsiveness, and improve attention span in children who have attention-deficit hyperactivity.

Oddly, Ritalin's effect on adults is just the opposite, resulting in increased stimulation. According to the *Drug Identification Bible*, "Eventually, the excess supply of released neurotransmitters is depleted, and the user experiences a crash. The crash generally includes a deep depression, followed by fatigue, difficulty in sleeping, headaches, decreased energy, and strong desire to use the drug again." (Marnell 1997, 541)

In a December 1996 issue of *Pediatrics*, the journal of the American Academy of Pediatrics, researchers reported that doctors were using two-and-a-half times more Ritalin for hyperactive and nonattentive children than they did in 1990. This report and others issued by the U.S. Drug Enforcement Administration and United Nations raised concerns on the part of some politicians and policy-making officials in the United States that Ritalin was being overprescribed for youngsters. In 1995 the press was also reporting that Ritalin was being widely used by teenagers who viewed the drug as a safe, socially acceptable alternative to cocaine.

See also: Amphetamines
References: Bromfield, Richard. 1996. "Is Ritalin Overprescribed for Behavior?" *Washington Times*, 3 December. Marnell, Timothy, ed. 1997. *Drug Identification Bible*.

Robert Wood Johnson Foundation Substance Abuse Policy Research Program

A $29 million research program administered through the national program office at the Wake Forest University Library School of Medicine. The program funds multidisciplinary research related to tobacco, alcohol and illicit drug policy. In the mid-1980s the foundation invited communities to accept proposals to set up community partnerships that would work together to help reduce substance abuse. So many communities responded that the U.S. government provided $100 million in assets siezed from drug dealers, which allowed even more communities to set up partnerships.

Reference: Robert Wood Johnson Foundation website at http://www.rwjf.org/.

Jose Rodriguez Gacha, late leader of the Medellin Cartel (Courtesy of the Colombian National Police)

Rodriguez Gacha, Jose Gonzalo (1947–1989)

Known as *El Mexicano* (The Mexican) for his love of things Mexican, Rodriguez Gacha was a leader of the Medellin Cartel and one of its most violent members. Born in 1947 in Pacho in central Colombia, the future drug kingpin ran away from home at age ten to lead a life of street crime. He served as a bodyguard to Gilberto Molina, the godfather of Colombia's emerald-smuggling underworld, and is believed to have joined Pablo Escobar Gaviria in drug trafficking about 1976. He gradually worked his way up to a mid-level cocaine dealer, helping to establish smuggling routes through Mexico and into the United States.

Public knowledge of his role in the Colombian drug trade came to light in July 1984 when evidence from informant Barry Seale led to the indictment of Rodriguez Gacha and several other leaders in the Medellin Cartel on racketeering and drug-trafficking charges. He was suspected of ordering the October 1987 killing of Jamie Pardo, a prominent leftist politician, and the December 1987 murder of journalist Guillermo Cano Isaza, who wrote editorials condemning the influence of the Colombian drug traffickers on Colombian society.

Rodriguez Gacha used the enormous money he made from the drug trade to buy horses, soccer teams, and vast tracts of land in Colombia to finance the importation of expensive technology that could serve the Medellin Cartel's needs. The Colombian government offered $625,000 for information leading to his arrest, but each time the authorities got close, Rodriguez Gacha would get away in the nick of time. On one occasion, police raided his palatial estate, only to watch him flee in a helicopter. International officials froze millions of dollars in Rodriguez Gacha's bank accounts, but he still managed to transfer $20 million to safety in a Panama bank.

Rodriguez Gacha's son Freddy had been arrested on drug-trafficking charges, but in December 1989 Colombian authorities released him, and he unwittingly led them to his father. In a bloody confrontation southwest of Cartagena, authorities killed

Rodriguez Gacha, Freddy, and several bodyguards in a wild shootout. It was unclear whether Rodriguez Gacha blew himself up with a hand grenade or died in the hail of gunfire.

See also: Cano Isaza, Guillermo; Escobar Gaviria, Pablo; Low Murtra, Enrique; Medellin Cartel; Mera Mosquera, Eduardo; Narcoterrorism; Seale, Barry Alderman

References: Strong, Simon. 1995. *Whitewash: Pablo Escobar and the Cocaine Wars.*
Lane, Charles. 1989. "Colombia: A Drug Lord's Last Shootout." *Newsweek*, 25 December.
"Gotcha!" 1989. *U.S. News and World Report*, 25 December.

Rodriguez Orejuela, Gilberto (1939–)

The younger brother of Miguel Rodriguez Orejuela and one of the cofounders of the Cali Cartel. Gilberto is believed to have been responsible for the drug-trafficking organization's strategic long-term planning. Nicknamed the "Chess Player" because of his criminal brilliance, Rodriguez Orejuela, was born in Mariquita, Colombia, a city in the Department of Tolima, but he and his brother were raised in the Balcazar neighborhood of Cali. Both Gilberto and Miguel spent their youth as juvenile delinquents and joined a gang that became known as Los Chemas. About 1970 Gilberto was arrested as a suspect in the kidnapping of two Swiss nationals, but he and the other suspects were released, apparently because of a lack of evidence.

It is believed that the ransom garnered from the kidnappings helped the brothers Rodriguez Orejuela finance a sizeable drug-smuggling operation. In the early 1970s Gilberto was moving small amounts of coca base from Peru to cocaine-refining laboratories in the Colombian departments of Narino, Cuaca, and Valle. With the profits he earned as a mule, Gilberto bought a small plane that allowed him to traffic in even larger drug shipments. By 30 September 1975 Gilberto and his brother were ranked fifty-eight and sixty-two respectively on a list of 113 top Colombian drug traffickers compiled by the intelligence section of the Colombian Customs Service.

In November 1975 Gilberto was arrested on a secret airstrip in Peru after authorities discovered that his plane was loaded with coca paste. For unexplained reasons, the case never came to court. In 1975 Gilberto sent Hernando Giraldo Soto to New York City to develop a cocaine distribution network

Gilberto Rodriguez Orejuela, a leader of the Colombian Cali Cartel (Courtesy of the Colombian National Police)

that would operate between Colombia and the New York City borough of Queens. Between 1976 and 1979 the pipeline was refined and enlarged, and it became the Cali Cartel's primary money maker in the United States. During the 1970s, Gilberto tried to establish and maintain a front of respectability by investing his drug proceeds in legitimate enterprises. By 1980 he owned an entire chain of popular drug stores in Colombia known as *La Rebaja*.

During the 1980s, Gilberto Rodriguez Orejuela, as leader of the Cali Cartel, became one of the world's most powerful drug traffickers. As security forces concentrated on shutting down the Medellin Cartel drug pipeline, the Cali Cartel quietly exported tons of cocaine from Colombia to the world, principally the United States and Europe and grabbed the lion's share of the market. By the time of Pablo Escobar Gaviria's death in December 1993, U.S. officials estimated that Gilberto Rodriguez Orejuela and the other Cali Cartel godfathers were responsible for shipping 80 percent of the cocaine entering the United States.

In the late 1980s, Gilberto dropped out of sight after his deep involvement in Colombia's drug-trafficking trade became clear to the country's authorities. After Escobar's death, the Colombian government, under pressure from the United States, began a hunt for Gilberto, his brother, and other top Cali Cartel leaders.

A Colombian drug task force, known as *Bloque de Busqueda*, that was originally set up to hunt for Pablo Escobar carried out raids on property known to be owned by Gilberto. Meanwhile, a reward of $1.2 million was offered for his capture. In June 1995 the world's most wanted criminal was found hiding in a closet in a house in Cali. "Don't kill me. I'm a man of peace," Gilberto reportedly begged police as they opened the door to his hidden compartment behind a television. (Farah 1996)

The godfather was imprisoned, but Colombian authorities reported that he and other jailed leaders of the Cali Cartel continued to conduct drug business while in jail via cellular phones that had been smuggled in. For his prominent role in the drug-trafficking trade, Gilberto Rodriguez Orejuela is serving a fifteen-year sentence in a Colombian prison.

See also: Cali Cartel; Giraldo, Alberto; Gomez Patino, Denis; Henao Montoya, Jose Orlando; Moran, William C.; Mule; Rodriguez Orejuela, Miguel; Santacruz Londono, Jose

References: Castillo, Fabio. 1988. *Los Jinetes de la Cocaina* (The Jockeys of Cocaine).

De Grazia, Jessica. 1991. *DEA: The War Against Drugs.*

Farah, Douglas. 1996. "Colombia's Jailed Drug Barons Said to Carry on Business." *Washington Post*, 13 January.

Morgenthau, Tom, and Robert Sandza. 1991. "Cocaine's Dirty 300." *Newsweek*, 1 July.

Strong, Simon. 1995. *Whitewash: Pablo Escobar and the Cocaine Wars.*

Rodriguez Orejuela, Miguel (1944–)

The older brother of Gilberto Rodriguez Orejuela and cofounder of the Cali Cartel who, as one of the group's managers, helped organize the shipment of hundreds of tons of cocaine to North America and Europe. Miguel and brother Gilberto accrued a fortune that at one time was estimated to be around $5 billion. Like his younger brother, Miguel was born in the Colombian Department of Tolima, but grew up in the tough Balcazar neighborhood of Cali. He, too, was a member of the Los Chemas street gang, but unlike Gilberto, was never arrested for kidnapping.

Miguel Rodriguez Orejuela, a leader of the Colombian Cali Cartel (Courtesy of the Colombian National Police)

By 1975 Colombian intelligence had listed him as sixty-second among the top 115 drug traffickers known to Colombian authorities.

As the Cali Cartel grew in wealth and power, Miguel became the equivalent of the chief executive officer, with responsibility for the gang's legal business ventures. This helps explain why so little is known about him. But like his brother, Miguel became the object of a massive manhunt in 1995, and the Colombian government put a $1.2 million reward on his head.

The U.S. government also wanted him on racketeering, drug-trafficking, and money-laundering charges. Colombian authorities said that in the weeks before Gilberto's capture, the two brothers were divided over tactics and were living apart. Miguel favored a strategy that involved corrupting the Colombian government in the hope of receiving lighter sentences, while Gilberto preferred one that involved attempting to intimidate the Colombian Congress through threats and violence in the hope of clearing their names without having to confess to any crimes.

Miguel was captured on 6 August 1995. In June 1996 Miguel, Gilberto, and seventy-two associates were charged with drug trafficking in a 207-page federal indictment in Miami. In October 1996 Miguel was also charged with illegally funding the 1994 presidential campaign of Ernesto Samper Pizano. As of December 1998 Miguel was incarcerated in a Colombian prison, serving a twenty-one-year sentence.

See also: Cali Cartel; Giraldo, Alberto; Henao Montoya, Jose Orlando; Moran, William C.; Rodriguez Orejuela, Gilberto; Sanchez, Orlando; Santacruz Londono, Jose

References: Castillo, Fabio. 1988. *Los Jinetes de la Cocaina* (The Jockeys of Cocaine).

"Drug Lord Charged." 1996. *MacLean's*, 6 October.

Farah, Douglas. 1996. "Colombia's Jailed Drug Barons Said to Carry on Business." *Washington Post*, 13 January.

Schreiber, David. 1996. "Sins of the Father: The Children of Cali Cartel Godfathers Can't Shake the Family's Past." *Newsweek*, 12 August.

Rohypnol

Described as the new date-rape drug of the 1990s, Rohypnol is officially known as flunitrazepam and belongs to a class of drugs called benzodiazepines. Its nicknames include rophies, ropies, roofies, rib, rope, ruffies, R-2s, la rocha, roofenol, rophs, Mexican valium, and mind erasers.

Although its illicit use originated in Europe in the 1970s, the substance did not appear in the United States until the early 1990s. In 1992 a South Florida hotline began receiving calls that reported abuse of the drug. Around this time the drug appeared in Texas as well. Today, Rohypnol is one of the fastest growing drug problems in both areas and is spreading across the United States. As of April 1995 the Drug Enforcement Administration had documented 1,000 cases of Rohypnol possession in thirteen states.

Rohypnol is manufactured legally in many European and South American countries, but is neither manufactured nor approved for medical use in the United States. The drug produces sedative effects, including amnesia, muscle relaxation, and the slowing of psychomotor performance. Sedation occurs twenty to thirty minutes after administration of a two milligram tablet and lasts for about eight hours.

The use of Rohypnol is dangerous and can lead to physical and psychological dependence, which increases with dose and duration of use. It is considered to be eight to ten times more powerful than valium, but a lethal overdose is unlikely.

The drug's cheapness ("hits" or tablets cost between $2 and $3) makes it popular among teenagers, college students, and, in fact, youths of all socioeconomic stratas. High school students have reportedly used the drug as a cheap drunk and as a cure for alcohol hangovers. In some areas, it is associated with gangs and is becoming known as a club drug.

The number of Rohypnol tablets seized increased from 42,269 in 1995 to 136,107 by September 1996, a 322 percent increase. Writing in the *International Drug Report* newsletter, Chris McKissick of Florida's Port Orange Police Department said, "Although a newly enacted Florida law makes it a felony to possess Rohypnol, legislation is still needed to make sure Rohypnol is classified as Schedule I Controlled Substance and that legislation is passed addressing the traffickers engaged in smuggling large amounts of the drug into the U.S." (McKissick 1996, 7)

Rohypnol has since been listed as a Schedule I drug under the Controlled Substances Act, which allows for the scheduling or classification of drugs depending on potency or impact. Known officially as the Comprehensive Drug Abuse Prevention and Control Act of 1970, this federal act provides the modern basis for reducing the consumption of illegal drugs. Meanwhile, Rohypnol does not have U.S. Food and Drug Administration (FDA) approval. Today, Mexico and Colombia are the primary sources for smuggling the drug into the United States.

Reference: Marnell, Timothy, ed. 1997. *Drug Identification Bible*.

McKissick, Chris. 1996. Rohypnol. *International Drug Report* (July-September): 3.

Romero de Vasco, Flavio

A former governor of the Mexican state of Jalisco, Romero de Vasco was jailed on 24 January 1998 in connection with alleged ties to drug lords Rigoberto Gaxiola Medina and Jorge Abrego Reyna Castro. Romero was accused of laundering drug money, accepting bribes, and providing a safe haven in Jalisco for the drug traffickers between 1977 and 1983.

Reference: U.S. Senate Committee on Foreign Relations. 1998. *International Organized Crime Syndicates and Their Impact on the United States: Hearings before the Subcommittee on Western Hemisphere, Peace Corps, Narcotics and Terrorism*, 26 February (statement of Thomas A. Constantine, Director, DEA). See DEA website http:www.usdoj/dea/pubs/congrtest.

Romero Gomez, Alfonso

An aide to General Ramon Guillen Davila, the former head of the Venezuelan National Guard, Romero Gomez was accused of smuggling up to twenty-two tons of cocaine into the United States between 1987 and 1991 while he was chief of Venezuela's National Guard antidrug force. In September 1997 Romero Gomez went on trial in Venezuela on drug conspiracy charges. He faced ten years in prison and a $4 million fine. Venezuela's government declined to extradite Guillen Davila, who lives in Venezuela, but Colombia extradited Romero Gomez to the United States after his arrest there. Guillen Davila acknowledged that he had helped ship 2.3 tons of cocaine through Venezuela, but he claimed he was part of a CIA-sanctioned operation that targeted Colombian drug cartels. Romero Gomez's lawyer claimed his client was only a very low-level informant for Guillen Davila.

See also: Extradition; United States Central Intelligence Agency

Reference: "Well-Traveled Miamian Joins Libyan Agent's Defense." 1998. *Miami Herald*, 27 August.

Rothstein, Arnold (1883–1928)

Rothstein was a prominent figure in the early history of American crime and is credited with organizing the modern illicit narcotics trade. The son of orthodox Jews, Rothstein made his name and fortune during Prohibition working the traditional rackets (stolen bonds, rum smuggling and labor racketeering). By the mid-1920s, seeing that the Harrison Act had restricted the previously easy access to morphine, cocaine, and heroin, he moved quickly to establish an illicit narcotics market.

Rothstein sent a number of employees with experience buying liquor in Europe to the Continent to locate major sources of narcotic supplies. They found that legitimate pharmaceutical firms in France, Germany, and Holland were eager to sell big orders of heroin, morphine, and cocaine, no ques-

Federal agents inspect the large drug cache worth a million or two dollars left by Arnold Rothstein. Rothstein was one of twentieth century America's first major drug dealers. (Corbis/Bettmann)

tions asked. Rothstein used only his own people to arrange giant orders and overseas shipments sent back to the United States as innocuous sea freight. Once in the United States, the drugs were distributed by Rothstein's people to the wide network operated by the big-city Prohibition gangsters. The U.S. government was preparing an indictment against Rothstein on drug-trafficking charges when he was murdered on 4 November 1928 by a small-time gangster.

See also: Cocaine; Harrison Narcotic Act; Heroin; Morphine; Prohibition

References: Chepesiuk, Ron. 1999. *Hard Target*.
Katcher, Leo. 1994. *The Big Bankroll: The Life and Times of Arnold Rothstein*.

Ruiz Massieu, Mario

In March 1997 a U.S. civil jury found Ruiz Massieu, the former deputy attorney general of Mexico, guilty of accepting $7.9 million in bribes in exchange for allowing drug cartels to make illegal shipments of drugs to the United States from Mexico. The verdict highlighted problems in Mexico's judicial and law enforcement systems, which critics described as corrupt and ineffective. Ruiz Massieu had also been charged with obstruction of justice and other crimes in Mexico, but the United States rejected four requests from Mexico for the attorney general's extradition. Observers felt it unlikely that the United States would ever deport him.

See also: Extradition

References: Guillermoprieto, Alma. 1995. "Whodunit?: Unsolved Assassinations Contribute to National Insecurity in Mexico." *New Yorker*, 25 September.
Morison, Scott. 1995. "Blood Ties: A Widening Murder Scandal Claims One-Time Mexican Political Hero." *MacLean's*, 20 March.

Russian Organized Crime

The struggle to move from a rigid totalitarian regime to a stable and viable capitalist society has been a difficult one for Russia. In fact, since the breakup of the former Soviet Union, Russia has changed from one of the world's safest and most orderly societies to a country almost overwhelmed with crime. Indeed, the range of criminal activity is astounding: forgery, arms trafficking, smuggling, extortion, bank fraud, the movement of all kinds of contraband, and, of course, drug trafficking.

Even hard drugs are beginning to get a foothold in a society where vodka has traditionally been the Russian drug of choice. Russia's increasing importance as a transhipment point for Colombian cocaine has created a growing domestic market for drugs. Russian police told the press that Russians were using fifteen times more narcotics in 1992 than they did in 1987. What adds to this disturbing scenario is that the former Soviet Union has huge resources that can be used in the production of narcotic drugs. There are, for example, vast poppy fields in former Soviet Republics such as Kazakstan, Uzbekistan, Tadjikstan, Turkmenistan, the Ukraine, Central Asia, and southern European Russia, and millions of hectares of wild hemp, including 4 million in Kazakstan alone. Russia has opened up its society, and now that Russians can travel freely, crime has been the country's biggest export. Journalist Claire Sterling's investigation of organized crime revealed that, within two or three years of the dissolution of the Soviet Empire, "[Russian organized crime] leaders [had] established contact with their Western counterparts, and thousands of [Russian Mafia] members had expanded operations in the United States and Western Europe. It was moving into the international drug trafficking arena and had masterminded the complexities of shady international finance." (Sterling 1994a, 95) That is not to say that organized crime and drug trafficking emerged in the former Soviet Union overnight. The old Communist system was one of total corruption, involving bribes, thefts, and organized crime on a vast scale. The mafia was the Communist Party and crime was a necessary part of doing business in the former Soviet Union.

After the emergence of the black market in the 1960s, large criminal organizations took shape in many Russian cities, led by powerful mobsters known as Thieves in Law, who began to work with government officials in the pursuit of criminal activities. By the time the Soviet communist system collapsed, an estimated 600 such groups were operating throughout the former empire, and the illegal underground economy accounted for as much 50 percent of its personal income.

Soon after the dissolution of the Soviet Empire, Russian criminal groups were active in many major European cities, including Paris, Amsterdam, and London, and their reach extended around the world to cities with growing communities of Russian émigrés. According to the Russian Interior Ministry, by the mid-1990s, an estimated 200 or more Russian organized crime groups were operating in twenty-nine cities in Europe, the United States, and such far flung places as Macao in East Asia. So who are these criminal entrepreneurs who are spreading like a cancer throughout the world? Experts reveal that organized crime Russian style includes about 9,000 gangs with a membership of about three million, and a reach that, in the words of Claire Sterling, "extends into all fifteen of the former Soviet Republics, across five time zones, and one-sixth of the earth's land mass." (Sterling, 1994b, 19–20) Among its members are many former KGB officers, Communist Party members, and military officers, who have given the Russian criminal gangs inside access to the workings and wealth of the former Soviet Union.

The term *Russian mafia* may actually be a misnomer, because there is no godfather or ruling council as in the Italian organization of that name, and often the groups are independent entities that may have as few as two members. Moreover, most of the groups are not Russian at all; in fact, the most powerful and best-organized groups are the Chechens from the Caucasian mountain region, with the Georgians a close second. The international growth of these criminal organizations has been explosive. In Poland, heroin seizures jumped tenfold between 1992 and 1994 after one huge seizure of 1,750 pounds of cocaine. Polish law enforcement agencies

Special armed police arrest suspected Mafia figures during an operation in Moscow, 19 February 1993. With the breakup of the Soviet Union, Russian organized crime has become a major player in international drug trafficking (Reuters/ Corbis-Bettmann)

reportedly have only thirty-five full-time drug enforcement officials for the entire country, and its annual budget was between a paltry $100,000 to $200,000 a year. During the early 1990s, Poland also began to play an important role in the amphetamine drug trade, moving what was described as currently the highest quality drug in Europe, with purity levels often ranging from 97 to almost 100 percent.

Between August and December 1994, about $1 billion per month was deposited in offshore accounts set up by Russian organized crime groups, according to Russian Central Bank estimates. (Banerjee 1994) "In the CIS [Commonwealth of Independent States] and most East European states, money laundering is not illegal," write Lee and MacDonald. "Banks are not legally required to report deposits transfers or withdrawals, and banking authorities have no incentive to screen their clients or report suspicious transactions. In Poland the convertibility of local currency and the absence of control on importing and exporting foreign exchange generate additional incentives to launder drug profits there." (Lee & MacDonald 1993, 93–94)

What disturbs many Western law enforcement officials is evidence showing that the Russian mafia is looking to expand its base of operations by forging alliances with other powerful criminal organizations around the world. Russian groups are reportedly involved with the Colombian cartels, and other reports indicate that criminal gangs in Russia and some of the other former Soviet republics were holding "summits" with the Sicilian Mafia. In May 1997 President Yeltsin moved to counter the growing criminal threat by implementing an anticrime measure that called for new laws, improved monitoring of banking transactions, and the strengthening of law enforcement. A month later, he signed another measure that expanded the investigative powers of the police, allowing them to do such things as detain suspects for thirty days without filing charges. Initially, U.S. law enforcement was slow to react to the growth of Russian criminal activity within U.S. borders. In 1990 the *Washington Post* writer James Rosenthal concluded that "Since the [U.S.] Justice Department does not consider the Russian mob to be organized crime, it doesn't treat it with the seriousness that it reserves for more VIP criminals." (Rosenthal 1990)

In conducting a 1991 strategic assessment of Russian organized crime, the U.S. Immigration and Naturalization Service reportedly relied on information obtained from the *New York Times*. Internationally, however, it has been a different story. Beginning in 1988, the U.S. signed a series of antidrug cooperation agreements with the Russian government, and the U.S. Drug Enforcement Administration began to help by organizing seminars for Soviet customs and law enforcement officials. In 1990 the Russian government invited DEA officials on a helicopter tour of the huge marijuana fields in Kazakhstan. In 1994 FBI Director Louis Freeh was in Moscow to sign an agreement with the Russian government to fight Russia-based organized crime more effectively. The agreement allowed FBI agents to gather records and evidence in the former Soviet Union and to interview witnesses, while trying to solve and prevent a variety of crimes, including drug trafficking. "We can honestly say that our two nations have more in common than ever before," Sergei V. Stephasin, head of the Russian Federal Counter Intelligence Service, the successor to the KGB, told the press at a conference to celebrate the Russian-U.S. agreement. "Together, we're invincible." (Grigg 1996, 4)

That, however, remains to be seen. The Russian gangs in the United States are expanding their influence after learning much from the Italian Mafia. So far, they have been content to play second fiddle to La Cosa Nostra, but that relationship has a good chance of changing. "They are now like the [Italian] Mafia was back in the Twenties and Thirties, but I think that they will far surpass it," predicted Terry Minton of the Los Angeles Police Department's organized crime intelligence division. (Cullen 1994, 70–72)

See also: Italian American Mafia; Offshore Financial Centers

References: Banerjee, Neela. 1994. "Russian Organized Crime Goes Global." *Wall Street Journal*, 22 December.

Cullen, Robert. 1994. "Comrades In Crime." *Playboy* (April): 70–72.

Goldberg, Carey. 1993. "Russian Police Warn of Cocaine Blizzard." *Los Angeles Times*, 27 February.

Grigg, William Norman. 1996. "Russia's New Export: Crime." *New American*, 27 May.

Handelman, Stephen. 1995. *Comrade Criminal: Russia's New Mafia*.

Klebnikov, Paul. 1993. "Joe Stalin's Heirs." *Forbes*, 27 September.

Lee, Rensselaer. 1991. "Soviet Narcotics Trade." *Society* (July–August), 1991.

Lee, Rensselaer, and Scott B. MacDonald. 1993. "Drugs in the East." *Foreign Policy* (Spring).

Rosenthal, James. 1990. "Russia's New Export: The Mob." *Washington Post*, 14 June, p. 1.

Sterling, Claire. 1994a. *Thieves' World: The Threat of the New Global Network of Organized Crime*.

Sterling, Claire. 1994b. "Redfellas." *The New Republic*, 11 April.

Tanner, Adam, and Pam Greer. 1995. "Russia's Notorious Mafia Spreads Tentacles of Crime around the Globe." *Christian Science Monitor*, 11 January.

U.S. Senate Committee on Foreign Relations. Subcommittee on Terrorism, Narcotics and International Operations. 1994. *Recent Developments in Transnational Crime Affecting U.S. Law Enforcement and Foreign Policy*.

S

Safe House

Different people are involved at various stages of the trafficking of illegal drugs. At the safe house, a centralized storage area for incoming drugs, people are hired to "babysit" the drugs, often remaining in the house twenty-four hours a day, for several days.

Reference: Chepesiuk, Ron. 1999. *Hard Target.*

Salinas de Gortari, Carlos (1948–)

Mexican political leader who served as the country's president from 1988 to 1994. During his election campaign, Salinas promised to launch an aggressive attack against the country's drug traffickers, but during his administration several top Mexican law enforcement officials were accused of active involvement in some of the country's biggest drug-trafficking organizations. Salinas himself became entangled

Presidential candidate Carlos Salinas votes in Mexico's July 1988 presidential election. Salinas' brother Raul would later be implicated and convicted in a corruption scandal and Carlos himself would leave Mexico for Ireland in self-imposed exile. (Underwood & Underwood/Corbis-Bettmann)

in a corruption scandal involving his brother and other members of his family. His brother Raul Salinas de Gortari was incarcerated in a Mexican jail on charges of illegal enrichment and murder in connection with the 1994 assassination of Jose Francisco Ruiz Massieu, the secretary general of the ruling Institutional Revolutionary Party (PRI).

See also: Garcia Abrego, Juan; Pallomari, Guillermo Alejandro "Reagan"; Salinas de Gortari, Raul; Ramos, Jose Manuel; Ruiz Massieu, Jose Francisco
Reference: Hughes, Sallie. 1995. "A Family's Value: Huge Bank Deposits Further Blacken Salinas Name." *MacLean's*, 11 December.

Salinas de Gortari, Raul (1947–)

In a February 1997 letter to his Mexican counterpart, Jorge Madrazo, Swiss Attorney General Carla du Ponte charged that Raul Salinas de Gortari, the brother of former Mexican President Carlos Salinas de Gortari, received, "enormous" sums of money from a major drug cartel. This was the first hint that a massive Swiss investigation was underway of the estimated $100 million in Raul Salinas's Swiss bank account. Salinas, who is in a Mexican jail on charges of murder and illegal enrichment, angrily denied that his Swiss bank account is linked to drug trafficking, as did his brother Carlos, who is currently in self-imposed exile in Ireland. Several Mexican and U.S. officials expressed skepticism that there was a drug connection in the case, pointing out that several of the witnesses who had testified may not have been reliable.

But in February 1997 the two Salinas brothers had to issue separate statements in response to the publication of several documents by the Mexican news magazine *Proceso*. The documents indicated that witnesses in a U.S. drug-trafficking case could link both brothers to drug smuggling. Early in 1998 authorities investigating the source of the $160 million held in Swiss bank accounts said they had proof that Raul Salinas de Gortari had received tens of millions of dollars from Colombian drug traffickers. The investigators, however, said that none of the evidence implicated Carlos Salinas.

In October the Swiss announced that they had seized more than $90 million from Raul Salinas's bank account, and they also made a request to the British government, asking it to seize another $23.4 million that Salinas had deposited there. Salinas's

lawyers said they would go before Switzerland's Supreme Court to demand the return of the money. In January 1999 a federal judge in Mexico sentenced Salinas to fifty years in jail for orchestrating the 1994 murder of his former brother-in-law, Jose Francisco Ruiz Massieu.

See also: Garcia Abrego, Juan; Pallomari, Guillermo Alejandro "Reagan;" Salinas de Gortari, Carlos; Ramos, Luis Manuel
References: "Closing in on Salinas." 1998. *MacLean's*, 23 March.
Oppenheimer, Andres. 1997. "R. Salinas Linked to Drug Trade." *Miami Herald*, 3 April, international satellite edition.

Samper Pizano, Ernesto (1950–)

The president of Colombia from 1994 to 1998, who on 10 June 1994 won the Colombian presidential election as the Liberal party candidate by the narrowest margin in the country's history. He was inaugurated to a four-year term on 8 August, pledging to negotiate Colombia's entry into the North American Free Trade Agreement and to vigorously combat the country's drug-trafficking industry. Samper was well educated for the post of head of state, earning economics and law degrees from Colombia's University of Javeriana School of Law and Economy in 1972 and 1973, respectively, and earning a doctorate from Columbia University in New York City in the early 1980s. He also authored three books, including *For Whom the Coffee Bonanza?*

A drug-trafficking scandal, however, rocked Samper's administration soon after he took office. The president faced accusations that his election campaign had been funded by more than $6 million in Cali Cartel drug money in exchange for the Samper administration's assurance that leaders of the Cali Cartel would be treated leniently in the future. Samper denied the accusation, but the United States obtained wiretapped telephone conversations (known as the narcocassettes) between officials in Samper's presidential campaign and Cali Cartel leaders.

Several members of Samper's administration resigned and the president faced a series of congressional investigations. Samper's credibility had been severely damaged. The president's critics pointed out that the investigations were conducted by his Liberal Party allies, many of whom themselves faced various

Former Colombian president Ernesto Samper at a press interview (Courtesy of Ernesto Samper's press office, photo by Roberto Bernal)

charges of corruption. In June 1996 the Colombian Congress cleared Samper of all charges, but the United States continued to put pressure on Colombia, decertifying the country for not doing enough in the War on Drugs, and calling on Samper to resign. Ironically, Samper himself was a victim of drug-related violence, having been shot accidently in a 1989 assassination attempt on another individual at the Bogotá airport.

See also: Botero Zea, Fernando; Certification; Giraldo, Alberto; Gonzalez, Guillermo Alberto; Narcocassettes; Pastrana Arango, Andres; Toft, Joe
References: Chepesiuk, Ron. 1999. *Hard Target.*
"Colombia, Still There." 1996. *The Economist,* 1 June.
Strong, Simon. 1995. *Whitewash: Pablo Escobar and the Cocaine Wars.*

Sanchez, Orlando

A Colombian drug trafficker who operates in the rural area north of Cali. Colombian authorities identified Sanchez as the man who shot William Rodriguez Orejuela, the son of Cali Cartel founder Miguel Rodriguez Orejuela, on 24 May 1996 at an upscale restaurant in the city of Cali. It is believed that Sanchez was settling a score with William Rodriguez's security chief, who was one of five people killed in the attack. Sanchez became known as "the Overalls Man" after Miguel Rodriguez Orejuela identified him by that name in telephone conversations with another Cali Cartel leader, Helmer "Pacho" Herrera Zuleta. Colombian authorities viewed Sanchez's brash attempt to challenge the leaders of the Cali Cartel as evidence that a new group of drug traffickers were taking over control of Colombia's drug trade from the wounded criminal organization.

See also: Cali Cartel; Herrera Zuleta, Helmer "Pacho"; Rodriguez Orejuela, Miguel
Reference: Torchia, Christopher. 1996. "Cali Cartel Leader Faces a Ruthless Rival: The Overalls Man." *Colombian Post,* 21–27 October.

Santa Cruz Mafia

Named for the city of Santa Cruz, Bolivia, this drug-trafficking organization is at the center of the country's illegal drug trade.

Reference: Shannon, Elaine. 1989. *Desperadoes.*

Santacruz Londono, Jose (1944–1996)

A founding member of the Cali Cartel who had several nicknames, including El Chepe, El Gordo (The

Fat One), and El Estudiante (The Student). Santacruz Londono's early life is sketchy. Colombian authorities believe that he is a native of Pereira, Colombia, and according to his wife, Amparo Castro Santacruz, who talked about her husband's background to the *El Espectador* newspaper, he attended the University of Valle until 1967, when he dropped out as he was about to finish his fourth year in the engineering program. Santacruz Londono then enrolled at the University of the Andes, where, while a student, Jose made money on the side as a kidnapper and drug smuggler. He, Gilberto and Miguel Rodriguez Orejuela, and several others founded a gang of kidnappers and drug smugglers known as Los Chemas. During the mid-1960s and early 1970s, gang members served as underlings to Fernando Tamayo Garcia, a member of the emerald-smuggling underworld in Colombia.

In 1969 Santacruz Londono and other members of Los Chemas were arrested in the kidnapping of two Swiss nationals. Gang members were tried but acquitted, apparently because of a lack of evidence. It was reported that following the kidnappings, Santacruz Londono bought a taxi cab company in Bogotá for which he paid $192,000 in cash. He was implicated in two more kidnappings.

Santacruz Londono also worked as a mule, meaning that he physically transported cocaine. As the Cali Cartel evolved, he played a key role in the organization's phenomenal growth and success, devising a number of ways to transport cocaine via cargo ships and using banks in a number of countries to launder Cali Cartel drug profits.

Santacruz Londono's U.S. cocaine and money-laundering distribution network was centered in the New York City metropolitan area. In 1992 the U.S. Drug Enforcement Administration seized two cocaine conversion laboratories in Brooklyn, New York, that were directly linked to him. Records indicate two known U.S. arrests for the drug kingpin. The first occurred in 1976 when he traveled from New York City to Costa Rica on a fake passport. The second took place in 1977 for a weapons charge in Queens, New York.

Santacruz Londono became somewhat of a legend in the New York City underworld—a godfather who would show up in the middle of a drug deal, exchange small talk, and then disappear into the night. In 1983 DEA agents learned that Santacruz Londono had been occupying an apartment from which he could see the agency's Manhattan field office.

Despite having bank accounts as far away as Hong Kong, Santacruz Londono rarely ventured outside Cali, but in the mid-1990s, when the Colombian government began putting pressure on the Cali Cartel in its home city of Cali, El Estudiante fled to Bogotá.

General Rosso Jose Serrano Cadena, the director major general of the Colombian National Police, knew that El Gordo liked to eat, so he ordered his men to stake out several good restaurants in the northern part of the city. On 14 July 1995 the authorities nabbed Santacruz Londono at the upscale Carbon de Palo steak house. "He was a bit fatter than in the pictures and videos we had of him," Serrano told the press. "He was in a very shocked state." Given his key role in the Cali Cartel, Santacruz Londono's capture was seen as decimating the powerful criminal organization. He was killed by police in 1996 after escaping from prison.

In addition to drug-trafficking charges, Santacruz Londono was also wanted for the 1989 killing of former Antioquia, Colombia, governor Antonio Roldan Betancur and for the 1992 murder of New York city-based journalist Manuel de Dios Unanue.

See also: Cali Cartel; de Dios Unanue, Manuel; Mule; Rodriguez Orejuela, Gilberto; Rodriguez Orejuela, Miguel; Serrano Cadena, Rosso Jose
References: Castillo, Fabio. 1988. *Los Jinetes de la Cocaina* (The Jockeys of Cocaine).
Fedarko, Kevin. 1995. "Outwitting Cali's Professor Moriarty." *Time*, 17 July.

Schmoke, Kurt (c. 1940–)

Three-term mayor of Baltimore, Maryland, who is one of the United States' most highly visible public officials favoring drug decriminalization. Schmoke believes that drug prohibition keeps the prices of illegal drugs much higher than they would be in a decriminalized system and that this leads to the high level of violence associated with the illegal drug trade. The mayor has implemented a number of innovative antidrug programs, including the Baltimore Substance Abuse System, which uses money from government and community sources to strengthen drug abuse and treatment programs, and a needle exchange program, the largest in the United States, which has reduced the AIDS infection rate among drug users by 40 percent. The mayor is also a strong supporter of the Drug Court System and is in favor of allowing doctors to prescribe maintenance levels of heroin, cocaine, and other narcotics drugs to hard-core addicts.

See also: Decriminalization.
References: Simon, Roger. 1994. "Where There's Schmoke." *Playboy* (May): 122+.
Dreyfuss, Robert. 1997. "Hawkes and Doves: Who's Who in the World of Drugs." *Rolling Stone*, 7 August.

Seale, Barry Alderman

A former special forces pilot in Vietnam and a TWA 747 captain who flew cocaine shipments from Colombia to the United States for Colombian drug traffickers during the 1970s and early 1980s and then became a top U.S. government drug informant. Seale claimed his top fee for smuggling a kilogram of cocaine was $5,000 and that he earned as much as $1.5 million for a single flight. His testimony led to an indictment in July 1984 against Federico Vaughn, a top Nicaraguan official in the Sandinista government, and ten others, charging that the Sandinista government was involved with Colombian drug traffickers. Seale also presented testimony before a federal grand jury that implicated Colombian drug traffickers Carlos Lehder Rivas, Pablo Escobar Gaviria, and Jorge Luis Ochoa Vasquez.

Seale refused government protection, even though he knew drug traffickers had put a price on his head. In January 1986, as part of a plea bargain agreement with the U.S. government, Seale began serving a six-month sentence at the Salvation Army House in his home town of Baton Rouge, Louisiana. At about 6 p.m. on 19 February 1986 as Seale pulled his white Cadillac Fleetwood into the Salvation Army parking lot, two men approached his car carrying Ingram Mac-10 guns and killed him instantly.

At the time of Seale's death, U.S. officials said that Colombian drug traffickers had put a contract of $500,000 on his head, or $1 million for getting him alive to Colombia. After the killing, a major federal manhunt was launched and several suspects were captured and arrested. Two weeks before Seale's death, thirty-five IRS agents raided Seale's home and seized boats, furniture, aircraft, and other property, as well as records, claiming that Seale owed the U.S. government $29,437,718 in taxes on illegal income derived from trafficking during the period 1981 to

Rosso Jose Serrano, head of Colombian National Police (Courtesy of the Colombian National Police)

1983. Federal agents later said Seale had been extremely valuable to the Drug Enforcement Administration and had a memory that was close to photographic.

See also: Escobar Gaviria, Pablo; Lehder Rivas, Carlos; Mermelstein, Max; Ochoa Vasquez, Jorge Luis; Operation Screamer; Rodriguez Gacha, Jose Gonzalo
Reference: Gugliotta, Guy, and Jeff Leen. 1990. *Kings of Cocaine.*

Serrano Cadena, Rosso Jose (1942–)

The director major general of the Colombian National Police who has played a major role in Colombia's battle against drug trafficking in the 1990s. Serrano has personally directed several of the operations that led to the capture of the leaders of the Cali Cartel.

See also: Cali Cartel; Cartelitos
Reference: Strong, Simon. 1995. *Whitewash: Pablo Escobar and the Cocaine Wars.*

Shanghai Conference

Considered the first step in the international campaign against drug trafficking, this 1909 conference was organized on the initiative of the United States, which was concerned about the problem of addiction in the Philippines. The United States and twelve other countries (China, Austro-Hungary, Portugal, Germany, France, Russia, Italy, Siam, Japan, Persia, Great Britain, and the Netherlands) sent representatives. The conference chose the Protestant Episcopal Bishop Charles Henry Brent to preside. He had been instrumental in organizing the conference.

The United States called for the immediate worldwide prohibition of opium, but the other participating countries were not willing to go that far. The Convention did, however, adopt nine resolutions unanimously, agreeing that "the use of opium in any form other than for medical purposes is held by almost every participating country to be a matter of prohibition or for careful regulation and that the duty of all countries is to adopt reasonable measures as to prevent all points of departure...the shipment of opium, its alkaloids, derivatives and properties." (Taylor 1969, 101)

See also: United States Opium Exclusion Act
References: Musto, David. 1991. "Opium, Cocaine and Marijuana in American History." *Scientific American* (July) 40+.
Taylor, Arnold H. 1969. *American Diplomacy and the Narcotics Trade, 1900–1939.*

Shining Path Guerrilla Movement (Sendero Luminoso)

The Shining Path movement was founded in 1970 in Peru at Ayacucho University by former philosophy instructor Abinael Guzman Reynoso (alias "Comandante Gonzalo"). It began as a small group committed to the radical communist policies of the late Mao Zedong, and by 1987 its campaign against the Peruvian government had resulted in the deaths of 10,000 people, mostly members of the government forces.

About 1983 the Shining Path started to establish a presence in Peru's Upper Huallaga Valley, which is located about 400 miles from Lima and is an immensely important area for coca leaf production and a principal artery of the Colombian drug empire. The guerrillas offered the local peasants "protection"

against the drug traffickers and police. Beginning about 1987 the Shining Path was able to gain a strong influence in the Upper Huallaga Valley and increase its resources enormously. During this period, the production of the drug crop increased significantly. Guzman, however, was captured in 1992 and sentenced to life in prison, a major development that stripped the Shining Path of its catalyst. Since 1992 the Peruvian government, under its president Alberto Fujimori, has all but destroyed Shining Path.

See also: Narcoguerrilla; Upper Huallaga Valley (Peru)
References: Guillermoprieto, Alma. 1993. "Down the Shining Path." *New Yorker*, 8 February.
Ricci, Jose Lopez. 1994. "Shining Path after Guzman." *NACLA Report on the Americas* (November–December): 6+.

Shultz, George P. (1920–)

U.S. secretary of state from 1982 until 1989, and later a distinguished fellow at the Hoover Institution at Stanford University in California. Schultz also served in the administration of President Richard Nixon as secretary of labor, director of the Office of Management and Budget, and secretary of the Treasury. Schultz's experience in two drug wars under the leadership of presidents Richard Nixon and Ronald Reagan led him to conclude in the late 1980s that decriminalization should be discussed as a viable option in the War on Drugs.

The White House's reaction to Schultz's change of opinion was expressed by one of its spokesmen who said, "The president [George Bush] feels very strongly that legalization is the wrong direction. The guy [Schultz] slips into retirement and right away he starts saying things that are strange." (Converts to Curiosity 1989)

See also: Bush, George Herbert Walker; Decriminalization; Legalization; Nixon, Richard Milhous; Reagan, Ronald
Reference: "Converts to Curiosity." *Economist*, 18 November.

Sicarios

The term used to describe the teenage killers from the slums of the neighborhoods of Colombia's Medellin City, whom drug traffickers employed as assassins during the drug-trafficking-induced killing spree that terrorized Colombia during the 1980s and early 1990s. The sicarios cared little for their personal safety and as Simon Strong described, "The adolescent contract killers preferred to live one minute as somebody than thirty years as nobody. They liked to ride their motorcycles through clogged traffic and pull alongside a target's car and empty their guns at the victims and their bodyguards. Sicarios loved their mothers and consumer goods and were religiously superstitious. As one sixteen-year-old sicario said in an interview, 'I am going to die, but my mother will remember me because I got her a beautiful new refrigerator.'" (Strong 1995, 158–159) Given the poverty in Colombia, sicarios still operate.

See also: Medellin Cartel; Narcoterrorism
References: Bugliosi, Vincent. 1995. *Drugs in America.*
Strong, Simon. 1995. *Whitewash: Pablo Escobar and the Cocaine Wars.*

Silvo Vivas, Raul (1950–)

An Argentine national and metals dealer who was suspected of laundering more than $1 billion via Los Angeles jewelry stores for his employer, the Medellin Cartel. Uruguay extradited Silo Vivas to the United States in December 1989. Vivas's arrest was part of the U.S. government's Polar Cap Operation that resulted in the indictment of thirty-three Los Angeles wholesale jewelers suspected of money laundering for Colombian drug traffickers. At the time of Vivas's arrest, U.S. officials said that he had been personally responsible for the movement of $1 billion in drug profits out of the United States.

Thomas R. Parker, assistant agent in charge of criminal investigations and organized crime activities in Los Angeles, told the press that Vivas's extradition "marked yet another turning point in the willingness of the international community, particularly in South America, to work with us in bringing to an end the tyranny and impunity of these drug empires." (Cartel Extradition 1989)

See also: Extradition; Medellin Cartel, Money Laundering; Operation Polar Cap
References: "Cartel Extradition." 1989. Associated Press, 11 December.
Reckard, E. Scott. 1989. "Money Laundering." Associated Press, 12 December.

Society for Prevention Research (U.S.)

Incorporated as a nonprofit organization in 1992, the Society for Prevention Research is committed to "the fostering and support of scientific efforts related to the prevention of problematic psychological, social, and physical outcomes and disorders in individuals across the lifespan and conducted at any phase of the prevention research cycle." (website: http://www.oslc.org.spr)

Reference: Society for Prevention Research website at http://www.oslc.org.spr.

Sokolowski, Salah Robert James

A Colombian American who was one of two drug traffickers (the other being Manuel Julio Palma Molina) extradited to the United States in November 1989 as a result of the war against Colombian drug traffickers initiated by Colombian President Virgilio Barco Vargas. Sokolowski had been indicted in North Carolina in November 1984 on a charge of murder conspiracy.

See also: Barco Vargas, Virgilio; Extradition; Palma Molina, Manuel Julio
Reference: Coleman, Joseph. 1989. "Colombians Extradite Two More." United Press International, 18 November.

Somnafac
See Methaqualone

Sonora Cartel (Mexico)

Headed by drug trafficker Miguel Caro-Quintero and his two brothers, Jorge and Genaro, this drug-trafficking organization is based in Sonora, Mexico, and specializes in the trafficking of marijuana. Like other Mexican drug-trafficking organizations, however, it has diversified, which means that the cartel also traffics in cocaine and methamphetamine.

The Cartel uses several ranches in the northern border state of Sonora to store drugs before smuggling them to the United States, principally through routes extending into California, Arizona, Texas, and Nevada. Although Miguel Caro-Quintero has been the subject of several arrest warrants in the United States, he has denied being a drug trafficker and claims to be an innocent rancher. Miguel was arrested in 1992 in Mexico, but he was able to use a combination of threats and bribes to get a Mexican judge to dismiss the charges against him. Miguel's brother Rafael is currently in jail for his part in the brutal torture and murder of Drug Enforcement Administration special agent Enrique Camarena Salazar.

See also: Camarena Salazar, Enrique; Mexican Federation
Reference: U.S. Senate Committee on Foreign Relations.
   1997. *Mexico and the Southwest Border Initiative*. 12
   March (statement of Thomas A. Constantine, Director,
   DEA). *See* DEA website at
   http://www.usdoj/dea/pubs/congrtest.

Soros, George (1933–   )

A billionaire U.S. investor who has made hundreds of millions of dollars by playing the stock market. Soros is best known for his financial support of political and economic reform in Eastern Europe and the former Soviet Union, but since about 1991 he has contributed more than $15 million toward drug policy reform and research.

He financially supported the New York City–based Lindesmith Institute, Drug Policy Foundation in Washington, D.C., and Drug Strategies, Washington, D.C., groups that support drug abuse education, treatment, and prevention strategies. In 1996 Soros played a key role in the successful medical-marijuana initiative in Arizona and California by contributing $1.1 million to the campaign.

See also: Lindesmith Institute; Drug Policy Foundation;
   Drug Strategies
Reference: Dreyfuss, Robert. 1997. "Hawks and Doves:
   Who's Who in the World of Drugs." *Rolling Stone*, 7
   August.

South Florida Task Force

In November 1981 a delegation of prominent leaders from Miami, which included former astronaut Frank Borman, chairman of Eastern Airlines, and Alvah Chapman, chairman of the Knight Ridder newspaper chain, the corporate owner of the *Miami Herald,* went to see President Ronald Reagan at the White House. The delegation, which called itself Citizens Against Crime, wanted federal help to deal with an epidemic of violent crime and a flood of illegal drugs that was wreaking havoc on South Florida, the prosperous and lush center of the Sunshine State. The problem was not new. As early as May 1972 the *New York Times,* based on information provided by federal law enforcement officials, reported that entrepreneurial French, South American, Puerto Rican and Cuban refugees were turning South Florida into a premier entry point for smuggled heroine and cocaine.

On 1 March 1982 Reagan responded to the visit of the delegation and to reports about increased drug trafficking in South Florida and the problems it was creating by establishing the South Florida Task Force. Vice President George Bush was put in charge of the Task Force, and it quickly became known as the Vice President's Task Force on South Florida.

Within weeks of its formation, the South Florida Task Force began to score some stunning successes. On 9 March 1982 the U.S. Customs Service at the Miami International Airport seized 3,906 pounds of cocaine valued at $1.3 million aboard a cargo plane arriving from Bogotá, Colombia. It was the largest amount of cocaine ever impounded by the federal agency. Then in April, authorities intercepted a Cessna 402B aircraft and seized another 115 pounds of cocaine worth $166 million.

The seizures of marijuana were equally impressive. Customs agents intercepted a 65–foot trawler called the *Misfit,* which was bound for Florida, and found 70,000 pounds of marijuana aboard, valued at $5.4 million. Law enforcement officers intercepted a 110–foot coastal freighter heading toward Florida with about 103,000 pounds of marijuana worth $77 million hidden inside a secret compartment of the boat. Then in November 1982 still another interdiction uncovered 61,500 pounds of marijuana aboard the 130–foot *Shooting Star.* Between 15 February and 30 September 1982, the Task Force reported the seizure of 1.7 million pounds of marijuana and 6,565 pounds of cocaine, a significant increase over a corresponding figure the first year.

Meanwhile, during the first year of the Task Force's operation, drug traffickers were being hauled into court. At the federal level the U.S. Attorney General's Office prosecuted a total of 664 drug-related cases, up 64 percent from the previous year. Ronald Reagan was quick to gain political capital from what appeared to be the government's win in the war against international drug trafficking.

Reagan journeyed to Miami and at a press conference stood before the seizures of his War on Drugs and called the South Florida Task Force "a brilliant example of working federalism." (Eddy, Sabogal, & Walden 1988, 37)

Critics charged that the president's well-orchestrated visits to South Florida were giving away the Task Force's operational plans to the enemy. (Eddy 1988, 98) "Every move was telegraphed to the smuggling community," one task force official told *Newsweek* magazine. "The only doper who doesn't know about it has been away somewhere." (Starr 1992, 15) But even before the first year ended, it appeared that the ever resourceful drug traffickers were shifting the battlefield of the War on Drugs, bringing to other parts of the country the violence, the drug addiction, the corruption, and the dirty money that had plagued South Florida. Still, the federal government did set up South Florida-style task forces wherever a new drug smuggling route seemed to be developing. The so-called El Dorado units soon began operation in Chicago, Houston, Philadelphia, New York, and Los Angeles.

See also: Bush, George Herbert Walker
References: Freemantle, Brian. 1985. *The Fix*.
Eddy, Paul, Hugh Sabogal, and Sarah Walden. 1988. *The Cocaine Wars*.
Gugliotta, Guy, and Jeff Leen. 1990. *Kings of Cocaine*.
Starr, Mark. 1992. "Reagan's War on Drugs." *Newsweek*, 9 August.

SOUTHCOM
See United States Southern Command

Southern Air Transport
A former CIA proprietary company based in Miami, Florida, that serviced aircraft for the "Enterprise," a secret covert operation established in mid-1984 by Oliver North to supply the Nicaraguan guerillas known as the Contras with financial and military support in their fight against the ruling Sandinista government. Southern Air Transport was suspected of being used to transport guns to the Contras, and on their return flights, cocaine to the United States. No one from the company was ever charged.

See also: Contras
Reference: Shannon, Elaine. 1989. *Desperadoes*.

Southwest Border Initiative
A joint program of the U.S. Drug Enforcement Administration and the FBI in which their special agents work together to disrupt Mexican drug-trafficking organizations and bring their leaders to jail. At a hearing before the Committee on Foreign Affairs in 1995, DEA Administrator Thomas A. Constantine said, "For the first time, the DEA, FBI, the Department of Justice Criminal Division and respective U.S. attorneys in every state along the southwest border are coordinating both the intelligence and

manpower resources against a common enemy— the poly-drug-trafficking organizations that are transporting increasing amounts of cocaine, heroin, marijuana and methamphetamine across our borders. Both the DEA and FBI have high expectations for the success of this operation." (Drug Trafficking in Mexico, 1996)

See also: Operation Zorro
Reference: U.S. Senate Committee on Banking, Housing and Urban Affairs. 1996. *Drug Trafficking in Mexico*, 28 March (statement of Thomas A. Constantine, administrator of the Drug Enforcement Administration).

Spanish American War
The United States' move towards the regulation and ultimately the prohibition of drugs was largely guided by its foreign policy, including the acquisition of the Philippines in 1898, after it won a four-month war with Spain. As a result of the peace treaty, Spain agreed to give up Cuba and cede Puerto Rico and Guam to the United States. American forces would occupy Manila, the capital of the Philippines, pending a peace treaty that would decide the fate of that country. The United States, however, considered the Filipinos incapable of immediate self-rule and took control of the welfare of the local population.

The Spanish had allowed Chinese residents in the Philippines to purchase opium and taxed its sale, but drug addiction had spread to the native population, which began to use the drug for its constipative effects in order to stave off cholera. Under pressure from clergy and others in the growing and increasingly active U.S. antiopium movement, President William Taft formed the Philippines Commission to investigate the opium trade and report back to him. The Commission's conclusion that the opium trade was one of the most serious problems in the Orient led Congress to ban opium use in the Philippines in 1905. Developments in the Philippines sparked an antiopium crusade that became an international movement that lobbied successfully for a series of treaties restricting the opium trade. In 1909 the United States and twelve other countries met in Shanghai, China, to examine the opium trade, and they agreed in principle that they should make a stronger effort to control opium and its derivatives, particularly morphine. Twelve of the thirteen countries then reconvened two years later at The Hague, Netherlands, where they agreed, among other mea-

Scene from the Spanish American War, 1898, United States troops on San Juan Hill in Cuba. The acquisition of the Philippines as a result of the war sparked a movement to control opium production and distribution at the international level. (UPI/Corbis-Bettmann)

sures, to regulate the production and distribution of opium with the goal of eventually suppressing the trade altogether.

See also: Brent, Charles; Shanghai Conference
References: Chepesiuk, Ron. 1999. *Hard Target.*
Morgan, H. Wayne. 1981. *Drugs in America: A Social History, 1800–1980.*
Weir, William. 1995. *In the Shadow of the Dope Fiend.*
Taylor, Arnold H. 1969. *American Diplomacy and the Narcotics Trade, 1900–1939.*

Special Action Office for Drug Abuse Prevention (U.S.)

In 1971 President Richard Nixon established this office to coordinate all federal drug prevention and treatment activities.

Reference: Bertram, Eva, Kenneth Sharpe, and Peter Anders. 1996. *Drug War Politics: The Price of Denial.*

Speed
See Methamphetamine.

Speed Balling

A term used when heroin is mixed or used in connection with cocaine. This practice has been in use since the 1930s. Speed ballers report that they love the rush or "flash" of cocaine that goes with the mellowing effect of heroin. The death of actor John Belushi in 1982 brought the practice of speed balling to public notice.

See also: Overdose, Victims of
Reference: Abel, Ernest L. 1994. *A Dictionary of Drug Abuse Terms and Terminology.*
Marnell, Tim, ed. 1997. *Drug Identification Bible.*

Steinberg, Donald

A major marijuana drug smuggler of the 1970s who called his drug-trafficking organization "The Company." While serving in the U.S. military in Vietnam, Steinberg started dabbling in marijuana smuggling for personal use and to service his friends. Returning to the United States, Steinberg made a Mexican connection and began smuggling larger amounts of marijuana from Mexico. But he was caught and convicted of smuggling 500 pounds of marijuana to Texas.

Steinberg received probation and moved to Fort Lauderdale, Florida, where he organized another marijuana-smuggling enterprise. Between 1976 and 1978 Steinberg made thirty-seven trips to Colombia to purchase marijuana for between $50 and $70 a pound.

According to a Drug Enforcement Administration memo, seized financial records of the Steinberg organization showed that for one three-month period (April-June 1978) the organization's net profits from only one source of supply, for marijuana alone, was $35 million. Steinberg eventually became a fugitive, but he was caught in 1979. In exchange for leniency, Steinberg agreed to testify against his associates. Steinberg was one of history's biggest marijuana traffickers, but he said after his capture, "I never saw a gun the whole time I was in the business. (Traub 1983, 102)

See also: Marijuana.
References: Mills, James. 1986. *The Underground Empire: Where Crime and Justice Embrace.*
Traub, James. 1983. *The Billion Dollar Connection: The International Drug Trade.*

Spence, Richard
See Weinig, Harvey

Strategic Alliance against Drugs

An agreement signed between the United States and Venezuela on 13 October 1997 at Miraflores Palace in Caracas. The agreement has as its goal the adoption of measures that will effectively combat the problems of production, consumption, and illicit trafficking of drugs and psychotropic substances, money laundering, and related crimes that undermine democracy. Among other steps, the two governments announced that they planned to reduce the demand for drugs through the strengthening of educational prevention programs and public campaigns especially aimed at youth. They also agreed to intensify efforts at enhancing the effectiveness of governmental institutions, including customs, intelligence, and the law enforcement and security agencies of the states, by means of increasing educational opportunities and technical cooperation through the exchange of experts.

Reference: Text: Clinton/Caldera Declaration in Caracas at website http://www.usemb.se/regional/ar/lattr:plodocs.dec13.htm.

Spike
See Tabuthium

Summit of the Americas

Hosted by the U.S. government in Miami in December 1994, this summit was attended by all the heads of major countries in the Western Hemisphere and was a response to the need for action by participating governments, individually and collectively, to address the problem of drug production, distribution, and use. Plans were made to hold another summit to develop instruments to combat money laundering and to implement under Organization of American States auspices a multilateral antidrug evaluation mechanism.

See also: Organization of American States; Summit of the Americas Ministerial Conference on Money Laundering
Reference: "The United States International Crime Control Strategy." 1998. *Trends in Organized Crime* (Fall): 1–87.

Summit of the Americas Ministerial Conference on Money Laundering

As a follow-up to the 1994 Summit of the Americas in Miami, Florida, the U.S. secretary of the treasury convened a conference of finance and justice ministers representing twenty-nine countries from Latin America in December 1995. The purpose was to develop and coordinate a joint strategy to combat money laundering. Among other measures, conference participants agreed to criminalize laundering of the proceeds from drug trafficking and to adopt measures to increase cooperation in money-laundering investigations.

In July 1997 Raymond V. Kelly, undersecretary of the Treasury Department, reported before the House Judiciary Subcommittee on Crime that "over a third of the Summit nations had passed legislation criminalizing money laundering or have issued anti-money laundering regulations. Many others are considering doing so. . . . Cooperation across national lines appears to be increasing." (U.S. House Judiciary Subcommittee on Crime 1997)

See also: Summit of the Americas
Reference: U.S. House of Representatives Judiciary Commit-

tee. *Hearings before the Subcommittee on Crime*. 1997. 24 July (statement of Raymond V. Kelly, undersecretary of the Treasury Department).

Sweet, Robert (1922–)

A federal judge in New York City who has been out-spoken in his opposition to current U.S. government policy on drugs and is on record as favoring the legalization of drugs. An unlikely "radical" on the drug issue, Sweet has been a long-time Republican and served as a deputy mayor of New York City under Mayor John Lindsey. Sweet believes the United States must have a more humane drug policy in place. The judge has said, ""We're a caring nation. The law must speak to justice." (Baer 1990)

See also: Legalization
References: Baer, Donald. 1990. "A Judge Who Took the Stand." *U.S. News and World Report*, 9 April.
Tovares, Robert W. 1989. "How Best to Solve the Drug Problem." *National Catholic Reporter*, 22 December.

Syndenham, Thomas

A prominent seventeenth-century English physician who developed a popular laudanum recipe that was used by such famous writers as Thomas De Quincey and Samuel Taylor Coleridge. Syndenham's mixture was actually an early cocktail—opium dissolved in a sherry flavored with cloves, saffron, and cinnamon. According to historian David Musto, "Syndenham considered opium 'one of the most valued medicines of the world [that] does more honor to medicine than any remedy whatsoever.'" (*The American Disease*, p. 69)

See also: De Quincey, Thomas; Laudanum
References: Musto, David F. 1987. *The American Disease: Origins of Narcotics Control*.
Sigerist, H. G. 1941. "Laudanum in the Words of Paracelsus." *Bulletin of Historical Medicine*.

Synthetic Drugs

A term used to refer to drugs synthesized and made in the laboratory. Examples of synthetic drugs are amphetamine, ecstasy, and methamphetamine. According to the United Nations International Drug Control Program, "In 1991, synthetic drugs were thought to account for less than 5 percent of the money spent on illicit drugs in the U.S. Since then, the share has grown rapidly. Consumption of two synthetic drugs, methamphetamine and ecstasy, has grown particularly rapidly." (United Nations International Drug Control Program 1997, 129)

Many critics of the current prohibitionist policy toward illegal drugs say that even if interdiction efforts were hugely successful in shutting down the production of coca and poppy plants, it would only result in an increase in synthetic drugs. Today, the consumption of ecstasy and amphetamine exceeds that of cocaine and heroin in many European countries.

See also: Amphetamine; Ecstasy; Methamphetamine; Perez, Augusto; United States Act of 8 March 1946
References: Abadinsky, Howard. 1990. *Organized Crime*.
Abel, Ernst L. 1994. *A Dictionary of Drug Abuse Terms and Terminology*.

T

Taboada, Gabriel

Drug trafficker and key informant for the U.S. government against Colombian drug cartels. While serving a twelve-year sentence for conspiracy to import cocaine in 1992, Taboada provided important testimony that helped convict Panamanian General Manuel Noriega. According to Senator John Kerry, "[Taboada's] first-hand testimony of behind the scenes in the Medellin and Cali cartels provided us [the U.S. government] with new insights into the cartels' operations and fleshed out a great deal of what was already said." (Kerry 1997, 71)

See also: Kerry, John F.
Reference: Kerry, John F. 1997. *A New Kind of War: National Security and the Globalization of Crime.*

Tambs, Lewis

U.S. Ambassador to Colombia from 1983 to 1985. Tambs was a hard-line anticommunist who had formulated the Santa Fe Report, a plan to contain communism in Latin America that was adopted by the Republican National Committee in 1980. According to journalists Guy Gugliotta and Jeff Leen, Tambs was "not bashful about voicing his opinion-—about drugs, guerrillas, politics, and almost anything else—and from the beginning of his term, he established a combative public persona that frequently irritated his Colombian hosts and made his aides cringe." (Gugliotta & Leen 1990, 183)

Tambs is credited with coining the term *narcoterrorism*, and given his strident anticommunist disposition, he made an effort to link drugs with the Colombian guerrilla movement. At that time, however, Colombian officials downplayed the connection. In July 1985 Tambs received a new assignment as U.S. Ambassador to Costa Rica. The following year, the U.S. Attorney's Office in Miami began investigating a rumor that Contra rebels in Nicaragua had accepted a Medellin Cartel contract to murder Tambs. The hit was never carried out, but Tambs had to resign in July 1987 when he was implicated in the illegal Contra resupply network in Costa Rica.

See also: Contras; Narcoguerrillas; Narcoterrorism
References: Gugliotta, Guy, and Jeff Leen. 1990. *Kings of Cocaine.*
Strong, Simon. 1995. *Whitewash: Pablo Escobar and the Cocaine Wars.*

Taylor, William Desmond (1877–1922)

A director and the president of the Screen Actor's Guild who was one of Hollywood's most colorful characters during its formative years. On 2 February 1922 he was shot dead under mysterious circumstances in his Hollywood mansion. Because Taylor opposed local drug dealers, there was speculation that he had been an object of a drug hit.

Reference: Jonnes, Jill. 1996. *Hep-Cats, Narcs and Pipe Dreams.*

Tijuana Cartel (Mexico)

Headed by the brothers Ramon, Benjamin, and Francisco Arellano Felix, this is one of Mexico's most powerful, aggressive, and violent drug-trafficking organizations. As Drug Enforcement Administration head Thomas A. Constantine described the Cartel, "More than any other major trafficking organization from Mexico, it extends its tentacles directly from high-echelon figures in the law enforcement and judicial systems in Mexico, to street-level individuals in the United States." (U.S. Senate Committee on Foreign Relations 1997)

The Arellano Felix brothers took control of the organization after the incarceration of Miguel Felix Gallardo in 1989 for his part in the torture-murder of DEA special agent Enrique Camarena Salazar. The Tijuana Cartel mainly operates in the Mexican state of Sinaloa, where the Arellano Felix brothers were born, as well as the states of Jalisco, Chiapas, and Michoacan. Its U.S. base is the southern and northern regions of Baja, California, from which the organization ships multiton quantities of cocaine and marijuana, as well as heroin and methamphetamine.

The Tijuana Cartel is well organized and it uses heavily armed and well-trained paramilitary security forces and a team of international mercenaries as advisors to train its members. The organization employs violent street gangs from towns in both Mexico and the United States to kill individuals who ship drugs through their territory without paying a special transportation tax demanded by the Cartel. A sophisticated criminal organization, the Cartel uses radio scanners, cellular phones, and other technology to carry out espionage against law enforcement. The group reportedly spends a million dollars a week in bribes to gain the complicity of Mexican drug enforcement officials. The DEA and FBI have set up a joint task force in San Diego, California, to target the Cartel for investigation.

See also: Arellano Felix, Ramon; Camarena Salazar, Enrique; Colosio Murrieta, Luis Donaldo; Logan Heights Calle 30; Mexican Federation; Navarro Lara, General Alfredo
Reference: U.S. Senate Committee. 1997. *Mexico and the Southwest Border Initiative*, Before the Senate Foreign Relations Committee, 12 March (statement of Thomas A. Constantine, head of the Drug Enforcement Administration). *See* DEA website: http://www.usdoj/dea/pubs/congrtest.

Toft, Joe

The head of the U.S. Drug Enforcement Administration office in Bogotá, Colombia, from 1987 to 1994 who, upon his retirement in September 1994, caused a furor when he labeled Colombia a "narcodemocracy" and insisted in a television interview that the electoral campaign of the country's president, Ernesto Samper Pizano, had taken money from the Cali Cartel. Samper's administration angrily charged that Toft had offended the country's national dignity, and the former DEA agent was denounced by several leading Colombian political figures. U.S. Ambassador Myles Frechette said Toft's comments did not represent the views of the U.S. government, but many Colombians expressed skepticism that Toft would have spoken without the knowledge, if not the consent, of his superiors.

See also: Cali Cartel; Frechette, Myles; Narcocassettes; Narcodemocracy; Samper Pizano, Ernesto
Reference: Sheridan, May Beth. 1994. "Colombia Rages Over Allegations by Former U.S. Anti-Drug Official." Knight Ridder/Tribune Service, 30 September.

Tongs
See Triads

Trafficante, Santo, Jr. (1886–1954)

The powerful godfather of a major narcotics and gambling empire based in Tampa, Florida, Trafficante, Jr., formed alliances with other leading organized crime figures, including Charles "Lucky" Luciano, and crime bosses in St. Louis and Kansas City. Upon Santo, Sr.'s death, his narcotics empire was taken over by his son Santo, Jr., who was later involved in a CIA plot to assassinate Cuban leader Fidel Castro.

See also: Italian American Mafia; Luciano, Charles "Lucky"
Reference: Blumenthal, Ralph. 1989. *Last Days of the Sicilians.*
Davis, John H. 1989. *Mafia Kingfish.*
Weir, William. 1995. *In the Shadow of the Dope Fiend.*

Tranquilandia (Colombia)

The site of one of the biggest drug busts in Colombian history, which occurred on 10 March 1984, when a task force spearheaded by the Colombian National Anti-Narcotics Unit and consisting of forty-five officers descended on this cocaine laboratory named Tranquilandia, located in the country's east-

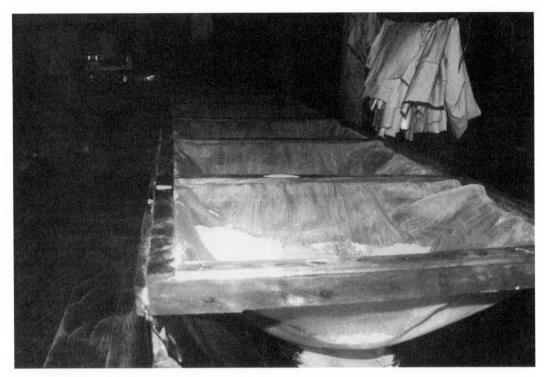

Colombian Nation Police bust a cocaine laboratory (Courtesy of the Colombian National Police)

ern Llanos region. The task force arrested several workers and confiscated an enormous inventory of cocaine-making material that included 305 drums of acetone, 482 jugs of gasoline, 363 drums of ether, and 133 jugs of aviation fuel. The fuel log books, moreover, showed that Tranquilandia had received 15,539 metric tons of cocaine paste and base between 15 December 1983 and 2 February 1984.

After the raid, U.S. and Colombian authorities realized for the first time the huge size of the Colombian cocaine trade. In retaliation for the drug bust, the Medellin Cartel ordered the killing of Jaime Ramirez Gomez, the head of the Colombian National Anti-Narcotics Unit, whom the Cartel held responsible for the raid.

See also: Ramirez Gomez, Jaime
References: Strong, Simon. 1995. *Whitewash: Pablo Escobar and the Cocaine Wars*.
Gugliotta, Guy, and Jeff Leen. 1990. *Kings of Cocaine*.

Tranquilizers

A term introduced in 1953 to describe drugs that have a calming, muscle-relaxing effect. There are two types of tranquilizers: one used for sedation and the other for the treatment of psychiatric disorders. Examples of such drugs include diazepam and chlordiazepoxide.

See also: Depressants; United Nations Convention on Psychotropic Substances of 1971; Valium
Reference: Marnell, Tim. 1997. *Drug Identification Bible.*

Treatment Alternatives to Street Crime (TASC)

One of the early U.S. federal government initiatives to combat drug-related crime. Begun in 1972 as a federally funded program, TASC has been continued by most states through block grants. In the program, suspended drug offenders are screened and referred to treatment. Today, TASC programs operate in every state, although they are sometimes known by other names.

Reference: Schmalleger, Frank, ed. 1997. *Crime and the Justice System in America: An Encyclopedia.*

Triads

Southern Asia is the world's biggest producer of raw opium and its refined product, heroin. To get the

The Boo How Doy Tong War during the 1930s in China-town, New York had many people worried that the "hatchet men" would once again bring out their cleavers after two decades of silence. Pictured is Eddie Gong, leader of the Hip Song Tong, inspecting his trust knives. (Corbis/Bettmann-UPI)

heroin from the remote jungle laboratories of southern Asia to the transhipment points in Bangkok, Taiwan, and Hong Kong, and on to the streets of the United States and Europe is the job of well-organized ethnic Chinese criminal groups known as Triads.

The Chinese connection in international drug trafficking came to public attention in the mid-1980s, when Chinese criminal gangs began to replace the Italian crime syndicates as the dominant force in heroin trafficking. In New York City, the country's biggest heroin market, federal prosecution of mob leaders in the famous Pizza Connection case weakened the Italian mob's hold of the wholesale distribution of the drug and allowed the Chinese to grab control of 65 to 85 percent of the market.

Beginning in 1986 Customs officials at international airports in cities like New York, Los Angeles, and San Francisco began to notice a huge increase in heroin trafficking involving Chinese nationals from Thailand, Taiwan, Hong Kong, and mainland China. By September of that year the modus operandi was

changing, as the Chinese traffickers began to shift from the use of couriers to the use of cargo ships to smuggle heroin. Within the next six months, the authorities intercepted shipments totaling 133 pounds of heroin.

By February 1989 one investigation was being called the biggest heroin bust in U.S. history. Twenty-six people who worked for a powerful Hong Kong-based international heroin ring were arrested and 800 pounds of pure high-grade heroin seized. The following year, cases implicating Chinese traffickers had become routine, and law enforcement agencies around the world were confiscating many thousands of pounds of heroin.

Who are the Chinese criminal entrepreneurs responsible for transporting and distributing hundreds of pounds of heroin to consumers in the United States, Europe, and other parts of the world? According to extensive research conducted by the Center for the Study of Asian Organized Crime, the global infrastructure for the distribution of heroin has been set up by the Taiwanese and the remnants of the Chinese Nationalist army that fled to Laos, Myanmar, Cambodia, and Thailand after the communists under Mao Tse Tung took control of mainland China in 1949.

Many of the Taiwanese leaders in the international drug-trafficking business are members of the Triads, Chinese secret societies that organized in China in the early seventeenth century as resistance groups to the Manchu dynasty that ruled China from the seventeenth century to 1911. After the Manchus were deposed, some Triad members moved into crime, including the lucrative opiate trade from the Golden Triangle.

The nationalists under Dr. Sun Yat Sen tried to disband the Triads in the 1910s, but were unsuccessful. When the Communists took over mainland China in 1949, a large group of Triads followed General Chiang Kai-Shek to Taiwan; others moved to Hong Kong, strengthening the large Triad population in what was then a British colony.

Today, Hong Kong is the nerve center for the Triad organization, which has spread all over the world and is involved not only in drug trafficking but also protection, loan sharking, illegal gambling, and extortion rackets, among other criminal activities. The Triads have a tradition, organization, initiations, and rituals that remind many law enforcement officials of the Italian Mafia. For example, to be a Triad, new members must be recommended by existing members in good standing, and, if admitted, they must go through a complicated initiation ceremony and observe many rituals. The Triads, however, differ from La Cosa Nostra in that they have no godfathers or no ruling council and are decentralized in nature.

The Triads have grown into one the world's biggest criminal organizations with as many as fifty gangs and membership that has been put as low as 50,000 and as high as 180,000. In 1994, the Center for the Study of Asian Organized Crime estimated that the Triads' earnings from the international heroin trade were a staggering $200 billion per year. Major markets for the Triad drug distribution pipeline include Taiwan, the Netherlands, Asia, and the United States.

In the 1970s Triad gang leaders began to see the new criminal opportunities presented by the growing Chinese communities of the United States. Between 1970 to 1980 the number of Chinese immigrants to the U.S. jumped 85 percent, from 435,062 to 806,027, thanks to the changes in the 1965 Immigration Act, which helped make the Chinese the second largest immigrant group in the United States after the Mexicans. This figure does not include the estimated 100,000 plus Chinese who are smuggled into the United States annually.

According to many law enforcement officials, the Triads have infiltrated local groups and associations in Chinese communities throughout the United States. The extent of Triad involvement in drug trafficking in the United States has been a contentious issue among experts. Some FBI and Drug Enforcement Administration officials have said that, while it is true that individual gang members have come from Hong Kong to the United States, no organized Triad criminal activity exists here.

Ko-lin Chin, a noted scholar of Chinese subculture, believes that the "Chinese mafia" does not exist and has maintained that "there was little evidence to support the contention that Hong Kong Triad societies are responsible for the bulk of heroin smuggled into the United States." (Chin 1986, 39)

Law enforcement officials in the streets have disagreed with the skeptics and warned that it would be a mistake to underestimate the Triad presence in the United States. "The wave of corruption has already occurred," Sergeant Tom Perdue of the San Francisco Police Department told one publication. "They [the Triads] have already filtered out the money into the U.S. High-level Triads are already here, and they are spreading out a lot of money, gathering their forces." (Carter 1991, 73)

Analysis by the U.S. Justice Department appears to back up what many of the police operating in the streets are saying. According to one of the government agency's reports, "Some ordinary Triad members are entering the U.S. and some of their former leaders are moving significant portions of their assets here as a hedge against the future. Both of these trends should accelerate in the next ten years." (Chinese Triads Pushing the Mafia Aside 1989, 4) Reports in the early 1990s indicated that the Triads were established in many U.S. cities with large Chinese populations, including Chicago, New York, San Francisco, Boston, and Monterey Park, California. Most of the Triads immigrating to the United States come from Hong Kong.

References: Carter, Hodding III. "Day of the Triads." *M INC.*, June 1991, 68.

Chin, Ko-lin. 1990. *Chinese Subcultural Criminality*, 39.

———. 1986. "Triad Societies, Tongs, Organized Crime and Street Gangs in Asia and the United States."

"Chinese Triads Pushing the Mafia Aside." 1989. *Organized Crime Digest*, 7 August, 4.

U

UCLA Drug Abuse Research Center (DARC)

The Drug Abuse Research Center is affiliated with UCLA's Neuropsychiatric Institute and investigates a wide array of issues relating to U.S. drug policy and to drug abuse and treatment, including methadone maintenance, cocaine and crack use and abuse, and the history of opiate use. In addition to its research activities, the Center also disseminates information about drug use and provides training for prospective researchers and scientists in affiliated disciplines.

See also: Cocaine; Crack Cocaine; Methadone Treatment Programs
Reference: UCLA Drug Abuse Research Center website at http://www.medsch.ucla.edu/som/npi/DARC.

UNESCO

See United Nations Scientific and Cultural Organization

United Nations Commission on Narcotic Drugs

Established in 1946, the Commission is composed of thirty members that are selected by the U.N.'s Economic and Social Council, and is the main United Nations policy-making agency for the control of narcotic drugs and psychotropic substances. As one of the working commissions of the U.N.'s Economic and Social Council, the Commission makes recom-

mendations to the Council regarding the control of those drugs and substances. It is also responsible for reviewing the global drug situation and making recommendations, including advice on how to strengthen international drug control.

See also: Psychotropic
References: Osmanczyk, Edmund Jan. 1985. *Encyclopedia of the United Nations and International Agreements.*
United Nations Department of Public Information. 1995. *Basic Facts about the U.N.*

United Nations Comprehensive Multi-Disciplinary Outline (CMO)

Adopted in 1987 at an international conference on drug abuse and drug trafficking, the CMO establishes the United Nation's drug strategy framework as the basis by which national, regional, and international drug strategies are to be coordinated. It sets forth a group of recommendations that address areas relating to drug abuse and drug trafficking: treatment and rehabilitation; and the reduction of demand and the control of supply.

Reference: United Nations International Drug Control Program. 1997. *World Drug Report.*

United Nations Conference on Drug Control

Held in Vienna from 21 through 26 June 1987, the conference was convened at the ministerial level and dealt with all aspects of drug control, including demand reduction, crop eradication, extradition, and the treatment and rehabilitation of addicts.

See also: Eradication; Extradition
Reference: United Nations Department of Public Information. 1986. *Everyman's United Nations.*

United Nations Convention on Psychotropic Substances of 1971

The World Health Organization General Assembly adopted this convention in 1971 as an international measure to control drugs that were not covered by previous treaties. The drugs included amphetamines, tranquilizers, barbiturates, nonbarbiturate substitutes, and lysergic acid diethylamide (LSD), and they were put under even stricter controls than narcotic drugs. The treaty came into force on 16 August 1976. As of November 1997 the number of states party to the 1971 Convention stood at 156.

See also: Amphetamines; Barbiturates; LSD; Tranquilizers; United Nations International Drug Control Program
References: Osmanczyk, Edmund Jan. 1985. *Encyclopedia of the United Nations and International Agreements.*
United Nations Department of Public Information. 1986. *Everyman's United Nations.*

United Nations Convention against the Illicit Traffic in Narcotic Drugs and Psychotropic Substances of 1988

This convention is designed to deprive international drug traffickers of their freedom of movement and illegally obtained profits from the drug trade. Among other measures, the thirty-four-article treaty prescribes that bank secrecy cannot be invoked when courts are asked to make available bank, financial, or commercial records; that states provide mutual legal assistance on drug-related investigations; and that parties make a concerted effort to reduce and eventually eliminate the demand for drugs. As of 1 November 1997, 142 states or 74 percent of all countries were party to the Convention.

See also: Certification; Money Laundering; Psychotropic; United Nations International Drug Control Program
Reference: United Nations Department of Public Information. 1995. *Basic Facts about the U.N.*

United Nations Crime Prevention and Criminal Justice Division (CPCJD)

This international agency focuses on the connection between crime and illegal drugs, including their impact on areas such as money laundering and judicial system reform.

See also: Money Laundering
Reference: United Nations International Drug Control Program. 1997. *World Drug Report.*

United Nations Decade against Drug Abuse (1991–2000)

Proclaimed during a special session of the U.N. General Assembly devoted to international drug control, the period covered by this proclamation is to focus on implementing the Global Program of Action to combat drug abuse and drug trafficking, which was adopted at the session.

See also: United Nations Political Program; Global Plan of Action
Reference: United Nations Department of Public Information. 1995. *A Guide To Information at the United Nations.*

United Nations Declaration on Enhanced Regional Cooperation for Drug Abuse Control for Asia and the Pacific

This declaration, which resulted from a meeting of senior officials on drug abuse issues in the Asian and Pacific region, was hosted by the Economic and Social Commission for Asia and the Pacific (ESCAP) and was held in Taipei in February 1991. The declaration called for development of regional and subregional antidrug programs and encouraged a proposal that would organize a coordinating antidrug center within the United Nations International Drug Control Program.

Reference: United Nations International Drug Control Program. 1997. *World Drug Report.*

United Nations Development Program

Established in 1965, this program is the main source of grants for sustainable development projects, and it promotes the inclusion of appropriate drug control elements in development activities.

Reference: United Nations Department of Public Information. 1995. *Basic Facts about the United Nations.*

United Nations Drug Abuse and Illicit Trafficking International Day

The United Nations General Assembly voted on 11 December 1988 that such a day should be declared on 26 June of each year.

Reference: Osmanczyk, Edmund Jan. 1990. *Encyclopedia of the United Nations and International Agreements.*

United Nations Educational, Scientific, and Cultural Organization (UNESCO)

Established in 1946, UNESCO'S primary function is to foster peace and security in the world by promoting collaboration among nations in the areas of education, science, and culture. To fulfill its mandate, the agency attempts to integrate drug use prevention and education-related programs and activities within both school and out-of-school programs.

References: United Nations International Drug Control Program. 1997. *World Drug Report.*
United Nations Department of Public Information. 1986. *Everyman's United Nations.*

United Nations Food and Agriculture Organization

Founded in 1945, this international agency helps with projects that attempt to reduce incentives for cultivating illicit drug crops while raising the income levels of farmers. It also is exploring the potential use of satellite imagery and remote sensing techniques to help detect illegal crop cultivation.

See also: Alternative Development
Reference: United Nations International Drug Control Program. 1997. *World Drug Report.*

United Nations Fund for Drug Abuse Control

Established by the U.N. General Assembly in 1991, the fund is a major source within the U.N. system for financing programs aimed at supporting national and interstate drug control initiatives. It is supported by the volunteer contributions of member states and private organizations.

See also: Betancur Cuartas, Belisario
References: Osmanczyk, Edmund Jan. 1985. *Encyclopedia of the United Nations and International Agreements.*
United Nations Department of Public Information. 1995. *Basic Facts about the United Nations.*

United Nations Industrial Development Organization

Established by the U.N. General Assembly in 1966, the organization's mandate is to promote industrial development and cooperation and to act as a central coordinating body for industrial activities within the U.N. system. In doing so, it assists governments and the private sector in establishing and managing agro-industries in illicit crop areas.

Reference: United Nations Department of Public Information. 1995. *Basic Facts about the United Nations.*

United Nations International Children's Fund (UNICEF)

Created by the U.N. General Assembly in 1946 to address the emergency needs of the children in Europe and Asia, this fund now works with agencies anywhere in the world to improve the lives of children. As part of its mission, UNICEF has drug prevention programs that focus on children and young people, especially those who are vulnerable.

Reference: United Nations Department of Public Information. 1995. *Basic Facts about the United Nations.*

United Nations International Drug Control Program (UNDCP)

Established in 1990 to enhance the effectiveness of the U.N. structure for drug control, the UNDCP became operational the following year and today has several offices that provide information, expertise, and technical assistance on drug abuse control to countries around the world. The UNDCP is guided by the following U.N. treaties: The Single Convention on Narcotic Drugs, 1961; The Convention as Amended by the 1972 Protocol; the 1971 Convention on Psychotropic Substances; and the 1988 United Nations Convention against Illicit Traffic in Narcotic Drugs and Psychotropic Substances.

See also: Arlacchi, Pino; United Nations Convention against Illicit Traffic in Narcotic Drugs And Psychotropic Substances of 1988; United Nations Convention On

Psychotropic Substances of 1971; United Nations Office at Vienna; United Nations Single Convention on Narcotic Drugs of 1961; World Customs Organization

References: United Nations Department of Public Information. 1995. *Basic Facts about the United Nations.*
United Nations Department of Public Information. 1995. *A Guide to Information at the United Nations.*

United Nations International Labor Organization (ILO)

Established in 1918 under the Treaty of Versailles, the ILO seeks to promote social justice for working people worldwide. This mandate includes focusing on drug-related problems and their prevention in the workplace, as well promoting social reintegration and vocational rehabilitation programs.

Reference: United Nations Department of Public Education. 1995. *Basic Facts about the United Nations.*

United Nations International Narcotics Board

See International Narcotics Board of the United Nations

United Nations Interregional Crime and Justice Research Institute

Established in 1968 and headquartered in Rome, Italy, the Institute is mandated to formulate and implement "improved" policies in the field of crime prevention and control, which includes international drug trafficking.

Reference: United Nations International Drug Control Program. 1997. *World Drug Report.*

United Nations Joint Program on AIDS (UNAIDS)

UNAIDS mandate is to address the connection between the spread of the HIV virus and intravenous drug use.

Reference: United Nations International Drug Control Program. 1997. *World Drug Report.*

United Nations Office at Vienna

The headquarters for United Nations activities in the field of international drug abuse, the Office's administrative units include the United Nations International Drug Control Program.

Reference: United Nations Department of Public Information. 1995. *A Guide to Information at the United Nations.*

United Nations Political Program and Global Plan of Action

This program was adopted by the UN General Assembly in 1990 as a response to the concern that many member states could not adequately address the worldwide drug problem on their own. It calls upon the United Nations to give its highest priority to allocating the personnel, financial, and other resources needed to facilitate international cooperation in drug control and calls on member states to strengthen the United Nation's role as an information center and to give the highest priority to adopting measures that reduce the demand for drugs. The U.N. General Assembly also declared the period from 1991 to 2000 to be the United Nations Decade Against Drug Abuse.

See also: United Nations Decade against Drug Abuse (1991–2000)
Reference: United Nations International Drug Control Program. 1997. *World Drug Report.*

United Nations Population Fund

Established in 1966, this agency is now the largest provider of population assistance to developing nations, and it incorporates drug abuse prevention messages into its educational programs.

Reference: United Nations Department of Public Information. 1995. *Basic Facts about the United Nations.*

United Nations Research Institute for Social Development (UNRISD)

Founded in 1963, the UNRISD is involved in researching the social dimensions of problems affecting development, including the political and socioeconomic consequences of illegal drug trafficking.

Reference: United Nations Department of Public Information. 1995. *A Guide to Information about the United Nations.*

United Nations Single Convention on Narcotic Drugs of 1961

The Convention's purpose was to simplify and consolidate the international drug control machinery and replace the treaties passed before World War II.

An important new step in international drug control was the Convention's decision to include as punishable offenses the cultivation of poppies, hemp, and coca leaves as raw material for drug production. Seventy-four countries adopted the Convention, which came into force on 13 December 1964. In 1972 the United Nations adopted a supplementary instrument, the Single Protocol Amending the Single Convention on Narcotic Drugs, 1961, to highlight the need for the treatment and rehabilitation of drug addicts. The Protocol went into force in 1975. By 1 November 1997 the number of states adopting the Convention stood at 160, of which 145 were parties to the Convention in its amended form.

See also: Hemp; United Nations International Drug Control Program
References: Osmanczck, Edmund Jan. 1985. *The Encyclopedia of the United Nations and International Agreements.*
United Nations Department of Public Information. 1986. *Everyman's United Nations.*

United Nations Vienna Convention

Signed in December 1988 and put into effect in November 1990, this convention compelled ratifying nations to cooperate more fully at the international level by introducing the crime of money laundering and providing for the means to confiscate proceeds from drug trafficking. The Convention also recommends that bank secrecy be abolished.

See also: Money Laundering
Reference: Jamieson, Alison. 1994. *Terrorism and Drug Trafficking in Europe in the 1990s.*

United Nations World Health Organization
See World Health Organization

United States Act of 8 March 1946

This act established an administrative procedure for controlling newly discovered synthetic drugs shown to possess the addicting qualities of cocaine or morphine.

See also: Cocaine; Synthetic Drugs
Reference: Bacon, Donald C., Roger H. Davidson, and Morton Keller. 1995. *The Encyclopedia of the United States Congress.*

United States Act of 14 June 1930

This act established the Bureau of Narcotics within the U.S. Treasury Department, moved to facilitate cooperation between the federal government and the individual states in battling drug abuse, and directed the U.S. attorney general to conduct research on narcotic drug use.

Reference: Bacon, Donald C., Roger H. Davidson, and Morton Keller. 1995. *The Encyclopedia of the United States Congress.*

United States Agency for International Development

Established in 1961 during the presidential administration of John F. Kennedy (1961–1963), the United States Agency for International Development is an independent agency that plays a role in the United States' War on Drugs by providing economic development and humanitarian assistance to support U.S. economic and political institutions overseas.

Reference: United States Agency for International Development website at http://www.info.usaid.gov.

United States Alcohol and Drug Abuse Education Act Amendments of 1974

This act extended the grant and contract authorities of the Drug Abuse Education Act of 1970 for three years and authorized the expenditure of $90 million over those three years. The Act also placed greater focus on prevention and early intervention programs. According to the President's Commission on Organized Crime, "In enacting the 1974 Alcohol and Drug Abuse Education Act Amendments, Congress noted that most of the previously adopted federal programs to reduce demand had inevitably been directed primarily toward the person who is already in serious trouble with alcohol and/or drugs, but that the focus of the Drug Abuse Education Act of 1970 has been different in that it was directed to those who had not yet experimented with drugs or to those who had just begun to do so. In passing the 1974 amendments, Congress applauded the focus on prevention, reaffirming the philosophy that suffused the 1970 Education Act." (President's Commission on Organized Crime 1986, 246–247)

Reference: President's Commission on Organized Crime. 1986. *America's Habit: Drug Trafficking and Organized Crime.*

United States Antidrug Abuse Act of 1988

This act provided various means to increase the U.S. government's role in and commitment to the War on Drugs, both domestically and internationally. Specifically, it provided support for increased drug interdiction efforts by providing additional funding for antidrug initiatives, making changes in criminal procedures, implementing new and expanded penalties for drug-trafficking offenses, providing for a so-called national drug czar, and supporting increased maintenance and treatment efforts. To show its commitment, the U.S. Congress provided an additional appropriation in 1989 of $2.7 billion to meet these objectives.

See also: Drug Czar
References: Bacon, Donald C., Roger H. Davidson, and Morton Keller. 1995. *The Encyclopedia of the United States Congress.*
President's Commission on Organized Crime. 1986. *America's Habit: Drug Trafficking and Organized Crime.*

United States Bank Secrecy Act of 1970

This act required financial institutions to maintain records and report certain financial transactions to the U.S. Department of the Treasury and reflected the government's new focus on going after the profits generated by illegal criminal activities, including drug trafficking. Among other measures, the act requires banking institutions to set up a record-keeping system that reports on current financial transactions of more than $10,000 or involving an individual at one time and multiple transactions if, for the same depositor, the transactions total more than $10,000 in a single day.

The Bank Secrecy Act also was designed to assist authorities in tracking the movement of illegally acquired money in financial institutions and across international borders.

See also: Currency Transaction Reports (CTRs); Operation Greenback; People's Liberty Bank (U.S.)
References: Ehrenfeld, Rachel. 1992. *Evil Money.*
Powis, Robert E. 1992. *The Money Launderers.*

United States Board of Drug Abuse Control (BDAC)

In February 1966 this board was established to carry out the new enforcement obligations imposed by the Drug Abuse Control Amendments of 1965. The Bureau of Customs, however, retained responsibility for the enforcement of laws relating to the importing and exporting of depressant drugs. With the BDAC's establishment, the Department of the Treasury's monopoly over enforcement of federal drug laws ended.

See also: United States Drug Abuse Control Amendments of 1965
Reference: President's Commission on Organized Crime. 1986. *America's Habit: Drug Trafficking and Organized Crime.*

United States Boggs Act

Enacted in 1951 in response to growing concerns about a perceived drug problem in the United States, this law established mandatory minimum sentences for narcotics and marijuana offenses and denied probation or a suspended sentence for a drug offense.

See also: Marijuana
References: Bacon, Donald C., Roger H. Davidson, and Morton Keller. 1995. *The Encyclopedia of the United States Congress.*
Morgan, H. Wayne. 1981. *Drugs in America: A Social History, 1800–1980.*

United States Border Patrol

The Border Patrol's overall mission is to prevent illegal entry of people into the United States. Specifically, the Border Patrol is the primary agency for drug interdiction between ports of entry, directly assisting other federal and local law enforcement agencies in preventing illegal drugs from entering the United States. At the same time, the Patrol works with Customs Service officials to stop drug traffickers from entering the country's ports of entry.

The Border Patrol attempts to fulfill its mission by detaining, interdicting, and apprehending illegal aliens and the smugglers of contraband, including those involved with illegal drugs. Since 1988 the Border Patrol has worked with federal, state, and local law enforcement agencies in the United States' War on Drugs. The Border Patrol carries out its mission

Agents of the Bureau of Narcotics and Dangerous Drugs run from their helicopter in California where a federal narcotics agent shot and killed Dirk Dickenson, a suspected drug dealer, 4 April 1973. (Corbis/Bettmann-UPI)

at 145 stations located throughout the United States and the Commonwealth of Puerto Rico and is responsible for patrolling 8,000 miles of border with vehicles, aircraft, boats, and on horseback, as well as by foot.

See also: United States Customs, Department Of
Reference: Border Patrol web site at http://www.usbp.com.

United States Bureau of Drug Abuse Control

The Bureau was established with the purpose of carrying out the new enforcement responsibilities imposed by the Drug Abuse Control Amendments Act of 1965. The Bureau of Customs, however, retained responsibility for the enforcement of laws relating to the importing and exporting of depressant drugs. When the Bureau of Drug Abuse Control (BDAC) was established on 1 February 1966, the Department of the Treasury's monopoly over the enforcement of the federal drug laws ended.

See also: Giordano, Henry L.; United States Drug Abuse Control Amendments of 1965
Reference: President's Commission on Organized Crime. 1986. *America's Habit: Drug Trafficking and Organized Crime.*

United States Bureau of Narcotics and Dangerous Drugs (BNDD)

In 1968 U.S. President Lyndon Johnson implemented Reorganization Plan Number 1, which consolidated the Federal Bureau of Narcotics (FBN) and the Bureau of Drug Abuse Control (BDAC) and created within the Food and Drug Administration a new drug enforcement unit called the Bureau of Drug Abuse Control (BDAC). The Bureau of Narcotics and Dangerous Drugs had responsibility for controlling stimulants such as methamphetamines and various hallucinogens. John Finlator was appointed the agency's director on 12 August 1968.

By 1972 the BNDD's budget had more than quadrupled; its agent force had increased to 1,361;

and its domestic and foreign arrests had doubled. It had regulatory control over more than a half million registrants licensed to distribute licit drugs. The following year, however, President Richard Nixon created a new federal agency—the Drug Enforcement Administration (DEA), in which the BNDD, along with six other agencies, were abolished and their functions placed under the DEA.

See also: Methamphetamines; National Drug Enforcement Officers Association; Nixon, Richard Milhous; United States Bureau of Drug Abuse Control; United States Drug Enforcement Administration; United States Federal Bureau of Narcotics; United States Office of Drug Abuse Law Enforcement

References: Courtwright, David T. 1982. *Dark Paradise.* Weir, William. 1995. *In the Shadow of the Dope Fiend.*

United States Central Intelligence Agency (CIA)

Established by the National Security Act of 1947 as a subdivision of the National Security Council, the CIA advises the National Security Council in matters concerning such intelligence activities of government agencies that relate to national security. The director of the CIA is the president's principal adviser on intelligence matters. To fulfill its mandate, the CIA collects, produces, and disseminates intelligence on foreign aspects of narcotic production and trafficking.

The alleged CIA connection to the international drug trade has been one of the most controversial aspects of the nation's War on Drugs. Critics have charged—and the CIA has denied—that the agency has been involved with drug smuggling since at least the period of U.S. involvement in the Vietnam War from the early 1960s to 1975 and that it has never fully and honestly shared that record with the American people. Some have charged that the Office of Strategic Services (OSS), the CIA's predecessor, was involved during the 1940s in smuggling heroin grown in Myanmar to the United States. With regard to the Vietnam War, critics say that the CIA flew shipments of heroin around Asia on CIA proprietary planes owned under the cover of a company named Air America.

By the early 1970s, American GIs were spending an estimated $88 million annually on heroin and bringing their habit home with them once they finished their tours of duty. The official U.S. response during the Cold War was to blame the communist enemy in Southeast Asia and, today, the CIA continues to deny any responsibility. CIA critics, however, note that given the covert nature of the CIA and the fact that there has been little government oversight of the agency, it has been difficult to prove the CIA connection with international drug trafficking.

The CIA, say the critics, has continued to be involved in drug trafficking even with the end of the Vietnam War. In the late 1970s during the Jimmy Carter administration, for example, the CIA was accused of supplying weapons to the Afghanistan rebels, the Mujahideen, who were fighting the country's pro-Soviet government. Afghanistan is one of the world's leading opium producers, and much of the territory where the crop is grown was under Mujahideen control. At the time, government reports indicated that there was an alarming rise in the amount of heroin entering the United States and that the number of drug-related deaths soared in many U.S. cities.

The United States government and the CIA have also been accused of complicity in the so-called "cocaine coup" in Bolivia in 1980, toleration of General Manuel Noriega's drug-related activities for more than twenty years because he was a good ally in the war against communism, and in 1990 and 1991, support of special Venezuelan antidrug units, which have been suspected of smuggling more than 2,000 pounds of cocaine into the United States with the CIA's knowledge.

The most controversial questioning of the suspected CIA-drug trafficking connection occurred in 1996 when a series of articles in the *San Jose Mercury News* written by journalist Gary Webb claimed that a drug pipeline from Colombia to the San Francisco area had financed the Nicaragua Contras by selling tons of cocaine to Los Angeles street gangs. In effect, the series contended that the U.S. government, through one of its agencies, may have fueled the crack cocaine boom that began in the mid-1980s and sparked the violence and the crime wave that came to permeate American society.

The series caused a public uproar. The mainstream press devoted large amounts of space to debunking the series' thesis and the *Mercury News* issued a major clarification, saying that parts of the story did not meet its journalistic standards. Later, reporter Webb was transferred to another beat. Public pressure, however, forced the CIA and the U.S. Justice Department to launch internal inquiries, release thousands of pages of classified documents, and issue three major reports.

CIA supporters, as well as many newspapers, said these reports convincingly rebutted the *Mercury News* article series. Critics, on the other hand, insisted that the reports advanced the series' main thesis: that the CIA and the Reagan administration tolerated drug trafficking so that they could promote the covert war against Nicaragua.

In July 1998, a CIA internal study found that CIA personnel continued to work with almost two dozen members of the Nicaraguan Contras who may have been involved in drug trafficking during the 1980s. The study noted that none of the suspected drug traffickers were in the top leadership of the Contra rebels and that no one in the agency aided the drug trade. Then, in October 1998, a newly declassified study by the CIA's inspector general reported that the CIA had failed to fully inform Congress and law enforcement agencies that Nicaraguan contras were involved in drug trafficking.

In 1998 the role of the CIA in the War on Drugs remained as controversial as ever.

See also: Carter, Jimmy; Contras; Kerry, John F.; McCoy, Alfred J.; Noriega, Manuel Antonio; Reagan, Ronald; Romero Gomez, Alphonso; Vaughn, Federico; Vietnam War; Webb, Gary

References: Chepesiuk, Ron. 1999. *Hard Target*.
"Contra Drug Links Broader than CIA Said, Study States." 1998. *The Rock Hill Herald*, 10 October.
Lamour, Catherine, and Michael J. Lamberti. 1974. *The International Connection: Opium from Growers to Pushers*.
McCoy, Alfred J. 1991. *The Politics of Heroin: CIA Complicity in the Global Drug Trade*.
Risen, James. 1998. "CIA Ignored Contra Drug Allegations." *Miami Herald*, 17 July.
"Secret CIA Report Notes Contra Drug Suspicions." 1998. *Charlotte Observer*, 18 July.
Webb, Gary. 1998. *Dark Alliance: The CIA, The Contras and the Crack Cocaine Explosion*.
Weir, William. 1995. *In the Shadow of the Dope Fiend*.

United States Chemical Diversion and Trafficking Act of 1988 (CDTA)

Signed into law in November 1988, this act placed under federal control the distribution of twelve precursor chemicals that are essential in the production

A United States Coast Guard officer guards a group of men arrested when their fishing trawler was found to be carrying 900 bales of marijuana worth up to $12 million, 29 June 1982. (Corbis/Bettmann-UPI)

of illicit drugs. Additional chemicals have since been added to the CDTA, bringing the total number of listed essential precursor chemicals to thirty-four.

The CDTA requires all firms handling regulated chemicals to maintain adequate records and makes mandatory the reporting of suspicious orders. Also, all firms that import or export regulated chemicals that exceed a threshold amount must notify the Drug Enforcement Administration fifteen days prior to action. The law also gives the DEA the power to seize or detain in the United States any suspected chemicals.

See also: Precursor Chemicals; United States Drug Enforcement Administration

Reference: United States Department of Justice, DEA. *The Supply of Illicit Drugs to the United States*.

United States Coast Guard

Established in 1915 and operating today under the U.S. Department of Transportation, the U.S. Coast Guard is the country's main maritime law enforcement agency and, as such, "enforces or assists in the enforcement of applicable federal laws and treaties and other international agreements to which the United States is party, on, over, and under the high seas and waters subject to the jurisdiction of the United States, and may conduct investigations into suspected violations of such laws and international agreements." (National Archives and Records Service 1997–1998, 97–98 and 417)

See also: Operation Frontier Lace; Operation Frontier Shield
References: Coast Guard website at http://www.uscg.gov/.
National Archives and Records Service. Office of the Federal

Registry. 1997–1998. *The United States Government Manual, 1997–1998.*

United States Comprehensive Crime Control Act of 1970

Popularly known as the Controlled Substances Act, this U.S. law replaced the Harrison Narcotics Act, the Marijuana Tax Act, the Boggs Act, and other existing—but scattered—federal drug laws. It provides the current legal foundation for federal drug control. It includes provisions for governing the distribution, possession, and manufacture of illegal drugs. Signed by President Richard Nixon in 1970, the law went into effect in 1971.

The Act places drugs in one of five categories and defines specific offenses and sanctions for drugs within them. A drug's placement depends on its potential for abuse, physical and psychological dependence, and current accepted medical use. Schedule I, the most tightly regulated category, includes drugs such as LSD, marijuana, and heroin, which the U.S. government considers to have a high potential for abuse and no recognizable medical use. Schedule II differs from Schedule I in that the category includes drugs such as morphine, methadone, and amphetamines, which are considered to have accepted medical uses in the United States.

Schedule I includes drugs that have a high potential for abuse, have no currently accepted medical use for treatment in the United States, or lack accepted safety for use of the drug. Schedule II drugs are those having a high potential for abuse, have a currently accepted use in treatment in the United States or currently accepted medical use with severe restrictions, or where the abuse of the drug will lead to psychological and physical dependence.

Schedule III drugs have less potential for abuse than drugs on Schedules I and II, the drug has currently accepted medical use in treatment in the United States, and abuse of the drug will lead to low physical dependence or high psychological dependence.

Schedule IV drugs have low potential for abuse relative to the drugs in Schedule III, have a currently accepted medical use in treatment in the United States, and abuse of the drug may lead to limited physical psychological dependence relative to drugs under Schedule III.

Schedule V includes drugs that have a low potential for abuse relative to the drugs or other substances in Schedule IV, have currently accepted medical use in treatment in the United States, and abuse of the drug may lead to limited physical or psychological dependence relative to the drugs in Schedule IV.

The Comprehensive Crime Control Act of 1984 amended this act, modifying the five schedules and establishing jail sentences with regard to the distribution of drugs in and near schools. The U.S. Justice Department enforces the United States Comprehensive Crime Control Act's provisions.

See also: Amphetamines; Barbiturates; Codeine; Harrison Narcotic Act; Heroin; LSD; Marijuana; Methaqualone; Morphine; Methadone Treatment Programs; National Commission on Marijuana and Drug Abuse; Opium; Psilocybin; United States Addict Treatment Act of 1971; United States Crime Control Act of 1984

References: Bertram, Eva, Kenneth Sharpe, and Peter Anders. 1996. *Drug War Politics: The Price of Denial.* President's Commission on Organized Crime. 1986. *America's Habit: Drug Trafficking and Organized Crime.*

United States Comprehensive Crime Control Act of 1984

This act derives its impetus from Ronald Reagan's War on Drugs and involved a major revision of the Omnibus Crime Control Act of 1968 and other federal laws. Three other important statutes came out of this act: The Controlled Substances and Penalties Act, The Comprehensive Forfeiture Act, and the National Narcotic Act. Amendments to the act in 1987 gave even greater authority to federal agencies to become involved in drug investigations and the War on Drugs.

See also: Reagan, Ronald

References: Bacon, Donald C., Roger H. Davidson, and Morton Keller. 1995. *The Encyclopedia of the United States Congress.* Cooper, Mary H. 1990. *The Business of Drugs.*

United States Comprehensive Crime Control Act of 1990

This act provided for additional measures aimed at the seizure and forfeiture of drug traffickers' assets. They include expanding the regulations governing the precursor chemicals used in the manufacture of illegal drugs, doubling the appropriations authorized for drug law enforcement grants to states and localities, and authorizing $220 million in matching grants to states for projects that develop alternatives to criminal incarceration.

See also: Asset Forfeiture; Precursor Chemicals
Reference: Bacon, Donald C., Roger H. Davidson, and Morton Keller. 1995. *The Encyclopedia of the United States Congress.*

United States Comprehensive Methamphetamine Control Act of 1996

Signed into law on 3 October 1996 by President Bill Clinton, this act provides for increased controls on the chemicals used in the production of methamphetamine and represents a concerted effort to target the highest level of methamphetamine violators. The act also increases the penalties for trafficking and manufacturing methamphetamine and listed chemicals.

See also: Methamphetamine
Reference: U.S. Drug Enforcement Administration website at www.usdoj.gov/ (Provisions of the Comprehensive Methamphetamine Control Act of 1996).

United States Controlled Substance Analogue Enforcement Act of 1986

This act is an effort by the U.S. government to deal with the growing problem of synthesized drugs that are chemically and pharmacologically similar to substances listed in the Controlled Substances Act, but which themselves are not specifically controlled by name. These substances are now commonly known as designer drugs. According to the Drug Abuse Handbook, implementation of this act was expected to "minimize the quantity of useable substances to those who are likely to abuse them. At the same time, the CSA provides for legitimate medical, scientific, and instructional needs of those substances in the U.S." (Karch 1998, 21)

See also: Controlled Substance; Designer Drugs; Synthetic Drugs; United States Comprehensive Crime Control Act of 1970
Reference: Karch, Steven. 1998. *Drug Abuse Handbook.*

United States Controlled Substances Act of 1970

See United States Comprehensive Crime Control Act of 1970

United States Customs, Department of

This federal agency is charged with policing the nation's borders against drugs. This task is formidable, given that in 1996 alone 3.5 million trucks, 75 million cars, and 254 million people crossed the U.S. border. To do its job, the Customs Service has only 1,800 inspectors working along the borders. Customs launched Operation Hardline in 1975 to strengthen its inspection along the southwest border points of entry to combat drug smuggling. Nearly 165 experienced special agents and intelligence analysts were reassigned under Operation Hardline to the southwest border to work on narcotics cases. The fiscal year 1997 budget provided for another 650 positions and $65 million for the operation.

Customs has credited Operation Hardline with substantially increasing the number of drug seizures along the southwest border. In fiscal year 1996, for example, narcotics seizures as measured by number increased 29 percent and by total weight increased 24 percent. Customs also launched Operation Gateway, which expanded the scope of Operation Hardline to include Puerto Rico. Another U.S. Customs antidrug initiative is the Land Border Courier Initiative Program, which involves Customs receiving pledges from more than 836 trucking companies on the southwest border to better police their trucks and warehouses in order to prevent the exploitation of legitimate carriers by drug cartels.

See also: Operation Autumn Harvest; Operation Bahamas, Turks and Caicos (OPBAT); Operation Bluefire; Operation Global Sea; Organized Crime Task Force; United States Border Patrol; United States Office of Drug Abuse Law Enforcement
Reference: U.S. Department of Customs website at http://www.customs.ustreas.gov/index.htm.

United States Department of Defense Act

Passed in 1982, this act amended the Posse Comitatus Act of 1878 by allowing the U.S. military to provide military training, intelligence, and equipment to civilian law enforcement agencies and to allow members of the army, navy, air force, and marines to operate military equipment for civilian agencies responsible for enforcing the nation's laws. For the first time in U.S. history, U.S. naval vessels began directly to interdict suspected drug-smuggling ships in international waters. The move sparked fierce debate in the U.S. Congress as some of its members questioned the wisdom of using the military as Posse Comitatus.

See also: Operation Thunderbolt; United States Posse Comitatus Act

References: Bacon, Donald C., Roger H. Davidson, and Morton Keller. 1995. *The Encyclopedia of the United States Congress.*
Chepesiuk, Ron. 1999. *Hard Target.*

United States Department of Justice, Drug Court Program Office

This office administers the drug court grant program as authorized by Title V of the Violent Crime Control and Law Enforcement Act of 1994 and is responsible for supporting, developing, and implementing effective drug court programming at the state, local, and tribal levels.

See also: Drug Courts

References: National Archives and Records Service. Office of the Federal Registry. 1997–1998. *The United States Government Manual, 1997–1998.*
U.S. Department of Justice website at http://www.usdoj.gov/.

United States Department of Justice, Narcotics and Dangerous Drugs Section

This section has supervisory jurisdiction for those laws pertaining to controlled substances. Senior section personnel participate in antidrug activities in a number of ways. For example, they develop and implement domestic and international narcotics law enforcement programs and policies and provide legal support to the Organized Crime Drug Enforcement Task Force (OCDETF), the High Intensity Drug Trafficking Areas (HIDTA) programs, and the Southwest Border Initiative. The section chief serves on several bodies involved with domestic and international antinarcotics initiatives.

See also: High Intensity Drug Trafficking Areas, Southwest Border Initiative; United States Department of Justice. Organized Crime Drug Enforcement Task Force

References: National Archives and Records Service. Office of the Federal Registry. 1997–1998. *The United States Government Manual, 1997–1998.*
U.S. Department of Justice website at http:www.usdoj.gov/.

United States Department of Justice, Organized Crime Drug Enforcement Task Force

In existence since 1982, the OCDETF is a federal drug enforcement agency that focuses its resources and attention on disrupting and weakening drug-trafficking organizations. The program is under the direction of the U.S. attorney general and provides a framework for federal, state, and local law enforcement agencies to work together on antidrug activities. As of 1997, the U.S. Department of Justice claimed that the OCDETF has been responsible for the successful prosecution and conviction of 44,000 members of drug-trafficking organizations and the seizure of cash and assets totaling more than $3 billion.

References: National Archives and Records Service. Office of the Federal Registry. 1997–1998. *The United States Government Manual, 1997–1998.*

United States Department of Labor

This Department is actively involved in the U.S government's War on Drugs through its Working Partners for an Alcohol- and Drug-Free American Workplace and its Substance Abuse Information Database (SAID). The Working Partners program attempts to make an impact on substance abuse in the workplace by providing quality substance abuse prevention information to small businesses. SAID helps the Working Partners fulfill its objectives by serving as a fully searchable database, which provides information on how to prevent drug abuse in the workforce.

References: Substance Abuse Information Database (SAID) website at http://www.dol.gov:8001/said.nsf/.
Working Partners website at http://www.dol.gov.dol.asp/public/programs/drugs/about/htm.

United States Department of State, Bureau of Narcotics and Law Enforcement Affairs

Organized in 1978, this agency is responsible for developing programs and policies to combat international narcotics and crime. Initially, the narcotics control program was the sole function of the Bureau, but in 1994 it also became responsible for developing programs and policies that can deter international criminal activities that threaten U.S. national interests. The narcotics program has three primary goals: to use the full range of U.S. diplomacy to persuade foreign governments of the importance and relevance of narcotics control to bilateral and multilateral relations; to promote cooperation within the United States; and to use the Bureau's various programs to help stop the flow of drugs to the United States.

References: National Archives and Records Service. Office of the Federal Registry. 1997–1998. *The United States Government Manual, 1997–1998.*

U.S. Department of State website at http://www.state.gov/.

United States Department of State, International Narcotics Drug Control Strategy Report (INCSR)

This is a primary source of information on production estimates and drug control efforts in foreign countries. The INCSR is prepared annually in accordance with provisions of § 481 of the Foreign Assistance Act of 1961.

See also: Operation Blast Furnace
Reference: U.S. Department of State web site at http://www.state.gov/.

United States Department of Transportation, Drug and Alcohol Policy and Compliance, Office of

This office works to ensure that national and international drug and alcohol policies and the goals of the secretary of transportation are "delivered and carried out in a consistent and efficient manner within the transportation industry." (National Archives 1997–1998, 414) The office does this by assisting the secretary of transportation in making sound policy regarding drug testing within the Department of Transportation and the transportation industry.

Reference: National Archives and Records Service. Office of the Federal Registry. 1997–1998. *The United States Government Manual, 1997–1998.*

United States Department of the Treasury, Bureau of Alcohol, Tobacco and Firearms

Established by the Department of the Treasury Order No. 221 on 1 July 1972, the Bureau has as its mission to collect revenue, reduce violent crime, and protect the public through tax collection, criminal law enforcement, and regulatory enforcement. The Bureau works in partnership with various federal, state, and local law enforcement agencies to investigate drug traffickers who might use firearms and explosives to further their criminal objectives. The Bureau is headquartered in Washington, D.C., but because of its operational nature, many of its personnel are stationed throughout the country.

Reference: National Archives and Records Service. Office of the Federal Registry. 1997–1998. *The United States Government Manual, 1997–1998.*

United States Domestic Chemical Diversion Control Act of 1993 (DCDCA)

The DCDCA, which became effective on 16 April 1994, amended the Controlled Substances Act and the Controlled Substances Import and Export Act with regard to selected illegal chemicals used in the production of certain chemical substances, such as methamphetamine and methacathinone. It established a registration system for imports, exports, and distributors of listed chemicals subject to diversion in the United States. The act was primarily a move to regulate ephedrine, an over-the-counter drug that is used in the manufacture of methamphetamine.

See also: Methacathinone; Methamphetamine; Precursor Chemicals; United States Comprehensive Crime Control Act of 1970
References: Miller, Gary J. 1997. *Drugs and the Law— Detention, Recognition and Investigation.*
United States Department of Justice, DEA. *The Supply of Illicit Drugs to the United States.*

United States Drug Abuse Control Amendments of 1965

These amendments to the Food, Drug, and Cosmetic Act placed special restrictions on depressant and stimulant drugs in an effort to curb the direct diversion of legal amphetamines to the U.S. black market. But according to Edwin Brecher, "It opened the door for the smuggling of exported amphetamines back to the United States. By 1969, law enforcement efforts had raised black market amphetamine prices and curbed amphetamine smugglers sufficiently to open the door for renewed cocaine smuggling." (Brecher 1972, 63).

See also: Amphetamines; Cocaine; United States Bureau of Drug Abuse Control
References: Brecher, Edwin M. 1972. *Licit and Illicit Drugs: The Consumers Union Report on Narcotics, Stimulants, Depressants, or Inhalants, Hallucinogens, and Marijuana—Including Coffee, Nicotine and Alcohol.*
President's Commission on Organized Crime. 1986. *America's Habit: Drug Trafficking and Organized Crime.*

United States Drug Abuse Epidemiology Center

The U.S. National Institute on Drug Abuse (NIDA) and the U.S. Department of Health, Education, and Welfare founded this center to preserve the original data of major drug surveys and records and to help formulate further analysis, to develop and maintain a library of drug research, and to implement and maintain a computer file for the retrieval of drug literature based on a refined taxonomy.

See also: United States National Institute on Drug Abuse
Reference: National Institute on Drug Abuse website at http://www.nida.gov.

United States Drug Abuse Warning Network (DAWN)

The Drug Abuse Warning Network is an on-going national survey of hospital emergency departments. Since the early 1970s, this program has collected information on patients seeking hospital emergency department treatment related to the use of an illegal drug or the nonmedical use of a legal drug. DAWN was established by the U.S. Drug Enforcement Administration in 1972 and transferred to the National Institute on Drug Abuse in 1972.

See also: United States National Institute on Drug Abuse (NIDA)
Reference: Drug Abuse Warning Network website at http://www.health.org/pubs/93DAWN.

United States Drug Enforcement Administration (DEA)

The DEA was formed on 1 July 1973, as a result of the U.S. government's implementation of Reorganization Plan Number 2, which put all federal antidrug agencies under a single unified command under the direction of the U.S. Department of Justice. The reorganization was the U.S. government's response to the growth of cocaine processing in Latin America and heroin refining in Southeast Asia and had as its objectives the unification of drug investigations and the establishment of a clear division between federal drug agents and their local, state, and foreign counterparts. Today, the DEA is the sole U.S. agency responsible for combating drug trafficking and has the responsibility for the development of overall federal drug strategy, programs, planning, and evaluation.

By 1998 the DEA had grown from a 1,470-agent operation in 1973 to a $1.3 billion a year organization in 1998 with 4,231 agents in offices around the world. According to a 1998 DEA press report "Just five years ago, Vice President Al Gore and other federal officials were touting a cost cutting plan that would have had the FBI taking over the DEA. Mr. Thomas A. Constantine [the DEA's head] fought off the effort, and today few people talk seriously about a takeover or merger." (Eaton 1998)

See also: Bartels, John R.; Bensinger, Peter; Bonner, Robert C.; Constantine, Thomas A.; Lawn, John C.; Mullen, Frances; National Drug Enforcement Officers Association; Nixon, Richard Milhous; Operation College Farm; Operation Global Sea; Operation Jalisco; Operation Reciprocity; Operation Red River; Operation Snow Cap; Operation Steeple; Operation Swordfish; Operation Tandem; Operation Thai-In; Operation Vanguard; Organized Crime Task Force; United Chemical Diversion and Trafficking Act of 1988; United States Department of Justice; United States Drug Abuse Warning Network; United States Federal Bureau of Investigation; United States Office of Drug Abuse Law Enforcement
References: De Grazia, Jessica. 1991. *DEA: The War against Drugs.*
Gugliotta, Guy, and Jeff Leen. 1990. *Kings of Cocaine.*
Eaton, Tracy. 1998. "After 25 years, DEA Finds Drug War Still a Mine Field." *Dallas Morning News,* 5 October.
Drug Enforcement Administration website at http://www.usdoj.gov.dea/.

Drug Enforcement Administration and local law enforcement officials speak at a news conference with 1,263 pounds of Colombian cocaine seized at Phoenix airport after an extensive six month undercover investigation of the Botero smuggling organization, 6 March 1987. (UPI/Corbis-Bettmann)

United States Drug Free America Act

Enacted in October 1986, this act has several provisions that attack drug trafficking and drug abuse on many fronts. Among other measures, the act provides for the funding of a school-based drug abuse education and prevention program, for a study of the nature and effects of drugs in the workplace, and for grants to schools, which went to implement drug prevention treatment and rehabilitation programs. The Alcohol, Drug Abuse and Mental Health Association was mandated to consolidate the antidrug prevention activities of the Drug Abuse and Alcohol Institutes under an Office of Drug Abuse Prevention, and the media and entertainment industries were urged to refrain from producing products that glamorized the use of illegal drugs.

Reference: Miller, Gary J. 1997. *Drugs and the Law— Detention, Recognition and Investigation.*

United States Drug-Induced Rape Prevention and Punishment Act of 1996

This act provides for additional penalties for persons using controlled substances to drug people, usually women, for the purpose of a violent crime. The act also provides for additional penalties relating to the drug flunitrazepan (also known by the brand name of Rohypnol and the street names of "roofies" and "date rape drug") that includes penalties for its distribution, simple possession, and its import and export. A study was also to be undertaken to see whether Rohypnol should be rescheduled as a Schedule I controlled substance. Under the U.S. Comprehensive Crime Control Act of 1970, drugs that are put in Schedule I are those that have a high potential for abuse, or have no currently accepted medical use in the United States, or have a lack of accepted safety for the use of the drug under medical supervision.

See also: Controlled Substance; Rohypnol
Reference: Miller, Gary J. 1997. *Drugs and the Law— Detention, Recognition and Investigation.*

United States Federal Bureau of Investigation (FBI)

Established in 1908, the FBI is the principal investigative arm of the U.S. Department of Justice. Among other duties, it is charged with investigating all violations of federal law, including drug-trafficking offenses, except those that have been assigned concurrent jurisdiction with the DEA for the enforcement of the Comprehensive Crime Control Act of 1970. The DEA reports to the attorney general through the FBI director.

See also: Constantine, Thomas A.; Operation College Farm; Operation Global Sea; United States Comprehensive Crime Control Act of 1970; United States Drug Enforcement Administration
Reference: Federal Bureau of Investigation website at http://www.fbi.gov/.
National Archives and Records Service. Office of the Federal Registry. 1997–1998. *The United States Government Manual, 1997–1998.*

United States Federal Bureau of Narcotics (FBN)

In 1930 responsibility for enforcing U.S. federal drug laws was transferred from the Bureau of Prohibition to the newly created Federal Bureau of Narcotics, which was located within the Department of the Treasury and headed by a commissioner of narcotics. The Bureau was to be mainly responsible for enforcing the Harrison Narcotic Act and related laws, while the Bureau of Customs would oversee the job of preventing the importation and smuggling of illegal drugs.

In the period from the 1930s to the 1950s, drug trafficking was not a major priority and the FBN was often handicapped by a shortage of agents and inadequate budgets, but according to the President's Commission on Organized Crime, "Despite the handicaps the FBN operated under this period, it nevertheless enjoyed a great degree of success." (President's Commission 1986, 208) By the 1960s, Eva Bertram and her coauthors noted that "the FBN had a really modest budget of $6 million (about twice its 1972 budget) and a staff of some 300 (roughly the same number as in 1932)." (Bertram, et al. 1996, 107) In 1968, the FBN was merged with the Bureau of Drug Abuse Control, which had been created in 1965 to regulate stimulant drugs. The new agency was called the Bureau of Narcotics and Dangerous Drugs, and it was overseen by the U.S. Justice Department.

See also: Anslinger, Harry; Mullen, Frances; Organized Crime Task Force; Prettyman Commission; *Reefer Madness*; United States Bureau of Drug Abuse Control; United States Federal Bureau of Narcotics (FBN)
References: Bertram, Eva, Kenneth Sharpe, and Peter Anders. 1996. *Drug War Politics: The Price of Denial.*
President's Commission on Organized Crime. 1986. *America's Habit: Drug Trafficking and Organized Crime.*

United States Food and Drug Administration (FDA)

Established in 1995 as an operating division within the Department of Health and Human Services, the FDA is responsible for protecting the health of the nation against drugs, impure and unsafe foods, and other health hazards. It includes the Center for Drug Evaluation and Research, which is charged with developing effective policies that investigate new drug applications, monitors the quality of new drug products, and reviews all drug products for human use.

Reference: Food and Drug Administration website at http://www.fda.gov/88.

United States General Accounting Office (GAO)

The GAO was established by the U.S. Budget and Accounting Act of 1921 to independently audit government agencies. Today, it meets this objective by evaluating government programs and activities. The agency had done numerous reports on all aspects of the War on Drugs, many of which have been critical, and virtually all of which are available to the public.

See also: Central Tactical Units (CENTAC)
References: General Accounting Office website at www.gao.gov.
National Archives and Records Service. Office of the Federal Registry. 1997–1998. *The United States Government Manual, 1997–1998.*

United States House Select Narcotics Abuse and Control Committee

Established on 26 July 1976 as a response to the drug problem of the early 1970s, this legislative committee of the House of Representatives was charged with reviewing recommendations made by the president or any agency of the federal government that related to narcotic drug programs and policies. The Speaker of the House appointed members, with at least one member to be chosen from one of the following standing committees with jurisdiction over important activities of the drug issue: Judiciary; Agriculture; Armed Services; Government Operations; Foreign Affairs; Energy and Commerce; Merchant Marine and Fisheries; Veteran's Affairs; and Ways and Means.

According to Donald C. Bacon and the coauthors of *The Encyclopedia of the United States Congress*, the committee's continued existence was "periodically challenged, principally on the grounds that a Select Committee should be a temporary entity, created for specific purposes and re-authorized indefinitely. However, it was always reconstructed by a comfortable margin until the opening of the 103rd Congress, when, along with other select committees in the House, it fell victim to a movement for congressional reform and was abolished." (Bacon, et al. 1995, 1,431–1,432)

Reference: Bacon, Donald C., Roger H. Davidson, and Morton Keller. 1995. *The Encyclopedia of the United States Congress*.

United States International Narcotics Control Act of 1990

This act provides for the continued funding of international narcotics control initiatives, particularly those that provide economic assistance for programs pertaining to the administration of justice in Peru, Colombia, and Bolivia. The objective is to support the U.S. government's Andean Strategy of reducing the flow of cocaine from those countries to the United States.

See also: Bush, George Herbert Walker
Reference: Miller, Gary J. 1997. *Drugs and the Law— Detention, Recognition and Investigation*.

United States International Narcotics Control Act of 1992

This act provided for increased reporting on money laundering and the whereabouts of precursor chemicals, and for the continued funding of international narcotics control activities and programs. Specifically, under the act, the United States could withhold bilateral loans and other forms of assistance, if it

was determined that a country was not cooperating in achieving the objectives of bilateral agreements the requirements of which were listed in the act. In other words, under the act foreign countries have to show that they are making efforts to reduce the production and distribution of illicit drugs before they may claim the benefit of loan and other agreements with the United States.

See also: Money Laundering; Precursor Chemicals
Reference: Miller, Gary J. 1997. *Drugs and the Law— Detention, Recognition and Investigation*.

United States Marijuana Tax Act

Passed in 1937, this act was essentially a revenue measure patterned after the Harrison Narcotic Act, and it required people importing, selling, or producing marijuana to register themselves and to pay a tax on earnings from the marketing of marijuana. The transferor was also held liable for the transfer tax if a transfer was made without an order form and without payment of the tax by the transferee. Also, the transference of marijuana had to be pursuant to a written order on a form used by the secretary of the treasury and the transferee was required to pay a tax of $1 per ounce, if he or she reported, and $100 per ounce, if he or she had not.

See also: Harrison Narcotic Act
References: Courtwright, David T. 1982. *Dark Paradise*.
Bacon, Donald C., Roger H. Davidson, and Morton Keller. 1995. *The Encyclopedia of the United States Congress*.

United States Marshal Service

An agency of the U.S Department of Justice, the Marshal Service is the country's oldest federal law enforcement agency. Today, the Service includes about 3,700 deputy marshals and administrative personnel, who are located in 427 office locations in all federal judicial districts nationwide, from Florida to the Canadian border, and from Guam to Puerto Rico. As part of its mission, the Service is responsible for seizing, managing, and selling property forfeited to the U.S. government by drug traffickers. It helps apprehend federal drug-trafficking fugitives, and through the Federal Witness Security Program, which it operates, ensures the safety of endangered government witnesses testifying against drug traffickers.

See also: Asset Forfeiture; United States Department of Justice

Reference: National Archives and Records Service. Office
of the Federal Registry. 1997–1998. *The United States
Government Manual, 1997–1998.*

United States Money Laundering Control Act of 1986

A part of the Antidrug Abuse Act of 1986, this law made money laundering itself a criminal offense when it was connected to another illegal activity. As Jeffrey Robinson explained, "If you simply want to move your own money through a whole series of jurisdictions, in and out of shell companies, to see what comes out the other end, that's your business. But if you're doing it in conjunction with a crime—insider trading, fraud, drug trafficking, income tax invasion, theft, whatever—then money laundering gets tagged onto the charge sheet." (Robinson 1990, 32)

This act puts substantial pressure on financial institutions to keep better informed about their clients and to cooperate with and refer appropriate matters to law enforcement agencies within the purview of the Financial Privacy Act whenever transactions seem atypical. The act states that people can be guilty of money laundering if they attempt to hide the source, location, nature, and ownership of proceeds that they have derived from illegal activity.

It is also a violation of the Money Laundering Control Act to knowingly and unlawfully transport monetary funds out of the United States. Money laundering is now a separate federal offense, punishable by a fine of $500,000 or twice the value of the property involved (whichever is greater) and twenty-five years imprisonment.

See also: Money Laundering; United States Money
Laundering Improvement Act of 1988
References: Kelly, Robert J., Ko-lin Chin, and Rufus
Schatzberg. 1994. *Handbook of Organized Crime in the
United States.*
Robinson, Jeffrey. 1990. *The Laundrymen.*

United States Money Laundering Control Act of 1988

This act authorized the U.S. Department of the Treasury to require financial institutions to verify the authority of people who purchase bank checks, traveler's checks, or money orders in excess of $3,000. This provision enabled the federal government to target certain geographic areas or types of institutions for special reporting requirements, and the act became another important legal instrument in combating money laundering.

See also: Money Laundering; Money Laundering Control
Act of 1986
Reference: Kelly, Robert J., Ko-lin Chin, and Rufus
Schatzberg. 1994. *Handbook of Organized Crime in the
United States.*

United States Narcotic Addict Rehabilitation Act

Enacted in 1966, this measure was one of the first major legislative changes resulting from recommendations made by President John F. Kennedy's President's Advisory Commission on Narcotics and Drug Abuse, the so-called Prettyman Commission. The act authorized the first public health service grants to communities for the sole purpose of treating people addicted to drugs.

See also: Prettyman Commission
Reference: Bertram, Eva, Kenneth Sharpe, and Peter
Anders. 1996. *Drug War Politics: The Price of Denial.*

United States Narcotic Addict Treatment Act of 1971

This act amended the 1970 Controlled Substances Act and required annual registration by practitioners dispensing drugs, including methadone, for maintenance or detoxification purposes.

See also: Methadone Treatment Programs and United States
Comprehensive Crime Control Act of 1970
Reference: President's Commission on Organized Crime.
1986. *America's Habit: Drug Trafficking and Organized
Crime.*

United States Narcotic Control Act of 1956

This act greatly strengthened the mandatory and minimum sentences for drug traffickers and allowed juries to impose the death penalty to any adult who sold heroin to a minor.

See also: Heroin
Reference: Bertram, Eva, Kenneth Sharpe, and Peter
Anders. 1996. *Drug War Politics: The Price of Denial.*
Morgan, H. Wayne. 1981. *Drugs in America: A Social History,
1800–1980.*

United States National Institute on Drug Abuse

This institute was established in 1974 as a federal focal point for research, training services, treatment and prevention, and data collection on the nature and extent of drug abuse. In October 1992 the agency became part of the National Institutes of Health, of the Department of Health and Human Services. Today, the institute is organized into divisions, each of which plays a part in programs involving drug abuse research.

See also: Community Epidemiology Work Group; United States Drug Abuse Warning Network (DAWN); United States Office and Treatment Act
Reference: President's Commission on Organized Crime. 1986. *America's Habit: Drug Trafficking and Organized Crime.*
National Institute on Drug Abuse website at http://www.nida.nih.gov/.

United States National Narcotics Information Board

A government body set up by Richard Nixon on 27 July 1972 to coordinate antidrug initiatives and activities within the U.S. government.

See also: National Inter-Agency Civil Military Institute; Nixon, Richard Milhous; United States National Drug Control Strategy
Reference: Lamour, Catherine, and Michael R. Lamberti. 1974. *The International Connection: Opium from Growers to Pushers.*

United States National Narcotics Control Act

Passed by the U.S. Congress in July 1956, this act established minimum sentences for selling narcotics and prohibited probation as a sentencing option in those cases. It even allowed the death penalty in certain cases for narcotics offenders. The act put travel restrictions on drug addicts as a way to reduce drug trafficking and created a Division of Statistics and Records to gather and disseminate information on narcotics that could help law enforcement efforts in the drug control area.

Reference: Bacon, Donald C., Roger H. Davidson, and Morton Keller. 1995. *The Encyclopedia of the United States Congress.*

United States Office and Treatment Act

This 1972 law established several national drug programs, including the Special Action Office of Drug Abuse Prevention, the National Institute on Drug Abuse, and the National Drug Abuse Training Center, as well as a council to develop a national antidrug abuse strategy. In addition, the act also set up a program for state drug abuse prevention grants.

See also: United States National Institute on Drug Abuse
References: Bacon, Donald C., Roger H. Davidson, and Morton Keller. 1995. *The Encyclopedia of the United States Congress.*
President's Commission on Organized Crime. 1986. *America's Habit: Drug Trafficking and Organized Crime.*

United States Office of Drug Abuse Law Enforcement (ODALE)

An executive order signed by President Richard Nixon in January 1972 created this office as an effort to quiet the public clamor for the U.S. government to do more to attack crime in the nation's streets. ODALE established nine regional offices to combat street pushers through special grand juries and by pooling intelligence from federal, state, and local law enforcement agencies.

But as each agency entered the War on Drugs, the effort was fragmented and weakened as they failed to communicate and promoted their own competing agendas. This led to the establishment of another agency, the Office of National Narcotics Intelligence (ONNI), to collect, analyze, and identify drug intelligence.

According to Eva Bertram and the coauthors of *Drug War Politics: The Price of Denial,* "the harsh enforcement tactics of ODALE's agents...gained it notoriety and eventually helped lead to its dissolution." (Bertram, et al. 1996, 20) ODALE was consolidated, along with three other federal antidrug agencies (the Bureau of Narcotics and Dangerous Drugs, the Office of National Narcotics Intelligence, and the Customs Service Investigation Unit) into the Drug Enforcement Administration (DEA).

See also: Nixon, Richard Milhous; United States Drug Enforcement Administration
Reference: Bertram, Eva, Kenneth Sharpe, and Peter Anders. 1996. *Drug War Politics: The Price of Denial.*

United States Office of National Drug Control Policy (ONDCP)

This federal agency was created by the National Narcotics Leadership Act of 1988 and became effective 29 January 1989. Its purpose is to coordinate federal, state, and local efforts involved in the control of illegal drug abuse and to formulate national strategies that effectively carry out the government's antidrug activities. In all, ONDLP is responsible for overseeing and coordinating drug control efforts of more than fifty federal agencies and programs. The director of the Office is appointed by the president with the advice and consent of the U.S. Senate.

Initially, Congress authorized the Office for a five-year period that extended to November 1993, but the reenactment of the Violent Crime Control and Law Enforcement Act of 1994, reauthorized it until 30 September 1997. In 1993, just after entering office, President Bill Clinton tried to downsize the ONDLP, as he reacted to criticism that the Office had become a dumping ground for Republican appointments.

In February 1993 Clinton reduced the agency's 146 positions by 83 percent, but Congress rejected the move and Clinton came under attack from both Democratic and Republican members who wanted to know how the president could fight an effective drug war, given the cuts. Congress then pushed Clinton into accepting a proposal that would retain forty staff members (up from twenty-five), while doubling his proposed budget for the agency.

See also: Bennett, William; Clinton, Bill; Community Action Coalition of America; Counterdrug Technology Assessment Center; Monitoring the Future; National Drug Control Strategy; National Youth Antidrug Media Campaign
Reference: Bertram, Eva, Kenneth Sharpe, and Peter Anders. 1996. *Drug War Politics: The Price of Denial.*

United States Opium Control Act

See World War II

United States Opium Exclusion Act

Enacted in 1909, this law banned the importation of opium into the United States except for medical reasons. The measure was the culmination of the steady number of antiopium smoking acts passed by the U.S. Congress. The bill was signed into law a little more than a week after the Shanghai Conference met. Antidrug crusader Hamilton Wright told those present at the Shanghai Conference that the Opium Exclusion Act was the beginning of a "new era in the United States." (Courtwright 1982, 83)

See also: Opium; Shanghai Conference; Wright, Dr. Hamilton
References: Bacon, Donald C., Roger H. Davidson, and Morton Keller. 1995. *The Encyclopedia of the United States Congress.*
Courtwright, David T. 1982. *Dark Paradise.*

United States Posse Comitatus Act

This act was originally passed after the U.S. Civil War to calm Southern fears that the U.S. Army might act as an occupying force. It prohibits military personnel from having police power over civilians. Soon after taking office in 1981, President Ronald Reagan declared war on drug trafficking, and one of his first actions was to push for amendments to this act so he could use the armed forces in the fight against drugs. The U.S. Congress readily obliged by amending the Posse Comitatus Act and authorizing the Department of Defense to provide military training, intelligence, and equipment to civil law enforcement agencies and to allow members of the army, navy and marines to operate military equipment for civil agencies responsible for enforcing the nation's laws. The move sparked a fierce debate in Congress, as some congressmen and women questioned the wisdom of using the military as posse comitatus.

See also: Operation Thunderbolt; United States Department of Defense Act
Reference: Chepesiuk, Ron. 1999. *Hard Target.*

United States President's Commission on Organized Crime

Created on 28 July 1983 by the executive order of President Ronald Reagan, this commission was charged with the responsibility of working to improve law enforcement efforts directed against organized crime and to make recommendations concerning appropriate administrative and legislative improvements in the administration of justice. The Commission was given $5 million and mandated to complete its charge within three years of its creation.

The Commission held seven public hearings and called several alleged organized crime figures to testify, most of whom invoked the Fifth Amendment or presented other arguments for not answering the Commission's questions. The hearings were controversial and generated much media coverage, which led to the criticism that the public hearings were mere publicity stunts. Still, the Commission produced five lengthy reports, three of which had relevance to drug trafficking: *The Cash Connection: Organized Crime, Financial Institutions and Money Laundering* (1984), *America's Habit: Drug Trafficking and Organized Crime* (1986), and *The Impact of Organized Crime Today* (1986). The Commission concluded that drug trafficking and abuse are the most serious organized crime problems today.

America's Habit: Drug Trafficking and Organized Crime was published in early 1986, and according to criminologist Howard Abadinsky, "the President's Commission created hardly a ripple—new legislation was not forthcoming, nor did new initiatives result. The policy that was in place before the Commission was established remained in place." (Abadinsky 1990, 97)

See also: Carter, James Earl; Cuban Connection; Vietnamese Gangs
Reference: Abadinsky, Howard. 1990. *Organized Crime.*

United States Pure Food and Drug Act

The U.S. Congress passed this act in 1906 to prohibit the interstate shipment of food or soda water containing cocaine and to ensure that packages and labels of medicine must state the contents of any narcotic ingredient, including marijuana. The act is considered to be the first piece of major antidrug legislation in U.S. history.

See also: Cocaine; Marijuana
References: Courtwright, David T. 1982. *Dark Paradise.*
Musto, David F. 1991. Opium, Cocaine and Marijuana in U.S. History. *Scientific American* (July): 40+.

United States Southern Command

Also known as Southcom, the Southern Command is the nerve center for nearly all U.S. military operations in Latin America and the Caribbean and hence plays an important role in the country's antidrug operations. In September 1997 Southcom was physically moved from the Panama base where it had been located for thirty-four years to an official complex in the Miami area in South Florida. With the

move from Panama, Southcom took over new duties, becoming responsible for the Caribbean region, which had been previously under the Atlantic Command in Norfolk, Virginia.

See also: McCaffrey, Barry
References: Marquis, Christopher. 1998. "U.S. Soldiers Find Military Wages Don't Go Far In Civilian World." Knight-Ridder Tribune News Service, 13 May.
"Goodbye Quarry Heights?" 1990. *The Economist*, 24 March.

United States Substance Abuse and Mental Health Data Archive (SAMHDA)

This is an institute of the Office of Applied Studies at the Substance Abuse and Mental Health Services Administration of the U.S. Department of Health and Human Services. SAMHDA's goal is to provide easy access to substance abuse and mental health research data and to promote the sharing of this information among academics, researchers, and policy makers. The Archives has a website featuring an online data analysis system that allows users to conduct analyses on selected data sets within it. SAMHDA is part of a larger project of the National Archives and Analytic Center for Alcohol, Drug Abuse and Mental Health Data.

Reference: Substance Abuse and Mental Health Data Archive website at http://www.samshsa.gov.aos. oasflp.htlm/.

United States Uniform Narcotics Drug Act

Enacted in 1932, this law criminalized possession of illegal drugs and was an example of how the laws were now beginning to sanction users as well as suppliers. Nearly every state in the Union adopted this act within the next decade. Eva Bertram and her coauthors noted that twenty years later, "possession of drugs was a felony punishable under federal law by a minimum sentence of two years for the first offense." (Bertram, et al. 1996, 77)

Reference: Bertram, Eva, Kenneth Sharpe, and Peter Anders. 1996. *Drug War Politics: The Price of Denial.*
President's Commission on Organized Crime. 1986. *America's Habit: Drug Trafficking and Organized Crime.*

United States v. Behrman

In the aftermath of the passage of the 1914 Harrison Narcotic Act, there was a question about whether addicts could be treated like patients and have drugs prescribed to them to help relieve the problems of withdrawal, or whether such prescriptions were unlawful. In this 1922 court case, *United States v. Behrman* (No. S2 1922 SCt. 111, LS8 U.S. 280, 66L.ed., 619, 4LS CT303), the U.S. Supreme Court ruled that a prescription for an addict was illegal, even if the drugs had been prescribed as part of a cure program. As a result of this decision, it became almost impossible for addicts to get drugs legally.

See also: Harrison Narcotics Act; *Linder v. United States*
References: Courtwright, David T. 1982. *Dark Paradise.*
President's Commission on Organized Crime. 1986. *America's Habit: Drug Trafficking and Organized Crime.*

United States v. Doremus

This 1919 U.S. Supreme Court decision, 249 U.S. 86 (1919) No. 367, addressed the constitutionality of the 1914 Harrison Narcotic Act. Dr. Charles T. Doremus of San Antonio had been charged with violating the act after providing 500 tablets of morphine to a known addict. By one vote, the high Court ruled in favor of the government, declaring that a doctor might not prescribe for "the purpose of providing the user with morphine sufficient to keep him comfortable by maintaining his customary use." (Courtwright 1982, 31)

References: Courtwright, David T. 1982. *Dark Paradise.*
Jonnes, Jill. 1996. *Hep-Cats, Narcs and Pipe Dreams.*

United States v. Jim Fuey Moy

With the passage of the 1914 Harrison Narcotic Act, the International Revenue Bureau of the Treasury Department decided that a physician who wrote a prescription that was not for the sole purpose of maintenance was acting illegally, and it undertook an aggressive antimaintenance program. In *United States v. Jim Fuey Moy,* 1910 S.Ct. 612, 254 U.S. 189, 65 L.ed. 214, 41 S.Ct. 98 (1916), the U.S. Supreme Court "rebuked the government for construing a revenue statute as a sweeping prohibition." (Courtwright 1982, 106)

See also: Harrison Narcotic Act
References: Bugliosi, Vincent. 1995. *Drugs in America.*

United States Violent Crime Control and Law Enforcement Act of 1994

This act contains numerous drug-related provisions, including the establishment of drug courts, drug testing of federal offenders on postconviction release, alternative methods for young drug offenders, and residential substance abuse treatment programs for eligible convicts who have been released from federal or state prisons. The act also increased the penalties for drug trafficking and drug use in prisons and for drug dealing in drug free zones.

The law also imposed the "three strikes and you're out" rule, which provides for mandatory imprisonment for prisoners convicted of one or more serious violent felonies related to drug offenses. A special provision of the act, known as the "Drive-By Shooting Prevention Act," imposed the death penalty for a person, who, in an effort to avoid arrest as the result of a major drug offense, fires his or her gun into a group of two or more persons with the intention of harming or maiming them. The act also reauthorized the Office of Drug Abuse Control Policy.

Reference: Miller, Gary J. 1997. *Drugs and the Law—Detention, Recognition and Investigation.*

Upper Huallaga Valley (Peru)

The major region in Peru for the growing of the coca plant. Analysts have estimated that the Valley is the source for as much as 65 percent of all the coca grown in the country. Peru has had a national plan for eradicating the coca plant in the valley since the 1980s, but the country has been hampered by economic instability, a high inflation rate, guerrilla activity, and corruption.

See also: Shining Path Guerrilla Movement
References: Jamieson, Alison. 1994. *Terrorism and Drug Trafficking in Europe in the 1990s.*

Urdinola Grajales, Ivan

A major drug trafficker who, along with his brother Julio Fabio Urdinola, operates out of the Norte de Valle (Northern Valley) del Cauca in Colombia and controls a loose-knit group of Colombian cocaine drug traffickers who rose to prominence through a vicious campaign of terror in the late 1980s and early 1990s. Among the atrocities committed by the group was the massacre of thirty peasants from the town of Trujillo, who were cut to pieces with chain saws, and the murder of hundreds of other people, whose decapitated bodies were found in a river, hacked open and filled with stones.

The only murder directly linked to Urdinola was that of Ricardo Peterson, one of his bodyguards, who allegedly angered his boss by flirting with his wife. Newspaper accounts said Peterson's genitals had been hacked off. In October 1997 Urdinola was serving a seventeen-and-one-half year prison term for drug trafficking when he was acquitted of Peterson's murder by one of Colombia's so-called "faceless judges," who ruled that there was insufficient evidence to convict the trafficker of the torture murder and ordered his release. The judge said his decision was in line with Colombia's "benevolent" treatment of drug traffickers who cooperated with authorities, and revealed that Urdinola Grajales got time off for good behavior and for confessing to the drug charges against him. Urdinola Grajales is related to the Henao Montoya family by marriage.

See also: Henao Montoya, Jose Orlando
Reference: "Colombia's Drug Kingpin Released of Murder Charges." 1997. Reuters, 2 October.

Urrego, Jose Nelson (1955–   )

At the time of Urrego's capture in February 1998 at his country estate outside Medellin City, where he was holed up with two bodyguards and two female companions, Colombian authorities believed that the drug trafficker had assumed the leadership of the Cali Cartel after the capture of its founding members and leaders in the mid 1990s. Nicknamed El Loco, ("The Crazy One"), Urrego had earned a fortune in drug trafficking, evident in the number of hotels, ranches, and other real estate he owned. General Rosso Jose Serrano told the press that Urrego was practically the "highest ranking person left in the (Cali) cartel. I don't want to say that it's over, but for us, the cartel has totally died with Urrego." (Man Believed to Head Drug Cartel Held in Colombia 1996)

See also: Cali Cartel; Serrano Cadena, Jose Rosso
Reference: "Man Believed To Head Drug Cartel Held in Colombia." 1996. *Charlotte Observer*, 20 February.

V

Valdez, Mainero Emilio

A hired assassin of the Tijuana cartel, who was wanted by Mexican authorities but fled to the United States, where he was arrested. On 19 February 1998 he pled guilty in San Diego on conspiracy charges and possession of fifty kilos of cocaine.

See also: Tijuana Cartel

Reference: U.S. Senate Committee on Foreign Relations. Subcommittee on the Western Hemisphere, Peace Corps, Narcotics and Terrorism. 1998. *International Organized Crime Syndicates and Their Impact on the United States.* 26 February (statement of Thomas A. Constantine, head of the Drug Enforcement Administration). *See* DEA website http://www.usdoj.dea/pubs/congrtest.

Valdivieso Sarmiento, Alphonso (c. 1950–   )

In 1994, when Valdivieso was appointed Colombia's attorney general, few thought that he would make an impact on the country's political system. Barely five feet four inches in height and soft spoken, Valdivieso appeared to most observers to be too timid and reserved to lead Colombia's investigation and prosecution of some of the world's most powerful drug traffickers—until, that is, the advent of Operation 8000.

In August 1995 Valdivieso launched this intensive drug corruption investigation of the Colombian government and swiftly attained national prominence, earning him the nickname of "Mr. Clean." Within a year, twenty politicians were under investigation, in-

Alphonso Valdivieso Sarmiento (Courtesy of Magdalena Chepesiuk)

cluding President Ernesto Samper Pizano, who was accused of bankrolling his 1994 presidential election campaign with money from the Cali Cartel. Although in June 1996, Samper was cleared of corruption charges by the Colombian Congress, which was dominated by his ruling Liberal Party, the United States canceled his tourist visa. Valdivieso also launched an intensive investigation of the Cali cartel, which eventually led to the surrender or capture of all its top leaders.

In less than two years, thanks to his aggressive tactics, Valdivieso was heralded as a beacon of hope who would compel Colombia to shed its image as a narcodemocracy. His heightened political visibility led him to resign his position as Colombia's prosecuting attorney general in May 1997 in order to run for president in the 1998 national elections. Valdivieso later dropped out of the race.

See also: Cali Cartel; Narcodemocracy; Samper Pizano, Ernesto
Reference: Chepesiuk, Ron. 1997. "Mr. Clean Goes to Bogotá." *Bostonia* (Fall): 26–27.

Valium

The brand name for the tranquilizer known as diazepam, Valium is generally not sold on the illegal market but is abused through what is generally termed "legal" physician prescription writing—that is, some patients take Valium freely when they find doctors and medical personnel who are willing to keep them well supplied. Valium is a Schedule IV drug under the U.S. Comprehensive Crime Control Act, which means that Valium has either a low potential for abuse relative to the drugs or other substances in Schedule III, or that the drug has a currently accepted medical use in treatment in the United States, or abusing the drug may lead to physical dependence or psychological dependence relative to other drugs or other substances in Schedule III.

See also: Tranquilizers; United States Comprehensive Crime Control Act of 1970; Vietnamese Gangs
References: Blum, Kenneth. 1984. *Handbook of Abusable Drugs.*
O'Brien, Robert, and Sidney Cohen. 1984. *The Encyclopedia of Drug Abuse.*

Vasquez, Orlando

Colombian interior minister during the presidential administration of Virgilio Vargas Barco (1986–1990) who, in October 1989, became the third cabinet minister to resign from the government after the country's drug cartels declared a war on the government. The previous July, Vasquez had been appointed to re-

place Raul Orejuela, who was forced to resign as a result of accusations that he had been involved as a spy for drug traffickers. Justice Minister Monica de Grieff had also resigned on 21 September after she received death threats against her and her family. After resigning, Orlando Vasquez told the press that he would return to the Senate to work for constitutional reform.

See also: Barco Vargas, Virgilio; De Grieff, Monica
Reference: "Colombian Interior Minister Resigns as Drug War Grows." 1989. United Press International, 5 October.

Vaughn, Federico

An elusive Nicaraguan who reportedly told U.S. drug informant Barry Seale in 1984 that he was an assistant to Tomas Borge, the Nicaraguan interior minister in the Sandinista government, and that the Sandinista government was willing to process all the cocaine that the Medellin Cartel could supply.

Photos taken in May 1984 by a CIA camera hidden in Seale's plane purportedly caught Seale loading twenty-five kilogram duffel bags filled with cocaine onto the plane with the help of Pablo Escobar and Federico Vaughn. The authenticity of the photo, however, would later be questioned. Writers Peter Dale Scott and Jonathan Marshall, for example, claimed that the photo wasn't even taken in Nicaragua.

In July 1984 Seale made another trip to Nicaragua from the United States to bring supplies for a new cocaine-processing center that was under construction. When Seale's undercover operation was exposed, Vaughan disappeared, and he, along with ten other persons, was indicted in the United States by a federal grand jury on drug-trafficking charges. In 1985 Vaughn was implicated in another drug-smuggling ring in which the Sandinistas had allegedly made a deal with Robert Vesco in 1983 to process cocaine and ship it to the United States. Tomas Borge and Federico Vaughn were to be in charge of the operation.

Today, Vaughn's identity is still a mystery, and no proof exists that he was involved in drug trafficking, although he did issue a statement acknowledging that he was an aide to Borge. Some observers even believe that Vaughn might have been a CIA "asset."

See also: Cocaine; Contras; Escobar Gaviria, Pablo; Kerry, John F.; North, Oliver; Seale, Barry Alderman; United States Central Intelligence Agency; Vesco, Robert

Two GIs exchange vials of heroin in their living quarters during the Vietnam War despite an anti-drug crackdown in all of South Vietnam's five northern provinces. Heroin use in Vietnam sparked a heroin epidemic in the United States in the early 1970s as thousands of GIs who had used the drug returned from the battlefield. (Corbis/Bettmann-UPI)

References: Ehrenfeld, Rachel. 1994. *Narcoterrorism.*
Gugliotta, Guy and Jeff Leen. 1990. *Kings of Cocaine.*
Scott, Peter Dale, and Jonathan Marshall. 1999. *Cocaine Politics, Drugs, Armies, and the CIA in Central America.*

Vesco, Robert (1935–   )

A prominent American financier who fled the United States in 1972 and spent nearly thirty-three years as a fugitive until his arrest by Cuban authorities in 1995. He had been indicted in the United States for financial crimes that involved swindling mutual fund investors out of $200 million. On 12 September 1985 U.S. federal officials claimed that Vesco, after fleeing the country, had set up a drug-trafficking ring that involved smuggling cocaine into the United States with the help of Nicaraguan Sandinistas and the Colombian coast guard.

Colombian drug traffickers also later testified in court about meetings that were purportedly held in Havana, Cuba, with Fidel Castro's brother, defense minister Raul Castro, to arrange for the transshipment of drugs to the United States. Observers speculated that Cuba would extradite Vesco to the United

States in order to foster better diplomatic relations with Uncle Sam, but on 31 May 1995 the Cuban authorities arrested Vesco, and the following year a Cuban court sentenced him to thirteen years in prison for economic crimes against the state.

See also: Cuban Connection; Vaughn, Federico
References: Bardach, Ann Louise. 1996. "Vesco's Last Gamble." *Vanity Fair* (March).
"Sentenced: Robert Vesco." 1996. *MacLean's,* 9 September.

Vietnam War

A conflict in Southeast Asia, primarily fought in South Vietnam between the government forces aided by the United States and guerrilla insurgents aided by North Vietnam. The approximate dates of U.S. involvement in the Vietnam War are 1961–1975. U.S. soldiers in Vietnam used drugs as no other soldiers in United States military history. The problem began about 1968 with the soldiers using marijuana, and by 1972 the problem had been exacerbated by epidemic heroin use. Drug abuse in the Vietnam War became such a concern that the military worried about the combat effectiveness and readiness of U.S.

troops. The drug situation in the Vietnam War was affected by the heroin traffic in Southeast Asia, which was concentrated in the Golden Triangle, an area of rugged terrain occupying parts of Laos, Thailand, and Burma, which today is known as Myanmar. The Drug Enforcement Administration estimates that today the Golden Triangle may be the source of as much as 70 percent of the world's heroin and opium.

First the French during their colonial rule of Southeast Asia and then the CIA during the Vietnam War supported the war lords in the area as allies and as a buffer against communist expansion in the region and turned a blind eye to their involvement in the cultivation and trafficking of the local opium crop.

The 1964 coup that toppled South Vietnam leader Ngo Dinh Diem gave a big boost to the narcotics trade in the Golden Triangle, because corrupt South Vietnamese government officials and generals were given a free hand to use Vietnamese and Laotian planes, paid for by the U.S. government, to ship heroin from the Triangle. Once the loads arrived in South Vietnam, the traffickers bribed corrupt customs officials not to inspect the bags and bundles carrying the heroin. Later, after the United States invaded Cambodia in 1970, the heroin was carried from the Golden Triangle to Cambodia by mule and then flown or shipped to South Vietnam. According to reports, the CIA or the U.S. embassy in Laos did nothing to discourage its Laotian or Vietnamese allies from moving heroin to South Vietnam.

Around 1968 Hong Kong chemists, under the protection of the CIA's local allies, including the commander in chief of the Royal Laotian Army, opened heroin laboratories in the Golden Triangle that produced large quantities of a new kind of 90 percent pure heroin called Number Four, which has the nickname of "China White." This heroin was ideal for injecting and was superior in quality to the type of heroin being sold at the time in the United States, which was only 25 to 50 percent pure.

By the early 1970s GIs were spending an estimated $88 million a year on heroin and bringing their habit home with them, once they had finished their tours of duty. A 1973 survey revealed that the U.S. heroin trade was worth $4 billion, making it the country's "largest single consumer import." (Weir 1995, 65) U.S. engagement in the Vietnam War ended in 1973, and two years later North Vietnam won the war and unified the country.

See also: China White; Contras; Golden Triangle; Heroin; Marijuana; Narcoguerrillas; Opium; United States Central Intelligence Agency; Vietnamese Gangs

References: Inglis, Brian. 1975. *The Forbidden Game: A Social History of Drugs.*
Karnow, Stanley. 1983. *Vietnam: A History.*
McCoy, Alfred J. 1991. *The Politics of Heroin: CIA Complicity in the Global Drug Trade.*
Nash, Jay Robert. 1994. *World Encyclopedia of Organized Crime.*
Weir, William. 1995. *In the Shadow of the Dope Fiend.*

Vietnamese Gangs

Vietnamese gangs are among the fastest growing ethnic criminal groups in America today and could become a major force in the lucrative business of international drug trafficking. The gangs are as ruthless and violent as any criminal group currently operating in the United States, and this trait, combined with their constant mobility, have made them a difficult target for U.S. law enforcement officials. According to testimony before U.S. Congress on 3 October 1991, Sergeant Douglas Zwemke of the San Jose Police Department said that the Vietnamese criminal gangs have left "virtually no illegal stone undisturbed" and identified their major criminal activities as narcotics trafficking, fraud, extortion, prostitution, gambling, home invasion robberies, high-tech theft, and political and criminal terrorism.

Vietnamese criminal gang activity in the United States has its roots in the Vietnam War and the fall of Saigon in 1975, when many Vietnamese criminals with experience in drug trafficking and other criminal activities fled Vietnam and became part of a massive influx of 650,000 Asian immigrants to the United States.

Many law enforcement experts believe the oligarchy that ruled South Vietnam before the Communist takeover also played a role in the development of Vietnamese criminal activity in the United States. Marshall Nguyen Cao Ky, the former prime minister of the Republic of Vietnam who settled in California, has been accused of involvement in drug trafficking during the Vietnam War and then working as a head of an international organization of Vietnamese gangs in the United States after his immigration. Ky has strongly denied the charges, and the 1984 President's Commission on Organized Crime went on record as saying, "We accept this denial." (President's Commission 1986, 96)

The Vietnamese gangs got their criminal start in the United States in the 1970s preying on their fellow countrymen in numerous violent and often brutal so-called home invasion robberies. But by the 1980s, Vietnamese criminal gangs were diversifying and becoming heavily involved in a number of illegal activities, including drug trafficking. Law enforcement officials suspected that Vietnamese criminals are involved in the illegal importation and distribution of prescription drugs, including codeine and Valium, which they smuggle in from France and sell illegally in the Vietnamese community, either on the street or in unlicensed businesses. "I have seen signs in the windows of Vietnamese non-drug stores advertising in Vietnamese the sale of prescription drugs without prescriptions," detective James R. Badey explained in an article in *Organized Crime Digest*. "This is done openly since most law enforcement officials can't read Vietnamese." (Badey 1987, 5)

Although Vietnamese gangs are known for their decentralized nature, the Vietnamese gang, Born to Kill, rose to notoriety in New York City with strong leadership and well-defined structure. Born to Kill was founded in 1988 by David Thai, who had left another gang known as the Vietnamese Flying Dragons. At its zenith, the gang Born To Kill, also known as the Canal Street Boys, had about fifty to one hundred members and branches in other cities in New York state, as well as New Jersey, Connecticut, and Canada. Even though David Thai and six of his top assistants in the gang were convicted in 1992 of committing numerous violent crimes, U.S. law enforcement believes the gang is still active.

Vietnamese gangs in the United States appear to be becoming more organized and structured, and law enforcement authorities worry that they will pose an increasingly powerful criminal threat in the future. They point out that law enforcement faces many of the same problems as they do in investigating Chinese criminal organizations, including the language barrier, lack of resources, and poor interagency and police department coordination. Moreover, the gangs' ambition and criminal talent means that they will want a greater share of the tremendous amount of money to be made from international drug trafficking.

See also: Vietnam War

References: Badey, James R. 1987. "Federal Coordination is Needed to Head Off the Growing Threat from Vietnamese Criminals." *Organized Crime Digest*, 11 March.

English, T. J. 1994. *Born To Kill: America's Most Notorious Vietnamese Gang, and the Changing Face of Organized Crime.*

Huston, Peter. 1995. *Tongs, Gangs and Triads: Chinese Criminal Gangs in North America.*

Kleinknecht, William. 1996. *The New Ethnic Mobs: The Changing Face of Organized Crime in America.*

President's Commission on Organized Crime. 1986. *The Impact of Organized Crime Today.*

U.S. House Committee on Government Affairs, Permanent Subcommittee on Investigations. 1992. *The New International Criminal and Asian Organized Crime.* 18 June–4 August 1992. Congress Session 102-2, Doc-Nos. Hrg-102-940 CIS-No. 93-S401-g.

Vin Mariani

A coca and wine mixed beverage produced and marketed by Angelo Mariani of Corsica that was popular during the latter part of the nineteenth century. Advertised as a beverage that frees the body from fatigue and uplifts the spirits, the drink was popular all over the world and made Mariani rich. Pope Leo XIII, who used the drink himself, even gave Mariani a medal of appreciation. Many other prominent personalities, including U.S. President William McKinley and inventor Thomas Edison also drank Vin Mariani.

References: Inciardi, James A. 1984. *The War on Drugs: Heroin, Cocaine, Crime and Public Policy.*

Jonnes, Jill. 1996. *Hep-Cats, Narcs and Pipe Dreams.*

W

War on Drugs

The term is used to describe the efforts of governments around the world to enforce the drug laws of their countries. Many government leaders believe that, in order to deal effectively with the negative consequences of drug trafficking and drug abuse, the problem of illicit drugs must be dealt with as if the countries are at war. When U.S. President Ronald Reagan declared War on Drugs in 1982, he said, "Drug abuse is one of the gravest problems facing us as a nation," and he vowed to establish a foreign policy that "vigorously seeks to interdict and eradicate illegal drugs, wherever cultivated, processed, and transported." (Chepesiuk 1999, 27)

As in a real war, large numbers of drug dealers, users, and abusers are treated as enemies of the

Colombian troops ready part of a two-ton cocaine haul for burning at a farm owned by Medellin Cartel baron Jorge Luis Ochoa. Troops later burned the cocaine and dismantled a cocaine processing lab on the farm, 28 August 1989. (Reuters/Corbis-Bettmann)

Colombia police battle narcoguerrillas (Courtesy of the Colombian National Police)

state. The laws are changed to provide severe penalties and those convicted are often imprisoned for long stretches of time. In the United States, for example, the War on Drugs has led to a situation in which the country has more people behind bars than at any time in its history. As in war, civil liberties are given a lower priority in order to achieve the military objective. Witness how the status of civil liberties and due process in the United States has evolved under the impact of the War on Drugs.

Some observers of the War on Drugs say the metaphor "leads to an 'us against them' climate and feeds the illusion that illegal drug trafficking and drug use can be stopped and that 'victory' can be achieved." (Chepesiuk 1999, 268) In 1987, Arnold S. Trebach of the Drug Policy Foundation actually coined a new word to replace the metaphor War on Drugs: Drugpeace. "We must stop thinking about drugs and drug users in terms of war and hate." (Trebach 1993, 75)

References: Chepesiuk, Ron. 1999. *Hard Target.*
Trebach, Arnold S., and James A. Inciardi. *Legalize It? Debating American Drug Policy.*

Web of Addictions

Produced by Andres L. Homer and Dick Dillon, the Web of Addictions in an Internet site that seeks to provide accurate information about drug addictions in order to correct what the creators believe is the vast amount of misinformation on the Internet, particularly in some news groups. Homer and Dillon have received several awards for this web site.

Reference: Web of Addictions website at
http://www.well.com/user/woa.

Webb, Gary

A journalist with the *San Jose Mercury News* from 1988 to 1997, who stunned the world in August 1996 with the publication of a series of articles based on his year-long investigation into the origins of the crack cocaine epidemic in America. Titled "Dark Alliance," the series concluded that, for the better part of the 1980s, a San Francisco area drug ring sold tons of cocaine to Los Angeles street gangs and funneled millions of dollars in drug profits to the CIA-backed Nicaraguan Contras, rebels who were fighting a guerrilla campaign against Nicaragua's Sandanista government.

The article caused an immediate sensation and much controversy. Public demonstrations were led in Los Angeles, New York City, and Washington, D.C., and the senators from California made formal requests for investigations into the U.S. government's relationship with the cocaine ring. Webb's investigation, however came under sharp criticism from the press, which questioned his findings and methods. In 1997 the *San Jose Mercury News* saw fit to issue a public apology. Jerry Ceppos, the newspaper's editor, said that Webb's article series "fell short of my standards for the *Mercury News*."

Webb was pulled off his beat and exiled to a job at a small *Mercury News* bureau in Cupertino, California. Webb defended his findings, but he left the *Mercury News* and moved to Sacramento to work as a consultant to the California State Legislative Task Force on Government Oversight. The CIA conducted an internal review of Webb's allegations in 1998 and issued a 149-page report that cleared itself of the drug charge. Three years after the publication of his three-part series in the *San Jose Mercury News* entitled "Dark Alliance on the Origins of the Crack Cocaine Epidemic in Los Angeles," Webb's investigation remains controversial. Webb published a book, *Dark Alliance*, which was an effort to tell his side of the story and set the record straight. Webb stands by his evidence: that two Los Angeles drug dealers named Juan Norwin Menese Cantero and Oscar Danito Blandon, both Nicaraguan and Contra politicians, began the crack cocaine epidemic that eventually swept the United States. Critics of Webb's investigation mention that investigations conducted by other major news sources such as the *Washington Post, New York Times,* and *Los Angeles Times* undermine Webb's thesis. Unless additional sources can be found that support Webb's thesis, it will continue to be controversial.

See also: Contras; Crack Cocaine; United States Central Intelligence Agency

References: Rothschild, Mathew. 1997. "Drugs, CIA and the Media." *The Progressive* (May): 4+.

Webb, Gary. 1998. *Dark Alliance: The CIA, the Contras and the Crack Cocaine Explosion.*

Weinig, Harvey (1948–   )

A New York City lawyer who was involved in a $100 million money-laundering scheme that law enforcement officials described as one of the biggest operations ever uncovered in New York City. The money-laundering ring, which was busted in 1995, included Weinig's law partner, Robert Hirsch, a former law professor, a beer distributor named Richard Spence, a police officer, and a former fireman, all working with a group of drug traffickers from the Colombian Cali Cartel. Members of the group picked up cash from the street sale of cocaine and deposited the money in bank accounts controlled by the Hirsch-Weinig law firm, or by Spence, and from those accounts the money was wired into private Swiss bank accounts operated by two other members of the group. Safely laundered, the money was then transferred from Switzerland to the Cali Cartel. In March 1996, Harvey Weinig was sentenced to eleven years and three months in prison.

The *Wall Street Journal* noted that the case showed that "traffickers now prefer to avoid filtering cash through banks, moving their funds instead through wire transfers and checks that are forwarded overseas. And because so many financial transactions can now be handled outside of banks, the front for such activities can be anything from a retail business to a brokerage firm account. Even a law firm will do." (O'Brien 1995)

See also: Money Laundering

References: O'Brien, Timothy. 1995. "Law Firm's Downfall Exposes New Methods of Money Laundering." *Wall Street Journal*, 26 May, eastern edition.

Teaster. Joseph B. 1995. "U.S. Says It Uncovered a $100 Million Drug Money Laundry." *New York Times*, 1 December.

Weld, William F. (1945–   )

In April 1997 the Clinton administration announced that it would name William Weld, a Republican and former governor of Massachusetts, to the post of ambassador to Mexico. But soon after, Jesse Helms, a Republican senator from North Carolina and the powerful chairman of the Senate Foreign Relations Committee, announced that the Committee would not give Weld a confirmation hearing. In other words, Weld would not get Senate approval as required by the Constitution before an appointment could be valid. Helms opposed Weld's nomination because he believed the nominee was "soft" on drugs and favored the medical use of marijuana.

Helms's decision caused an uproar, but he stood firm. As the *Economist* magazine pointed out: "The uncomfortable fact is Mr. Helms, as chairman of the Senate Foreign Relations Committee, has a voice in foreign policy almost as loud as that of the president himself, and sometimes louder." (Not By Helms Alone 1997, 20) Weld did not help his nomination either when he pointedly attacked Helms and the Senate, and he lost a great deal of support, even from Democrats. On 15 September 1997 Weld withdrew his name for consideration.

See also: Davidow, Jeffrey

References: Cassata, Dana. "Helms Lashes Back at Critics, Holds Firm on Blocking Weld." *Congressional Quarterly Weekly Report*, 20 September.

"The Helms-Weld War: In the Same Party You Said?" 1997. *Economist*, 2 August.

"Not By Helms Alone." 1997. *Economist*, 20 September.

White House Conference on Narcotics and Drug Abuse

Held in September 1962, this conference was the first ever to deal with the problem of narcotics and drug abuse. It lasted two days and was attended by an estimated 500 people who had a variety of backgrounds and included police, psychiatrists, and government officials. The meeting showed how little the United States knew about narcotics and drug abuse. Seeking to make an initiative to deal with the problem, President John F. Kennedy appointed an official President's Advisory Commission on Narcotics and Drug Abuse on 16 July 1963, which became known as the Prettyman Commission.

See also: Prettyman Commission

References: Jonnes, Jill. 1996. *Hep-Cats, Narcs and Pipe Dreams.*

President's Commission on Organized Crime. 1986. *America's Habit: Drug Trafficking and Organized Crime.*

World Customs Organization (WCO)

Formerly known as the Customs Cooperation Council, the WCO is an international intergovernment organization that deals with issues and concerns pertaining to international customs and trade. Since its founding in 1953, the organization has been aware of the need to take measures against smuggling, particularly of illicit drugs. The WCO has worked with the United National Drug Control Program on joint projects that have had as their objective the improvement of law enforcement cooperation at the national, regional, and international levels. The two organizations have worked to do this by developing a regular drug enforcement reporting and analysis mechanism among participating countries, as well as with other regional offices.

See also: United Nations International Drug Control Program
Reference: United Nations International Drug Control Program. 1997. *World Drug Report.*

World Health Organization (WHO)

Established in 1948, the WHO works to give people a level of health that will allow them to live socially and economically productive lives. As part of its mandate, it seeks to reduce the abuse of all narcotic and psychotic substances through the promotion of global health.

Reference: Osmanczyk, Edmund Jan. 1985. *Encyclopedia of the United Nations and International Agreements.*

World Narcotic Defense Association

Organized in 1927 and based in the United States, this antidrug organization was one of many similar such groups organized during the 1920s. To achieve the group's objectives, its members lobbied for federal funds to support national campaigns against drugs, sponsored so-called Narcotic Education Weeks, and provided speakers and printed material for schools, churches, and other organizations across the United States. But as historian H. Wayne Morgan writes, these programs, "cared little for sophisticated theories about the causes and treatment of addicts, and critics attacked their statements about the effects of opiates and cocaine, and their estimates of the number of users." (Morgan 1981, 132–133)

See also: International Narcotics Education Association
Reference: Morgan, H. Wayne. 1981. *Drugs in America: A Social History, 1800–1980.*

World Narcotics Conference

Founded in 1926, this group was one of several antinarcotic organizations created in the early 1920s by crusader Richard P. Hobson. The conference and other antinarcotic organizations like it were given a boost by the passage of the 1919 Prohibition Amendment against alcohol.

See also: Hobson, Richard P.; Prohibition
Reference: Bertram, Eva, Kenneth Sharpe, and Peter Anders. 1996. *Drug War Politics: The Price of Denial.*

World War II (1939–1945)

As World War II engulfed Europe, it crippled the international drug trade by cutting off the supply line between drug pushers and users, suppressing the traffic to the point that in 1940, heroin sold in the United States had dropped to a purity level of about 5 percent. This reportedly forced many addicts to search for and use paregoric, an antidiarrheal drug containing powdered opium. The resulting heroin shortage led to thefts of the drug from hospitals, pharmacies, and other sources of legitimate drugs. For a time, barbiturates became a potential drug problem. An increasing number of Americans began to try so-called goof balls (a mixture of amphetamines and barbiturates) for relaxation and diversion.

The major piece of U.S. antidrug legislation passed during World War II was the Opium Control Act, which prohibited the domestic production of poppies without the Federal Bureau of Narcotics approval. For propaganda purposes, the United States made an effort to tie the enemy to international drug trafficking. In 1946 the *New York Times* wrote: "Of all the indictments against Japan, that of the use of opium and its derivative heroin, as deliberate government policy to control the minds of conquered people, or all of Japan's enemies, is perhaps the most damning." (Morgan 1981, 144)

During World War II, some important developments occurred regarding international drug trafficking. Representatives from several countries met with U.S. officials in Washington in 1942 to discuss the question of the discontinuance of government monopolies for opium smoking after the war, when territories held by Japan would be returned to the

European Allies that formerly controlled them. In 1943 the Allies announced that the system of opium smoking under government license would end with the return of the liberated territories, In June 1944 the U.S. Senate and House passed a joint resolution introduced by Walter Judd, a Minnesota congressman and former missionary to China, authorizing the president to urge opium-producing countries to limit their production of opium strictly to meet the world's scientific and medical needs. With the defeat of the Axis powers in 1945, drug trafficking once again became the focus of international attention.

See also: Amphetamines; Barbiturates; Heroin; Opium
References: Chepesiuk, Ron. 1999. *Hard Target.*
Courtwright, David T. 1982. *Dark Paradise.*
Morgan, H. Wayne. 1981. *Drugs in America: A Social History, 1800–1980.*

Wright, Dr. Hamilton (1867–1917)

A prominent American spokesman for international drug control in the latter part of the nineteenth century, who served as a major catalyst in the United States' move for domestic drug control and as a force in the international antiopium movement. In 1909 U.S. President Theodore Roosevelt appointed Wright a member of the International Opium Commission, and as an antidrug crusader, Wright conducted surveys and campaigned for regulatory legislation that led to the passage of the Harrison Narcotic Act in 1914.

See also: Harrison Narcotic Act; Opium; United States Opium Exclusion Act
References: Morgan, H. Wayne. 1981. *Drugs in America: A Social History, 1800–1980.*
Taylor, Arnold H. 1969. *American Diplomacy and Narcotics Trafficking, 1900–1939.*

Y

Yakuza

Most organized crime syndicates do their best to operate in secrecy out of the public spotlight; the Japanese Yakuza is not one of them. With his semi-dark sunglasses, white shoes, polyester suit, and short military-style haircut, a Yakuza gang member can easily be picked out in a crowd. Get closer and take a look at his hands and you will notice the missing tips of his little fingers, the result of having been snipped off in one of the gang's initiation rituals. If his shirt is open, you might get a glimpse of the near total body tatoos consisting of elaborate dragons and cherry blossoms. He may even hand you a business card, if you happen to stop and chat with him. Pay him a visit and you will most likely see his name on his office door plate when you enter.

This high profile, though, has not stopped the Yakuza from being one of organized crime's most successful criminal syndicates. With a membership that has been put at from 88,000 to as high as 110,000, the Yakuza may be the world's oldest and largest criminal organization. The term *yakuza* is actually a generic name applied to about 2,500 different crime groups operating in Japan and several other countries, including Hawaii and the United States West Coast.

Like La Cosa Nostra in Italy, the Yakuza has a strong tradition and a well-defined structure that is based on hierarchial systems of elders and younger brothers in a kind of familial paternalism. A great emphasis is placed on ritual and ceremonial initia-

tives, such as the finger-snipping practice. The gang's hierarchy includes a *kaicho*, a type of boss or godfather, who is the absolute authority; the *wakato*, a deputy chairman; and the *wakaishu*, the soldiers who make up most of the membership.

By 1980 in Tokyo, Japan, alone, there were fifty drug-trafficking syndicates known as the Tekiya, which had names like Koshu-Ya, Kyokuto-Rengo and Hashi-Ya and formed a closed, powerful and well-organized society.

The Yakuza got their big break after Japan's defeat in World War II, when adverse political and economic conditions allowed them to expand into a number of illicit enterprises, including narcotics trafficking. Before World War II, Japanese criminals were drug suppliers to the United States, providing huge amounts of heroin to America's biggest drug rings. As David Kaplan and Alec Dubro described their role, "Early in the 1930s, some Japanese in America were driven to the narcotics trade for the simple reason that the Japanese Empire, in its conquest of East Asia, had acquired much of the opium, morphine and heroin business there. Connections between the drug distributors in Asia and America were logical and fairly easily made." (Kaplan & Dubro 1986, 232) The outbreak of the war, however, severed the connection.

There were as many as 70,000 Yakuza in Japan by 1958, but that figure jumped five years later to 184,000, when the crime organization began its modern expansion. In the early 1970s, the Yakuza

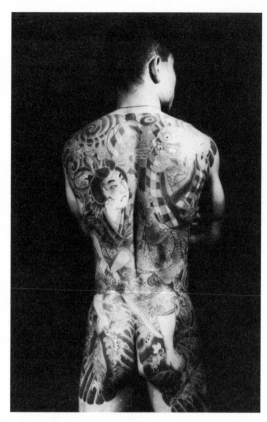

Tattooed back of a Japanese Samurai Swordsman (Corbis/Underwood & Underwood)

diversified and began moving into the growing international narcotics trade, establishing links with the powerful Chinese Triads and becoming active in Hong Kong, Taiwan, and Southeast Asia.

U.S. authorities began to get concerned about the Yakuza in the 1970s, after it became apparent that the group had made the United States its prime target for criminal activity. By 1986 the President's Commission on Organized Crime published a report in which it noted that the Yakuza are active in drug trafficking, primarily smuggling amphetamine from the United States to Japan.

Although it is difficult to gather information about the Yakuza, U.S. officials do know that the Yakuza's role in drug trafficking is different from the one played by other organized crime groups that target the huge U.S market for distribution. The Yakuza work primarily as exporters of drugs from the United States to Japan, and principally traffic in amphetamines. Methamphetamine, a type of amphetamine, became hugely popular in Japan in the early

1980s. By 1983 the number of speed-related arrests in Japan tripled, and the number of amphetamine abusers was estimated to be at between 300,000 and 600,000.

The Yakuza may focus on exporting drugs from the United States, but this does not mean that the organization has not contributed to the growth of drug use and abuse in the United States. "One might think that because the Yakuza is exporting drugs from the U.S. to Japan that they are not contributors to the U.S. drug problem," explained criminologist Michael D. Kelley. "In fact, the reverse may very well be true, as the Yakuza acts as a wholesale customer of local drug manufacturers, thus creating a giant demand for production of the drug as a large drug using population would." (Kelley 1988, 121)

The demand in Japan for methamphetamine is so great and the sales so lucrative that Japanese authorities believe the trade in the drug accounts for fully half of the Yakuza's income—an amount believed to be worth in the billions of dollars. At the 1991 congressional hearings on the New International Criminal and Asian Organized Crime, then-FBI Director William Sessions reported that in 1988 the Yakuza grossed almost $10 billion in revenue, one-third from crystal methamphetamine, according to statistics provided by Japan's National Police Agency.

Crystal methamphetamine (more popularly known as "ice") is a stimulant that became highly popular in Hawaii and the West Coast of the United States during the 1980s, thanks to the Yakuza. The drug is cheaper than cocaine, has a long-lasting high, is extremely harmful, and has been known to put users into a violent, paranoid state. The Yakuza produce "ice" in secret laboratories in Korea and Taiwan, and Filipino criminals help to smuggle the drug into the United States.

What the Yakuza does with its huge amount of illegally earned income may pose a greater threat to the United States. The FBI estimated that the Yakuza may have laundered as much as $1 billion in the United States in the 1980s. Jim G. Moody, chief of the FBI's organized crime and drug section, told *Business Week* magazine, "There was more money laundering activity by them [the Yakuza] than drug trafficking." (Grover 1993, 38)

In the early 1990s the Japanese authorities began to crack down on the Yakuza and reverse Japan's long tradition of official toleration of organized crime, which had led to a high level of corruption in Japanese society. Yet, despite the recent concerted anti-Yakuza campaign, Japanese authorities continue to worry about the corrupting threat of the criminal group on Japanese society, especially the gang's efforts to take over the country's far right-wing organizations.

Masayuki Takagi, a professor of sociology at Teikyo University and an expert on Japan's political right wing, told one newspaper that the Yakuza had taken over 80 to 90 percent of the country's extreme right-wing groups, although police have put the figure at between 25 and 50 percent. The professor also attributed thirty-nine incidents "of terrorism and guerilla activity" to such groups in the previous three years. (Radin 1994) The U.S. government has been skeptical of Japanese law enforcement's willingness to seriously investigate the Yakuza. "While the Japanese Government has recently adopted new anti-organized crime laws, the effect of these laws remains to be seen," concluded the 1991 congressional hearings on Asian organized crime. "What is clear is that heretofore anemic Japanese law enforcement efforts against Boryokudan [Yakuza] gangs have had an adverse impact on the United States and other countries where the Boryokudan have begun to extend their influence and investments. The failure of Japanese law enforcement officials to share information and intelligence about the Boryokudan members in a timely fashion and in a form which is legally admissible has severely handicapped U.S. law enforcement efforts." (U.S. Senate Committee on Governmental Affairs 1991, 54)

See also: Amphetamine; Heroin; Methamphetamine; Money Laundering; Triads

References: Grover, Ronald. 1993. "A Japanese Laundry Worth $1 Billion." *Business Week,* 24 May.

Kaplan, David E., and Alec Dubro. 1986. *Yakuza: The Explosive Account of Japan's Criminal Underworld.*

Kelley, Michael D. 1988. *Gangland: Drug Trafficking by Organized Criminals.*

Kelley, Robert J., ed. 1986. *Organized Crime: A Global Perspective.*

President's Commission on Organized Crime. 1986. The Impact of Organized Crime Today.

Radin, Charles A. 1994. "Japanese Political Gangsters." *Charlotte Observer,* 10 June.

U.S. Senate Committee on Governmental Affairs, Permanent Subcommittee on Investigations. 1992. *The New International Criminal and Asian Organized Crime.* Doc Nos. Hrg 102940, 18 June–4 August 1992. SVDOC: 44.G74119: S.Hrg, 102940.

Young Boys Inc. (YBI)

A Detroit, Michigan, gang of the 1980s that is credited with pioneering many of the techniques currently used by other drug gangs across the United States, such as moving drugs via underage youngsters who cannot be sentenced to prison, the use of brand names on drug products, and the use of brutal and indiscriminate violence to capture an increasingly larger share of the drug market. The Young Boys recruited employees by driving down the street with loud speakers blaring advertisements for their group, and they became so famous that their jackets were sold at local malls to enthusiastic teenagers. Young Boys Inc. leader Butch Jones and forty other gang members were indicted in 1983 and given long prison sentences.

Reference: Kleinknecht, William. 1996. *The New Ethnic Mobs: The Changing Face of Organized Crime in America.*

Z

Zero Tolerance Policy Program (U.S.)

Initiated by the Reagan administration on 21 March 1988, this program was aimed at reducing the supply of illegal drugs entering the United States by targeting the consumers as well as the suppliers. As part of the policy, law enforcement authorities were to go after casual users as well heavy users of drugs, including those who smoked marijuana. Federal officials were ordered to seize vessels within a twelve-mile radius of the U.S. coastline if they found any trace of a banned substance on board.

Several well-publicized incidents, however, caused controversy. In one incident in May 1988, for example, the U.S. Coast Guard seized a $2.5 million yacht after discovering a tenth of an ounce of marijuana on board. The critics of Zero Tolerance Policy charged that the program was unfair because it made innocent people pay for the others' behavior, over which they had no control. Within two months of initiating the program, the federal government began relenting to public pressure and started to relax the zero tolerance standard.

See also: Reagan, Ronald
Reference: Cooper, Mary H. 1990. *The Business of Drugs.*

Chronology

1916   *United States v. Jim Fuey Moy* is decided by Supreme Court

1917   U.S. Congress passes Eighteenth Amendment, which imposes prohibition of alcohol

1919   Mescaline first synthesized in laboratory

Eighteenth Amendment to the U.S. Constitution ratified

Supreme Court decides *Linder v. United States*

Supreme Court decides *United States v. Doremus*

League of Nations established Committee on Traffic in Opium and Other Dangerous Drugs

Supreme Court decides *Webb v. United States*

International Labor Office (ILO) created

1920   Eighteenth Amendent goes into effect

League of Nations creates Advisory Committee on Traffic in Opium and Other Dangerous Drugs

United Kingdom passes Dangerous Drug Act

American Civil Liberties Union founded

1921   U.S. General Accounting Office and U.S. Treasury Department's Bureau of Alcohol, Tobacco and Firearms established

1922   U.S. Congress passes National Drug and Export Act

Noted movie director William Desmond Taylor dies under suspicious circumstances, believed to be from a drug overdose

United States v. Behrman Supreme Court decision

U.S. Congress passes Narcotic Drug and Import Act

1923   Interpol formed

International Narcotics Education Association established

Actor Wallace Reid dies from drug addiction

1925   Geneva International Opium Convention of 1925 held

1926   PCP synthesized

World Conference on Narcotics Education established

1927   World Narcotic Defense Association established

U.S. Customs Service established

1928   Pioneer drug trafficker Arnold Rothstein is murdered

1930   Harry Anslinger appointed head of Federal Bureau of Narcotics (FBN)

Interpol initiates first antidrug program

Actress Mabel Normand dies from drug abuse

Geneva International Opium Convention of 1925 goes into force

1931   Under Italian mobster Lucky Luciano's leadership, La Cosa Nostra establishes "National Commission"

Limitation Convention of 1931 held

1932   Codeine synthesized

United States Uniform Narcotics Drug Act passed

1933   Eighteenth Amendment repealed

Limitation Convention of 1931 goes into force

1937   U.S. Congress passes Marijuana Tax Law

Movie *Reefer Madness* released

1939   Convention for Suppression of Illicit Traffic in Dangerous Drugs goes into force

1940   As result of World War II, heroin in United States drops to purity level of only 5 percent

1941   Marijuana is dropped from official compendia of drugs in United States, Pharmacopeia and National Formulary

1942   U.S. Congress passes Opium Control Act

1943   Dr. Albert Hoffman, codiscoverer of LSD, accidentally ingests it and experiences a "trip."

United States has 350,000 acres of marijuana under cultivation in support of U.S. war effort

1944   National Council on Alcoholism and Drug Dependence Inc. founded

United Nation's Children's Fund founded

1945   Lucky Luciano deported to Italy

United Nations Food and Agricultural Organization and United Nations Educational, Scientific and Cultural Organization (UNESCO) established

1946   League of Nations dissolved

United Nations Commission on Narcotic Drugs established

United States enacts Act of 8 March 1946

1948   Chinese Revolution gives boost to international drug trade

World Health Organization (WHO) established

1949   General Chiang Kai-Shek's Third and Fifth armies flee China for Burma and communists take over on mainland

LSD introduced to United States

1951   U.S. Congress passes Boggs Act

Methaqualone first synthesized

U.S. Senate Kefauver Committee begins investigation of Italian Mafia

1952   Chiang Kai-Shek's forces become powerful drug traffickers in Myanmar (Burma)

1953   Signing of U.N. Protocol for Limiting and Regulating Cultivation of Poppy Plant, Production of International and Wholesale Trade In and Use of Opium

World Customs Organization (WCO) founded

1954   Aldous Huxley publishes *Doors of Perception*

1955   Aldous Huxley publishes *Heaven and Hell*

Movie *Man with the Golden Arm* is released

Jazz musician Charles Parker dies of drug abuse

1956   U.S. Congress passes Narcotics Control Act of 1956

1957   La Cosa Nostra meets in Appalachian Mountains in New York state

Italian Mafia summit held in Palermo, Sicily

Mexican Mafia organized

1958   Great Sicilian Mafia War begins

1959   Cuban Revolution brings Fidel Castro to power

Pagans and Outlaws motorcycle gangs established

1960   U.S. Congress passes Narcotics Control Act

1961   Bay of Pigs invasion fails

United Nations Single Convention on Narcotic Drugs signed

Chiang Kai-Shek's forces push into Thai portion of Golden Triangle

1962   First White House Conference on Narcotics and Drug Abuse held

1963   Joseph Valachi testifies against Italian Mafia, making American public aware for the first time of the workings of the Mafia

Prettyman Commission issues first report

United Nations Research Institute for Social Development established

United Nations Protocol for Limiting and Regulating Cultivation of Poppy Plant, Production of International and Wholesale Trade In and Use of Opium enters into force

Harvard University fires Timothy Leary and Baba Ram Dass

1964   Coup in South Vietnam topples Ngo Dinh Diem

U.S. Congress passes Violent Crime Control and Law Enforcement Act

United Nations Single Convention on Narcotics Drugs goes into force

Methadone treatment programs begin

Outlaw motorcycle gang founded

1965   U.S. Immigration Act passed

New York City heroin kingpin Leroy "Nicky" Barnes is sent to prison where he meets Italian Mafia godfather Joseph "Crazy Joe" Gallo

United Nations Development Program established

U.S. Congress passes Drug Abuse Control Amendments

U.S. launches Operation Tradewinds

Watts riots in Los Angeles lead to formation of Bloods and Crips gangs

1966   U.S. President Lyndon Johnson establishes President's Commission on Law Enforcement and Administration of Justice. Johnson also creates Bureau of Drug Abuse Control (BDAC)

Hippy movement born in Haight-Ashbury district of San Francisco, California

United States National Addict Rehabilitation Act is passed

Revolutionary Armed Forces of Colombia (FARC) founded

Bandidos motorcycle gang founded

United Nations World Population Fund and Industrial Development Organization founded

1967   Phoenix House founded

United Nations Conference on Drug Abuse Control held

PCP becomes popular in United States

Monterrey Pop Festival held

1968   President Richard Nixon creates Bureau of Narcotics and Dangerous Drugs

1968
cont.

International Narcotics Board of United Nations established

United Nations Interregional Crime Justice Research Institute established

Operation Intercept launched along United States–Mexican border

Operation Cooperation launched in Mexico

Bureau of Narcotics and Dangerous Drugs established with Henry L. Giordano as director

1969

International Narcotics Research Conference established

1970

Shining Path (Sendero Luminoso) founded in Peru

Film *Easy Rider* released

U.S. Congress passes Bank Secrecy Act and Organized Crime Control Act of 1970

Operation Dinero launched

U.S. Congress establishes National Commission on Marijuana and Drug Abuse

National Drug Enforcement Officers Association formed

U.S. Congress passes Drug Abuse Prevention and Control Act

U.S. Congress passes Bank Security Act and Controlled Substances Act

President Richard Nixon calls Timothy Leary "most dangerous man in America"

Under Comprehensive Crime Control Act of 1970 (more popularly known as Controlled Substances Act), heroin and marijuana are classified as Schedule I drugs; prescriptions containing morphine, as Schedule II and III drugs; medicine containing opium, Schedule II, III and IV drugs; and barbiturates, Schedule V drug

Rock stars Janis Joplin and Jimi Hendrix die from overdoses

Federal legislation in United States reduces penalty for first-time possession of marijuana from felony to misdemeanor punishable by less than one year in jail

1971

United Nations Convention on Psychotropic Substances ratified

U.S. National Institute on Drug Abuse established

Rock star Jim Morrison dies from drug abuse

Bank of Credit and Commerce International

(BCCI) founded

1972

U.S. Congress passes Drug Abuse and Treatment Act

National Association of Alcoholism and Drug Abuse Counselors founded

U.S. Bureau of Alcoholism, Tobacco and Firearms established

U.S. Drug Abuse Office and Treatment Act passed

New York Times notes South Florida's increasing importance for smuggling of heroin and cocaine

United Nations adopts amendment to 1961 Single Convention on Narcotics Drugs

Executive order of President Nixon creates Office of Drug Abuse Law Enforcement

1973

Drug Enforcement Administration established

General Augusto Pinochet launches successful coup in Chile

Colombian guerrilla group, M-19 (Movimiento 19 Abril), founded

Oregon becomes first state to legalize marijuana

New York City drug kingpin Frank Mathews is arrested, let out of jail on bond, and never seen again

French Connection drug distribution network smashed

Centac established

U.S. immigration laws favoring Russian political refugees enacted

1974

U.S. Congress enacts Narcotic Addict Treatment Act of 1974

El Paso Intelligence Center established

U.S. National Institute on Drug Abuse founded

1975

With the fall of Saigon, North Vietnamese and Viet Cong allies win the Vietnam War, playing an important part in the rise of the heroin epidemic in the United States in the early 1970s

National Institute on Drug Abuse establishes Monitoring Future Study

Protocol Amending United Nations 1961 Single Convention on Narcotic Drugs enters into force

Operation Condor/Trigo launched in Mexico

Cali Cartel drug lord Gilberto Rodriguez Orejuela sends Hernando Giraldo Soto to New York City

1976   Jeff Fort is released from prison and resumes control of Blackstone Rangers, which he renames El Rukns

National Institute on Drug Abuse establishes Community Epidemiology Work Group

United States Select Narcotic Abuse and Control Committee established

1977   Chemical Bank of New York becomes first bank indicted under Bank Secrecy Act of 1970

National Families in Action founded

1978   Medellin Cartel founded

Bureau of International Narcotics Matters and Law Enforcement Affairs organized under U.S. State Department

National Intelligence Consumers Committee established in United States

New York City crime kingpin Leroy "Nicky" Barnes goes to prison

Bureau of International Narcotics and Law Enforcement Affairs of the U.S. State Department organized

1979   Soviet Union invades Afghanistan; Afghan rebels later accused of drug trafficking in order to purchase guns

Operation Raccoon launched

Dadeland massacre takes place in Miami

1980   U.S. Customs and IRS launch Operation Greenback

Mariel boatlift undertaken from Cuba

Drug Abuse Warning Network (DAWN) transferred to U.S. National Institute on Drug Abuse from Drug Enforcement Agency

Pizza Connection operation begins

In Bolivia, General Luis Garcia Meza stages coup, which is believed to be run by drug traffickers

1981   Prominent delegation of Miamians goes to see President Reagan in White House to ask the U.S. government to do something about drug-related crime epidemic in South Florida

The United Nations General Assembly adopts International Drug Abuse Control Strategy and a five-year (1982–1986) Action Plan

General Luis Garcia Meza deposed as Bolivian leader, ending control of Bolivian government by drug traffickers

U.S. Congress passes amendments to Posse Comitatus Act

Marta Nieves Ochoa kidnapped by M-19 guerrillas from university campus in Antioquia, Colombia, and Colombian drug traffickers subsequently form MAS (Death to Kidnappers)

Frances Muller appointed DEA director

DEA establishes Centac 26

Operation Thunderbolt launched

Bank officials for Garfield Bank in Los Angeles found guilty of money laundering

DEA agent Johnny Phelps arrives in Colombia

1982   Drug trafficker Pablo Escobar elected as alternate to Colombian Congress

Beginning of indictments against Great American Bank of Dade County, Florida

Comedian John Belushi dies of drug overdose

Indictments handed down in Pizza Connection case

Antidrug program DARE founded

Drug trafficker Jaime Guillot-Lara indicted

Case of money launderer Eduardo Orozco-Prado goes to trial

American entrepreneur John DeLorean arrested on drug smuggling charge

Cocaine Anonymous founded

Operation Swordfish concluded

President Ronald Reagan creates President's Commission on Organized Crime by executive order

Campaign Against Marijuana Planting (CAMP) organized

Financier Robert Vesco flees United States

Ronald Reagan launches U.S. War on Drugs

People's Liberty Bank of Lexington, Kentucky, becomes involved in international money-laundering scheme

South Florida Task Force becomes operational

U.S. launches Operation Red River, Operation Fountainhead, and Operation Padrino

Colombian drug trafficker Carlos Lehder Rivas founds National Latin Party

1982
cont.

New York City heroin kingpin Leroy "Nicky" Barnes is sent to jail for the second time

M-19 guerrillas release Marta Nieve Ochoa unharmed

Pablo Escobar creates social action program, Medellin Without Slums

U.S. Congress passes Department of Defense Authorization Act

Shining Path establishes presence in Peru's Upper Huallaga Valley

Lewis Tambs appointed ambassador to Colombia

1984

Colombian Justice Minister Rodrigo Lara Bonilla assassinated

Medellin cartel offers to pull out of international drug trade in return for amnesty

U.S. Congress passes Comprehensive Crime Control Act

United States Congress makes possession of quaaludes illegal

Johnny Phelps leaves Colombia

Operation Vanguard launched in Mexico

Raid on Tranquilandia, Colombia, takes place

Medellin Cartel bombs U.S. embassy in Colombia

United States pushes Colombia to start marijuana eradication campaign

U.S. Army and Transportation Department initiate drug testing programs

United Nations General Assembly adopts Declaration on the Control of Trafficking and Drug Abuse

Quito Declaration Against Traffic in Narcotics Drugs made

United States creates drug courts

Oliver North establishes "The Enterprise"

Spanish police arrest Medellin Cartel drug lord Jorge Luis Ochoa

Dr. Snow (Larry Lavin) indicted but flees to Virginia

1985

DEA agent Enrique Camarena Salazar murdered in Mexico

Paul Castellano, godfather of the Italian American Mafia Gambino family, indicted, indicating weakening of power of Italian American Mafia

Miami Rivers scandal uncovered

John Gotti assumes control of the Italian American Mafia Gambino family

U.S. Department of Justice creates National Assets Seizure and Forfeiture Fund

U.S. Senate approves bill requiring random drug testing of airline pilots

Nancy Reagan starts "Just Say No" campaign

Drug Abuse Control Amendments of 1985 passed

Colombian guerrillas attack Palace of Justice in Bogotá

Drug Ecstasy made illegal in United States

1986

Operation Blast Furnace launched in Bolivia

Maxi Trial in Italy held

U.S. authorities capture Dr. Snow

Attempted assassination of Enrique Parejo Gonzalez, Colombian ambassador to Hungary

U.S. government launches Operation Snow Cap, Operation Caribbean Cruise, and Operation Alliance

U.S. Congress passes Drug Free America Act

United States begins investigating BCCI for possible money-laundering ties to Colombian drug traffickers

United States launches Operation C-Chase, Operation Screaming Eagle, and Operation Jalisco

President Ronald Reagan signs National Security Directive Number 221

U.S. government launches Operation Blue Fire along U.S.-Mexican border

Spain extradites Jorge Luis Ochoa Vasquez to Colombia

Operation Alliance launched along the United States' southwest border

President's Commission on Organized Crime issues report, which reveals the nature and wide extent of drug trafficking in the United States

Drug Policy Foundation founded in Washington, D.C.

Barry Alderman Seale murdered

U.S. Congress passes Controlled Substance Analogue Act of 1986 and Comprehensive Methamphetamine Control Act

Ochoa brothers, members of Medellin Cartel, indicted in United States for conspiring to bring cocaine into country

City of Washington, D.C. launches Operation Clean Sweep

Colombian newspaper editor Guillermo Cano Isaza murdered

U.S. Congress passes Money Laundry Control Act of 1986

U.S. Congress passes Anti-Drug Abuse Act

Organization of American States ratifies Hemisphere Anti-Drug Plan

Jaime Ramirez Gomez, head of Narcotics Unit of Colombian National Police, assassinated

Ronald Reagan calls for "Zero Tolerance" towards drug use

1987   Carlos Lehder captured in Colombia

U.S. government initiates Drug Use Forecasting (DUF)

DEA creates Operation Calico to go after Cali Cartel

Best Friends antidrug program established in Washington, D.C.

Leading Mexican drug trafficker Pablo Acosta killed by narcotics strike force

United Nations Comprehensive Multidisciplinary Outline (CMO) adopted at international conference

Robert B. Anderson goes to jail

Colombian judge releases Jorge Luis Ochoa from jail

U.S. National Guard and Customs Service launch Operation Autumn Harvest

United Nations holds conference on drug abuse

Jeff Fort, leader of El Rukns, is sent to jail

U.S. Operation Desert Stop culminates

U.S. government establishes Operation Hat Trick

215 members of at least eight separate rings of Chicago-based heroin drug-trafficking syndicate are arrested and many more become fugitives

1988   U.S. launches Operation Rum Punch

Organization of American States (OAS) establishes Inter-American Drug Abuse Commission

Ernesto Fonseca Carrillo indicted for murder of Enrique Camarena Salazar

U.S. Congress passes Chemical Diversion and Trafficking Act of 1988

United States begins High Intensity Drug Trafficking Areas (HIDTA) program

Cuban general Arnaldo Ochoa Sanchez executed by firing squad for drug trafficking

Soviet government relaxes restrictions on travel, and many members of the Russian Mafia go to the United States to establish criminal operations

U.S. Congress passes Anti-Drug Abuse Amendment Act

Seventeen-member drug ring with ties to Medellin Cartel charged with smuggling cocaine to United States via Cuba

New York becomes first U.S. city to use public money to fund needle exchange programs

Reagan administration introduces Zero Tolerance Policy program

Vietnamese gang Born To Kill founded in New York City by David Thai

Fortune magazine names Pablo Escobar one of world's richest men

War breaks out between Medellin and Cali Cartels

U.S. Congress passes Money Laundering Prosecution Improvement Act of 1988

Colombian drug kingpin Carlos Lehder drug trial begins in United States

Bank of Credit and Commerce International (BCCI) indictment made

U.S. Congress passes Chemical Diversion and Trafficking Act

United Nations passes United Nations Convention Against Illicit Traffick in Narcotics Drugs and Psychotropic Substances

Congressional hearings on Asian organized crime held

U.S. Congress passes National Narcotics Leadership Act, which authorizes Office of National Drug Control Policy (ONDLP)

U.S. launches Operation C-Note, money-laundering sting operation, in several U.S. cities

United Nations sponsors International Day Against Drug Abuse and Illicit Trafficking

1988
cont.

Basel Declaration signed

United Nations Vienna Convention signed

Drug traffickers murder Colombian attorney general Carlos Mauro Hoyos Jiminez and kidnap Bogotá mayor Andres Arango Pastrana

1989   Colombia presidential candidate Luis Carlos Galan and leading Colombian police official colonel Waldeman Franklin Quintero assassinated

William Bennett appointed first U.S. drug czar

U.S. government issues first National Drug Control Strategy report

Rand's Drug Policy Research Center established

U.S. Congress establishes Financial Crimes Enforcement Network (FINCEN)

DEA launches Operation Snowcap and Operation Polar Cap

Mexican drug trafficker Miguel Angel Felix Gallardo arrested in Guadalajara, Mexico

Bolivian drug trafficker Juan Carlos Lisboa Medgar arrested

Nigerian government creates National Drug Enforcement Agency

Colombia concludes Operation Primavera

U.S. Supreme Court upholds U.S. government's right to demand urine tests of workers in "sensitive" positions

U.S. Kerry Commission report released

George Bush announces first National Drug Control Strategy report

Colombia arrests and extradites to United States Luis Fernando Mejia Palaez, Eduardo Mera Mosquera, Severo Escobar, Eduardo Martinez Romero, Nelson Cuevas Ramirez, Jorge de La Cuesta Marquez, and Manuel Palma

G-7 establishes Financial Action Task Force

Colombian Minister of Justice Monica de Grieff quits and flees Colombia

United States invades Panama and arrests General Manuel Noriega, one-time spy for the United States government, who is accused of being part of international drug-trafficking trade

Medellin Cartel bombs Bogotá-to-Medellin airplane flight, killing all aboard

U.S. Andean Strategy unveiled

U.S. launches Operation Tandem

Soviet Union withdraws from Afghanistan; Afghan guerrillas subsequently became a more powerful part of international drug trade

Group of Seven (G-7) Economic Summit meets in Paris and establishes Financial Action Task Force

European Committee to Combat Drugs organized

1990   Operation Green Sweep launched

Cartagena Summit held

United Nations Decade Against Drug Abuse (1991–2000) proclaimed by United Nations

U.S. Food and Drug Administration (FDA) bans sales of GHB

U.S. government indicts several BCCI bankers and dozens of individuals on drug-trafficking and money-laundering charges

United Nations International Drug Control Program established

Raymond Bonner appointed head of DEA

President Bush signs Andean Trade Preference Act into law

National Institute on Drug Abuse initiates Drug Abuse Treatment Outcome Study (DATOS)

City councillors of nine European cities sign Frankfurt Resolution

DEA sting implicates Washington, D.C., Mayor Marion Barry in crack cocaine case

Edgar Garcia, so-called "accountant" of Cali Cartel leader Jose Santacruz Londono, arrested in Luxembourg

Operation Green Sweep launched

United Nations General Assembly adopts Political Declaration and Global Program of Action

1991   Soviet Union collapses and Russian Mafia becomes a more powerful force in the international drug trade

Mexican drug trafficker Baltazar Diaz Vega arrested

Fabio, Jorge Luis, and Juan David Ochoa surrender to Colombian authorities

European Cities on Drug Policy formed

Bob Martinez appointed U.S. drug czar

Declaration on Enhanced Regional Cooperation for Drug Abuse Control in Asia and Pacific

Eight countries join together to seize assets of BCCI

Drug traffickers murder Enrique Low Murtra, Colombia's former justice minister

Dennis Peron founds Cannabis Buyer's Club in San Francisco

U.S. government establishes Counter Drug Technology Assessment Center

Operation Cornerstone launched

Dr. Lester Grinspoon publishes *Marijuana Reconsidered*

1992 Giovanne Falcone, crusading prosecutor of Mafia members, is murdered by Italian Mafia

National Inhalant Prevention Coalition founded

Former Panamanian dictator Manuel Noriega convicted in U.S. court and sentenced to forty years in prison

Colombian drug trafficker Ivan Urdinola Grajales arrested

Officials of American Express Bank are indicted in money-laundering case

U.S. government's Pulse Check first conducted

Fund of United Nations International Drug Control Program established

Federal prosecutors in Miami consider indicting entire Cuban government as criminal enterprise

Sixty youths in United States die from sniffing inhalants

Twenty-six members of Philadelphia-based gang, Junior Black Mafia, sent to jail

Operation Thai-In culminates in arrest of Brian Daniels

Italian Government launches Operation Clean Hand

North American Free Trade Association (NAFTA) formed

U.S. Congress passes Domestic Chemical Diversion Control Act

U.S. Government launches Operation Green Ice II

President Bill Clinton appoints Dr. Joycelyn Elders as surgeon general of United States, and her statements about the War on Drugs become controversial

Surveys show an estimated 17 million Americans smoke marijuana

Lee Brown appointed U.S. drug czar

Cardinal Juan Jesus Posada Ocampo shot and killed in Guadalajara, Mexico

Pablo Escobar killed

Sammy Gravano testifies against Italian American Mafia godfather John Gotti

European Union established

Raymond Bonner resigns as head of DEA

1994 United States decertifies Nigeria as helpful partner in War on Drugs

European Commission adopts European Action Plan on drugs for period 1995 to 1999

Dr. Joycelyn Elders, U.S. surgeon general, is fired

Bureau of International Narcotics Matters becomes Bureau of International Narcotics and Law Enforcement Affairs

U.S. FBI Director Louis Freeh signs agreement in Moscow with Russian government to fight Russian-based organized crime

Mexican presidential candidate Luis Donaldo Murrietta assassinated

Marion Barry elected mayor of Washington, D.C., for the second time

Lindesmith Center founded

Operation Dinero and Operation Blue Thunder launched

Summit of Americas conference held in Buenos Aires

U.S. Congress passes Violent Crime Control and Law Enforcement Act of 1994

Summit of Americas meeting in Miami, Florida

Gilbert Taboada testified before U.S. Congress

U.S. Congress enacts Violent Crime Control and Law Enforcement Act, which reauthorizes Office of National Drug Control Policy

Thomas Constantine appointed head of DEA

U.S. prisoners in state and federal prisons top one million

Colombian President Ernesto Samper Pizano presidential campaign accused of accepting money from Cali Cartel

1995 U.S. decertifies Colombia as a helpful partner in the War on Drugs

1995
cont.

International Law Enforcement Academy (ILEA) established in Budapest

U.S. authorities seize 650 pounds of methamphetamine in Las Cruces, New Mexico, believed to belong to Juarez Cartel.

Fifteen countries ratify three conventions: European Convention on Drug Trafficking, Illegal Immigration, Vehicle Crime and Traffic in Human Beings; Convention on Protection of Financial Interests of Community; and Customs Information Systems Convention

Guillermo "Reagan" Palomari, Cali Cartel accountant, flees to United States

Henry Loaiza Cebellos, Cali Cartel leader, surrenders to Colombian authorities in Bogotá

U.S. Senator Orrin Hatch releases report, *Losing Ground Against Drugs*

DEA begins assigning METs to its divisions across United States

Authorities bust $100 million New York City-based money-laundering operation that includes Harvey Weinig, Robert Hirsch, and Richard Spence.

Atlanta Agreement announced

Colombian authorities capture Gilberto Rodriguez Orejuela

U.S. Supreme Court upholds legality of drug testing of student athletes in public schools

Colombian drug lord Jose Santacruz Londono captured

Summit of Americas Ministerial Conference on Money Laundering held

1996

Khun Sa, Burmese war lord and drug trafficker, surrenders to Burmese authorities

Mexican drug trafficker Juan Garcia Abrego arrested and deported to United States for trial, where he is convicted of drug-trafficking charges and sentenced to life in prison

Timothy Leary dies

Colombia decertified by United States for second straight year

Colombia passes assets forfeiture law

Gilberto Rodriguez Orejuela confesses to authorities his involvement in narcotics trade and agrees to pay $105 million fine

San Jose Mercury News publishes Gary Webb's investigative series of articles on CIA, Contras, and crack cocaine epidemic in Los Angeles

Barry McCaffrey appointed U.S. drug czar

Adrian Carrera Fuentes sentenced to jail

Helmer Pacho Herrera, major figure in Cali Cartel, turns himself in to Colombian authorities

Orlando Sanchez, so-called Overalls Man, attempts to kill son of Cali Cartel leader Miguel Rodriguez Orejuela

U.S. Supreme Court upholds constitutionality of forfeiture laws

Colombian drug trafficker Efrain Hernandez Ramirez killed

Cannabis Buyer's Club in San Francisco closed

Cuban government sentences U.S. fugitive Robert Vesco to jail in absentia

University of Michigan survey shows marijuana use among young people rising

Colombian police kill Jose Santacruz Londono

U.S. government launches Operation Global Sea

Colombian drug lord Helmer "Pacho" Herrera arrested

Arizona and California vote to ease restrictions on medical use of marijuana

1997

Great Britain returns Hong Kong to People's Republic of China

Two U.S. congressional panels conduct hearings on drug-related corruption along U.S. border

Former Mexican deputy attorney general Mario Ruiz Messieu found guilty

Swiss authorities reveal drug-related investigation of Raul Salinas de Gortari

Top Mexican antidrug official Jesus Guiterrez Rebello arrested

Jesus Blancornelas, prominent Mexican newpaper editor and critic of Mexican drug traffickers, murdered

United States and European Union sign Chemical Precursor Agreement

U.S. Southern Command is transferred from Panama to location outside Miami area

Mariano Salvetti Herran appointed to head Mexican National Institute to Combat Drugs

United States and Venezuela form Strategic Alliance Against Drugs

Colombian drug kingpin Jose Orlando Henao Montoya surrenders to Colombian authorities

William Weld withdraws his nomination for post of U.S. ambassador to Mexico

Colombian judge releases drug trafficker Ivan Urinola Grazales from jail

Ten members of Diablos motorcyle gang indicted on various charges, including drug trafficking

Operation Desert Stop, U.S. government initiative, culminates in several arrests and seizures of drugs

U.S. law enforcement launches Operation Reciprocity and Operation Limelight

U.S. and Colombia sign antidrug maritime agreement

Members of Outlaw motorcycle gang indicted on drug-trafficking charges

Colombian drug kingpin Pastor Perafan captured in Venezuela and extradited to United States

Group of Rio denounces U.S. certification program

Connecticut consideres revision of its state antidrug laws

Allen Ginsberg dies

DEA reports that ketamine use is increasing in United States

Comedian Chris Farley dies of drug abuse

1998   Researchers claim drug buprenorphine as breakthrough in treatment of heroin addiction

Members of San Diego-based street gang indicted in 1994 murder of Juan Jesus Posada Ocampo

Jesus Gutierrez Rebello found guilty of corruption and sent to jail

Jose Nelson Urrego and Alberto Orlandez Gamboa, Cali Cartel leaders, are arrested

DEA announces successful completion of Operation Casablanca

Jeffrey Davidow appointed U.S. ambassador to Mexico

U.S. grand jury indicts Jorge Castro, high-ranking member of Mexican Arellano-Felix drug-trafficking organization

World Press Review magazine selects Mexican newspaper editor Jesus Blancornelas as "Editor of the Year"

Andres Pastrana Arango wins Colombian presidential election, ending the controversial four-year term of Ernesto Samper Pizano, who is accused of corruption and collaboration with Cali Cartel

Clinton administration launches National Youth Media Campaign as part of antidrug strategy

Victor Patino-Fomeque, Cali Cartel leader, sentenced to eighteen years in jail in Colombia for drug trafficking

Justo Pastor Perafan found guilty in U.S. court of drug-trafficking charges

Declaration of European Cities on Drug Policy passed

Drug trafficker Fernando Jose Flores captured

U.S. federal court closes down Oakland Cannabis Buyer's Cooperative, and Oakland city council votes to allow city officials to develop other means of selling marijuana

Helmer Pacho Herrera, major figure in Cali Cartel, murdered in prison

Europol officially opens

Incoming Colombian president Andres Arango Pastrana establishes antidrug office headed by "drug czar"

Marion Barry announces he won't run for another term as mayor of Washington, D.C.

United Nations AIDS conference urges that needle exchange programs worldwide be increased to halt rising spread of AIDS virus through illicit drug injections

Switzerland holds referendum on legalization of drugs

Alberto Giraldo, key figure in Colombia's "narco-cassette" scandal goes to jail

Selected Websites

Advocacy

American Civil Liberties Union (ACLU)
http://www.aclu.org

American Council on Drug Education
http://www.acde.org/

Asset Forfeiture
http://www.fear.org/

Common Sense for Drug Policy
http://www.csdp.org/

Cops Against the Drug War
http://www.drcnet.org/cops.cops.html/

Drug Abuse Resistance Education (DARE)
http://www.dare-america.com/

Drug Watch International(DWI)
http://www.drugwatch.org/

Harm Reduction Coalition (HRC)
http://www.harmreduction.org/

Join Together
http://www.jointogether.org/

Lindesmith Institute
http://www.lindesmith.org/

Marijuana Policy Project(MPP)
http://www.mpp.org/

National Association of Methadone Advocates
http://www.methadone.org/

National Center on Addiction and Substance Abuse
http://www.casacolumbia.org/

National Families in Action
http://www.emory.edu/NFIA/

National Inhalant Prevention Coalition (U.S.)
http://www.inhalants.org/

National Organization for the Reform of Marijuana Laws
http://www.norml.org/

North American Syringe Movement
http://www.nasen.org/

Parent Resource Institute for Drug Education (PRIDE)
http://www.prideusa.org/

Partnership for a Drugfree America
http://www.drugfreeamerica.org/

Partnership for Responsible Drug Information
http://www.prdi.org/

Human Rights

Amnesty International
http://www.amnesty.com/

Colombia Support Network
http://igc.apc.org/csn/

Human Rights Watch's Drugs and Human Rights Project
http://www.hrw.org

Washington Office on Latin America
http://www.wola.org/

International

Europol
http://www.europol.eu.int/home.htm/

Financial Action Taskforce
http://www.oecd.fr/fatf

Interpol
http://193.123.144.14/interpol.com/

Observatoire Geopolitique Des Drogues
http://www.ogd.org/

Organization of American States
http://www.oas.org/

United Nations Office for Drug Control & Crime Prevention
http://www.odccp.org

Libraries

Drug Reform Coordination Network
http://www.drcnet.org/
http://www.druglibrary.org/

Drug Sense
http://www.drugsense.org/

Drugtext Europe
http://www.drugtext.nl/

Schaffer Drug Library
http://druglibrary.org

Stanton Peele Addiction Web Site
http://www.frw.uva.nl/cedro/peele/

Medical Marijuana

Medical Marijuana Magazine
http://www.marijuanamagazine.com/

News Sources

DRCNet Bulletin
http://www.drcnet.org/rapid/

Media Awareness Project
http://www.mapinc.org/

National Drug Strategy Network (NDSN)
http://www.ndsn.org/

United States Information Agency
http://www.usia.gov/

Prisons and Sentencing

Families against Mandatory Minimums
http://www.famm.org/

Federal Judicial Center
http://www.fjc.gov/

November Coalition
http://www.november.org/

United States Sentencing Commission
http://www.ussc.gov/

Professional Associations

National Association of Alcohol and Drug Abuse Counselors
http://www.naadac.org/

National Drug Enforcement Officers Association
http://www.ndeoa.org/

Research and Policy

Addiction Resources Foundation
http://www.arf.org/

Center for Substance Abuse Research
http://www.caesar.umd.edu/

College of Problems of Drug Dependence
http://www.views.ucu.edu.cpdd/

Drug Policy Foundation
http://www.drugpolicy.org/

Drug Strategies
http://www.drugabuseprevention.com/ds/

European Cities on Drug Policy
http://www.ecdp.net/

Multidisciplinary Association for Psychedelic Studies
http://www.maps.org/

National Clearinghouse for Alcohol and Drug Abuse
Information
http://www.health.org/

National Council for Alcohol and Drug Dependence
http://www.ncadd.org/

Partnership for Responsible Drug Information
http://www.prdi.org/

Rand Corporation Drug Policy Research Center
http://www.rand.org/centers/dprc/DPRCpubindex.html/

Robert Wood Johnson Foundation Substance Abuse Policy
Research Program
http://www.rwjf.org/

Sentencing Project
http://www.sproject.com/

Society for Prevention Research
http://www.oslc.org.spr/

UCLA Drug Abuse Research Center
http://www.medsch.ucla.edu/som/npi/DARC/

Web of Addictions
http://www.well.com/user/woa/

Treatment and Self-Help

Cocaine Anonymous
http://www.ca.org/

Narcotics Anonymous
http://www.wsoinc.com/

Phoenix House
http://www.phoenixhouse.org/

Project Craft
http://www.unmi.edu/~craft

United States Government

See also Federal Judicial Center, the United States Sentencing
Commission, and the United States Information Agency

Agency for International Development
http://www.info.usaid.gov/

Border Patrol
http://www.usbp.com/

Central Intelligence Agency (CIA)
http://www.odci.gov.cia/

Coast Guard
http://www.uscg.mil/hello.html

Customs Department
http://www.customs.ustreas.gov/

Department of Justice
http://www.usdoj.gov/

Department of Labor
http://www.dol.gov

Substance Abuse Information Database (SAID)
http://www.dol.gov/dol/asp/public/programs/drugs/said.ht
m

Working Partners Program
http://www.dol.gov/dol/asp/public/programs/drugs/working
partners/main.htm

Department of State
http://www.state.gov/

Drug Abuse Epidemiology Center
http://www.nida.gov/

Drug Abuse Treatment Outcome Study
http://www.datos.org

Drug Abuse Warning Network
http://www.health.org/pubs/93DAWN

Drug Enforcement Administration (DEA)
http://www.usdoj.gov/dea

Federal Bureau of Investigation (FBI)
http://www.fbi.gov/

Food and Drug Administration
http://www.fda.gov/

General Accounting Office
http://www.gao.gov/

Marshals Service
http://www.usdoj.gov/marshals/

National Criminal Justice Reference Service
http://www.ncjrs.org/

National Institute on Drug Abuse
http://www.nida.nih.gov/

National Inter-Agency Civil-Military Institute
http://www.nici.org/

Office of National Drug Control Policy (ONDCP)
http://www.whitehouse.drug.policy.gov/

Bibliography

Abadinsky, Howard. *Organized Crime*. Chicago: Nelson-Hall, 1990.

ABC News. "America's War on Drugs—Searching for Solutions." 7 April 1995. Denver: Journal Graphics (transcript).

Abel, Ernst L. *Marijuana, the First Twelve Thousand Years*. New York: Plenum Press, c. 1980.

———. *A Dictionary of Drug Abuse Terms and Terminology*. Westport, CT: Greenwood Press, 1994.

Abrams, Elliott. "Drug Wars: The New Alliance against Traffickers and Terrorists." *Department of State Bulletin* (April 1986): 89–92.

Abrams, Jim. "U.S. Drug Czar Defends Mexico Certification." *Miami Herald*, 4 March 1997, international satellite edition.

Adams, James. *The Financing of Terror*. New York: Simon and Schuster, 1986.

Adams, James Ring. "Losing the Drug War." *American Spectator* (September 1988): 20–24.

———.. "Medellin's New Generation." *American Spectator* (December 1991): 22.

AFP. "Los Drugs Ganan Terreno en Europa" (Drugs Gain ground in Europe). *El Tiempo* (Bogota, Colombia), 9 October 1996.

Agency for International Development and the Foundation for Higher Education. *Justice Sector Reform Program*. Bogota, Colombia: Agency for International Development, 1996.

Albini, Joseph. *The American Mafia: Genesis of a Legend*. New York: Appleton-Century-Crofts, 1971.

Albor, Teresa. "Burma's Heroin Trade Picks Up Despite U.S. Isolation Policy." *Christian Science Monitor*, 29 July 1992.

Alexander, Bruce K. "Alternatives to the War on Drugs." *Journal of Drug Issues* (Winter 1990): 1–27.

"Alleged Drug Boss Captured in Colombia." *Charlotte Observer*, 8 June 1998, 6A.

Alzate, Jorge Cardona. "Catarsis de una Epidemia" (Catharsis of an Epidemic). *El Espectador* (Bogota, Colombia), 20 October 1996.

"Amado Carrillo Fuentes: El Pablo Escobar de Mexico" (The Pablo Escobar of Mexico). *El Tiempo* (Bogota, Colombia), 20 February 1997.

Ambrus, Stephen. "Pablo Escobar Dies in Shootout." *Los Angeles Times*, 3 December 1993.

Amburn, Ellis. *Pearl: The Obsessions and Passions of Janis Joplin: A Biography*. New York: Warner, 1992.

"American Express Unit Found Officially Guilty in U.S. Case." *Wall Street Journal*, 3 June 1994.

"The Annals of Permanent War." *U.S. News and World Report*, 28 August 1989, 21.

Anastasia, George. "That Last Civil War." *Playboy*, September 1994, 66–68.

"Andean Trade Pact of 1991." *U.S. News and World Report*, 2 March 1992, 166.

Andelman, David A. "The Drug Money Maze." *Foreign Affairs* (July 1994): 94–108.

Anderson, Helmer. "Alleged Colombian Launderer Captured." United Press International, 1 November 1989.

Anderson, John Ward. "Mexican Cartels Diversify: Drug Dealers Cornering U.S. Speed Market." *Washington Post*, 12 August 1996.

Anderson, Malcolm, and Monica De Boer. *Policing the European Union*. Oxford: Clarendon Press, 1995.

Anderson, Patrick. *High in America: The True Story behind NORML and the Politics of Marijuana*. New York: Viking Press, 1981.

Annas, George J. "Reefer Madness: The Federal Response to California's Medical Marijuana Law." *The New England Journal of Medicine*, 7 August 1997, 435 (5pp.).

Anslinger, Harold Jacob. *The Protectors*. New York: Farrar, Straus, 1964.

Anslinger, Harold Jacob, and W. F. Tomkins. *The Traffic in Narcotics*. New York: Funk and Wagnalls, 1953.

Anslinger, Harold Jacob, and Will Oursler. *The Murderers: The Story of the Narcotics Gangs*. New York: Farrar, Straus and Culahy, 1964.

"Antigua and Barbados Combat Drug Trafficking." *Americas* (March 1996): 52–53.

Arana, Ana. "El Pablo Escobar de Mexico" (The Pablo Escobar of Mexico). *El Tiempo* (Bogota, Colombia), 20 October 1996.

———. "Saul Sanchez Sabia Demasiado" (Saul Sanchez Knew Too Much). *El Tiempo* (Bogota, Colombia), 22 October 1996.

Arlacchi, Pino. *Mafia Business: The Mafia Ethic and the Spirit of Capitalism*. New York: Verso, 1987.

———. *Men of Dishonor: Inside the Sicilian Mafia: An Account of Antonio Calderone*. New York: William Morrow, 1993.

Aronson, Bernard W. "Andean Trade Preference Pact: Essential to Combating Narcotics Traffic." *U.S. Department of State Dispatch*, 5 August 1991, 584–586.

"Asesinado Narco Alias 'Don Efra'" (A Narco Alias "Don Efra"). *El Espectador* (Bogota, Colombia), 7 November 1996.

"Asi Se Cayo El Ministro De Defensa." *El Tiempo* (Bogota, Colombia), 18 March 1997, 8A.

"Asian Gangs Move into Drugs." *Newsday* 29 September 1987.

Assad, Hafex Al, and Charles R. Schwab. "Syria." *Wall Street Journal*, 23 November 1992.

"Associate Director H. L. Giordano Retires as Head of U.S. Narcotics Bureau." *New York Times*, 1 March 1969.

Auld, John. *Marijuana Use and Social Control*. New York: Academic Press, 1981.

"Bacchus Asked Why ExProsecutor Not Charged." *Miami Herald*, 22 March 1997, International Satellite edition.

Bacon, Donald C., Roger H. Davidson, and Morton Keller. *The Encyclopedia of the United States Congress*. New York: Simon and Schuster, c. 1995.

Badey, James R. "Federal Coordination Is Needed To Head Off Growing Threat from Vietnamese Criminals." *Organized Crime Digest*, 11 March 1967, 1–6.

Baer, Donald. "A Judge Who Took a Stand." *U.S. News and World Report*. 9 April 1990, p. 26 (2pp.).

Bagley, Bruce. "The New Hundred Years War? U.S. National Security and the War on Drugs." *Journal of Interamerican Studies and World Affairs* (Spring 1988): 164+.

———. "U.S. Foreign Policy and the War on Drugs: An Analysis of Policy Failure." *Journal of Interamerican Studies And World Affairs* (Summer/Fall 1988): 189–212.

———. "Dateline Drug Wars: Colombia: The Wrong Strategy." *Foreign Policy* (Winter 1989–1990): 54+.

Bagley, Bruce, and William O. Walker, III. "Special Issue: Drug Trafficking Research Update." *Journal of Interamerican Studies and World Affairs* (Fall 1992): 35+.

———. *Drug Trafficking in the Americas*. New Brunswick, NJ: Transaction, 1994.

Bajak, Frank. "Colombian Drug Lord Is Slain." *Charlotte Observer*, 6 November 1998.

Bak, David J., and Robert C. Fourier. "New Weapons in the War on Drugs." *Design News*, 4 September 1989, 117+.

Bake, Allan. "Drugged to the Eyeballs." *New African* (June 1995): 16–19.

Baker, James. "Narcotics: Threat to Global Security." *U.S. Department of State Dispatch*, 3 September 1990, 15.

Bandow, Doug. "Perverse Effects of the War on Drugs." *New York Times*, 23 August 1992.

Banerjee, Neela. "Russian Organized Crime Goes Global." *Wall Street Journal*, 2 December 1994.

"Banker Pleads Innocent to Laundering Charges." *Wall Street Journal*, 17 January 1994.

"Barry R. McCaffrey." *Current Biography* (July 1997): 31 (4pp.).

Bastone, William. "The Mob Is Dead! Long Live the Mob!" *Village Voice*, 21 September 1993, 25–32.

Baum, Dan. "The War on Civil Liberties." *Nation*, 29 June 1992, 886–888.

———. *Smoke and Mirrors: The War on Drugs and the Politics of Failure*. Boston: Little and Brown, 1996.

Bayona Vargas, Mauricio. "Clinton Reparte Los Dolores." *El Espectador* (Bogota, Colombia), 25 September 1996.

Beasley, James O. "Forensic Examination of Money-Laundering Records." *FBI Enforcement Bulletin* (March 1993): 13–17.

Beaty, Jonathan, and Richard Hornick. "A Torrent of Dirty Dollars." *Time*, 18 December 1989, 50+.

Beaty, Jonathan, and S. C. Gwynne. "Too Many Questions." *Time*, 11 November 1991, 42+.

Bedford, Sybil. *Aldous Huxley: A Biography*. New York: Random House, 1974.

Behr, Elwood. *Prohibition*. New York: Arcata Publishing, 1997.

Bennett, William. *The Devaluing of America*. New York: Summit Books, 1992.

Bensinger, Peter B. "World Drug Traffic." *Society* (May-June 1982): 78–79.

Bentsen, Lloyd. "National Can Pull Plug on Money Laundering." *USA Today*, 8 December 1994.

Berkeley, Bill. "Dead Right." *Columbian Journalism Review* (March-April 1993, 36+ (9pp.).

Bertram, Eva, Kenneth Sharpe, and Peter Anders. *Drug War Politics: The Price of Denial*. Berkeley, CA: University of California Press, 1996.

Bertram, Eva, and Kenneth Sharpe. "The Drug War's Phony Fix; Why Certification Doesn't Work." *Nation*, 28 April 1997, 18+ (4pp.).

Bierderman, Christine. "The Commandante." *Texas Monthly* (July 1997): 18+ (30pp.).

"Birth of a Narco Democracy." *Time*, 11 April 1994, 19.

"Bishop Brent Dies at 66 in Lausanne." *New York Times*, 28 March 1929.

Blackman, Morris, and Kenneth Sharpe. "The War on Drugs: American Democracy under Assault." *World Policy Journal* (Winter 1989): 35+.

Blair, Doniphan. "Drug War Delusions, Unrealistic, Unfeasible and Logistical Nightmare." *Humanist* (September-October 1990): 7+.

Blakesley, Christopher L. *Terrorism, Drugs, International Law and the Protection of Human Liberty*. New Brunswick, NJ: Transactional Press, 1992.

Blum, Kenneth. *Handbook of Abusable Drugs*. New York: Gardner Press, 1984.

Blumenthal, Ralph. "How Tapes and Turncoat Helped Win the War Against Gotti." *New York Times*, 5 April 1992.

———. *Last Days of the Sicilians*. New York: Pocket Books, 1989.

Bolgar, Catherine. "Colombian Drug Money Distortion." *Wall Street Journal*, 25 March 1994.

"Bolivian 'Fat Fish' Cocaine Trafficker Freed." United Press International, 9 December 1989.

Bonner Richard J., and Charles H. Whitehead, II. *The Marijuana Conviction: A History of Marijuana Prohibition in the United States*. Charlottesville, VA: University Press of Virginia, 1974.

Booth, William. "Drug War Locks Up Prisons." *Washington Post*, 7 July 1993.

Boudreaux, Richard. "Russian Police Back Plan for Joint Anti-Mob Effort." *Los Angeles Times*, 5 July 1994.

Boutros-Ghali, Boutros. "Transnational Crime: The Market and the Rule of Law." *Vital Speeches*, 15 December 1991, 130.

Bowden, Mark. *Doctor Dealer*. New York: Warner Books, 1987.

Boyce, Daniel. "Narco Terrorism." *FBI Law Enforcement Bulletin* (October 1987): 1–32.

Boyum, David. "No: Swift and Sure Sanctions Work Better." *Insight on the News*, 12 June 1995, 19.

Branigan, William. "Sting Snares Asian Drug Ring, but Mass Heroin Flows to U.S." *Washington Post*, 12 December 1993.

Brant, Martha. "Most Wanted Kingpin?" *Newsweek*, 10 March 1997, 12.

Brauchli, Marcus W. "Pakistan's Wild Frontier Breeds Trouble." *Wall Street Journal*, 3 June 1993.

Brecher, Edwin M. *Licit and Illicit Drugs: The Consumers Union Report on Narcotics, Stimulants, Depressants, or Inhalants, Hallucinogens, and Marijuana—Including Coffee, Nicotine and Alcohol*. Boston: Little and Brown, 1972.

Brianchon, Pierre. "Russian Mob Scene." *World Press Review* (October 1995): 28–29.

Briscoe, David. "Senators Won't Seek Mexico Vote." *Miami Herald*, 15 March 1997, International Satellite edition.

Bromfield, Richard. "Is Ritalin Overprescribed for Behavior?" *Washington Times*, 3 December 1996.

Brooke, James. "Strong Drug Foe Wins in Colombia By Wide Margin." *New York Times*, 28 May 1990.

———. "Gaviria's Gamble." *New York Times*, 13 October 1991.

———. "Crackdown Has Cali Drug Cartel on the Run." *New York Times*, 27 June 1995, 1.

Brookes, Stephen. "Drug Money Soils Clean Hands." *Insight on the News*, 21 August 1989, 8.

Brown, Claude. *Manchild in a Promised Land*. New York: Simon and Schuster, 1990.

Bugliosi, Vincent. *Drugs in America*. 1995.

Burgess, Harvey. "Drug Ring Suspected in Double Slaying." *Rock Hill (S.C.) Herald*, 6 June 1991.

Burks, John. "Hendrix: An Appreciation." *Rolling Stone*, 15 October 1970, 8.

Burnstein, P. "The Deadly Politics of Heroin." *MacLeans*, 6 December 1992, 10.

Buruma, Ian, and John McBeth. "Asia's Crime Syndicates." *World Press Review* (March 1985): 55+.

Butturini, Paula. "Italy Slowly Breaking Mafia's Iron Grip." *Boston Globe*, 16 January 1994.

Byrne, John J. "How the Feds Beat the Money Launderers." *ABA Banking Journal* (January 1995): 55–56.

"Cae Capo de la Mafia Colombo Italiano" (Godfather of Colombo Italian Mafia Captured). *El Espectador* (Bogota, Colombia), 8 February 1997.

"Cali Mafia." *DEA Drug World* (March-April 1996): 6–9.

"Cali Quiere Jubilarse" (Cali Wants to Retire). *La Semina* (11 May 1993, 44–47.

Califano, Joseph A. "Legalization of Narcotics: Myths and Reality." *USA Today* Magazine, 1997.

Cannon, Angie. "Is Drug War DARE Worth Teaching?" *Charlotte Observer*, 30 September 1997 (March 1997): 46+ (2pp.).

Cannon, Angie, Vanessa Gallman, and Steven Thomma. "Surgeon General Jocelyn Elders Is Fired after Remarks on Masturbation." Knight-Ridder/Tribune News Service, 9 December 1994.

Carey, Donald J., and H. Indelicarto. "Indications and Warnings and the New World Environment: The Drug War Example." *Defense Intelligence* (Spring 1994): 89–105.

Carrigan, Ana. *The Place of Justice: A Colombian Tragedy*. New York: Four Walls Press, 1993.

———. "Victims of the Dirty War." *The Progressive* (November 1996): 39–41.

Carter, Hodding III. "Day of the Triads." *M INC.* (June 1991): 68+.

Carter, Mark R. "How To Win the Drug War Quickly." *Wall Street Journal*, 2 December 1992.

"Cash at Any Price." *Economist*, 9 May 1992, 100.

Casper, Juliet M. Review of *Organized Crime in America*, by Dennis Jay Kennedy and James O. Finkenauer. *Journal of Criminal Law and Criminology* (Winter 1995): 837.

Cassata, Donna. "Helms Lashes Back at Critics, Holds Firm on Blocking Weld." *Congressional Quarterly Weekly Report*, 20 September 1997, 2,240.

Cassidy, Peter. "The Banker Who Said No to the CIA." *Progressive* (June 1992): 24+.

Castillo, Fabio. *Los Jinetes de la Cocaina* (The jockeys of cocaine). Bogotá, Colombia: Documentos Periodisticos, 1988.

Castro, Janice. "The Cash Cleaners: A Major Bank Is Indicted in Running a Global Drug-Money Network." *Time*, 24 October 1988, 65.

———. "A Worrisome Brand of Japanese Investor." *Time*, 20 April 1992, 21.

Cavalier Castro, Andre. "Droga: Debate Artificiel in E.U." (Drugs: Artificial Debate in the United States). *El Tiempo* (Bogota, Colombia), 14 September 1996.

"Cayo El Dueno de las Tonnelades de Coca." (The Owner of Tons of Cocaine Captured) *El Tiempo* (Bogota, Colombia), 15 December 1998.

Center for Strategic and International Studies. *The Transnational Drug Challenge*. Washington, DC: Center for Strategic and International Studies, 1993.

"Change in Colombia." *MacLean's*, 6 July 1998, 35.

"Change in Swiss Bank Laws." *New York Times*, 3 March 1994.

Chapman, Stephen. "The Awful Price of Fighting the War on Drugs." *Chicago Tribune*, 21 May 1992.

———. "A Weapon of the Drug War Provokes Growing Disgust." *Chicago Tribune*, 1 July 1993.

"The Charms of Coca." *Economist*, 28 October 1995, 52.

Chauvin, Lucien. "Bolivian Farmers Open Markets to Show Coca Is Not a Drug Problem." *National Catholic Reporter*, 26 March 1993, 15.

Chepesiuk, Ron. *Hard Target: The U.S.'s War with International Drug Trafficking*. Jefferson, NC: McFarland Publishing, 1999.

———. "Colombian Connection: Country Battles Drug Mafia's Vicious Terror." *Charlotte Observer*, 14 June 1987.

———. "Kingpin's Trial: A Small Win in Losing War on Drugs." *Orlando Sentinel*, 4 October 1987.

———. "Colombia's Cocaine Convulsion." *New Leader* 27 June 1988, 11–14.

———. "Colombian Drug Lords Try to Turn Wealth into Respect." *Orlando Sentinel*, 10 March 1989.

———. "Colombia: A Nation Descends into Anarchy as Drug-Fueled Violence Escalates." *Defense and Diplomacy* (September 1989) 1D+.

———. "The War on Drugs: A Latin American Perspective." *Defense and Diplomacy* (September 1989): 48–51.

———. "A Country under Siege: Fighting Anarchy in Colombia." *New Leader*, 18 September 1989, 5–8.

———. "To Live and Die in Colombia." *St. Petersburg Times*, 24 September 1989.

———. "Tales of the Drug Wars." *Creative Loafing*, 11 November 1989, 1–2.

———. "Colombian Drug Lords Try to Buy Legitimacy." *Orlando Sentinel*, 18 March 1990.

———. "Undermining Democracy: Drug Lords versus the Press." *New Leader*, 30 April 1990, 9–10.

———. "Colombia under Siege." *Defense and Diplomacy* (September 1990): 41–45.

———. "America's Other War." *Creative Loafing*, 16 March 1991, 1.

———. "Colombia's Better-Run Kingdom." *Orlando Sentinel*, 7 February 1994.

———. *Sixties Radicals, Then and Now: Candid Conversations with Those Who Shaped an Era*. Jefferson, NC: McFarland Publishing, 1995.

———. "Colombia's Guerrillas Cultivate a Different Kind of Power Base." *Orlando Sentinel*, 26 January 1996.

———. "War on Drugs: A Government Sham." *Rock Hill (S.C.) Herald*, 21 December 1996.

———. "A War of Attrition: Narco-Paralysis in Colombia." *New Leader*, 13–27 January 1997, 6–7.

———. "Are CIA's Hands Clean on Drugs?" *Rock Hill (S.C.) Herald*, 30 January 1997.

———. "The New Drug Threat in Colombia." *Rock Hill (S.C.) Herald*, 15 March 1997.

———. "Colombian Press under Siege." *Editor and Publisher*, 11 May 1997, 10.

———. "Mr. Clean Goes to Bogota." *Bostonia* (Fall 1997): 26–27.

———. "Guilty by Association?" *Student Lawyer*, 1997.

———. "Guerrillas in the Midst." *National Review*, 1 September 1998, 27.

Chin, Ko-lin. "Triad Societies, Tongs, Organized Crime and Street Gangs in Asia and the United States." Unpublished Ph.D. dissertation, University of Pennsylvania, 1986.

———. *Chinese Subculture and Criminality*. Westport, CT: Greenwood Press, 1990.

"Chinese Triads Pushing the Mafia Aside: Focusing on Heroin Smuggling, Extortion." *Organized Crime Digest*, 9 August 1989, 3–4.

Christensen, Mike. "FBI May Help Russia Fight Cocaine Wave." *Atlanta Journal* and *Atlanta Constitution*, 28 May 1994.

Clawson, Patrick, and Rensselaer Lee, III. *The Andean Cocaine Industry*. New York: St. Martin's Press, 1996.

"Clinton Pressured to Decertify Mexico after Drug Arrest." *USA Today*, 28 February 1997.

"Closing in on Salinas." *MacLean's*, 23 March 1998, 37.

Cloud, John. "Is Your Kid on K?" *Time*, 20 October 1997, 9 (2pp.).

———. "A Way Out For Junkies." *Time*, 19 January 1998, 59.

"CMA Defends Industry on Drug Charges." *Chemical Marketing Reporter*, 12 February 1990, 3.

"Cocaine Extradition." Associated Press, 6 December 1989.

Cody, Edward. "Sunfish Avoid a Net Set by Boss." *Washington Post*, 16 October 1982.

Cohen, Laurie, and Kenneth H. Bacon. "Banker at American Express Affiliate Faces Money-Laundering Investigation." *Wall Street Journal*, 8 November 1993.

Cole, Richard. "Asian Gangs a Rising Threat." *Chicago Tribune*, 6 July 1994.

———. "Kurdish Group Reportedly Uses Heroin to Finance Terrorism." *Miami Herald*, 17 December 1998, International Satellite edition.

Coleman, Bill, and Patty Coleman. "Church Queried in Mexican Murder Probe." *National Catholic Reporter*, 31 March 1995, 12.

Coleman, Joseph. "Colombia Extradites Two More." United Press International, 18 November 1989.

———. "Police: Slain Bodyguard Was Drug Cartel Leader." Associated Press, 19 December 1989.

Colford, Steven W. "New Surgeon General Backs Condom Ads: Elders Wants TV Networks To Abandon Prohibition." *Advertising Age*, 11 January 1993.

Collette, Merrill. "The Myth of the Narco Guerrilla." *Nation* (August 1988): 130+.

Collier, Robert. "Matta, the Honduran Hero." *St. Petersburg Times*, 10 April 1988.

"Colombia." *Miami Herald*, 17 September 1996, 4.

"Colombia, Still There." *Economist*, 1 June 1996, 41 (2pp.).

Colombian Baron Surrenders under Offer of Lenient Treatment. *New York Times*, 16 January 1991.

"Colombian Drug Kingpin Cleared of Murder Charges." Reuters, 2 October 1997.

"Colombian Drug Lord Extradited to Detroit." United Press International, 15 October 1989.

"Colombian Interior Minister Resigns as Drug War Grows." United Press International, 5 October 1989.

"Colombian Pushing Anti-Drug Plan." *Miami Herald*, 2 December 1996, International Satellite edition.

"Colombian Terror." *Economist*, 30 September 1995, 50–52.

"Colombian Traffickers Enter Heroin Market." *Rock Hill (S.C.) Herald*, 10 December 1990.

"Colombian War Hero, 3 Others Executed by Firing Squad." *Los Angeles Times*, 14 July 1989.

"Colombians Look for a Change." *Economist*, 27 June 1998, 35.

"Colombia's Drug Business." *Economist*, 24 December 1994, 21–24.

"Colombia's Other Gangsters." *Economist*, 25 March 1995, 48.

Concar, David, and Laura Spinney. "The Highs and Lows of Prohibition." *New Scientist*. 1 October 1994, 38 (4pp.).

Conlon, Edward. "Mob Stories." *American Spectator* (November 1992): 78.

Conner, Roger, and L. Burns. "The Winnable Drug War: How Communities Are Eradicating Local Drug Markets." *Brookings Review* (Summer 1992): 26–29.

Constantine, Thomas A. DEA Congressional Testimony Regarding Mexico and the Southwest Border Initiative, 12 March 1997.

———. "Drug Trafficking in Mexico." Statement Before the Senate Committee on Banking, Housing and Urban Affairs, 28 March 1996.

———. "International Organized Crime Syndicates and their Impact on the United States." DEA Congressional Testimony Before the Senate Foreign Relations Committee Subcommittee on Western Hemisphere, Peace Corps, Narcotics and Terrorism, 26 February 1998.

———. "Mexico and the Southwest Border Initiative." Statement Before the Senate Foreign Relations Committee, 12 March 1997.

"Contra Drug Links Broader than CIA Said, Study States." *Rock Hill Herald*, 10 October 1998.

"Converts to Curiosity." *Economist*, 18 November 1989, 33.

"Convicted, Juan Garcia Abrego." *Time*, 28 October 1996, 31.

Cooper, Mary H. *The Business of Drugs*. Washington, DC: *Congressional Quarterly*, 1990.

Cordoba, José de. "Testimony Says President Knew of Contributions by Cali Cartel." *Wall Street Journal*, 4 August 1995.

———. "Ex-General Venezolano: La CIA Aprobo Envio de Cocaina a EE.UU." (CIA Approves Sending Cocaine to the U.S.) *El Tiempo* (Bogota, Colombia), 22 November 1996.

Cormier, Jim. "Booking the Mafia." *Saturday Night* (March 1990): 19+.

Corn, David. "The CIA and the Cocaine Coup." *Nation*, 7 October 1991, 404.

———. "CIA Clears Itself of a Drug Charge." *Nation*, 7 March 1998.

Cotton, Paul. "'Harm Reduction' Approach May be Middle Ground." *Journal of the American Medical Association*, 1 June 1994, 164 (4pp.).

Courtnay, Daniel. "Washing Dirty Money." *Police Chief* (October 1985): 74.

Courtwright, David T. *Dark Paradise: Opiate Addiction in America before 1940*. Cambridge, MA: Harvard University Press, 1982.

———. "Should We Legalize Drugs? History Answers." *American Heritage* (February-March 1993): 43+.

Cowall, David. "Laundering of Crime Cash Troubles UN." *New York Times*, 25 November 1994.

Cox, Caroline. "Glyphosate." *Journal of Pesticide Reform* (Summer 1991): 121+.

Craig, Richard B. "Are Drug Kingdoms South America's New Wave?" *World and I* (November 1989): 160–165.

Crook, Farrell. "Drug Smuggler Jailed 12 Months." *Toronto Star*, 24 June 1993.

Crozier, William. "The New World Disorder." *National Review*, 19 December 1994, 47.

Cullen, Robert. "Comrades in Crime." *Playboy* (April 1994): 70–72.

Culley, Harriet. "International Narcotics Control." *Department of State Dispatch* (October 1984): 39.

Cusack, Michael. "Where the Drug Trade Begins, How It Must End." *Scholastic Update*, 10 May 1985, 6.

Cyrix, Oliver. *Crime: An Encyclopedia*. North Pomfret, VT: Trafalgar Square, 1995.

Dalton, David. *Piece of My Heart: The Life, Times, and Legend of Janis Joplin*. New York: St. Martin's Press, 1985.

D'Amato, Alphonse. "How To Stamp Out Money Laundering." *USA Today* magazine (September 1991): 16–18.

Dane, Abe. "High Tech Drug Busters." *Popular Mechanics* (February 1990): 49+.

Darling, Juanita. "Accused Mentor of Imprisoned Drug Kingpin Arrested." *Los Angeles Times*, 28 March 1991.

Dass, Baba Ram. *Be Here Now, Remember.* New York: Crown, 1974.

Dass, Baba Ram, and Stephen Levine. *Grist for the Mill.* Santa Cruz, CA: California University Press, 1977.

Davies, Frank. "New Ways to Launder Cash." *Miami Herald,* 28 September 1977.

———. "Guilty Verdict Ends Massive Money-Laundering Trial." *Miami Herald,* 14 January 1998.

Davis, John H. *Mafia Kingfish.* New York: NAL/Dutton, 1989.

"The Days Dwindle Down for Ed Meese." *U.S. News and World Report,* 11 April 1988, 11 (2pp.).

De Borchgrave, Arnaud. "The Bubonic Plague of International Crime." *Insight on the News,* 23 October 1995, 40.

De Grazia, Jessica. *DEA: The War against Drugs.* London: BBC Books, 1991.

De Palma, Anthony. "Drug Traffickers Smuggling Tons of Cash from the U.S. Through Mexico." *New York Times,* 25 January 1996.

———. "A $50 Million Payment Fuels Mexican Scandal." *New York Times,* 1 February 1996.

———. "Mexico: General Tied to Drugs Gets Fifteen Years." *New York Times,* 26 October 1998.

Deangelis, Mary Elizabeth. "Teen Dies After Inhaling Chemical." *Charlotte Observer,* 21 June 1995.

"A Defector in the Drug War: Mexico's Drug Czar Is Arrested for Selling Out the Cause." *Newsweek,* 3 March 1997, 54.

DeGeorge, Gail. "Confessions of a Money Launderer." *Business Week,* 30 May 1994, 119.

DeLuca, V. H. *Thomas De Quincey: The Prose of Vision.* Toronto: University of Toronto Press, 1980.

"Democracy and Drugs." *Christian Science Monitor,* 6 October 1995.

Departemento Administrativo de Seguridad Direccion. *Aspectos de Interese sobre el Cultivo de Amapola* (Aspects of Interest on the Cultivation of the Poppy). Bogotá, Colombia: Departamento Administrativo de Seguridad, Direccion, 1991.

Dermota, Ken. "When You Order Steak—and a Stallion." *Business Week,* 27 March 1995, 32E–35E.

"Detecting Illegal Drugs." *USA Today* magazine (June 1993): 8+.

Deveney, Paul J. "The U.S. Fills Posting in Mexico." *Wall Street Journal,* 29 June 1998.

"Died, Virgilio Barco." *Time,* 2 June 1977.

Doerner, William R. "The Chemical Connection." *Time,* 20 February 1989, 44–45.

Dolphin, Rick. "A Global Struggle: Drug Police Are Fighting the Odds." *MacLean's,* 3 April 1989, 48.

"Don't Wait: Reintegrate." *Economist,* 29 February 1992, 46–47.

"El Dossier de Efrain Hernandez Ramirez" (The Background of Efrain Hernandez Ramirez). *El Espectador* (Bogota, Colombia), 7 November 1996.

Dougherty, Steve. "What a Long Strange Trip." *People Weekly,* 21 August 1995, 64 (6pp.).

Dowd, Maureen. "Resurrection." *New York Times* (Magazine), 11 September 1994.

Dreyfuss, Robert. "Hawks and Doves: Who's Who in the World of Drugs." *Rolling Stone,* 7 August 1997, 42 (8pp.).

Drozdiak, William. "European Unit For Organized Crime." *Washington Post,* 2 August 1994.

"Drug Busters' Aim: Hit the Big Boys." *National Observer* (May 1996): 1, 16.

"Drug Czar Escapes Post to Become Sociology Professor at Rice University in Houston." *Jet,* 8 January 1996, 22.

"Drug Found to Curb Craving for Cocaine." *Charlotte Observer,* 6 August 1998.

Drug Interdiction in the Caribbean and Other Areas. *International Drug Report* (April/May/June 1998).

"Drug-Linked Currency Irregularities at Florida Banks." *International Currency Review* no. 4 (1980): 44–49.

Drug Lord Charged. *MacLean's,* 6 October 1996.

"A Drug Tale of Two Cities." *Economist,* 6 April 1996, 41–42.

"Drug War Begins." *CQ Researcher,* 19 March 1993, 250.

"Drug Wars." *U.S. News and World Report,* 11 February 1991, 12.

"Drugs and Civil Rights." *Christian Science Monitor,* 16 December 1993.

"Drugs $400 Billion; Second Only to Arms Trade." *Chicago Tribune,* 15 December 1994.

"Drugs in Switzerland." *Economist,* 28 November 1998, 51.

"Drugs, Latin America and the United Sates," *Economist,* 7 February 1998, 35 (2pp.).

Duffy, Brian. "The Old Man and the Seizures: A Key informant and Good Police Work Produce the Biggest Case against the Cali Cartel." *U.S. News and World Report,* 19 June 1995, 36 (3pp.).

Duke, Steven B., and Albert Cross. "The Drug War: Prohibition Has Shot Gaping Holes in the Bill of Rights." *Reason* (February 1994): 20+.

Du Lac, J. Freedom. "Free Fall—In the Rough through Bedminister." *Fortune,* 25 December 1995, 48.

"Duros Golpes a Mafia Colombos-Italianos" (Hard Blows to Italian Colombo Mafia). *El Tiempo* (Bogota, Colombia), 9 February 1997.

Duzan, Maria Jimena. *Death Beat: A Colombian Journalist's Life inside the Cocaine Wars.* New York: HarperCollins, 1994.

Dvorak, Rich. "Clinton's New Tack in War on Drugs: Reduce Demand." *Chicago Tribune,* 17 September 1993.

Dye, David R. "Nicaraguan Cocaine Bust Reveals New Cartel Route." *Christian Science Monitor,* 26 January 1994.

Eaton, Tracy. "Mexico Fights Its Own Police in Drug War." *Dallas Morning News,* 18 August 1996.

———. "Mexico's Drug Eradication Agents Hail Success Against Pot, Poppies." *Miami Herald,* 23 November 1996, International Satellite edition.

———. "After 25 Years DEA Finds Drug War Still a Minefield." *Dallas Morning News,* 5 October 1998.

Eddy, Paul, Hugh Sabogal, and Sarah Walden. *The Cocaine Wars.* New York: Norton, 1988.

Editorial Amnistia Internacional. *Violencia Politica en Colombia: Mito y Realidad* (Political Violence in Columbia: Myth and Reality). Washington, DC: Editorial Amnistia Internacional, 1994.

Ehrenfeld, Rachel. "Narco-Terrorism and the Cuban Connection." *Strategic Review* (Summer 1988): 55–63.

———. *Evil Money*. New York: HarperCollins, 1992.

———. *Narcoterrorism and the Cuban Circuit*. New York: William Morrow, 1994.

Eisner, Peter. *America's Prisoner: The Memoirs of Manuel Antonio Noriega*. New York: Random House, 1997.

Elliott, Michael. "Global Mafia." *Newsweek*, 13 December 1993, 22–31.

Elliott, Patricia. "A Life in the Drug Trade." *Saturday Night* (December 1993): 20.

Ellis, David. "Open Borders, Sealed Accounts." *Time*, 29 April 1991, 21.

Elsasser, Glen. "Court Rules U.S. May Abduct Foreigners." *Chicago Tribune*, 16 June 1992.

Emshwiller, John R. "IRS Dispatches Agents on Business in Crackdown on Money Laundering." *Wall Street Journal*, 2 May 1995.

English, T. J. "Rude Boys." *Playboy* (October 1991): 86.

———. *Born To Kill: America's Most Notorious Gang and the Changing Face of Organized Crime*. New York: William Morrow, 1994.

Epstein, Gerald, Julie Graham, and Jessica Nembhard, eds. *A New World Economy: Forces of Change and Plans of Action*. Philadelphia: Temple University Press, 1993.

"Equity and Addiction." *Nature*, 30 March 1995, 39.

Erlanger, Stephen. "Southeast Asia Is Now Number One Source of U.S. Heroin." *New York Times*, 11 February 1990, 26A.

Estrada, Louis. "Renegades in the Drug War: A Lord of Jamaican Posses." *Times of the Americas*, 26 June 1991, 16–19.

Estrada, Richard. "Drug War Alliance with Mexico Has Its Limits," *Dallas Morning News*, 25 September 1998.

Etheridge, Eric. "The Drug War Fails Again." *Rolling Stone*, 11 August 1994, 44.

"E.U. No Se la Rebaja a Capo Mexicano" (The United States Is Not Afraid of Mexican Godfather). *El Espectador* (Bogota, Colombia), 17 October 1996.

"E.U. Teme al Poder Corruptor de los Narcos" (U.S. Fears Corrupting Power of Drug Traffickers). *El Tiempo* (Bogota, Colombia), 15 May 1997.

"European Markets in Cocaine." *Contemporary Crisis* (March 1989): 35–52.

Executive Intelligence Review. *Dope, Inc.* Washington, DC: Executive Intelligence Review, 1992.

"Ex-Mexican Police Chief Sentenced." Associated Press, 1 September 1998.

"Extradited Colombian Get Fifteen Years in 1984 Conviction." United Press International, 7 November 1989.

"Fact Sheet: Controlling Chemicals Used in Drug Trafficking." *U.S. Department of State Dispatch*, 2 March 1992, 164.

Farah, Douglas. "Colombian Chain-Saw Gang Pushes Heroin, Prospers." *Washington Post*, 27 July 1992, 17.

———. "Colombia's Jailed Drug Barons Said To Carry on Business." *Washington Post*, 13 January 1996.

———. "The Crack Up." *Washington Post* (Magazine), 21 July 1996.

———. "Drug Traffickers Build Central American Route to U.S." *Washington Post*, 28 March 1993.

———. "Illicit Dollars Flow via Unique Network." *Washington Post*, 19 September 1993.

———. "U.S.-Bogota: What Went Wrong?" *Washington Post*, 3 March 1996.

———. "U.S.-Colombian Split over Cali Cartel." *Washington Post*, 8 March 1994.

Farley, Dixie. "Illegal Use of Vet Drug Results in Fine, Probation." *FDA Consumer* (April 1996): 28.

Farley, Hugh. "To Catch a Drug Kingpin, Follow the Money." *Governing* (October 1990): 94.

Farragher, Thomas. "Ex-Contra Chief Scoffs at CIA Drug Link." *Miami Herald*, 27 November 1996, International Satellite edition.

Fay, P. W. *The Opium War, 1840–1842*. Chapel Hill, NC: University of North Carolina Press, 1975.

Fedarko, Kevin. "Outwitting Cali's Professor Moriarty." *Time*, 17 July 1995, 30–31.

Federa, Sid. *The Luciano Story*. New York: Popular Library, 1986.

"Fed's Big Catch: Man at the Center of Cali Cartel." *Miami Herald*, 6 October 1995.

Felsenthal, Edward, and Laurie P. Cohen. "Legal Beat: Bank Employees Charged." *Wall Street Journal*, 22 December 1993.

Ferguson, Jeffrey M. "Investigation and Prosecution of Methamphetamine Manufacture." *NarcOfficer* (January-February 1998): 17–22.

Fialka, John J. "Drug Dealers Export Billions of Dollars to Evade Laws on Currency Reporting." *Wall Street Journal*, 7 April 1994, Eastern edition.

———. "DEA's Sting Bank in the Caribbean Uncovers Laundering of Drug Money." *Wall Street Journal*, 19 December 1994.

———. "Computers Keep Tabs on Dirty Money." *Wall Street Journal*, 8 May 1995.

Fineman, Mark. "Swiss Link Raul Salinas to $100 Million." *Los Angeles Times*, 7 December 1995.

———. "Mexico's Drug Czar Called Man of Integrity." *Miami Herald*, 6 December 1996, International Satellite edition.

Fish, Jefferson. "Discontinuous Change and the War on Drugs." *Humanist* (September-October 1994): 14+.

Fitz-Simmons, Daniel W. "Sendero Luminoso—Case Study in Insurgency." *Parameters* (Summer 1993): 64–73.

Flood, Susan. *International Terrorism: Policy Implications*. Chicago: Office of Criminal Justice, University of Illinois at Chicago, 1991.

Florez, Carl P., and Bernardette Boyce. "Colombian Organized Crime." *Policy Studies* (1990): 81–88.

———. "Laundering Drug Money." *FBI Law Enforcement Bulletin* (April 1990): 22–25.

Flynn, Steven. "Worldwide Drug Scourge: The Expanding Traffic in Illicit Drugs." *Brookings Review* (Winter 1993): 6–11.

Follain, John. *A Dishonored Society: The Sicilian Mafia's Threat to Europe.* New York: Warner, 1976.

"Follow the Money." *Economist*, 21 October 1989, 29.

Forbes, Steve. "Deadly Deceit." *Forbes*, 8 September 1997, 27 (2pp.).

Foust, Dean. "The New, Improved Money Launderers." *Business Week*, 28 June 1993, 90–91.

Fowler, Thomas B. "Winning the War on Drugs: Can We Get There from Here?" *Journal of Social, Political and Economic Studies.* (Winter 1990): 403–421.

Fox, Stephen R. *Blood and Power: Organized Crime in Twentieth-Century America.* New York: William Morrow, 1989.

Frankel, Max. "O.K., Call It a Drug War." *New York Times* (Magazine), 18 December 1994, 30.

Freedman, Dan. "Congress to Probe U.S.-Mexican Border Corruption." *Miami Herald*, 22 November 1996, International Satellite edition.

Freemantle, Brian. *The Fix: Inside the World Drug Trade.* 1985.

Freud, Sigmund. *The Cocaine Papers.* Reprint. New York: Stonehill Publishing Company, 1974.

Friedman, Alan. "BCCI's Deadly Secrets." *Vanity Fair* (February 1992): 36.

Friedman, Robert I. "The Organizatsiya." *New York*, 7 November 1994, 50–58.

"From the Money-Laundering Front." *ABA Banking Journal* (March 1990): 16.

Gallego, Leonardo. "Coca Growers and Guerrillas." *Wall Street Journal*, 15 December 1994.

Galliher, John F., David P. Keys and Michael Elsner. "Lindesmith versus Anslinger: An Early Government Victory in the Failed War on Drugs." *Journal of Criminal Law and Criminology* (Winter 1998): 661–683.

Gambatta, Diego. *The Sicilian Mafia: The Business of Private Protection.* Cambridge, MA: Harvard University Press, 1993.

"Gangster's Story, A." *Economist*, 5 December 1992, 33.

Gans, David, and Peter Simon. *Playing in the Band. An Oral History and Visual Portrait of the Grateful Dead.* New York: St. Martin's Press, Griffin, 1996.

"Garcia Abrego Attorneys Rest Case." *Miami Herald*, 11 October 1996, International Satellite edition.

Garcia, G. D. "Running Pot Where It's Not as Hot." *Time*, 29 November 1982, 20.

Garretty, Deborah J., et al. "Benzodiazepine Misuse by Addicts." *Journal of Substance Abuse* (1977): 68–73.

Garrison, Lloyd. "Let Them Shoot Smack." *Time*, 19 March 1984, 35.

Gatjanis, Greg. Cocaine's Latest Victim: "The Water Runs Red." *U.N. Chronicle* (June 1995).

Gedda, George. "Amnesty: U.S. Aide to Colombia Used for Repression." *Miami Herald*, 30 October 1996, International Satellite edition.

Gelbard, Robert S. "International Crime Fighting Strategies." *Department of State Dispatch* (December 1995): 924–927.

Gene, J. P. "Losing Battles in the War on Drugs." *World Press Review* (June 1992): 16–17.

"Getting the Boot: Italy, Unfinished Revolution." *Virginia Quarterly Review* (Spring 1996): SS59–SS60.

Gilbert, Murray. *From the League of Nations to the U.N.* London, Oxford: University Press, 1948.

"Gilberto Rodriguez Quedo Abogado a Pagar $105.00 Millones a la Justicia" (Gilberto Rodriguez Asks Lawyer to Pay $105 Million to Justice). *El Tiempo* (Bogota, Colombia), 30 October 1996.

Gobierno de la Republica de Colombia et Gobierno de Los Estados Unidos de America. *Programa para la Modernizacion de la Administracion de Justicia* (Program for the Modernization of the Administration of Justice). Bogota, Colombia: U.S. Embassy, 1996.

Gold, M. S. *Marijuana.* New York: Plenum Press, 1989.

Goldberg, Carey. "Russian Police Warn of Cocaine Blizzard." *Los Angeles Times*, 27 February 1993.

Goldman, Albert. "Outlaw Strongholds of Colombia." *High Times* (July 1978): 45–48.

"Goodbye Quarry Heights?" *Economist*, 24 March 1990, 27.

Goode, Erich, ed. *Marijuana.* New York: Atherton Press, 1969.

Goodson, Roy, and William J. Olson. "International Organized Crime." *Society* (January 1995): 18–29.

Gordon, Dinah. *The Return of the Dangerous Classes: Drug Prohibition and Politics.* New York: W. W. Norton, 1994.

Gordon, Michael R. "U.S. Military Long a Part of the Drug Battle." *New York Times*, 2 August 1992.

"Gotcha!" *U.S. News and World Report*, 29 December 1989, 10.

Gray, John. "The Rise of Russia's Crime Commissars." *World Press Review* (June 1994): 13–15.

Green, Eric. "Constantine Warns of New Drug Menace in the United States." *U.S.I.A. Press Release*, 12 August 1997.

"Green Ice II: Money Launderers Caught." *DEA World* (Spring/Summer 1995) 214–215.

Greenberger, Robert S. "China Becomes Major Transit Point in Heroin Trade." *Wall Street Journal*, 20 May 1992.

Greenburg, Michael. *British Trade and the Opening of China, 1800–1842.* Cambridge, UK: Cambridge University Press, 1951.

Grigg, William Norman. "Russia's New Export: Crime." *New American*, 27 May 1996.

Gross, Richard C. "Dutch Claim Drug Policy Works, but Agree to Strict Enforcment." *Insight on the News,* 17 March 1997, 40.

Grover, Ronald. "A Japanese Laundry Worth $1 Billion." *Business Week*, 24 May 1993, 38.

Gugliotta, Guy, and Jeff Leen. *Kings of Cocaine*. New York: Harper, 1990.

Guillermoprieto, Alma. "Down the Shining Path." *New Yorker*, 8 February 1993, 64 (11pp.).

———. "Who Done It? Unsolved Assassinations Contribute to National Insecurity in Mexico." *New Yorker*, 25 September 1995, 44–53.

Gunst, Laura. "Johnny-Too-Bad and the Sufferers." *Nation*, 13 November 1989, 54.

———. *Born Fi': A Journey through the Jamaican Posse*. New York: Henry Holt, 1995.

Guthrie, Steven. "Colombia Enters Heroin Market." *Charlotte Observer*, 13 October 1991.

Gutierrez, Edwin. "Colombia: 500 Mil Consumidores de Drogas" (Colombia: 500,000 Consumers of Drugs). *El Tiempo* (Bogota, Colombia), 21 December 1998.

Hall, Kevin J. "Truckers: Business as Usual." *Journal of Commerce*, 22 October 1988, 5A.

Hallett, Carol Boyd. "Drugs, Diplomacy, Trade." *Washington Post*, 27 August 1993.

Handelman, Stephen. "The Russian 'Mafiya.'" *Foreign Affairs* (March 1994): 83–94.

———. *Comrade Criminal: Russia's New Mafia*. New Haven, CT: Yale University Press, 1995.

Hannun, Phil, with Al Lotz. *Nightmare: Vietnamese House Invasion Robberies*. Falls Church, VA: International Association of Asian Crime Investigators, 1991.

Hanson, David J. "Chemical Industry, Drug Agency Sort Out Chemical Diversion Issues." *Chemical and Engineering News*, 29 January 1990, 18–19.

———. "Industry Rebuts Chemical Diversion Charges." *Chemical and Engineering News*, 12 February 1990, 5–6.

———. "Narcotics Commission: Novel Initiatives for Growing Crisis." *UN Chronicle* (September 1992): 72.

Hargreaves, Claire. *Snowfields: The War on Cocaine in the Andes*. New York: Holmes and Meir, 1992.

Harrison, Eric. "Jamaicans: New Face of U.S. Crime." *Los Angeles Times*, 3 January 1989.

Harrison, Faye V. "Jamaica and the International Drug Economy." *Transafrican Forum* (Fall 1990): 49–57.

Harrison, Hank. *The Dead Book: A Social History of the Grateful Dead*. New York; Links, 1973.

Heald, Bonnie. "Former Surgeon General Speaks at Local Conference." Knight-Ridder/Tribune News Service, 9 December 1994, p. 1209K7901.

Healy, Melissa. "New Anti-Drug Plan Would Use Military." *Los Angeles Times*, 1 June 1992.

Hellman, Peter. "Reagan Gets Tough on Drugs." *Rolling Stone*, 15 April 1982, 13–14.

"Helms-Weld War: In the Same Party, You Said?" *Economist*, 2 August 1997, 18–19.

Herman, E., and G. O'Sullivan. *The Terrorism Industry: The Experts and Institutions That Shape Our View of Terror*. New York: Pantheon, 1989.

"Heroina Colombiana Alarma a la DEA" (Colombian Heroin Alarms DEA). *El Espectador* (Bogota, Colombia), 14 September 1996.

Hertling, Mark P. "Narcoterrorism: The New Unconventional War." *Military Review* (March 1990): 28–45.

"High in the Andes." *Economist*, 13 February 1993, 45.

Higham, Charles. *The Adventures of Conan Doyle: The Life of the Creator of Sherlock Holmes*. New York: Norton, 1996.

Himmelstein, Jerome. *The Strange Career of Marijuana: Politics and Ideology and Drug Control in America*. Westport, CT: Greenwood Press, 1983.

Hinckle, Pia. "The Grip of the Octopus." *Newsweek*, 8 June 1992, 32.

Hockstader, Lee. "Russia's Criminal Condition: Gangsters Spreading Web from Moscow to the West." *Washington Post*, 26 February 1995.

Hohler, Bob. "Crime Gangs Imperil Regimes, CIA Says." *Boston Globe*, 21 April 1994.

Holmstrom, David. "War on Drugs, Two Decades Later." *Christian Science Monitor*, 27 August 1992.

"Honduran Trafficker First U.S. Conviction for DEA in Camarena Case." Associated Press, 27 July 1990.

"Honorable Mob." *Economist*, 27 January 1990, 19.

Hopkins, Jerry, and Danny Sugarman. *No One Gets Out of Here Alive*. New York: Warner, 1980.

Horvitz, Leslie Alan. "U.S. Gamble May Pay Off in High Stakes Crime Battle." *Insight on the News*, 25 July 1994, 6.

"Hot Money; City of Angels." *U.S. News and World Report*, 10 April 1989, 14.

"How BCCI Grew and Grew." *Economist*, 27 January 1990, 84.

Hudson, Tim. "South America High: A Geography of Cocaine." *Focus* (January 1985): 22.

Huff, Ronald. *Gangs in America*. Newbury Park, CA: Sage, 1990.

Hughes, Sallie. "A Family's Value: Huge Bank Deposits Blacken Salina's Name." *MacLean's*, 11 December 1995, 52.

Huston, Peter. *Tongs, Gangs, and Triads: Chinese Crime Gangs in North America*. Boulder, CO: Paladin Press, 1995.

"In the Land of the Rising Sun." *Economist*, 26 August 1989, 23.

Inciardi, James A. *History and Crime: Implications for Criminal Justice Policy*. Newbury Park, CA: Sage, 1980.

———. *The War on Drugs: Heroine, Cocaine, Crime and Public Policy*. Palo Alto, CA: Mayfield, 1984.

———. *The Drug Legislation Debate*. Newbury Park, CA: Sage, 1991.

Inciardi, James A., and Karen McElrath. *The American Drug Scene: An Anthology*. Los Angeles: Roxbury Publishing Company, 1995.

Inglis, Brian. *The Forbidden Game: A Social History on Drugs*. New York: Scribner's, 1975.

"An Insider's Look at Drug Enforcement." *Scholastic Update*, 19 May 1985.

"International Assistance for U.S. Police." *Police Chief* (October 1993): 40.

"International Cartels Expand Influence." *UN Chronicle* (June 1994): 68.

"International Narcotics Control." *Department of State Dispatch*, 3 September 1990, 15.

"International Narcotics Control: The Challenge of Our Decade." *Police Chief* (October 1985): 42.

"An Interview with John C. Lawn." *Narcotics Control Digest*, 28 March 1990.

Intriago, Charles A. "Money Laundering: New Penalties, Risks, Burdens for Bankers." *Banker's Magazine* (March-April 1990): 50–55.

Irvin, Richard. "12 Busted in E. Baltimore Raids." *Baltimore Sun*, 8 September 1994.

"Is the Mafia in Retreat or in Defeat?" *Economist*, 29 July 1995, 33.

Isikoff, Michael. "War on Drugs Mobilizes National Guard: Raiders Attack Domestic Marijuana Boom in Remote Patches." *Washington Post*, 14 August 1990.

———. "U.S. May Widen Anti-Drug Drive in the Caribbean." *Washington Post*, 1 June 1992.

———. "U.S. Considers Shift in Drug War." *Washington Post*, 16 September 1993.

———. "U.S. Probes Narcotics Unit Funded by CIA." *Washington Post*, 20 November 1993.

———. "DEA Chief Has Harsh Words for Clinton Anti-Drug Policy." *Washington Post*, 31 October 1995.

"Italy: Mafia Looks East." *International Management* (European edition) (May 1990): 14.

Ivins, Molly. "War on Drugs Makes Some Cops Act Like Criminals." *Sacramento Bee*, 6 September 1998.

Jackson, Robert L. "219 Jamaicans Held in Gang Arrest." *Los Angeles Times*, 14 October 1988.

Jaffe, Jerome H., editor-in-chief. *Encyclopedia of Drugs and Alcohol.* New York: Simon and Schuster, 1995.

James, George. "Suspected Head of Heroin Network Is Arrested." *New York Times*, 30 March 1993.

Jamieson, Alison. *Terrorism and Drug Trafficking in Europe in the 1990s.* London: Dartmouth Publishing, 1994.

"Japanese Gangs Invade U.S." *Boston Globe*, 6 February 1994.

Jensen, Holger. "The Laundering Game: Cleaning Dirty Money Is Crucial." *Economist*, 24 June 1989, 22.

Jiminez, Michael J. Review of *Death Beat: A Colombian Journalist's Life Inside the Cocaine Wars*, by Maria Jimena Duzan. *Nation*, 5 September 1994, 246.

Johnson, Peyton, and Philip Lealey. "Tackling Drug Trafficking at Its Source." *Ceres* (July-August 1980): 27–35.

Johnson, Tim. "Pastrana Cool to Coca Policy." *Miami Herald*, 16 October 1998.

Jones, Colin. "What's in a Suitcase?" *Banker* (London) (April 1990): 12.

Jonnes, Jill. "Founding Father: One Man Invented the Modern Narcotics Industry." *American Heritage* (February-March 1993): 48–49.

Jonnes, Jill. *Hep-Cats, Narcs and Pipe Dreams.* New York: Scribner, 1996.

"Justo Pastor Parafan Guilty!" *Global Crime Update*, 27 July 1998, 2.

Kaplan, David E., and Alec Dubro. *Yakuza: The Explosive Account of Japan's Criminal Underworld.* Reading, MA: Addison-Wesley, 1986.

Karch, Stephen, ed. *Drug Abuse Handbook.* Boca Raton, FL: CRC Press, 1998.

Karnow, Stanley. *Vietnam: A History.* New York: Viking, 1983.

Katcher, Leo. *The Big Bankroll: The Life and Times of Arnold Rothstein.* New York: Da Capo Press, 1994.

Katz, Gregory. "Russian Underworld Flourished in Police Wake." *Atlanta Journal and Atlanta Constitution*, 18 June 1995.

Keating, Michael. "Breaking the Taboo on Drugs." *World Today* (July 1997): 178 (2pp.).

Kelly, Orr. "Feds versus Drug Runners: Game Gets Trickier." *U.S. News and World Report*, 4 October 1982, 54.

Kelly, Robert J. "Organized Crime: Past, Present, and Future." *USA Today* magazine (May 1992): 78.

Kelly, Robert J., Ko-lin Chin, and Rufus Schatzberg. *Handbook of Organized Crime in the United States.* Westport, CT: Greenwood Press, 1994.

Kelly, Robert J., ed. *Organized Crime: A Global Perspective.* Totowa, NJ: Rowman and Littlefield, 1986.

Kendall, Sarita. "Colombia Poll Victor Denies Drug Cartel Link." *Financial Times* (London), 23 June 1994.

Kennedy, Kenneth. "Drug Corruption in South Florida." *NarcOfficer* (January-February 1998): 26–32.

Kenney, Dennis J., and James O. Finckenauer. *Organized Crime in America.* London: International Thompson, 1990.

Keough, Caroline. "The General Is In." *Miami Herald*, 27 September 1997.

Kerf, Peter. "Chinese Dominate New York Heroin Trade." *New York Times*, 9 August 1987.

Kernovsky, Eva. "Chaos in Colombia." *World Press Review* (December 1996): 5.

Kerry, John F. *National Security and the Globalization of Crime.* New York: Simon and Schuster, 1997.

Kesey, Ken. *Further Inquiry.* New York: Viking, 1990.

King, R. *The Drug Hang Up: America's Fifty Year Folly.* New York: Norton, 1972.

"Kingpin Falls, A." *U.S. News and World Report*, 30 May 1988, 9.

Kirkpatrick, Sidney. *Turning the Tide: One Man against the Medellin Cartel.* New York: E. P. Dutton, 1991.

Klare, Michael T. "Fighting Drugs with the Military." *Nation*, 1 January 1990, 8–12.

Klebnikov, Paul. "Joe Stalin's Heirs." *Forbes*, 27 September 1993, 124–134.

Kleiman, Mark A. R. "Snowed in the Cocaine Blizzard." *New Republic*, 23 April 1990, 45–67.

Kleinknecht, William. *The New Ethnic Mobs: The Changing Face of Organized Crime in America.* New York: Free Press, 1996.

Kotler, Jared. "Fatso May Be Big Break against Cali Cartel Bosses." *Seattle Times*, 28 July 1997.

Kowalski, B. J. "Taking on the Drug Lords." *World Press Review* (April 1998): 12 (2pp.).

Krauss, Clifford. "One Cartel Dies and the Drugs Go On." *New York Times*, 13 August 1995.

Krauss, Clifford, and Douglas Frantz. "Cali Drug Cartel Using U.S. Business to Launder Cash." *New York Times*, 30 October 1985.

Ku, Min-Chuan. *A Comprehensive Handbook of the United States*. New York: Monarch Press, 1979.

"La Fortuna de El Senor de los Mares." *El Tiempo* (Bogota, Colombia), 8 November 1996.

"La Fortuna del 'Don Efra'" (The Fortune of Don Efra). *El Espectador* (Bogota, Colombia), 8 November 1996.

La Velle, Philip J. "Drug Money Launderers to Dry Out in Prison." *San Diego Union Tribune*, 4 July 1993.

Laats, Alexander, and Kevin O'Flaherty. "Colombia's Human Rights: Implications of the War on Drugs Control Policy." *Harvard Human Rights Journal* (Spring 1990): 87.

———. "Is U.S. Narcotics Assistance Promoting Human Rights Abuse in Colombia?" Human Rights Working Paper, 1 (March 1990): 102.

Labaton, Stephen. "Review of *Dirty Laundry*." *New York Times* Book Review, 11 December 1994, 33.

Lader, M. " History of Benzodiazepine Dependence." *Journal of Substance Abuse Treatment* (1991): 53–59.

LaFranchi, Howard. "Cali Cartel Shows Drug Fight Isn't Over." *Christian Science Monitor*, 9 March 1995.

———. "Cali Cartel Stretches Out Tentacles." *Christian Science Monitor*, 8 February 1996.

LaFraniere, Sharon. "150 Arrests in 6–Nation Drug Sting." *Washington Post*, 29 September 1992.

Lamar, Jacob V. "The Crusading Attorney General." *Time*, 9 September 1985, 41.

Lamour, Catherine, and Michael R. Lamberti. *The International Connection: Opium from Growers to Pushers*. New York: Pantheon, 1974.

Lane, Charles. "Colombia: A Drug Lord's Last Shootout." *Newsweek*, 25 December 1989, 48.

Langer, John H. "A Preliminary Analysis: Drug Trafficking." *Police Studies* (Spring 1986): 42–56.

Langford, Terri. "Ruiz Massieu: No Drug Bribes on My Watch." *Miami Herald*, 15 March 1997, International Satellite Edition.

———. "U.S. Gets to Seize $7.9 Million from Mexican Prosecutor." *Miami Herald*, 16 March 1997, International Satellite edition.

Lardner, George. "FBI Withholds Files It Had on Donovan." *Washington Post*, 6 June 1982.

Larmer, Brooke. "A Leap of Faith." *Newsweek*, 10 March 1997, 10–12.

Lasagna, Louis, and Gardner Lindzey. "Marijuana Policy and the Drug Mythology." *Society* (January-February 1983): 67.

Latimer, Dean, and Jeff Goldberg. *Flowers In the Blood: The Story of Opium*. New York: Franklin Watts, 1981.

Leary, Timothy, and William S. Burroughs. *Flashbacks*. New York: J. P. Tarcher, 1997.

"Lee Brown Elected Houston's First Black Mayor." *Jet*, 22 December 1997, 4 (2pp.).

Lee, Martin, and Bruce Shlain. *Acid Dreams, The CIA, LSD, and The Sixties Rebellion*. New York: Grove Press, 1985.

Lee, Rensselaer W., III. "South America's Cocaine: Why the U.S. Can't Stop It." *Current History* (June 1989): 23.

———. "Soviet Narcotics Trade." *Society* (July-August 1991).

———. "Global Reach: The Threat of International Drug Trafficking." *Current History* (May 1995): 207–211.

Lee, Rensselaer W., and Scott B. MacDonald. "Drugs in the East." *Foreign Policy* (Spring 1993).

Leeds, Barry H. *Ken Kesey*. New York: F. Ungar Publishing Company, 1981.

Lehmann-Haupt, Christopher. "Corralling the Brutes and Boobs of the Mob." *New York Times*, 8 February 1996.

Leitzel, Jim, Clifford Gaddy and Michael Alexeev. "Mafiosi and Matrioshki." *Brookings Review* (Winter 1995): 26–29.

Levine, Michael. *Deep Cover*. New York: Delacorte, 1990.

Levitsky, Melvyn. "Progress in the International War against Illicit Drugs." *Department of State Dispatch*, 2 March 1992, 156–162.

———. "Review of U.S. Efforts to Combat the Narcotics Trade." *Department of State Dispatch*, 24 May 1993, 386–387.

Lewis, Neil A. "In Washington, A Sicilian Mafia Trial without the Glass Cages." *New York Times*, 18 July 1992.

Lewis, Paul. "Nancy Reagan at U.N. Says U.S. Must Do More to Combat Drugs." *New York Times*, 26 October 1988, A1.

Lieberman, Howard. "New Cartel Brazil." *Christian Science Monitor*, 8 February 1996.

Lifshultz, L. "Bush, Drugs and Pakistan: Inside the Kingdom of Heroin." *Nation*, 14 November 1987, 492–496.

Lilley, Jeffrey. "Russian Revolution." *Sports Illustrated*, 10 January 1994, 56–61.

Linden, Dana Wechsler. "Closing In." *Forbes*, 7 June 1993, 52.

Linnemann, J. H. "International Narcotics Control Strategy." *Department of State Bulletin* (February 1982): 46–51.

Lintner, Bertil. "Hooked on the Junta: U.S. Drug Policy Assailed for Links to Burmese Generals." *Far Eastern Economic Review*, 18 November 1993, 23–24.

———. "Khun Sa: Asian Drug King on the Run." *Far Eastern Economic Review*, 20 January 1994, 22–24.

———. "Pusher with a Cause: Khun Sa Stresses His Role as Shah Leader." *Far Eastern Economic Review*, 20 January 1994, 24.

Lippin, Todd. "Drug War versus Development." *Technology Review* (January 1991): 17–19.

Lodwick, Kathleen L. *Crusades Against Opium: Protestant Missionaries in China*. Lexington, KY: University Press of Kentucky, 1996.

Long, Robert Emmet. *Drugs and American Society*. New York: Wilson, 1985.

"Lopez Acepto Aportes de Escobar." *El Tiempo* (Bogota, Colombia), 28 December 1998.

Lowry, Tom, "Chasing the Dragon." *USA Today*, 7 August 1996, A1A2.

Lubasch, Arnold H. "Drug Dealing Was Banned by Mob, U.S. Witness Says." *New York Times*, 15 April 1993.

Lubin, Nancy. "Central Asia's Drug Bazaar." *New York Times*, 16 November 1992.

Lubove, Seth. "Cash Capital." *Forbes*, 16 April 1993, 18.

Lupo, Alan. "A New Breed of Comrade(s) in Arms." *Boston Globe*, 10 December 1995.

Lupsha, Peter A. "Drug Trafficking: Mexico and Colombia in Comparative Perspective." *Journal of International Affairs* (Spring/Summer 1981): 95–115.

Lupsha, Peter, and Kip Shlegel. *The Political Economy of Drug Trafficking: The Herrera Organization (Mexico and the United States).* Albuquerque, NM: Department of Political Science, University of New Mexico, 1980.

Lyman, Michael D. *Gangland: Drug Trafficking by Organized Criminals.* Springfield, IL: Charles C. Thomas, 1989.

———. *Organized Crime.* Springfield, IL: Charles C. Thomas, 1990.

Lyons, David. "DEA Officer Faults Police in Mexico." *Miami Herald*, 14 March 1997, International Satellite edition.

Mabry, Donald J. *Latin American Narcotics Control and U.S. National Security.* Westport, CT: Greenwood Press, 1989.

MacCormack, John. "Border Crossing Access Likely to Be Curtailed." *Colombian Post*, 18–24 November 1996.

MacDonald, Scott B. *Dancing on a Volcano: The Latin American Drug Trade.* New York: Praeger, 1988.

———. *Mountain High, White Avalanche: Cocaine and Power in the Andean States and Panama.* Westport, CT: Praeger, 1989.

MacGregor, James. "The Opium War." *Wall Street Journal*, 29 September 1992.

Machalaba, Daniel. "Deadly Cargo." *Wall Street Journal*, 18 May 1989.

Mack, J. A. *The Crime Industry.* Lexington, MA: Lexington Books, 1975.

"The Mafia Again." *Economist*, 11 March 1995, 5.

Maingot, Anthony P. "Offshore Secret Centers and the Necessary Role of States: Bucking the Trend." *Journal of Interamerican Studies and World Affairs.* (Winter 1995): 1–24.

Mallowe, Mike. "Disorganized Crime." *Philadelphia Magazine* (January 1993): 72.

"Man Believed To Head Drug Cartel Held in Colombia." *Charlotte Observer*, 20 February 1996.

Marnell, Tim, ed. *Drug Identification Bible.* Boulder, CO: Drug Identification Bible, 1997.

Marquis, Christopher. "Decertification Could Result in Backlash." *Miami Herald*, 26 February 1997, International Satellite edition.

———. "U.S. Lawmakers Urge Sending Stern Warning." *Miami Herald*, 26 February 1997, International Satellite edition.

———. "House Rebuffs Mexico 251–175." *Miami Herald*, 14 March 1997, International Satellite edition.

———. "Senate Passes Mexico Bill." *Miami Herald*, 21 March 1997, International Satellite edition.

———. "U.S. Soldiers Find Military Wages Don't Go Far in the Civilian World." 13 May 1998, Knight-Ridder Tribune/News Service, p. 513K6578.

Marshall, Ingwerson. "Jamaican Drug Gangs Stake Out Turf in U.S." *Christian Science Monitor*, 13 August 1987.

"A Marshall Plan in Reverse." *UN Chronicle* (March 1990): 20–33.

Martin, John M., and Anne T. Romano. *Multinational Crime: The Challenge of Terrorism, Espionage, Drugs and Arms Trafficking.* Newbury Park, CA: Sage, 1992.

Martin, Justin. "John de Lorean: In the Rough in Bedminister." *Fortune*, 25 December 1995, 48.

Martin, Peter. "How We Can Control Narcotics." *American Legion.* 20 January 1994, 8.

"Mass Exodus of Triads Denied." *South China Morning Post* (Hong Kong), 8 June 1997.

Massing, Michael. "The New Mafia." *New York Review of Books*, 3 December 1992, 6.

———. "There's Always a New Kingpin." *Washington Post*, 25 June 1995.

Matheson, Mary. "Kings Jailed but Colombia's Drugs Roll On." *Christian Science Monitor*, 11 July 1995.

Maura, Christopher. "How the U.S. Battles Drugs on Three Fronts." *Scholastic Update*, 10 May 1985, 6.

MacCallum, J. "College Star Len Bias Barely Misses Realizing His Two Biggest Goals." *Jet,* 17 July 1986.

McCarroll, Thomas. "The Supply Side Scourge: Cocaine Is So Abundant That Interdiction Fails to Affect Prices." *Time*, 13 November 1989, 81.

McClintick, David. *Swordfish: A True Story of Ambition, Savagery, and Betrayal.* New York: Pantheon, 1993.

McCoy, Alfred J. *The Politics of Heroin: CIA Complicity in the Global Drug Trade.* Brooklyn, NY: Laurence Hill, 1991.

———. "What War on Drugs? The CIA Connection." *Progressive* (July 1991): 20–26.

McCoy, Alfred J., and Alan A. Block, eds. *War on Drugs: Studies in the Failure of U.S. Narcotics Policy.* Boulder, CO: Westview, 1992.

McDonald, R. Robin. "DEA Says Operation Exposed U.S.-Europe Drug Money Ties." *Atlanta Journal and Atlanta Constitution.* 17 December 1994.

McGarvey, Robert. "Global Organized Crime." *American Legion* magazine (February 1996): 16–17.

———. "Hard Time for the Mafia." *American Legion* magazine (April 1991): 32.

McGee, Jim. "Cartel Picks Wrong Bank for Drug Money." *Washington Post*, 17 December 1994.

———. "Fake DEA Bank Stings Cali Cartel." *Washington Post*, 17 December 1994.

———. "Ex-Prosecutors indicted in the Cali Cartel Probe." *Washington Post*, 4 July 1995.

McKissick, Chris. "Rohypnol." *International Drug Report* (July-September 1996): 3.

McNamara, Joseph. "The Drug War; Violent, Corrupt, and Unsuccessful." *Vital Speeches*, 15 June 1997, 537 (2pp.).

McPhee, John. "Death of an Agent." *New Yorker*, 26 June 1996, 60.

McQuade, Molly. "'On the Bus' with Kesey, Viking and Thunder's Mouth." *Publisher's Weekly*, 15 June 1990, 14 (2pp.).

McWeeney, Sean M. "The Sicilian Mafia and Its Impact on the United States." *FBI Law Enforcement Bulletin* (February 1997): 1–10.

Mecham, Michael. "Customs Integrates P-3B Orion into Surveillance Fleet." *Aviation Week and Space Technology*, 30 January 1989, 53.

———. "E-2C Aircraft Are Key to Coast Guard's Anti-Drug Smuggling Operations." *Aviation Week and Space Technology*, 30 January 1989, 37.

———. "Pentagon Offers 3As, Utility Helicopters for Anti-Drug Effort." *Aviation Week and Space Technology*, 30 January 1989, 45.

Meddis, Sam Vincent. "Cocaine Bust Links Mafia, Cali Cartel." *USA Today*, 29 September 1992.

———. "Colombians Enter Free-for-all for Heroin Trade." *USA Today*, 4 February 1994.

———. "A Big-Time Agenda for New Head of DEA," *USA Today*, 3 May 1994.

Medegaard, Erik. "Chris Farley, 1964–1997." *Rolling Stone*, 5 February 1998, 39 (7pp.).

"The Meese Record." *National Review*, 5 August 1998, 17.

"Mercenary Talks: How Drug Links Get Arms." *San Francisco Chronicle*, 28 February 1991.

Mermelstein, Max. *The Man Who Made It Snow.* New York: Simon and Schuster, 1990.

"Merrill Lynch Brokers in Panama Indicted in Laundering Case." *Wall Street Journal*, 7 March 1994.

"Mexican Military to Fight Drugs." *Miami Herald*, 15 December 1996, International Satellite edition.

"Mexicans Arrest Alleged Godfather of Drug Traffic." *Los Angeles Times*, 10 April 1989.

"Mexico Files New Charges Against Jailed Brother of Ex-Chief." *New York Times*, 4 December 1995.

"Mexico, Minado por los Narcos." *El Espectador* (Bogota, Colombia), 24 February 1997.

"Mexico, Principal Amenaza para E.U. en Trafico de Droga" (Mexico, Main Threat for United States in Drug Trafficking). *El Tiempo* (Bogota, Colombia), 22 November 1996.

"Mexico Rejects New Plan to Arm U.S. Drug Agents." *Miami Herald*, 27 August 1998.

"Mexico Reportedly Links Military, Drugs." Reuters, 28 July 1997.

"Mexico Wants to Charge U.S. Agents Over Probe." *Charlotte Observer*, 4 January 1998, 14A.

"Mexico's Drug Chief Arrested." *MacLean's*, 3 March 1997, 37.

"Mexico's Lozano Defends Tenure." *Miami Herald*, 5 March 1997, International Satellite edition.

Meyer, Dan C. "The Myth of Narco Terrorism in Latin America." *Military Review* (March 1990): 64–70.

Mica, John. "Did the Clinton Administration Drop Ball on Drug Interdiction Policy?" *Insight on the News*, 4 November 1996.

Michaelis, Laura. "Money-Laundering Bill Passes House." *Congressional Quarterly Weekly Report*, 26 March 1994, 725.

Miles, Barry. *William Burroughs: El Hombre Invisible: A Portrait.* New York: Hyperion, 1994.

"Military's Drug Interception Is Labeled Failure by Study." *New York Times*, 16 September 1993.

Miller, Gary J. *Drugs and the Law—Detention, Recognition and Investigation.* New York: Gould Publications, 1997.

Miller, Karen Lowry. "Suddenly, the Japanese Mob Is Out of the Shadows." *Business Week*, 8 July 1991, 29.

Miller, Marjorie, and Juanita Darling. "Thousands Honor Slain Cardinal." *Los Angeles Times*, 26 May 1993.

Mills, James. *The Underground Empire: Where Crime and Justice Embrace.* New York: Doubleday, 1986.

Mitchell, Alison. "U.S. Freezes Assets of Cartel in New Effort Against Drugs." *New York Times*, 23 October 1995.

"The Mob Fights Back: Kidnapping and Murder are the Drug Dealers' Weapons." *Economist*, 13 December 1997, 29.

"The Mob: Hit Hard but Still a Force." *U.S. News and World Report*, 25 May 1996, 32.

"Money Laundering Problems and Solutions." *Banker's Magazine* (March-April 1990): 50–55.

Montgomery, Jim. "Feds Crack Down on Laundering of Narcotics Money." *Wall Street Journal*, 12 March 1981.

Moody, John. "A Day with the Chess Player." *Time*, 1 July 1991, 34–37.

Moore, John W. "Global Reach To Grab Drug Smugglers, Stock Swindlers and Tax Cheats." *National Journal*, 11 February 1989, 326–331.

———. "A Lobbyist Who Packs Real Passion." *National Journal*, 25 February 1995, 500.

Moore, M. H. "Organized Crime as a Business Enterprise." Unpublished manuscript. J. F. Kennedy School of Government, Harvard University, 1989.

Moore, Robin. *The French Connection.* Paris: Presses Pocket, 1972.

Moorhead, Alan Howell. "International Narcotics Control, 1939–1946." *Foreign Policy Reports*, 1 July 1946, 94.

Morales, Edmundo. *White Gold Rush in Peru.* Tucson, AZ: University of Arizona Press, 1989.

Morgan, H. Wayne. *Drugs in America: A Social History, 1800–1980.* Syracuse, NY: Syracuse University Press, 1981.

Morgan, Robert. "Knock and Talk: Consent Searches and Civil Liberties." *FBI Law Enforcement Bulletin* (November 1991): 6–10.

Morgenthau, Tom. "The War Over Weed." *Newsweek*, 3 February 1997.

Morgenthau, Tom, and Douglas Waller. "The Widening Drug War." *Newsweek*, 1 July 1989, 32–34.

Morgenthau, Tom, and Mark Miller. "The Drug Warrior." *Newsweek*, 10 April 1989, 20 (5pp.).

Morgenthau, Tom, and Robert Sandza. "Cocaine's 'Dirty' 300." *Newsweek*, 1 July 1991, 3–7.

Morison, Scott. "Blood Ties: A Widening Murder Scandal Claims One-time Mexican Political Hero." *MacLean's*, 20 March 1995, 20 (2pp.).

Morley, Jefferson. "Barry and His City." *Nation*, 19 February 1990, 221.

Mosquera, Julia Navarrete. "Serrano Afirma Que Los Cartels Estan Unidos" (Serrana confirms that the cartels are united). *El Espectador* (Bogota, Colombia), 26 December 1996.

"Murder Charge Added to Murder Indictment." *Business Wire*, 27 October 1997.

Musto, David F. *The American Disease: Origins of Narcotics Control*. New York: Oxford University Press, 1987.

———. "Illicit Price of Cocaine in Two Eras." *Connecticut Medicine* (June 1990): 321–326.

———. "Opium, Cocaine and Marijuana in American History." *Scientific American* (July 1991): 40.

Myerson, Allen R. "American Express Unit Settles Laundering Case." *New York Times*, 22 November 1994.

Nadelmann, Ethan A. "International Drug Trafficking and U.S. Foreign Policy." *Washington Quarterly* (Fall 1985): 86–104.

———. "Drug Prohibition in the United States: Goals, Consequences, and Alternatives." *Science*, 1 Sept 1989, 939–997.

"El Narcotrafico Amenaza Con Destabilizar a Europa" (Drug Trafficking Threatens to Destabilize Europe). *El Tiempo* (Bogota, Colombia), 27 November 1996.

Nash, Jay Robert. *World Encyclopedia of Organized Crime*. New York: Marlowe, 1994.

Nash, Nathaniel C. "War on Drugs in Peru Shows Limited Gains." *New York Times*, 6 December 1992.

"The National and International Drug Problem." *Police Chief* (October 1985): 28.

National Archives and Records Service. Office of the Federal Registry. *The United States Government Manual, 1997–1998*. Washington, DC: United States Government Printing Office, 1997.

National Public Radio. "UN Conference in Naples Focuses on International Crime." *Morning Edition*, 21 November 1994. Washington, DC: National Public Radio (Transcript).

"National Youth Anti-Drug Media Campaign Launched." *International Drug Report* (July/August/September 1998).

Navarro, Mireya. "When Drug Kingpins Fall, Illicit Assets Buy a Cushion." *New York Times*, 19 March 1996.

———. "Lawyers Weigh Effect of Conviction of Missing Colleague." *New York Times*, 9 August 1998.

Navone, John J. "Italy's Re-Renaissance." *America*, 9 December 1989, 417–418, 425.

"El Negocio de la Droga Se Extiende en México" (The Drug Business Expands into Mexico). *El Tiempo* (Bogota, Colombia), 19 December 1996.

Nell, Edward. "The Dynamics of the Drug Market." *Challenge* (March-April 1994), 13.

"Nephew of Pablo Escobar Gaviria Arrested." Associated Press, 6 December 1989.

"New Drug Strategy Needed." *Colombian Post*, 18–24 November 1996.

"A New Front on the War on Drugs." *Economist*, 29 April 1995, 56.

"New UN Crime Commission Created." *UN Chronicle* (March 1992): 87.

Nicholl, Charles. *The Fruit Palace*. New York: St. Martin's Press, 1985.

Nielsen, Kirk. "Cali Cartel Stretches Out Tentacles: Miami Remains Corporate Office for Illicit Drug Barons." *Christian Science Monitor*, 8 December 1996.

"The Nigerian Connection." *Newsweek*, 19 October 1991, Asian edition, 19.

Northedge, F. S. *The League of Nations: Its Life and Times, 1920–1946*. New York: Holmes and Meir, 1986.

"Not By Helms Alone." *Economist*, 20 September 1997, 20–21.

O'Brien, Robert, and Sidney Cohen. *The Encyclopedia of Drug Abuse*. New York: Facts on File, 1984.

O'Brien, Timothy L. "Law Firm's Downfall Exposes New Methods of Money Laundering." *Wall Street Journal*, 26 May 1995, Eastern edition.

"Ocho Anos de Prision Para Alberto Giraldo" (Eight Years in Prison for Alberto Giraldo). *El Tiempo* (Bogota, Colombia), 23 December 1998.

O'Donnell, Santiago. "Former Nigerian Diplomat Charged in Heathrow-to-Dulles Drug Sting." *Washington Post*, 13 December 1992.

Olson, William J., and Samuel Francis. "Question: Should Crime Fighting Be Foreign Policy Priority?" *Insight on the News*, 17 July 1995, 18.

"The Opening Up of BCCI." *Economist*, 3 August 1991, 21.

"Operation Global Sea Nets Big Fish in Heroin Traffic." *DEA World* (May 1997): 7.

"Operation Red River Completes First Phase." *DEA World* (October 1992): 7–8.

"Operation Wipeout." *DEA World* (July–August 1991).

Oppenheimer, Andres. *Castro's Final Hour: The Secret Story Behind the Coming Fall of Communist Cuba*. New York: Simon and Schuster, 1993.

———. "Mexican Drug Lord Deported to U.S." Knight-Ridder/Tribune News Service, 15 January 1996.

———. "Rift Threatens Drug Probe." *Miami Herald*, 28 November 1996, International Satellite Edition.

———. "Salinas Inquiry Puts Mexico to the Test." *Miami Herald*, 1 December 1996, International Satellite Edition.

———. "Mexican Drug Suspect Freed." *Miami Herald*, 2 March 1997, International Satellite Edition.

———. "New Cartels Muscle In: Mexico, Not Colombia." *Miami Herald*, 15 March 1997, International Satellite Edition.

———. "R. Salinas Linked to Drug Trade." *Miami Herald*, 3 April 1997, International Satellite Edition.

———. "Are More Generals in Mexico Focus of Drug Probe?" *Seattle Times*, 28 July 1997.

———. "Swiss Pursue Links to Drug Money." *Miami Herald*, 14 July 1998.

Ormande, Tom. "Cracking Down on the Yakuza." *World Press Review* (May 1992): 48.

Osmanczyk, Edmund Jan. *Encyclopedia of the United Nations and International Agreements*. New York: Taylor and Francis, 1985.

Ostrow, Ronald J. "Leaders' Arrest Called Death of Cali Drug Cartel." *Los Angeles Times*, 7 August 1995.

Padgett, Tim. "Getting Off Drugs?" *Time*, 10 March 1997, 14–20.

Padilla, Felix M. *The Gang as an American Enterprise*. New Brunswick, NJ: Rutgers University Press, 1992.

"Panama—Del Cid." Associated Press, 12 December 1989.

Paternostro, Silvana. "Mexico as a Narco Democracy." *World Policy* (Spring 1995): 41–47.

Patten, Steve. "All-Out War on Heroin in Golden Triangle." *U.S. News and World Report*, 24 May 1982, 49.

Payne, Douglas W. "Why Drug Traffickers Love Free Trade." *Dissent* (Summer 1997): 59–64.

Peck, Grant. "McCaffrey Sees Case for Asian Cooperation." *Miami Herald*, 24 November 1996, International Satellite Edition.

Pendergrast, Mark. *For God, Country and Coca-Cola*. 1999.

Penn, Stanley. "Asian Connection." *Wall Street Journal*, 22 March 1990.

Penn, Stanley, and Edward T. Pound. "Havana Haven." *Wall Street Journal*, April 1984.

Perl, Raphael. *Drugs and Foreign Policy: A Critical Review*. Boston: Westview, 1994.

Philipsborn, Chris. "Cocaine Squeeze." *New Statesman and Society*, 12 February 1993, 10.

Pletka, Danielle. "Mafia Warfare Deadlier Than Ever." *Insight on the News*, 22 October 1990, 38.

———. "Heroin, Inc.: The Nigerian Connection (Drug Trafficking Through Nigeria)." *Insight on the News*, 30 September 1991, 22.

Plummer, William. *The Holy Goof: A Biography of Neal Cassady*. Englewood Cliffs, NJ: Prentice Hall, 1981.

Podesta, Don, and Douglas Farah. "Drug Policy in the Andes." *Washington Post*, 27 March 1993.

Podesta, Jane Sims. "William Bennett." *People Weekly*, 11 June 1990, 97 (4pp.).

"Police Gain Powers Against Crime." *Facts on File*, 19 March 1992, 200.

Policia Antinarcoticas (Colombia). *El Glifisato en la Erradicacion de Cultivos Illicitos* (Gliphosate in the Eradication of Illicit Cultivation). Bogota, Colombia: Policia Nacional de Colombia, 1992.

Polk, Peggy. "Informers Expose the Sicilian Mafia." *Chicago Tribune*, 6 February 1994.

Pons, Philippe. "China's Gang of Choice." *World Press Review* (February 1994): 51.

Poppa, Terrance E. *Drug Lord: The Life and Death of a Mexican Kingpin*. New York: Pharo Books, 1990.

"Por un General, Mexico Se Raja en Lucha Antidroga." *El Espectador* (Bogota, Colombia), 20 February 1997.

Posada Arizmendi, Ignacio. *Presidentes de Colombia, 1810–1990*. (Presidents of Colombia) Bogota, Colombia: Planeta, 1989.

Posner, Gerald. *Warlords of Crime: Chinese Secret Societies—The New Mafia*. New York: McGraw-Hill, 1988.

Post, T. "10 Acres, Valley View: Drug Lord's Jail." *Newsweek*, 1 July 1991, 34.

"Pot Shots Over a Drug Inquiry." *Time*, 13 February 1984, 33.

Potts, Mark, Nick Kochran, and Robert Whittlington. *Dirty Money: BCCI*. Washington, DC: National Press Books, 1992.

Powell, Bill. "Japan: The Fall of the Don." *Newsweek*, 26 October 1992, 42.

Powis, Robert E. *Money Launderers*. New York: Probus, 1992.

———. "Money Laundering: Problems and Solutions." *Banker's Magazine* November-December 1992, 72.

Pownall, Mark. *Heroin*. Oxford, UK: Heinemann, 1991.

Prager, Karsten. "Drugs, Money and a President's Ruin." *Time*, 5 February 1996, 37.

President's Commission on Organized Crime. *The Cash Connection: Organized Crime, Financial Institutions and Money Laundering*. Washington, DC: U.S. Government Printing Office, 1984.

———. *The Impact of Organized Crime Today*. Washington, DC: U.S. Government Printing Office, 1986.

———. *America's Habit: Drug Trafficking and Organized Crime*. Washington, DC: U.S. Government Printing Office, 1986.

Press, Robert M. "Drugs Strain U.S.-Nigeria Relations." *Christian Science Monitor*, 12 August 1992.

Preston, Gregory A. Review of *The New Ethnic Mobs: The Changing Face of Organized Crime*, by William Kleinknecht. *Library Journal*, 15 February 1996, 64.

Preston, Julia. "Drug Connection Links Mexican Military to Spate of Abductions." *Colombian Post*, 17–23 March 1997.

Price, Mark. "Redemption of Hemp: Weed to Wearable." *Charlotte Observer*, 11 October 1998.

"A Prision de la Nueva Generacion de la Mafia." *El Tiempo* (Bogota, Colombia), 30 December 1998.

"Pulse Check." *NarcOfficer* (September-October 1998), 36.

Pusey, Allen. "Asian Organized Crime Growing in Dallas." *Dallas Morning News*, 14 September 1986.

"Putting an Ear to the Wires." *Time*, 16 October 1989, 60.

Raab, Selwyn. "Influx of Russian Gangsters Trouble FBI in Brooklyn." *New York Times*, 23 August 1994.

Radin, Charles A. "Japan's Political Gangsters." *Charlotte Observer*, 10 June 1994.

Raine, Linnea P., and Frank J. Clilluffo. *Global Organized Crime: The New Empire of Evil.* Washington, DC: Center for Strategic and International Studies, 1994.

Ramo, Joshua Cooper. "Crime Online." *Time* Canada, 30 September 1996, 24.

Reckard, E. Scott. "Money Laundering." Associated Press, 12 December 1989.

Reding, Andrew. "The Fall and Rise of the Cartels." *Washington Post*, 17 September 1995.

Reiss, Spencer. "Jim Brown Is Still Dead." *Newsweek*, 6 April 1992, 41.

"Remarks by Thomas Constantine." *NarcOfficer* (July-August 1997): 18–19.

Renborg, Bertie A. *International Drug Control: A Study of International Administration By and Through the League of Nations.* Washington, DC: Carnegie Endowment of Peace, 1947.

"Respected Drug Lord Turns Himself in to Colombian Police." *Orange County Register*, 30 September 1997.

Reuter, Peter. "The Decline of the American Mafia." *Public Interest* (Summer 1995): 89–99.

Review of *A Dishonored Society: The Sicilian Mafia's Threat to Europe*, by John Follain. *New Statesman and Society*, 12 January 1996, 36.

Reyes, Geraldo, and Jeff Leen. "One-Time Venezuela Guard Chief Indicted on Drug Counts in the U.S." *Miami Herald*, 23 November 1996, International Satellite edition.

Ricci, Jose Lopez. "Shining Path After Guzman." *NACLA Report on the Americas* (November-December 1994), 6 (4pp.).

"Richard Pryor's Accident Spotlights Dangerous Drug Craze: Free Basing." *People Weekly*, 30 June 1980, 69 (3pp.).

Richburg, Keith B. "U.S.-Nigerian Relations Soured by Recriminations." *Washington Post*, 21 July 1992.

Riemer, Blanca. "The Drug War-European Style." *Business Week*, 2 October 1989, 31.

Riley, Kevin Jack. *Snow Job? The War Against International Drug Trafficking.* New Brunswick, NJ: Transaction Press, 1996.

Risen, James. "CIA Ignored Contra Drug Allegations, Report Says." *Miami Herald*, 17 July 1998.

"Rising Narcotics Danger Says Council." *UN Chronicle* (June 1982): 76–79.

Roark, Garland. *The Coin of Contraband: The True Story of United States Customs Investigator Al Scharff.* Garden City, NJ: Doubleday, 1964.

Robberson, Tod. "Mexico's Spreading Drug Stain: Mexican Cartels Expanding Role in Trafficking." *Washington Post*, 12 March 1995.

———. "Salinas In-Laws Linked to Drug Allegations." *Washington Post*, 25 November 1995.

Robinson, Eugene. "Israeli Mercenary Allegedly Provided Training and Services to the Medellin Cartel." *Washington Post* Foreign Service, 29 August 1989.

Robinson, Jeffrey. *The Laundrymen.* New York: Simon and Schuster, 1990.

Robinson, Linda. "New Target: Cali Cartel." *U.S. News and World Report*, 23 December 1991, 28–29.

Robinson, Linda, and Gordon Witkin. "Cracks in the Drug War." *U.S. News and World Report*, 2 March 1992, 49.

Robson, Michael. *Opium: The Poisoned Poppy.* New York: Weatherhill, 1994.

Rohter, Larry. "Seized Honduran: Drug Baron or Robin Hood?" *New York Times*, 16 August 1988.

———. "Mexicans Arrest Top Drug Figure and 80 Policemen." *New York Times*, 11 April 1989.

———. "Convicting Cali's Drug Boss May Be as Hard as Arresting Him." *New York Times*, 11 June 1995.

Rose, Jonathan. "The Sorry History of Drug Abuse in the U.S." *Scholastic Update*, 10 May 1985, 19.

Rosenberg, Anton. "A Hipster Ideal Dies at 71." *New York Times*, 22 February 1998.

Rosenthal, James. "Russia's New Export: The Mob." *Washington Post*, 14 June 1990, 1.

Rost, Curtis. "Weed the People." *People Weekly*, 21 October 1996, 75 (2pp.).

Rotella, Sebastian. "U.S., Mexico Join Forces against Drug Cartels." *Los Angeles Times*, 4 April 1995.

Rothschild, Mathew. "Drugs, CIA and the Media." *Progressive* (May 1997), 4.

Rowe, Chip. "Just Say?" *Playboy* (October 1998): 44.

Rowe, Dennis, ed. *International Drug Trafficking.* Chicago: University of Illinois at Chicago, Office of International Criminal Justice, 1988.

Rublowsky, John. *The Stoned Age: Drugs in America.* New York: Putnam, 1974.

Ryan, Patrick J. *Organized Crime.* Denver: ABC-CLIO, 1995.

Sabbage, Robert. "The Cartels Would Like a Second Chance." *Rolling Stone*, 4 May 1994, 35–38.

Sabourin, Serge. "From the Cold War to the Drug War." *New Perspectives Quarterly* (Fall 1989): 111–132.

Sack, Kevin. "26 Members of Chinese-American Groups in Atlanta Indicted." *New York Times*, 6 February 1996.

Sadoul, George. *Dictionary of Film.* Berkeley, CA: University of California Press, 1972.

Salerno, Ralph. *The Crime Confederation: Cosa Nostra and Allied Operations in Organized Crime.* Garden City, NJ: Doubleday, 1969.

"San Diego Street Gang Members Indicted in Connection with Cardinals' Murder." *CNN Interactive*, 1 February 1998.

Sanchez Fonseca, Marcelo. "CIA: Traficantes de Cocaina" (CIA: Traffickers of Cocaine). *El Tiempo* (Bogota, Colombia), 22 September 1996.

Sanger, David E. "Hemisphere Talks Open; U.S. Is Hedging Its Hopes." *New York Times*, 10 December 1994.

———. "Money Laundering New and Improved." *New York Times*, 24 December 1995.

Savage, David G. "New York Police Chief to Head DEA." *Los Angeles Times*, 14 January 1994.

Scheer, Robert. "Fighting the Wrong War." *Playboy,* October 1994, 49.

Schemann, Serge. "Russian Wise Guys." *New York Times Book Review,* 4 June 1995, 7.

Schemo, Diana Jean. "Heroin Proving a Growth Industry for Colombia." *Colombian Post,* 21–27 April 1997.

Scherer, Jane. *Crack: The Rock of Death.* Community Intervention Inc., 1988.

Schlosser, Eric. "Reefer Madness." *Atlantic Monthly* (August 1994): 45.

Schmalleger, Frank, ed. *Crime and the Justice System in America: An Encyclopedia.* Westport, CT: Greenwood Press, 1997.

Schmoke, Kurt. "Back to the Future." *Humanist* (September-October 1990): 28.

Schreiberg, David. "Sins of the Father: The Children of Cali Cartel Godfathers Can't Shake the Family's Past." *Newsweek,* 12 August 1996.

———. "Birth of the Baby Cartels." *Newsweek,* 21 August 1995, 37.

Schulteis, Rob. "Chinese Junk: My Search for the Red Tiger General." *Mother Jones* (March 1982): 34.

Sciolino, Elaine. "State Department Report Labels Nigeria Major Trafficker of Drugs to U.S." *New York Times,* 5 April 1994.

Scott, George. *The Rise and Fall of the League of Nations.* New York: Macmillan, 1974.

Scott, Peter Dale, and Jonathan Marshall. *Cocaine Politics, Drugs, Armies and the CIA in Central America.* Los Angeles: University of California Press, 1999.

"The Scourge of Drug Trafficking." *New Times* (December 1985): 18–23.

"Se Reanude La Extradicion" (Extradition Denied). *El Tiempo* (Bogota, Colombia), 15 December 1998.

"Secret CIA Report Notes Contra Drug Suspicions." *Charlotte Observer,* 18 July 1998.

Sene, P. M. "Africa and the Drug Threat." *World Health* (December 1981): 10–13.

Senigallia, Silvio F. "Challenged by the Mafia: Italian Justice on the Run." *New Leader,* 4 September 1989, 10–11.

"Sentenced: Robert Vesco." *MacLean's,* 9 September 1996, 11.

Serrill, Michael S. "Mexico's Black Mood." *Time,* 7 October 1991, 14–19.

Sessions, William. "International Crime in the 90s and the 21st Century." *Vital Speeches,* 15 November 1990, 69.

———. "Combating Organized Crime: The American Experience." *Vital Speeches,* 15 February 1993, 262.

Shannon, Elaine. *Desperadoes.* New York: NAL-Dutton, 1989.

———. "New Kings of Cocaine." *Time,* 1 July 1991, 28–33.

———. "Narco-Gnomes of Mexico: Where Drug Money Goes to Hide." *Washington Post,* 17 March 1996.

Shapiro, Harry, and Caesar Glebbek. *Jimi Hendrix: Electric Gypsy.* New York: St. Martin's Press, 1995.

Shenon, Philip. "Clinton Picks a Career Diplomat for Disputed Mexican Vacancy." *New York Times,* 29 April 1998.

Sheridan, May Beth. "Colombia Rages Over Allegations by Former U.S. Anti-Drug Official." Knight-Ridder/Tribune News Service, 30 September 1994.

Sheriman, Dick. "Prof, Crew May Have Key To Unlock Drug Addiction." *New York Daily News,* 21 August 1998.

Short, M. *Crime Inc.: The Story of Organized Crime.* London: Thomas Methuen, 1984.

Shultz, George. "The Campaign Against Drugs: The International Dimension." *Department of State Bulletin* (November 1984): 29–34.

"The Sicilian Mafia: A State within a State." *Economist,* 24 April 1993, 21–22.

Sides, W. Hampton. "This Is War: In the Shadowy World of Drugs, Police Battle Violent Jamaican Posses." *Washingtonian* (April 1988): 137–139.

Sierra, Sonia. "El Senora de los Narcos" (The Woman of the Narcos). *El Tiempo* (Bogota, Colombia), 23 February 1997.

Sifakis, Carl. *The Mafia Encyclopedia.* New York: Facts on File, 1987.

Sigerist, H. G. "Laudanum in the Words of Paracelsus." *Bulletin of Historical Medicine,* 1941.

Silberman, Charles. *Criminal Violence, Criminal Justice.* New York: Random House, 1978.

Simon, Roger. "Where There's Schmoke." *Playboy* (May 1994): 122.

Sinha, Maya. "The New Mafia Order." Review of *Thieves' World: The Threat of the New Global Network of Organized Crime,* by Claire Sterling. *Mother Jones* (May 1995): 78.

"Six Top Colombian Drug Traffickers Still at Large." Reuters, 10 June 1995.

Skornek, Carolyn. "New York Police Chief Picked to Head DEA." Associated Press, 13 January 1994.

"Slaying Ignites Fear of Mexican Drug War." *Miami Herald,* 12 September 1998.

Slevin, Peter. "Outlaw Cowboy Relished His Fame." *Miami Herald,* 3 December 1993, International Satellite Edition.

———. "Clinton Rebuffed on Mexico." *Miami Herald,* 7 March 1997, International Satellite Edition.

———. "A One-Sided War on Drugs." *Miami Herald,* 16 March 1997, International Satellite Edition.

Sloane, Wendy. "Russian Organized Crime Infiltrates Economy, Threatens Foreign Investment." *Christian Science Monitor,* 14 June 1994.

———. "FBI's Moscow Mission: The Mob, Nuclear Theft." *Christian Science Monitor,* 5 July 1994.

Sloman, L. *Reefer Madness: The History of Marijuana in America.* Indianapolis: Bobbs Merrill, 1979.

Slosser, Bob. "Courage to Fight: Drug Abuse May Destroy the Heart of America Unless We Are Willing to Go After Organized Crime." *Saturday Evening Post* (May-June 1989): 34 (2pp.).

Smith, H. E. *Transnational Crime: Investigative Responses.* Chicago: University of Illinois at Chicago, Office of International Criminal Justice, 1989.

Sniffer, Michael J. "U.S. To Post Reward for Drug Kingpin." *Seattle Times*, 24 September 1997.

"Sniffing Out Illicit Drugs and Explosives." *USA Today* magazine (June 1993): 8.

Snow, Anita. "Shakeup in Mexico's Ruling Party." *Miami Herald*, 15 December 1996, International Satellite Edition.

———. "Mexico Drug Scandal Widens with Arrest of Second General." *Miami Herald*, 19 March 1997, International Satellite Edition.

Snyder, Robert L. "Thomas de Quincey." *Bicentenary Studies Quarterly* of Oklahoma Press, 1986.

———. *Thomas De Quincey: The Prose of Vision*. Norman, OK: University of Oklahoma Press, 1986.

"Solving a Journalist's Murder." *Editor and Publisher*. 15 May 1993, 11.

Sondheimer, Adrian. "Cocaine-Exposed Infants: Social, Legal, and Public Health Issues." *Journal of the American Academy of Child and Adolescent Psychiatry* (April 1998): 453 (2pp.).

Spaeth, Anthony. "When the Barbarians Overrun the Gate." *Time*, 20 March 1995, 51.

Spencer, David. "Liability under U.N. Drug Trafficking Convention: Do the New Measures to Combat Money Laundering Go Far Enough?" *International Financial Review* (March 1990): 16–19.

Stahl, Marc B. "Asset Forfeiture, Burdens of Proof and the War on Drugs." *Criminology and Criminal Law* (Summer 1992): 274–337.

Stares, Paula B. *Global Habit: The Drug Problem in a Barbarous World*. Washington, DC: Brookings Institution, 1996.

———. *The Problem of Drugs in a World Without Frontiers*. Washington, DC: Brookings Institution, 1996.

Starr, Mark. "Reagan's War on Drugs." *Newsweek*, 9 August 1982, 14–15.

Stelle, Charles C. *America and the Chinese Opium Trade in the Nineteenth Century*. North Straford, NH: Ayer, 1981.

Sterling, Claire. *Octopus: The Long Reach of the International Sicilian Mafia*. New York: W. W. Norton, 1990.

———. *Crime without Frontiers*. New York: Little and Brown, 1994.

———. "Redfellas." *New Republic*, 11 April 1994, 19–22.

———. *Thieves' World: The Threat of the New Global Network of Organized Crime*. New York: Simon and Schuster, 1994.

Sternberg, Steve. "Funding Urged for Needle Exchanges." *USA Today*, 13 June 1997.

Sterne, Jane, and Michael Sterne. *Sixties People*. London: Macmillan, 1990.

Stevenson, Mark. "Ex-Mexico City Prosecutor New Drug Czar." *Miami Herald*, 11 March 1997, International Satellite Edition.

Stewart, Gail B. *Drug Trafficking*. San Diego, CA: Lucent, 1990.

Stille, Alexander. "The Mafia's Biggest Mistake." *New Yorker*, 1 March 1993, 66.

Stoessel, Walter J., Jr. "U.S. Policy on International Narcotics Control." *Department of State Dispatch* (September 1982): 46–48.

Storr, Anthony. *Freud*. Oxford, UK: Oxford University Press, 1989.

Strobel, Warren. "U.S. Moves to Extradite Drug Trafficker." *Washington Times*, 23 August 1989.

Strong, Simon. *Whitewash: Pablo Escobar and the Cocaine Wars*. London: Macmillan, 1995.

Stuttaford, Genevieve. "Review of *Gangland: How the FBI Broke the Mob*, by Howard Blum." *Publisher's Weekly*, 20 September 1993, 52.

Sullivan, Mary Ellen. "Drugs: The World Picture." *Current Health* (February 1990): 4–5.

Sutton, James. "Colombian Drug Cartels." Unpublished Report to the U.S. Department of Justice, ca. 1993.

———. "A Brief Overview of the Collaboration between Colombian and Mexican Drug Trafficking Operations." Unpublished Report to the U.S. Department of Justice, ca. 1994.

Sweeney, John. "A Culture of Corruption," *World and I* (August 1997): 34–39.

Swisher, Karen, ed. *Drug Trafficking*. San Diego, CA: Greenhaven, 1991.

Symons, William C., et al. "The Sicilian Mafia Is Still Going Strong." *Business Week*, 18 April 1988, 43.

"Taking on the Drug Lords." *World Press Review*, 28 April 1998, 12 (2pp.).

Tanner, Adam, and Pam Grier. "Russia's Notorious Mafia Spreads Tentacles of Crime Around Globe." *Christian Science Monitor*, 11 January 1995.

Tanner, Stephen L. *Ken Kesey*. Boston: Twayne Publishing, c. 1983.

Tarazona-Sevillano, Gabriela. *Sendero Luminoso and the Threat of Narcoterrorism*. Westport, CT: Praeger, 1990.

Tarshis, Lauren. "From Coca-Cola to Cartels: Battling Drugs in America." *Scholastic Update*, 17 November 1989, 10.

Taylor, Arnold H. *American Diplomacy and Narcotics Trafficking, 1900–1939*. Durham, NC: Duke University Press, 1969.

Taylor, Clyde D. "Links Between International Narcotics Trafficking and Terrorism." *Department of State Bulletin* (August 1985): 68–74.

Tedford, Deborah, and Jo Ann Zuniga. "Cocaine Kingpin Is Guilty, Cartel Chief Could Get Life." *Houston Chronicle*, 17 October 1996.

Thomas, Jon R. "International Campaign against Drug Trafficking." *Department of State Dispatch* (January 1985): 50.

———. "Narcotics Control in Latin America." *Department of State Dispatch* (April 1986): 77–80.

Thomas, Pierre. "Rules Target Chemical Sales in Colombia." *Washington Post*, 18 March 1996.

Thornton, Mark. *Economics of Prohibition*. Salt Lake City, UT: University of Utah Press, 1991.

"Three Found Guilty in Son of Lehder Case." United Press International, 26 October 1989.

"Time for a Global Criminal Court." *New York Times*, 21 November 1994.

Toner, Robin. "Parties Seek to Cast Blame in Teenage Drug Use." *New York Times*, 22 August 1996.

Toosi, N. "Saying 'Yes' to 'No'." *Charlotte Observer*, 21 May 1998.

Torchia, Christopher. "Cali Cartel Leader Faces Ruthless Rival: The Overalls Man." *Colombian Post*, 24–27 October 1996.

Toro, Maria C. *Mexico's War on Drugs: Causes and Consequences*. Boulder, CO: Lynne Rienner, 1995.

Tovares, Robert W. "How Best to Solve the Drug Problem." *National Catholic Reporter*, 22 December 1989.

"Tracking the International Drug Trade." *Scholastic Update*, 10 May 1985, 37–41.

Traub, James. *The Billion Dollar Connection: The International Drug Trade*. New York: Julian Messner, 1983.

Travis, Jeremy. "National Institute of Justice: Research in Brief." *NarcOfficer* (March-April 1998).

Treaster, Joseph B. "Exiting Drug Chief Warns of Cartels." *New York Times*, 31 October 1993.

———. "U.S. Says It Uncovered a $100 Million Drug Money Laundry," *New York Times*, 1 December 1995.

Trebach, A. S. *The Great Drug War*. New York: Macmillan, 1986.

Trebach, Arnold S., and James A. Inciardi. *Legalize It? Debating American Drug Policy*. Washington, DC: American University Press, 1993.

Treniowski, Alex. "Requiem for a Heavyweight." *People Weekly*, 12 January 1997, 46 (6pp.).

Trotta, Dan. "U.S.-Mexican Border Becomes Fertile New Killing Ground." Reuters, 24 October 1996.

Troy, Sandy. *One More Saturday Night: Reflections With the Grateful Dead, Dead Family and Dead Heads*. New York: St. Martin's Press, 1991.

"True Confessions: A Gang Member's Story." *U.S. News and World Report*, 18 January 1988.

True, Philip. "Mexico's New Anti-Drug Czar Vows to Reorganize, Deepen Investigation." *Miami Herald*, 23 March 1997, International Satellite Edition.

Tullis, Lamond. *Handbook of Research on the Illicit Drug Traffic: Socioeconomic and Political Consequences*. Westport, CT: Greenwood Press, 1991.

Tutsathit, Tapin, and Yinder Lertcharoechok. "Khun Sa Network Dismantled." *Sunday Nation*, 18 December 1994, 1A, 2A.

Twersky, David. "The Risks of Cozying Up to Syria." *New York Times*, 28 July 1992.

"Two Gentlemen of Verona." *Economist*, 11 November 1989, 59.

"2 (One-Half) Tons of Cocaine Seized." *Los Angeles Times*, 25 January 1992.

Tytell, John. *Naked Angels: The Lives and Literature of the Beat Generation*. New York: McGraw-Hill, c. 1976.

Uhlig, Mark A. "Cuba Replaces Top Security Officer." *New York Times*, 30 June 1989.

Unanue de Dio, Manuel. *Los Secretos de Cartel de Medellin (The Secrets of the Medellin Cartel)*. Jackson Heights, NY: Cobra Editorial, 1988.

"Uncertain Origins." *CA Researcher*, 27 March 1992, 272–273, 283.

United Nations Department of Public Information. *Everyman's United Nations*. New York: United Nations, 1986.

———. *Basic Facts about the U.N.* New York: United Nations, 1995.

———. *A Guide to Information about the United Nations.* New York, United Nations, 1995.

United Nations International Drug Control Program. *World Drug Report*. Oxford, UK: Oxford University Press, 1997.

"The United States International Crime Control Strategy." *Trends in Organized Crime* (Fall 1998): 1–87.

"Upheaval Won't Stop War on Drugs, McCaffrey Says." *Miami Herald*, 8 December 1996, International Satellite Edition.

U.S. Attorney General. *Drug Trafficking: A Report to the President of the United States*. Washington, DC: U.S. Government Printing Office, 1989.

"U.S. Brings Colombian to New York on Drug Charges." United Press International, 15 December 1989.

"U.S. Crime Notebook: California." *Global Crime Network*, 27 July 1998, 8.

U.S. Department of Justice. *Oriental Organized Crime: A Report on Research Conducted by the Organized Crime Section*. Washington, DC: U.S. Government Printing Office, 1985.

———. *Report on Asian Organized Crime*. Washington, DC: U.S. Government Printing Office, 1988.

———. *Drug Trafficking: A Report to the President of the United States*. Washington, DC: U.S. Government Printing Office, 1994.

———. DEA. *The Supply of Illicit Drugs to the United States*.

———. "Methamphetamine and Methacathinone: New Threats to Law Enforcement." *Drug World* (February 1994): 17–23.

U.S. Department of State. *Estudio Conciso de Medio Ambiente para la Erradicacion de la Amapola y Marijuana en Guatemala* (Concise Study of the Environment for the Eradication of the Poppy and Marijuana in Guatemala). Washington, DC: U.S. Department of State, 1987.

———. "Treaty between the U.S. and the Federal Republic of Nigeria on Mutual Assistance in Criminal Matters." 20 May 1992. TREATY DOC. 10226.

———. *Country Report on Human Rights: Colombia*. Bogota, Colombia: U.S. Information Service, 1996.

"U.S. Drug Chief Stresses Reduction of Use." *New York Times*, 15 August 1993.

U.S. General Accounting Office. *Drug Courts: Overview of*

Growth, Characteristics and Results. Washington, DC: General Accounting Office, 1987.

———. *Emerging Drug Problems.* Washington, DC: U.S. Government Printing Office, 1998.

———. *Money Laundering: Treasury's Financial Crimes Enforcement Network.* Washington, DC: U.S. Government Printing Office, 1991.

———. *Money Laundering: The U.S. Government Is Responding to the Problem.* Washington, DC: U.S. Government Printing Office, 1991.

———. *Money Laundering: Characteristics of Currency Transaction Reports in Calendar Year 1992.* Washington, DC: U.S. Government Printing Office, 1992.

———. *Coordination of Intelligence Activities: Briefing Report to the Chairman on Governmental Operations, House of Representatives.* Washington, DC: General Accounting Office, 1993.

———. *Illicit Narcotics: Recent Efforts to Control Chemical Diversion and Money Laundering.* Washington, DC: U.S. Government Printing Office, 1993.

———. *Money Laundering: Progress Report on Treasury's Financial Crimes Enforcement Network.* Washington, DC: U.S. Government Printing Office, 1993.

———. *War on Drugs: Arrests Burdening Local Criminal Justice System.* Washington, DC: U.S. Government Printing Office, 1994.

———. *Drug Control: Counter Narcotics Efforts in Mexico.* Washington, DC: General Accounting Office, 1996.

———. *Drug Control: Threats and Roles of Explosives and Narcotics Technology: Briefing Report to Congressional Requesters.* Washington, DC: General Accounting Office, 1996.

———. *Drug Control: U.S. Heroin Program Encounters Many Obstacles in Southeast Asia.* Washington, DC: General Accounting Office, 1996.

———. *Drug Control: U.S. Interdiction Efforts in the Caribbean Decline.* Washington, DC: General Accounting Office, 1996.

———. *Drug War: Observations on the U.S. International Drug Control Strategy: Statement of Joseph E. Kelly, Director in Charge, International Affairs Division.* Washington, DC: General Accounting Office, 1996.

———. *Money Laundering: A Framework for Understanding U.S. Efforts Overseas.* Washington, DC: U.S. Government Printing Office, 1996.

———. *Drug Control: Status of U.S. International Counternarcotics Activities.* Washington, DC: General Accounting Office, 1998.

———. *Planned Activities Should Clarify Counter Technology Assessment Center's Impact.* Washington, DC: U.S. Government Printing Office, Feb. 1998.

———. *Drug Interdiction: Operation Autumn Harvest: A National Guard-Customs Anti-Smuggling Effort.* Washington, DC: U.S. Government Printing Office, 1989.

U.S. House Judiciary Committee. *Hearings before the Subcommittee on Crime.* 105th Congress, 1st session, 24 July 1997 (statement of Raymond W. Kelly, Commissioner, U.S. Customs).

U.S. House Committee on Foreign Affairs. *The Threat of International Organized Crime: Hearings before the Subcommittee on International Security, International Organizations and Human Rights.* 103rd Congress, 1st session, 4 November 1993.

U.S. House Judiciary Committee on Crime. July 24, 1997.

Hearings before the Subcommittee on Western Hemisphere Affairs. Review of the 1992 International Narcotics Control Strategy Report Hearings, 3–12 March 1992. Washington, DC: U.S. Superintendent of Documents, 1992.

———. Select Committee on Narcotics Abuse and Control. International Narcotics Control Study Mission to Hawaii, Hong Kong, Thailand, Burma, Pakistan, Turkey and India. Washington, DC: U.S. Government Printing Office, 1984.

———. Testimony of Robert Newbery, U.S. Defense Department's Director of Drug Enforcement Policy and Support. *Hearing before the Subcommittee on National Security, International Affairs, and Criminal Justice.* 105th Congress, 1st session, 9 July 1997.

U.S. House Committee on Foreign Affairs. *The Andean Initiative: Hearings before the Subcommittee on Western Hemisphere Affairs.* 101st Congress, 2nd session, 6 June 1990 and 20 June 1990.

———. "Operation Snowcap: Its Present and Future." 23 May 1990.

U.S. House Committee on Government Affairs. Permanent Subcommittee on Investigations. 1991. "The New International Criminal and Asian Organized Crime." 18 June–4 August 1992. Congress Session 102-2, Doc-Nos. Hrj-102-940 CIS-No. 93-S401-g.

U.S. House Committee on Foreign Affairs. *Hearing before the Task Force on International Narcotics Control.* 101st Congress, 2nd session, 10 October 1990.

U.S. House Committee on Government Operations. *Federal Strategies to Investigate and Prosecute Major Narcotics Traffickers: Hearings before the Justice and Agricultural Subcommittee.* 101st Congress, 1st session, 4 April 1989.

U.S. House Committee on the Judiciary. *Hearings on International Drug Supply, Control and Interdiction.* 103rd Congress, 1st session, 15 July 1993.

U.S. House Committee on the Judiciary. Subcommittee on Crime and Criminal Justice. 104th Congress, 1st session. *Heroin Trafficking.* Washington, DC: U.S. Government Printing Office, 1995.

U.S. Senate Committee on Commerce, Science, and Transportation. *U.S. Chemical Exports to Latin America: Hearing before the Subcommittee on Foreign Commerce and Tourism,* 101st Congress, 2nd session, 6 February 1990.

U.S. Senate Committee on Foreign Relations. "Treaty Between the U.S. and the Federal Republic of Nigeria on Mutual Legal Assistance in Criminal Matters." (Treaty

Doc. 102–26). Washington, DC: U.S. Superintendent of Documents, 20 May 1992, p. 7.

———. Wankel, Harold D. "Drug Control Along the Southwest Border." DEA Congressional Testimony Before the House Judiciary Committee, 31 July 1996.

U.S. Senate Committee on Foreign Relations, Subcommittee on Terrorism, Narcotics and International Operations. *Recent Developments in Transnational Crime Affecting U.S. Law Enforcement and Foreign Policy.* Washington, DC: U.S. Superintendent of Documents, 20–21 April 1994.

———. *Report: Drugs, Law Enforcement and Foreign Policy.* Washington, DC: U.S. Government Printing Office, 1989.

U.S. Senate Committee on Governmental Affairs. *Asian Organized Crime.* Washington, DC: U.S. Government Printing Office, 1992.

U.S. Senate Committee on Governmental Affairs, Permanent Subcommittee on Investigations. *Arms Trafficking, Mercenaries and Drug Cartels, Hearings of February 27–28, 1991.* Washington, DC: U.S. Superintendent of Documents, 1991.

U.S. Senate Committee on the Judiciary. *U.S. Drug Control Policy: Recent Experience, Future Options: Seminar Proceedings, February 2, 1994.* Washington, DC: U.S. Superintendent of Documents, 1994.

U.S. Senate Committee on the Judiciary, Subcommittee on Improvements in the Federal Criminal Code. *Illicit Narcotics, Hearings of June 2–November 25, 1955.* Washington, DC: U.S. Government Printing Office, 1955.

"U.S. To Reveal Mafia Drug Link." *New York Times,* 6 December 1994.

"U.S. Warns of Possible Heroin Epidemic." *Rock Hill (S.C.) Herald,* 4 April 1994.

Valentine, Paul W. "Eight Nigerians Found Guilty in Heroin Smuggling Ring." *Washington Post,* 21 July 1992.

"Verdadero Poder de los Narcos Mexicanos" *El Espectador* (Bogota, Colombia), 23 February 1997.

"Vesco's Last Gamble." *Vanity Fair* (March 1996).

"Vietnamese Gangs Active in Florida." *New York Times,* 25 November 1985.

Villamarin, Polido, and Luis Alberto. *El Cartel de las FARC* (The Cartel of FARC). Bogota, Colombia: Ediciones El Faraon, 1996.

"Virginia ROHR System Covers Caribbean Drug Smuggling Routes." *Aviation and Space Technology,* 27 November 1989, 76.

Viviano, Frank, and Holly Lloyd. "The New Mafia Order." *Mother Jones* (May-June 1995): 44–55.

Von Raab, W. "How the U.S. Is Cracking Down on Drug Smugglers." *U.S. News and World Report,* 7 June 1982, 45–46.

Vulliany, Ed. "Mafia Inc." *World Press Review* (December 1992): 11.

"The Wages of Prohibition." *Economist,* 24 December 1994, 21–24.

Wagner, Dennis. "Crackdown Shifted Drug Trafficking to Mexico." *Colombian Post,* 18–24 November 1996.

Wall, Tim. "Transnational Crime Busters Agree on New Action Plan." *UN Chronicle* (March 1985): 89.

"Wall-to-Wall Drug Traffickers." *U.S. News and World Report,* 19 June 1989, 14.

Wardlaw, Grant. "Linkages Between Illegal Drug Traffic and Terrorism." *Conflict Quarterly* (Summer 1988): 5–26.

Washington Office on Latin America. *Colombia Besieged: Political Violence and State Responsibility.* Washington, DC: Washington Office on Latin America, 1989.

Watts, Harold H. *Aldous Huxley.* New York: Twayne Publishers, c. 1969.

Webb, Gary. *Dark Alliance: The CIA, The Contras and the Crack Cocaine Explosion.* New York: Seven Stories Press, 1998.

Weiner, Tim. "Anti-Drug Unit of CIA Sends Tons of Cocaine to U.S." *New York Times,* 20 November 1993.

Weir, William. *In the Shadow of the Dope Fiend.* New Haven, CT: Archon, 1995.

Weisberg, Jacob. "The Mafia and the Melting Pot." *New Republic,* 12 October 1987, 33.

Well, Tom. "Pilot of Pablo Escobar Captured." Associated Press, 19 October 1989.

Wankel, Harold D. "Drug Control along the U.S. Border."

West, Stan. "Home of the Brave." *Hispanic* (December 1991): 58.

West, Woody. "A Farewell to the Dead." *Insight on the News.* 11 September 1995, 40.

"Why Do You Think They Call It Dope?" *Time,* 18 October 1993, 25.

Wiant, Jon. "Narcotics in the Golden Triangle." *Washington Quarterly* (Fall 1985): 125–140.

Williams, Daniel. "Revival of Terrorism in Italy Intensifies Aversion to Mafia, State." *Washington Post,* 6 June 1993.

Williams, Dennis A. "When Cocaine Can Kill." *Newsweek,* 23 June 1980, 30.

Williams, William F. "Terrorism in the Nineties: The Skull and Crossbones Still Flies." *Police Chief* (September 1990): 47–50.

Wirpsa, Leslie. "U.S. Coalition Calls on Bush to Redirect Drug War Dollars." *National Catholic Reporter,* 15 September 1991, 13.

———. "U.S. Militarization of Anti-drug Campaign in Bolivia Fires More Peasant Opposition." *National Catholic Reporter,* 26 March 1993, 15.

Witkin, Gordon. "The New Opium Wars: The Administration's Plan to Attack the Lords of Heroin." *U.S. News and World Report,* 10 October 1994, 39.

———. "The Troubled Reign of the Nation's Drug Czar; the Elusive Quest for Real Power and Respect." *U.S. News and World Report,* 8 September 1997.

Wood, Christopher. "Limitless Discretion." *Economist,* 24 June 1989, S22.

Woodward, Bob. *Wired: The Short Life and Fast Times of John Belushi.* New York: Faber and Faber, 1985.

Woolner, Ann. *Washed in Gold: The Story Behind the Biggest*

Money-Laundering Investigation. New York: Simon and Schuster, 1994.

"World Conference on Organized Crime, Money Laundering to Be Hosted by Italy." *UN Chronicle,* 1 September 1993, 71.

World, Frank S. "Oakland Marijuana Club Closed by Feds." Associated Press, 19 October 1998.

The World This Week. "Fighting International Organized Crime." 14 October 1993. Transcript. Denver, CO: Journal Graphics.

Wren, Christopher. "Colombians Taking Over Heroin Trade." *New York Times,* 11 February 1996.

———. "Two Democrats Say Mexico Is No U.S. Ally in Drug War." *Colombian Post,* 3–9 March 1997.

———. "U.N. Aide Would Fight Drugs With Better Life For Growers." *New York Times,* 7 June 1998.

"Yankee Drug Busters Head South." *Economist,* 23 May 1998, 31.

Yarbro, Stan. "Authorities Capture Drug Trafficker." Associated Press, 15 October 1989.

Yelin, Lev. "Why the Golden Crescent Still Flourishes." *New Times* (February 1985): 28–30.

York, Byron. "Clinton's Phony Drug War." *American Spectator* (February 1994): 40.

York, Michael. "Security Tightens as Italian Trial Begins." *Washington Post,* 17 July 1992.

Young, Charles M. "Son of Samurai." *Rolling Stone,* 11 June 1992, 124 (3pp.).

Index